A Source Book for Russian History from Early Times to 1917

A SOURCE BOOK FOR RUSSIAN HISTORY

FROM EARLY TIMES TO 1917

VOLUME 1
Early Times to the Late Seventeenth Century

George Vernadsky, SENIOR EDITOR
Ralph T. Fisher, Jr., MANAGING EDITOR
Alan D. Ferguson
Andrew Lossky
Sergei Pushkarev, COMPILER

New Haven and London: Yale University Press

1972

Library of Congress catalog card number: 70-115369.
ISBN: 0-300-01625-5 (3-volume set); 0-300-01286-1 (vol. 1);
        0-300-01602-6 (vol. 2); 0-300-01612-3 (vol. 3).

Designed by John O. C. McCrillis
and set in IBM Press Roman type.
Printed in the United States of America by
The Murray Printing Co., Forge Village, Mass.

Published in Great Britain, Europe, and Africa by
Yale University Press, Ltd., London.
Distributed in Canada by McGill-Queen's University
Press, Montreal; in Latin America by Kaiman & Polon,
Inc., New York City; in Australasia and Southeast
Asia by John Wiley & Sons Australasia Pty. Ltd.,
Sydney; in India by UBS Publishers' Distributors Pvt.,
Ltd., Delhi; in Japan by John Weatherhill, Inc., Tokyo. ·

CONTENTS   VOLUME 1

CONTENTS VOLUMES 2 AND 3

PREFACE

Our purpose in this book is to provide, in English, an illustrative sample of the wealth of primary source material that exists for the study of Russia from early times to 1917.

Source books in American and general European history have existed in abundance. They have proved their value as teaching tools to supplement a comprehensive textbook. The need for source books in Russian history has been felt by a great many teachers, to judge from those who offered suggestions to us. It was thanks in large part to their encouragement that we pushed ahead.

As we worked we have had in mind the teacher and especially the purposeful student—the student who is seeking not merely entertainment or native color but solid information as well; the student who does not want to have interpretations handed to him ready-made, but likes to do some evaluating for himself.

Accordingly, in the introductory notes we have avoided either summarizing the document or repeating the background that a text would provide, but we have tried to identify the source and to give enough data to enable the reader to place the document in its historical setting and to figure out what sorts of questions the selection helps to answer.

In the same spirit, we have retained the use of many Russian terms, especially where there is no direct or specific English equivalent, as in the case of territorial divisions, terms of office, and units of measure and money. We believe the hardship this causes to some will work to the net advantage of all of the book's readers— including even the beginner, especially if he is persistent enough in turning to the *Dictionary of Russian Historical Terms* compiled by Mr. Pushkarev.*

In our choice of selections we have sought to achieve a balanced mixture of various types of sources. Along with spirited first-person accounts, there are official documents and other sober fare which require intensive reading. We have included representative samples of the sources that are important enough to be alluded to in the standard textbooks. Often our excerpts are shorter than we would have preferred if expense were no problem, but they are, we think, not too short to convey significant points to the thoughtful reader who is alert to the uses of various kinds of historical evidence.

In response to the wishes of our colleagues, we have emphasized sources not previously published in English translation. About 81 percent of our selections were in that category in 1956 when we began. That proportion is now down to around 75 percent, owing to the new translations that have appeared in recent years. We have cited these new translations in our reference notes for the pertinent items (about 6 percent of our total), so that the reader may locate them easily for further study. About 8 percent of our selections came from publications in English which

---

*A companion volume to this set, the *Dictionary of Russian Historical Terms from the Eleventh Century to 1917* was published by Yale University Press in 1970.

we simply reproduced. Most of these are English in origin, from Richard Chancellor in the sixteenth century to Sir James Buchanan in the twentieth. The remaining selections, about 12 percent, are from sources that had been translated into English but for which we used both the original language and the published translation to produce the version included in this book. In some cases we revised the previous translation only slightly—in other cases, considerably. Our reference notes explain how much.

Scope and coverage. Although our excerpts represent about seven hundred distinct sources (the number could be raised or lowered depending on how one decided to count certain kinds of documents of various dates grouped under one heading), these are of course only a minute fraction of the published sources available. Our original prospectus had to be sharply cut. And although we incorporated about two hundred items from among the additions to our prospectus that were suggested by the letters of our teacher-colleagues, their suggestions totaled around three times that many. It is obvious, then, that much that is worthwhile could not be included here and that many of our choices had to be made on the basis of convenience and availability. At the same time our selections were guided by certain general principles, and these we should explain.

We have felt it necessary to exclude the vast realm of belles lettres, despite its vital importance for the historian. We did not see any way of doing justice to it within the scope of this work. Fortunately that category of source material is widely available in anthologies as well as in translations of individual works.

We have given relatively little space to documents in foreign relations. While we have included some documents bearing on Russia's territorial expansion or on Russian views of certain questions beyond the frontiers, we have generally shunned diplomatic documents which, falling within the scope of general European or world history, are available already in English or are so well summarized in most texts that the marginal gain from an excerpt would be slight.

We have tried to provide sources for political and social history in the broad sense, and have therefore included numerous selections from such fields as intellectual history, church history, economic history, and legal history. We have followed the practice of most textbooks in focusing primarily on the dominant Great Russians, even though by the late nineteenth century they constituted not much over half of the population. We have allotted space to other peoples and areas especially during those periods when they were being brought into the empire. We have not systematically followed the fate of each national element or geographical region thereafter, but have provided occasional illustrations and reminders of the multinational nature of the empire and the problems resulting therefrom.

We have held to a fairly narrow definition of "primary," resisting the temptation to include historical writings that, although "primary" as expressions of the attitudes of their own time, would not generally be classified as such. Our introductions give enough data to enable the student to discern varying degrees of primariness.

In our chronological divisions we have followed the prevailing practice of increasing the coverage as we move closer to the present, but we have given more than the usual emphasis to the 1500s and 1600s, believing, along with many of our colleagues, that we should help to broaden the time span of Russian history beyond that usually taught. On the contemporary end, some of our fellow teachers wanted us to go beyond March 1917. We agree that this would make the book more widely usable in survey courses, but so many sources for Russian history since 1917 had already been translated that we believed such an extension would not be justifiable.

Beyond the problem of achieving a suitable mixture of kinds of sources and a suitable topical and chronological distribution is the at least equally vexing problem of which excerpts to select when, as in most cases, a source is far too long to be included in its entirety. Here, as elsewhere, we have tried not to be unduly influenced by our own preconceptions and have sought to include a wide spectrum of viewpoints from among the voices of the past.

Arrangement, form, style. Our goal in arranging the material has been to make it easy to use this source book along with any textbook in Russian history. Our chapter units thus follow traditional lines. Within them we have arranged the items in a combination of chronological and topical groupings, much as a text might treat them. Particularly where one document touches several topics, our placement has had to be arbitrary. Occasionally—as in the case of the early chronicles—we have broken one source down into separate excerpts by date and topic, but we did not want to overdo this, lest we deemphasize the distinct nature of each source. This means that while it is possible to read the book straight through like a narrative, we have expected, rather, that most users would be reading it by sections or groups of documents, in conjunction with a text or after becoming generally familiar with the period in question. In order to assist both teacher and student in adapting these source readings to any lesson plan, we have provided a Guide to Major Topics.

Our reference notes acknowledge the works we have used as the basis for each item; they are by no means a catalog of all available sources for the same selection. All dates are in the old style or Julian calendar unless labeled N.S. Spaced ellipsis dots indicate that passages in original documents have been omitted in this book; closed-up ellipsis dots represent ellipses contained in the original; double-length dashes represent lacunae—mutilated or otherwise illegible passages—in the original. Unless a selection is identified in our introductory note as a full text, it is an excerpt.

All translators of nonmodern materials understand the compromises required between modern English usage and older expressions which have their counterparts in the Russian of various periods of the past. We felt it unreasonable, in working with so many different kinds of documents, to strive for complete uniformity of style. But even in seeking accuracy we were forced into decisions that will not fully satisfy everyone. Take the example of *tsarskii,* the adjective formed from "tsar." The common rendering, "tsarist," may properly be condemned as now having in English a pejorative connotation that is inappropriate to our uses. But after considering such possibilities as "tsarly" (on the model of "kingly"), "tsarial" (after "imperial"), or "tsarish" (used as "czarish" a few generations back), we returned to "tsarist"—not without dissent in our own ranks. The similar problem of rendering adjectives especially when used as proper names is one familiar to every translator. (Should it be "Resurrection Chronicle" or "Voskresensk Chronicle"? And what about the full adjectival ending and the gender?) We have tried in such cases to follow what seems to be common usage in college textbooks, even though this has led to inconsistencies that may annoy the specialist.

Some of the most frequently used Russian terms have been Anglicized: soft signs have been dropped and plurals have been formed with "s" (for example, "dumas"). In the majority, however, the soft sign and Russian nominative plurals have been retained (*pomest'ia, strel'tsy*). Sometimes this produced results irritating to the Russian speaker, especially when numbers are followed by a nominative case. But the use of genitive forms would have complicated matters unduly for the student who has had no Russian. Where, as an aid to those who have studied Russian, we have added transliterations of Russian words in brackets after the English, we have made some changes toward the modern orthography. But where no confusion would occur we have simply transliterated a term as it stood, thereby preserving changes in spelling, sometimes even within the same document. Our transliterations follow the Library of Congress system with minor modifications.

Family names and patronymics have been simply transliterated. First names have been transliterated except when the English equivalent is very widely used for the person in question (e.g. Tsar Paul). Place names have been transliterated, except where English substitutions are current (Moscow, Archangel). One politically touchy problem is that of rendering place names in the non-Great-Russian parts of the empire. We have in general chosen the solution, favored by English-language texts, of using the Russian form, but we have often added the other names in parentheses.

DIPLOMATIC HISTORY
HISTORY OF RUSSIAN FOREIGN RELATIONS

From early times to the late seventeenth century, see:

From Peter the Great to Nicholas I, see:

From Alexander II to the February Revolution, see:

LIST OF ITEMS BY CHAPTERS, VOLUME 1

LIST OF ABBREVIATIONS

AAE — *Akty sobrannye v bibliotekakh i arkhivakh Rossiiskoi Imperii arkheograficheskoiu ekspeditsieiu Imperatorskoi Akademii Nauk.* 4 vols. St. Petersburg, 1836.

AN BSSR — Akademiia Nauk Belorusskoi Sovetskoi Sotsialisticheskoi Respubliki.

AN SSSR — Akademiia Nauk Soiuza Sovetskikh Sotsialisticheskikh Respublik.

AOIZR — Arkheograficheskaia Komissiia, ed. *Akty otnosiashchiesia k istorii zapadnoi Rossii,* 5 vols. St. Petersburg, 1846-51.

CIOIDRMU — Obshchestvo Istorii i Drevnostei Rossiiskikh. *Chteniia v Imperatorskom Obshchestve Istorii i Drevnostei Rossiiskikh pri Moskovskom Universitete.* 264 vols. Moscow, 1846-1918.

DAI — Arkheograficheskaia Komissiia, ed. *Dopolneniia k aktam istoricheskim.* 12 vols. St. Petersburg, 1846-72.

Gosiurizdat — Gosudarstvennoe Izdatel'stvo Iuridicheskoi Literatury.

Gosizdat — Gosudarstvennoe Izdatel'stvo.

Goslitizdat — Gosudarstvennoe Izdatel'stvo Khudozhestvennoi Literatury.

Gospolitizdat — Gosudarstvennoe Izdatel'stvo Politicheskoi Literatury.

OGIZ — Ob"edinenie Gosudarstvennykh Izdatel'stv.

PBIPV — *Pis'ma i bumagi Imperatora Petra Velikogo.* 11 vols. Vols. 1-7, St. Petersburg: Gosudarstvennaia Tipografiia, 1887-1918. Vols. 8-11, Moscow: AN SSSR, 1948-64.

PRP — *Pamiatniki russkogo prava.* 8 vols. Moscow: Gosiurizdat, 1952-61.

PSRL — Arkheograficheskaia Komissiia, ed. *Polnoe Sobranie Russkikh Letopisei.* 31 vols. St. Petersburg, 1841-1968.

PSZRI — *Polnoe Sobranie Zakonov Rossiiskoi Imperii . . . 1649-1913.* 134 vols. St. Petersburg, 1830-1916 (1st ser., 46 vols., containing laws of 1649-1825; 2d ser., 55 vols., covering 1825-81; 3d ser., 33 vols., covering 1881-1913).

PVL — V. P. Adrianova-Peretts and D. S. Likhachev, eds. *Povest' vremennykh let.* Moscow: AN SSSR, 1950.

RIB — Arkheograficheskaia Komissiia, ed. *Russkaia istoricheskaia biblioteka.* 39 vols. St. Petersburg, 1872-1927.

RPC   Samuel H. Cross and Olgerd P. Sherbowitz-Wetzor, eds. and trans.
               The Russian Primary Chronicle, Laurentian Text. Cambridge, Mass.:
               Mediaeval Academy of America, 1953.

SIRIO   *Sbornik Imperatorskogo Russkogo Istoricheskogo Obshchestva.*
               148 vols. St. Petersburg: Imperatorskoe Russkoe Istoricheskoe
               Obshchestvo, 1867–1916.

Tsentrarkhiv   Tsentral'nyi Gosudarstvennyi Istoricheskii Arkhiv v Moskve.

VOLUME 1

Early Times to the Late Seventeenth Century

CHAPTER 1

Pre-Kievan Beginnings

Historical research and writing are based on primary sources which enable us to reconstruct "what happened in history"—the development of the main political events; the political, economic, and social structure of nations; the intellectual, artistic, and religious currents; the manner of life; in short, the whole course of evolution of mankind in its various aspects.

The main types of primary sources used by the historian are written: manuscripts and publications of manuscripts. However, the student of history needs also monumental and pictorial sources to visualize more vividly the life of the past. We like to know, not only what our ancestors did and how they thought, but also how they lived—in what houses they dwelt, what weapons and tools they made and used, what kinds of clothes and ornaments they wore, how they worshiped, how they buried their dead.

It is in answering these questions that archaeology proves invaluable for the study of history. For the ancient periods of the history of mankind archaeology constitutes our main, and more often than not our only, historical source. This is especially true in regard to the earliest epoch of Russian history, since the relevant written sources for that age in Russia are scant.

Archaeological evidence, especially of distant lands, is made available to the student mainly through photographic reproduction of old monuments and artifacts. An album of illustrative plates containing the representations of typical archaeological materials for the study of Russian history would constitute a desirable companion volume to the present *Sourcebook*. It is, however, obviously impossible to include such materials here. In order that students of Russian history, using this *Sourcebook*, may obtain some idea of the scope of archaeological research in Russia and of the kind of archaeological evidence available for the study of the early periods of Russian history, a few remarks on this aspect of sources seem necessary.

The development of archaeological research in Russia makes a fascinating story. Peter the Great was the first of the Russian rulers to understand the importance of archaeological finds for science. The first collection of Siberian antiquities was established in the museum of the Academy of Sciences in 1725. Some archaeological research work was done in Russia in the eighteenth century. It was, however, only in the nineteenth century, and especially in the second half of it, that archaeological research assumed wider significance in Russia. At first, the attention of both scholars and amateurs was attracted to spectacular finds in south Russia—the barrows of the Scythian era which yielded quite a number of the gold and silver objects of the brilliant Greco-Scythian art and its rich jewelry. The Hermitage Museum in Saint Petersburg (Leningrad) became the main depository for these artifacts; it continues to attract throngs of sightseers in our day.

Closer to the end of the nineteenth century scholars became aware of the importance, for the study of Russian history, of archaeological exploration of the barrows and sites of old settlements in central, western, and northern Russia, in the area of habitation of East Slavic, Lithuanian, Finnish, and Turkish tribes. The Historical Museum in Moscow serves as an important center of antiquities of this type. For the Ukraine, the Kiev Museum of Art and Archaeology fulfills the same task. In addition, there is quite a number of provincial and local archaeological museums both in Russia and the Ukraine.

The rapid influx of antiquities into the Russian museums enabled the great Russian archaeologist Nikodim P. Kondakov to publish, in cooperation with Count Ivan I. Tolstoi, the first systematic survey of the archaeological aspects of Russian history, from the Scythian period down to the thirteenth century, under the title *Russkie drevnosti* (Russian antiquities, 6 vols. 1889-99). The First World War, the Russian Revolution of 1917, and the civil war in Russia (1918-20) could not but temporarily disrupt many cultural activities in Russia, including archaeological research. Many Russian archaeologists had to leave Russia to continue their work abroad. Among them, the distinguished historian and archaeologist Michael I. Rostovtzeff went to England and published there his convincing interpretation of the archaeological background of Russia in his remarkable book *The Iranians in South Russia* (1922). Later Rostovtzeff emigrated to the United States and became Sterling Professor at Yale University. (He died in 1952.)

In Russia, meanwhile, archaeological research was gradually resumed and its methods modernized. The political terror of the late 1930s painfully affected the work of Russian and Ukrainian archaeologists, a number of whom were imprisoned or exiled. Then came the devastating German invasion during which so many old Russian and Ukrainian monuments and museums were completely or partially destroyed. However, the war did not stop the work of Russian archaeologists in the eastern regions of Russia not immediately affected by the war. After the end of the Second World War, archaeological research in the Soviet Union vastly expanded, and many new excavations were made in a thorough way, following a systematic plan. While the interpretation of the finds given by the editors of recent Russian archaeological publications may not be convincing in some cases, the finds speak for themselves, and their importance is obvious.

As a result of all this archaeological work— past and present— our knowledge of Old Russia has grown substantially and continues to grow every year. We now know more of the Russian way of life in both the pre-Kievan and the Kievan periods than could have been dreamed of fifty years ago. It has become obvious that even in the early Middle Ages the Slavic civilization achieved a much higher level than had been supposed before. Moreover, the continuity of that civilization, from the Scythian age down to the Kievan period, is being made much clearer to us than before.

The products of archaeological research are obviously of immense importance for the study of Russian history, especially that of Old Russia. The main categories of antiquities made available for the observation of the historian may be sketchily summarized as follows:

> Antiquities illustrating the arrangement of old Slavic rural settlements, types of dwellings, barns, storerooms, bathhouses, furniture
> Remnants of city architecture (civil and military) such as foundations of buildings, towers, defense walls, bridges, wood pavement of the streets
> Funeral houses (for ashes of cremated bodies) and objects found in funeral mounds
> Monuments and remnants of monuments of religious architecture (heathen sanctuaries and old Christian churches)
> Antiquities illustrating agricultural and industrial activities (tools of various kinds, remnants of smithies and other workshops)
> Dress and ornaments
> Samples of old writing on tree bark and ceramics
> Paintings, mosaic, sculpture (mostly in bas-relief), wood carving, jewelry, enamels, glass, ceramics, embroidery
> Old musical instruments

Selected Bibliography

Field, Henry. "Contributions to the Anthropology of the Soviet Union." *Smithsonian Miscellaneous Collections*, vol. 110, no. 13. Washington: Smithsonian Institution, 1948.

Gimbutas, Marija. "The Prehistory of Eastern Europe," pt. 1. In *American School of Prehistoric Research*, bulletin no. 20. Cambridge: Peabody Museum, 1956.

Grabar, Igor. *Istoriia russkogo isskustva* [History of Russian art]. Vol. 1, 2d ed. Moscow: AN SSSR, 1953.

Grekov, B. D., and M. I. Artamonov, eds. *Istoriia kul'tury drevnei Rusi* [History of Old Russian culture]. 2 vols. Moscow: AN SSSR, 1948-51.

Hensel, Witold. *Slowianszczyzna wczesnosredniowieczna* [The Slavs in the early Middle Ages]. 2d ed. Warsaw: Panstwowe Wydawn. Naukowe, 1956.

Ianin, V. L. *Ia poslal tebe berestu* [I sent you a birchbark letter] (the story of the discovery and survey of the inscriptions on birchbark and of other objects of the eleventh to fifteenth centuries found in Novgorod in 1951-63). Moscow: Moskovskii Gos. Universitet, 1965.

In the land of Scythia to the westward dwells, first of all, the race of the Gepidae, surrounded by great and famous rivers. For the Tisia [Tisza, Theiss] flows through it on the north and northwest, and on the southwest is the great Danube. On the east it is cut by the Flutausis [Aluta, Olt], a swiftly eddying stream that sweeps whirling into the Ister's [Danube's] waters. Within these rivers lies Dacia, encircled by the lofty Alps as by a crown. Near their left ridge, which inclines toward the north, and beginning at the source of the Vistula, the populous race of the Venethi dwell, occupying a great expanse of land. Though their names are now dispersed amid various clans and places, yet they are chiefly called Sclaveni and Antes. The abode of the Sclaveni extends from the city of Noviodunum and the lake called Mursianus to the Danaster [Dniester], and northward as far as the Vistula. They have swamps and forests for their cities. The Antes, who are the bravest of these peoples dwelling in the curve of the Sea of Pontus, spread from the Danaster to the Danaper [Dnieper], rivers that are many days' journey apart.

. . .

. . . After the slaughter of the Heruli, Hermanaric also took arms against the Venethi. This people, though despised in war, was strong in numbers and tried to resist him. But a multitude of cowards is of no avail, particularly when God permits an armed multitude to attack them. These people, as we started to say at the beginning of our account or catalogue of nations, though off-shoots from one stock, have now three names, that is, Venethi, Antes, and Sclaveni. Though they now range in war far and wide, in consequence of our sins, yet at that time they were all obedient to Hermanaric's commands.

I:4. MAURICIUS ON THE SLAVS, CA. 600

In the reign of the Byzantine emperor Mauricius (582-602), a manual of the art of war (*Strategicon*) was written; some scholars attribute it to the emperor himself. The manual contains data on the organization, strategy, and tactics of the Byzantine army of that time and also gives information about the neighboring peoples with whom the Byzantines were at war, including the ancient Slavs. It is to them that the following comments refer.

Reference: A. V. Mishulin, ed., "Drevnie slaviane v otryvkakh greko-rimskikh i vizantiiskikh pisatelei po VII v. n. e.," *Vestnik drevnei istorii,* No. 14 (1941, no. 1), suppl., pp. 253-54.

Fragment 44

Numerous as these barbarians are, they lack military organization and unified leadership. Such are the Slavs and the Antes, as well as other barbarian tribes, who can neither obey nor fight in formation.

Fragment 45

The Slavic and Antian tribes are similar in their way of life, their customs, and their love of freedom. It is impossible by any means to force them into slavery or subordination in their own country. They are numerous and hardy, and they easily endure heat, cold, rain, nakedness, and lack of food. They are friendly to foreign visitors and, showing them tokens of favor, protect them whenever necessary [in their travels] from place to place. So that, should the foreigner suffer any harm because of the negligence of his host, his previous host goes to war [against the guilty one], considering it a debt of honor to avenge the stranger. They do not keep their captives in slavery indefinitely, as do other tribes, but, limiting [the term of slavery] to a definite period, they offer them a choice: to return home in exchange for a certain ransom or to remain [where they are] as free men and friends.

They have large quantities of livestock of all kinds and fruits of the land, piled up in heaps, especially millet and wheat.

The modesty of their women exceeds all human nature, so that most of them consider their husband's death their own and voluntarily strangle themselves since they do not regard widowhood as [a befitting way of] life.

They settle in forests, along impassable rivers, swamps, and lakes, and build their homes with many exits, because of the many dangers that naturally occur in their lives. They bury the things they need in secret places, do not openly possess any superfluous belongings, and lead a nomadic life.

. . .

Having no chief and warring among themselves, they do not recognize military formation and are incapable of fighting in regular battle or proving themselves in level and open places. If they happen to venture into battle, they move slowly forward in a body throughout its duration, yelling constantly; if the enemy is shaken by their yells, they advance strongly; otherwise, they turn to flight, reluctant to try their strength in hand-to-hand fighting with the enemy. Having a great ally in the woods, they withdraw there, since they are excellent fighters in narrow space. Often they will drop their booty [as if] in confusion and run into the woods; but then, when the attackers throw themselves upon the booty, they rise without difficulty and inflict damage on the enemy. All this they do with great skill in a variety of ways which they invent to lure the enemy.

Fragment 46

In general, they are deceitful and do not keep their word in regard to agreements; they are more easily subjugated by fear than by gifts. Since there is no unanimity of thought among them, they do not gather together; and if they should gather, then their decision is immediately broken by others, since they are all hostile toward one another, and none is willing to yield to the next one.

I:5. IBN-KHURDADHBIH ON THE ROUTE OF RUSSIAN MERCHANTS, CA. 846-847

Among early descriptions in Arabic of the Russians, that of Ibn-Khurdadhbih, in his "Book of Routes and Kingdoms," has this to say about the route of Russian merchants.

Reference: Tadeusz Lewicki, *Zrodla arabskie do dziejow slowianszczyzny*, vol. 1 (Wroclaw and Krakow: Wyd. Polskiej Akademii Nauk, 1956), pp. 76-77. For a useful collection of Russian translations of Arabic sources, see L. E. Kubvele and V. V. Matveeva, eds., *Arabskie istochniki VII-X vv.* (Moscow: AN SSSR, 1960).

[The Russians] are a tribe of Slavs. They bring furs of beavers and black foxes, as well as swords, from the most distant parts of the land of the Slavs to the Black Sea where the ruler of the Greeks collects the tithe [from their goods]. If they like, they go via the Slavic River [the Don] to Hamlih [on the Volga], a city of the Khazars, where the latter's ruler collects the tithe from them. Then they reach the Sea of Jurjan [the Caspian Sea] and land at the shore they like. . . . Sometimes they bring their wares on camels from Jurjan to Baghdad, where Slavic eunuchs serve as interpreters for them. They profess to be Christians, and they pay [only] the head tax.

I:6. IBN-RUSTA ON THE RUSSIANS, CA. 903-913

Ibn-Rusta was an Arab scholar who wrote early in the tenth century. Other accounts available to him at that time presumably formed the basis for these remarks of his about the Russians.

Reference: Carlile A. Macartney, *The Magyars in the Ninth Century* (Cambridge: At the University Press, 1930), pp. 213-15. Arabic text in "Kitab al-Alak an Nafisa," ed. M. J. de Goje, *Bibliotheca Geographorum Arabicorum*, vol. 7 (Leyden: E. J. Brill, 1892).

Russia is an island around which is a lake, and the island in which they dwell is a three days' journey through forests and swamps covered with trees and it is a damp morass such that when a man puts his foot on the ground it quakes owing to the moisture.

They have a king who is called Khaqan Rus, and they make raids against Saqlaba [the Slavs], sailing in ships in order to go out to them, and they take them prisoner and carry them off to Khazar and Bulkar [Bulgar] and trade with them there. They have no cultivated lands; they eat only what they carry off from the land of the Saqlaba.

When a child is born to any man among them, he takes a drawn sword to the newborn child and places it between his hands and says to him: "I shall bequeath to thee no wealth and thou wilt have naught except what thou dost gain for thyself by this sword of thine."

They have no landed property nor villages nor cultivated land; their only occupation is trading in sables and grey squirrel and other furs, and in these they trade and they take as the price gold and silver and secure it in their belts [or saddlebags].

They are cleanly in regard to their clothing,

and the men wear bracelets of gold. They are kind to their slaves and clothe them well for they engage in trade.

The Russians have many cities, and they expend much money on themselves. They honour their guests and are kind to strangers who seek shelter with them, and everyone who is in misfortune among them. They do not allow anyone among them to tyrannise over them, and whoever among them does wrong or is oppressive, they find out such a one and expel him from among them. They have Sulaymani swords, and when there is any call to war, they go out all together, and do not scatter, but are as one hand against their foes until they have conquered them.

If one of them has a complaint against another, he summons him before their king and they plead their case against each other, and if he settles their differences it will be as he wishes, but if they disagree with his opinion, he orders them to settle it with their swords, and whichever sword is the sharper will be victorious, and the two sets of kindred go out, and they two [both] take up their weapons, and the dispute is adjudged in favour of the one who gets the better of his friend.

. . .

These people are vigorous and courageous and when they descend on open ground, none can escape from them without being destroyed and their women taken possession of, and themselves taken into slavery. The Russians are strong and observant, and their raids are not made riding, but their raids and fights are only in ships.

. . .

When a great man among them dies, they erect for him a tomb like a spacious house, they place him in it and with him his body-clothes and the gold bracelets which he used to wear, and abundance of food and jars of wine and money also, and they place with him in the tomb his wife whom he loved, while she is still alive, and the door of the tomb is sealed upon her and she dies there.

I:7. MASUDI, CA. 956

Masudi, born in Baghdad, wrote his comprehensive treatise on history and geography around 956, drawing upon some earlier reports.

Reference: Avraam Ia. Garkavi, *Skazaniia musul'manskikh pisatelei o slavianakh i russkikh* (St. Petersburg, 1870), pp. 125, 129-31. See also Masudi, *Les Prairies d'Or*, text and trans. C. Barbier de Meynard and Pavet de Courteille, 9 vols. (Paris, 1861-77), 2: 9-12, 15, 18-25; 3: 61-65.

The Slavs are divided into many clans; some of them are Christians, but among them are also pagans, as well as sun worshipers.

. . .

As for the pagans dwelling in the land of the Khazar khaqan [emperor], some of their tribes are Slavs and Russians. They live in one of the two halves of this city [Itil] and burn their dead with their pack animals, weapons, and ornaments. When a man dies, his wife is burned alive with him; if the woman dies first, the husband is not burned; and if an unmarried man dies, he is given a spouse after death. Their women desire to be burned with their husbands so as to follow them to paradise.

. . .

The Khazar River has a branch that discharges into an inlet [the Sea of Azov] of the Sea of Naitas [Pontus], which is called a Russian sea; they (the Russians) are the only ones who sail on it and they live on one of its shores. They form a numerous nation, which submits neither to a king nor to a revealed religious law; among them are found merchants who maintain relations with the Bulgars. There is a silver mine in the land of the Russians. . . .

The Russians comprise many tribes. . . . After the three-hundredth year of the Hegira [A.D. 912-13] it happened that around five hundred [Russian] ships, each with a hundred men, entered the inlet of the Naitas which connects with the Khazar Sea [via the Don and the Volga]. . . .

After the Russian vessels arrived at the mouth of the canal, where Khazar men were stationed, they [the Russians] sent to the Khazar khaqan to ask that they be allowed to cross into his country, enter his river, and emerge into the Khazar [Caspian] Sea which laves the shores of Jurjan, Tabaristan, and other barbarian countries . . . on the condition that they give him half of everything they might plunder from the peoples living along this sea. He [the khaqan] agreed to this. Following this they entered the branch [the Don River] which they ascended to the river [Volga] itself. They sailed down it, passed the city of Itil, and reached the place where the river discharges into the Khazar [Caspian] Sea. [The expedition was successful, but on their way back the Russians were treacherously attacked by the Khazars and completely defeated.]

I:8: IBN-FADHLAN, CA. 922

This fragment is from Ibn-Fadhlan's "Report on the Mission to the Volga Bulgars," written in Arabic around 922.

Reference: Ignati Iu. Krachkovskii, ed., *Puteshestvie Ibn-Fadlana na Volgu* (Moscow: AN SSSR, 1939), p. 78.

I saw the Russians when they came for commerce and pitched their camp on the bank of the Atil River [the Volga]. Never did I see men with more perfect bodies than they. They resemble palm trees and are florid and ruddy. They wear neither jackets nor caftans. A man wears a garment of cloth which is thrown back on one side so that one of his hands remains free. Everyone carries a battle-ax, a sword, and a knife, and he never parts with these weapons. Their swords are broad, grooved, and of Frankish make.

I:9. THE BERTINIAN ANNALS CONCERNING RUSSIANS IN GERMANY, 839

The so-called *Annales Bertiniani* (Annals of Saint Bertin) deal with the years from 830 to 882. They were written by three different authors. The author of the part covering the period from 835 to 861 was the bishop of Troyes, Prudentius. The following excerpt is from the year 839.

Reference: G. Waitz, ed., *Annales Bertiniani* (Hannover: 1883), pp. 19-20.

There came [to Ingelheim] the Greek envoys sent by Emperor Theophilus. . . . He also sent with them certain men who said that they [i.e. their tribe] were called Rhos [Russians], and that their king, known as chacanus [kagan], had dispatched them to him [Theophilus], for the sake of friendship, as they had asserted. He [Theophilus] asked . . . that the emperor [Louis the Pious] allow them to return home across his possessions since the roads by which they had come to Constantinople were cut by wild and ferocious tribes and he [Theophilus] did not want them to face danger in case of returning by the same route. The emperor [Louis] investigated diligently the cause of their [the kagan's envoys'] coming and discovered that they were Swedes by origin.

I:10. PATRIARCH PHOTIUS ON THE RUSSIAN ATTACK ON CONSTANTINOPLE IN 860-861

In a sermon he delivered after the Russian departure, Patriarch Photius characterized their attack in these words.

Reference: A. A. Vasiliev, *The Russian Attack on Constantinople in 860* (Cambridge: Harvard University Press, 1946), p. 201.

Indeed [this disaster] does not resemble other inroads of barbarians; but the unexpectedness of the incursion and its extraordinary speed, the mercilessness of the barbarous race and the harshness of their temper and the savagery of their habits, prove that this blow has been sent from heaven like a thunderbolt. . . . They [the Russians] despoiled the surroundings and plundered the suburbs, cruelly massacred captives and safely established themselves around all this [city], showing in their greed for our wealth such conceit and arrogance that the inhabitants did not even dare to look on them with level and undaunted eyes. . . . [This people] poured upon our frontiers all at once, in the twinkling of an eye, like a billow of the sea, and destroyed the inhabitants on the earth, as the wild boar [destroys] grass or reed or crop.

I:11. PATRIARCH PHOTIUS ON THE ACCEPTANCE OF CHRISTIANITY BY SOME OF THE RUSSIANS, CA. 866

A few years after the Russian attack of 860-61, in a letter to the Oriental patriarchs, dated 867, Patriarch Photius of Constantinople included this optimistic report.

Reference: Vasiliev, *Russian Attack on Constantinople,* pp. 229-30.

[The Russians] have changed their Hellenic and godless religion for the pure and unadulterated faith of the Christians, and have placed themselves under the protection of the Empire, becoming good friends instead of continuing their recent robbery and daring adventures.

I:12. THE RUSSIAN PRIMARY CHRONICLE ON SAINTS CYRIL AND METHODIUS,
CA. 863 AND AFTER

The Russian Primary Chronicle (concerning which, see the section on Kievan Russia, below) gives this account of the ninth-century labors of Saints Cyril and Methodius. This story, with its theme of the cultural unity of the Slavs, seems to be of West Slavic (Moravian) origin and gives evidence of intellectual ties between the Western and Eastern Slavs in this period. Scholars remain uncertain about some of the details in this and other accounts, but all agree that Constantine (Saint Cyril) invented one of the two early Slavic alphabets, Glagolithic or Cyrillic (most, but not all, think it was the Glagolithic), and there is a consensus that he and his brother translated from the Greek the Gospels, the Psalter, and selected lections from the Acts and Epistles of the Apostles.

It should be noted that in this and the other excerpts from the Russian Primary Chronicle in this section, the expression *Rus',* which denotes both the land and the people, is translated "Russia" and "Russian," according to its meaning in each case, while the expression *Slovene,* with variations, is translated either "Slav," "Slavic," and so forth, or "Slovenian" (i.e. the tribe around Novgorod), depending on the connotation.

Reference: *PVL,* pt. 1, pp. 21-23; the English translation is taken, with slight changes, from *RPC,* pp. 62-63 (see List of Abbreviations).

There was at that time but one Slavic race, including the Slavs who settled along the Danube and were subjugated by the Magyars, as well as the Moravians, the Czechs, the Lyakhs [Poles], and the Polianians, the last of whom are now called Russians. It was for these Moravians that Slavic books were first written, and this writing prevails also among the Russians and the Danubian Bulgarians.

When the Moravian Slavs and their princes were living in baptism, the Princes Rostislav, Sviatopolk, and Kotsel sent messengers to the emperor Michael, saying, "Our nation is baptized, and yet we have no teacher to direct and instruct us and to interpret the Sacred Scriptures. We understand neither Greek nor Latin. Some teach us one thing and some another. Furthermore, we do not understand written characters nor their meaning. Therefore send us teachers who can make known to us the words of the Scriptures and their sense." The Emperor Michael, upon hearing their request, called together all the scholars and reported to them the message of the Slavic princes. . . . The emperor prevailed upon them [Constantine and Methodius] to undertake the mission and sent them into the Slavic country to Rostislav, Sviatopolk, and Kotsel. When they arrived [in 863], they undertook to compose a Slavic alphabet and translated the Acts and the Gospels. The Slavs rejoiced to hear the greatness of God extolled in their native tongue. The apostles afterward translated the Psalter, the Oktoechos, and other books.

Now some zealots began to condemn the Slavic books, contending that it was not right for any other nation to have its own alphabet, apart from the Hebrews, the Greeks, and the Latins, according to Pilate's superscription, which he composed for the Lord's cross. When the pope at Rome heard of this situation, he rebuked those who murmured against the Slavic books. . . . Constantine then returned again and went to instruct the people of Bulgaria, but Methodius remained in Moravia.

Prince Kotsel appointed Methodius bishop of Pannonia in the see of Saint Andronicus. one of the Seventy, a disciple of the holy apostle Paul. Methodius chose two priests who were very rapid writers and translated the whole Scriptures in full from Greek into Slavic in six months. . . . Now Andronicus is the apostle of the Slavic race. He traveled among the Moravians, and the apostle Paul taught there likewise. . . . Since Paul is the teacher of the Slavic race, from which we Russians too are sprung, even so the apostle Paul is the teacher of us Russians, for he preached to the Slavic nation and appointed Andronicus as bishop and successor to himself among them. But the Slavs and the Russians are one people, for it is because of the Varangians that the latter became known as Russians, though originally they were Slavs. While some Slavs were termed Polianians, their speech was still Slavic, for they were known as Polianians because they lived in the fields [*pole* means "field" in Russian]. But they had the same Slavic language.

I:13. CONSTANTINE'S PROLOGUE TO THE GOSPELS, CA. 863-867

The Moravian mission of Constantine the Philosopher and his brother Methodius—"the two Teachers of the Slavic Nation," as they were called—was an event of tremendous significance in the history of Slavic literature, religion, and culture in general. Owing to the Orthodox church policy of allowing the use of the vernacular in the church service, it was the Eastern Slavs for whom the legacy of Saints Cyril and Methodius proved the most fruitful. The motivation that underlay their work was expressed in Constantine's poem prepared as a prologue to the Slavic rendition of the Gospels. A portion follows.

Reference: Roman Jakobson, "Saint Constantine's Prologue to the Gospels," *Saint Vladimir's Seminary Quarterly*, n.s. vol. 7 (1963), pp. 14-19.

1. I am the Prologue to the Holy Gospels:
2. As the prophets prophesied of old—
3. "Christ comes to gather the nations and tongues,
4. Since He is the light of the world"—
5. So it has come to pass in this seventh millennium.
6. Since they have said, "The blind shall see,
7. The deaf shall hear the Word of the Book,
8. For it is proper that God be known."
9. Therefore hearken, all ye Slavs!
   · · ·
14. Matthew, Mark, Luke, and John
15. Teach all the people, saying:
16. "If you see and love the beauty of your souls,
    · · ·
22. Then hear now with your own mind,

23. Since you have learned to hear, Slavic people,
24. Hear the Word, for it came from God,
25. The Word nourishing human souls,
26. The Word strengthening heart and mind,
27. The Word preparing all to know God."
    · · ·
47. So that you will not have intellect without intelligence,
48. Hearing the Word in a foreign tongue,
49. As if you heard only the voice of a copper bell.
50. Therefore St. Paul has taught:
51. "In offering my prayer to God,
52. I had rather speak five words
53. That all the brethren will understand
54. Than ten thousand words which are incomprehensible."
55. What man will not understand this?

I:14. THE RUSSIAN PRIMARY CHRONICLE ON THE EXPANSION OF THE EASTERN SLAVS

The Russian Primary Chronicle gives this account of the territory and tribes of the Eastern Slavs, as well as of the trade route from the Varangians to the Greeks through Russia.

Reference: *PVL*, pt. 1, pp. 11-13; the English translation is based on *RPC*, pp. 52-55, somewhat revised.

Over a long period the Slavs settled beside the Danube, where the Hungarian and Bulgarian lands now lie. From among these Slavs, [tribes] scattered throughout the country and were known by appropriate names, according to the places where they settled. . . . Certain Slavs settled also on the Dnieper and were called Polianians. Still others were named Derevlians, because they lived in the forests. Some also lived between the Pripet' and the Dvina and were known as Dregovichians. Other tribes resided along the Dvina and were called Polotians, after a small stream called the Polota, which flows into the Dvina. . . . The Slavs also dwelt about Lake Il'men' and were known there by their [particular] name [Slovenians]. They built a city which they called Novgorod. Still others had their homes along the Desna, the Sem', and the Sula and were called Severians. Thus the Slavic race was divided, and its language was known as Slavic.

When the Polianians lived by themselves among the hills, a trade route connected the Varangians with the Greeks. Starting from Greece, this route proceeds along the Dnieper, above which a portage leads to the Lovat'. By following the Lovat', the great lake Il'men' is reached. The river Volkhov flows out of this lake and enters the great lake Nevo [Ladoga]. The mouth of this lake opens into the Varangian Sea. Over this sea goes the route to Rome, and on from Rome overseas to Tsar'grad ["Imperial City," i.e. Constantinople]. The Pontus, into which flows the river Dnieper, may be reached from that point. The Dnieper itself rises in the upland forest and flows southward. The Dvina has its source in this same forest but flows northward and empties into the Varangian Sea. The Volga rises in this same forest but flows to the east and discharges through seventy mouths into the Caspian Sea. It is possible by this route to the eastward to reach the Bulgars and the Caspians. . . . But the Dnieper flows through various mouths into the Pontus. This sea, beside which taught Saint Andrew, Peter's brother, is called the Russian Sea.

· · ·

The Polianians lived apart and were governed by their clans. For the Polianians had already existed even before the time of these brothers [to be mentioned presently], and

each one lived with his clan on his own place, belonging each to his clan. And there were three brothers, Kiy, Shchek, and Khoriv, and their sister was named Lybed'. . . . They built a town and named it Kiev after their elder brother. Around the town lay a wood and a great pine forest in which they used to catch wild beasts. These men were wise and prudent; they were called Polianians, and there are Polianians descended from them living in Kiev to this day.

· · ·

After the deaths of these three brothers, their clan assumed supremacy among the Polianians. The Derevlians possessed a principality of their own, as did also the Dregovichians, while the Slovenians had their own authority in Novgorod, and another principality existed on the Polota, where the Polotians dwell. Beyond them reside the Krivichians, who live at the headwaters of the Volga, the Dvina, and the Dnieper, and whose city is Smolensk. It is there that the Krivichians dwell, and from them are the Severians sprung. At Beloozero are situated the Ves', and on the Lake of Rostov, the Meria [i.e. Finnish tribes, along with the Chud'].

I:15. THE RUSSIAN PRIMARY CHRONICLE ON THE CUSTOMS OF THE EASTERN SLAVS

Reference: *PVL*, pt. 1, pp. 14-15; translation is based on *RPC*, pp. 56-57.

And the Polianians, the Derevlians, the Severians, the Radimichians, and the Croats lived at peace. The Dulebians dwelt along the Bug, where the Volynians now are found, but the Ulichians and the Tivertsians lived by the Dniester and extended as far as the Danube. There was a multitude of them, for they inhabited the banks of the Dniester almost down to the sea, and to this day there are cities in that locality which still belong to them. Hence they are called "Great Scythia" by the Greeks.

These Slavic tribes preserved their own customs, the law of their forefathers, and their traditions, each observing its own usages. For the Polianians retained the mild and peaceful customs of their ancestors and showed respect for their daughters-in-law and their sisters, as well as for their mothers and fathers. For their mothers-in-law and their brothers-in-law they also entertained great reverence. They observed a fixed custom, under which the groom's brother did not

fetch the bride, but she was brought to the bridegroom in the evening, and on the next morning her dowry was turned over.

The Derevlians, on the other hand, existed in bestial fashion and lived like cattle. They killed one another, ate every impure thing, and there was no marriage among them, but instead they seized upon maidens by the water. The Radimichians, the Viatichians, and the Severians had the same customs. They lived in the forest like any wild beast and ate every unclean thing. They spoke obscenely before their fathers and their daughters-in-law. There were no marriages among them, but simply festivals among the villages. When the people gathered together for games, for dancing, and for all other devilish amusements, the men on these occasions carried off wives for themselves, and each took any woman with whom he had arrived at an understanding. In fact, they even had two or three wives apiece. Whenever a death occurred, a funeral feast was held over the corpse, and then a great pyre was constructed, on which the deceased was laid and burned. After the bones were collected, they were placed in a small urn and set upon a post by the roadside, even as the Viatichians do to this day. Such customs were observed by the Krivichians and the other pagans, since they did not know the law of God but made a law unto themselves.

I:16. THE RUSSIAN PRIMARY CHRONICLE ON RIURIK'S INVITATION TO NOVGOROD, CA. 855

The story of Riurik's invitation to Novgorod was apparently compiled by the authors of the Russian Primary Chronicle on the basis of two different versions. According to one of these versions, the Russians were among the tribes who invited Riurik: "Said the Russians . . ." (*resha Rus'*). According to the other, Riurik himself belonged to the "Varangian Russians" (*Variagi-Rus'*). Because of this confusion, we find in some manuscripts, instead of "Said the Russians" (resha Rus'), the reading "Said [the other tribes] to the Russians" (resha Rusi). The basic codices (Laurentian and Hypatian) have resha Rus'. Concerning Riurik himself, a number of scholars identify him as Roric of Jutland, but there is no consensus on this point. As to the date of Riurik's arrival in north Russia, the actual year was probably around 855 rather than 862, the date given in the Chronicle.

Reference: *PVL,* pt. 1, p. 18; translation based in part on *RPC,* pp. 59-60.

The tributaries of the Varangians [in north Russia] drove them back beyond the sea and, refusing them further tribute, set out to govern themselves. There was no justice among them, but tribe rose against tribe. Discord thus ensued among them, and they began to make war one against another. They said to themselves, "Let us seek a prince who may rule over us and judge us according to the law." They accordingly went overseas to the Varangian Russians; these particular Varangians were known as Russians, just as some are called Swedes, and others Norsemen, English, and Gotlanders, for they were thus named. Said the Russians, the Chuds, the Slovenians, the Krivichians, and the Ves' [to the Varangians], "Our land is great and rich, but there is no order in it. Come to rule and reign over us." And three brothers, with their kinsfolk, chose [to come], took with them all the Russians, and migrated. The oldest, Riurik, located himself in Novgorod; the second, Sineus, at Beloozero; and the third, Truvor, in Izborsk. On account of these Varangians, the Russian land received its name. [As to] the Novgorodians, they are of Varangian origin although formerly they were Slovenians.

After two years, Sineus and his brother Truvor died, and Riurik assumed the sole authority. He assigned cities to his followers, Polotsk to one, Rostov to another, and to another Beloozero. In these cities there are thus Varangian colonists, but the first settlers were, in Novgorod, Slovenians; in Polotsk, Krivichians; at Beloozero, Ves'; in Rostov, Merians; and in Murom, Muromians. Riurik had dominion over all these districts.

Minns, Ellis H. *Scythians and Greeks*. Cambridge: At the University Press, 1913.
Niederle, Lubor. *Manuel de l'antiquité Slave*. 2 vols. Paris: E. Champion, 1923–26.
Rice, Tamara T. *The Scythians*. New York: Thames and Hudson, 1957.
Rostovtzeff, Michael I. *Iranians and Greeks in South Russia*. Oxford: Clarendon Press, 1922.
Rybakov, B. A. *Remeslo drevnei Rusi* [The handicraft of Old Russia]. Moscow: AN SSSR, 1948.

Reports of recent excavations and current archaeological research are published in Moscow in the *Kratkie Soobshcheniia* [Brief communications] of the Institute of the History of Material Culture (Academy of Sciences) and in the review *Sovetskaia Arkheologiia* [Soviet archaeology]. See also *Materialy i issledovaniia po arkheologii SSSR* [Materials and research on archaeology of the USSR], vols. 1 ff., Moscow: AN SSSR, 1940-.

I:2. PROCOPIUS ON THE SLAVS AND ANTES, MID-SIXTH CENTURY

Procopius of Caesarea was a noted Byzantine historian of the sixth century (d. after 560).

Reference: Procopius, *History of the Wars*, trans. H. B. Dewing, Loeb Classical Library, vol. 4, bk. 7 (Cambridge: Harvard University Press, 1924), pp. 269–73. For a recent collection of Russian translations of this and other Byzantine sources, see L. A. Freiberg, ed., *Pamiatniki vizantiiskoi literatury IV-IX vv. Sbornik perevodov* (Moscow: Nauka, 1968).

For these nations, the Sclaveni and the Antae, are not ruled by one man, but they have lived from of old under a democracy, and consequently everything which involves their welfare, whether for good or for ill, is referred to the people. It is also true that in all other matters, practically speaking, these two barbarian peoples have had from ancient times the same institutions and customs. For they believe that one god, the maker of the lightning, is alone lord of all things, and they sacrifice to him cattle and all other victims. ... They reverence, however, both rivers and nymphs and some other spirits, and they sacrifice to all these also, and they make their divinations in connection with these sacrifices. They live in pitiful hovels which they set up far apart from one another, but, as a general thing, every man is constantly changing his place of abode. When they enter battle, the majority of them go against their enemy on foot carrying little shields and javelins in their hands, but they never wear corselets. Indeed some of them do not wear even a shirt or a cloak, but gathering their trews up as far as their private parts they enter into battle with their opponents. And both the two peoples have also the same language, an utterly barbarous tongue. Nay further, they do not differ at all from one another in appearance. For they are all exceptionally tall and stalwart men, while their bodies and hair are neither very fair or blonde, nor indeed do they incline entirely to the dark type, but they are all slightly ruddy in colour. And they live a hard life, giving no heed to bodily comforts, just as the Massagetae do, and, like them, they are continually and at all times covered with filth; however, they are in no respect base or evildoers, but they preserve the Hunnic character in all its simplicity. In fact, the Sclaveni and Antae actually had a single name in the remote past; for they were both called Spori in olden times, because, I suppose, living apart one man from another, they inhabit their country in a sporadic fashion. And in consequence of this very fact they hold a great amount of land; for they alone inhabit the greatest part of the northern bank of the Ister [Danube].

I:3. JORDANES ON THE SLAVS, MID-SIXTH CENTURY

Jordanes, a Goth of Alanic origin, wrote in Latin in the middle of the sixth century.

Reference: Jordanes, *The Gothic History*, trans. C. C. Mierow (Princeton: Princeton University Press, 1915; photographically reprinted, Cambridge [Eng.] and New York, 1960), pp. 59–60, 84–85. The Latin text is in *Romana et Getica*, ed. T. Mommsen, *Monumenta Germaniae historica ...*, 4th ser., vol. 5, *Auctores Antiquissimi* (Berlin, 1882), and in E. Ch. Skrzhinskaia, ed., *Iordan* (Moscow: Izd. Vostochnoi Literatury, 1960), with Russian translation.

CHAPTER II

Kievan Russia
Tenth to Twelfth Centuries

Note: For the Kievan period of Russian history (tenth to twelfth centuries) the principal sources are the chronicles or annals which were kept in various princely and religious centers throughout Russia. Those annals that have survived seem to have based their account of events up to the early twelfth century upon one homogeneous account which is usually called "The Tale of Bygone Years" (Povest' vremennykh let), or the Russian Primary Chronicle. This narrative was compiled around the year 1110 by one or more persons associated with the Monastery of the Caves, near Kiev. The author or authors, and their informants, evidently possessed personal knowledge of political events from about 1050 to 1110. For events before 1050 the chronicle evidently was based upon oral tradition and upon still older records which have not been recovered. The chronicle has come down to us not in the original but in several versions copied at later dates. These differ somewhat, depending on the time, abilities, and circumstances of work of each monastic copyist. The oldest codex still extant was prepared in 1377. It is called the Laurentian version since it was transcribed by a monk named Lawrence, who performed this work for the prince of Suzdal'. The Laurentian codex belongs to the State Public Library in Leningrad. Another reliable version was preserved in the so-called Hypatian codex written in the early fifteenth century. The Hypatian codex belongs to the Academy of Sciences of the Soviet Union. (Originally it was in the library of the Hypatian Monastery in Kostroma.)

II:1. THE LAURENTIAN CHRONICLE CONCERNING OLEG'S ESTABLISHMENT IN KIEV IN 882 AND CAMPAIGN AGAINST BYZANTIUM IN 907

In the second excerpt below, concerning the Russo-Byzantine commercial convention of 907, we may suppose that the chronicler used a résumé of the document kept in the princely archives. (In this and subsequent selections the noun "Rus'" and its derivations—referring to the state and people associated with Kiev—have in most cases been translated simply as "Russia" and "Russian," but the editors do not necessarily imply thereby a verdict on the much-debated historiographical problems raised by this practice.)

Reference: *PVL*, pt. 1, pp. 20, 23–25; see also ibid., pp. 216–17 and 220–21, for a translation into modern Russian by D. S. Likhachev and B. A. Romanov, and pt. 2, pp. 252–54 and 262–70 for commentary by Likhachev. The present translation is based largely on *RPC*, pp. 61, 64–65, considerably revised.

[In the year 882] Oleg set himself up as prince in Kiev and declared: "May this be the mother of Russian cities." He had with him Varangians, Slavs [Slovenians of Novgorod], and others called Russians. Oleg began to build stockaded towns and imposed tribute on the Slovenians, the Krivichians, and the Merians. He commanded that Novgorod should pay the Varangians tribute in the amount of three hundred grivny a year for the sake of peace [i.e. to pay the Varangians not to attack Novgorod]. This tribute was paid to the Varangians until the death of Iaroslav.

. . . .

The year 6415 [from the supposed Creation; equivalent to A.D. 907]: Leaving Igor' in Kiev, Oleg set off against the Greeks. He took with him a multitude of Varangians, Slovenians, Chuds, Krivichians, Merians, Derevlians, Radimichians, Polianians, Severi-ans, Viatichians, Croats, Dulebians, and Tivertsians, who are famous as interpreters. All these tribes the Greeks called "Great Scythia." With this entire force, Oleg sallied forth by horse and by ship, and his vessels numbered two thousand. He arrived before Tsar'grad [Constantinople], and the Greeks closed [with a chain] the Sud [the harbor, at the Golden Horn] and locked up the city. Oleg disembarked upon the shore and began to wage war, and he accomplished much slaughter of the Greeks around the city, and [his troops] destroyed many palaces and burned churches. Of the prisoners they captured, some they beheaded, some they tortured, some they shot, and still others they threw into the sea. The Russians inflicted many other woes upon the Greeks after the usual manner of soldiers. Oleg commanded his warriors to make wheels and to place the ships upon them, and, when the wind was favorable, they raised the sails and bore down upon the city from the open plain. When the Greeks saw this they were afraid, and through messengers they said to Oleg: "Do not destroy the city. We agree to pay whatever tribute you desire." . . . So Oleg demanded that they pay tribute for his two thousand ships at the rate of twelve grivny per man, and there were forty men to a ship.

The Greeks assented to these terms and began to beg for peace lest Oleg should conquer the land of Greece. Oleg, retiring a short distance from the city, began peace talks with the Greek emperors Leo and Alexander and sent into the city to them Karl, Farlof, Velmud, Rulav, and Stemid, saying, "Pay the tribute." And the Greeks said: "Whatever you want, we will give you." Oleg demanded that they should give to the troops on the two thousand ships twelve grivny per oarlock and pay in addition tribute to the Russian cities: first Kiev, then Chernigov, Pereiaslavl' . . . and other towns, for in those cities lived great princes subject to Oleg.

[The Russians proposed the following terms:] "When Russians come here as emissaries they shall receive as much maintenance as they require. When they come as merchants they shall receive monthly allowances for six months, including bread, wine, meat, fish, and fruit [including vegetables]. Baths shall be prepared for them in any volume they require. When the Russians return homeward, they shall receive from your emperor food, anchors, cord-age, sails, and whatever else is needed for the journey."

The Greeks accepted these stipulations, and the emperors and all courtiers declared:

"If Russians come here without merchandise, they shall receive no provisions. Your prince shall personally forbid such Russians as journey here to do harm to our towns and our territory. Such Russians as come here shall dwell near Saint Mamas's Church. Our government will send officers who will record their names. After that they shall receive their monthly allowance, first the natives of Kiev, then those from Chernigov, Pereiaslavl', and the other cities. They shall enter the city through one gate only, unarmed and fifty at a time, escorted by an agent of the emperor. They may conduct as much trade as they need to without paying taxes."

Thus the emperors Leo and Alexander made peace with Oleg, and, after agreeing upon the tribute and mutually binding themselves by oath, they kissed the cross and invited Oleg and his men to swear an oath likewise. According to Russian custom, they swore by their weapons and by their god Perun, as well as by Volos, the god of cattle, and thus confirmed the treaty.

Oleg said: "Make sails of brocade for the Russians and canvas ones for the Slavs [the Novgorodians]," and this was done. Oleg hung his shield upon the gates as a sign of victory and then departed from Tsar'grad.

II:2. THE TREATY OF OLEG WITH BYZANTIUM AS TRANSMITTED IN THE LAURENTIAN CHRONICLE, 911

Reference: *PVL*, pt. 1, pp. 25-28, 222-24; pt. 2, pp. 272-78; translation based on *RPC*, pp. 65-68, with some revisions.

[In the year 911] Oleg sent his men to make peace and to draw up a treaty between the Greeks and the Russians. His envoys thus made this declaration:

"This is an exact copy of the treaty concluded under the emperors Leo and Alexander. We of the Russian nation—Karly, Inegeld, Farlof, Veremud, Rulav, Gudy, Ruald, Karn, Frelav, Ruar, Aktevu, Truan, Lidul, Fost, and Stemid—are sent by Oleg, the Russian grand prince [velikii kniaz' ruskii], and by all the serene and great princes and the great boyars under his sway, to you, Leo and Alexander and Constantine, great autocrats in God, emperors of the Greeks, for the maintenance and affirmation of the long-standing amity between Christians and Russians, in accordance with the desires of our great princes and at their command, and in behalf of all those Russians who are subject to [Oleg's] hand. . . . As we previously agreed in the name of God's peace and amity, the articles of this convention are as follows:

"First, that we shall conclude a peace with you Greeks, and love each other with all our heart and will, and, as far as lies in our power, prevent any subject of our serene princes from committing any fraud or crime. . . . May you Greeks on your part maintain henceforth and forever the same irrevocable and immutable amity toward our serene Russian princes and toward all the subjects of our serene prince.

"Concerning any crime that may occur, we agree as follows: . . .

"Any Russian who kills a Christian [i.e. a citizen of Byzantium] or any Christian who kills a Russian shall die at the place of the murder. If a man flees after committing a murder, and if he has property, the nearest relative of the victim shall receive a legal portion of his property, while the wife of the murderer shall receive as much as is legally due to her. But if the defendant is propertyless and has escaped, he shall remain under the court's jurisdiction until he returns, and then he shall be executed.

"If any man strikes another with a sword or assaults him with any other sort of weapon, he shall, according to Russian law, pay five pounds of silver for such blow or assault. If the defendant is propertyless, he shall pay as much as he is able and shall be deprived even of the very clothes he is wearing. Concerning the unpaid remainder he shall declare upon oath that he has no one to aid him. Thereafter the case against him shall be discontinued.

. . .

"Whenever it is necessary [for you] to go to war, and some Russians wish to serve your emperor, then, no matter how many of them come at such a time and wish to remain in the service of your emperor, their desire shall be granted."

II:3. THE TREATY OF IGOR' WITH BYZANTIUM AS TRANSMITTED IN THE LAURENTIAN CHRONICLE, 944

Reference: *PVL*, pt. 1, pp. 34-39; see also ibid., pp. 231-36, and pt. 2, pp. 289-94; translation based on *RPC*, pp. 73-77, somewhat revised.

[In the year 944] Roman [Romanos], Constantine, and Stephen sent envoys to Igor' to restore the former peace. Igor' spoke with them about peace and sent his own envoys to Roman. Roman called together his boyars and his dignitaries. The Russian envoys were introduced and bidden to speak, and it was commanded that the remarks of both parties should be inscribed upon parchment. A copy of the agreement concluded under the most Christian rulers Roman, Constantine, and Stephen follows:

"We are the envoys and merchants [gosti] from the Russian nation: Ivar, envoy of Igor', the Russian grand prince, and the general envoys [a list of about fifty mixed Slavic and Scandinavian names] . . . sent by Igor', the Russian grand prince, and by each prince and all the people of the Russian land; we [i.e. the envoys] have been instructed to renew the former peace, which has been violated for many years by the good-hating and discord-loving Devil, and to establish concord between Greeks and Russians.

"Our grand prince Igor', and his princes and his boyars, and the whole Russian people have sent us to Roman, Constantine, and Stephen, the mighty emperors of Greece, to establish a bond of friendship with the emperors themselves, as well as with all their boyars and the entire Greek nation forever,

as long as the sun shines and the world endures. . . ."

[The Greeks stipulated:] "The grand prince of Russia and his boyars shall send to the Greek land, to the great Greek emperors, as many ships as they desire with their envoys and merchants, according to the prevailing usage. The envoys heretofore carried gold seals, and the merchants silver ones. But your prince has now proclaimed that he will forward a certificate to our government, and any envoys or merchants thus sent by the Russians shall be provided with such a certificate to the effect that a given number of ships has been sent. By this means we shall be assured that they come with peaceful intent. . . . Your prince shall moreover prohibit his envoys and any Russians who come here from molesting our villages and territory. Such Russians as come here shall dwell in the vicinity of Saint Mamas's Church. Our authorities shall note their names, and they shall then receive their monthly allowance, the envoys the amount proper to their ambassadorial position, and the merchants the usual amount; first, those from Kiev, then those from Chernigov and Pereiaslavl' and from the other cities. They shall enter the city through one gate in groups of fifty without weapons, in the company of one of the emperor's men, and shall conduct as much trade as they need to, after which they shall depart. An officer of our government shall guard them, in order that, if any Russian or Greek does wrong, he may redress it. When the Russians enter the city . . . they shall not have the right to buy silk above the value of fifty bezants.

. . .

"Concerning the region of Kherson [i.e. the Crimea]: Whatever cities there are in that part of the country which is not under the authority of the Russian prince, let him wage war in those localities, and if a locality does not submit to him, then, if the Russian prince asks us for troops [to help him] to wage war, let me give him as many as he needs. [Note: The meaning of this passage is disputed. The foregoing translation is the one favored by Vernadsky, and is close to that supported by Shakhmatov. Cross gives the following: "In the matter of the country of Kherson and all the cities in that region, the prince of Rus' shall not have the right to harass these localities, nor shall that district be subject to you. If the prince of Rus' calls on us for soldiers wherewith to wage war, we agree to supply him with any number required." Likhachev supports the latter interpretation.]

. . .

"If Russians meet with Khersonian fishermen at the mouth of the Dnieper, they shall not harm them in any way. The Russians, moreover, shall not have the right to winter at the mouth of the Dnieper, either at Belobereg or by Saint Eleutherius, but when autumn comes they shall return home to Russia.

. . .

"If a Christian kills a Russian or a Russian a Christian, he who committed the murder shall be held by the relatives of the deceased,

and they shall kill him.

. . .

"If our government should desire of you troops for use against our enemies, we shall communicate with your grand prince, and he shall send us as many as we require. From this fact, other countries shall learn what amity the Greeks and the Russians entertain toward each other."

. . .

[The Russians thus bound themselves:] "Those of us who are baptized shall swear in the Cathedral Church of Saint Elias [in Kiev] upon the holy cross set before us, and upon this parchment, to abide by all that is written herein and not to violate any of its stipulations. And if any one of our compatriots, prince or any other, baptized or unbaptized, does so violate them, may he have no help from God, but may he be slave in this life and in the life to come, and may he die by his own weapons.

"The unbaptized Russians shall lay down their shields, their naked swords, their armlets, and their other weapons and shall swear to all that is inscribed upon this parchment, to be faithfully observed by Igor', by all his boyars, and by all the people from the land of Russia forever. If any of the Russian princes or subjects, whether Christian or non-Christian, violates the terms of this document, he shall merit death by his own weapons and be accursed of God and of Perun because he violated his oath. And if Prince Igor' confirms this treaty, then shall he maintain this righteous friendship, that it may never be broken now and forevermore, as long as the sun shines and the world endures."

II:4. THE LAURENTIAN CHRONICLE ON IGOR'S DEATH IN THE LAND OF THE DEREVLIANS, 945

Reference: *PVL*, pt. 1, pp. 39-40; see also ibid., pp. 236-37, and pt. 2, pp. 294-95; translation based on *RPC*, p. 78, considerably revised.

[A.D. 945:] In this year, Igor's retinue [druzhina] said to him, "Sveneld's servicemen are adorned with weapons and fine raiment, but we are naked. Go forth with us, Prince, after tribute [dan'], that both you and we may profit." Igor' heeded their words, and he attacked Dereva in search of tribute, and to the old tribute he added a new tribute and collected it by violence from the people, with the assistance of his followers. After thus

gathering the tribute, he departed for his city. On his homeward way, he said to his retinue after some reflection, "Go on home with the tribute. I shall turn back and collect some more." He let his retinue proceed on its journey homeward, and, with a few of his retainers, he turned back, seeking more booty.

The Derevlians, having heard that he was again approaching, consulted with Mal, their prince, saying, "If a wolf comes among the sheep, he will take away the whole flock one by one, unless he is killed. So it is with this man: if we do not kill him now, he will destroy us all." They then sent messengers to Igor', saying, "Why are you returning? You have collected all the tribute." But Igor' did not heed them, and the Derevlians, having come forth from the city of Iskorosten', slew Igor' and his retainers, for they were few.

II:5. CONSTANTINE PORPHYROGENITUS ON THE RUSSIANS, CA. 950

Emperor Constantine Porphyrogenitus (912-59), writing around 948-52, left this oft-quoted account of the process by which the Russians of the tenth century traveled from the Kievan hinterland to Constantinople.

Reference: Constantine Porphyrogenitus, *De administrando imperio,* Greek text ed. Gy. Moravcsik, Eng. trans. R. J. H. Jenkins (Budapest: Institute of Greek Philology of Peter Pazmany University, 1949), pp. 57-63. Republications of Jenkins's translation have been issued by Oxford University Press (1962) and Dumbarton Oaks Center (Harvard University, 1967).

Of the coming of the Russians
in single-straked ships from
Russia to Constantinople

The single-straked ships [i.e. dugouts] which come down from outer Russia to Constantinople are from Novgorod, where Sviatoslav, son of Igor, prince of Russia, had his seat, and others from the city of Smolensk and from Teliutza and Chernigov and from Busegrad. All these come down the river Dnieper, and are collected together at the city of Kiev, also called Sambatas. Their Slav tributaries, the so-called Krivichians and the Lenzanines and the rest of the Slavonic regions, cut the single-strakers on their mountains in time of winter, and when they have fastened them together, as spring approaches, and the ice melts, they bring them on to the neighboring lakes. And since these lakes debouch into the river Dnieper, they enter thence onto this same river, and come down to Kiev, and draw the ships along to be fitted out, and sell them to the Russians. The Russians buy these bottoms only, furnishing them with oars and rowlocks and other tackle from their old single-strakers, which they dismantle; and so they fit them out. And in the month of June they move off down the river Dnieper and come to Vitichev, which is a tributary city of the Russians, and there they gather during two or three days; and when all the single-strakers are collected together, then they set out, and come down the said Dnieper river. And first they come to the first barrage [rapids], called Essoupi, which means in Russian and Slavonic "Do not sleep!"; the barrage itself is as narrow as the width of the Polo-ground [in Constantinople]; in the middle of it are rooted high rocks, which stand out like islands. Against these, then, comes the water and wells up and dashes down over the other side, with a mighty and terrific din. Therefore the Russians do not venture to pass between them, but put in to the bank hard by, disembarking the men on to dry land but leaving the rest of the goods on board the single-strakers; they then strip and, feeling with their feet to avoid striking on a rock — . This they do, some at the prow, some amidships, while others again, in the stern, punt with poles; and with all this careful procedure they pass this first barrage, edging round under the river-bank. When they have passed this barrage, they re-embark the others from the dry land and sail away, and come down to the second barrage, called in Russian Oulvorsi, and in Slavonic Ostrovouniprach, which means "the Island of the Barrage." This one is like the first, awkward and not to be passed through. Once again they disembark the men and convey the single-strakers past, as on the first occasion. Similarly they pass the third barrage also, called Gelandri, which means in Slavonic "Noise of the Barrage," and then the fourth barrage, the big one, called in Russian Aeifor, and in Slavonic Neasit, because the pelicans nest in the stones of the barrage. At this barrage all put into land prow foremost, and those who are deputed to keep the watch with them get out, and off they go, these men, and keep vigilant watch for the Pechenegs. The remainder, taking up the goods which they have on board the single-strakers, conduct the slaves in their chains past by land, six miles, until they are through the barrage. Then, partly dragging their single-strakers, partly porting them on their shoulders, they convey them to the far side of the barrage; and then, putting them on the river and loading up their baggage, they embark themselves, and again sail off in them. When they come to the fifth barrage, called in Russian Varouforos, and in Slavonic Voulniprach, because it forms a large lake, they again convey their single-strakers through at the edges of the river, as at the first and second barrages, and arrive at the sixth barrage, called in Russian Leanti, and in Slavonic Veroutzi, that is "the Boiling of the Water," and this too they pass similarly. And thence they sail away to the seventh barrage, called in Russian Stroukoun, and in Slavonic Naprezi, which means "Little Barrage." This they pass at the so-called ford of Krarion, where the Chersonites cross over from Russia and the Pechenegs to Cherson; which ford is as wide as the Hippodrome [in Constantinople], and is as high from below up to where the friends of the Pechenegs survey the scene as an arrow might reach of one shooting from bottom to top. It is at this point, therefore, that the Pechenegs come down and attack the Russians. After traversing this place, they reach the island called St. Gregory, on which island they perform their sacrifices because a gigantic oak-tree stands there; and they sacrifice live cocks. Arrows, too, they peg in round about, and others bread and meat, or something of whatever each may have, as is their custom. They also throw lots regarding the cocks, whether to slaughter them, or to eat them as well, or to leave them alive. From this island onwards the Russians do not fear the Pecheneg until they reach the river Selinas. So then they start off thence and sail for four days, until they reach the lake which forms the mouth of the river, on which is the island of St. Aitherios. Arrived at this island, they rest themselves there for two or three days. And they re-equip their single-strakers with such tackle as is needed, sails and masts and rudders, which they bring with them. Since this lake is the mouth of this river, as has been said, and carries on down to the sea, and the island of St. Aitherios lies on the sea, they come thence to the Dniester river, and having got safely there they rest again. But when the weather is propitious, they put to sea and come to the river called Aspros, and after resting there too in like manner, they again set out and come to the Selinas, to the so-called branch of the Danube river. And until they are past the river Selinas, the Pechenegs keep pace with them. And if it happens that the sea casts a single-straker on shore, they all put in to land, in order to present a united opposition to the Pechenegs. But after the Selinas they fear nobody, but, entering the territory of Bulgaria, they come to the mouth of the Danube. From the Danube they proceed to the Konopas, and from the Konopas to Constantia, and from Constantia to the river of Varna, and from the Varna they come to the river Ditzina, all of which are Bulgarian territory. From the Ditzina they reach the district of Mesembria, and there at last their voyage, fraught with such travail and terror, such difficulty and danger, is at an end. The severe manner of life of these same Russians in winter-time is as follows. When the month of November begins, their chiefs together with all the Russians at once leave Kiev and go off on the "poliudie," which means "rounds," that is, to the Slavonic regions of the Vervians and Drugovichians and Krivichians and Severians and the rest of the Slavs who are tributaries of the Russians. There they are maintained throughout the winter, but then once more, starting from the month of April, when the ice of the Dnieper river melts, they come back to Kiev. They then pick up their single-strakers, as has been said above, and fit them out, and come down to Romania.

II:6. THE LAURENTIAN CHRONICLE ON SVIATOSLAV'S CAMPAIGNS, 964-971

Reference: *PVL*, pt. 1, pp. 46, 48, 50; see also ibid., pp. 244, 246, 248, and pt. 2, pp. 309, 314-15, 317, translation based on *RPC*, pp. 84, 86, 88, considerably revised.

In the year 6472 [964]: When Prince Sviatoslav had grown up and matured, he began to collect a numerous and valiant army. Stepping light as a leopard, he undertook many campaigns. On his expeditions he carried with him neither wagons nor kettles, and boiled no meat, but cut off thin slices of horseflesh, game, or beef, and ate them after roasting them over the coals. Nor did he have a tent, but he spread out a horse blanket under him, and he set his saddle under his head; and all his retine did likewise. He sent messengers to the other lands, saying, "I wish to march against you."

. . .

In the year 6477 [969]: Sviatoslav announced to his mother and his boyars, "I do not want to remain in Kiev but want to live in Pereiaslavets on the Danube, since that is the center of my realm and all merchandise is brought there: gold, silks, wine, and various fruits from Greece, silver and horses from Hungary and Czechia, and from Russia furs, wax, honey, and slaves."

. . .

In the year 6479 [971]: . . . Sviatoslav advanced against the Greeks, who came out to oppose the Russians. When the Russians saw them they were terrified at the multitude of the Greek soldiery. And Sviatoslav said, "Now we have no place to flee to—whether we want to or not, we must fight. Let us not disgrace the Russian land but rather die in battle, for being dead we shall suffer no dishonor. If we flee, we shall be disgraced. So let us not run away, but stand firmly, and I will march before you. If my head falls, then take care of yourselves." And his warriors replied, "Wherever your head falls, there we too will lay down our own." So the Russians took up battle positions, and the carnage was great. Sviatoslav came out the victor, and the Greeks fled.

II:7. THE LAURENTIAN CHRONICLE ON VLADIMIR AND THE CHRISTIANIZATION OF RUSSIA, 980-988

Vladimir's baptism may have taken place in Kiev rather than Kherson and in 989 rather than 988, but the story told here is nevertheless significant as a legend. (For Vladimir's church statute, see Item 20 in this chapter.)

Reference: *PVL*, pt. 1, pp. 56, 74-77, 80-81; see also ibid., pp. 254, 272-75, 279-80, and pt. 2, pp. 324-25, 335-37, 341; translation based on *RPC*, pp. 93, 110-13, 116-17, considerably revised.

[In the year 980] Vladimir began to reign alone in Kiev, and he set up idols on the hills outside the castle: one of Perun, made of wood with a head of silver and a moustache of gold, and others of Khors, Dazh'bog, Stribog, Simar'gl, and Mokosh'. The people sacrificed to them, calling them gods, and brought their sons and their daughters to sacrifice them to these devils. They desecrated the earth with their offerings, and the Russian land and this hill were defiled with blood.

. . .

In the year 6495 [987] Vladimir summoned together his boyars and the city elders and said to them, "Behold, the Bulgars came before me, saying, 'Accept our religion.' Then came the Germans and praised their own faith. After them came the Jews. Finally the Greeks appeared, disparaging all other faiths but praising their own, and they spoke at length, telling the history of the whole world from its beginning. Their words were wise, and it was marvelous to listen and pleasant for anyone to hear them. They preached about another world. 'Anyone,' they said, 'who adopts our religion and then dies shall arise and live forever. But anyone who embraces another faith shall in the next world be consumed by fire.' What is your opinion on this subject, and what do you answer?" The boyars and the elders replied, "You know, Prince, that no man condemns what is his own but praises it instead. If you desire to make certain, you have servants at your disposal. Send them to inquire about the ritual of each and how he worships God."

Their counsel pleased the prince and all people, so that they chose ten good and wise men.

[They visited foreign lands, and] then they returned to their country. The prince called together his boyars and the elders, and he said: "The envoys who were sent out have returned. Let us hear what took place." He said, "Speak in the presence of my retinue." The envoys then reported, "When we journeyed among the Bulgars, we observed how they worship in their temple. . . . Their religion is not good. Then we went among the Germans and saw them performing many ceremonies in their temples, and we saw no beauty there. Then we went to Greece, and the Greeks led us to where they worship their

God, and we did not know whether we were in heaven or on earth. For on earth there is no such splendor or such beauty, and we are at a loss to describe it. We know only that God dwells there among men, and their service is better than the ceremonies of other nations. For we cannot forget that beauty. Every man, after tasting something sweet, is afterward unwilling to accept that which is bitter, and therefore we can no longer remain here [in paganism]." Then the boyars said in reply, "If the Greek faith were evil, it would not have been adopted by your grandmother Olga, who was wiser than anyone else." Vladimir then responded, asking, "Where shall we accept baptism?" and they replied, "Wherever you wish." . . .

After a year had passed, in 6496 [988], Vladimir proceeded with an armed force against Kherson, a Greek city [by the Black Sea]. . . . [After a siege] the inhabitants . . . surrendered.

Vladimir and his retinue entered the city, and he sent messages to the emperors Basil and Constantine, saying, "Behold, I have captured your glorious city. I have also heard that you have an unwedded sister. Unless you give her to me in marriage, I shall deal with your own city as I have with Kherson." When the emperors heard this message they were troubled, and they issued this statement: "It is not proper for Christians to give women in marriage to pagans. If you are baptized, you shall have her for your wife, inherit the kingdom of God, and be our co-believer. If you do not do so, however, we cannot give you our sister in marriage." When Vladimir learned of their response, he said to the emperors' envoys, "Tell the emperors I will accept baptism, since I have already given some study to your religion, and the Greek faith and ritual, as described by the emissaries I sent to examine it, has pleased me well." When the emperors heard this report they rejoiced and persuaded their sister Anna [to consent to the match]. They then sent word to Vladimir, "Be baptized, and then we shall send you our sister." But Vladimir said, "Let your sister

herself come [with the priests] to baptize me." The emperors complied with his request and sent their sister, accompanied by some dignitaries and priests. . . . The bishop [episkop] of Kherson, together with the princess's priests . . . baptized Vladimir.

. . .

As a bride price in exchange for the princess, he gave Kherson back to the Greeks and then went back to Kiev.

When the prince arrived at his capital, he directed that the idols should be overturned and that some should be cut to pieces and others burned up. . . .

Thereupon Vladimir sent heralds throughout the whole city, proclaiming, "If anyone, whether rich or poor, beggar or slave, does not come tomorrow to the river, he will be an enemy of mine." When the people heard this they went gladly, rejoicing and saying, "If this were not good, the prince and his boyars would not have accepted it." On the morrow the prince went forth to the Dnieper with the priests of the princess and those from Kherson, and a countless multitude assembled. They all went into the water; some stood up to their necks, others to their breasts, and the younger up to their breasts near the bank, some people holding children in their arms, while the adults waded farther out. The priests stood by and offered prayers. There was joy in heaven and upon earth at the sight of so many souls saved. But the Devil groaned, "Woe is me! They are driving me out of here!" . . .

He [Vladimir] ordered that wooden churches should be built and established where [pagan] idols had previously stood. He founded the Church of Saint Basil on the hill where the idol of Perun and the other images had been set, and where the prince and the people had offered their sacrifices. He began to found churches, to assign priests throughout the cities and towns, and to bring people in for baptism from all towns and villages. He began to take the children of the best families and send them for instruction from books.

II:8. THE LAURENTIAN CHRONICLE ON IAROSLAV THE WISE, 1019-1054

Concerning Iaroslav's rise to power in Kiev, see Item IV:1. Iaroslav's church statute is given at the end of the present chapter, Item II:21. See also Iaroslav's Pravda Russkaia, Item II:18, below.

Reference: *PVL*, pt. 1, pp. 102-03, 108; see also ibid., pp. 302-03, 308, and pt. 2, pp. 374-77, 387-89; translation based on *RPC*, pp. 137-38, 142-43, considerably revised.

In the year 6545 [1037], Iaroslav built the great citadel [at Kiev], near which stands the Golden Gate. He built also the metropolitan Church of Sancta Sophia, the Church of the Annunciation over the Golden Gate, and also the Monastery of Saint George and [the Convent of] Saint Irene. During his reign the Christian faith began to bear fruit and to spread; the number of monks [*chernoriztsy*] began to increase, and new monasteries came into being. Iaroslav loved the religious way of life and was devoted to priests, especially to monks. He applied himself to books, often reading them day and night. He assembled many scribes, and they translated from Greek into Slavic. They wrote many books through which true believers receive pleasure in religious education. For as one man plows the land, and another sows, and still others reap and eat food in abundance, so it was in this case. His father Vladimir plowed and softened [harrowed] the soil, that is, enlightened the [Russian] land through baptism, while this prince sowed the hearts of the faithful with the written word, and we in turn reap the harvest by receiving the teaching of books.

Great is the profit from the study of books. Through the medium of books we are shown and taught the way of repentance, for we gain wisdom and self-restraint from the written word. Books are like rivers that water the whole earth; they are the springs of wisdom. For books have an immeasurable depth; by them we are consoled in sorrow. . . . He who often reads books converses with God or with saints. From reading the words of the prophets, the teachings of the evangelists and the apostles, and the lives of the holy fathers, our souls will derive great profit.

Thus Iaroslav, as we have said, was a lover of books, and, having written [or transcribed] many, he deposited them in the Church of Sancta Sophia which he himself had founded. He adorned it with gold and silver and religious vessels. . . . He founded other churches in the cities and other localities, appointing priests and paying them out of his personal fortune, and directing them to teach the people, since that is the duty God has assigned to them, and to go often into the churches. And priests and Christian laymen increased in number.

. . .

In the year 6562 [1054], Iaroslav, the Russian grand prince, passed away. While he was still alive, he admonished his sons, saying, "I am about to leave this world, my sons. Love one another, since you are brothers by one father and mother. If you maintain love among yourselves, God will dwell among you and will vanquish your enemies for you, and you will live in peace. But if you live in hatred and dissension, quarreling with one another, then you yourselves will perish, and you will ruin the land of your ancestors, which they won at the price of great effort. Therefore remain at peace, brother heeding brother. The throne of Kiev I bequeath to my eldest son, your brother Iziaslav. Obey him as you have obeyed me, so that he may take my place among you. To Sviatoslav I give Chernigov, to Vsevolod Pereiaslavl', to Igor' the city of Vladimir [in Volynia], and to Viacheslav Smolensk." Thus he divided the cities among them, commanding them not to violate one another's boundaries and not to oust one another [from their respective thrones]. He told Iziaslav: "If anyone begins to harm his brother, help the one being wronged." And thus he admonished his sons to dwell in harmony.

II:9. METROPOLITAN HILARION'S EULOGY OF PRINCE VLADIMIR, CA. 1050

An eloquent appraisal of the significance of Russia's conversion to Christianity is contained in this eulogy, which Hilarion (or Ilarion) delivered in the Church of the Dormition (the so-called Church of the Tithe, which Vladimir built and where he was buried) in the presence of Vladimir's son Iaroslav, sometime between 1037 and 1050. From 1051 to 1054 Hilarion was metropolitan of Kiev. Vladimir was officially canonized only in the thirteenth century, ca. 1263. The eulogy comes from the "Sermon on Law and Grace" (Slovo o zakone i blagodati) which, although unsigned and extant only in manuscripts dating from the fourteenth century, has been traced by scholars to Metropolitan Hilarion.

Reference: A. I. Ponomarev, ed., *Pamiatniki drevnerusskoi tserkovno-uchitel'noi literatury*, pt. 1 (St. Petersburg, 1894), pp. 69-71, 73, 75. For a translation of another version of the sermon, see Serge A. Zenkovsky, ed. and trans., *Medieval Russia's Epics, Chronicles, and Tales*

(N.Y.: Dutton, 1963), pp. 78-83. Recently the sermon has been published in Russian with English annotations and glossary in John L. I. Fennell and Dimitri Obolensky, eds., *A Historical Russian Reader. A Selection of Texts from the XIth to the XVIth Centuries* (Oxford: At the Clarendon Press, 1969), pp. 1-20, 154-58.

Let us, too, lift our feeble voices to praise with all our might him who has done great and wonderful things, our teacher and preceptor, the great kagan of our land, Vladimir, grandson of old Igor' and son of the glorious Sviatoslav, who in the years of their reign were renowned in many countries for their courage and bravery and are even now remembered and esteemed. Not in a poor or unknown land did they reign, but in the Russian [land], which is known and heard of in every corner of the earth. . . . His was the great deed of ordering all throughout his land to be baptized in the name of the Father and of the Son and of the Holy Ghost, and to praise the Holy Trinity clearly and loudly in all the towns, and to be Christians all, great and small, slaves and freemen, young and old, rich and poor; and [he ordered] that none should oppose his pious command, even if some were baptized not in love but in fear of their ruler, since his orthodoxy was conjoined with power; and all at once our entire land glorified Christ with the Father and with the Holy Ghost. Then the darkness of idolatry began to leave us, and the dawn of orthodoxy arose; then the blackness of demon worship lifted and the sun of the Gospels shone over our land; the heathen temples were destroyed and churches were erected; idols were cast down and icons of the saints appeared; the devils fled; the cross cast its sanctity over the towns; and the shepherds of the figurative sheep of Christ took their stand, bishops and presbyters and deacons, bringing out the uncontaminated Sacrifice; and the clergy decorated and adorned the holy churches in splendor.

· · ·

What great praise goes to you, who have not only confessed that Christ is the Son of God but have also established the faith through-

out this land, and erected churches of Christ, and brought in His ministers, as did the great Constantine, whom you equaled in wisdom, in love for Christ, and in honoring His ministers. He [Constantine], together with the holy fathers of the Nicean Council, prescribed the law for men; while you often gathered and took counsel in great humility with our new fathers, the bishops, asking how to establish the law among these newly cognizant men.

· · ·

Arise, revered ruler, from your grave; arise, shake off sleep, for you are not dead but only sleeping until the general resurrection. Arise, for you are not dead; it is not fitting for you to die, you who have believed in Christ, the life of all the world. Shake off sleep, lift your eyes, that you may see what honor the Lord has here bestowed upon you in preserving your memory on earth through your son [Iaroslav the Wise]. Arise, see your child Georgii [Iaroslav the Wise], see your scion, see your beloved, see him whom the Lord has drawn forth from your loins; see him gracing the throne of your land, and rejoice and be glad. See too your daughter-in-law Irina, true in her faith; see your grandchildren and great-grandchildren, how they live, how the Lord protects them, how they maintain the true faith according to your testament, how they frequent the holy churches, how they glorify Christ, how they bow before His name. See how the city shines in majesty, see how the churches flourish, see how Christianity spreads, see how the city glitters, illumined by the icons of the saints and fragrant with incense, and resounding with praise and divine holy singing; and having seen all these things, rejoice and be glad and praise the good God, the creator of all these things.

II:10. THE LAURENTIAN CHRONICLE ON THE MONASTERY OF THE CAVES, IN KIEV, FROM CA. 1054

Other accounts, including the *Life of Theodosius*, by Nestor, differ from the following account in some details. For example, it appears that Antonius died in 1072 or 1073 and hence could hardly have spent even twenty years in his crypt, let alone forty.

Reference: *PVL*, pt. 1, pp. 105-07; see also ibid., pp. 305-07, and pt. 2, pp. 383-86; translation based on *RPC*, pp. 140-42, somewhat revised.

[The chronicle recounts that before Hilarion was named metropolitan in Kiev in 1051, his favorite place of prayer was a small cave about ten feet deep which he had dug in the bank overlooking the Dnieper, just south of Kiev. Shortly after Hilarion's elevation, the chronicle goes on, there came to Kiev a certain Antonius, who had recently taken monastic vows at Mount Athos in Greece.] Antonius came to Kiev and reflected on where he should live. He went about the monasteries and liked none of them, since God did not so will, and subsequently wandered about the woods and hills seeking the place that God would show him. He finally came to the hill where Hilarion had dug the little cave, and he liked this site. . . . He took up his abode there, praying to God, eating dry bread every other day, drinking water moderately, and digging the cave. He gave himself rest neither day nor night but endured in his labors, in vigil, and in prayer. . . . When Grand Prince Iaroslav died, his son Iziaslav came to power and was installed in Kiev. Antonius was celebrated throughout the Russian land. Iziaslav, having learned of his manner of life, came with his retinue to request his blessing and prayers. The great Antonius was thus known and revered by everyone. Brethren began to join him, and he welcomed and tonsured them. Brethren gathered about him to the number of twelve, and they dug a large cave, and a church, and cells, which exist to this day in the crypt under the old monastery. . . . So he appointed Varlaam as their prior [*igumen*], and he himself went to the hill, where he dug a crypt which is under the new monastery, and in which he ended his life, enduring in virtue and for the space of forty years never going out of the crypt in which his bones lie to the present day. . . .

God began to augment the number of the brotherhood . . . and the brethren took counsel with the prior about constructing a monastery. . . . Antonius rejoiced and . . . sent one of the brotherhood to Prince Iziaslav with the message, "My Prince! Behold, God strengthens the brotherhood, but their abode is small. Give us therefore the hill which is above the cave." When Iziaslav heard this he rejoiced, and sent one of his men, and gave them the hill. The prior and the brethren founded there a great church and fenced in the monastery with a palisade. They constructed many cells, completed the church, and adorned it with icons. Such was the origin of the Monastery of the Caves, which was so named because the brethren first lived in a cave. The Monastery of the Caves thus issued from the benediction of the Holy Mount [Athos]. . . . Many monasteries have indeed been founded by emperors and nobles and rich men, but they are not such as those founded by tears, fasting, prayer, and vigil. . . .

When Varlaam had departed to Saint Demetrius' . . . the brethren, being twenty in number, appointed Theodosius to be their prior. When Theodosius took over the monastery, he began to practice abstinence, fasting, and tearful prayer. He undertook to assemble many monks and thus gathered together brethren to the number of one hundred.

He also interested himself in searching out the monastic rules. There was in Kiev at the time a monk from the Studion Monastery [in Constantinople] named Michael, who had come from Greece with Metropolitan George [the second successor of Hilarion], and Theodosius inquired of him [Michael] concerning the practices of the Studion monks. He obtained their rule from him, copied it out, and established it in his monastery. . . . From this monastery all others adopted the same regulations. Therefore the Monastery of the Caves is honored as the oldest of all.

II:11. THE LAURENTIAN CHRONICLE ON THE FIRST KIEVAN REVOLUTION, 1068

As the last line of this excerpt suggests, this "revolution" brought little change in the political structure of the Kievan state.

Reference: *PVL*, pt. 1, pp. 112, 114-15; see also ibid., pp. 312, 314-15, and pt. 2, pp. 397-99; translation based on *RPC*, pp. 146-49, considerably revised.

In the year 6576 [1068], foreigners—a multitude of Polovtsians—invaded the Russian land. Iziaslav, Sviatoslav, and Vsevolod went forth against them on the Al'ta [a confluent of the Trubezh, an eastern tributary of the Dnieper below Kiev]. . . . The Russian princes fled and the Polovtsians were victorious.

. . .

When Iziaslav, accompanied by Vsevolod, had fled to Kiev, while Sviatoslav had taken refuge in Chernigov, the men of Kiev who had escaped to their native city held a veche [assembly] in the marketplace and sent word to the prince: "The Polovtsians have spread over the country. Give us arms and horses, Prince, so that we may fight them again." Iziaslav, however, paid no heed to this request. Then the people began to murmur against his general [voevoda], Constantine. From the place of the veche they mounted the hill and arrived before the house of Constantine. Not finding him, they then . . . said: "Let's free our friends from the prison." They then separated into two parties: half of them went to the prison and half . . . went to the prince's palace. As Iziaslav was sitting with his retinue on his balcony, the crowd standing below began to threaten him. As the prince and his retainers were watching the crowd from a small window, Tuky, the brother of Chudin, remarked to Iziaslav: "Look, Prince, the people are aroused; men had better be sent to guard Vseslav [of Polotsk, who had been captured after a war against Iziaslav]." While he was thus speaking, the other half of the crowd approached from the prison, which they had thrown open. . . . The mob then gave a shout and went to Vseslav's dungeon. When Iziaslav saw this, he fled with Vsevolod from the palace. So the people freed Vseslav from his dungeon —this was on September 15—and set him up in the midst of the prince's palace. The palace itself they pillaged, seizing a huge amount of gold and silver in coins and other articles of value. Iziaslav fled to Poland [where he could seek asylum with his cousin, Boleslaw the Bold].

. . .

And Vseslav ruled in Kiev for the space of seven months.

II:12. THE LAURENTIAN CHRONICLE ON THE REVOLT OF THE PAGANS IN NOVGOROD, 1071

Reference: *PVL*, pt. 1, pp. 120-21; see also ibid., p. 321, and pt. 2, pp. 405-06; translation based on *RPC*, p. 154, considerably revised.

[In the year 1071], during the rule of Gleb [as prince] in Novgorod, a magician [*volkhv*] appeared. He conversed with the people, representing himself as a god, and deceived many of them, almost the entire city. For he claimed to be able to prophesy all things, and he blasphemed against the Christian faith, announcing, "I will walk across the Volkhov River in the presence of everyone." There was finally an uprising in the city, and everyone believed in him, and they wanted to murder their bishop. But the bishop took his cross, and clad himself in his vestments, and stood forth, saying, "He who wants to believe in the magician, let him follow him, but he who is a true believer [in Christianity], let him come to the cross." So the people were divided into two factions; Gleb and his retainers took their stand beside the bishop, while the common people all followed the magician. And there was a great conflict between them.

Then Gleb, having taken an ax under his cloak, approached the magician and asked, "Do you know what is to happen tomorrow and what before evening?" The magician replied, "I know everything." Then Gleb asked, "Do you then know what is to happen to you today?" The magician answered, "I shall perform great miracles." But Gleb, pulling out the ax, cleaved him so that he fell dead, and the people dispersed.

II:13. THE LAURENTIAN CHRONICLE ON THE DEVASTATION OF RUSSIA BY THE CUMANS, CA. 1093

The following passage appears in the Laurentian Chronicle under the year 1093, but it apparently relates to conditions during a span of years toward the close of the eleventh century, when the Cumans or Polovtsians were ravaging Kievan Russia.

Reference: *PVL*, pt. 1, pp. 146-47; see also ibid., pp. 347-48; translation based on *RPC*, pp. 178-79, considerably revised.

We are punished for our sins; we suffer in proportion to our misdeeds. All our cities and villages are laid waste. We traverse the meadows where horses, sheep, and cattle once grazed in herds and see them desolate. The fields are grown wild and have become the lairs of wild beasts. . . .

The Polovtsians harried widely and then returned to Torchesk ["Turk town," apparently on the edge of Polovtsian territory, near the river Ros', about sixty-five miles south of Kiev]. The inhabitants were weakened by hunger and therefore surrendered to the enemy. The Polovtsians, upon taking the city, destroyed it by fire, divided up the inhabitants among themselves, and led them away to their tents to their relatives and kin. A multitude of Christian people were thus led away to an unknown land, sorrowing, tormented, stiff with cold, hungry and thirsty and miserable, their faces pinched and their bodies black, their tongues inflamed, naked and barefoot, their feet pierced with thorns.

II:14. THE LAURENTIAN CHRONICLE ON THE MEETINGS OF PRINCES AT LIUBECH (1097) AND DOLOBSK (1103)

The Laurentian Chronicle here recounts instances of princely cooperation in the Kievan state. The Liubech meeting is significant for the relationship between princes and territorial units; the Dolobsk meeting illustrates one kind of quasi-parliamentary council. (Concerning Kiev's relations with Novgorod at this time, see Chapter IV, Section A.)

Reference: *PVL*, pt. 1, pp. 170-71, 183-84; see also ibid., pp. 372-73, 385-86, and pt. 2, pp. 459-60, 467-68; translation based on *RPC*, pp. 187-88, 200, somewhat revised.

In the year 6605 [1097], Sviatopolk, Vladimir [Monomakh], David, son of Igor', Vasilko, son of Rostislav, David, son of Sviatoslav, and Oleg his brother met at Liubech [on the Dnieper about ninety miles north of Kiev] to make peace. They said to one another, "Why do we ruin the Russian land by quarreling with one another? The Polovtsians plunder our country and rejoice that we wage war among ourselves. Let us rather hereafter be united in spirit and watch over the Russian land, and let each of us guard his own domain—Sviatopolk retaining Kiev, the heritage of Iziaslav, while Vladimir holds the domain of Vsevolod, and David, Oleg, and Iaroslav between them possess that of Sviatoslav. Let the domains apportioned by Vsevolod stand, leaving the city of Vladimir [in Volynia] in the hands of David, while the city of Peremyshl' belongs to Volodar', son of Rostislav, and Vasilko, son of Rostislav, holds Terebovl'." On this covenant they kissed the cross: "If any one [of us] should hereafter attack another, then all the rest, with the aid of the holy cross, will be against the aggressor." Thus they all said, "May the holy cross and the entire Russian land be against him," and having taken the oath, returned each to his domain. Accompanied by David, Sviatopolk arrived in Kiev, and all the people rejoiced. Only the Devil was distressed by this agreement.

. . .

In the year 6611 [1103], God inspired the hearts of the Russian princes Sviatopolk and Vladimir [Monomakh], and they met for consultation at Dolobsk [on the east bank of the Dnieper, opposite Kiev]. Sviatopolk with his retinue and Vladimir with his own took their seats in the same tent. The retainers of Sviatopolk began the discussion, and remarked, "It is not advisable to go on campaign now, in the spring, since [by mobilizing the peasants' horses for the campaign] we will ruin the peasants and their plowing." Vladimir then replied, "I am surprised, comrades, that you concern yourselves for the horses with which the peasant plows. Why do you not bear in mind that as soon as the peasant begins his plowing, the Polovtsian will come, shoot him down with his arrow, seize his horse, ride on into his village, and carry off his wife, his children, and all his property? Are you concerned for the horse and not for the peasant himself?"

Sviatopolk's retainers could find no answer, and Sviatopolk himself said, "I am already prepared [to fight]," and he stood up. And Vladimir said to him, "Then you will be doing a great service to the Russian land." They then sent to Oleg and David, saying, "Go [with us] against the Polovtsians, whether we emerge dead or alive." David accepted, but Oleg refused, explaining, "I am in poor health." Vladimir then embraced his cousin, and proceeded to Pereiaslavl', followed by Sviatopolk, David, son of Sviatoslav, David, son of Vseslav, Mstislav, grandson of Igor', Viacheslav, son of

Iaropolk, and Iaropolk, son of Vladimir.
They advanced on horseback and by boat.

[The expedition ended in victory over the Polovtsians.]

II:15. THE HYPATIAN CHRONICLE ON THE KIEVAN REVOLUTION OF 1113

This is an account of the accession, by the people's demand, of one of Old Russia's most revered rulers. (Concerning the Hypatian Chronicle or codex, see the note at the beginning of this chapter.)

Reference: *PVL*, pt. 1, pp. 196-97; see also ibid., pp. 398-99, and pt. 2, pp. 477-80; translation based on *RPC*, pp. 319-20, somewhat revised.

Thus on April 16 [1113] near Vyshgorod [just upstream from Kiev], Sviatopolk [son of Iziaslav] passed away. He was brought on a boat to Kiev, where they adorned his body and laid it on a sledge [i.e. for the funeral ceremonies]. . . . On the morrow, April 17, the inhabitants of Kiev took counsel and sent word to Vladimir [Monomakh]: "Come, Prince, and ascend the throne of your ancestors." On hearing their message, Vladimir wept and refused to accept, mourning for his brother. But the men of Kiev plundered the palace of Putiata the tysiatskii [thousandman] and attacked and plundered the Jews. The citizens of Kiev then again sent messengers to Vladimir, saying, "Come, Prince, to Kiev; and if you do not come, know that much evil will occur. For it will not be merely a matter of robbing the palace of Putiata, or the hundredmen [*sotskii*], or even the Jews, but they will attack your sister-in-law and the nobles and the monasteries, and if they plunder the monasteries, you will be responsible for it." When Vladimir heard this, he went to Kiev.

. . . Vladimir Monomakh arrived at Kiev on Sunday and was met with great honor by Metropolitan Nicephorus, the bishops, and all the inhabitants. He thus assumed the throne of his father [Vsevolod] and his ancestors, and all the people rejoiced, and the rioting was quelled.

II:16. VLADIMIR MONOMAKH'S TESTAMENT, CA. 1115

This set of instructions from Vladimir Monomakh to his sons is found in the Russian Primary Chronicle under the year 1096, but it probably was written about twenty years later.

Reference: *PVL*, pt. 1, pp. 153, 155, 157-58, 162-63; see also ibid., pp. 354, 356, 358-59, 363-64, and pt. 2, pp. 425-39, 450-54; cf. *RPC*, pp. 206, 208, 210-11, 214-15 (translation considerably revised). Recently this document was published in Russian with English annotations and a glossary in Fennell and Obolensky, eds., *Historical Russian Reader*, pp. 52-62, 165-72.

I, wretched man that I am . . . named at baptism Vasilii and with the Russian name Vladimir . . . sitting upon my sledge [i.e. "as I approach death"], have meditated in my heart and praised God, who has guided me, a sinner, even to this day. Let not my sons or anyone else who happens to hear this document laugh at its contents. But rather let any one of my sons who likes it take my words to heart and not be lazy, but work hard.

First, for the sake of God and your own souls, retain the fear of God in your hearts and give alms generously, for such liberality is the root of all good.

. . .

Our Lord has shown us how to vanquish and overcome through three good deeds: repentance, tears, and almsgiving.

. . .

Above all things, do not forget the poor but feed them to the extent of your means. Give alms to the orphan, protect the widow, and do not permit the mighty to destroy anyone. Do not kill [execute] the just or the unjust person or permit him to be killed. Do not destroy any soul even if he deserves death. . . . Whenever you kiss the cross to your brothers or anyone else . . . then take care not to violate your oath, lest you destroy your souls. Receive with affection the blessing of bishops, priests, and priors, and do not shun them, but rather, according to your means, love and help them, so that you may receive from them their prayers . . . [for help] from God. Above all things admit no pride in your hearts and minds. . . . Honor the old as your father, and the young as your brothers.

Do not be lazy in your own households, but keep watch over everything. Do not depend upon your steward or your servant lest they who visit you ridicule your house or your table. When you set out to war, do not be lazy, do not depend upon your voevody [commanders], do not indulge yourself in drinking, eating, or sleeping. Set the sentries yourselves, and at night go to sleep only after you have posted them on all sides of your troops, and get up early. Do not put down your weapons without a quick glance about you, for a man may thus perish suddenly through his own carelessness. Guard against lying, drunkenness, and lechery, for thus perish soul and body. When journeying anywhere [probably meaning "in the collecting of tribute"] through your domain, do not permit your attendants or anyone else's to damage the villages or the fields, lest men curse you. Wherever you go and wherever you stay, give food and drink to the needy. Furthermore, honor the visitor, if not with a gift, at least with food and drink, wherever he comes from and whether he is a commoner, a nobleman, or an ambassador; for travelers spread the word everywhere as to whether a man is good or bad.

Visit the sick and walk in funeral processions, for we are all mortal. Pass no man without a greeting; give him a kindly word. Love your wives, but grant them no power over you. Most important for you is to hold the fear of God above everything else.

. . .

Do not forget what useful knowledge you possess, and learn what you do not know, just as my father [Vsevolod I], though he remained at home in his own country, still learned five languages. For by this means honor is acquired in other lands. Laziness is the mother of all evil; what a man knows, he forgets, and what he does not know, he does not learn. In the practice of good works, you cannot neglect whatever pertains to good conduct. . . .

Let not the rising sun find you in your bed. . . . [First, say morning prayers.] Then sit and deliberate with your retinue, or render justice to the people, or ride out for hunting. . . . Sleep is decreed by God for noontime, since birds and beasts and men then rest from their labors.

I now narrate to you, my sons, the fatigue I have endured on journeys and hunts ever since the age of thirteen [he was born in 1053].

. . .

Among all my campaigns there are 83 long ones, and I do not count the minor adventures. I concluded 19 peace treaties with the Polovtsians both while my father was living and since then. . . .

I devoted much energy to hunting as long as I reigned in Chernigov. . . . At Chernigov, I even bound wild horses with my bare hands. . . . Two aurochs tossed me and my horse on their horns, a stag once butted me, an elk stamped upon me and another butted me with his horns, a boar once tore my sword from my thigh, a bear on one occasion bit the saddlecloth beside my knee, and another wild beast jumped on my thigh and knocked over my horse with me. But God preserved me unharmed. . . .

In war and at the hunt, by night and by day, in heat and in cold, I did whatever my servant had to do, and gave myself no rest. Without relying on governors [posadniki] or bailiffs [birichi], I did whatever was necessary; I looked after things myself and did the same in my own household. At the hunt I posted the hunters, and I looked after the stables, the falcons, and the hawks. I did not allow the mighty to distress the common peasant [smerd] or the poverty-stricken widow, and I interested myself in the church administration and service.

Let not my sons or whoever else reads this disparage me, for I am not praising my own boldness, but I praise God and glorify his mercy because he guarded me, a sinful and wretched man, for so many years. . . . Without fear of death, or war, or wild beasts, do a man's work, my sons, as God sets it before you. . . . None of you can be harmed or killed unless that is destined by God. But if death comes from God, then neither father, nor mother, nor brothers can prevent it, and though it is prudent to be constantly upon one's guard, the protection of God is better than the protection of man.

II:17. THE HYPATIAN AND SUZDALIAN CHRONICLES ON THE VECHE OF KIEV IN 1146-1147

The following excerpts illustrate the role of the people's assembly or veche (often alluded to as simply "the people") in twelfth-century Kiev, first in accepting a prince, then in ousting him, and then in aiding the new prince against his enemies, the princes of Chernigov. The first version is from the Kievan Chronicle of the mid-twelfth century, as brought to us in the Hypatian codex of the early 1400s. The second is from the Suzdalian (hence north Russian) Chronicle of about 1200 and later, as copied by the monk Lawrence about 1377. (Concerning the veche in Novgorod, see Chapter IV.)

Reference: Arkheograficheskaia Komissiia, ed., *Letopis' po Ipatskomu spisku* (St. Petersburg, 1871), pp. 229-30; *PSRL,* vol. 1, pt. 2, 2d ed. (1927), cols. 313-14, 316-17 (see List of Abbreviations).

[From the Kievan Chronicle:]
[A.D. 1146:] Vsevolod [ruling prince of Kiev] came to Kiev and fell sick, and sent for his brothers Igor' and Sviatoslav, and was very sick and encamped on an island near Vyshgorod [just north of Kiev]; and Vsevolod summoned [prominent] Kievans and began to speak: "I am very sick; here is my brother Igor'; accept him [as prince]." They said: "Gladly, Prince, will we accept him." And they took Igor' to Kiev; he went with them to Ugorskoe [a suburb of Kiev] and called all the people of Kiev together; and they all kissed the cross to him, saying, "You shall be our prince," but they accepted him deceitfully; on the following day Igor' went to Vyshgorod, and the people of Vyshgorod kissed the cross to him. . . . On the following day Vsevolod departed this life, on the first day of the month of August [1146], and they prepared his body and buried it in the Church of the Holy Martyrs [Boris and Gleb]. Igor' went to Kiev and called all the people of Kiev together on the hill in the courtyard of the palace of Iaroslav [*Iaroslavl' dvor*], and they kissed the cross to him; and the people of Kiev assembled again at the Turov temple and sent for Igor', saying: "Prince, come to us." Igor' took his brother Sviatoslav and went to them, and encamped with his druzhina [retinue], and sent his brother Sviatoslav to them at the veche. And the people of Kiev began to cast accusations against Vsevolod's tiun [judge] Ratsha and against the other tiun, Tudor of Vyshgorod, saying: "Ratsha has brought Kiev to ruin, and Tudor, Vyshgorod; but now, Prince Sviatoslav, kiss the cross to us for your brother, that if any of us suffers injury, you shall render justice." Sviatoslav said to them: "I kiss the cross for my brother, that you shall not be oppressed in any way, and that you shall have the tiun whom you desire." Sviatoslav dismounted and

swore to this upon the cross to them at the veche; the people of Kiev dismounted and began to say: "Your brother shall be prince and you also." And the people of Kiev all kissed the cross to this, with their children [i.e. including adult offspring of the household heads who were in the veche], so that they would engage in no deceit under the rule of Igor' and Sviatoslav. And Sviatoslav took Kievan men of quality [*luchshie muzhi*] and went with them to his brother Igor' and said: "Brother, I have kissed the cross to them that you shall rule them justly and love them." Igor' dismounted and swore to them upon the cross to everything they and his brother had agreed upon, and went to dine. They [the people of Kiev] set forth to pillage Ratsha's house and attack the *mechniki* [assistants of the tiun]; and Igor' sent his brother Sviatoslav to them with the druzhina, and [the druzhina] were barely able to restrain [the people]. . . . And Igor' did not suit the people of Kiev, and they sent to Pereiaslavl' [an important city about fifty miles southeast of Kiev] for Iziaslav, saying: "Come to us, Prince, we want you." When he heard this, Iziaslav [grandson of Vladimir Monomakh] assembled his troops and went against him [Igor'] from Pereiaslavl'. . . . The people of Belgorod and Vasilev [small towns near Kiev to the southwest and south] sent to him . . . saying: "Come and be our prince; we don't want the Olgovichi" [i.e. sons of Oleg; Igor' and his brother Vsevolod were sons of Oleg of Chernigov]; at the same time men came from the Kievans, saying: "Come and be our prince; we don't want to be the legacy of the Olgovichi; we are ready to go with you wherever your banner flies."

[From the Suzdalian Chronicle:]
[A.D. 1146:] And Igor' entered Kiev and did not suit the people, and they sent to

Pereiaslavl' for Iziaslav [son of Mstislav, grandson of Vladimir Monomakh], saying: "Come, Prince, we want you." And hearing this, Iziaslav took pity and went with his druzhina and with the people of Pereiaslavl'. . . . And Iziaslav entered Kiev, praising and glorifying God for helping him thus; and there came forth to greet him a multitude of people, and abbots [igumeni] with monks, and priests from the entire city of Kiev in their vestments; and four days later they seized Igor' in a swamp and brought him before him [Iziaslav], and he sent him to a monastery . . . and thrust him in a dungeon, in the Monastery of Saint John, and put guards to guard him; and thus ended the rule of Igor'.

.   .   .

[A.D. 1147:] Iziaslav [prince of Kiev] . . . sent two men ahead, Dobrynka and Radilo, to his brother Vladimir and to Lazar' the tysiatskii in Kiev, with the message: "Brother, go to the metropolitan and call all the Kievans together; let these men tell of the deceit of the princes of Chernigov." And Vladimir went to the metropolitan, summoning the Kievans; and a great multitude of Kievans came, seating themselves before [the Cathedral of] Sancta Sophia [to listen]. And Vladimir said to the metropolitan: "My brother has sent two Kievan men; let them speak to their brethren." And Dobrynka and Radilo came forward and said: "Your brother greets you, and bows to the metropolitan, and greets Lazar' and all the Kievans." And the Kievans said: "Tell us why the prince has sent you." They spoke: "Thus said the prince: 'The Davydovichi [sons of David] and Sviatoslav Vsevolodich have kissed the cross to me, and for them I have done many good things; and now they wanted to kill me by deceit, but God, and the most holy cross upon which they swore to me, have spared me; and now, brethren, you should come to me, to Chernigov, on horseback or, lacking horses, by boat; for they did not want to kill me alone, but to destroy you also.'" The Kievans said: "The prince summons us to Chernigov, but we have here the prince's enemy and ours [i.e. Igor', languishing in prison]; we wish to kill him, and [then] we wish to go with our children [i.e. those of military age but not participating in the veche] and fight for our prince." [And the crowd of resentful Kievans killed Igor'.]

II:18. THE PRAVDA RUSSKAIA OR RUSSIAN LAW OF THE ELEVENTH CENTURY

The Pravda Russkaia, in the so-called Short Version, is the earliest comprehensive document of Russian jurisprudence. It contains a section issued by Iaroslav the Wise (1019-54) and a supplement approved by his sons at a meeting in Vyshgorod in 1072. In later centuries these two parts were copied together. The earliest copies still extant, like the one used for this translation, date from the 1400s. (The *Dictionary of Russian Historical Terms* explains the monetary terms used in this and other documents.)

Reference: George Vernadsky, *Medieval Russian Laws* (New York: Columbia University Press, 1947), pp. 26-35. Russian text in Boris D. Grekov, ed., *Pravda Russkaia*, vol. 1 (Moscow: AN SSSR, 1940), pp. 70-73; and in *PRP*, 1:77-85 (see List of Abbreviations). The translation has been slightly revised. (The Vernadsky volume also exists in reprints of 1965 and 1969.)

[Iaroslav's Pravda:]

ARTICLE 1. If a man kills a man [the following relatives of the murdered man may avenge him]: the brother is to avenge his brother; the son, his father; or the father, his son; and the son of the brother [of the murdered man] or the son of his sister [their respective uncle]. If there is no avenger, [the murderer pays] 40 grivny wergild. Be [the murdered man] a [Kievan] Russian—a palace guard, a merchant, an agent, or a sheriff—be he an izgoi [i.e. of alien stock], or a [Novgorodian] Slav, his wergild is 40 grivny. . . .

ART. 5. If [anyone] cuts [another's] arm, and the arm is cut off or shrinks, 40 grivny. . . .

ART. 7. If a finger is cut off, 3 grivny for the offense.

ART. 8. And for the moustache, 12 grivny; and for the beard, 12 grivny.

ART. 9. He who unsheathes his sword, but does not strike, pays 1 grivna. . . .

ART. 12. If anyone rides another's horse without asking the owner's permission, he has to pay 3 grivny.

ART. 13. If anyone takes another's horse, or weapon, or clothes, and [the owner] identifies [the object] within his township, he receives it back and 3 grivny for the offense. . . .

ART. 17. And if a slave [*kholop*] strikes a freeman and hides in [his master's] house, and his master is not willing to give him up, the master has to pay 12 grivny, and the offended freeman beats the slave whenever he finds him.

[The Pravda of Iaroslav's Sons:]

[PREAMBLE.] The Law of the Russian land enacted when [the princes] Iziaslav, Vsevolod, Sviatoslav, [and their councillors] Kosniachko Pereneg, Nikifor the Kievan, [and] Chudin Mikula met together [presumably in 1072].

ART. 19. If they kill the [prince's] bailiff, deliberately, the [actual] murderer has to pay 80 grivny [as bloodwite or *vira*], and the guild is not liable. And for the prince's adjutant, 80 grivny.

ART. 20. And if the bailiff is killed in a highway attack, and they do not search for the murderers, that guild within the boundaries of which the body has been found has to pay the bloodwite. . . .

ART. 23. And for the master of the stable, 80 grivny, as constituted by Iziaslav in the case of his master of the stable whom the Dorogobuzhians killed.

ART. 24. And for [the murder of] the prince's farm manager as well as of the field overseer, 12 grivny.

ART. 25. And for the contract laborer on princely estates, 5 grivny.

ART. 26. And for a peasant, or a herdsman, 5 grivny. . . .

ART. 29. And if anyone abducts another man's male or female slave, he has to pay 12 grivny for the offense. . . .

ART. 33. And if they inflict pain on a peasant without the prince's order, 3 grivny for the offense; and for the bailiff, and the assistant steward, and the sheriff, 12 grivny.

ART. 34. And if anyone plows beyond the boundary [of his property] or beyond a hedge, 12 grivny for the offense.

II:19. THE PRAVDA RUSSKAIA OF THE TWELFTH CENTURY

The Pravda Russkaia in its Expanded Version is a twelfth-century revision of the earlier one, plus the statute of Vladimir Monomakh (prince in Kiev, 1113-25) and other supplementary ordinances. Vladimir Monomakh's additions reflect the reforms he initiated when he came to power after the revolt in Kiev. In other respects, too, the Expanded Version suggests some of the social and economic changes in the Kievan state of the eleventh and twelfth centuries. The present translation is based on a copy that dates from the 1200s.

Reference: Vernadsky, *Medieval Russian Laws*, pp. 35-56. Russian text in Grekov, *Pravda Russkaia*, 1:104-17, and in *PRP*, 1:108-37. Translation slightly revised.

[The Expanded Version:]

ARTICLE 1. If a man kills a man [the following relatives of the murdered man may avenge him]: the brother is to avenge his brother, or the father [his son], or the son [his father]; or the son of the brother, or the son of the sister [their respective uncle]. If there is no avenger the wergild is set at the amount of 80 grivny in case [the murdered man] was a prince's councillor or a prince's steward; if he was a [Kievan] Russian—a palace guard, a merchant, a boyar's steward, or a sheriff— or if he was an izgoi, or a [Novgorodian] Slav, [the wergild is] 40 grivny.

ART. 2. And after Iaroslav his sons, Iziaslav, Sviatoslav, and Vsevolod, and their councillors, Kosniachko Pereneg and Nikifor, met in a conference and canceled the [custom] of blood revenge, and [instead ordered] composition of [the crime] by money. And as to anything else, all that Iaroslav had decreed, his sons confirmed accordingly. . . .

ART. 3. If anyone kills a prince's man in a highway attack, and the [local people] do not search for the murderer, the guild within the territory where the body lies has to pay the bloodwite [which, for the prince's official, is] 80 grivny, and for a commoner, 40 grivny.

ART. 4. And if a guild [*verv'*] has to pay a "dark" bloodwite [i.e. for an unknown offender], its members [are allowed] to pay [in installments] for several years, since they pay on behalf of [an unknown] murderer. . . .

ART. 11. And [the wergild] of the prince's page, or groom, or [man] cook is 40 grivny.

ART. 12. And for the palace steward and the stable steward, 80 grivny.

ART. 13. And for the farm steward or the field overseer, 12 grivny.

ART. 14. And for a contract laborer, 5 grivny; and as much for a boyar's contract laborer. . . .

ART. 15. And for the handicraftsman or handicraftswoman, 12 grivny.

ART. 16. And for a peasant or a slave, 5 grivny; and for a female slave, 6 grivny. . . .

ART. 21. And if [the defendant] is unable to produce witnesses but [in his turn] accuses his accuser of the homicide, let them be given an ordeal by iron.

ART. 22. And the same refers to all lawsuits, including theft and other accusations. If the [stolen] thing is not produced, give him [that is, the plaintiff] [ordeal by] iron even against his will [in case the amount of the damages] is over one half of a grivna gold. If [the amount] is less [than a half grivna gold] but over 2 [silver] grivny, [the ordeal is] by water. And if the amount is less [than 2 silver grivny], then let him [the plaintiff] take the oath concerning his money. . . .

ART. 35. . . . If the guilty one is a horse thief, he shall be surrendered to the prince for banishment; if he is a house thief, he pays 3 grivny [to the prince]. . . .

ART. 46. If slaves, be they the prince's or the boyars' or the monasteries', happen to be thieves, the prince does not fine them since they are not freemen, but they are to pay double for the offense to the plaintiff. . . .

ART. 49. If anyone stores his goods at another's house, there is no need of witnesses; but if he extends claims for a large amount, he who stored the goods has to swear [as follows]: "You stored at my house such and such volume only." Because [he who accepted goods for storage] did a favor to [the owner of the goods] and kept them safe. . . .

ART. 50. If anyone lends money [kuny] at interest [rez], or honey or grain on accruement, he has to produce witnesses; he receives interest or accruement according to the rate agreed upon. . . .

ART. 51. As to the monthly interest, [the lender] shall collect it on short-term [loans] only; if the money has been used for a year, let him [the lender] receive the interest at the third-of-the-year rate, and the monthly rate interest is annulled. . . .

[Vladimir Monomakh's Statute:]

ART. 53. After the death of [Prince] Sviatopolk, [Prince] Vladimir [Monomakh], son of Vsevolod, called his councillors [for a meeting] at Berestov. . . . [The following were present:] Ratibor, tysiatskii of Kiev; Prokopii, tysiatskii of Belgorod; Stanislav, tysiatskii of Pereiaslavl'; Nazhir; Miroslav; and Ivanko Chudinovich, of [Prince] Oleg's retinue. And they ordered that he who lends money at third-of-the-year rates be limited by the third collection of interest. If he has collected interest for two [third-of-the-year] terms, he receives [also] his money back; but if he has collected interest for three terms, he cannot get his money back. . . .

ART. 54. If a merchant with another's money in his hands is shipwrecked or loses [his goods] in war or in fire, they should not apply pressure on him, nor sell his entire property, but let him repay [the lender] in yearly installments; because his ruin is from God, and he is not guilty. If he squanders another's goods on drink or [wrecks them] in a brawl, or damages them through his foolishness, then the lenders may choose: if they so wish, they wait for their goods; if not, they sell his entire property.

ART. 55. If anyone is indebted to many creditors, and there comes a merchant from another town, or a foreigner, and without knowing [of the man's indebtedness] lends him goods, and he will not pay him and [if when the last lender claims his money back] the former lenders object to his being satisfied first, they [all the lenders] shall bring the man to the marketplace and sell his entire property. From the proceeds, they shall first repay the [out-of-town or foreign] merchant, and the balance shall be divided among his hometown creditors. If the prince's money was involved, they shall first pay the prince, and the balance shall be divided among the others. And he who had [already] collected much interest, [now] receives nothing. . . .

ART. 56. If an indentured laborer [zakup] runs away from his lord, he becomes the latter's slave. But if he departs openly, to sue for his money [and goes] to the prince, or to the judges, to complain of the injustice on the part of his lord, they shall not reduce him to slavery but give him justice. . . .

ART. 59. If the lord offends the indentured laborer and seizes his money or his movables, he has to return all this and pay 60 kuny for the offense. . . .

ART. 61. If the lord sells the indentured laborer into slavery, the laborer is free from all obligations for the money [he had received from the lord], and the lord pays a 12-grivna fine for the offense.

ART. 62. If the lord beats the indentured laborer for good reason, he is without fault; but if he beats the indentured laborer foolishly, being drunk, and without any fault on the part of the indentured laborer, he has to pay for the offense to the indentured laborer the same fine as it would be for a freeman. . . .

ART. 65. And if a slave [kholop] strikes a freeman and hides in the house, and his lord will not surrender him, the lord pays for him a 12-grivna [fine]; and then whenever and wherever the injured man meets the offender who struck him, [Prince] Iaroslav ordered [to allow him] to kill the offender, but his sons, after their father's death, ordered the matter to be settled with the alternative of payment: either to bind the slave [to a post] and beat him, or to accept 1 grivna for the offense to his honor. . . .

ART. 66. And the slave cannot serve as a witness; however, at need, when there is no freeman, a boyar's steward [even if he is a slave] may be a witness, but no other [slave]. And in a minor litigation, at need, an indentured laborer may serve as a witness. . . .

ART. 72. If anyone cuts an apiary boundary [hedge], or plows through a field boundary, or bars [another's] yard boundary by paling, a 12-grivna fine.

ART. 73. If anyone cuts a landmark oak, a 12-grivna fine. . . .

ART. 78. If a peasant inflicts pain on another peasant without the prince's authorization, a 3-grivna fine, and 1 grivna of kuna [amends] for the pain. If he inflicts pain on the prince's bailiff, a 12-grivna fine, and 1 grivna [amends] for the pain. . . .

ART. 83. If anyone sets fire to a threshing court, he is to be banished and his house confiscated; first, the damages are paid, and the prince takes care of the rest. The same for setting fire to anyone's homestead. . . .

ART. 85. In all the above litigations the trial is with freemen as witnesses. If the witness is a slave, he is not to take [a direct] part in the trial. . . .

ART. 88. If anyone kills a woman, he is to be tried in the same way as if he killed a man. If he is found guilty [he shall pay] one half of the bloodwite, 20 grivny.

ART. 89. And there is no bloodwite for either a male or a female slave; but if a slave is killed without any fault of his, [the killer] has to pay amends for the male as well as for the female slave; and to the prince, a 12-grivna fine. . . .

ART. 90. If a peasant dies [without male descendants], his estate goes to the prince; if there are daughters left in the house, each receives a portion [of the estate]; if they are married, they receive no portion. . . .

ART. 91. In regard to the boyars and the members of the princely retinue, the estate does not go to the prince, but, if there are no sons left, the daughters inherit.

ART. 92. If anyone, before dying, makes a settlement dividing his estate between his children, his will stands. If he dies without a will, the estate is divided between his children [in equal shares], except for a portion which goes [to a monastery] for prayers for the soul [of the deceased]. . . .

ART. 110. Full slavery [kholopstvo obel'no] is of three kinds: [first] if anyone buys [a man] willing [to sell himself into slavery], for not less than half a grivna, and produces witnesses and pays [the fee of] 1 nogata in the presence of the slave himself. And the second kind of slavery is this: if anyone marries a female slave without special agreement [with her lord]; if he marries her with a special agreement, what he agreed to stands. And this is the third kind of slavery: if anyone becomes [another's] steward or housekeeper without a special agreement; if there has been an agreement, what has been agreed upon stands.

ART. 111. The recipient of a [money] grant is not a slave. And one cannot make a man one's slave because [he received] a grant-in-aid in grain, or [failed to furnish] additional grain [when repaying the grant]; if he fails to complete the term of work [for the grant], he has to return the grant; if he completes the term, he stands cleared. . . .

ART. 117. If anyone authorizes his slave to trade and the latter falls in debt, the owner redeems him but does not lose him.

II:20. THE CHURCH STATUTE OF SAINT VLADIMIR, CA. 988-1015

This selection presents the basic articles of the statute of Prince (and later Saint) Vladimir (who ruled Kievan Russia from 977 or 980 to 1015) concerning relations between church and state. The text has come down to us in six variants. The earliest extant manuscript copy, which is used here, dates from the thirteenth century.

Reference: *PRP*, 1:244-46.

Statute of the Saint Prince Vladimir,
Who Baptized the Russian Land,
on the Church Courts

1. In the name of the Father and the Son and the Holy Ghost.

2. I, Prince Vasili, called Vladimir, son of Sviatoslav, grandson of Igor' and of the blessed Princess Olga, received the holy baptism from the Greek emperor [and from the patriarch].
. . .

3. Within [a few] years I erected the Church of the Holy Virgin [in Kiev] and granted to that church, all over the Russian land, the tithe of all princely court fees . . . of all market sales . . . and of all cattle and grain [from princely and private estates].

4. Then, having opened the Greek Nomocanon [manual of canon and civil law], we found in it that it is not proper for either the prince, or his boyars, or his judges to conduct these [church] courts and lawsuits. And I, having consulted my princess Anna and my sons, granted [the administration of] these courts to the metropolitan and to all bishoprics [in some variants, "bishops"] throughout the Russian land.

5. And therefore neither my children, nor grandchildren, nor any of my descendants for all time shall interfere with the church people or with their court cases. I have turned over [to the church] all these matters in all the cities and pogosty [rural districts] and slobody [settlements], wherever there are Christians. . . .

6. The following are church court cases: divorces; *smil'noe* [perhaps meaning adultery on the part of a husband]; adultery on the part of a wife; rape; kidnapping of a girl; dis-

putes over property between husband and wife; marriage between persons closely related by blood or marriage; sorcery; use of magic drugs; preparation of such drugs; witchcraft; soothsaying; calling [a person] by any of the three shameful epithets—whore, user of magic drugs, and heretic; biting during a fight; a son or daughter beating his father or mother, or a daughter-in-law her mother-in-law; litigations between brothers (sons of a deceased man) over an inheritance; theft of church property; desecration of graves; cutting down a cross; bringing cattle or dogs or fowl [into church] except in an emergency, or doing anything else unseemly in church. . . .

7. All these court cases have been given over to the church; the prince and the boyars and the judges shall not interfere in these court cases. All this I have given in accordance with the enactments of the former [Greek] emperors and of the seven ecumenical councils. . . .

12. And these are church people: abbots, priests, deacons, their children, wives of priests, choir singers, monks, nuns, bakers of communion bread, pilgrims, physicians . . . slaves freed by their masters and given to the church . . . the blind, the lame, [the attendants of] monasteries, hospitals, inns, and places of asylum.

13. The above are church people taken care of in the name of God; the metropolitan or bishop shall have jurisdiction over trials between them, or offenses, disputes, fights, or legacies. But if a layman is involved in a lawsuit with one of these men, then a joint court's trial [by the prince's and the bishop's judges] shall be held.

II:21. THE CHURCH STATUTE OF IAROSLAV THE WISE, 1019-1054

Iaroslav's father Vladimir (see above) laid down the basic regulations concerning the church, which was placed under the prince's protection. Iaroslav confirmed the principles of his father's statute and added sanctions such as those excerpted here. Iaroslav's charter is known to us in a revised form of ca. 1400.

Reference: *PRP*, 1:259-62. Among the many collections of documents on Kievan Russia in addition to those cited in this chapter and the next, see especially vol. 1 of *Khrestomatiia po istorii SSSR*, listed in the Bibliography, and G. E. Kochin, ed., *Pamiatniki istorii Kievskogo gosu-darstva IX-XII vv. Sbornik dokumentov* (Leningrad: Gosudarstvennoe Sotsial'no-Ekonomicheskoe Izdatel'stvo, 1936).

I, Grand Prince Iaroslav, son of Vladimir, following the enactments of my father, have taken counsel with Metropolitan Hilarion and have copied from the Greek Nomocanon the principle that it is not fitting for the prince and boyars to try such lawsuits [as are listed below]. I have given over to the metropolitans and bishops those court cases that are written down in the rules, in the Nomocanon, throughout all the cities and all the regions where Christians live.

1. If anyone should abduct or violate a maiden, if she is a boyar's daughter, [he must pay] 5 grivny in gold to her for her shame, and 5 grivny in gold to the bishops; [if she is the daughter] of a lesser boyar, 1 grivna in gold [to her], and 1 grivna in gold to the bishop; [if she is the daughter] of worthy people [*dobrye liudi*], 5 grivny in silver [to her] for her shame, and 5 grivny in silver to the bishops; and those who aided the abductor [must pay] one grivna in silver to the bishop, and the prince shall punish them. . . .

6. If a husband should commit adultery, he shall be at fault before the bishop, and the prince shall punish him.

7. If a husband should take a second wife without divorcing the first, that man shall be at fault before the bishop, the second wife shall be sent to a nunnery, and he shall live with his first wife.

8. If a wife should suffer from a grievous sickness, or blindness, or a prolonged illness, her husband must not separate from her because of this; nor likewise may a wife separate from her husband. . . .

22. If a maiden should refuse to marry, and her father and mother give her away by force, and she should attempt to do away with herself, her father and mother shall be at fault before the bishop, and they shall pay damages; likewise with a son. . . .

31. If a maiden should wish to marry, and her father and mother refuse to give her away, and she should attempt to do away with herself, the father and mother shall be at fault before the bishop; likewise with a son. . . .

35. The prince's volosteli [agents in charge of volosti or rural districts] shall not interfere in the affairs of people under the jurisdiction of church prelates, both in churches and monasteries; but they shall be governed by their bishop's volosteli, and property left without heir shall go to the bishop.

CHAPTER III

The Russian Lands
(except Novgorod and Pskov)
From the Late Twelfth
through the Fourteenth Century

The significance of the veche in the Russian northeast, the region of Rostov and Suzdal', is illustrated in this excerpt from the Chronicle of Suzdal' (Laurentian version; see note in Chapter II). The passage also provides a glimpse of the fratricidal conflict that kept Russia fragmented in the decades before the Mongol conquest. When Andrei Bogoliubskii, prince of the town and principality of Vladimir and dominant prince of the Volga-Oka region, was assassinated in 1174, he was succeeded in Vladimir by his brother Mikhalko (Michael) Iur'evich. Mikhalko, supported by the people of Vladimir, was attacked by his nephews Mstislav and Iaropolk Rostislavich, who had the support of the people of Rostov, at that time the "senior" or ranking city of the Volga-Oka region.

Reference: *PSRL,* vol. 1, pt. 2, 2d ed. (1927), cols. 373-79.

[In the year 1175] the people of Vladimir, unable to endure starvation, said to Mikhalko: "Either make peace, Prince, or else look after yourself." He replied, saying: "You are right. Why should you perish because of me?" He left for Rus' [the southwest], and the people of Vladimir saw him off with tears; and then the people of Vladimir swore a compact with the Rostislavichi, kissing the cross that they would do them no evil in the city. They came forth from the city with crosses to greet Mstislav and Iaropolk, and when [the princes] entered the city, they consoled the people of Vladimir and, dividing the Rostov domain, began to rule. And the people of Vladimir joyfully seated Prince Iaropolk on the throne in the city of Vladimir and arranged all the terms in [the Cathedral of] the Holy Virgin. . . .

[In the year 1176] the Rostislavichi, upon becoming rulers of the Rostov land, had distributed the posts of posadnik [town official, mayor] in the towns to *detskie* [younger members of the druzhina] from Rus'. They imposed great burdens upon the people in the form of monetary fines for criminal offenses; and the princes themselves, being young, heeded [the wishes of] the boyars; and the boyars took much property for themselves. On the first day they took the gold and silver from the [Cathedral of the] Holy Virgin in Vladimir; they took away the keys to the church sacristy and took away the towns and gifts which the blessed Prince Andrei had given to that church. And the people of Vladimir began to say: "We received the princes of our own free will and kissed the cross to every-

thing; but they act as if this were not their own domain, as if they were not our princes; they not only plunder the entire domain but even the churches; brethren, let us look after ourselves." And they sent to the people of Rostov and Suzdal', telling them of their resentment. The latter were with them in word but far from them in deed; while the boyars sided firmly with the prince. The people of Vladimir, having agreed among themselves, sent to Chernigov for Mikhalko, saying: "You are the eldest of your brothers; come to Vladimir; and if the people of Rostov and Suzdal' should plan any action against us because of you, let it be as God and the Holy Virgin shall will it." . . . Mikhalko won the battle . . . and went to Vladimir with great honor and glory. . . .

[The chronicler then digresses:] From the very beginning, whenever the people of Novgorod, and of Smolensk, and of Kiev, and of all the domains have gathered in the veche for deliberation, whatever the senior [town] decided has had a binding force upon its subordinate towns [*prigorody*]. . . .

[The chronicler then resumes his story:] Then the people of Suzdal' sent to Prince Mikhalko, saying: "We, Prince, were not with Mstislav in that battle; it was the boyars who were with him; do not be angry with us, but come to us." Mikhalko went to Suzdal', and from Suzdal' to Rostov, and arranged all the terms with the people, confirming his compact with them by kissing the cross, and he accepted their honors and took many gifts from the people of Rostov, and placed his brother Vsevolod in Pereiaslavl', and himself returned to Vladimir.

III:2. THE GALICIAN-VOLYNIAN CHRONICLE, 1187-1240

As Kiev declined, the provinces of Galicia (or Galich, which was the name of its capital) and Volynia (with its capital, Vladimir, near the Western Bug) flourished in their own right—sometimes divided, sometimes under one rule. The following indications of princely strife in this region are from the Hypatian transcription (early 1400s) of the Galician-Volynian Chronicle, which appears to have been composed late in the 1200s by an educated retainer of the Galician-Volynian princes.

Reference: Arkheograficheskaia Komissiia, ed., *Letopis' po Ipatskomu spisku* (St. Petersburg, 1871), pp. 441-42, 444-45, 508, 525.

[A.D. 1187:] Prince Iaroslav of Galich, son of Vladimir, departed this life. . . . And before his death he realized that he was weak from his grievous illness, and called together his men and the entire land of Galich, and summoned [the clergy of] all the churches and monasteries, and the poor, and the strong and the weak. . . . And he spoke thus to his men: "I have held together the entire land of Galich with my weak head alone; and now I bequeath my place to Oleg, my youngest son, and give Peremyshl' to Vladimir." And after arranging with them he brought Vladimir and the men of Galich to kiss the cross that he would not seek to take Galich from his brother. Oleg was the son of Anastasia [Iaroslav's concubine, burned by the people of Galich in 1173] and was dear to him, while Vladimir did not obey his will, and for this reason he [Iaroslav] did not give him Galich. Upon the death of Iaroslav, there was great turmoil in the land of Galich. And the men of Galich, conspiring with Vladimir, violated their sworn oath and drove Oleg from Galich; and Oleg fled from there to Riurik in Vruchii; and Vladimir began to rule in Galich, on the throne of his grandfather and father.

. . .

[A.D. 1188:] Vladimir, ruling in the land of Galich, was much addicted to drink and did not like to take counsel with his men; and he took the wife of a priest and made her his wife, and two sons were born to her. Roman Mstislavich of [the town of] Vladimir [in Volynia, north of Galich] . . . seeing that the men of Galich did not live well with their prince . . . was not afraid to send word to the men of Galich, urging them to oppose their prince and drive him from his patrimony, and take him [Roman] as prince. The men of Galich took the advice of Roman, assembled their forces and swore a compact on the cross, and rose against their prince, but did not dare to seize him or kill him, since not all were of that mind, fearing the friends of [Prince] Vladimir; and after considering this they sent word to their prince: "Prince! We have not risen against you, but we don't want to bow to a priest's wife, and we want to kill her; and we will get you a wife wherever you want." And they said this knowing that he would not let the priest's wife go, just so that they might drive him out somehow, and they threatened him with this. He was afraid, and taking much gold and silver with his druzhina, he took his wife and two sons and went to Hungary to the king.

. . .

Following this we shall speak of much turmoil, great treachery, and countless battles.

[A.D. 1230:] In the year 6738, there was sedition among the godless boyars of Galich.

. . .

[A.D. 1240:] The boyars of Galich called Danilo [son of Roman] their prince but governed the entire land themselves . . . and there was great turmoil in the land and plunder on their part. Danilo, seeing this, sent his stol'nik Iakov to Dobroslav [the leading boyar of Galich] in great woe, saying to him: "I am your prince, [but] you do not carry out my command; you plunder the land." [Note: Concerning Daniel and the Tatars, see below.]

III:3. THE VOSKRESENSK CHRONICLE CONCERNING THE MONGOL INVASION OF 1237-1238

Although a Mongol reconnaissance force had invaded southern Russia some fifteen years earlier and had defeated Russians and Polovtsians in the battle at the Kalka River, the Mongols' systematic conquest of Russia was begun only in 1237, with the capture of Riazan'. Here is that incident as related by the Voskresensk Chronicle, which is represented in several excerpts in this and also in subsequent chapters. The Voskresensk Chronicle [Letopis' po Voskresenskomu spisku] is a work of the last half of the 1500s (two of the surviving versions end with the year 1541; others go somewhat farther). The authors, whose identity is unknown, evidently lived and worked within the territory of the Muscovite state. Their account stems in part from the Hypatian codex of the Russian Primary Chronicle (see Chapter II), but it also contains much about Kievan affairs that is not included in that Kievan source. Other identifiable sources used in the Voskresensk Chronicle include the Suzdalian Chronicle (Laurentian codex; see Chapter II) and the Nikonian Chronicle (see below); however, it contains details about events within Muscovy that are not given in either of those. Presumably the authors had access to various documents of their own century. The Voskresensk Chronicle is thus a valuable source, especially for Muscovy in the 1400s and 1500s.

Reference: *PSRL,* 7:139.

[A.D. 1237. By the reckoning of that time it was already 1238, since the new year was counted from the first of September.] That same winter the godless Tatars, with their tsar Batu, came from the east to the land of Riazan', by forest . . . and . . . sent their emissaries . . . to the Princes of Riazan', asking from them one-tenth of everything: of princes, of people, of horses. . . . And the princes replied: "When we are gone, then all will be yours." And from there [the Tatars] sent an emissary to the grand prince, Iurii, in Vladimir, and began to devastate the land of Riazan'. . . . The princes of Riazan' sent to Prince Iurii of Vladimir, asking him to send help or to come himself; but Prince Iurii did not come himself nor did he heed the entreaty of the princes of Riazan', but rather he wished to defend himself separate-ly. But there was no opposing the wrath of God; he brought bewilderment, and terror, and fear and trepidation upon us, for our sins. Then the foreigners besieged the town of Riazan', on December 16, and surrounded it with a palisade; the prince of Riazan' shut himself up in the town with his people. The Tatars took the town of Riazan' on the twenty-first of the same month, and burned it all, and killed its prince, Iurii, and his princess, and seized the men, women, and children, and monks, nuns, and priests; some they struck down with swords, while others they shot with arrows and flung into the flames; still others they seized and bound. . . . They delivered many holy churches to the flames, and burned monasteries and villages, and seized property, and then went on to Kolomna.

III:4. THE FIRST NOVGORODIAN CHRONICLE, CONCERNING THE MONGOL INVASION, 1238

The First Novgorodian Chronicle (thirteenth to fifteenth centuries; see Chapter IV) continues the story, under the year 1238.

Reference: *Novgorodskaia pervaia letopis'* (Moscow: AN SSSR, 1950), pp. 75-76. Cf. Robert Michell and Nevill Forbes, eds. and trans., *The Chronicle of Novgorod* (London: Royal Historical Society, 1914), pp. 82-84 (translation somewhat revised).

Having taken Riazan', the pagan and godless Tatars—a host of shedders of Christian blood—then went to Vladimir. Prince Iurii left Vladimir and fled to Iaroslavl', while his son Vsevolod, with his mother and the bishop and the whole [population] of the province, shut themselves up in Vladimir. The lawless Ishmaelites approached the town, and surrounded the town in force, and fenced it all round with a stockade. And the next morning Prince Vsevolod and Bishop Mitrofan saw that the town would be taken, and they entered the Church of the Holy Virgin, and Bishop Mitrofan sheared them all into monasticism and into the *skhima* [the strictest monastic vows] — the prince and the princess their daughter and daughter-in-law, and good men and women. And when the lawless ones had already come near and set up battering rams, they took the town and set it on fire on Friday before Sexagesima Sunday. The prince and the bishop and the princess, seeing that the town was on fire and that the people were already perishing, some by fire and others by the sword, took refuge in the Church of the Holy Virgin and shut themselves in the sacristy. The pagans, breaking down the doors, piled up wood, and set fire to the sacred church, and slew them all. Thus they perished, giving up their souls to God. . . . And [the people of] Rostov and Suzdal' dispersed in various directions. Having come from there, the accursed ones took Moscow, Pereiaslavl', Iur'ev [northeast of Moscow], Dmitrov, Volok [Volokolamsk], and Tver'. . . . Then the accursed, godless ones pushed on from Torzhok, cutting down everyone like grass, to within one hundred versty [about sixty-six miles] of Novgorod. God, however, and the great and sacred apostolic cathedral Church of Sancta Sophia . . . protected Novgorod.

III:5. GIOVANNI DE PLANO CARPINI DESCRIBES KIEV, 1246

This eyewitness report of Kiev six years after the Mongols had sacked it comes from a Franciscan friar, Giovanni de Plano Carpini, Pope Innocent IV's envoy to the Mongol khan. Friar Giovanni left Lyon, France, in April 1245, passed through Kiev in February 1246, and, after visiting the Mongol capital of Karakorum, passed through Kiev again on his return in 1247.

Reference: Giovanni de Plano Carpini, *The Mongol Mission,* ed. and intro. Christopher Dawson (New York: Sheed and Ward, 1955), pp. 29, 70-71.

They [the Mongols] attacked Russia, where they made great havoc, destroying cities and fortresses and slaughtering men; and they laid siege to Kiev, the capital of Russia; after they had besieged the city for a long time, they took it and put the inhabitants to death. When we were journeying through that land we came across countless skulls and bones of dead men lying about on the ground. Kiev had been a very large and thickly populated town, but now it has been reduced almost to nothing, for there are at the present time scarce two hundred houses there and the inhabitants are kept in complete slavery. Going on from there, fighting as they went, the Tartars destroyed the whole of Russia.

. . .

When the inhabitants of Kiev became aware of our arrival, they all came to meet us rejoicing and they congratulated us as if we were risen from the dead. We met with the same reception throughout the whole of Poland, Bohemia and Russia.

Daniel [Prince of Galicia] and his brother Vasilko [Prince of Volynia] made a great feast for us and kept us, against our will, for quite eight days. In the meantime they discussed between themselves and with the bishop and other worthy men the matter about which we had spoken to them when we were setting out for the Tartars. They answered us jointly declaring that they wished to have the Lord Pope as their special lord and father, and the Holy Roman Church as their lady and mistress, and they also confirmed everything which they had previously despatched by their abbot concerning this matter. In addition they sent with us a letter and envoys.

III:6. FRIAR WILLIAM OF RUBRUCK ON RUSSIA, CA. 1253

Friar William of Rubruck, sent by Louis IX of France to Batu's headquarters in south Russia and then to the great khan in Mongolia, left these and other fragmentary observations on Russia.

Reference: W. W. Rockhill, ed. and trans., *Journey of William of Rubruck to the Eastern Parts of the World, 1253-1255, as Narrated by Himself* (London: Hakluyt, 1900), pp. 93-94, 98.

Alania extends . . . from the Danube to the Tanais [Don] (which is the boundary between Asia and Europe). . . . To the north of this province lies Russia, which is everywhere covered with forests, and extends from Poland and Hungary to the Tanais, and it was all ravaged by the Tartars, and is still being ravaged every day. For the Tartars prefer the Saracens to the Ruthenians, who are Christians, and when the latter can give no more gold or silver they drive them off to the wilds, them and their little ones, like flocks of sheep, there to herd their cattle.

. . .

We found ourselves here [in Russia] in great straits, for we could procure neither horses nor oxen for money. Finally, when I had proved to them that we were working for the common good of all Christendom, they obliged us with oxen and horses; but we ourselves had to go on foot.

It was the season when they were cutting the rye. Wheat thrives not there; but they have great abundance of millet. The Ruthenian women arrange their heads as among us, but their outside gowns they trim from the feet to the knee with vaire [squirrel pelts] or minever [miniver]. The men wear capes like the Germans; on their heads they wear felt caps, pointed and very high.

III:7. JUWAINI ON THE IMPERIAL CODE OF CHINGIS KHAN, IN THE EARLY 1200s

The closest approach to a constitution for the Mongol Empire was the Great Yasa or code prepared by Chingis Khan and promulgated by his Kuriltay or council in the first quarter of the thirteenth century. The Yasa was assumed to have supernatural power, and all decrees of Chingis Khan's successors were expected to be in harmony with it; hence it constitutes an important key to Mongol life, attitudes, and institutions. Although the original has not come down to our day, we have several thirteenth-century summaries and partial quotations from which to reconstruct the original. The following excerpts are from the version of Juwaini, a Persian historian who died in 1283.

Reference: George Vernadsky, "Juwaini's Version of Chingis-Khan's Yasa," *Annales de l'Institut Kondakov,* 11 (1939): 39, 42–44. Cf. Juvaini, 'Ala-ad-Din 'Ata-Malik, *The History of the World Conqueror,* trans. John A. Boyle, 2 vols. (Cambridge: Harvard University Press, 1958), 1: 23–34.

I. In those messages which he [Chingis Khan] used to send to neighboring countries urging their obedience to him he never used intimidation and threats, although it was customᵃry for [other] rulers to threaten [their enemies] with the size of their respective countries and the extent of their might and supplies. On the contrary, by way of extreme warning, he wrote them that if they would not submit to him, "What do we know? The Ancient God, he knows." On that occasion we should consider the saying concerning those who trust God: "Thus spoke God the Allhighest: whoever trusts God, this is enough to him"; and surely they found and obtained whatever they had in their heart and were asking for.

II. Whereas Chingis Khan did not belong to any religion and did not follow any creed, he avoided fanaticism and did not prefer one faith to the other or put the ones above the others. On the contrary, he used to hold in esteem beloved and respected sages and hermits of every tribe, considering this a procedure to please God. Thus he respected the Moslems and favored both the Christians and Idolaters.

As to his sons and grandsons, a number of them chose some definite creed for themselves: some imposed Islam on their necks, others followed the Christian community, some selected Idolatry; some others kept the old customs of their fathers and grandfathers and did not bend their mind to any side, but these are now few.

In spite of the fact that they have adopted [different] religions, they [still] avoid fanaticism and do not swerve from Chingis Khan's Yasa which enjoins [them] to respect all of the creeds equally and makes no difference between them. . . .

V. . . . The inspection of the army is so organized that there is no need for the existence of a special inspection Department and no need to employ special officials and clerks for it. All of the men are divided into units of ten, and among each ten one man is appointed chief of the other nine; and among ten chiefs of the ten units one is called centurion and the whole century is under his command. And so it goes through the unit of one thousand up to the unit of *tuman* [ten thousand; in Russian, *t'ma*], and the chiefs are called chiliarch [and *temnik,* respectively].

In accordance with this arrangement, as soon as there is some matter to be settled and there is need of any man or thing, the matter is referred to the *temnik,* and by him to a chiliarch and so on down to the decurion.

There is equality. Each man works as much as the other; there is no difference. They do not pay attention to wealth or importance of a man. In case soldiers are needed, an order is issued: "so many men [have to report] at such and such an hour"; and on the day or evening appointed they do appear in the place [appointed]. "They come neither earlier nor later than the hour [appointed]." There is never any haste or delay. . . .

VI. And there is another Yasa as follows. Let no one shift from the thousand, century and the unit of ten to which he has been ascribed, to another unit, or try to take refuge in another unit. And no [chief of some other unit] shall admit this man [to his unit]. And if anybody violates this order let the man who would shift [from one unit to another] be publicly executed and the [chief of the other unit] who would give him refuge [be] imprisoned and punished. Therefore nobody shall accept a stranger [into his unit]. If for example, [the chief] be a prince, he [still] has no power to admit the lowest ranking man [to his unit] and shall restrain himself from any violation of the Yasa. Therefore no one shall take liberties with his chief, and other [chiefs] shall not entice him away. . . .

VII. And one more [Yasa]: if there be found in the horde moonlike girls, they collect them and pass them from the tens to the centuries and each chief makes his choice up to the myriarch. After that selection the girls are brought in to the Khan or the princes, and they make their choice again. To the girl who proves fit and beautiful the announcement is made: "To be kept according to the laws"; and to the others: "To be dismissed with kindness," and they are appointed as maids for the *Khatuns* (Royal Dames). If the Khan or the princes like they will present them as gifts [to their associates]; [and again] if they like, they will sleep with them.

VIII. And one more [Yasa]: When the [Mongol] Kingdom expanded itself widely, and important events began to take place, obtaining news about the location of the enemies became essential. Also, valuables had to be sent from the West to the East and from the Far East to the West. Therefore, *iamy* [post-horse stations] were established across the countries, and provisions were made for supplies and expenditures of each *iam;* a fixed number of men and beasts as well as food and drink and other necessities [were provided for] and adjusted to the taxation per *tuman* [ten thousand]: each two *tumany* had to provide for one *iam,* the expenditures being apportioned and collected accordingly; and the stations had to be so located that there would be no [unnecessary] detours for the envoys [and messengers], and, on the other hand, that neither the soldiers nor the serfs would be constantly annoyed [by excessive demands].

And he [Chingis Khan] gave strict orders to the envoys and messengers on the sparing of mounts, etc. It would be too long to discuss it in detail. Each year there is an inspection of the *iamy.* In case of some deficiency, the serfs have to make it good.

III:8. THE NIKONIAN CHRONICLE CONCERNING MONGOL ADMINISTRATION, CA. 1257

The Tatar system of administration was based on a census and on the establishment of regions for taxation and military recruiting. The smallest unit was a "ten," so called because it was obliged to furnish ten recruits. Larger territorial subdivisions were the "hundred," "thousand," and "ten-thousand." Church personnel were spared, as shown in the following excerpt from the Nikonian Chronicle. The unknown author of this chronicle compiled his account in the second half of the 1500s, using chronicles known to us such as the Kievan, Volynian, Suzdalian, and Novgorodian, as well as others that have not survived and for which the Nikonian Chronicle is now our only source. He also apparently had access to various other documents of his own time. This chronicle is therefore especially valuable as a source for the reign of Vasilii III and the first part of the reign of Ivan IV (up to 1559).

Reference: *PSRL,* 10:141.

[A.D. 1257:] That same winter census takers came from the Tatar land, and took a census of the entire land of Suzdal', Riazan', and Murom, and posted *desiatskie, sotniki, tysiatskie,* and *temniki* [respectively, chiefs of 10, 100, 1,000, and 10,000], and, having made all the arrangements, returned to the Horde, enumerating all except archimandrites, abbots, monks [*inoki*], priests, deacons [*diakony*], church servitors, and the entire church retinue, whosoever obeys the Lord God and the most pure Virgin and lives in the house of the Lord and serves the churches of God.

III:9. A DECREE ON FREE TRADE IN THE MONGOL REALM, CA. 1266-1272

One of the means by which the Mongols assured free trade throughout their realm is seen in this message sent between 1266 and 1272 by Iaroslav Iaroslavich, prince of Novgorod, to the people of Riga. What follows is the complete text as preserved on parchment.

Reference: Sigizmund N. Valk, ed., *Gramoty velikogo Novgoroda i Pskova* (Moscow: AN SSSR, 1949), p. 57.

The word of Mengu-Temir to Prince Iaroslav: give foreign merchants passage into your domain. From Prince Iaroslav to the people of Riga, and to the great and the small [bol'shie i molodye], and to those who come to trade, and to everyone: you shall have free passage through my domain; and if anyone comes to me with arms, him I shall deal with myself; but the merchant has free passage through my domain.

III:10. A MONGOL CHARTER CONCERNING PROTECTION OF THE RUSSIAN CHURCH, CA. 1308

The privileged status of the Russian church, especially during the first century of Mongol rule, was formalized in *iarlyki* or charters, including one issued by Khan Mengu-Temir in about 1308. Although the original document has not been recovered, the existence of several secondary versions in the chronicles and elsewhere enabled the historian Priselkov to attempt a reconstruction, here translated almost in its entirety.

Reference: Mikhail D. Priselkov, *Khanskie iarlyki russkim mitropolitam* (St. Petersburg: Nauchnoe Delo, 1916), pp. 58-59.

And this third iarlyk Tsar [Khan] Mengu-Temir gave to Metropolitan Peter, in the year 6816 [1308].

. . .

Tsar [Khan] Chingis [ordered] that in the future: [in exacting] tribute [*dan'*] or subsistence for officials [*korm*], do not touch [the clergy]; may they pray to God with righteous hearts for us and for our tribe, and give us their blessing. . . . And past tsars [khans] have granted [privileges] to priests and monks by the same custom. . . . And we who pray to God have not altered their charters and, in keeping with the former custom, say thus: let no one, whoever it may be, demand tribute, or tax on land [*popluzhnoe*], or transport [*podvoda*], or korm; or seize what belongs to the church: land, water, orchards, vineyards, windmills . . . ; and if anything has been taken, it shall be returned; and let no one, whoever he may be, take under his protection what belongs to the church: craftsmen, falconers, huntsmen; or seize, take, tear, or destroy what belongs to their faith: books, or anything else; and if anyone insults their faith, that man shall be accused and put to death. Those who eat the same bread and live in the same house with a priest—be it a brother, be it a son—they shall likewise be granted [privileges] by the same custom, so long as they do not leave them; if they should leave them, they shall give tribute, and everything else. And you priests, to whom we granted our previous charter, keep on praying to God and giving us your blessing! And if you do not pray to God for us with a righteous heart, that sin shall be upon you. . . . Saying thus, we have given the charter to this metropolitan; having seen and heard this charter, the *baskaki* [tax inspectors], princes, scribes, land-tax collectors, and customs collectors shall not demand or take tribute, or anything else from the priests and from the monks; and if they should take anything, they shall be accused and put to death for this great crime.

III:11. THE SUZDALIAN AND VOSKRESENSK CHRONICLES CONCERNING RUSSIAN PRINCES AS SUBJECTS OF THE GOLDEN HORDE, 1243-1341

The relations between the Russian princes and their Tatar overlords in the thirteenth and fourteenth centuries are illustrated by these excerpts from the chronicles.

Reference: *PSRL*, vol. 1, pt. 2, 2d ed. (1927), cols. 470-73; ibid., 7:205-06.

[From the Suzdalian Chronicle:]

[A.D. 1243:] Grand Prince Iaroslav went to the Tatar land to Batu and sent his son Konstantin to the khan [in Mongolia]. Batu honored Iaroslav and his men with great honor and in dismissing him said: "Iaroslav, be you the senior among all the princes of the Russian people." Iaroslav returned to his land with great honor.

[A.D. 1244:] The princes Vladimir Konstantinovich, Boris Vasilkovich, and Vasilii Vsevolodovich went with their men to the Tatar land to Batu, concerning their patrimony [*otchina*]. Batu honored them with due honor and dismissed them, adjudging to each his patrimony; and they returned to their lands with honor.

[A.D. 1245:] . . . Grand Prince Iaroslav

went to the Tatar land to Batu, with his brothers and sons.

[A.D. 1246:] ... Mikhailo, prince of Chernigov, went to the Tatar land with his grandson Boris, and while they were in the camp, Batu sent to Prince Mikhailo, ordering him to bow to the fire and to their idols. Prince Mikhailo did not obey his command but reproached his false gods, and thus was slain without mercy by the heathen and reached the end of his life.

. . .

[A.D. 1249:] Prince Gleb Vasilkovich went to the Tatar land to Sartak. Sartak honored him and dismissed him to his patrimony. That same winter, Aleksandr and Andrei returned from the khan, who ordered that Kiev and the entire Russian land be given to Aleksandr and that Andrei sit on the throne in Vladimir.

. . .

[A.D. 1252:] Aleksandr Iaroslavich [Aleksandr Nevskii], prince of Novgorod, went to the Tatar land, and they dismissed him with great honor, giving him seniority over all his brothers. . . . Grand Prince Aleksandr returned from the Tatar land to the city of Vladimir, and the metropolitan and all the abbots and the townspeople met him with crosses at the Golden Gate and seated him on the throne of his father Iaroslav . . . and there was great rejoicing in the city of Vladimir and in all the land of Suzdal'.

[From the Voskresensk Chronicle:]

[A.D. 1339:] Grand Prince Ivan Danilovich [called Kalita or "Purse"] went to the Horde, and with him his sons Semen [Simon] and Ivan. . . . That same autumn, on October 29, the accursed Tatars killed Prince Aleksandr Mikhailovich of Tver' and his son Feodor in the Horde, by command of the godless tsar Azbiak; and he had summoned him [the Russian prince] deceitfully, saying: "I want to bestow my favor upon you"; and he [the Russian] had obeyed the deceitful words of the pagan, and upon their arrival they were killed and their bodies dismembered. That same winter the sons of Grand Prince Ivan Danilovich, Semen, Ivan, and Andrei, were dismissed from the Horde in favor and in peace.

. . .

[A.D. 1341:] Grand Prince Ivan Danilovich departed this life. . . . And all the Russian princes went to the Horde: Prince Semen Ivanovich with his brothers, and Prince Vasilii Davydovich of Iaroslavl', Prince Konstantin of Tver', Prince Konstantin Vasilievich of Suzdal', and other Russian princes. . . . That same autumn Prince Semen Ivanovich left the Horde as grand prince, and with him his brothers Ivan and Andrei; and all the Russian princes were placed under his rule, and he took his place upon the throne in Vladimir.

III:12. THE VOSKRESENSK CHRONICLE CONCERNING OPPOSITION TO MOSLEM TAX-FARMERS IN 1262

The difficult role of the Russian prince as a Tatar subject is suggested in this passage from the Voskresensk Chronicle, dealing with the period when Moslems were serving in Russia as the chief tax-farming agents of their as yet not Moslemized Tatar overlords.

Reference: *PSRL*, 7:162–63.

[A.D. 1262:] God delivered the people of the Rostov land from the savage torture of the Moslems through the prayers of the Holy Virgin and instilled fury in the hearts of Christians, unable to endure any longer the oppression of the pagans; and they convoked a veche and drove them from the towns: from Rostov, from Vladimir, from Suzdal', from Iaroslavl', from Pereiaslavl'; these accursed Moslems had farmed tribute from the Tatars and had brought much ruin upon men thereby, enslaving Christian men for [nonpayment of] interest [on loans], and many men were taken to various places; but God, who loves mankind, in his mercy delivered his people from great misfortune. . . . That same summer Grand Prince Aleksandr [Nevskii] decided to go to the tsar in the Horde, so that his entreaties might avert misfortune from his people.

III:13. THE GALICIAN-VOLYNIAN CHRONICLE ON PRINCE DANIEL AND THE TATARS, 1250-1263

From the Galician-Volynian Chronicle (see above) come these further excerpts concerning the reign of the celebrated Prince Daniel or Danilo and his relations with the Tatar overlords.

Reference: Arkheograficheskaia Komissiia, *Letopis' po Ipatskomu spisku*, pp. 536-37, 548-49, 558, 570.

[A.D. 1250:] [Danilo] came to Batu, to the Volga, in order to do homage to him. . . . He was summoned by Batu . . . and bowed according to their custom and entered their tent. [Batu] said to him: "Danilo! Why did you not come long ago? But since you have now come, that is good. Do you drink black milk, our drink, mare's kumiss?" He replied to him: "I have never drunk it before, but if you order it now, I will." [Batu] said: "You are already one of us Tatars: drink our drink." After drinking it [Danilo] bowed according to their custom and, uttering his words, said: "I shall go bow to the great princess Barakchin." [Batu] said: "Go." He went to bow according to the custom. And [Batu] sent him a dipper of wine with the message: "You are not used to drinking milk; drink wine." Oh, eviler than evil is the honor of the Tatars! Great was Prince Danilo Romanovich, who ruled over the Russian land, Kiev and Vladimir [in Volynia] and Galich, and other lands, with his brother: now he kneels and calls himself a slave, and they want tribute; he risks his life and is threatened with danger. O evil Tatar honor! His father was tsar in the Russian land, who subjugated the land of the Polovtsians and fought against all other countries; if no honor is shown to his son, then who else can expect it? There is no end to their hatred and deceit: they killed Iaroslav, the grand prince of Suzdal', with poison; Mikhail, prince of Chernigov, and his boyar Fedor, who would not bow to the bush, were slain with knives . . . and won a martyr's crown; many other princes and boyars have been slain. After being with them for twenty and five days, the prince [Danilo] was dismissed and the land that had been his was charged to him, and he went to his land, and his brother and sons met him, and there was grief for his insult, and there was great rejoicing for his safety.

. . .

[A.D. 1255:] The pope sent worthy envoys, bearing a wreath and scepter and crown, which are called kingly regalia, saying: "Son! Accept from us the crown of kingship." He had previously sent to him the bishop of Beren [Brno, in Moravia]. . . saying to him: "Accept the crown of kingship." At that time he had not accepted, saying: "The evil Tatar war does not cease but remains with us: how then can I accept a crown, without your help?" Opizo [the papal legate] came bearing a crown, promising that "you will have help from the pope"; although he again did not want [to accept the crown], he was persuaded by his mother, and Boleslav and Semovit, and the Polish boyars, who said: if he would accept the crown, "then we will help against the pagans." He accepted the crown from God, from the church of the holy apostles and from the throne of Saint Peter, and from his father Pope Innocent [IV], and from all his bishops. For Innocent cursed those who blasphemed against the orthodox Greek faith, and he wanted to hold a council concerning the true faith and the unification of the church. Danilo accepted the crown from God in the city of Dorogychin.

. . .

[A.D. 1259:] The city of Kholm was founded thus: by the will of God, when Danilo was ruling in Vladimir [in Volynia], he founded the city of Ugoresk [evidently Ugroveisk, on the Western Bug northeast of Vladimir] and installed a bishop in it. While riding through a meadow during a hunt, he saw a beautiful and wooded place on a hill, encircled by a meadow, and he asked the local dwellers: "What is this place called?" They said: "It is called Kholm [hill]." And he took a liking to this place and resolved to build a small city there; he vowed to God and to Saint John Chrysostom that he would erect a church in his name. And he founded a small city. . . . Prince Danilo, seeing that God favored the place, began to invite newcomers, Germans and Russians, foreigners and Poles; day after day they came, both young people [apprentices?] and craftsmen of various sorts who were fleeing from the Tatar land—saddlers, and bow makers, and quiver makers, and blacksmiths and coppersmiths and silversmiths; and there was life, and they filled the courtyards and the fields and villages around the city. He erected the Church of Saint John, beautiful and splendid.

. . .

[A.D. 1263:] The king [Danilo] then fell into a great sickness, from which he died, and they buried him in the Church of the

Holy Virgin, in Kholm, which he himself had founded. This King Danilo was a good, brave, and wise prince, who founded many cities, and erected churches, and decorated them with varied ornaments; he shone with brotherly love for his brother Vasilko; this Danilo was second only to Solomon.

III:14. MARCO POLO ON RUSSIA IN THE EARLY 1290s

After serving seventeen years at the Mongol court of the great Khan Kubilay, Marco Polo traveled back to Venice (1292-95). On the way he had occasion to talk with merchants who had visited Russia, and he made notes about it.

Reference: L. F. Benedetto, *The Travels of Marco Polo,* trans. Aldo Ricci (London: G. Routledge and Sons, 1931), pp. 388-89, 391.

Russia is a very large province. . . . They are Christians, and follow the Greek rite. They have many Kings, and a language of their own. They are a very simple people, but are quite handsome, both the men and the women, for they are all white and fair. . . . They pay tribute to no one, except a section of them, who give something to a King of the Ponent, who is a Tartar, and whose name is Toctai. To him they do pay tribute but it is very little.

It is not a land of trade. True it is, however, that they have quantities of precious and costly furs, such as sables, ermines, vairs, *erculins,* and foxes, among the best and most valuable in the world. Moreover, they have many silver-mines, from which they extract quantities of silver.

. . .

You must know that in Russia the cold is greater than anywhere else, so that it can hardly be borne. Such great cold as reigns there is not to be found in any other part of the world, and, were it not for the many "stoves" they have, the inhabitants could not but die of the extreme cold. These stoves, however, are very numerous, and the noble and powerful have them built as a deed of charity, as in our countries they build hospitals.

. . .

We will now tell you of a custom that they have. They make an excellent wine with honey and panic, which is called *cervisia,* or ale; they have great drinking-bouts of this, as you shall hear. They frequently assemble in companies of men and women, especially noblemen and magnates, 30, 40, or even 50 people together, husbands taking their wives and children with them. Each company elects a king or leader, and fixes rules, as for example, that if some one utters an improper word, or somehow breaks the rules, he is to be punished by the king the company has elected. Now, there are certain men, like our taverners, who keep that ale for sale. The companies go to these taverns, and pass the whole day drinking.

III:15. THE VOSKRESENSK AND TVER' CHRONICLES CONCERNING THE UPRISING IN TVER' IN 1327

The 1327 uprising in Tver' serves as an example of the occasional Russian outbursts that occurred as Tatar rule wore on. Also, a comparison of merely these two of the surviving versions of this incident will demonstrate the difficulties historians have encountered as they have labored to unravel the story of medieval Russia. The Tver' Chronicle was written in 1534 by an unknown inhabitant of Rostov, who was evidently without formal schooling. Scholars have deduced that he based part of his account on a manuscript of the 1450s.

Reference: *PSRL,* 7:200; vol. 15, cols. 415-16.

[From the Voskresensk Chronicle, under the year 1327:]

A mighty envoy named Shchelkan [Shevkal] came from the Horde to Tver' with a multitude of Tatars, and began to do great violence, and wanted to kill Prince Aleksandr Mikhailovich and his brothers, and wanted to become prince in Tver' himself, and wanted to install his other princes in other Russian cities, and wanted to force Christians to accept the Moslem faith. Being in the city of Tver' on the very feast day of the Dormition [*uspenie,* corresponding to, but not identical with, the Assumption] of the Virgin [i.e. August 15], he planned then to kill everyone there. . . . Learning of the accursed one's plan, Prince

Aleksandr Mikhailovich called together all the people of Tver', took up arms, and went against Shchelkan. . . . Shchelkan, hearing that Prince Aleksandr was coming against him with an army, went out to meet him with his multitude of Tatars, and they came together at sunrise and fought the whole day, and toward evening Prince Aleksandr won out, and Shchelkan fled to the hall [of the palace]; Prince Aleksandr set fire to his father's hall and the whole palace, and Shchelkan and the other Tatars burned to death.

[From the Tver' Chronicle, under the year 1326:]

God permitted the Devil to instill evil in the hearts of the godless Tatars, to say to the lawless tsar [i.e. the Tatar khan]: "Unless you destroy Prince Aleksandr [Mikhailovich] and all the Russian princes, you will not have power over them." And Shevkal [called Shchelkan in the Voskresensk Chronicle], the lawless and accursed instigator of all evil, the scourge of Christians, opened his foul mouth and began to say as the Devil had taught him: "Lord Tsar, if you command, I will go to Rus', and destroy Christianity, and kill their princes, and bring their princesses and children to you." And the tsar commanded him to do thus. The lawless Shevkal, scourge of Christians, went to Rus' with many Tatars, came to Tver', and drove the grand prince from his palace, and himself, in his great insolence, stayed in the palace of the grand prince;

and he stirred up a great persecution of Christians, with violence, and plunder, and killing, and desecration. The people, constantly hurt in their pride by the pagans, complained many times to the grand prince that he should defend them; but he, although he saw the injuries done to his people, could not defend them and ordered them to be patient; but the people of Tver' could not endure this and waited for a suitable moment. And it happened that on the fifteenth day of August, in mid-morning, during the market hours, a certain deacon, Tveritin, surnamed Diudko, was leading a small and very fat mare to drink the water of the Volga; the Tatars saw her and carried her away. The deacon was grieved and began to cry out loudly, saying: "Oh men of Tver', do not let me down!" And a fight took place between them; the Tatars, relying on their unlimited authority, began to use weapons, and straightway men gathered, and the people arose in tumult, and sounded the bells, and assembled in a veche; and the entire city turned [against the Tatars], and the people all gathered right away, and there was agitation among them, and the men of Tver' gave a shout and began to kill the Tatars, wherever they found them, until they had killed Shevkal himself and all of them in turn. . . .

[A.D. 1327:] And after he had heard this, the lawless tsar [khan] sent an army in winter into the Russian land, with the voevoda Fedorchiuk, and five temniki [commanders of units of 10,000 soldiers each]; and they killed many people, and took others captive, and put Tver' and all the towns to flame.

III:16. THE TESTAMENT OF IVAN I, CA. 1339

The founder of Moscow's power in the Russian northeast, Ivan Danilovich—called Kalita ("Purse") for his concern over material wealth—is revealed in his testament as a believer in the old Russian custom of dividing his principality among his sons and giving only a modest advantage to the eldest. The city of Moscow itself was bequeathed to the three sons jointly.

Reference: *PRP*, 3:253-56. This and other similar documents have recently been republished in the Russian texts, together with translations and commentary, in Robert C. Howes, ed. and trans., *The Testaments of the Grand Princes of Moscow* (Ithaca: Cornell University Press, 1967). Two versions of the Russian text are given on pp. 115-19; a full English translation is on pp. 182-87.

In the name of the Father and of the Son and of the Holy Ghost. I, the sinful, unworthy servant of God, Ivan, about to journey to the Horde, write my testament of my own free will, in sound mind and in full health. In case God should decide anything concerning my

life, I give this testament to my sons and my princess.

I bequeath to my sons my patrimony of Moscow and apportion it as follows. To my eldest son Semen I give: Mozhaisk with all its volosti [rural districts], Kolomna with all the Kolomna volosti [a list follows]. . . . And during my lifetime I have given to my son Semen: four gold chains, three gold belts, two gold goblets with pearls, a gold plate with a pearl and precious stones, and two large gold bowls; and of the silver vessels I have given him three silver plates. To my son Ivan I give: Zvenigorod [and a slightly less impressive list of other settlements and properties]. . . . To my son Andrei, I have given: [a similar list]. . . . And to my princess and the younger children I give: [a similar list]. . . . And if for my sins the Tatars should covet any of these volosti and take them away, then you, my sons and my princess, should again divide these [remaining] volosti among yourselves in place of those [that have been taken]. And my sons shall govern jointly the peasants listed in the [Tatar] census, and my sons shall divide among themselves the peasants whom I have bought, [listed] in the great scroll. . . .

And of my clothing, [I give] to my son Semen my red fur coat [*kozhukh*] with pearls and my gold cap . . . [there follows another list of articles to be distributed among his children, his widow, and church beneficiaries].

Besides the Moscow villages, I give to my son Semen the villages I have bought . . . [a list follows, as well as other villages for Ivan and Andrei].

And as to the village Bogoroditskoe, that I bought in Rostov and gave to Borisko Vorkov: If he serves any one of my sons, the village will be his; but if he does not serve my children, the village shall be taken away from him. . . .

And you, my son Semen, I designate you as the guardian, under God, of your younger brothers and my princess with the smaller children.

And if anyone should violate this my testament, let God judge him. To which have witnessed: my spiritual father Efrem, my spiritual father Feodosii, my spiritual father the priest Davyd.

III:17. MOSCOW'S TREATY WITH TVER', 1368

The growing influence of Moscow and of the grand principality it headed under Tatar suzerainty may be seen in this treaty of 1368 (possibly 1375) between Dmitrii Donskoi and the prince of nearby Tver'. As in earlier times, such expressions as "elder brother," "brother," and "younger brother" often denoted not a blood relationship but a political order of precedence.

Reference: *Dukhovnye i dogovornye gramoty velikikh i udel'nykh kniazei* XIV-XVI *vv.* (Moscow: AN SSSR, 1950), pp. 25-28.

In accordance with the blessing that our [spiritual] father Aleksei, metropolitan of all Russia, has given to this, you, my younger brother, Grand Prince Mikhail Aleksandrovich [of Tver'], should kiss the cross [for yourself], and for your children and your nephews as well, to me, your elder brother, Grand Prince Dmitrii Ivanovich, and to my brother, Vladimir Andreevich [prince of Serpukhov, just south of Moscow; Dmitrii's cousin and ally], and to our patrimony of Novgorod the Great.

You must consider me as your elder brother and my brother, Prince Vladimir, as your brother. You must wish us well everywhere and in everything without deceit; and if you hear good or bad tidings concerning us from a Christian or from a foreigner, you must inform us of it truthfully, in accordance with your oath, without deceit. . . . And if I or my brother Vladimir Andreevich should go to war, you too must mount your horse together with us, without deceit; and if we send voe-vody, you too must send your voevody. And you must protect our patrimony of Moscow and the entire grand principality and Novgorod the Great, and do it no harm; and you and your children and nephews must not covet our patrimony of Moscow and the entire grand principality and Novgorod the Great before our death. And you must protect our people of Moscow and of the entire grand principality and of Novgorod the Great and Novyi Torzhok as your own, and do them no harm. And you must not hold anyone in pledge to you or give out deeds in our patrimony, in the grand principality. And if the Tatars should try to make us quarrel and start giving you our patrimony, the grand principality, you must not take it before [our] death; and if they start giving us your patrimony of Tver', we likewise shall not take it before [your] death. . . . We shall live, brother, in accordance with this treaty: if we have peace with the Tatars, it shall be upon consultation; if we pay tribute, it shall be upon consultation; if we do not pay tribute, it shall likewise be upon consultation. If the Tatars should attack us or attack you, then we shall fight jointly with you against them; if we should attack them, then you shall attack them jointly with us. You must renounce your oath to Olgerd [of Lithuania], and to his brothers, children, and nephews. If Lithuania should attack either us or the grand prince of Smolensk or any of our brother princes, we shall defend them, and you together with us jointly; if they should attack you, we shall likewise help you and all defend ourselves jointly — .

And if any boyar or servitor has left us to come to you, or has left you to come to us, and their villages are either in our patri-mony, the grand principality, or in your patrimony in Tver', neither you nor we shall interfere in these villages–– and the boyars and free servitors shall be free. . . . The administration of justice and the levying of taxes [*sud i dan'*] shall belong to him to whom the land and water belong. . . .

The oath shall be binding until death. . . . And you shall collect tolls and customs duties from our merchants and traders as in former times; and they shall be given free passage, as was in the reign of our grandfather, Grand Prince Ivan [I], in the reign of our uncle, Grand Prince Semen, and in the reign of my father, Grand Prince Ivan [II]; and new tolls and customs duties shall not be introduced.

III:18. THE VOSKRESENSK CHRONICLE CONCERNING MOSCOW'S DEFEAT OF THE TATARS, SEPTEMBER 8, 1380

The famous battle at Kulikovo Pole (Snipes' Meadow) on September 8, 1380, which earned for Grand Prince Dmitrii the epithet Donskoi ("of the Don"), is here depicted in excerpts from one of the shortest of several surviving accounts, that of the Voskresensk Chronicle. What it lacks in precision (for example, it exaggerates the actual number of Russian troops) it may make up in enthusiasm.

Reference: *PSRL*, 8:34-35, 38-39. For another version of this event, see Roman Jakobson and Dean S. Worth, eds., *Sofonija's Tale of the Russian-Tatar Battle on the Kulikovo Field* (The Hague: Mouton, 1963), and Zenkovsky, *Medieval Russia's Epics*, pp. 185-98.

In the year 6888 [1380] the prince of the Horde, Mamai, came from the Horde with his adherents, with all the princes of the Horde, and with the entire force of the Tatars and Polovtsians, and also hired troops [of several south Russian and Caucasian peoples]. . . . And together with Mamai, with the same thought and of the same mind, was also the Lithuanian prince Iagailo Olgerdovich with his entire army of Lithuanians and Poles; also in agreement with them was Prince Oleg Ivanovich of Riazan': and [Khan Mamai] with all these allies went against Grand Prince Dmitrii Ivanovich.

. . .

[Dmitrii] arose from prayer, left the church, and sent for his brother [i.e. ally and cousin] Prince Vladimir Andreevich [of Serpukhov], and for all the Russian princes and for the great voevody. And the grand prince said to his brother, Prince Vladimir Andreevich, and to all the Russian princes: "Let us go against this accursed, godless, impious, and dastardly eater of uncooked flesh, Mamai, for the orthodox Christian faith, and for the holy churches and for all Christians." . . . And he assembled all the Russian princes and the entire army, and quickly went from Moscow to meet them, wishing to defend his patrimony, and came to Kolomna . . . since the beginning of the world there had never been such an army of Russian princes . . . as under this grand prince, Dmitrii Ivanovich. There was a total strength and a total army of 150,000 or 200,000. . . . And they went beyond the Don into the far regions of the land; and soon they crossed the Don . . . so that the bowels of the earth shook from the great number of the Russian force. Grand Prince Dmitrii Ivanovich crossed the Don into an open field, into the land of the Horde, to the mouth of the Nepriadva River; the Lord God alone guided him. . . . And it was in the sixth hour of the day that the accursed Moslems began to appear in the open field, and the godless Tatars arrayed their regiments against the Christians, and both armies began to regard each other; and there was a great multitude of each, so that the earth thundered, and the mountains and

hills trembled; and on both sides they un-
sheathed their weapons, sharp in their hands.
. . . And straightway both great forces joined
battle for many an hour, and the armies
covered the field for a distance of ten versts
because of the multitude of warriors; and
there was a great slaughter, and a hard battle,
and a very great tumult, so that since the beginning of the world no Russian grand prince
had been in such a slaughter as was this grand
prince, Dmitrii Ivanovich. They fought from
the sixth hour to the ninth, and the blood
of both Christians and Tatars flowed as in a
cloudburst, and a great multitude, a countless
number, fell dead on both sides, and many
Russians were killed by the Tatars, and Tatars
by Russians, and corpse fell upon corpse, the
body of a Christian falling upon a Tatar, likewise the body of a Tatar upon a Christian;
elsewhere could be seen a Russian pursuing
a Tatar and a Tatar overtaking a Russian;
they were in confusion and mixed together,
each one seeking to slay his adversary. . . .
In the ninth hour, as they were fighting, the
faithful saw angels helping the Christians,
and hosts of the holy martyrs, and the great
soldier of Christ Georgii, and the glorious
Dmitrii, and the Russian grand princes, Saints
Boris and Gleb, and among them the voevoda
of the perfect army of the heavenly host, the
great Archistrategus [Supreme Commander]
Mikhailo [Archangel Michael]. . . . All the
temniki and the entire Tatar army fled, and
seeing this the other foreigners, both great
and small, being pursued by the wrath of God
and overcome with fear, set forth in flight.

III:19. THE VOSKRESENSK CHRONICLE TELLS HOW THE TATARS PUNISHED MOSCOW, 1382

When Dmitrii Donskoi, emboldened by his victory at Kulikovo Pole in 1380, evinced unwilling-
ness to resume Muscovy's tribute to the Golden Horde, he brought upon his people the punishment described here.
    Reference: *PSRL*, 8:42–43, 45–47.

[A.D. 1382:] Grand Prince Dmitrii Ivanovich heard tidings that the tsar himself
[Tokhtamysh, khan of the Golden Horde]
was advancing upon him in great force, and
began to assemble his regiments of soldiers,
and rode from the city of Moscow, wishing
to go against the [khan's] soldiers; and Grand
Prince Dmitrii Ivanovich began to take
counsel with all the Russian princes, and dissension arose among them, and they did not
wish to help. . . . There was discord and mis-
trust among them, and when he learned of
and realized this, Grand Prince Dmitrii Ivanovich was perplexed and concerned, not wishing to oppose the tsar himself; but he went
to his city of Pereiaslavl', and from there past
Rostov . . . to Kostroma. . . . There was great
turmoil in the city of Moscow; the people
were in confusion, like sheep without a
shepherd; the townspeople were agitated:
some wanted to remain and shut themselves
up in the city, while others thought of fleeing, and there were great disputes between
them; some rushed into the city with their
belongings, while others fled from the city
after being robbed; and they called together
a veche and sounded all the bells, and the
rebels and traitors gathered in a crowd; not
only did they not permit those who wished
to leave the town to do so, but even robbed
them. . . . Then a certain Lithuanian prince
named Ostei, grandson of Grand Prince Olgerd,
came into the city to them; he heartened the
people, and put down the turmoil in the city,
and shut himself up in the city with them,
and together with a multitude of people came
under siege. . . . [The townspeople beat off
the Tatar assaults for three days; then, tricked
by the persuasions and promises of the princes
of Suzdal' and Nizhnii-Novgorod who were in
the Tatar camp, they opened the gates to the
Tatar "tsar":] The Tatars entered the city,
killing, . . . and a great slaughter took place
inside the city. . . . The Christians who were
in the city ran to and fro in the streets, rush-
ing about in throngs, with great cries; . . .
some shut themselves up in the stone churches,
but this did not save them either, for the godless ones broke open the church doors by
force and slaughtered them with swords;
there was great and fearful shouting and crying everywhere, so that one person could not
call to another; while a multitude of people
shouted, they led the Christians out, and,
after beating and stripping them, they slaughtered them. And they plundered the cathedrals,
defiled the altars and holy places, and tore
down the venerated crosses and miraculous

icons, decorated with gold and silver and pearls and precious stones. . . . Many books had been brought from the entire city and from the villages, and a great number had been placed in the cathedrals, sent there for safekeeping, and [the Tatars] destroyed everything without trace. . . . Thus soon did the evil ones take the city of Moscow, on the twenty-sixth day of August . . . and the city was set aflame, and they plundered all the goods and the wealth and put people to the sword; on one side there was fire and on the other side the sword: some who fled from the flames died by the sword, and others who fled from the sword burned in the flames; and doom faced them in four forms: (1) by the sword, (2) by fire, (3) by water, (4) by being taken captive. Heretofore the city of Moscow had been great and wonderful to see, and there were many people in it; it abounded in wealth and glory, it surpassed all the cities in the Russian land in its great honor, and princes and primates dwelled in it; but now its beauty changed and its glory left it, and in a single hour all its honor was gone, when it was taken and burned: nothing could be seen but smoke and earth and the corpses of many dead lying about; the holy churches had burned and fallen in, while the stone [churches] stood burned out within and blackened without; there was no singing or ringing of bells to be seen in them, no one entering a church, and there was no voice raised in song, nor paeans of praise to be heard in church; but everything to be seen was empty, there was not a soul to be seen where the fire had passed. And Moscow was not the only city to be taken; other cities and lands were captured by the pagans as well.

III:20. THE WILL OF DMITRII DONSKOI, APRIL OR MAY, 1389

This testament of Grand Prince Dmitrii is a significant departure from the earlier custom of treating all sons more or less equally. At this time Dmitrii was still under Tatar rule. Dmitrii speaks of his two portions or shares of Moscow, referring both to that third he inherited directly from his father, Ivan II, and that third he inherited from his brother, Ivan of Zvenigorod, when in 1364 that brother died.

Reference: *PRP*, 3:258-60, 262-64. For a recent translation of the whole document, fully annotated, see Howes, ed., *Testaments of the Grand Princes of Moscow*, pp. 208-17 (Russian text on pp. 126-30).

In the name of the Father and of the Son and of the Holy Ghost. I, the sinful and unworthy servant of God Dmitrii Ivanovich, write my testament in sound mind. I make my bequest to my sons and to my princess.

I place my children in my princess's charge. And you, my children, live in harmony, and obey your mother in everything.

And I bequeath my patrimony [*otchina*] of Moscow to my children, Prince Vasilii, Prince Iurii, Prince Andrei, and Prince Petr. And my brother [really a cousin] Prince Vladimir shall govern his third, with which his father, Prince Andrei, blessed him. And I bless my son Prince Vasilii with the larger income [consisting of] a half of my two portions [i.e. my two-thirds] in the city and in the stany [rural districts] of my appanage; [the other] half [shall go] to my three [other] sons, along with a half of the customs duties from the towns. . . .

And I bless my son Prince Vasilii with my patrimony, the Grand Principality [of Vladi-

mir].

. . .

And if for my sins God should take away any of my sons, my princess shall divide his appanage among my [other] sons. Whatever she gives to each, that he shall have, and my children shall not disobey her will.

. . .

And if the patrimony with which I blessed any of my sons should be diminished, my princess shall give him a share from the appanages of my [other] sons. And you, my children, obey your mother.

And if for my sins God should take away my son Prince Vasilii, whoever of my sons shall be next in line, this son of mine shall have the appanage of Prince Vasilii, and my princess shall divide his appanage [among the other sons]. And you, my children, obey your mother; whatever she gives to each, that he shall have.

. . .

And if God should change the Horde [i.e.

should liberate us from the Horde] and my children do not have to give tribute to the Horde, then whatever [tribute] each of my sons collects in his appanage, that shall be his.

. . .

And I have placed my children in my princess's charge. And you, my children, obey your mother in everything; do not disobey her will in anything. And if any of my sons shall not obey his mother, and shall disobey her will, he shall not have my blessing.

And my younger children, brothers of Prince Vasilii, honor and obey your elder brother Prince Vasilii, in your father's place. And my son Prince Vasilii shall treat his brother Prince Iurii and his younger brothers in brotherly fashion, without injustice.

. . .

And I have written this testament in the presence of my fathers, Abbot Sergii and Abbot Savast'ian.

And our boyars were present [a list follows].

CHAPTER IV

Novgorod the Great
and Pskov
Twelfth to Fifteenth Centuries

A. THE POLITICAL STRUCTURE OF NOVGOROD

IV:1. THE FIRST NOVGORODIAN AND RUSSIAN PRIMARY CHRONICLES ON IAROSLAV
AND NOVGOROD IN THE STRUGGLE AGAINST SVIATOPOLK, 1015-1019

At the time of Prince (later Saint) Vladimir's death in 1015, his son Iaroslav was his vicegerent
or lieutenant (*namestnik*) in Novgorod. Iaroslav's elder brother Sviatopolk killed three of his
brothers and seized the Kievan throne. The following excerpts from the chronicles give some
glimpses of the ensuing struggle, as a result of which Iaroslav rewarded the Novgorodians for
their essential help by giving them certain privileges. Unfortunately, the details of the privileges
remain lost to us, but many a subsequent prince of Novgorod was obliged to swear to observe
"the will of Novgorod and all the charters of Iaroslav."

Reference: The first and third excerpts are from *Novgorodskaia pervaia letopis'* (Moscow:
AN SSSR, 1950), pp. 174-76; the English translation is based on Robert Michell and Nevill
Forbes, eds. and trans., *The Chronicle of Novgorod* (London: Royal Historical Society, 1914),
pp. 1-2, slightly revised. The excerpt dated 1018 is from *PVL*, pt. 1, p. 97; translation based on
RPC, p. 132, slightly revised. (The *Novgorodskaia pervaia letopis'* was reprinted by Mouton in
1970.)

[From the First Novgorodian Chronicle:]

[A.D. 1016:] And the same night Iaroslav's
sister Peredslava sent word to him from Kiev,
saying: "Your father [Vladimir] is dead, and
your brothers slain." And having heard of this,
Iaroslav the next day gathered a multitude of
Novgorodians, and held a veche in a field. . . .
And he said to them: "Brethren! My father
Vladimir is dead, and Sviatopolk is prince in
Kiev; I want to go against him. Come with
me and help me." And the men of Novgorod
said to him: "Yes, Prince, we will follow you."
And he gathered 4,000 soldiers: there were
1,000 Varangians, and 3,000 of the men of
Novgorod; and he went against [Sviatopolk].

[From the Russian Primary Chronicle:]

[A.D. 1018:] [After Sviatopolk and King
Boleslaw of Poland had gained the upper
hand,] Iaroslav fled with four men to Novgorod, and Boleslav entered Kiev in company
with Sviatopolk. . . . When Iaroslav arrived
at Novgorod in his flight, he planned to
escape across the sea, but the posadnik [gov-
ernor-mayor of the whole city-state] Konstantin, son of Dobrynia, together with the
men of Novgorod, destroyed his boats, saying:
"We wish to fight once more against Boleslav

and Sviatopolk." They set out to gather
money at the rate of four kuny per freeman
[*muzh*], ten grivny from each elder [*starosta*—
the elected chief of each borough (*konets*)
and street (*ulitsa*)], and eighteen grivny from
each boyar. [Note: For the value of these
monetary units see the *Dictionary of Russian
Historical Terms.*]

And they brought in Varangians and paid
them, and thus Iaroslav collected a large
army. . . . And Iaroslav attacked Sviatopolk
again, and Sviatopolk fled to the Pechenegs.

[From the First Novgorodian Chronicle:]

[Told under A.D. 1016, but evidently
refers to 1019.] And Iaroslav went to Kiev
and took his seat on the throne of his father
Vladimir. And straightway he began to
distribute pay to his troops: to the elders
[*starosta* here could also mean "captain"]
ten grivny each, to the peasants [*smerd*] one
grivna each, and to all the men of Novgorod
ten grivny each, and he dismissed them all
to their homes; and he gave them a law code,
and wrote it down, and said to them: "Live
in accordance with this charter which I have
written for you, and observe it."

IV:2. THE RUSSIAN PRIMARY CHRONICLE ON NOVGORODIAN ENVOYS IN KIEV, 1102

In this as in other excerpts from the Russian Primary Chronicle, the personalized narrative of the
annalist gives little hint of the larger forces at play—in this case the economic and political growth
of Novgorod, which by 1102 enabled its leaders to deal with the grand prince of Kiev in the manner related here.

Reference: *PVL*, 1:182; see also pp. 384-85 for modern Russian translation. English translation based on *RPC*, pp. 199-200, considerably revised.

On December 20 of the same year [1102], Mstislav, the son of Vladimir [Monomakh], arrived at Kiev with men from Novgorod, since Sviatopolk [grand prince of Kiev] had made an agreement with Vladimir [Monomakh, at that time prince of Pereiaslavl'] whereby Sviatopolk should have Novgorod and appoint his own son prince there, and Vladimir should appoint his son [Mstislav, at that time prince of Novgorod] prince in [the town of] Vladimir [in Volynia]. And Mstislav came to Kiev [accompanied by Novgorodian envoys], and they sat [for parley] in [Sviatopolk's] palace. . . . And the men from Novgorod said to Sviatopolk, "We were sent to you, Prince, and they told us [in Novgorod to convey this message]: 'We do not want either you or your son. If your son has two heads, you might send him. But Vsevolod [Vladimir Monomakh's father] assigned us that one [Mstislav, as our prince]. We brought him up as our prince, while you abandoned us.'" Sviatopolk then had a long argument with them, but the Novgorodians did not want him, and they took Mstislav and departed for Novgorod.

IV:3. THE FIRST NOVGORODIAN CHRONICLE ON THE EXPULSION OF PRINCE VSEVOLOD BY THE NOVGORODIANS, 1136

Not long after the deaths of the strong and popular Kievan princes Vladimir Monomakh (d. 1125) and Mstislav (d. 1132), the Novgorodians began to behave as their chronicler indicates below. The so-called First Novgorodian Chronicle, which is the source of this and many other items in this section, survives in one version on parchment, partly in the handwriting of the thirteenth century and partly in that of the first half of the fourteenth, and in another version in a fifteenth-century hand.

Reference: *Novgorodskaia pervaia letopis'*, p. 24; translation based on Michell and Forbes, *Chronicle of Novgorod*, p. 14, considerably revised.

[A.D. 1136:] The men of Novgorod summoned the men of Pskov and Ladoga and took counsel [deciding] to expel their prince, Vsevolod [son of Mstislav], and they confined him in the bishop's palace together with his wife, children, and mother-in-law on May 28, and armed guards guarded him day and night, thirty men each day; he was a prisoner for two months, and on July 15 they allowed him to leave the town. . . . And they cited these faults of his: (1) that he had no care for the peasants; (2) that he wished to rule in Pereiaslavl'; (3) that he rode away and left the army behind; and much else besides.

IV:4. THE VOSKRESENSK AND FIRST NOVGORODIAN CHRONICLES ON THE CITIZENRY AND THE PRINCE, 1149-1270

The following excerpts from the chronicles deal with the relationship between the citizens of Novgorod, or their veche, and several of the princes of the twelfth and thirteenth centuries.

Reference: *PSRL*, 7:45 [excerpt from the Voskresensk Chronicle]; *Novgorodskaia pervaia letopis'*, pp. 43, 50, 59, 260, 68, 278, and 88 [excerpts from the First Novgorodian Chronicle, respectively]. The translations of all but the first excerpt are based on Michell and Forbes, *Chronicle of Novgorod*, pp. 39, 49, 60-61, 72, 75, 104, somewhat revised.

[From the Voskresensk Chronicle:]

[A.D. 1149:] And Iziaslav [Mstislavich, grand prince 1146-54] went from there to Novgorod with a small retinue [druzhina], wanting to lead them against Iurii [Dolgorukii of Suzdal']. . . . The people of Novgorod, hearing that Iziaslav was coming to them, were very glad and went out three days' journey from the city to meet him, and others went one day's journey; he entered the city on Sunday, and his son Iaroslav met him here with the boyars of Novgorod, and they went to Sancta Sophia for mass. Iziaslav and his son Iaroslav sent constables [*podvoiskie*] and criers [*birichi*] to call in the streets, summoning everyone, great and small, to dine with the prince; and everyone came to the Gorodishche [the prince's residence] to dine with the prince, and so after dining and making merry they dispersed, each going his own way. On the following day Iziaslav sent to Iaroslav's Courtyard [the veche meetingplace and also the veche chancellery, in a square in the Commercial Quarter on the right bank] and ordered the veche to be summoned; and all the people of Novgorod and Pskov gathered at the veche, and Iziaslav said to them: "My son and you, brethren, have sent to me, [saying] that my uncle Iurii has injured you, and I have come here because of your injuries, leaving the Russian land [the Kiev region]; so take counsel, how to go against him: either we shall make peace with him, or decide the matter by arms." They said: "We will all gladly go with you, great and small, because of our injuries." And all the men of Novgorod, and Pskov, and the Karelians went with him.

[From the First Novgorodian Chronicle:]

[In 1196] all the princes set Novgorod at liberty: they might take to themselves a prince from wherever they wished.

. . .

[A.D. 1209:] From Kolomna he [Vsevolod III, "Big Nest"] let the men of Novgorod go to Novgorod, after giving them countless presents, and he gave [confirmed] them all their liberties and the decrees of their former princes, all that the men of Novgorod had wished for, and he said to them: "Love him who is good to you, but punish the bad."

. . .

[A.D. 1218:] Prince Sviatoslav sent his tysiatskii to the veche, and said: "I cannot be with Tverdislav; and I take away the office of posadnik from him." But the men of Novgorod said: "Is he at fault?" And he answered: "Faultless." Tverdislav said: "I am glad that I am not to blame; and you, brethren, are free to choose posadnik and prince." And the men of Novgorod answered: "Prince! As he is without blame, and you swore on the cross to us not to deprive a man [of office] without cause: therefore, we bow down to you, but this is our posadnik, and we will not yield in this." And there was peace.

. . .

[A.D. 1229:] Prince Mikhail came from Chernigov to Novgorod . . . and the men of Novgorod were glad at their choice; and he swore upon the cross to all the liberties of Novgorod and to all the charters of Iaroslav.

. . .

[A.D. 1230:] And they [the Novgorodians] showed young Prince Rostislav the road from Torzhok and [sent him] to his father in Chernigov, [saying]: ". . . go hence, and we will provide a prince for ourselves." And they sent for Iaroslav, with [i.e. reserving to themselves] all the liberties of Novgorod. And Iaroslav quickly came to Novgorod on December 30 and held a veche in Iaroslav's Courtyard and swore upon [the icon of] the Holy Virgin in [confirmation of] all the charters of Iaroslav and all the liberties of Novgorod.

. . .

[In 1270] there was a tumult in Novgorod; they set about expelling Prince Iaroslav from the town, and they summoned a veche in Iaroslav's Courtyard and killed Ivanko, and others ran into the Church of Saint Nicholas; and on the morrow the tysiatskii Ratibor, Gavrilo Kiianinov, and others of his friends fled to the prince in the Gorodishche; and [the Novgorodians] took their houses for plunder and destroyed their buildings, and they sent to the prince in the Gorodishche a document with all his faults: "Why have you taken up the Volkhov with snarers of wild ducks and taken up the fields with catchers of hares? Why have you taken Aleksei Mortkinich's homestead? Why have you taken money away from Nikifor Manuskinich, Roman Boldyzhevich, and Varfolomei? And another thing, why do you send away from us the foreigners who dwell among us?" and many faults of this kind. "And now, Prince, we cannot suffer your violence. Depart from us; and we will find a prince for ourselves." And the prince sent Sviatoslav and Andrei Vrotislavich to the veche with greetings: "I renounce all that, and I swear upon the cross to all that you desire." But the men of Novgorod answered: "Prince, go away, we do not want you; or else we shall come, the whole of Novgorod, to drive you out." And the prince left the town against his will.

IV:5. THE FIRST NOVGORODIAN CHRONICLE ON ALEKSANDR NEVSKII IN THE 1240s

Aleksandr Iaroslavich, called "Nevskii" for his victory over the Swedes on the river Neva in 1240, was the most famous and popular Russian prince of the thirteenth century. The chronicle here depicts his dealings with the Swedes, the Livonian Germans, and the Tatar overlords.

Reference: *Novgorodskaia pervaia letopis'*, pp. 290-93, 295-97, 303-04; translation based in part on Michell and Forbes, *Chronicle of Novgorod*, pp. 86-87, considerably revised.

In truth his [Prince Aleksandr's] rule would not endure unless God willed it; his stature exceeds that of other men, his voice is like a trumpet among men, his face is a face like Joseph's, whom the Egyptian caesar [*tsesar'*, i.e. the pharaoh] made a second caesar in Egypt; his strength is like the strength of Samson the Strong; and God has given him the wisdom of Solomon, and the courage of the Roman caesar Vespasian, who took captive the entire land of Judea.

· · ·

[In 1240, after hearing of the invasion of a large army of Swedes, Aleksandr, having prayed and received the bishop's blessing] began to hearten his retinue [druzhina], and said: "God is not with the strong, but with the just. . . ." And he went to meet them [on the banks of the Neva] with a small retinue, without waiting for his large army, but trusting in the Holy Trinity. . . . And there was a great battle with the Romans [Catholics], and [Aleksandr] killed a countless multitude of them. . . .

· · ·

In the year 6750 [A.D. 1242]: Prince Aleksandr went in winter with men from Novgorod and with his brother Andrei and with men of the Volga region [the Niz], in great force, to the Chud land [Estonia] against the Germans, lest they boast and say: "We will subject the tribe of Slovenes [*Slovenskii iazyk,* the people of the Novgorod region] to ourselves"; for Pskov had been taken, and their own bailiff [tiun] installed. And Prince Aleksandr seized all the roads to Pskov, stormed the city by a sudden attack, and seized the Germans and Chuds, and, shackling them, imprisoned them in Novgorod, and himself went against the

Chuds. . . . The Germans and Chuds advanced toward them. Learning of this, Prince Aleksandr and the men of Novgorod drew up their forces on Lake Chud . . . and an army of Germans and Chuds came upon them, and they fought their way through his army in a wedge; and there was a great battle with the Germans and Chuds, with the crash of shattering spears and the sound of clashing swords, so that even the frozen sea moved and the ice could not be seen: for all was covered with blood. . . . And the Germans fell there, and the Chuds took to flight; they were pursued and slain on the ice for seven versty, up to the Sobolitskii shore; and countless Chuds fell, and five hundred Germans, and fifty others were taken prisoner and brought to Novgorod. . . . And the name of Aleksandr became famed in all the lands . . . as far as Rome itself.

· · ·

In the year 6754 [1246]: The stern prince Aleksandr went to the Tatar land to the caesar [i.e. the khan] Batu. For the caesar had spoken to him thus: "God has subjugated all the nations to me; you alone do not wish to subjugate yourself to me, nor to my power; but if you wish to preserve your land, come to me and perceive the glory of my realm." . . . Prince Aleksandr went straightway to Bishop Kiril and spoke these words to him: "Father, I want to go into the Horde to the caesar." Bishop Kiril, with all the clergy, blessed him, and he went to the caesar Batu. . . . The caesar Batu gave great honor and gifts to the Russian prince Aleksandr and dismissed him with great affection.

IV:6. THE FIRST NOVGORODIAN CHRONICLE ON THE TATARS IN NOVGOROD, 1257 AND 1259

Although the Tatars had missed Novgorod during their first sweep across the Russian plain, they wished to collect tribute from the Novgorodians as well as from the Russians further to the south. In these excerpts the chronicle suggests the varied responses of prince, boyars, common people, and the chronicler himself to the Tatars who came, as was their custom, to take a census in order to assess the area for the paying of tribute or the drafting of recruits.

Reference: *Novgorodskaia pervaia letopis'*, pp. 82-83; translation based on Michell and Forbes, *Chronicle of Novgorod*, pp. 95-96, somewhat revised.

[A.D. 1257:] Evil news came from Russia that the Tatars wanted the customs tax [*tamga*] and tithe [desiatina] from Novgorod; and people were disturbed the entire summer. . . .

The same winter Tatar envoys came with [Prince] Aleksandr [Nevskii] . . . and the envoys began to ask for the tithe and the customs tax, and the men of Novgorod did not agree to this, and gave presents to the [Tatar] caesar [tsesar', i.e. the khan], and let [the envoys] go in peace.

. . .

[A.D. 1259:] And the men of Novgorod agreed to be counted [for the payment of tribute]. The same winter the accursed raw-eating Tatars Berkai and Kasachik came with their wives and many others, and there was a great tumult in Novgorod, and they did much evil in the rural districts [volosti], taking tuska [a special tax] for the accursed Tatars. And the accursed ones began to fear death; they said to [Prince] Aleksandr: "Give us guards, lest they kill us." And the prince ordered the son of the posadnik and all the deti boiarskie to protect them by night. And the Tatars said: "Give us the tribute, or we will run away [presumably to return in greater strength]. And the common people would not submit to the census but said: "Let us die honorably for Sancta Sophia and for the holy temples." Then the people were divided: the worthy stood by Sancta Sophia and by the true faith, and there was an argument, with the greater men bidding the lesser to submit to the census. . . . And the next morning the prince left the Gorodishche, and the accursed Tatars with him, and by the counsel of evil men they agreed to be counted [and to pay tribute]; for the boyars thought to make it easy for themselves but hard on the lesser men. And the accursed ones began to ride through the streets, registering the Christian houses. . . . And having taken the census [and the tribute], the accursed ones went away, and Prince Aleksandr left afterward, having set his son Dmitrii on the throne.

IV:7. NOVGOROD'S TREATIES WITH ITS PRINCES, 1270 AND 1371

One expression of Novgorod's independence was the treaty or contract it customarily made with the man it agreed to acknowledge as its prince, and whose namestniki or vicegerents it would permit to reside in Novgorod. The following examples, of 1270 and 1371, show in what ways and to what extent Novgorod was able to limit the prince's interference in its internal affairs. The treaty of 1371 also shows how Novgorod, uncertain whether Dmitrii of Moscow or Mikhail of Tver' would win the Horde's endorsement, strove to assure that the city-state would in any event be on the side of the victor.

Reference: Sigizmund N. Valk, ed., *Gramoty velikogo Novgoroda i Pskova* (Moscow: AN SSSR, 1949), pp. 11–13, 28–30.

[Treaty between Novgorod and the grand prince of Tver', Iaroslav Iaroslavich, 1270. (Item IV:4, above, on the election of princes tells how Iaroslav worked out.)]

The bishop's blessing, and greetings from the *posadnik* Pavsha [Pavel Onan'inich], from all the great and the small and from all of Novgorod to the lord, Prince Iaroslav. Swear upon the cross, Prince, to all of Novgorod, what your forefathers and your father Iaroslav swore. You shall govern Novgorod as of old, in accordance with its ancient privileges. As for all the territories [volosti, here meaning lands beyond the original five provinces] of Novgorod, you, Prince, shall not govern these territories through your own men, but shall govern them through men of Novgorod; but you, Prince, shall receive gifts [*dar*] from these territories. And you, Prince, shall not hold trials, assign territories, or issue court decisions, without the posadnik. . . . And, as has been the custom for you, Prince, in Torzhok and Volok [Volokolamsk], your bailiff [*tiun*] shall govern in your section [*chast'*], and a Novgorodian [bailiff] in his section. And in Bezhitsy and in the entire land of Novgorod neither you, Prince, nor your princess, nor your boyars, nor your servitors shall own villages or buy them or accept them as gifts. And these, Prince, are the territories of Novgorod: Volok [Volokolamsk] with all its districts [volosti], Torzhok, Bezhitsy, the town of Palits, Melecha, Shipino, Egna, Zavoloch'e, Tre, Perm', Pechora, Iugra, Vologda. To [Staraia] Rusa, Prince, you shall go every third winter, and in summer, Prince, you shall go to Ozvado [a village near Staraia Rusa] to hunt wild animals. To Ladoga, Prince, you shall send a sturgeon fisherman and a mead brewer in accordance with the charter of your father Iaroslav. . . . To Ladoga, Prince, you shall go every third year. And you, Prince, shall not transfer people from Bezhitsy, or from any other territory of Novgorod, into your own land [volost'; i.e. Tver']; nor shall you issue documents; nor shall you, nor your princess, nor your boyars, nor your servitors, take in pledge [or, indenture] either peasants or merchants. You, Prince, shall not deprive a man of his territory [i.e. remove him from office] without cause, nor repeal court decisions. As for the meadowland that has belonged of old to you, Prince, and to your men, that shall belong to you and your men. . . . And as for the violence your brother Aleksandr did in Novgorod, you shall renounce this. Your dvoriane [here meaning the prince's servitors] shall receive travel payment [pogon] as before, five kuny [literally "martens," but here a metal currency] from the prince, and two kuny from a [prince's] bailiff. And throughout the land of Suzdal' and in your land [Tver'], Prince, you shall take as customs duties [myt] two vekshi ["squirrels," the smallest monetary unit] from each cartload, barge, and basket [korob, a unit of dry measure] of hops or flax. Your dvoriane shall not require transport service [povoz] from the merchants, unless there is news of war. You shall not establish tax-exempt settlements [slobody] or customs duties in the Novgorod land. . . . If a man or woman slave should make a complaint against his master, you shall not give credence to this. And you, Prince, shall not judge men of Novgorod in the Volga-Oka basin [the Niz] or grant revenues [i.e. grant financial and administrative jurisdiction over Novgorodian lands]. And as for the wrath which you, Prince, held against the posadnik and against all of Novgorod, you, Prince, must lay aside all enmity, and not take vengeance on anyone, great or small, either by trial or in any other way; and if anyone should make complaint to you, you shall not give credence to this. . . . You shall trade in the German settlement [dvor] through our own brethren, and you shall not close the settlement or appoint constables [pristavy]. . . . To all this, Prince, you

shall swear upon the cross to all of Novgorod. And our merchants shall trade throughout the land of Suzdal' without hindrance, in accordance with the tsar's [i.e. the Tatar khan's] charter. You shall send bailiffs on Saint Peter's day [June 29], as has been the custom. And you, Prince, shall not transfer men between the Suzdal' land and Novgorod. And as for those who are in pledge [indentured; zakladniki] to Prince Iurii [Iaroslav's nephew] in Torzhok or to you, or to the princess, or to your men: if he is a merchant, he shall return to his hundred [sto, an administrative unit], and if he is a peasant, he shall return to his pogost [rural administrative unit]. This has been the custom in Novgorod; release them all hence.

[Treaty between Novgorod and the grand prince of Tver', Mikhail Aleksandrovich, 1371:]

Greetings from the posadnik, and from the tysiatskii, and from all the great, and from all the small, and from all of Novgorod to the lord Grand Prince Mikhail. To this, Sire, all of Novgorod swears upon the cross. We shall maintain your rule faithfully, in accordance with your ancient rights, without injury; and you, Sire, shall likewise govern Novgorod in accordance with its ancient privileges, without injury. . . . And as for your villages, Prince, and those of the prelate [the bishop of Tver'], and the princess, and your boyars, and your servitors, in the land of Novgorod: whatever village has been obtained without payment [bez kun], it shall go [back] to Novgorod without payment; and if someone has bought [a village], he must find the second party [istets, i.e. from whom the village was bought], or his children; if there is no second party, or children, then he shall swear upon the cross that he knows of no second party, and he shall take, upon investigation, as large a payment as he gave, and the land [shall go] to Novgorod. And you, Prince, shall maintain the old boundary between the land of Suzdal' and Novgorod, as was under your grandfather and your great-grandfather Iaroslav. And as for the Novgorod territories [volosti], Prince, you shall not govern these territories through your men but through men from Novgorod; but you shall receive gifts from those territories. And you, Prince, shall not hold trials, assign territories, or issue court decisions without the posadnik. And you shall not deprive a man of his territory without cause. And you, Prince, shall go to [Staraia] Rusa in the autumn, as has been the custom. And in summer you shall go to Ozvado to hunt animals. . . . And neither you, Prince, nor your princess, nor your boyars, nor your servitors shall own villages, or buy them, or accept them as gifts, in Bezhitsy and throughout the entire land of Novgorod. . . . And throughout the land of Suzdal' and in your land [Tver'], Prince, you shall take as customs duties [myt] two vekshi from each cartload, barge, and basket of hops and flax. And your dvoriane shall not require transport service from the merchants, unless there is news of war. And you shall not establish tax-exempt settlements nor customs duties in the Novgorod land. And if a man or woman slave should make complaint against his master, you shall not give credence to this. And you, Prince, shall not judge men of Novgorod in the Volga-Oka basin [the Niz], or assign territories. And if anyone should make complaint to you, you shall not give credence to this. And you, Prince, shall trade in the German settlement through our brethren only, you shall not close the settlement, and you shall not appoint constables [pristavy]. And our merchants shall trade with the land of Suzdal' without hindrance, in accordance with the tsar's [i.e. the Tatar khan's] charter. And you shall send your judges on Saint Peter's day as has been the custom. And you, Prince, shall not transfer men between the land of Suzdal' and Novgorod. . . . And if there should be an outbreak of hostilities between Novgorod and the Germans or Lithuania or anyone else, you, Prince, shall help Novgorod without deceit. And you, Prince, shall not plan to make war without the consent of Novgorod. You shall not send constables from the Volga-Oka basin into any part of the Novgorod land. And [as for those who have been indentured,] if they are merchants, they shall return to their hundred, and if they are peasants, to their pogost; this has been the custom in Novgorod; release them hence. And you, Prince, must not bear wrath against anyone in Novgorod. And you, Prince, and your judges shall not repeal any legal decisions in the Novgorod land. You shall not hold arbitrary trials. And neither male nor female slaves shall be tried by your judges without their master. And your dvoriane shall not hold trials, nor remove them beyond the borders of the Novgorod land. And you shall give up the settlements [slobody] and villages [that you now possess]. And the grand prince has sworn upon the cross to all of this. And as for the sworn treaties [krestnaia gramota] between Novgorod and all the German cities, you, Prince, shall not violate those treaties, and shall preserve the men of Novgorod from sin. And if the [Tatar] Horde confers the grand principality upon you, you shall be our grand prince; but if the Horde does not confer the grand principality upon you, your vicegerents must leave Novgorod and the dependent towns [prigorody] of Novgorod, and this shall not be [considered] treachery on the part of Novgorod.

IV:8. THE CHARTER OF NOVGOROD, 1471

The legal code of the Novgorodian city-state was in a way a continuation of and supplement to the Russkaia Pravda of old Kiev. These excerpts are from the oldest extant version of this code or "charter," which was approved by the veche in 1471. (Concerning Novgorod's relations with Ivan III at this time, see the last five selections in Section B of this chapter, below.)

Reference: PRP, 2:212-18, with modern Russian translation on pp. 219-27; English translation based on George Vernadsky, Medieval Russian Laws (New York: Columbia University Press, 1947), pp. 83-92, slightly revised.

[PREAMBLE.] Having referred the matter to the lords, the grand princes—Grand Prince Ivan [III] Vasil'evich of all Russia and his son Grand Prince Ivan Ivanovich—for their approval, and having received the blessing of the archbishop-elect of Novgorod the Great and Pskov, Hieromonk [priest-monk] Feofil [Theophilus], we, the posadniki of Novgorod and the tysiatskie of Novgorod, and the boyars, and the well-to-do burghers [zhit'i liudi], and the merchants, and the common people [chernye liudi—"black people," the petty artisans and hired laborers], all the five boroughs [kontsy, "ends"], the whole of Lord Novgorod the Great, at the veche in Iaroslav's Courtyard, have completed and confirmed the following:

ARTICLE 1. The archbishop-elect of Novgorod the Great and Pskov, Hieromonk Feofil, in his court—the ecclesiastical court—shall conduct trials in accordance with the rules of the holy fathers, the Nomocanon. And he shall give equal justice to every litigant, be he a boyar, or a middle-class [zhit'i] burgher, or a lower-class [molodshii] burgher.

ART. 2. The posadnik in his court shall conduct trials jointly with the grand prince's vicegerents [namestniki], according to the old customs; and without the concurrence of the grand prince's vicegerents the posadnik may not conclude any lawsuit.

ART. 3. The grand prince's vicegerents and justices [tiuny] have authority to reexamine cases in appeal proceedings, according to the old customs.

ART. 4. The tysiatskii conducts trials in his court. And all of them must conduct trials justly according to the oath they swear upon the cross.

ART. 5. Each contestant may elect two assessors to sit in the court. And once the assessor is chosen by the contestant, he must continue to deal with him. But the authority of the posadnik, the tysiatskii, the archbishop's vicegerent, and their judges in the conduct of the trials must not be interfered with.

ART. 6. The litigant must not bring along with him his partisans for intimidating the other litigant, or the posadnik, or the tysiatskii, or the archbishop's vicegerent, or other judges, or the members of the court of reexamination [or court of appeals, dokladshiki]. And whoever brings his partisans for intimidating the posadnik, or the tysiatskii, or the archbishop's vicegerents, or other judges, or the members of the court of reexamination, or the other litigant, be it at the trial, or at the reexamination of the case, or on the duel field, stands guilty, and the grand princes and Novgorod the Great fine the culprit, for bringing his partisans, in the following amounts: the boyar, 50 rubles; the middle-class [zhit'i] burgher, 20 rubles; the lower-class [molodshii] burgher, 10 rubles; and in addition he pays damages to the other litigant. . . .

ART. 9. The posadnik, the tysiatskii, the archbishop's vicegerent, and their judges, and the borough judges shall complete the conduct of each trial within a month; and they may not prolong the conduct of any case beyond that term.

ART. 10. If anyone sues another for the forcible seizure and robbery of his land, the court tries first the case about the forcible seizure and robbery and then that about [the ownership of] the land. And whoever is accused in the forcible seizure of land and robbery, the grand princes and Novgorod the Great fine the culprit to the amount as follows: the boyar, 50 rubles; the middle-class burgher, 20 rubles; and the lower-class burgher, 10 rubles. . . .

ART. 14. Anyone commencing a lawsuit [after the promulgation of this charter] must swear upon the cross once [promising to obey the law]; and if he comes to the court hall without having sworn upon the cross, he must swear upon it and only then is allowed to sue; and if the defendant has not yet sworn upon the cross after the promulgation of this charter, he likewise must swear upon the cross and only then may sue; and if either litigant refuses to swear upon the cross he loses his case. . . .

ART. 25. At the court presided over by the grand prince's justice [tiun] there shall be an assessor for each litigant; the assessors must be reliable men and must conduct the trial honestly, after being sworn to obey the law according to this charter.

ART. 26. And if the case has been referred to the superior court [on the judge's recommendation], the court of reexamination meets in the archbishop's hall, with one boyar and one middle-class burgher from each borough [konets] present; also present are those judges and assessors who had tried the case in the lower court, as well as the assessors representing the litigants; and no one else is admitted.
. . .

ART. 27. The posadnik and tysiatskii, and the archbishop's vicegerent, and their judges, and the borough judges all have to swear upon the cross that they will conduct the trials justly

ART. 28. The trial of any lawsuit about land has to be completed within two months; and its conclusion may not be delayed over two months. . . .

ART. 29. If a judge has not completed a lawsuit about land within two months, the plaintiff shall receive, for his assistance, sergeants at arms [or "constables," pristavy] from Novgorod the Great, and the judge shall complete the case in the presence of these sergeants at arms.

B. OTHER ASPECTS OF LIFE IN NOVGOROD

IV:9. PRINCE VSEVOLOD'S STATUTE FOR THE MERCHANTS OF SAINT JOHN'S, CA. 1135

From Prince Vsevolod Mstislavich, whose rule in Novgorod ended in 1136 (see item IV:3), a statute (called *rukopisanie,* "testament") was transmitted, known to us in the form it took in the course of the thirteenth and fourteenth centuries (to ca. 1385). The document is the confirmation, by the prince, of the privileges of a powerful corporation ("Ivanskoe" kupechestvo) of Novgorodian merchants engaged in foreign trade. The corporation, being exempted from interference as these excerpts show, served as the main commercial tribunal under the authority of the tysiatskii.
Reference: *PRP,* 2:174-77.

I, Grand Prince Gavriil, called Vsevolod . . . have erected the Church of Saint John the Baptist on Petriatina Court . . .

1. To [the Church of] Saint John the Baptist I give for all time, from my great wealth, for the maintenance of the church, the duties [*ves*] on wax; and of the duties [*pud*] on wax in Torzhok, [I give] half to [the Church of] the Holy Savior [in Torzhok], and half to Saint John the Baptist on Petriatina Court. . . .

2. And I, Grand Prince Vsevolod, have installed three elders [starosty] in Saint John's from among the well-to-do burghers [zhit'i liudi], a tysiatskii to represent the common people [chernye liudi], and two elders from among the merchants, to manage all the affairs of Saint John's relating to trade, foreign merchants, and commercial courts; and the posadnik Miroslav, and the other [i.e. old but still active] posadniki, and the boyars of Novgorod, shall not interfere in any of the affairs of Saint John's.

3. And if anyone should wish to enter the ranks of the merchants of Saint John's, he shall pay an entrance fee of fifty grivny in silver to the corporate [*poshlye*] merchants, and of Ypres cloth to the tysiatskii, and [from this entrance fee] the merchants shall allot twenty-five grivny in silver to Saint John's. And if he does not enter the merchant ranks, and does not give fifty grivny in silver, he shall not be a corporate merchant. And [the status of] corporate merchant shall be obtained by heredity and by [paying] the entrance fee.

4. And weights shall be measured in the vestibule of Saint John's, to be done where it is prescribed. And weights shall be measured by the elders of Saint John's, by two corporate merchants, worthy men; and noncorporate merchants shall not be elders, nor measure the weights of Saint John's.

IV:10. A TREATY OF NOVGOROD WITH GOTLAND AND THE GERMAN CITIES, CA. 1190

Novgorod's flourishing trade with the German and Scandinavian towns in the Baltic area, through which Novgorodian merchants supplied furs, leather, wax, pitch, and other wares to western Europe, was regularized by occasional treaties. The oldest extant treaty between Novgorod and the German towns dates from the period 1189-99; among other things, it bespeaks the early role in Novgorod of merchants from the island of Gotland.
Reference: Valk, *Gramoty velikogo Novgoroda i Pskova,* pp. 55-56. See also *PRP,* 2:124-31.

I, Prince Iaroslav Vladimirovich, having taken counsel with the posadnik Miroshka, with the tysiatskii Iakov, and with all the people of Novgorod, have confirmed the existing agreement with the envoy Arbud, with all the Germans, with the people of Gotland, and with all the Latin [Catholic] peoples. I have sent my envoy Griga to [conclude] these terms. First: The envoys of Novgorod and all the people of Novgorod shall go in peace to the German land and to Gotland; likewise the Germans and the people of Gotland shall go to Novgorod without harm, without suffering injury from anyone. If the prince of Novgorod should try [a German merchant] in Novgorod, or a German [prince should try a Novgorodian] in the German land, by this agreement the merchant shall return home without harm. And this agreement shall be confirmed with whomever God ordains as prince, or else the land shall be without peace. If an envoy of Novgorod should be killed beyond the sea, or a German envoy in Novgorod, twenty grivny in silver [shall be paid] for that man. And if a

Novgorodian merchant should be killed [in the German land], or a German merchant in Novgorod, ten grivny in silver [shall be paid] for that man. If a man should be put in chains without cause, twelve grivny in old kuny [equals three grivny in silver] [shall be paid] for this dishonor. . . . If a lawsuit that does not involve bloodshed should arise, and witnesses gather, both Russians and Germans, then lots shall be cast; whoever the lot falls upon shall, after swearing an oath, take what is his right. If a Varangian [Scandinavian] should sue a Russian for a debt, or a Russian sue a Varangian, and he denies the debt, then [the plaintiff must produce] twelve men as witnesses and, after swearing an oath, shall take what is his. If a lawsuit should arise in the German land involving a Novgorodian, or involving a German in Novgorod, [the defendant] shall not be detained at the border, but the complaint shall be renewed the following year. . . . Germans shall not be put in prison in Novgorod [for debt], nor a Novgorodian in the German land; what is due shall be exacted from the guilty one instead. . . . If a hostage or priest from Novgorod should be killed [in the German land], or a German [hostage or priest] in Novgorod, twenty grivny in silver [shall be paid] for that man.

IV:11. THE FIRST NOVGORODIAN CHRONICLE ON THE ELECTION OF ARCHBISHOPS BY THE VECHE OF NOVGOROD, 1156-1415

The archbishop of Novgorod, the leading church official of the Novgorodian realm, governed the extensive lands of the church and was an important political figure. Beginning with the middle of the twelfth century, the archbishop's office was no longer filled simply by appointment from the metropolitan of Kiev. Instead, the "people of Novgorod" exercised their will, in ways suggested by these excerpts from the chronicle.

Reference: *Novgorodskaia pervaia letopis'*, pp. 29-30, 40, 68, 365, 405; translation based on Michell and Forbes, *Chronicle of Novgorod*, pp. 21-22, 36, 72-73, 147, 183-84, somewhat revised.

[In 1156] Archbishop [actually "Bishop"] Nifont died. . . . The same year all the townspeople gathered together and decided to appoint as their bishop Arkadii, a man chosen by God; and all the people went and took him out of the Monastery of the Holy Virgin, [in the presence of] Prince Mstislav Iur'evich, all the clergy of Sancta Sophia, all the town priests, and the abbots and the monks; and they installed him, entrusting him with the bishopric in the court of Sancta Sophia, until there should be a metropolitan in Russia [the see was vacant at that time], and then he should go to be consecrated.

· · ·

[In 1193] Gavrilo, archbishop of Novgorod, died. . . . And the men of Novgorod, having consulted with Prince Iaroslav, the abbots, the retainers of [the Cathedral of] Sancta Sophia, and the priests, decided on Marturii, chosen by God, and sent for him and brought him from [Staraia] Russa, and installed him as bishop; and they sent [word] to the metropolitan and he sent for him with honor; and he [Marturii] went [to Kiev] with the foremost men; and Prince Sviatoslav and the metropolitan received him with love; and they consecrated him on December 10 . . . and he returned to Novgorod on January 16.

· · ·

. . . The same year [1229], Prince Mikhail said: "Behold, you have no bishop and it is not seemly for this town to be without a bishop; . . . you should look for a suitable man, whether from among priests, abbots, or monks." And some said to the prince: "There is a monk, a deacon at Saint George's [Monastery] named Spiridon; he is worthy of it!" And others named Ioasaf [Joasaph], bishop of Vladimir in Volynia, and yet others a Greek: "Whomever the metropolitan shall give, that one shall be our father." And Prince Mikhail said: "Let us cast three lots; let it be whom God will give us." And having written out the names, they laid them on the altar and sent out young Prince Rostislav from the bishop's council chamber [to draw lots]. God chose a servant for himself and a shepherd for the flock in Novgorod and in its entire region, and [the name of] Spiridon was drawn; and they sent to the monastery for him, and having brought him, they installed him in the court [of Sancta Sophia], until he should go to Kiev to be consecrated.

. . .

[In 1359] . . . Archbishop Moisei left his office of his own free will on account of ill health . . . and all Novgorod implored him to remain, but he would not; but he blessed them saying: "Choose a man for yourselves, whomever God gives you."

And having deliberated much, the posadnik and the tysiatskii and all Novgorod and the abbots and priests decided not to make a choice for themselves by human means, but decided to accept God's decision and to trust in his mercy, and let God designate whomever he and Sancta Sophia should desire. And they selected three men: the monk Aleksei, steward [kliuchnik] of the Cathedral of Sancta Sophia; Savva, abbot of the Monastery of Saint Anthony; and Ivan, a priest of Saint Barbara's Church; and they placed three lots on the altar in Sancta Sophia, declaring: "Whomsoever God and Sancta Sophia, the Wisdom of God, may desire to have as a servant at His altar, his lot will He leave on

His altar." And God and Sancta Sophia chose as prelate the good, wise, and perspicacious monk Aleksei and left his lot on His altar; and all Novgorod brought him with honor to the episcopal palace on September 15 . . . and installed him until the metropolitan should summon him for consecration.

. . .

[In 1415, when Archbishop Ivan resigned his office] the men of Novgorod, after deliberating in Iaroslav's Courtyard and holding a veche at Sancta Sophia, placed three lots upon the altar with the [following] names: Samson, monk of the Holy Savior [Monastery] in Khutin; Mikhail, abbot of Saint Michael's in Skovorodka [near Novgorod]; and Lev, abbot of the [Monastery of the] Holy Virgin in Kolmovo [near Novgorod]. And at the end of the holy service the old archpriest [protopop] Vasilii brought out to the veche first Lev's lot, then Mikhail's, and Samson's remained on the altar; then the posadnik, Andrei Ivanovich and the tysiatskii, Aleksandr Ignat'evich, with the men of Novgorod, installed Samson with honor in the Cathedral of Sancta Sophia.

IV:12. THE FIRST NOVGORODIAN CHRONICLE ON CIVIL VIOLENCE IN NOVGOROD, 1228-1418

The city-state of Novgorod, with its democratic ways, suffered economic and social strife between competing boyar interests, between rich and poor, and between shifting alliances of various elements. In these excerpts from the First Novgorodian Chronicle the reader will perceive some of the modes of conflict and settlement, even if he may not always be certain who is fighting whom, or why.

Reference: *Novgorodskaia pervaia letopis'*, pp. 67, 70, 356, 365-66, 379, 382, 409-10; translation based on Michell and Forbes, *Chronicle of Novgorod*, pp. 71, 75, 138, 147-48, 160, 162, 187-88, considerably revised.

[In 1228] the whole town rose in tumult, and they went from the veche in arms against the tysiatskii Viacheslav and plundered his homestead and those of his brother Boguslav, of Andrei the archbishop's steward, of Davydko [the steward] of Sancta Sophia, and of Sudimir [a boyar]. And they sent [men] to plunder Dushilich, the elder [starosta] of Lipno [a village near Novgorod] and were going to hang him, but he escaped to [Prince] Iaroslav. But they seized his wife, saying: "These people incite the prince to evil," and there was great tumult in the town.

. . .

[In 1230] . . . they killed Semen Borisovich [a former posadnik], plundered his whole house and his villages, and seized his wife; and they buried him at the Saint George

monastery. Similarly the homesteads and villages of Vodovik [the incumbent posadnik] and of his brother Mikhail, of Danislav [a boyar], of Boris the tysiatskii, and of Tvorimir, and many other homesteads [were plundered]. And Vodovik, having heard of this evil, fled from Torzhok with his brothers, and the tysiatskii Boris with the men of Torzhok [fled] to [Prince] Mikhail [Vsevolodovich] in Chernigov. And they gave the office of posadnik to Stepan Tverdislavich, and to Nikita Petrilovich the office of tysiatskii, and the property of Semen and Vodovik was distributed among the hundreds. [Note: Each borough (konets) was divided into two "hundreds"—*sotnia* or *sto*.] Where others had labored and harvested, these [people] had gotten the fruit of their labors.

. . .

[In 1342] . . . the common people [chernye liudi] rose against Andrei and the posadnik Fedor Danilov. . . . And Onisifor and Matvei [both former posadniki] summoned a veche at Sancta Sophia, while Fedor and Andrei summoned another in Iaroslav's Courtyard. And Onisifor and Matvei sent the archbishop to the veche, but, not waiting for the archbishop's return from that veche, they attacked Iaroslav's Courtyard and there seized Matvei Koska and his son Ignatii, and they imprisoned them in a church, while Onisifor fled with his confederates. That was in the morning; and by midday the whole town was up in arms, one side against the other, until Archbishop Vasilii with the vicegerent [namestnik] Boris made peace between them. So the cross was exalted and the Devil vanquished.

. . .

. . . The same spring [1359], God permitting it on account of our sins, and through the actions of the Devil, and by the advice of wicked men, there was a great tumult in Novgorod; they took the office of posadnik away from Adrian Zakharich, [by the will of] not all Novgorod, but only the Slavenskii borough, and they gave the office of posadnik to Sil'vestr Leontievich. And a great disturbance arose in Iaroslav's Courtyard, and there was a fight because the men of the Slavenskii [borough] attacked with arms and dispersed the men from across the river [the left bank] who were without arms, and they wounded and robbed many boyars and killed Ivan Borisov Likhinin.

Then the two sides armed themselves against each other; the Sophia side [the left bank of the Volkhov] sought to avenge the dishonor of its brothers, and the Slavenskii side [the right bank] fought for their lives and property. They stood opposite each other for three days, for the Slavenskii men had wrecked the bridge. And [the former] Archbishop Moisei [who had just resigned his office] and Aleksei [the newly appointed archbishop] came out of the monastery, taking with them the archimandrite and the abbots, and blessed them, saying: "My children, do not bring triumph to the pagans and desolation to the sacred churches and to this place; engage not in battle." And they accepted his word, and dispersed.

[A.D. 1384:] The townsmen of Orekhov and of Korela [both on Lake Ladoga] came to Novgorod complaining of Prince Patrikii [a Lithuanian prince who had been given these two towns as *kormlenie*]. And Prince Patrikii incited the Slavenskii [borough] to rise and created turmoil in Novgorod. And the Slavenskii people sided with the prince and they held a veche in Iaroslav's Courtyard, while another veche met at Sancta Sophia; and both were armed as for battle, and they wrecked the great bridge [across the Volkhov]; but God and Sancta Sophia preserved us from internal strife. They took away those towns from the prince, and they gave him [the two towns of] [Staraia] Russa and Ladoga.

. . .

[In 1388] . . . the three boroughs of the Sophia side rose against Posadnik Osip Zakhar'evich, and, summoning a veche at Sancta Sophia, they went like a large army, every one armed, to his homestead, and seized his house, and destroyed the buildings. Posadnik Osip fled across the river to the Plotnitskii borough; and the entire Commercial Quarter [the right bank of the Volkhov] rose up for him, and began to rob people, and to beat off the ferry-men from the shore, and to destroy the boats; and so they were without peace for two weeks, and then they came together in agreement, and gave the office of posadnik to Vasilii Ivanovich.

. . .

[1418:] And the people, learning that Stepanko [a citizen who had assaulted a boyar] had been seized [by the boyar], began to summon a veche in Iaroslav's Courtyard, and a multitude of people assembled, and they kept shouting and crying for many days: "Let us go against that boyar and plunder his house." And they came armed and with a banner to the Street of Saints Cosmas and Damian, [and] they sacked his house and many other homesteads. . . . And again they became enraged, as if drunk, against another boyar, Ivan Ievlich, of Chudintseva Street, and pillaged a great many boyar's houses along with his; and they pillaged the Monastery of Saint Nicholas in the Fields, crying out: "Here is the treasure house of the boyars." And again the same morning they plundered many homesteads in Liudgoshcha Street, calling out: "They are our enemies." And they came to Prusskaia [Prussian] Street, but there they beat them off successfully. From that hour the animosity began to increase. Returning to their own district, the Commercial Quarter, they decided that the Sophia side was going to arm against them and plunder their houses. And they began to ring throughout the whole town, and armed men began to pour out from both sides [of the river] as for war, fully armed, to the great bridge. And men perished, some from arrows, others from firearms. They died as in war; the whole town trembled at this terrible storm and great insurrection, and a dread fell upon the people on both sides. And Archbishop Simeon shed tears from his eyes on hearing of the internecine strife between his children. . . . And the prelate came and stood in the middle of the bridge, and raised the lifegiving cross, and began to bless both sides. And those who looked at the glorious cross wept. The men of the Commercial Quarter heard of the prelate's arrival, and the posadnik Fedor Timofeevich came with the other posadniki and tysiatskie and bowed to the archbishop. . . . And they dispersed, through the prayers of the Holy Virgin and with the blessing of Archbishop Simeon, and there was peace in the town.

IV:13. THE VOSKRESENSK CHRONICLE ON THE NOVGORODIAN RIVER RAIDERS, 1375

Among the favorite pastimes of the tough young men of Novgorod was to go raiding, many boatloads strong, all over the Russian plain, wherever the rivers could carry them. One of the more famous exploits of these "brave lads," as the Novgorodians called them, is reported here in the less admiring words of the Voskresensk Chronicle.
    Reference: *PSRL*, 8:23-24.

That same summer [1375] when the grand prince [of Muscovy] was in the vicinity of Tver', at that same time brigands came from Novgorod the Great, in seventy boats, with their leaders Prokofii and Smolnianin; and they came to Kostroma and began to prepare their forces for battle, and the townspeople came out to meet them in battle. . . . They [the brigands] came to the city and saw that there was no one guarding it, and that it had no defense from any side, and they entered it and plundered everything that was in it; they remained there a whole week, and found everything that was hidden there, and carried out all the goods into an open place, and took what was best and lightest, and threw what was heavy and unneeded into the Volga, and burned other things, and took a great number of Christians captive—men, and women, and children, youths and maidens—and set forth with them. They went downstream to Nizhnii-Novgorod and did much evil there; they killed Moslems and Christians too, and led others into captivity with their wives and children, and plundered their goods. And they went downstream and turned up the Kama, and plundered much going along the Kama, and then returned to the Volga, and reached the land of the Bulgars, and here they sold all their Christian captives and then went downstream to Sarai, killing Moslems and foreign merchants, seizing their goods, and plundering Christians. And they reached the city of Khaztorokan' [Astrakhan'] at the mouth of the Volga near the sea, and there the prince of Khaztorokan', named Salchei, killed them by deceit; thus they were all killed without mercy; not one of them remained alive. The Moslems took all their wealth, and thus perished these evil brigands.

IV:14. THE FIRST NOVGORODIAN CHRONICLE ON A NOVGORODIAN
MILITARY EXPEDITION, 1398

The chronicle here relates an interesting and characteristic episode in the struggle between Novgorod and Moscow for control of the northern Russian hinterland.
    Reference: *Novgorodskaia pervaia letopis'*, pp. 389-91; translation based on Michell and Forbes, *Chronicle of Novgorod*, pp. 169-70, considerably revised.

[1397:] And the men of the [Northern] Dvina [region], Ivan Mikitin, the boyars of the Dvina, and all the people of the Dvina gave their allegiance to the grand prince [Vasilii I of Moscow] and swore an oath upon the cross to the grand prince; and the grand prince, violating his oath, took Volok Lamskii [Volokolamsk] with its volosti, Torzhok with its volosti, and Vologda and Bezhitsy away from Novgorod; and then he renounced his oath to Novgorod and sent back the sworn charter. . . .

And the men of Novgorod with their father the archbishop sent envoys . . . to the grand prince. . . . And the grand prince did not accept the blessing and the good words of the archbishop, nor the petition from the Novgorod envoys; he did not withdraw his displeasure from Novgorod, and he did not make peace with them. . . .

[1398:] In the spring, after Easter, the men of Novgorod said to their lord [and] father, Archbishop Ivan: "We cannot, Lord Father, endure this violence from our grand prince, Vasilii Dmitrievich, who has taken away from Novgorod and Sancta Sophia the dependent towns [prigorody] and territories [here, volosti] that belonged to our fathers and grandfathers; but we intend to try to recover the dependent towns and territories of Sancta Sophia which belonged to our fathers and grandfathers." And they swore upon the cross as one man to try to recover

the dependent towns and territories of Sancta Sophia and Novgorod the Great. And the posadnik Timofei Iur'evich, the posadnik Iurii Dmitrievich, Vasilii Borisovich, the boyars, the deti boiarskie, the zhit'i liudi ["well-to-do people"], the merchants' sons [i.e. not yet themselves registered as guild merchants] and all the soldiers [voi] petitioned: "Bless us, Lord Father Archbishop, in our attempt to recover the dependent towns and territories of Sancta Sophia. We shall either regain our patrimony for Sancta Sophia and for Novgorod the Great, or we shall lay down our lives for Sancta Sophia and for our Lord Novgorod the Great." And Archbishop Ivan blessed his children and the voevody of Novgorod and all the soldiers, and Novgorod sent forth its brethren, saying to them thus: "Go, try to recover the dependent towns and the territories of Sancta Sophia and our patrimony." And the voevody of Novgorod, Posadnik Timofei, Posadnik Iurii, and Vasilii, and all the soldiers went off to the Dvina. [And the Dvina region was reconquered by the Novgorodians.]

IV:15. ENACTMENTS OF THE NOVGORODIAN VECHE, 1411, 1452, 1459-1469

The following excerpts from charters or enactments of the Novgorodian veche illustrate the all-embracing competence of this rather unwieldy instrument of democracy.

Reference: Valk, *Gramoty velikogo Novgoroda i Pskova*, pp. 146 [charter of 1411], 127 [1452], 152-53 [1459-69].

[Grant charter of ca. 1411:]

To the lord posadnik of Novgorod Vasilii Mikitin, to the Novgorod tysiatskii Avram Stepanovich, and to all of lord Novgorod the Great, to the veche in Iaroslav's Courtyard. [The following men] have made petition. . . . And the posadnik and the tysiatskii and all of lord Novgorod the Great have given a grant charter [zhalovannaia gramota], at the veche in Iaroslav's Courtyard, to the peasants [siroty] of Terpilov rural district [pogost]: that they should give the basic tax on plowland [poral'e] to the posadnik and the tysiatskii in accordance with the old charters: forty squirrels, and four sevy [unit of dry measure] of flour, and ten loaves of bread. . . . And if anyone should violate this charter, he shall give one hundred rubles to Novgorod.

[Charter of 1452:]

From the Novgorod posadnik Mikhail Onan'inich, and from the Novgorod tysiatskii

Onikii Vlasievich, and from all of lord Novgorod the Great, from the veche in Iaroslav's Courtyard, to Nikita Tinchov. As for the two rubles you took from the Kolyvan [Revel', or Tallinn] envoy Ivan and from Gostil, you shall return them. And do not disobey the command of Novgorod the Great; and if you should disobey, you shall be punished by Novgorod the Great.

[Grant charter to Solovki Monastery, ca. 1459-69:]

To His Grace the prelate Iona, lord archbishop of Novgorod the Great and Pskov, to the senior lord posadnik of Novgorod the Great, Ivan Lukinich, and the other posadniki, to the senior lord tysiatskii of Novgorod the Great Trufan Iur'evich and the other tysiatskie, and to the boyars, and to the well-to-do people and to the merchants, and to the common people [chernye liudi], and to all of lord sovereign Novgorod the Great, to all the five boroughs [kontsy], to the veche in Iaroslav's Court-yard. The abbot Ivonia and all the monks of the [Monastery of the] Holy Savior and Saint Nicholas, from Solovki, from the ocean sea, have petitioned, saying thus: "Sirs, the Monastery of the Holy Savior and Saint Nicholas, our hermitage, is very far away, a hundred versty from [the nearest] communities; [we petition,] sirs, that you grant to the Monastery of the Holy Savior and Saint Nicholas, and to us the needy, these islands of Solovki, and the island of Anzer, and the island of Nuksy, and the island of Zaichii, and the small islands." And with the blessing of His Grace the prelate Iona, archbishop of Novgorod the Great and Pskov, the senior lord posadnik of Novgorod the Great, Ivan Luki-nich, and the other posadniki, and the senior lord tysiatskii of Novgorod the Great, Trufan Iur'evich, and the other tysiatskie, and the boyars, and the well-to-do people, and the merchants, and the common people, and all of lord sovereign Novgorod the Great, all five boroughs, at the veche in Iaroslav's Court-yard, have granted to Abbot Ivonia and to all the monks, to the Monastery of the Holy Savior and Saint Nicholas, those islands of Solovki, and the island of Anzer, and Nuksy Island, and Zaichii Island, and the small

islands, and the land, the hunting grounds, the fisheries, the meadows, and the wooded lakes on those islands: they shall till the land, mow the meadows, and fish in the wooded lakes and in the fishing grounds freely. And neither the Novgorod boyars, nor the Karelians, nor anyone else shall interfere in these islands. . . . And if anyone should come to these islands for hunting or for fishing, for tallow or for hides, he shall give a tenth part of everything to the Monastery of the Holy Savior and Saint Nicholas. And the abbot and all the monks of the Monastery of the Holy Savior and Saint Nicholas shall keep these islands, the land and water, the hunting grounds, fisheries, and meadows, in accordance with this grant charter of Novgorod the Great for all time. And Novgorod the Great shall protect the abbot and all the monks. And if anyone should interfere in these islands in violation of this grant charter of Novgorod the Great, he shall give to the treasury of Novgorod the Great one hundred rubles. And His Grace the prelate Iona, lord archbishop of Novgorod the Great and Pskov, and the incumbent posadnik Ivan Lukinich and the incumbent tysiatskii Trufan Iur'evich have affixed their seals to this charter; by command of all of lord sovereign Novgorod the Great, all the five boroughs have affixed their seals.

IV:16. GHILLEBERT DE LANNOY ON NOVGOROD, 1413

The French diplomat and traveler Ghillebert de Lannoy (1386-1462) visited Novgorod as a young man in 1413. In the memoirs he wrote later in life, he made many acute observations, although in this passage his note on the selling of women should serve to remind us that the traveler is not always a reliable source.

Reference: Ghillebert de Lannoy, *Oeuvres de Ghillebert de Lannoy* . . . (Louvain, 1878), pp. 32-34, 36.

Novgorod the Great is a remarkably large city; it is situated on a beautiful plain, surrounded by great forests, and is located in a lowland amid waters and swamps. Through the afore-mentioned city flows a great river called the Volkhov. The city is encircled by poor walls, made of wattles and earth, while the towers are of stone. This city is free [*franche*] and has a communal government [*seignourie de commune*]. There is a bishop here who is like their sovereign [*souverain*]. And in common with all the other Russians in Russia, which is very extensive, they observe the Christian religion according to their own rites, which are the same as those of the Greeks. And in

the aforementioned city there are three hundred and fifty churches. They have a castle situated on the bank of the aforementioned river, and in it stands the Cathedral of Sancta Sophia, which they revere, and their afore-mentioned bishop lives there.

Likewise, inside the aforementioned city live many great seigneurs, whom they call boyars, and there are townspeople, remarkably rich and powerful, who own lands as much as two hundred leagues [*lieues*] in length. And the Russians of great Russia [*Russie*] have no other rulers except for these seigneurs, who are elected in succession as the commune [*le commun*] wishes. Their coins consist of pieces of silver without impressions, weighing about six ounces, since they do not strike gold coins at all; while their small coins consist of heads of squirrels and martens [i.e. actual coins with these names]. They have a market in their city, in which they sell and buy women for themselves, which they have a right to do (whereas we, as true Christians, would never dare to do this), and they buy their women, replacing one with another, for a piece or two of silver, whatever they agree upon—so that one would give the other a sufficient amount. They have two leaders: the duke [*duc*, referring here to the tysiatskii] and the burgrave [the posadnik], who govern the aforesaid city. These rulers are renewed from year to year. And I visited the afore-mentioned bishop and seigneurs there.

Likewise, the women wear their hair plaited in two braids, hanging in back, and the men, in a single braid. I was in this city nine days, and each day the aforementioned bishop sent more than thirty men to me with bread, meat, fish, hay, oats, beer, and mead, and the aforementioned duke and burgrave held for me the strangest and most remark-able banquet I have ever seen. That winter it was so cold that it would be entertaining to tell of the cold spell they had, because I had to travel during a cold spell.

. . .

The seigneurs of Novgorod together have forty thousand horsemen and countless foot soldiers. They often are at war with their neighbors, particularly with the Livonian knights, and in the past have won many great battles.

IV:17. A LETTER FROM NOVGOROD TO RIGA, CA. 1435

This Novgorodian business letter affords a glimpse of the employment procedures in cases where a skilled craftsman was needed and reveals a surprising willingness to overlook religious differences.
    Reference: Valk, *Gramoty velikogo Novgoroda i Pskova*, p. 108.

The blessing of His Grace [*preosviashchennyi*] the prelate of Novgorod the Great and Pskov, Archbishop Efimii, to the posadniki of Riga and to the magistrates [*ratmany*], and to the good people. I have sent to you my servitor Petr, in order [to procure] a master of the bell-making craft; and you, our neighbors, posadniki, and magistrates, and all the good

people, send a good master of the bell-making craft to us, for our sake, and thereby extend to us your friendship. And when your answer reaches us, we will gladly extend to you our friendship in return and perform a favor for you. And we will give the master whatever remuneration you give him for his work.

IV:18. A TREATY OF NOVGOROD WITH THE HANSEATIC TOWNS, JULY 16, 1436

This treaty is one of the many documents that provide clues to the nature of Novgorod's rela-tions with the Hanseatic League.
    Reference: Valk, *Gramoty velikogo Novgoroda i Pskova*, pp. 110-12.

The German envoys came to Novgorod the Great. . . . There also came envoys from Riga, Iur'ev [Dorpat], Kolyvan [Revel'], and Lübeck, from seventy-three towns on this seacoast and beyond the sea, and from all the merchantry. And the German envoys . . . concluded an agreement with the Novgorod posadnik Boris Iur'evich, and with the Nov-gorod tysiatskii Fedor Iakovlevich, and with the merchant elders [starosty], for all of Novgorod, to the effect that German mer-chants shall have free passage to come to Novgorod the Great and to leave, by water and by land, in accordance with the old treaties and in accordance with the old oaths sworn upon the cross, and in accordance with

this treaty and by this agreement, without any deceit. Likewise did the German envoys . . . conclude an agreement with the Novgorod posadnik Boris Iur'evich, and the Novgorod tysiatskii Fedor Iakovlevich, and the mer-chant elders Aleksandr and Efrem, and all the merchants' sons, and all of Novgorod the Great, for all the seventy-three towns and for all the merchantry, to the effect that the people of Novgorod should have free passage to travel to the German land and to the Ger-man towns, by land and by water, to come and go with their goods, in accordance with the old treaties and in accordance with the old oaths sworn upon the cross, and in ac-cordance with this treaty and by this agreement, without any deceit. And the German merchants shall trade with the merchants of Novgorod in Novgorod the Great or on the Neva, in accordance with the old oaths sworn upon the cross and in accordance with this treaty and by this agreement, without any deceit. The people of Novgorod shall give legal protection to the Germans as to their brother Novgorodians, and the Germans shall give legal protection to the people of Novgorod as to their brother Germans. And Novgorod the Great shall render justice to Germans who make complaint, in accordance with the old treaties, and in accordance with the old oaths sworn upon the cross, and in accordance with this treaty and by this agreement, without any deceit. Likewise shall the Germans render justice to people of Novgorod who make complaint, in accordance with the old treaties and in accordance with the old oaths sworn upon the cross, and in accordance with this treaty and by this agreement, without any deceit, on either side. . . . And if any Russian is on the German blacklist, he shall be taken off the blacklist and traded with as before. And as for the people of Novgorod who were under arrest in the German settlement, or who were themselves detaining Germans, the Germans shall not sue the people of Novgorod for this but shall trade with them as before. To all of this the Novgorod posadnik Boris Iur'evich, and the Novgorod tysiatskii Fedor Iakovlevich, and the merchant elders Aleksandr Matveevich and Efrem Iakovlevich have agreed, for all their towns and for their entire land, and have affixed their seals. Likewise have the German envoys . . . agreed for the seventy-three towns and for their entire land, and affixed their seals to this treaty.

IV:19. NOVGOROD'S TREATY WITH KING CASIMIR IV OF POLAND, 1470

In 1470, feeling that Novgorod's self-rule was threatened by the powerful Muscovite state of Ivan III, the Novgorodian leaders turned to Moscow's rival, Casimir [Kazimierz] of Poland and Lithuania, and arrived at the following terms.

Reference: Valk, *Gramoty velikogo Novgoroda i Pskova*, pp. 130-32.

I, the illustrious king of Poland and grand duke of Lithuania, have concluded a treaty with the archbishop-elect Feofil, and with the posadniki of Novgorod, and with the tysiatskie, and with the boyars, and with the well-to-do people [zhit'i liudi], and with the merchants, and with all of Novgorod the Great. And the envoys came to me. . . . I concluded a treaty with them and with all of Novgorod the Great, with its free men. [The terms of the Novgorodians follow:] You, illustrious King, shall govern Novgorod the Great in accordance with this sworn treaty. And you, illustrious King, shall maintain as your vicegerent in the Gorodishche a person of our Greek faith, Orthodox Christianity. And your vicegerent shall not hold trials without the Novgorod posadnik. . . . And your vicegerent shall hold trials in accordance with the customs of Novgorod. And your majordomo [dvoretskii] shall live in the palace in the Gorodishche, in accordance with the customs of Novgorod. . . . And your judge [tiun] shall sit in chamber [odrina] with the Novgorod constables [pristavy]. And your vicegerent, and steward, and judge shall have fifty men with them in the Gorodishche. And your vicegerent shall hold trials with the posadniki in the prelate's court, in the traditional place, whether judging boyars or well-to-do people or common folk [molodshie liudi] or villagers. And he shall hold fair trial, in accordance with the oath he has sworn, judging all equally. And he shall take the *peresud* [payment for appealing a case] in accordance with the sworn treaty of Novgorod, an equal amount with the posadnik; and he shall take no payment other than the peresud. And you shall not interfere in trials conducted by the prelate, or tysiatskii, or monasteries, as of old. And if the grand prince of Moscow, or his son or his brother, should attack Novgorod the Great, or incite another land against Novgorod the Great, you, Sire, our illustrious King, shall mount your horse for Novgorod the Great and go against the grand prince with your entire Lithuanian Council [rada], and defend Novgorod the Great. And if, Sire, illustrious King, you should go into the Polish or the German land without making peace between Novgorod the Great and the grand prince, and if in your absence, Sire, the grand prince, or his son, or his brother should attack Novgorod the Great or incite an-other land against it, your Lithuanian Council [of Lords] shall mount horses for Novgorod the Great, in accordance with the oath you have sworn on the cross, and shall defend Novgorod.

. . .

And as for the territories [volosti] of Novgorod, illustrious King, you shall not gov-ern them through your men, but through men of Novgorod. . . . And in the land of Novgorod neither you, illustrious King, nor your queen, nor your children, nor your princes, nor your lords [pany], nor your servitors shall erect villages, or buy them, or accept them as gifts. And if a male or female slave, or a peasant [smerd], should make a complaint against his master, you, illustrious King, shall not give credence to this. And a merchant shall return to his hundred [sto, or sotnia], and a peasant shall belong to his potug [administrative unit, apparently a new name for pogost] in Nov-gorod, as before. And you, illustrious King, shall not send constables into any of the provinces of Novgorod. And you, illustrious King, shall not take our Greek Orthodox faith away from us. and we shall appoint prelates of our free will, whomever it pleases us, Novgorod the Great, in our Orthodox Christianity. And you, illustrious King, shall

not erect Roman [Catholic] churches in Novgorod the Great, nor in the dependent towns of Novgorod, nor anywhere in the land of Novgorod. . . . And if you, Sire, illustrious King, should make peace between Novgorod the Great and the grand prince [of Moscow], you, illustrious King, shall collect *chernyi bor* [an extraordinary general requisition] in the provinces of Novgorod once only, as of old, in accordance with the former treaties, but you must not collect chernyi bor in subsequent years. And you shall not close the German settlement, or appoint your constables; and your merchants shall trade with the Germans through our brethren. And envoys and mer-chants shall have free passage on both sides, throughout the land of Lithuania and the land of Novgorod. And you, illustrious King, shall govern Novgorod the Great in accordance with the will of its free men, in accordance with our customs and in accordance with this sworn treaty. And swear to all of this upon the cross, illustrious King, for your entire realm and for the entire Lithuanian Council [of Lords], to all of Novgorod the Great, truly, without any deceit. And the envoys of Novgorod have sworn upon the cross sincerely as men of Novgorod to the illustrious king for all of Novgorod the Great, truly, without any deceit.

IV:20. THE THIRD NOVGORODIAN CHRONICLE ON THE CHASTISING OF NOVGOROD BY IVAN III, 1471

The reaction of Moscow to Novgorod's treaty of 1470 with Casimir was to attack. Casimir gave no help. The so-called Third Novgorodian Chronicle, which brings together accounts composed mostly in the sixteenth and seventeenth centuries, tells us what happened and how, at least from one viewpoint.

Reference: Arkheograficheskaia Komissiia, ed., *Novgorodskie letopisi (Novgorodskaia vtoraia i Novgorodskaia tret'ia letopisi)* (St. Petersburg, 1879), pp. 291-92.

Thus [in the year 1471] did the grand prince [of Moscow] advance with all his host against his patrimonial domain Novgorod the Great because of the treacherous spirit of the people, their pride, and their apostasy into Latinism. With a numerous and overpowering force he occupied the entire Novgorod country from border to border, visiting every part of it with the dread powers of his fire and sword. . . .

The Novgorod country was filled with lakes and swamps, for which reason mounted forces had never been employed in the sum-mertime against Novgorod by former grand princes; and the wicked people in their wonted

contumacy, following their own evil ways from the autumn to the winter, and even up to springtime, lived in security during the summer because of the inundation of the terrain.

But now, by the beneficence of God, vouchsafed by God from on high to Grand Prince Ioan Vasilievich of all Russia to the detriment of the Novgorod land, not a drop of rain had fallen during the summer, from the month of May to the month of Septem-ber, and the land dried out and the impas-sable swamps were dried up by the heat of the sun. The troops of the grand prince found no impediments and could ride in every direction over the country. . . . Thus did the Lord God through this desiccation of the earth punish the men of Novgorod for their evildoing and subject them to the strong hand of the pious sovereign and grand prince, Ioan Vasilievich of all Russia.

IV:21. THE VOSKRESENSK CHRONICLE ON NOVGOROD, POLAND, AND MOSCOW, 1470-1471

A somewhat different version of Novgorod's relations with Poland and with Moscow in 1470-71 is provided by the Voskresensk Chronicle.
Reference: *PSRL*, 8:159-61, 163.

Some of [the Novgorodians], the children of the posadnik Isaak Boretskii with their mother Marfa and with certain other traitors, taught by the Devil, who were worse than demons in using deceit to the ruination of their land and to their own destruction, began to say unseemly and pernicious things and, coming to the veche, to shout: "We don't want to be under the grand prince of Moscow, or to be called his patrimony, for we are free men of Novgorod the Great; and the grand prince of Moscow does us much injury, but we want to be under the king of Poland and grand duke of Lithuania, Casimir." And so their city became agitated and turbulent, as if drunk. Some wanted the grand prince and Moscow, as of old, while others wanted the king of Lithuania; these traitors began to bribe the poor men [*muzhiki*] in the veche, who were ready to do anything for this, as is their wont, and coming to their veche they rang all the bells and shouted: "We want to be under the king." Others said in answer to them: "We want to be under the grand prince as of old, as it was before." And those who were bribed by the traitors threw stones at those who wanted the grand prince. And there was great disorder among them, and they fought among themselves, taking up arms against each other; while many of them, former posadniki, and tysiatskie, and the worthiest men [*lutchii liudi*], and well-to-do people [zhit'i liudi], spoke to them thus: "It should not be done as you say, that we should place ourselves under the king, and that his metropolitan, who is a Latin [Catholic], should consecrate our archbishop. . . ." Those seducers, taught by the Devil as were the heretics of old, wanting to have their own way and scorning piety, and not wishing to submit to the grand prince, kept on crying: "We want to be with the king," while others said: "We want to be with Moscow, with Grand Prince Ivan and his father Metropolitan Philip, in Orthodoxy." The other evildoers made themselves enemies of Orthodoxy, not fearing God, and sent their envoys to the king with many gifts . . . saying: "We the free people of Novgorod the Great petition you, illustrious King, that you be the sovereign of our Novgorod the Great and be our lord, and order your metropolitan Grigorii to consecrate our archbishop, and give us a prince from your realm." The king accepted their gifts with benevolence, and was pleased with their words, and after rendering their envoys great honor, sent them back to them with all those things which they wanted, and sent Mikhail Olelkovich of Kiev to them as prince; and the people of Novgorod received him with honor. . . .

The grand prince [Ivan III] was saddened at hearing these things and grieved for what they had done, since even before they were Orthodox, from Riurik to Grand Prince Vladimir, they had never betrayed their allegiance for another sovereign, but from Vladimir up to this day knew only his lineage, and were ruled in everything by all the grand princes, first of Kiev, then of Vladimir; and now in the last few years they wished to destroy everything that was theirs, by forsaking Christianity for the Latin faith. . . . And after pondering these things much, he declared thus to his father, Metropolitan Philip and to his mother, Grand Princess Maria, and to his boyars who were with him that he would go to war against Novgorod. When they heard this, they counseled him to place his trust in God and to carry out his intention regarding the people of Novgorod, for their infidelity and apostasy. And the grand prince straightway sent to all his brothers, and to all the bishops of his land, and to the princes, and to his boyars, and to the voevody [military commanders], and to all his warriors; and when all had gathered together, then he announced to them his intention of going to war against Novgorod, "since they have been unfaithful in everything, and there is no truth to be found in them anywhere."

. . .

Grand Prince Ivan Vasil'evich . . . armed

himself against the enemy in great force. . . . And thus the grand prince went against them, not as Christians, but as foreigners and apostates from Orthodoxy.

IV:22. NOVGOROD'S PEACE TREATY WITH IVAN III, AUGUST 11, 1471

Ivan III's quick defeat of Novgorod led to the treaty translated in part here, which left the Novgorodians at least a measure of local autonomy.

Reference: Valk, *Gramoty velikogo Novgoroda i Pskova*, pp. 45-46.

With the blessing of the hieromonk [priestmonk] Feofil, nominated to the archbishopric of Novgorod the Great and Pskov, the [former] posadniki of Novgorod . . . have come to the grand prince of all Russia Ivan Vasil'evich and to his son the grand prince Ivan Ivanovich from the [senior] Novgorod posadnik Timofei Ostaf'evich, and from the Novgorod tysiatskii Vasilii Maksimovich, from all of Novgorod the Great . . . and have petitioned their lord, the grand prince, and in accordance with the sworn treaties have concluded peace with the grand prince Ivan Vasil'evich and with his son the grand prince Ivan Ivanovich. . . . You, Sire, shall govern Novgorod as of old, in accordance with its ancient rights, without injury; and we, the men of Novgorod, shall maintain your rule in honor and in fear, without injury. And we, the free men of your patrimony of Novgorod the Great, shall not by any deceit renounce you, the grand princes, to place ourselves under the rule of the king and the grand duke of Lithuania, whoever may be king or grand duke in Lithuania, and we shall not leave you, the grand princes, for anyone. And we shall not ask for princes from the king and grand duke of Lithuania for our dependent towns [prigorody], nor receive princes from Lithuania in Novgorod the Great. Likewise

we, your patrimony of Novgorod the Great, shall not receive in Novgorod the grand princes' enemies, Prince Ivan Mozhaiskii, and Prince Ivan Shemiakin, and Prince Vasilii Iaroslavich [princes who had resisted the extension of Muscovite power], and their children and their sons-in-law. And if after this agreement any men who do evil to the grand princes should come from the land of Moscow, from the grand principality, into Novgorod the Great, Novgorod shall not receive them; or if any men who do evil to the grand princes should flee from the land of Moscow to Lithuania or to the German land, and should come from Lithuania or from the German land to Novgorod, Novgorod shall not receive them. And we, Novgorod the Great, shall choose our prelate ourselves, in accordance with our ancient rights; but our prelate shall be consecrated in your city of Moscow, in the Church of the Dormition and before the tomb of Saint Peter the Miracle Worker [the former metropolitan of Moscow] . . . and our prelate shall not be consecrated by anyone save the metropolitan of Moscow. And you, the princes, shall collect taxes as of old, and your father the metropolitan shall take payment from the prelate [of Novgorod], as of old, and not add anything extra.

IV:23. THE FIRST PSKOV CHRONICLE CONCERNING THE END OF NOVGOROD'S INDEPENDENCE, 1478

The First Pskov Chronicle, versions of which are known to us through sixteenth- and seventeenth-century copies, tells what happened when Ivan III, in 1477, decided that Novgorod should lose its last traces of self-rule and become simply a province of his realm. The two versions from which excerpts are given here provide only a small hint of the variety of accounts the chronicles offer concerning this and many other important events.

Reference: *PSRL*, 4:260; *Pskovskie letopisi*, 2 vols. (Moscow: AN SSSR, 1941-55), 1:75.

[Version A:]

The grand prince thus began to besiege Novgorod and continued the siege for three and [then] four weeks, waiting to see if they

would petition him [for mercy]; meanwhile the people of Novgorod were likewise waiting to see if he would himself depart or would conclude an agreement with them preserving their ancient customs. But the grand prince was steadfast and wanted to have his will over them in everything; and eight weeks had passed since the forces of the grand prince had begun the siege, and turmoil broke out among the people under siege in the city, some wanting to fight the grand prince and others wanting to submit to the grand prince; and there were more of those who wanted to submit to the grand prince. Seeing their dissension and great turmoil, Prince Vasilii Shuiskii [their *kniaz' kormlenyi* or "hired prince," whom the Novgorodians hired as a military commander and to whom they gave certain towns or territories as kormlenie] bade them farewell, abjured the oath he had sworn, and left their city; and coming to the grand prince he petitioned him and swore an oath upon the cross to him; and he [the grand prince] received him. When all these things had taken place, the people of Novgorod saw that their voevoda and hired prince, with whom they were to take their stand and defend themselves, had left their city for the grand prince; and the people of Novgorod placed all their trust in God, submitted wholly to the will of the grand prince, and opened the city to him on January 13 [1478], a Tuesday, and all of them, great and small, swore an oath upon the cross [to submit] to his will and to his courts; and the ancient rights of Novgorod would be no more, nor would its veche, nor its [independent] courts, nor its incumbent [*stepennyi*] posadnik, nor its tysiatskie.

[Version B:]

And Grand Prince Ivan Vasil'evich was angered with his patrimony of Novgorod the Great and broke the peace with them; and the grand prince himself went against the land of Novgorod on November 30 [1477], in great force, and devastated the land of Novgorod; and the voevody of the grand prince ravaged the Zavoloch'e [the region "beyond the portage," i.e. along the Northern Dvina, Emtsa, and Vaga rivers] and the western border, and beyond Iam-town [Iamburg] and to the sea. . . . And the prelate Feofil came to petition Grand Prince Ivan Vasil'evich for Novgorod the Great, and the people of Novgorod shut themselves up in the city, and the army of the grand prince stood all around Novgorod; and the archbishop made petition many times: "Be merciful, sovereign Grand Prince; govern your patrimony as of old; and Novgorod the Great makes petition to you, its sovereign grand prince." And he did not accept their petition but forced Novgorod the Great to yield by siege; and the people of Novgorod opened Novgorod to Grand Prince Ivan Vasil'evich, on February 17 [1478]. . . . And Archbishop Feofil, and the posadniki, and tysiatskie, and all of Novgorod the Great, great and small, swore an oath upon the cross to the grand prince, that there should be no posadniki, or tysiatskie, or veche in Novgorod; and they removed the veche bell and took it away to Moscow; and he [the grand prince] installed his vicegerents in Novgorod the Great.

B. PSKOV

IV:24. THE THIRD NOVGORODIAN CHRONICLE ON SELF-GOVERNMENT IN PSKOV, 1347

Although Pskov was originally considered part of the city-state of Novgorod the Great, its people soon displayed a penchant for self-rule, and from 1137 on often exercised their own initiative in selecting and inviting a princely protector. The following excerpt from the Third Novgorodian Chronicle records the "elder brother's" belated acknowledgment of Pskov's self-governing status.

Reference: Arkheograficheskaia Komissiia, *Novgorodskie letopisi*, p. 224.

That same year [1347], when the men of Novgorod were going to Orekhovets [against the Swedes], they granted to the city of Pskov [these privileges]: that the Novgorod posadnik shall not dwell or hold trials in Pskov; [for the administration of church affairs] the archbishop [of Novgorod] shall appoint people from Pskov to dispense justice [in Pskov]; and neither gentry [dvoriane], nor constables [podvoiskie], nor retainers of the archbishop of Novgorod [sofiiane], nor bailiffs [izvetniki], nor criers [birichi] shall summon them to Novgorod; but Pskov shall be called the younger brother of Novgorod.

IV:25. THE FIRST PSKOV CHRONICLE ON THE ACCEPTANCE OF A NEW PRINCE, 1448

The chronicle here records one of the many instances during the twelfth to fifteenth centuries when the city of Pskov obliged its newly selected prince to swear to maintain its traditional self-government.
Reference: *Pskovskie letopisi,* 1:48.

That same year [1448] Prince Vasilii Vasil'evich, of the princes of Suzdal', came to Pskov from Novgorod the Great . . . and the people of Pskov received him worthily, installed him as prince in the [Cathedral of the] Holy Trinity, and gave the prince everything that was due him; and he swore to the people of Pskov upon the cross to maintain all the ancient rights of Pskov.

IV:26. THE FIRST PSKOV CHRONICLE ON THE ATTACKS OF THE LIVONIAN GERMANS, 1323 AND 1480

The tragic theme that dominates the First Pskov Chronicle from the thirteenth through the fifteenth century is that of the struggle against hostile neighbors to the west, especially the Livonian Germans. The situation of the city, at the confluence of the rivers Velikaia and Pskova, just before the Velikaia falls into Lake Chud, facilitated its development as a virtually impregnable frontier fortress.
Reference: *Pskovskie letopisi,* 1:15-16, 78.

That same spring [1323] the Germans came to Pskov, on the eleventh day of March, and besieged the city for three days, and retreated in shame. Eight weeks later, on the eleventh day of May, the godless Germans, grown proud, came to Pskov in great force, wanting to take captive the house of the Holy Trinity [i.e. Pskov]; they came in ships, in boats, and on horse, with battering rams, and with siege machines, and with many other devices. Then they killed the posadnik Solil Oleksinich [Alekseevich]. And they besieged the city for eighteen days, driving their battering rams, moving up their siege machines, advancing under cover, and using ladders to mount the walls; and they had many other devices. And many messengers hurried from Pskov to Prince Georgii [i.e. Iurii Danilovich of Moscow] and to Novgorod with much woe and grief; for it was a difficult time for the people of Pskov. . . . By God's favor Prince David arrived in time from Lithuania with his men. And through the help of the Holy Trinity and the prayers of Prince Vsevolod and Prince Timofei [two former princes and patron saints of Pskov], they arrayed themselves with the men of Pskov and drove [the Germans] beyond the Velikaia River, and captured their battering rams, and set fire to their siege machines and other devices; and the Germans fled in great shame and disgrace. But Grand Prince Georgii [Iurii] and the people of Novgorod did not give help.

. . .

That same summer [1480], on the eighteenth day of August, the master [of the Livonian Order] came with the Germans and with all his men to the town of Izborsk [a fortified town near Pskov] with an army, in great force, with many of his devices; the godless Germans directed their evil intentions at the house of the holy father Saint Nicholas [i.e. the town of Izborsk], wishing to seize it, bombarding the town with cannon, and setting fire to brushwood beneath the walls; and much did the madmen toil, but they could do no evil, since God protected the town and its people from the Germans, and they went from Izborsk to Pskov; and the Germans had besieged Izborsk for two days. That same summer, on August 28, the master came with the entire German force to Pskov, and encamped on Zavelich'e field [on the other bank of the Velikaia River], and the people of Pskov themselves burned Zavelich'e; on the second day, men from Iur'ev came in twenty-three German battle vessels, encamped in the meadow beyond Saint Stephen's and began to fire cannon at Zapskov'e [on the other bank of the Pskova River] and at Polonishche [the eastern part of the town, the third side of the triangle of which the rivers Velikaia and Pskova form the other two sides], with many other devices; and many messengers hurried from Pskov to Grand

Prince Ivan Vasil'evich with much woe and grief, and it was a very difficult time, and [the Germans] pushed toward Zapskov'e with zeal, advancing in their battle vessels and firing their cannon and using other devices; and God aided the people of Pskov and they captured a battle vessel from the Germans, and the Germans fled hence.

IV:27. THE CHARTER OF PSKOV, CA. 1467

Like the Charter of Novgorod, the Charter or legal code of Pskov was a descendant of the Kievan Russkaia Pravda. The charter is a digest of Pskov laws approved by the veche in the period from the mid-thirteenth century to the 1460s (revised ca. 1467). The only more or less complete extant copy of it was found in the library of Prince M. S. Vorontsov in Odessa in 1847. A close study of the charter reveals a great deal about relations between the social classes and numerous other aspects of life in Pskov. (The Charter of Pskov became one of the important sources of the Sudebnik of 1497, concerning which see Item VI:7, below.)

Reference: *PRP*, 2:286-301, with modern Russian translation on pp. 302-24; English translation based on Vernadsky, *Medieval Russian Laws*, pp. 61-82, slightly revised. See also I. D. Martysevich, *Pskovskaia sudnaia gramota* (Moscow: Izd. Moskovskogo Universiteta, 1951).

[PREAMBLE.] This charter is based on Grand Prince Alexander's charter, and on Prince Constantine's charter, and on records of Pskov's old customs. [It is issued] with the blessing of the fathers—the priests of all the five cathedrals, and the hieromonks, and the deacons, and the priests and all God's clergy—[as approved] by the whole of Pskov, at the veche in the year 6905. [Apparently should be 6975, i.e. 1467.] . . .

ARTICLE 3. When a posadnik is installed in his office, he shall swear that he will conduct the trials justly, in accordance with his oath; and will not embezzle municipal funds; and will not avenge through his court decisions; and will not favor his relatives; and will ruin no innocent person, nor help a culprit. And no man shall be punished either by the court or by the veche without due examination.

ART. 4. The prince and the posadnik shall not conduct trials at the veche; they shall conduct the trials in the prince's palace, consulting the law, according to their oath. . . .

ART. 7. Life is denied to one who commits theft in the Kremlin; and to the horse stealer; and to the spy; and to the incendiary. . . .

ART. 30. If anyone intends to loan money [to another], he may lend up to one ruble without a pledge and without a [certified] note, but no money to the amount over one ruble should be lent without security and without a note. . . .

ART. 36. If a woman sues a man for debts on the evidence of [noncertified] notes, or a child, or an old man, or a sick person, or a cripple, or a monk, or a nun, each of them may hire a substitute fighter [for the duel]; and the plaintiff takes an oath upon the cross but fights [the duel] through his substitute; and the defendant may hire a fighter of his against the plaintiff's fighter or may fight him personally. . . .

ART. 38. If anyone sues another for money he loaned him for commercial transactions on the basis of [noncertified] notes, and if the defendant produces a receipt in which it is mentioned that the money loaned to him for commerce [has been paid by him], but there is no copy of the receipt in the files at the Holy Trinity Cathedral, the receipt is not valid.

ART. 39. If a master carpenter or a hired laborer [*naimit*] accomplishes the work [and the employer refuses to pay him], he may sue the employer for his pay through an announcement [in the marketplace].

ART. 40. If a hired worker about the homestead leaves his employer before the completion of his appointed work, he receives wages in accordance with the amount [of time he worked]. And a worker may sue his employer for his wages only within one year after his leaving the work. . . .

ART. 42. If the landlord wants to terminate the lease of his tenant farmer [*izornik*], or vegetable gardener, or fisherman, the term for ending such leases is the day of the beginning of Saint Philip's fast [i.e. November 14]; likewise, if the farmer wants to terminate the lease on the farm, or the vegetable gardener, or the fisherman [wants to terminate the lease], the term is the same, and there shall be no other term, either for the landlord, or for the farmer, or the fisherman. . . .

ART. 51. If a farmer denies that he owes any money to his landlord and says thus, "I stayed on your land, but owe you nothing," the landlord must produce some outsiders, four or five of them, and those men must state the case justly as if facing God. [And if they say] that the farmer did occupy the plot [presumably receiving a subsidy from the lord], then it is left to the landlord's will: he may take the oath and then [if the court is satisfied] receive the subsidy back; or the farmer takes the oath. And if the landlord produces no men [to confirm the fact] that the farmer stayed on his land [receiving a subsidy], he loses [the right to claim back] the subsidy. . . .

ART. 68. No posadnik may be an attorney in another's lawsuit, but may only be [a litigant] in his own lawsuit, or an attorney in a lawsuit involving the church of which he is warden.

ART. 69. No other public official may serve as an attorney for another [citizen], but only as [a litigant] in his own lawsuit.

ART. 77. The Pskov judges, and the posadniki and elders of the dependent towns,

must swear that they will conduct the trials justly in accordance with their oaths. . . .

ART. 103. A lodger may sue his landlord for money loaned or for any other cause. . . .

ART. 106. If there is litigation about a landed property, or an apiary, and [the defendant] produces his old deed, and [the plaintiff] produces his [more recent] deed of sale, and if that deed affects many co-owners of the land, or of the apiary, and they all appear before the court, each defending his share of the land, or of the apiary, and present to the supreme court their [old] deeds and then call land surveyors, and the latter, taking into account old men's assertions, establish their boundaries, the plaintiff shall take the oath [to prove] that the contestable portion of the land duly belongs to him. . . .

ART. 108. If any provision of the customary law is missing in this charter, the posadniki may refer the matter to lord Pskov at the city veche, advising the insertion of a new clause accordingly. And if any clause in this charter is not satisfactory to lord Pskov [i.e. the people assembled in the veche], that clause may be deleted.

IV:28. THE FIRST PSKOV CHRONICLE ON PSKOV'S ANNEXATION BY MOSCOW, 1510

When Vasilii III annexed Pskov in 1510, abolishing its traditional self-rule, the people of Pskov did not put up armed resistance. The story is told here from the standpoint of the author or authors of the First Pskov Chronicle.

Reference: *PSRL*, 4:282-83, 286-87. Also found in *Pskovskie letopisi*, pp. 92-97. Among the collections of documents on Novgorod and Pskov in addition to those cited in this chapter, see G. E. Kochin, ed., *Pamiatniki istorii Velikogo Novgoroda i Pskova* (Leningrad: Gosudarstvennoe Sotsial'no-Ekonomicheskoe Izdatel'stvo, 1935; reproduced also Ann Arbor: Xerox, 1969).

In the year 7018 [1510]. Grand Prince Vasilii Ivanovich [of Moscow] came to Pskov on the twenty-fourth day of the month of January and abolished the usages of Pskov and violated its ancient ways, forgetting the promises of his father and forefathers, and their grants to the people of Pskov and the oaths they had sworn upon the cross; he instituted his own usages and new customs. He took patrimonies [*otchiny*] away from the people of Pskov, and installed two vice-gerents and the secretary [*d'iak*] Misiur' [-Munekhin], and removed 300 families from Pskov to Moscow, and brought his own people there; he drove the people of Pskov

from the old Zasten'e [area beyond the walls] and ordered the merchants whom he had brought in to live there, and there were 6,500 households in Zasten'e; he ordered the storehouses to be carried out of the Krem [Krom—central part of the city], and the Krem was empty. And there was great weeping and sorrow in Pskov over the separation. He seized 300 men of Pskov who had made complaint and imprisoned them in Novgorod. And [formerly] he had written soft words to Pskov: "I, Grand Prince Vasilii Ivanovich, wish to grant to you, my patrimony, your ancient ways, and wish to visit the [Cathedral of the] Holy Trinity, and wish to administer justice for you." ...

The taking of Pskov, how Grand Prince Vasilii Ivanovich took it: From the beginning of the Russian land this town of Pskov had never been the possession of any prince, but its people lived in it in freedom. ... Pskov is a town with strong walls, and there were a great number of people in it; and for this reason [the grand prince] did not go against them in war, fearing also lest they defect to Lithuania; for this reason he deceived them with evil wiles and made peace with the people of Pskov; and the people of Pskov swore an oath upon the cross to him, that they would not defect anywhere from the grand prince. The grand prince sent his princes to them in accordance with their request, sending whoever pleased them, but sometimes he sent his vicegerents to Pskov of his own will, whomever he pleased, and not of their will; they oppressed, plundered, and imposed fines on [the people of Pskov] through false accusations and unjust trials. The inhabitants of the town of Pskov and others in neighboring towns would send their posadniki to the grand prince to complain against them. And this happened many times.

. . .

[After Pskov's annexation by Vasilii III in January 1510,] they took down the veche bell at the [Cathedral of the] Holy Life-Giving Trinity, and the people of Pskov, looking at the bell, began to weep for their ancient ways and for their freedom. ... "Oh most glorious and great city of Pskov! Wherefore do you lament and weep?" And the fair city of Pskov answered: "How can I help but lament, how can I help but weep and mourn over my desolation? For a many-winged eagle has flown against me, his wings filled with lion's claws, and has taken from me the three cedars of Lebanon, and has carried off my beauty and my wealth and my children, God having permitted this because of our sins. And they have laid waste the land, and devastated our city, and taken my people captive, and leveled my market squares, and strewn other market squares with horses' dung, and led our fathers and brothers away into places where our fathers and forefathers had never been."

CHAPTER V

The Lithuanian-Russian State
(the Grand Duchy of Lithuania)
from the
Fourteenth to the Mid-Sixteenth Century

Solid facts are scarce concerning the process by which the Lithuanian state ruled by Grand Duke Gedimin (ca. 1316-41) extended its domain southward into Volynia and the Kiev region and laid the foundation for a vast Lithuanian-Russian realm extending from the Baltic to the Black Sea. The account given in this codex of the West Russian Chronicle (the codex owned by Count Rachinskii—apparently written about 1580 on the basis of earlier Polish as well as Russian annals) is in many respects inexact, but Liubavskii accepts it as basically true. It may be noted that the people of southwestern Russia (the Ukraine), whose lands had been devastated by the Tatars, might understandably have preferred Gedimin's suzerainty to Tatar domination.

In deference to common usage, the title of the Lithuanian rulers is translated in this book as "grand duke," although the words in Russian (*velikii kniaz'*) are the same as those rendered in this book as "grand prince" where the rulers of Kiev and Muscovy are concerned.

Reference: *PSRL*, vol. 17, cols. 311-14. Inaccuracies are pointed out in Vladimir B. Antonovich, *Monografii po istorii zapadnoi i iugozapadnoi Rossii*, vol. 1 (Kiev, 1885), pp. 46-58. See also Matvei K. Liubavskii, *Ocherk istorii litovsko-russkogo gosudarstva*, 2d ed. (Moscow: Moskovskaia Khudozhestvennaia Pechatnia, 1915), pp. 24-25 (reprinted by Mouton, 1966).

About Grand Duke Gedimin [Kgidimin, Gediminas] and the battle with Prince Vladimir of Vladimir [-Volynsk]:

Having safeguarded the land of Samogitia [Zhmud, the area between the lower reaches of the Niemen and the Windau] from the Germans [the Teutonic Order], he [Gedimin] set out against the Russian princes and came first to the town of Vladimir [Volodymer, in Volynia], whose Prince Vladimir assembled his men and began a great battle with Grand Duke Gedimin. God helped Grand Duke Gedimin, who slew Prince Vladimir of Vladimir [-Volynsk], and destroyed his entire army, and took the town of Vladimir.

Then [Gedimin] went forth against Prince Lev of Lutsk [Luck]. Prince Lev heard that Prince Vladimir had been slain by the Lithuanians and that the town of Vladimir had been taken; and he dared not withstand [Gedimin] but fled to his son-in-law Prince Roman in Briansk. And the princes and boyars of Volynia petitioned Grand Duke Gedimin to rule over them and to be their sovereign but to desist from ruining their lands. Grand Duke Gedimin bound them by an oath of allegiance and left his vicegerents [namestniki] with them to rule. Then he went for the winter to Brest [Berestie, i.e. Brest-Litovsk]; there he disbanded his troops and spent the winter in Brest. Easter Day soon came and went. He gathered all his forces, Lithuanian, Samogitian, and Russian, and in the second week after Easter set out

against Prince Stanislav of Kiev and captured the towns of Ovruch and Zhitomir [west of Kiev] . . . . There was a great battle and slaughter, and God helped Grand Duke Gedimin to inflict a total defeat upon all the Russian princes. . . . Grand Duke Gedimin invested [the town of] Belgorod. The townspeople, seeing that their sovereign [Prince Stanislav] had fled with his troops and that their troops were completely vanquished, and not wanting to oppose such a great Lithuanian force, gave themselves up, with their town, to [Grand] Duke Gedimin and took an oath to serve the Grand Duchy of Lithuania. Then Grand Duke Gedimin went with all his forces against Kiev and besieged the city of Kiev. The Kievans began to defend themselves against him. Gedimin remained before Kiev for a month. Then the townspeople of Kiev resolved among themselves that they could not withstand the might of the grand duke, especially in the absence of their sovereign, Grand Prince Stanislav of Kiev. . . . And they unanimously decided to yield to Grand Duke Gedimin. Their abbots, priests, and deacons went out of the city with crosses and opened the city gates. They met Grand Duke Gedimin worthily, paid him obeisance and engaged themselves to serve him, took an oath of allegiance thereupon to Grand Duke Gedimin, and petitioned him not to deprive them of their patrimonial estates. Grand Duke Gedimin granted them this and entered the city of Kiev with honor. Kiev's dependent towns [*prigorodki Kievskie*]—Vyshgorod, Cherkassy, Kanev, Putivl', [and] Slepovrod—heard that the Kievans had gone over with their city [to the Grand Duke Gedimin], and that their sovereign [Prince Stanislav] had fled to Briansk, and that all his army was vanquished; and they all went over to Grand Duke Gedimin and, with Kiev's above-mentioned dependent towns engaged to serve him, took an oath of allegiance thereupon to Grand Duke Gedimin.

The people of Pereiaslavl' heard that Kiev and its dependent towns had yielded to Grand Duke Gedimin and that their sovereign Prince Oleg had been slain by Grand Duke Gedimin; and they came and engaged with their city to serve Grand Duke Gedimin and swore an oath of allegiance thereupon. Having taken Kiev, Pereiaslavl', and all those dependent towns, Grand Duke Gedimin appointed as their ruler the son of [Grand] Duke Mindovg [Mindaugas], Grand Prince Ol'gimunt Gol'shanskii [Holszanski]. Meanwhile, he himself departed for Lithuania in great joy.

· · ·

Grand Duke Gedimin reigned for many years over the Duchy of Lithuania, Russia, and Samogitia, and was just, and fought many wars and won them all, and reigned happily to a ripe old age.

When he was very advanced in years, Grand Duke Gedimin endowed all his sons with appanages while he was still alive . . . [recites the division of Gedimin's provinces among his numerous heirs, including Ol'gerd:] and Ol'gerd [Algirdas] received Krevo, and since the prince of Vitebsk [Iaroslav Vasil'evich] had no sons, only a daughter, he gave her to Ol'gerd [in marriage] and received him in the land of Vitebsk. . . . [Ol'gerd became prince of Vitebsk upon the death of Iaroslav Vasil'evich in 1320.]

V:2. THE WEST RUSSIAN CHRONICLE ON OL'GERD'S WAR AGAINST MOSCOW, CA. 1370

The Evreinov codex of the West Russian Chronicle is quoted here in what appears to be a fictionalized synthesis of the campaigns Ol'gerd (who ruled Lithuania ca. 1345-77) waged against Moscow. Not once but three times (in 1368, 1370, and 1372) did Ol'gerd, in alliance with the grand prince of Tver', attack the Muscovite state of Dmitrii Donskoi.

Reference: *PSRL*, vol. 17, cols. 377-79.

Grand Duke Ol'gerd [Olkgird, Algirdas] Gediminovich of Lithuania diligently administered his state, and reigned for many years over the Grand Duchy of Lithuania, and was on peaceful and friendly terms with Grand Prince Dmitrii Ivanovich of Moscow [Dmitrii Donskoi]. That same Grand Prince Dmitrii Ivanovich terminated that friendship without any cause and sent to Grand Duke Ol'gerd an envoy with a message conveying fire and sword [i.e. a declaration of war]. . . . Grand Duke Ol'gerd . . . dismissed the envoy and assembled his Lithuanian and Russian troops and started out straightway from Vitebsk. And in the early morning on Easter Day, as Grand Prince [Dmitrii] was leaving church with all his princes and boyars . . . Grand Duke Ol'gerd appeared with all his army outside Moscow on Poklonnaia Hill. Grand Prince Dmitrii Ivanovich, seeing that Ol'gerd . . . stood in force and had come in force and that he could not offer any resistance, sent to him [asking] that Ol'gerd not expel him from his patrimony of Moscow, that he relent his wrath and take anything he might desire. Grand Duke Ol'gerd reached an accord with him, made peace with him, and then concluded a treaty. And Grand Prince Dmitrii Ivanovich himself rode out to meet him, gave Grand Duke Ol'gerd many gifts, and reimbursed him for the losses he had incurred while on his campaign. Then Duke Ol'gerd told the grand prince [Dmitrii] that, even though they had made peace, his desires would not be fulfilled, nor would it be worthy of him, unless he were to lean his spear against Moscow['s wall], so that it would be known that Grand Duke Ol'gerd of Lithuania, Russia, and Samogitia had leaned his spear against Moscow['s wall]. And mounting his horse, he took his spear in hand, and when he got up to the city [wall] he leaned his spear against the city [wall]. As he rode back he said in a loud voice that the grand prince of Moscow should remember that this Lithuanian spear had stood against Moscow['s wall]. Then Grand Duke Ol'gerd and all his troops fought a campaign with great glory and with great [and] incalculable booty and many prisoners; they took many towns, extended the frontiers [of Lithuania] to Mozhaisk and Kolomna, and took many prisoners.

V:3. WEST RUSSIAN CHRONICLE ON THE CONVERSION OF OL'GERD, 1377

Here, from a genealogical section of the West Russian Chronicle, is an account of Ol'gerd's conversion to Christianity. The existence of several versions has led scholars to wonder how much of the graphic detail comes from the chronicler's imagination.

(In this and subsequent selections, Ol'gerd's capital is referred to by its Russian form, "Vil'no." This is done for the sake of simplicity and uniformity. The city may be referred to also as Vilna, Vilnius, Vil'nius, or Wilno.)

Reference: *PSRL*, vol. 17, cols. 415-16.

Ol'gerd sent to Grand Prince Simeon Ivanovich [Semen the Proud, who ruled in Moscow from 1341 to 1353], asking to marry his sister-in-law, the daughter of Grand Prince Aleksandr Mikhailovich of Tver'. Grand Prince Simeon, with the blessing of his [spiritual] father Theognostus, metropolitan of all Russia, gave his sister-in-law Grand Princess Ul'iana to him in marriage. . . . The years went by, and Grand Duke Ol'gerd was overcome by a grievous illness and began to make arrangements for his sons. He loved his son Iakov best of all and gave him the Grand Duchy and city of Vil'no, while the other sons received appanages. The orthodox grand duchess Ul'iana, seeing that her husband Ol'gerd was breathing his last, and being anxious for his salvation, called together her sons and summoned her spiritual father

David, archimandrite of the Pecherskii [Monastery, i.e. the Monastery of the Caves, at Kiev], and persuaded her husband Ol'gerd with good counsel, and had him accept holy baptism with God's help. Ol'gerd was given the name of Aleksandr in holy baptism, after which he was elevated to the lofty dignity of a monk, took the strictest monastic vows [*skhima*], and was adorned in the great angelic image [*velikii angel'skii obraz,* another name for the skhima]; and he was given the monastic name of Aleksei in place of Aleksandr. A few days thereafter he departed this life, and his body was laid to rest in the Church of the Holy Virgin which he himself had erected in Vil'no. His spouse, the orthodox [grand] duchess Ul'iana, did not long survive him but departed this life; her body was interred in the same church.

V:4. GRAND DUKE IAGAILO'S DECLARATION CONCERNING THE UNION OF POLAND AND LITHUANIA, AUGUST 14, 1385

After the death of King Louis I of Hungary and Poland, the Polish part of his realm accepted as his successor his younger daughter Jadwiga. The Polish magnates then proceeded to negotiate with Iagailo (or Jogaila [Lithuanian] or Jagiello [Polish]), ruler of the extensive Lithuanian-Russian state, for a marriage that would unite the two countries. Iagailo was so keenly interested that, on August 14, 1385, at Krevo (near Vil'no), he undertook this difficult and portentous commitment.

Reference: Stanislaw Kutrzeba and W. Semkowicz, eds., *Akta unji Polski z Litwa, 1385-1791* (Krakow: Nakladem Polskiej Akademji Umiejetnosci i Towarzystwa Naukowego Warszawskiego, 1932), pp. 1-2.

We, Iagailo, by the grace of God grand duke of the Lithuanians and hereditary lord and master of Russia, make [this declaration] known by the present document to all whom it may concern. . . . Therefore, most serene Sovereign [Jadwiga's mother, Elizabeth, queen of Hungary and Poland], may Your Majesty most graciously deign to accept this lord Grand Duke Iagailo as a son, with your most beloved daughter, the most renowned Princess Jadwiga, queen of Poland, joined to him in lawful marriage. We believe that this will lead to the glory of God, the salvation

of souls, honor to men, and the enlargement of the kingdom. Moreover, in the meantime—until these things have been achieved [and] are crowned with the desired result—the lord Grand Duke Iagailo, together with all his brothers not yet baptized, his kinsmen, nobles, and gentry from the greatest to the least, who dwell in his lands, shall support the Catholic faith of the holy Roman church and seek and desire to extend it. . . . Finally, the oft-mentioned [Grand] Duke Iagailo promises to join [*applicare*] his lands of Lithuania and Russia to the crown of the kingdom of Poland for all time.

V:5. THE WEST RUSSIAN CHRONICLE ON THE MARRIAGE OF IAGAILO AND JADWIGA, 1386

The Academy codex of the West Russian Chronicle relates the following story of the marriage that united the crowns of Lithuania and Poland.
      Reference: *PSRL*, vol. 17, col. 148.

The Poles began to send [envoys] from Krakow to Grand Duke Iagailo [asking him] to be baptized in [the faith of] old Rome, to take their queen Jadwiga as his wife, and to become their king in Krakow and over all the Polish lands. Grand Duke Iagailo took counsel with his mother Grand Duchess Ul'iana, and with his brothers, and with all the princes and boyars of the Lithuanian land, and went to Krakow, to the land of the Poles. There he himself was baptized, and also his brothers and the princes and boyars of the Lithuanian land. And he took Queen Jadwiga as his wife, was crowned with the crown of that kingdom [Poland], and thereupon began to baptize the Lithuanians in the Latin faith. And the archbishop [of Gniezno, the primate of Poland] sent a bishop to the Lithuanian land, to Vil'no, and then they began to build Latin churches throughout the Lithuanian land.

V:6. A CHARTER GRANTED BY IAGAILO TO THE BISHOP OF VIL'NO, 1387

In compliance with the pledge he had made at Krevo in 1385, Iagailo proceeded in 1387 to authorize the establishment of a Roman Catholic bishopric in his principal city, Vil'no. His charter to the bishop spells out his firm intentions.
      Reference: Arkheograficheskaia Komissiia, ed., *Dokumenty ob"iasniaiushchie istoriiu zapadno-Russkogo kraia i ego otnosheniia k Rossii i Pol'she* (St. Petersburg, 1865), p. 2.

In the name of our Lord, amen. May this be forever remembered. We, Wladyslaw [the Christian name of Iagailo], declare that, touched by the grace of the Holy Ghost and reborn by the water of baptism, having renounced the errors of paganism and embraced the holy faith, we wish to propagate this same Catholic faith in our lands of Lithuania and Russia. With the approval and consent of our brothers the most renowned dukes and of all the nobles of the Lithuanian land, we have arranged, ordained, pledged, vowed, and sworn by the holy sacraments to persuade, attract, assemble, or indeed constrain all those of the Lithuanian nation, of either sex, of every rank, station, and dignity, and of whatever sect, who live in our domains of Lithuania and Russia, to profess the Catholic faith and swear obedience to the holy Roman church.

      Moreover, lest the Lithuanians, still neophytes in the Catholic faith, be drawn away in any manner from obedience to the Roman church and from its rites, we expressly forbid any Lithuanian of either sex to enter into marriage with any Ruthenian [Russian], unless first the latter truly submits to the obedience of the Roman church.

      If, however, in violation of this our prohibition, a marriage is contracted between a Catholic, obedient to the Roman church, and a follower of the Ruthenian [i.e. the Orthodox] rite, the union shall not be dissolved, but either the man or the woman who is of dissident faith shall be obliged to profess the Catholic faith, to promise it obedience and fidelity, even under compulsion of corporal punishment.

V:7. THE WEST RUSSIAN CHRONICLE ON THE ACHIEVEMENT OF AUTONOMY BY THE LITHUANIAN-RUSSIAN STATE UNDER VITOVT, 1392

Iagailo's ambitions of 1386 soon had to yield to reality, and in 1392 at Ostrow he was obliged to install his first cousin, Vitovt or Vytautas, as grand duke of the Lithuanian-Russian lands. The West Russian chronicler depicts the event as follows.
      Reference: *PSRL*, vol. 17, col. 275. See also Liubavskii, *Ocherk istorii litovsko-russkogo gosudarstva*, p. 49.

While [Grand] Duke Vitovt was in the German land, visiting the [grand] master [of the Teutonic Order] in Marienburg, the king of Poland [Iagailo] sent [envoys] to him, saying: "Dear brother, do not despoil the Lithuanian land, do not devastate your patrimony and ours;

but come to us for agreement and for great brotherly concord. Take for yourself the Grand Duchy of Vil'no [Lithuania] and ascend the throne of your uncle Grand Duke Ol'gerd [Algirdas], and of your father Grand Duke Keistut [Kestutis]." And Grand Duke Vitovt,

hearing this, convoked a council with his princes and lords of Lithuania. . . . And he returned to Lithuania and ascended the throne of the Grand Duchy of Lithuania in Vil'no and the entire Lithuanian and Russian land rejoiced.

V:8. THE CHARTER OF GORODLO, 1413

In 1413 Iagailo and Vitovt conferred, together with representatives of the aristocracy of both their realms, at the town of Gorodlo (Horodlo), on the Western Bug River not far south of Brest and east of Lublin. There they concluded a new treaty which, as can be seen from these excerpts, had profound significance for the future structure of the Lithuanian-Russian state. As regards article 9 of this charter, it should be noted that the grand dukes of Lithuania later (beginning with 1432) had to make concessions to the Orthodox Russians.

Reference: Liubavskii, *Ocherk istorii litovsko-russkogo gosudarstva*, pp. 319-22. See also the Charter of Vil'no, 1563, Item V:17, below.

We, Wladyslaw [Iagailo], by the grace of God king of Poland, . . . and Alexander, otherwise Vitovt [Vytautas, Withawdus], grand duke of Lithuania and lord and master of the lands of Russia . . . through the clemency [and] benevolence inherent in us, by the present document do confer and bestow upon them [i.e. "the lands of Lithuania and their inhabitants, who are subject to our rule"] the freedoms, immunities, favors, exemptions, and privileges customarily given to Catholics, as included in the articles following:

1. First of all, at the time when, under the inspiration of the Holy Spirit, having perceived the truth of the Catholic faith, we assumed the crown of the Kingdom of Poland, for the increase of the Christian religion and for the well-being and advantage of our aforesaid lands of Lithuania, we associated, incorporated, joined, united, connected, and confederated them, and the lands and dominions subordinated and bound to them, with our aforesaid Kingdom of Poland, unanimously by our own consent and that of our brothers, and with the voluntary agreement and assent of all the lords [*barones*], nobles, magnates [*proceres*], and boyars of this same land of Lithuania. . . . [Now this union of 1385-86 is renewed and confirmed.]

3. Let also the lords, nobles, and boyars of our aforesaid lands of Lithuania, as long as they are Catholics and obedient to the Roman church, and have been granted coats of arms, rejoice in, partake of, and enjoy the donations, privileges, and concessions we have granted, bestowed, and presented to them, just as they are possessed and enjoyed by the lords and nobles of the Kingdom of Poland.

4. Likewise may the aforesaid lords and nobles possess their own patrimonial estates on the same legal basis that the lords of the Kingdom of Poland are known to possess theirs; and may they similarly possess estates granted by us, for which they have a supporting document from us and which are secured by a title-deed of permanent validity; and may they be free to sell, exchange, alienate, or give them away, and likewise to use them for their own purposes, but only with our special consent in each case; in such wise, however, that in alienating, exchanging, or giving [them] away, they shall make the act of transfer in our presence or before our officials, in accordance with the customs of the Kingdom of Poland. . . .

8. Let this be said in a special manner: that all the lords and nobles of the lands of Lithuania must have and maintain toward us, Wladyslaw, king of Poland, and Alexander, otherwise Vitovt, grand duke of Lithuania, and to our successors, the fidelity and loyalty proper to the Christian faith, just as the lords and nobles of the Kingdom of Poland are accustomed to have and maintain toward their own kings. Besides which, the lords, boyars, and magnates of the aforesaid lands of Lithuania have already sworn an oath of allegiance to us. . . .

9. Likewise, the dignities, seats, and offices that are instituted in the Kingdom of Poland, shall be instituted and established to remain for all time to come: in Vil'no, namely, the offices of voevoda and castellan of Vil'no, and in Troki as well, and in other places, wherever it shall seem proper to us according to our will [and] pleasure. And no dignitaries

shall be chosen [for these offices] unless they are communicants of the Catholic faith and obedient to the holy Roman church. Nor shall any permanent offices [of the land], dignities such as castellanships, and so forth, be granted except to practitioners of the Christian faith; nor shall [non-Christians] be admitted to our counsels and be present at them when matters concerning the welfare of the state are discussed: because differences of faith often lead to differences of opinion, and counsels are revealed of such a kind as ought to be kept secret. . . .

11. Let this be added: that the aforesaid lords and nobles [and so forth] of Lithuania, after the death of Alexander, otherwise Vitovt, the reigning duke, shall have and elect no one as grand duke of Lithuania whom the king of Poland and his successors, in accordance with the advice of the prelates and lords of Poland and of the lands of Lithuania, have not deemed fit to be chosen, elevated, and installed. So likewise the prelate, lords, and nobles of the Kingdom of Poland, in the event

of the death of the king of Poland without children and legitimate heirs, may not elect a king and lord for themselves without our knowledge and counsel, i.e. of Grand Duke Alexander and the aforesaid lords and nobles of the lands of Lithuania. . . .

12. Moreover, only those lords and nobles of the land of Lithuania may use and enjoy the aforesaid liberties, privileges, and favors, to whom the insignia and coats of arms of the nobles of the Kingdom of Poland have been granted, and who are communicants of the Christian religion, obedient to the Roman church, and not schismatics or other unbelievers. . . .

14. Let this be added especially and expressly: that the aforesaid lords and nobles of the Kingdom of Poland and of the lands of Lithuania will convene meetings and diets whenever necessary, in Lublin or in Parczow or in other suitable places, with our consent and by our will, for the greater advantage and good of the Kingdom of Poland and the aforesaid lands of Lithuania.

V:9. THE WEST RUSSIAN CHRONICLE'S PANEGYRIC ON VITOVT, AFTER 1430

During the long reign of Vitovt, or Vytautas, as grand duke (1392-1430), the Lithuanian-Russian state may have achieved its apogee in both domestic and international spheres. The prolonged political troubles that followed his death (he fell from a horse at the age of eighty) made it natural that the West Russian chroniclers of the time, like the author of the Uvarov codex quoted here (as well as the authors of many of the other codices where similar panegyrics appear), should look back with particular nostalgia on the great days of his rule.

Reference: *PSRL,* vol. 17, cols. 102-04.

Panegyric [*pokhvala*] on Grand Duke Vitovt: It is good to keep a tsar's secrets; but it is likewise good to tell of the deeds of a great sovereign. I want to tell you of Grand Duke Alexander [the baptismal name] Vitovt, sovereign of Lithuania and Russia and of many other lands. . . . But it is not possible to relate or to put in writing the deeds of the great sovereign; just as it is impossible for anyone to scale the heights of heaven or plumb the depths of the seas, so is it impossible to describe the strength and bravery of that glorious sovereign. Grand Duke Vitovt ruled over the Grand Duchy of Lithuania and Russia, and over many other lands; I would simply say over the entire Russian land. And not only the Russian [land] but even the sovereign of Hungary, called the Roman caesar [Sigismund was both Holy Roman Emperor and king of Hungary], lived in great concord with him. . . . Once

when that great sovereign [Vitovt] was staying in his city of Lutsk the Great, he sent his envoys to the Hungarian king and Roman caesar [Sigismund] and bade him come and visit him. [Sigismund] did not disobey but soon came to him accompanied by his queen, and [the Lithuanians] paid them great honor and gave them many gifts. From that time great concord existed between them. We may well marvel at the honor paid the great sovereign [Vitovt], to whom the lands in the east and in the west would come and make obeisance, the glorious sovereign who was tsar over all the earth. The Turkish tsar, who had paid great honor and given many gifts to the glorious sovereign, the Orthodox and Christ-loving tsar of Tsar'grad [the Byzantine emperor], and who lived in great concord with him, likewise came and made obeisance to Tsar [and] Grand Duke Alexander [Vitovt]. The Czech kingdom

[Bohemia] likewise paid great respects to the great sovereign. The king of Denmark likewise paid great honor and gave many gifts to the glorious sovereign Grand Duke Vitovt. At that time his brother [actually cousin] Iagailo, called Wladyslaw in the Polish tongue, ruled over the Kingdom of Krakow [Poland]; and he lived in great concord with him [Vitovt].
. . . The grand prince of Moscow likewise lived in great concord with him. Other German grand dukes, called masters [masters of the Teutonic and Livonian Orders] in the German tongue, were at his service with all their cities and lands. And likewise the sovereigns of the lands of Moldavia and Bessarabia, called *voivodes* in the Wallachian [Rumanian] tongue; and likewise the sovereign of the Bulgarian land, called the despot in the Bulgarian tongue; and likewise other great princes: the grand prince of Tver', the grand prince of Riazan', the grand prince of Odoev, and Novgorod the Great, and Pskov; to put it simply, not a single castle, not a single city could be found along the Littoral [of the Baltic Sea] which would disobey that glorious sovereign Vitovt. Among those great sovereigns, tsars, grand princes, and mighty lands of which I have written here, some lived in great concord with him, and others served him faithfully, paid him great honor, and gave him many gifts, not merely once a year but every day. Whenever the glorious sovereign Grand Duke Vitovt was wrathful at some land and wanted to punish it, he would either go himself or send his mighty voevody, if he so desired; and whenever he commanded [the ruler of] a mighty land to come before him, he would soon come from his own land to him [Vitovt] without any disobedience. And if any sovereign were prevented from coming by some necessity, he would send all his army and forces to aid and serve him [Vitovt]. Grand Duke Vitovt lived in great honor and glory.
. . . And grand princes [khans] sent [envoys] to him from the [Golden] Horde; they came to serve him, and to ask for [Vitovt's approval of] a tsar [khan] for their tsardom. There were many great tsars [Tatar princelings] from the Horde serving him at his court.

V:10. AN APPANAGE PRINCE'S CONTRACT WITH THE GRAND DUKE, FEBRUARY 20, 1442

The West Russian appanage princes who entered the service of the grand duke of Lithuania concluded contracts that specified obligations on both sides. This sample, dated early in the reign of Casimir IV, was with the prince of Odoev and Novosil'—small principalities south of Tula and at that time roughly on the border of the Muscovite state. Thus the concluding part of this contract was not necessarily inoperative.

Reference: *AOIZR,* 1:55 (see List of Abbreviations). Also contained in L. V. Cherepnin and S. V. Bakhrushin, eds., *Dukhovnye i dogovornye gramoty velikikh i udel'nykh kniazei XIV-XVI vv.* (Moscow: AN SSSR, 1950), pp. 117-18.

February 20, 1442. Treaty of Prince Fedor L'vovich Novosil'skii and Odoevskii [of Novosil' and Odoev] with Grand Duke Casimir of Lithuania.

By the grace of God and of the sovereign grand duke Casimir, the king's son [Casimir was the son of King Jagiello (Iagailo) of Poland], I, Prince Fedor L'vovich Novosil'skii and Odoevskii, have petitioned Grand Duke Casimir, the king's son, to take me into his service; and Grand Duke Casimir, the king's son, in response to my petition, has granted my request and has taken me into his service in accordance with the treaty with Grand Duke Vitovt [which Prince Fedor had concluded when Vitovt was grand duke]. And I shall serve [Casimir] faithfully and without any trickery and shall be obedient in every-thing; and he shall maintain me in honor and in his favor according to the treaty, just as his uncle, the sovereign grand duke Vitovt, maintained me in honor and in his favor. And I shall pay a yearly tax [*poletnoe*] as before. And I shall act in accordance with Grand Duke Casimir's will: with whomever Grand Duke Casimir is at peace, I also shall be at peace; and with whomever Grand Duke Casimir is at war, I also shall be at war. And Grand Duke Casimir shall defend me against any [enemy] as his own. And without Grand Duke Casimir's permission I shall not conclude treaties with anyone, nor assist anyone in any way. . . . If God should cause anything to happen to Prince Fedor L'vovich, and any children survive him, they will rule over his patrimony; and after my death Grand Duke

Casimir shall conclude a treaty [with them] similar to this treaty, and he shall maintain them in the same way as the grand duke [agreed upon when he] took me into his service and concluded a treaty with me. But if any [grand duke] should refuse to render justice, and refuse to conclude a similar treaty [with them], and refuse to maintain them in the same way, then our oath shall be cast aside and we shall be free [from any obligation].

V:11. THE VOSKRESENSK CHRONICLE ON AN APPANAGE PRINCE'S TRANSFER TO MUSCOVY, 1500

One method by which Muscovy expanded under Ivan III is illustrated in this excerpt from the Voskresensk Chronicle. Mozhaisk, only about fifty miles west of Moscow, was the appanage of Semen's (Simeon's) father, who had abandoned the Muscovite service a half-century earlier and had sought refuge in Lithuania. Semen's appanage of Starodub, in the Grand Duchy of Lithuania, was some two hundred miles further to the southwest.
    Reference: *PSRL*, 8:239.

About [Prince] Starodubskii and [Prince] Shemiakin: After that, in the same month of April [1500], Prince Semen, son of Ivan Andreevich Mozhaiskii [of Mozhaisk], and Prince Vasilii, son of Ivan Dmitrievich She-miakin, sent a petition to Grand Prince Ivan [III] Vasil'evich of all Russia, [stating] that great pressure was being exerted upon them [to abandon] the Greek creed, and [requesting] that the sovereign [Ivan III] grant them his favor and receive them [into his service] with their patrimonies; for Grand Duke Alexander of Lithuania had violated his agreement [with them] in other matters as well. And Grand Prince Ivan Vasil'evich of all Russia, in view of that oppression, took Prince Semen and Prince Vasilii into his service with their patrimonies and sent Ivan Teleshev [to them] with his answer; and he [Ivan III] sent Afanasii Sheenk Viazmiatin to Grand Duke Alexander with a declaration of war; and to the princes [Semen and Vasilii] he sent his voevoda the boyar Iakov Zakharievich and other voevody with many men. And Iakov Zakharievich went ... to the princes and brought them to swear upon the cross that they would serve the sovereign grand prince of all Russia Ivan Vasil'evich, with their patrimonies.

V:12. A LETTER FROM PRINCE SEMEN BEL'SKII, 1500

Another facet of the process illustrated in the preceding item is seen in this excerpt from a letter to Grand Duke Alexander of Lithuania. The letter was evidently delivered by an emissary of Bel'skii's newly adopted sovereign, Ivan III of Russia.
    Reference: *SIRIO*, 35:295 (see List of Abbreviations).

Your Grace wishes to destroy our Greek [Orthodox] faith, and Your Grace wishes to convert [the Orthodox] to the Roman [Catholic] faith by force. And we, not wishing to see this done to us, have therefore left Your Grace and have petitioned the Orthodox Christian sovereign Grand Prince of All Russia Ivan Vasil'evich— and thus cast off our oath of allegiance [to you].

V:13. GENERAL LEGISLATION: CASIMIR'S CHARTER OF 1447

This charter issued by Casimir (Kazimir, Kazimierz) IV assured the nobles of the Lithuanian-Russian state of certain very important rights and privileges.
    Reference: Liubavskii, *Ocherk istorii litovsko-russkogo gosudarstva*, pp. 325-28.

1. First of all, therefore, to the aforementioned prelates, princes, lords, nobles, and towns of the aforesaid lands of the Grand Duchy of Lithuania, Russia, Samogitia, and so forth, we have given, granted, and irrevocably bestowed, and with renewed will we now give, grant, bestow, and generally dispense in perpetuity, all the same rights, liberties, and immunities that the prelates, lords, princes nobles, and towns of the Kingdom of Poland enjoy. . . .
    3. Likewise, to the aforementioned prelates princes, lords, nobles, and towns of the said lands of the Grand Duchy of Lithuania, Russia

Samogitia, and so forth, we have granted this: that we do not desire to chastise or inflict any punishment upon these same princes, lords, nobles, and towns, whether by seizure of estates, monetary fines, imprisonment, or execution, upon anyone's denunciation or accusation, public or secret, or upon suspicion, however grave, unless first they have truly been found guilty in open court, in keeping with the Catholic tradition of justice, with accuser and accused confronting each other in person. After such a trial and conviction according to the customs and laws of Poland, they should be punished and sentenced according to the degree and extent of their offenses.

4. Likewise, [we grant] that for the crimes of any person, only he who has sinned and transgressed and, always in keeping with the traditions of Catholic justice, has been judicially convicted and sentenced should be punished; thus, for example, a wife should not be punished for the crime of her husband, nor a father for the crime of his son and vice versa, nor any relative or servant, unless he has been a party to the offense, crimes of lese majesty alone excepted.

5. Likewise, we grant that the aforesaid princes, nobles, and boyars shall be free to leave our own lands of the grand duchy, and so forth, so as to acquire greater wealth and to perform military service for any foreign land, save only the states of our enemies; but nonetheless, service to us and to our successors from the estates of those who leave in this fashion shall not be neglected but shall be furnished and performed just as if they were present themselves, as often as the need arises. . . .

10. Likewise, each and every peasant and subject of the princes, lords, nobles, boyars, and townspeople of these same lands of the Grand Duchy of Lithuania shall be released, wholly freed, and totally exempted from giving and paying the tax or levy called

serebshchizna [silver collection], and the requisitions called diaklo [a tax in kind]; likewise from the burden of the [transport] obligation called podvody . . . and all other unjust labors . . . except for work on the building of new castles and the repair of old ones. . . .

11. Likewise [we declare] that we or our officials will not receive [into our service] rent-paying peasants [homines tributarii], long-term dwellers [originarii], peasants [cmetones], or dependent bondmen, of either sex or whatever status, of the aforesaid princes, lords, nobles, and townspeople of our lands of Lithuania, Russia, Samogitia, and so forth, nor will we allow our officials to do so; likewise the prelates, princes, lords, nobles, boyars, and townspeople of the Grand Duchy of Lithuania, Russia, Samogitia, and so forth, shall not receive [into their service] our peasants and those of our successors, similarly regardless of position, sex, or status, nor presume to receive [them] either themselves or through their agents in any way whatsoever.

12. Likewise, we shall not send [our] agents, otherwise called detskie, after the subjects of the above-mentioned princes, lords, nobles, and boyars [i.e. for trial] unless satisfaction has first been demanded from the master whose subject has done the wrong; if after a certain time satisfaction is denied, then our agent or [the agent] of our officials shall be instructed accordingly, and the offender who has merited punishment shall be punished by his master, and by no one else. . . .

14. Likewise, we promise and vouchsafe that in these our own lands of the grand duchy we shall grant no lands, castles [and] towns, or any kind of estates, possessions, and holdings, or any kind of offices and dignities to foreigners, but only to natives of our own lands of the aforesaid grand duchy; and our successors too will grant [them] to be held and possessed [only to natives of the grand duchy].

V:14. ALEXANDER'S CHARTER OF 1492

When Alexander succeeded Casimir as king of Poland and grand duke of Lithuania in 1492, he issued a charter which not only confirmed Casimir's charter of 1447 but made some significant additions to the privileges and political powers of the higher nobility. The following is an excerpt from it.

Reference: Liubavskii, *Ocherk istorii litovsko-russkogo gosudarstva*, pp. 331-33.

14. Likewise, whatever decisions and actions we shall take, decree, and prescribe with our lords in council, we shall not alter, amend, or annul with anyone else.

15. Likewise, when any proposals and matters emerge that are subject to discussion with our lords in council and are not approved by these same lords, we shall not force them on that account; rather we shall carry out whatsoever they advise us for our own and the common good.

16. Likewise, we shall not confer dignities, holdings, or any other offices or hereditary estates upon any foreigner or newcomer, but only upon natives [of the grand duchy]. Moreover, we shall demand no recompense for granting, conferring, or bestowing spiritual and temporal dignities, holdings, and offices of any kind. . . .

17. Moreover, no offices or holdings shall be conferred by us upon anyone without the advice of our councillors [the Council of Lords]. . . .

23. Likewise, the revenue from customs duties and the tavern tax, and that accruing to us from fines or any other source, shall be taken and placed in our treasury and shall be spent for the common good of the land, in accordance with the advice of our lords in council. If, however, there is no immediate need for the said revenues, they shall not be withdrawn from the treasury and reserved for our own use, or removed from the province, without permission of the lords themselves. . . .

25. Likewise, we shall not elevate common people above nobles but shall maintain the full dignity of the nobility.

V:15. SIGISMUND'S CHARTER OF 1506

In 1506 Sigismund II of Lithuania (Sigismund I in Poland) promulgated a charter confirming that of 1492 issued by his predecessor Alexander (1492-1506), but stating even more categorically, in article 7, the limitations on his own power by the Council of Lords.
Reference: Liubavskii, *Ocherk istorii litovsko-russkogo gosudarstva,* pp. 335-36.

7. Likewise, as for the approval and endorsement of statutes and customs, either old ones that should be preserved, or new ones that should be established and promulgated, as well as the many which in the future should be ordained for the general welfare of the state and our own welfare, we shall handle and settle [these matters] only upon careful consideration and with the knowledge, counsel, and agreement of our lords in council of the Grand Duchy of Lithuania.

V:16. THE FIRST LITHUANIAN STATUTE, 1529

The First Lithuanian Statute or code, promulgated in 1529, contained a confirmation and a systematic definition of the rights and liberties that had previously been granted by the grand dukes of Lithuania to separate groups and geographic entities. Here are some of the most important provisions of the statute.
Reference: Obshchestvo Istorii i Drevnostei Rossiiskikh, *Vremennik Imperatorskogo Moskov-skogo Obshchestva Istorii i Drevnostei Rossiiskikh,* 25 vols. (Moscow, 1849-57), 18:2, 12, 19-21, 40. See also K. I. Iablonskis, ed., *Statut velikogo kniazhestva litovskogo 1529 goda* (Minsk: AN BSSR, 1960), pp. 31-32, 42, 48-50, 69.

SECTION I. [Concerning accusations.]

The sovereign [king and grand duke Sigismund] promises not to punish anyone on the basis of an accusation not made in the presence of the accused, even if it concerns lese majesty against His Grace [the king]. And if anyone should accuse another unjustly, he shall be punished in the same way [as the accused would be if the accusation were true].

1. First of all, we grant to all the above-mentioned prelates, princes, standard-bearing lords [*pany khorugovnye,* magnates who went to war with their own large detachments of servitors and under their own banners], gentry [*szlachta*], and towns of the above-mentioned lands of the Grand Duchy of Lithuania, Russia, Samogitia, and so forth, that we shall not punish those princes, standard-bearing lords, gentry, and townspeople on the basis of anyone's complaint or accusation, open or secret, [or] of an unfounded suspicion, or sentence them to any punishment, [whether it be] a fine, death, imprisonment, or confiscation of property, unless first accuser and accused confront each other in an open Christian court of justice, which shall examine the evidence and determine, upon such trial and investigation and in accordance with the custom

of Christian justice, who shall be punished and sentenced according to the gravity of his offense. And if anyone should accuse another of a crime punishable by death, or [confiscation of] property, or any kind of punishment, and [thereby] subject [the accused] to [possible] dishonor or death, he who has made such an accusation and is unable to prove it shall be punished in the same way [as the accused would be if the accusation were true]. . . .

SEC. II. Concerning the defense of the land.

Everyone is obligated to serve in time of war.

1. We decree, with the consent of our entire Council [of Lords] and all our subjects, that every prince, lord, and nobleman [dvorianin], as well as every widow and every orphan, whether or not he is of age, and every such person who owns landed property is obliged in the hour of need to serve in war with us and our descendants, or under our hetmans [military commanders], and to furnish for military service as many men as required by the resolution of the land [i.e. of the diet], which shall indicate how many [soldiers] are necessary at a [given] time: that is, [men] from among both the patrimonial peasants [bound to the soil] and the mobile peasants [pokhozhie liudi, free to leave when their contract with the landowner expired] [living] on patrimonial, service-earned, or purchased estates, excluding only those [estates] of ours [the sovereign's] that someone holds in mortgage from us. Those men shall then be obliged to supply, in accordance with the resolution [of the diet] which shall be decreed at the time, servitors on good horses, [each] with a value of 240 groshi [4 kopy groshei; 1 kopa equalled 60 groshi, and a kopa groshei at this time apparently corresponded to one Muscovite poltina, or half a ruble], and armed with a breastplate, helmet, sword, and shield, and [carrying a] staff and banner. If some boyar or townsman does not have as many [men] on his estate as the resolution calls for, then he shall go himself and serve [with as many men] as the size of his estate [enables him]; and if a lord has not a single man, he shall himself go [to serve] as best he can. . . .

SEC. III. . . .

Tenures and dignities shall not be given to foreigners.

3. We likewise swear and promise that in our lands of this grand duchy we shall not give any lands, castles, or towns, or grant any property of any kind in ownership or in tenure, or bestow offices [urady], honors, and dignities of any kind on any outsiders; but we shall give them, and our descendants shall give them in tenure and as grants, only to natives and residents of those lands of ours in the above-mentioned grand duchy. . . .

The sovereign promises to maintain all the old decrees, and to promulgate new ones [only] with [the consent of] the Council of Lords [pany rady].

6. And we shall likewise safeguard the old charters of the land and the customs that have been written down, confirmed, and decreed in those charters; and if new [charters] should be granted or [old ones] amended, for our benefit and that of the commonwealth [rech', i.e. rzecz pospolita], then we shall gladly amend them with the knowledge, advice, and consent of our Council [of Lords] of the Grand Duchy of Lithuania.

His Grace the sovereign promises to maintain inviolate the liberties [granted] to the princes, lords, gentry, and townspeople.

7. We promise by our sovereign person that all the gentry, princes, standard-bearing lords, all the boyars jointly, the townspeople, and all their men will enjoy the freedoms and liberties granted to them by our ancestors and by us. . . .

Common people will not be raised above the gentry [shliakhta, i.e., szlachta].

10. We shall likewise not raise men not belonging to the gentry above the gentry [by appointing them to offices where the gentry would be subordinate to them], but shall maintain the full dignity of the gentry. . . .

SEC. VI. Concerning judges, that they should dispense justice in accordance with written law; and if they should do otherwise, they shall be punished.

1. We likewise decree that all our voevody, starosty, land marshals [marshalok zemskii, highest officer of the grand ducal household], court marshals [marshalok dvornyi, his assistant], and derzhavtsy [local administrators appointed by the grand duke], each in his own district [povet], will not hold trials or render justice to our subjects except in accordance with the written laws we have given to all our subjects in the grand duchy. But if either party in a lawsuit should consider a

trial to be unjust and decided not on the basis of the written laws, then at the first diet when we, the sovereign, are ourselves present with our entire Council of Lords, or when in our absence the Council of Lords is assembled, he who has been unjustly tried shall make complaint against our official [judge] to us or to our Council of Lords.

V:17. THE CHARTER OF VIL'NO, 1563

In 1563, by the Charter of Vil'no, Sigismund Augustus significantly extended the rights of the Lithuanian and Russian nobles of Orthodox faith. The following excerpt from this charter should be compared with the earlier excerpts from the Charter of Gorodlo, Item V:8, above.
    Reference: *AOIZR*, 3:119-20.

We have perceived, together with our Council of Lords, that . . . not only the followers of the Roman church but also those of the Greek [church] who have occupied the benches of our ancestors' Councils [of Lords] and ours, and all the other estates that have served us in various capacities, have always and unceasingly displayed their loyalty and constancy in willingly serving our ancestors and ourselves, as befits good and faithful subjects. Therefore, taking into consideration all these great services . . . and with the advice and consent of our Council of Lords spiritual and temporal, we decree and desire that henceforth not only those lords, nobles, and boyars who are followers of the Roman church and whose ancestors received insignia and coats of arms in the Kingdom of Poland [by the Charter of Gorodlo in 1413] should possess and enjoy the charters granted them and all the liberties and rights given them, but that also all others of knightly and noble estate, both Lithuanians and Russians, as long as they are of Christian faith, including those whose ancestors did not receive insignia or coats of arms from the Kingdom of Poland, shall similarly and equally possess and enjoy for all time to come those liberties, just as heretofore, from time immemorial and to this day, the knightly and noble estate of both nations, Lithuanian and Russian, has possessed and enjoyed all those liberties. Likewise, all the dignities and positions, including [membership in] our Council [of Lords] and court [*dvornye*] and state [*zemskie*, central administrative] offices, shall henceforth be filled and occupied, not by followers of the Roman faith alone, but similarly and equally by anyone of knightly estate, by noblemen of Christian faith, Lithuanians and Russians alike.

V:18. THE SECOND LITHUANIAN STATUTE, 1566

In 1563-65 reforms were enacted in the Grand Duchy of Lithuania aimed at making it into a gentry republic on the Polish model. The Second Lithuanian Statute, promulgated in 1566, not only confirmed the preceding statute but also, as the following excerpts show, incorporated many significant innovations. (Note: Curiously enough, the Third Lithuanian Statute, in 1588, retained the provisions of section III, article 9, below, concerning "foreigners," although it obviously contradicted the terms of the Union of Lublin in 1569, Item IX:1, below.)
    Reference: Obshchestvo Istorii i Drevnostei Rossiiskikh, *Vremennik Imperatorskogo Moskovskogo Obshchestva Istorii i Drevnostei Rossiiskikh*, 23:15, 30-32, 43, 45-48, 50, 63.

SECTION I, ARTICLE 1. All inhabitants of the Grand Duchy of Lithuania shall be tried according to the common written law which we have granted.
    First of all, we, the sovereign [Sigismund Augustus], promise and swear by the oath we took to all the inhabitants of all the lands of our realm, the Grand Duchy of Lithuania, that all the princes, lords temporal and spiritual of the council, standard-bearing lords, nobles, [inhabitants of the] towns, and all our subjects and all estates of our realm, the Grand Duchy of Lithuania, as well as of the Russian lands, Kiev, Samogitia [sic], Volynia, Podliash'e, and other lands belonging to our realm, from the highest estate to the lowest, shall be tried and judged according to the common written law that we have granted.
    ART. 2. We, the sovereign, promise and swear that no one will be punished on the basis of an accusation not made in the presence of the accused, even if it concerns lese

majesty against us, the sovereign; and if any-one should accuse another and be unable to prove his accusation, he shall be punished in the same way [as the accused would be if guilty].

Upon our sovereign word we promise to the above-mentioned prelates, princes, lords, lords spiritual and temporal of the council, standard-bearing lords, gentry, and [inhabitants of the] towns in the land of the Grand Duchy of Lithuania, [and] of Russia, Kiev, Samogitia, Volynia, Podliash'e, Smolensk, Polotsk, Vitebsk, Mstislavl', and other lands of the Grand Duchy of Lithuania, that we shall not punish [men of] the above-mentioned estates on the basis of anyone's complaint or accusation, open or secret, [or] of a mere suspicion, or sentence them to any kind of punishment, [whether it be] a fine, death, or deprivation of dignities, offices, or estates; unless first the plaintiff, that is, the accuser, and the defendant, [that is,] the accused, shall confront each other before an open court, which shall examine the evidence by due process of law and thereupon determine, upon such trial and investigation, who is guilty and subject to the punishments designated in the following articles. . . .

SEC. II, ART. 1. Concerning the obligations to which all inhabitants of the Grand Duchy of Lithuania are subject.

We likewise decree, with the consent of our entire Council [of Lords] and the subjects of every estate of our realm, the Grand Duchy of Lithuania, that all princes and spiritual lords, and likewise all noblemen [and] boyars, and all widows, and [men of] other estates, and our Tatars [i.e. Tatars who settled in Lithuania and entered the service of the grand duke] and the townspeople of our towns, who possess landed property and are of age, are obliged in the hour of need to serve in war with us and with our descendants, or under our hetmans [military commanders], and to furnish [men] for military service, whenever the need arises, in accordance with the resolution of the land, [adopted by] the diets of our Grand Duchy. . . . But if anyone among our subjects, of the nobility and knighthood [and] of every estate, should possess landed property but not perform military service . . . he shall lose all his [landed] property. . . .

ART. 2. The defense of the state shall be ordered only by the diets.

We promise and decree unalterably for all time to come that if the need arises for our realm, the Grand Duchy of Lithuania, to defend the land against some enemy, or to wage war, then neither we, the sovereign, alone, nor together with our Council of Lords, have or shall have the right to do this, or to impose any levy or tax, without first convoking a great general diet [*soim velikii val'nyi*] in our realm, the Grand Duchy of Lithuania, at which, in accordance with our order and proclamation, all the princes, and the lords spiritual and temporal of our council, [and] the marshals and other officials of the state [zemskie] and of the court, [and] the standard-bearing lords, [and] the deputies of the land from each district [*posly zemskie povetovye*] shall assemble; then only, at this great general diet, with our entire Council of Lords and with all the princes and lords and with the entire knighthood, upon their advice and consent, shall we decide such matters, and not otherwise. But if some enemy of ours should make a sudden attack upon our realm, the Grand Duchy of Lithuania, then even without the diet, [but simply] by our own proclamation, or in our absence by proclamation of our Council of Lords [or] of our grand hetman [*getman velikii,* the commander in chief], all the princes and lords [and] all our subjects shall be obliged to perform military service [and] to appear at the appointed time and place, as [they would respond] to an alarm, and for the love of the Commonwealth to defend their wives and children [and] the possessions of their fatherland. . . .

SEC. III, ART. 2. Concerning the liberties of the gentry.

Upon our word we, the sovereign, promise for ourselves and for our descendants, the grand dukes of Lithuania . . . that all the princes and lords spiritual and temporal of the council, and all the officials of the state and of the court, [and] the standard-bearing lords, the gentry, the knighthood, the townspeople, and all the men in common in the Grand Duchy of Lithuania and in all the lands of that realm shall be maintained by us in all their Christian freedoms and liberties, in which they have lived and been governed, following the example and manner of free

Christian realms, as free men who since ancient times [and] since the days of their most remote ancestors have freely elected their lords and sovereigns, the grand dukes of Lithuania, and who have shared equally, possessed, and enjoyed these liberties together with their neighbors [and] brethren, the knighthood and other estates of the people in the Kingdom of Poland. . . .

ART. 5. Concerning the district dietines [*soimik povetovyi*] and their sending and dispatch of deputies of the land [*posol zemskii*] to the general diet [*val'nyi seim*].

We decree . . . for all time to come that, prior to the great general diet which we and our descendants shall always convoke whenever the need arises for the commonwealth of the Grand Duchy, upon the advice of our Council [of Lords] of that realm [and] by our proclamation, district dietines shall assemble . . . four weeks before the great diet. At these dietines shall gather and appear the voevody and castellans [and] officials of the state, and likewise princes, lords, [and] gentry of that district and *voevodstvo* [province governed by a voevoda], to discuss those matters and needs of the land that we have made known to them in our towns, and likewise their own [needs] and all the needs of the land and the requirements of that district; and after agreeing by unanimous decision they shall choose their deputies, that is, two men from every land court [i.e. district; each district (povet) contained a single land court (*zemskii sud*)], from as many [districts] as there are in each voevodstvo [the number ranged from one to five], and shall dispatch them to the diet, after informing and instructing them to deliberate, discuss, and resolve all those matters mentioned in our sovereign proclamations, and likewise all the needs [of the land], [and] empowering them to determine and decide these and other pertinent matters at this general diet, as the times and needs require. And princes, lords, marshals, and all other officials of the state and of the court shall be summoned to such general diets by our [special] proclamations, in accordance with ancient custom. . . .

ART. 6. Concerning the general diet.

Moreover, we likewise decree, with the consent of our lords spiritual and temporal of the Council and of all the estates represented in the diet, at the present great diet in Vil'no, and wish it maintained for all time to come, that we and our descendants, the grand dukes of Lithuania, upon the need of the commonwealth [and] the advice of our Council [of Lords] of that realm, or upon the request of the knighthood, shall always convoke a general diet in that realm, the Grand Duchy of Lithuania, whenever the need should arise. . . .

ART. 9. That dignities [and] offices shall not be given into the possession of foreigners.

We, the sovereign, likewise promise and swear upon our oath . . . that in this realm, the Grand Duchy of Lithuania, and in all the lands belonging to it, we shall not bestow spiritual and temporal dignities, towns, homesteads, and estates, [or the office of] starosta upon any foreigners, aliens, or neighbors of this realm in tenure or use or eternal possession; but we and our descendants, the grand dukes of Lithuania, shall be obliged to bestow all this only upon Lithuanians and Russians whose forefathers for generations and who themselves were born in the Grand Duchy of Lithuania or in other lands belonging to that grand duchy. . . .

ART. 12. Concerning the maintenance of old decrees; that new [decrees] shall not be issued without the general diet.

We likewise affirm that all the ancient charters of the land and the freedoms newly granted by us and the worthy ancient customs shall be maintained by this statute and not violated in any way, and nothing new shall be established. And if it should be necessary to add something new for the good of the commonwealth, then we shall not do this or make any amendments except at the [session of the] general diet of our realm and in this realm of ours, the Grand Duchy of Lithuania, with the knowledge [and] advice of our Council [of Lords] and with the consent of all the lands of this realm of ours. . . .

ART. 15. Commoners shall not be elevated above the gentry.

We likewise shall not elevate commoners above the gentry, shall not appoint our commoners to dignities, and [shall not] grant them offices; but as for the gentry, because of our sovereign benevolence toward their services and abilities, we, the sovereign, promise to provide all men of knightly estate in our realm, the Grand Duchy of Lithuania, with dignities and offices in accordance with their abilities and to maintain them in our service as our faithful subjects. . . .

SEC. IV, ART. 1. . . . [Concerning the zemskii sud or land court, which settled disputes involving landed estates of the gentry:] In each district the princes, [members of] our Council of Lords [i.e. those members who owned estates in that district], and likewise the entire knighthood and gentry . . . shall all choose from among all the gentry of that district their brethren for each office as follows: for the office of judge [*sud'ia*], four worthy men; for the office of assistant judge [*podsudok*], another four men; and for the office of clerk [*pisar'*], still another four men; [these must all be] worthy, honest, and intelligent men with knowledge of law, and of noble birth, with landed property in that district, and of no other faith but the Christian; and after choosing [the candidates] they [the members of the dietine] shall inform us, the sovereign, by written deed as to whom they have chosen, and we shall select three of these twelve persons for land offices in that district: a judge, an assistant judge, and a clerk for the court. . . .

And the land clerk shall write all documents and writs in the Russian language, with Russian letters and words; and not in any other language and words.

V:19. REGIONAL CHARTERS: THE CHARTER OF VITEBSK, JULY 16, 1503

In addition to the general legislation, of which samples have just been given, the charters granted to various regional units help to indicate to what extent the Belorussian, Ukrainian, or West Russian lands which were absorbed into the Grand Duchy of Lithuania were able to retain their previous social and political structure and their own rights and privileges. The following are excerpts from a few of the many regional charters of the sixteenth century. It may be noted that the "boyars" mentioned in these documents were members of the landowning gentry class in Lithuania and not, as in Moscow, members of the highest aristocracy.

The first document is the charter of July 16, 1503, confirming the previous regional charter granted to the "land" or province of Vitebsk by Casimir IV.

Reference: *RIB*, vol. 27, cols. 846-49 (see List of Abbreviations).

Charter to all the boyars and townspeople of Vitebsk granting certain rights and liberties.

. . .

All the princes, boyars, and servitors [*slugi*, a group of people enjoying rights similar to those of the boyars, but of lower social status, living rather like peasants] of Vitebsk, and the mayor [*voit*, chief magistrate of a village or town] and townspeople of the town of Vitebsk, and the entire land of Vitebsk have petitioned us [Alexander, grand duke of Lithuania 1492-1506] and have told us that evildoers came from Novgorod the Great [and] robbed their Church of the Holy Virgin, and stole from that church the charter they had received from our father, His Grace the king [Casimir IV, king of Poland 1447-92, grand duke of Lithuania 1440-92]. They brought us a copy of this charter and petitioned us to give them a charter deed with the same terms [as the old one]. And we have granted this to them out of our benevolence because of their faithful service [and] have given them our deed with the same terms that our father, His Grace the king, had given to them. . . . [The terms follow:] We shall not interfere with their churches; and we shall not interfere with the purchased [estates] in Vitebsk which they purchase with our permission or [with estates left] without heirs or intestate; and we shall not give their wives [widows] in marriage forcibly. . . . We shall not give credence to [the testimony of] male or female slaves [against their masters]. We shall render justice for all offenses; and we shall not retry those cases that were tried by our ancestors, the grand dukes; we shall deal with the people of Vitebsk [in legal matters] only upon investigation and shall not punish them without trial; we shall not change our own verdicts in cases already tried; and if a crime should be committed, we shall impose punishment in accordance with the guilt; we shall accept petitions from the people of Vitebsk; if [an accused man] has a guarantor, we shall not put him in chains or torture him in any way; we shall not take away their patrimonies; we shall not interfere with the villages they have bought or with their fields; we shall not give credence to accusations that are not made in the presence of the defendant; and if anyone should make an accusation against a man of Vitebsk, we shall make this known to him [the accused]. We shall not send men of Vitebsk [to other towns] for garrison duty, but they shall be ready to go to war together with us. Our voevoda shall not travel through the land of Vitebsk [requisitioning food and services from the inhabitants]; but if he goes out to hunt, he shall not accept any gifts from the [inhabitants of the] stany [territorial divisions]. . . . And we shall not force *siabry* in the towns [siabry were peasants who owned a share, either by purchase or by long residence, of the property belonging to a large peasant family or commune] to do work for us, either as carters or as huntsmen. Likewise we shall not interfere with the weights and measures of Vitebsk; and if some inhabitant of Vitebsk should give fraudulent weight or measure, then he shall be punished by the people of Vitebsk themselves, in accordance with their own law, and we shall not interfere with this. . . . We shall not grant the people of Vitebsk to anyone [i.e. not grant their land as a patrimonial estate to anyone]. We have likewise absolved them for all time

to come from [paying] internal customs duties [*myto*] throughout our patrimony [Lithuania]. . . . We shall likewise appoint voevody as of old, in accordance with their wishes; and if a voevoda is unacceptable to them, and they make complaint against him, we shall give them another voevoda to suit their wishes. On the first day after his arrival in Vitebsk, the voevoda shall kiss the cross to the people of Vitebsk that he will not punish them on the basis of a mere accusation, without due process of law. And the people of Vitebsk are free to live in Vitebsk as of old, as long as they wish; and if we should offend any man of Vitebsk and he be unwilling [to remain], we shall not detain him by force, but he will be free to go wherever he wishes, without any hindrance. . . . As for any Lithuanians or Poles in Vitebsk who have been christened in the Russian faith [Orthodoxy], or whose descendants now live [there], we shall not persecute them, or violate their rights as Christians in any way.

V:20. REGIONAL CHARTERS: SMOLENSK, 1505

Here is another example of a charter issued by Grand Duke Alexander (who ruled from 1492 to 1506).

Reference: Liubavskii, *Ocherk istorii litovsko-russkogo gosudarstva*, pp. 369-70.

Bishop Joseph of Smolensk and the okol'-nichie [members of the administrative and judicial council] of Smolensk, and all the princes, lords, boyars, townspeople, and common people, and the entire population of the town [and] land of Smolensk have petitioned us and placed before us the august charter of our father, His Grace King Casimir of glorious memory, which our father [King Casimir IV of Poland, 1447-92, grand duke of Lithuania 1440-92] gave to them when he was only grand duke [i.e. before he became king in 1447], realizing and beholding their true and faithful service to His Grace and to our ancestors. . . . [The terms of the new charter follow:] First of all, we shall not violate the Christianity of the Greek law [Orthodoxy], shall not oppress [the people of Smolensk] for their religion, and shall not interfere with the lands and waters belonging

to the church, or with monasteries and intestate estates. After the death of a husband we shall not move his widow from her home and shall not give her in marriage against her will. . . . The volosti that were administered by the boyars of Smolensk shall be administered by them as of old, whichever volost' shall be granted to whichever boyar [to administer]. And as for those volosti that Svidrigailo [Svitrigaila, grand duke of Lithuania 1430-32 rival of Grand Duke Sigismund for the throne until 1438, autonomous prince of areas in the southwest until his death in 1452] detached from Smolensk, His Grace [Grand Duke Casimir] returned those volosti to Smolensk. . . . And His Grace [Casimir] granted the same rights to the princes, lords, and boyars of Smolensk as he gave to the [other] princes, lords, and boyars of Lithuania.

V:21. REGIONAL CHARTERS: KIEV, 1529

Sigismund, king of Poland and grand duke of Lithuania from 1506 to 1548, granted these rights and liberties to the "land" or province of Kiev in his charter of 1529. The phrase "we had confirmed" in the first sentence evidently refers to a charter Sigismund issued to Kiev on December 8, 1507.

Reference: Liubavskii, *Ocherk istorii litovsko-russkogo gosudarstva*, pp. 376-80. For the charter of 1507 see *AOIZR*, 2:33-36.

Our servants, the princes, lords, boyars, *zemiane* [name given to the gentry class, particularly in the southwest regions of the Grand Duchy of Lithuania], and all the szlachta [gentry] of Kiev, have petitioned us, [saying] that first our father Casimir of blessed memory, king of Poland and grand duke of Lithuania, and then our brother King Alexander, and we ourselves, had given them free rights as Christians; and we had confirmed this by our charters, in accordance with what our father had granted to them. . . . We grant anew to all of them and bestow upon ecclesiastics and laymen alike those rights that were granted before by our father and brother, Their Graces the kings [of Poland, Casimir and Alexander]. First of all, we shall not interfere with the churches of God, [or] with men living on church land, or with [church] lands, or with [church] incomes and revenues. And without due process of law we shall not punish or ruin anyone, or take away his property; but if anyone should commit a crime, a trial shall be held, and whoever is found guilty shall be punished according to his guilt. If anyone should accuse another or make a complaint against another, whether secretly or openly, the accused will not be punished, either by imprisonment or by death, until the accuser and the defendant have appeared before an open Christian court, which shall examine the case and render justice; and everyone shall be punished as he deserves, except for traitors who plot against us or our country: those will be punished by death and [confiscation of] property [this clause apparently means that traitors shall be tried by special courts and not by the normal "open Christian courts"]. Whoever deserves punishment shall be punished according to his guilt, but his wife and children shall not be deprived of their property; . . . only the guilty one and his accomplices shall be punished. And patrimonies or estates granted for service shall not be taken away. . . . Those princes and lords who hold estates granted for service, which we have confirmed by our documents, are free to bequeath them to churches for [the repose of] their souls and to exchange, sell, or give them away with our consent; whomever they bequeath their inheritance to, we shall not disturb him. . . . If any prince or lord should wish to travel to foreign lands, he must inform us or make petition to our voevoda and leave behind someone on his estate who can perform military service as well as he, and who can act as defendant if any litigation arises in his absence involving one of his men; then after making his report [to the grand duke or voevoda] he is free to go [abroad], provided there is no [current] military service. . . . And if a bondman or male or female slave should make complaint against his lord, no trial shall be held; the bondman or male or female slave shall be turned over to his lord. The people of Kiev shall be treated with honor and shall receive offices just like Lithuanians and shall not be degraded in any way; and Kievan towns and volosti shall be governed by [native] Kievans and by no one else; we shall assign them to those men who are suitable. . . . And men living on land of the church, or of princes and lords, shall not build weirs or mow hay or settle on our land; they must obey only the lords whom they serve; and our homesteads [*dvor*] shall be settled [only] by our men. . . . The fortifications of Kiev [shall be built] as before: everyone is obliged to work on the fortifications. . . . [The people of Kiev] shall not receive [on their estates] our men [peasants living on crown domains], whether they live locally or come from Lithuania; nor shall we, the grand duke, receive men living on lands of the church, or of princes and lords, patrimonial [*otchiznye*, belonging to private landowners] peasants who are bound to the soil [*nepokhozhie liudi*, who had lived on their land for generations and thereby lost the right to leave].

· · ·

And we shall firmly observe these rights, granted to them by us and by our ancestors, and shall not violate them in any way.

V:22. REGIONAL CHARTERS: POLOTSK, 1547

Sigismund Augustus, who granted the present charter, was the actual ruler of Lithuania from 1544 on, though his father did not die until 1548. The preceding charter confirming the rights of the voevodstvo or province of Polotsk was issued July 23, 1511.

Reference: Liubavskii, *Ocherk istorii litovsko-russkogo gosudarstva*, pp. 381-84. For the charter of 1511 see *AOIZR*, 2:86-90.

Charter to all the inhabitants of the voevodstvo [province, or administrative division governed by a voevoda] and town of Polotsk, outlining the rights and liberties granted to them.

. . . The boyars of Polotsk and the townspeople and the entire city [and] the entire land of Polotsk have petitioned us and placed before us the documents of Their Graces the kings [of Poland]: of our grandfather Casimir [grand duke of Lithuania 1440-92], and of our uncle Alexander [grand duke 1492-1506], and of our lord [and] father [Sigismund II of Lithuania, king of Poland as Sigismund I from 1506 to 1548]; [charters] that Their Graces had previously granted to [the people of Polotsk], giving them the rights [and] liberties it is fitting for Christians to have: liberties that exist in the Kingdom of Poland and which they were previously given [in Polotsk] by our ancestors the grand dukes [of Lithuania], by the grand dukes Vitovt and Sigismund [I, 1432-40] and Skirgailo [Skirgaila, brother of Iagailo and prince of Polotsk 1386-94]; and [the people of Polotsk] have asked us to confirm all these rights and freedoms by our charter. We . . . confirm by the present document, with special sovereign benevolence, all those liberties [and] documents of our ancestors, our grandfather, uncle, and father, Their Graces the kings and grand dukes; and by the present charter we grant for all eternity the rights [and] liberties it is fitting and just for Christians to have. First, we shall not interfere with the churches of God and with church estates.
. . . And if anyone should accuse another, either openly or secretly, we shall not punish [the accused] in any way, either by [confiscation of] property, or imprisonment, or monetary fine, or death, until accuser and accused shall confront each other face to face in an open Christian court, which shall then examine the matter and render justice. Whoever is found guilty shall be punished as he deserves, according to his guilt; but his wife and children shall not be touched, or their property disturbed. . . . Those who own patrimonial estates, or [estates] granted

to them by Grand Duke Vitovt, or by Grand Duke Svidrigailo, or which Their Graces the kings, our grandfather, uncle, or father had granted, or which we have granted, shall continue to own them just as princes, lords, and townsmen in the Kingdom of Poland own [estates]. If anyone should wish to sell his estate, or give it away, or exchange it with someone, he shall inform us or our vicegerent and then [shall be free to] sell or exchange it. We shall not interfere with purchased [estates] in Polotsk, nor shall we interfere with estates left without heirs or intestate. . . . And our voevoda in Polotsk shall not judge the townspeople by himself, but shall judge them [only] with the boyars and the townspeople. . . . We shall not give credence to [the testimony of] male or female slaves [in court]. . . . And they [the people of Polotsk] shall be ready to go to war together with us. And our voevoda shall not travel through the land of Polotsk [requisitioning food and services from the inhabitants]; if he goes out to hunt, he shall not accept any gifts from [the inhabitants of] the stany [territorial divisions].

. . .

We shall not grant the people of Polotsk to anyone [i.e. not grant their land as a patrimony to anyone]. . . . We, the sovereign, shall likewise appoint voevody for them, the people of Polotsk, in accordance with their wishes; and if a voevoda should be unacceptable to them, we shall appoint a voevoda in accordance with their wishes; and on the first day after his arrival in Polotsk the voevoda shall kiss the cross to the people of Polotsk that he will not punish a man of Polotsk in any way without due process of law. And the town [of Polotsk] shall not give gifts to the voevoda. All the people of Polotsk are free to live in Polotsk as long as they wish; and if we should offend any man of Polotsk [and he wishes to leave], we shall not detain him by force; he will be free to go wherever he wishes, without any hindrance; and he will be free [to do what he wishes] with his property when he leaves: to sell it, or entrust it to a friend; and we shall not interfere with this.

V:23. REGIONAL CHARTERS: VOLYNIA, 1547

Sigismund Augustus, evidently having before him a charter issued by his father to Volynia in 1509, granted it the following rights and liberties in 1547.

Reference: Liubavskii, *Ocherk istorii litovsko-russkogo gosudarstva*, pp. 388-91. For the charter of 1509 see *AOIZR*, 2:64-66.

The ecclesiastics and laymen [of Volynia]— the bishop of Vladimir [-Volynsk], the bishop of Lutsk, the princes, lords, and zemiane, and all the gentry [szlachta] of the land of Volynia—have petitioned us and brought before us the charter of His Grace the king and grand duke Sigismund the elder [Sigismund I of Poland and II of Lithuania]. . . . And so, having examined the charter of His Grace King [Sigismund] the elder, our lord [and] father, we have done as they requested and shall maintain inviolate those rights and liberties which they enjoyed in the reigns of our grandfather [Casimir IV of Poland] and of our uncle [Alexander, grand duke 1492-1506], Their Graces the kings [of Poland], and in the reign of our father, His Grace King [Sigismund] the elder; and we confirm [these rights] by our [present] charter. . . . If any servant or peasant of theirs [the gentry] should commit murder [the gentry] shall themselves impose the fine for murder [*golovshchina*] upon their servants and peasants; and our starosty and vicegerents [*namestniki*] shall not impose fines for murder upon their servants and peasants. And our starosty shall not dishonor princes, lords, and zemiane, nor arrest them or imprison them in the tower [of the starosta's castle]. If a prince or lord or zemianin should commit an offense, the starosta shall inform us: and as we instruct him [the starosta] in writing or by messenger to deal with [the offender], thus shall he deal with him in accordance with our instructions. . . . Our starosty and vicegerents shall not take fines or sureties from [the gentry] nor hold trials over their peasants; they [the gentry] shall hold trial themselves over their own peasants, each taking fines from his own peasants. . . . Further, our starosta shall hold trials in his castle over peasants of princes, lords, and zemiane, in matters involving apprehended robbery, assault, injury to a nobleman, and arson, lest such evildoing should multiply. . . . If any prince, lord, or zemianin who is being tried by a starosta or vicegerent should appeal to us, the sovereign, for trial by a higher court, our starosty or vicegerents shall not forbid this but shall let him come to us, setting a date for him to appear before us; and our starosty and vicegerents shall not hold trial over princes, lords, or zemiane by themselves, but shall have princes, lords, and zemiane sitting alongside them for the trial. . . . Out of benevolence to their humble request and petition, we have granted them [the gentry] our favor and exempted their peasants throughout the entire land of Volynia from paying the cattle tax [*volovshchina*, the chief agricultural tax in Volynia], which their peasants have paid since olden times, in the reigns of our ancestors; we have granted them this exemption eternally and for all time to come, and neither we, the sovereign, nor our descendants shall collect the cattle tax from their peasants. But if our Council of Lords [pany rada] of the Grand Duchy of Lithuania should agree to collect a levy from their peasants because of some great need of the state, then the princes and lords and all the gentry of the land of Volynia shall likewise collect for us that levy from their peasants.

V:24. THE CHARTER GIVING MAGDEBURG LAW TO BREST, AUGUST 15, 1390

To encourage the development of trade and industry, the Grand Duchy of Lithuania began, late in the fourteenth century, to grant some of its principal towns a form of self-government known as the Magdeburg law, after the pattern of Germany and Poland. Vil'no received the reform in 1387. The following passage is from the second such charter, issued August 15, 1390, to Brest (-Litovsk), by Iagailo, who had taken the Polish name of Wladyslaw.

Reference: *CIOIDRMU*, 1899, bk. 4, pp. 1-2.

In the name of our Lord, amen. May this be forever remembered. We, Wladyslaw, by the grace of God king of Poland . . . make known by the present document to all whom it may concern both now and hereafter: Desirous of improving the condition of our town of Brest, so that it may succeed in attracting more inhabitants, we transfer it from the Ruthenian law to the German law of Magdeburg for all time to come, nullifying at the same time all Polish and Ruthenian laws and general customs which have constantly been the cause of friction; moreover, we absolve and forever release the townspeople and inhabitants of our town of Brest, Germans as well as Poles and Ruthenians, Christians of whatever status, from any jurisdiction and authority of all the palatines, castellans, starosty [here called *capitanei*], voevody, burgraves, judges, assistant judges, officials, and their agents or detskie, so that [the townspeople] shall in no way be answerable to them or to anyone else for any offenses great or small, as, for example, theft, bloodshed, murder, mutilation, arson, or anything else; nor shall they be held to suffer any punishments; but rather, the townspeople and inhabitants of the aforesaid town, Ruthenians as well as Poles, Germans, and anyone else, shall be answerable to their own mayor [voit], whoever it may be at that time. This mayor, moreover, shall not be bound to answer anyone's charges before us or our general court unless summoned by our dispatch, sealed with our seal, and then only in accordance with the aforementioned German Magdeburg law. Moreover, in criminal and capital offenses of any kind, we give and confer to the mayor of the said town of Brest the full and unlimited power of judging, passing sentence, reprimanding, and punishing according to the custom of the land, as the German Magdeburg law demands and requires in all its points, provisos, and conditions.

V:25. THE CHARTER GIVING MAGDEBURG LAW TO POLOTSK, OCTOBER 7, 1498

The town of Polotsk, on the Western Dvina, received the Magdeburg form of government from Grand Duke Alexander on October 7, 1498. The following excerpts illustrate the process by which the towns gradually gained an increasing voice in their own economic and political affairs.

Reference: *RIB*, vol. 27, cols. 701-06. This and other similar charters are also given in *AOIZR*, 1:179-81 [Polotsk, 1498], 187-89 [Minsk, 1499]; 2:75-79 [Polotsk, 1510], 93-95 [Brest, 1511]; 3:110-14 [Mogilev, 1561], 202-06 [Mogilev, 1577], 255-58 [Polotsk, 1580], 261-64 [Pinsk, 1581].

Charter to the city of Polotsk granting it the Magdeburg law and other liberties:

. . . We, Alexander, by the grace of God grand duke and hereditary lord of Lithuania, Russia, Samogitia, and other [lands], make known through this charter of ours to all whom it may concern, to both present and future [generations], that with the intention of improving the general welfare and with the desire of raising to a higher level the condition of the town of Polotsk, so that our people living there would prosper as a result of good and just administration, we transfer for all time to come this town of ours from [the jurisdiction of] Lithuanian and Russian law, or whatever [law] may be observed there, to the German Magdeburg law; and in accordance with the general custom and all the statutes of that Magdeburg law, we abrogate forever all rights, statutes, and customs previously in force that contravene or conflict with that Magdeburg law. In accordance with that Magdeburg law we once again establish the office of mayor [voit] in the above-mentioned city, and through this charter grant [privileges] to the office of mayor, prescribing for the present mayor and for all who shall occupy this office after him a third part of all the court fees and taxes and court fines and other revenues of every kind, just as our ancestors have established in Vil'no and in other towns that observe the same law. . . . All these . . . men [the people of Polotsk] shall be subject to that Magdeburg law in all matters, and we exempt all these men from the authority of the castle [i.e. of the voevoda] and the boyars, before whose courts they shall not be obliged to stand; and if anyone should be guilty of any [crime], justice shall be administered to him by the mayor and burgomasters. But in a time of unrest or in the event of some other need of the land, and particularly when we enjoin it, they shall obey the orders of the vicegerent who is in our castle at that time and shall be ready to defend [the town] as long as necessary. . . . We likewise allow that above-mentioned town to hold a fair three times a year for its benefit, as is the custom in other towns. . . . We likewise permit that town of ours to keep a weighing scale, [the revenues from] which shall be turned over to the benefit of our treasury. They shall likewise keep a container for wax [*kapnitsa*], and they shall stamp with their own seal all the wax that is melted there and keep all the profit therefrom for the public good. We likewise enjoin the mayor and burgomasters, whoever may be [in office] at the time, to bring in settlers and increase the population in all uninhabited areas in and around the town. . . . All the townspeople of Polotsk shall be exempt from customs duties throughout the entire Grand Duchy of Lithuania, just as our ancestors granted to the people of Vil'no and Troki by special permission. They shall likewise choose a suitable spot to build and construct a public bath for the town's profit; they shall likewise erect a town hall, under which will be located dry goods stores and bakeries, that is, bakehouses, and drapers' shops; and in the town hall they shall likewise keep a measuring barrel [for dry measures] and a copper vessel [for liquid measures] with the city seal, from which the mayor and burgomasters shall use all the profits for public works within the town. The above-mentioned town shall have a permanent number of twenty council members [*radtsy*], who will be chosen by the mayor; one half [of the council members] shall be of Roman faith and the other half of Greek. These council members, together with the mayor, shall choose two burgomasters from among themselves each year, one of Roman faith and the other of Greek, who shall govern the population together with the mayor. The burgomasters and council members shall allow all appeals [from their decisions] to the mayor; but there shall be no appeals from [a decision of] the mayor except to us [the grand duke]. Likewise, the mayor shall have the authority to execute decisions without [consulting] the burgomasters or council members; but the burgomasters and council members shall not issue any decisions without the mayor or his deputy [*lentvoit*]. We likewise decree for all time to come that the above-mentioned town should deliver 400 *kopy* of *groshi* [1 kopa equalled 60 groshi] to our treasury each year, on Saint Michael's Day, without any excuses. By this charter of ours we likewise remove and exempt eternally all the people of this town from the courts and authority of all the voevody, lords, starosty, judges, assistant judges, and other vicegerents . . . so that they shall not be obliged to answer to them in any matters for which they may be summoned. But if the mayor or the burgomasters should appear unjust, then they shall be called before us and shall be answerable for this; and we shall judge them in accordance with the same [Magdeburg] law.

V:26. THE CHARTER CONFIRMING MAGDEBURG LAW FOR KIEV, MARCH 29, 1514

This charter, granted by Sigismund (1506-48) in confirmation of the grant of the Magdeburg system to Kiev, illustrates among other things the special defensive obligation that rested upon that border region.

Reference: Arkheograficheskaia Komissiia, ed., *Akty otnosiashchiesia k istorii iuzhnoi i zapadnoi Rossii,* 15 vols. (St. Petersburg, 1863-92), 2:126-28.

The mayor [voit] and townspeople of the town of Kiev have petitioned us and informed us that our brother, His Grace the king and grand duke Alexander of glorious memory, for the enhancement of the town of Kiev, had granted to them in his benevolence the German or Magdeburg law, to townspeople of Roman, Greek, and Armenian faith alike, so that in the future as well the townspeople would be governed in accordance with all the articles of that law. . . .

Therefore, taking into consideration their services and the losses they suffer from our enemies in the borderland [the Tatars], and desiring that this town of ours should increase in population and prosperity, out of particular benevolence we have done as they petitioned, that is, we have granted for all time to come the German law, called the Magdeburg [law], to our town of Kiev and to all [its] townspeople, present and future, of Roman, Greek, and Armenian faith; they shall observe this law in its entirety and govern themselves by it, just as our town of Vil'no possesses and is subject to that Magdeburg law; and we exempt them [the people of Kiev] from Polish, Lithuanian, and Russian laws and from all other customs that contravene that German Magdeburg law; and we likewise exempt all our townspeople from any authority, force, or coercion . . . on the part of voevody and judges and the entire body of our officials, so that . . . in matters great and small alike . . . the townspeople of the town of Kiev shall be answerable to their mayor, whoever he may be, and the mayor shall not be answerable to anyone but ourselves, and only in accordance with that same German law, and then only if he is summoned before us by our message. In criminal cases and in all other above-mentioned matters the mayor of that town of ours shall likewise have full authority to judge and sentence [men], to punish and behead and impale and drown [them], as contained and indicated in that German Magdeburg law in all its articles. . . .

. . . The weighing tax [*vazhnoe*] shall be paid to us as of old; likewise the silver tax [*serebshchizna* or *serebshchina*, collected

from all peasants and townspeople] shall be paid to us as it is in our other towns. [The people of Kiev] shall likewise keep guard in the field against the Tatars at all times, in accordance with ancient custom, in the same places where they kept guard before; and likewise whenever the need should arise, however many times a year, to set forth with us or with our subjects in pursuit of the Tatars, they shall all set forth mounted and armed and shall [furnish men] in accordance with their wealth, as they are obliged to do in case of war, without any delay or disobedience, as soon as we or our officials issue orders. They shall likewise keep guard and call the watch around our castle in Kiev, in accordance with ancient custom. In addition, they shall hold two fairs each year for the support of our town. . . .

And they shall observe this Magdeburg law in every respect and be governed by it, just as our town of Vil'no observes it and is governed by it; and by this charter of ours we confirm eternally and inviolably for all time to come, and for future townspeople of Kiev, all those above-mentioned rights and exemptions which we have granted to them [and] to our town.

CHAPTER VI

Muscovy
in the
Fifteenth Century

A. POLITICAL DEVELOPMENTS UNDER VASILII I AND II, AND IVAN III

*VI:1. MOSCOW AND THE TATARS: THE NIKONIAN CHRONICLE'S RECORD OF EDIGEI'S LETTER
TO VASILII I, 1409*

The fifteenth century witnessed substantial changes in Moscow's relations with the Tatars, as illustrated by this document and those immediately following. In 1408 Moscow withstood a siege led by Edigei, the power behind the throne in the Golden Horde, and even gave asylum to the sons of Tokhtamysh, who were claimants to the throne of the Horde in opposition to Edigei and his puppet khan. This is a statement of Edigei's grievances. (Concerning the Nikonian Chronicle, see Chapter III.)
Reference: *PSRL*, 11:209-10.

[A.D. 1409:] The prince of the [Golden] Horde, Edigei, sent [a letter] to Grand Prince Vasilii Dmitrievich, saying thus: "We have heard that the children of Tokhtamysh are with you, and for this reason we have come in war; and we have also heard that you act wrongfully in the towns: the tsar's [khan's] envoys and merchants come from the Horde to you, and you ridicule the envoys and merchants, and moreover they are subjected to great injury and persecution from you. This is not good; for in the past this was the tsar's [khan's] domain [*ulus*] and he held power; you respected the ancient customs and the tsar's envoys, and merchants were treated without persecution and without injury; and you should ask the old men how this was done in the past. Now you do not do this; but is this [change] good? Temir-Kutlui became tsar, and you became sovereign of your domain, and since that time you have not visited the tsar in the Horde; you have not seen the tsar with your own eyes, nor have you dispatched any princes, or elder boyars, or younger [boyars], or anyone else, nor have you sent a son or a brother with any message. Then Shadibek ruled for eight years, and you did not visit him either, or send anyone with any message. And the reign of Shadibek likewise came to an end, and now Tsar Bulat-Saltan [Pulad] has become tsar, and this is already the third year of his rule, and you have likewise failed to visit him yourself, or to send a son, or brother, or elder boyar. You are the eldest, the grand prince, over such a great domain, but all your deeds are evil and wrongful. . . . It would be well for you . . . to observe the ancient customs, and then you will live safely and rule in your domain. Whenever you suffer any harm either from Russian princes or from Lithuania, each year you send complaints to us against them and ask us for charters of protection from them, and you give us no respite on this account; and you say that your domain is destitute and that there is no means of paying tribute. Heretofore we have never seen your domain with our own eyes, but only heard reports of it; but as for your messages and letters which you have sent to us in the Horde, you have lied to us everywhere; and as for the [tribute of] one ruble per two *sokhi* ["plows"—taxation units] which you have collected from each region of your realm, where is that silver? It would be well for you to acknowledge this, [to give over] what was given over honestly in the past, lest evil befall your domain, and Christians meet their final doom, and our anger and war be upon you."

*VI:2. MOSCOW AND THE TATARS: THE VOSKRESENSK CHRONICLE ON EVENTS OF 1431,
1445-1446, AND 1451*

These excerpts suggest a few of the problems faced by the next prince of Moscow.
Reference: *PSRL*, 8:95-96, 113-14, 123-24.

[A.D. 1431:] Grand Prince Vasilii [II, Vasilievich] and his uncle Prince Iurii Dmitrievich, vying with each other for the title of grand prince, decided to go to the Horde to Tsar Makhmet. . . . The tsar ordered his princes to judge the Russian princes, and there was much dispute between them—the grand prince seeking his throne on the basis of inheritance from

113

his father [Vasilii I] and grandfather [Dmitrii Donskoi], Prince Iurii on the basis of the chronicles and ancient registers [*spiski*] and the testament of his father, Grand Prince Dmitrii [Donskoi]. And then a boyar of [the late] Grand Prince Vasilii [I] Dmitrievich spoke to the tsar [Makhmet] and to his princes, saying thus: "Free and sovereign Tsar! Permit me, a slave of the grand prince, to utter a word. Our sovereign, Grand Prince Vasilii, seeks the throne of the grand prince, in your realm [ulus], in accordance with your regal grant [*zhalovanie*] and your *devter* and *iarlyk* [two kinds of charters giving privileges], and your grant is here before you; while our master, Prince Iurii Dmitrievich, seeks to become grand prince in accordance with the testament of his father, and not by your grant, the grant of a free tsar; you are free in your realm and you may grant your favor to anyone you wish; but our sovereign, Grand Prince Vasilii Dmitrievich, passed the title of grand prince to his son, Grand Prince Vasilii [II], in accordance with your grant, the grant of a free tsar; he has now been sitting on his throne for many years, ruling by your grant, and fulfilling his obligations to you, his sovereign, the free tsar; and this is known to you." And then the tsar [Makhmet] gave the title of grand prince to Prince Vasilii Vasilievich and ordered Prince Iurii to lead the horse that [Prince Vasilii] rode; but the grand prince did not wish to dishonor his uncle thus.

. . .

[A.D. 1445:] The Tatars returned and again attacked the Christians and triumphed over them. They seized the grand prince [Vasilii II] himself, and likewise Prince Mikhail Andreevich and many other princes, boyars, deti boiarskie [lesser nobles], and other warriors. . . . And since the city [Mos-

cow] had been burned, Grand Princess Sofiia and Grand Princess Mariia went to the city of Rostov with their children and boyars, and the townspeople were in great anguish and alarm: those who were able to flee wanted to abandon the city and flee, while the common people assembled and began to fix the city gates first, and began to seize those who wanted to flee the city first, and beat and shackled them; thus the turmoil was put down, and they all began to fortify the city together and to get their own household equipment ready.
. . .

[A.D. 1446:] Tsar [Khan] Makhmet and his son Mamutek released the grand prince, arranging with him, by an oath upon the cross, that he would give [the khan] as great a ransom as he could. . . . The tsar [khan] was gracious and dismissed him to his patrimony, to rule as grand prince.

. . .

[A.D. 1451:] The grand prince [Vasilii II] . . . himself left the city of Moscow with his son Grand Prince Ivan [the future Ivan III], and sent off his grand princess with the younger children to Uglich. . . . And the Tatars . . . set out for Moscow . . . and set fire to all the posady [suburbs] in a single hour, and meanwhile began to approach the city from all sides. . . . So the townspeople were in great grief and sorrow and in much bewilderment. . . . Coming out of the city, they began to fight with their enemies; when it was twilight the Tatars retreated from the city, and the townspeople began to prepare the city's equipment for the morrow against the godless ones: cannon, guns, arbalests, weapons, shields bows and arrows, as are needed for battle with enemies. But when at sunrise the townspeople were readying themselves against the enemies, they could not see anyone.

VI:3. TREATIES OF IVAN III CONCERNING THE TATAR KHANATE OF KASIMOV, 1473 AND 1483

A significant step in Muscovy's relations with the Tatars was Vasilii II's establishment in 1452-53 of a new Tatar khanate under his tutelage. This "tsardom," as the Russians called it, was headed by Khan (or Tsarevich) Kasim; its capital, Gorodets—on the Oka not far from Riazan'—was renamed Kasimov after his death. The following excerpts from treaties of Ivan III in 1473 and 1483 help explain how he protected his satellite.
    Reference: *Dukhovnye i dogovornye gramoty velikikh i udel'nykh kniazei XIV-XVI vv.* (Moscow: AN SSSR, 1950), pp. 226, 284.

[From the Treaty of Ivan III with Prince Boris of Volotsk, February 13, 1473:]

You shall protect, together with us, Tsarevich Dan'iar [i.e. the son and successor of Kasim], or whoever else may be tsarevich there after him. And, brother, if I, the grand prince, and my son the grand prince, should receive from anywhere another tsarevich [like Khan Kasim] into our land, you shall protect him too, together with us, for our sake, and for Christianity's sake.

[From the Treaty of Ivan III with Prince Ivan of Riazan', June 9, 1483:]
Do not conclude any treaty with Tsarevich Dan'iar, or whoever else may be tsarevich there, or carry on negotiations harmful to us. You must live with them in accordance with our treaty. And what went from your land to Tsarevich Kasim and his son Tsarevich Dan'iar in the reign of your grandfather, Grand Prince [of Riazan'] Ivan Fedorovich, and in the reign of your father, Grand Prince [of Riazan'] Vasilii Ivanovich, and what went to the tsarevich's princes, and their treasurers and sealers [*dorogi*]—this you must give from your land to Tsarevich Dan'iar, or whoever else may be tsarevich there, and to their princes, and to the princes' treasurers and sealers, in accordance with those lists, as my father, Grand Prince Vasilii [II] Vasilievich, concluded a treaty for your father, Grand Prince [of Riazan'] Vasilii Ivanovich, with the tsareviches, the princes of Kasimov, with Kobak the son of Aidar, and with Isak the son of Akhmat. And you, Grand Prince Ivan, your boyars, and your men shall not receive tribute-paying men from the tsarevich, from Dan'iar or whoever else may be tsarevich there.

VI:4. THE VOSKRESENSK CHRONICLE ON THE INVASION OF KHAN AHMED IN 1480

Muscovy traditionally has been said to have "thrown off the Tatar yoke" in 1480, when the Tatar army under Ahmed, after threatening Moscow, retreated without a full-scale battle. Meanwhile, the Voskresensk Chronicle tells us in the following passage, Ivan III did not emerge unreproached.

Reference: *PSRL*, 8:206-08, 211. A partly overlapping excerpt has recently been translated in Basil Dmytryshyn, ed., *Medieval Russia: A Source Book, 900-1700* (N.Y.: Holt, Rinehart, and Winston, 1967), pp. 159-61. The text of Archbishop Vasian's letter has recently been republished in Russian with English annotations and a glossary in John Fennell and Dimitri Obolensky, eds., *A Historical Russian Reader: A Selection of Texts from the XIth to the XVIth Centuries* (Oxford: At the Clarendon Press, 1969), pp. 99-107, 191-94.

Akhmat [Ahmed] came to the Ugra [River] with all his forces, wanting to cross the river. And the Tatars came and began to shoot our men, while ours [began to shoot] at theirs ... and [our men] beat [the Tatars] back from the shore. For many days [the Tatars] advanced, fighting, but were not able [to cross the river]. And they stood waiting for the river to freeze over, for there were great frosts at that time, and the river had already begun to freeze over. There was fear on both sides, each being afraid of the other. . . . When our forces pulled back from the bank, then the Tatars, possessed by fear, fled, thinking that the Russians had ceded them the bank in order to fight them; while our people thought the Tatars had crossed the river and were pursuing them, and [so] they [the Russians] came to Kremenets. Then the grand prince with his son and brothers and all his voevody went to Borovsk, saying, "We will join battle with [the Tatars] on those fields." And [Ivan III] listened to evil people— misers, rich and pot-bellied men, Christian traitors, heathen-lovers—who were saying: "Run away! You cannot do battle against [the Tatars]!" The Devil himself was speaking through their mouths. . . .

[The chronicler continues:] O brave, courageous sons of Rus'! Take care to protect your fatherland, the Russian land, from the vile pagans; do not spare your heads, so that your eyes may not see the capture and plundering of your homes, the murdering of your children, and the violation of your wives and daughters.

That same autumn Archbishop Vasian of Rostov sent a letter to the Ugra to Grand Prince Ivan [III] Vasilievich of all Russia, that he should stand up firmly for Christianity against the infidels, and in this letter he wrote: "To the gracious, Christ-loving, noble, God-crowned, God-confirmed, glorious lord, Grand Prince Ivan Vasilievich of all Russia, whose piety shines to the ends of the universe. . . . It is our duty, great lord, to remind you [of your duty], and yours to listen. . . .

"Take courage and fortify yourself, my spiritual son! As a good warrior of Christ, according to the word of the Lord's Gospel, you are a good shepherd, and a good shepherd lays down his life for his sheep; while the hireling who is herding sheep that are not his own, seeing the approaching wolf, abandons his sheep and runs, and the wolf plunders them and drives them away. . . . But you, O my lord and spiritual son, not like a hireling, but rather like a true shepherd, must try to save the flock of Christ's sheep, which has been entrusted to you by God, from the wolf that is now approaching. . . . And what prophet or apostle or bishop taught you to obey this godless and evil one who calls himself a tsar, while you are the great Christian tsar of the Russian lands?"

VI:5. THE VOSKRESENSK CHRONICLE ON THE ANNEXATION OF TVER' IN 1485

The chronicler gives this description of an important step in the unification of central Russia under Ivan III.
Reference: *PSRL*, 8:216.

In the year 6994 [1485], on the eighth day of September, Grand Prince Ivan Vasilievich, with his son Grand Prince Ivan and all his brothers, and his voevody and all his forces, came up to the town of Tver' and surrounded it. The same month, on the tenth day, a Saturday, they set fire to the suburbs outside the town of Tver', and on the eleventh day, a Sunday, the princes and boyars of Tver' came out from the town of Tver' to the Grand Prince and petitioned him to take them into his service. And the same day, after dark, Grand Prince Mikhailo Borisovich [of Tver'], seeing that he was powerless, fled from the town into Lithuania. On the twelfth day, a Monday, there came to Grand Prince Ivan Vasilievich the bishop of Tver', Vasian, and Prince Mikhailo Kholmskoi with his brothers and his son, and other princes and boyars and all the local commoners [*zemskie liudi*], and they opened the town. And the grand prince sent his boyars Iurii Shestak and Konstantin Malechkin and his clerks into the town . . . and ordered them to make all the townspeople kiss the cross [take the oath of allegiance] to him, and to protect them [the townspeople] from any pillaging by his own troops.

VI:6. THE CHARTER OF BELOOZERO, 1488

The following charter was issued for the city and region of Beloozero or White Lake, almost three hundred miles north of Moscow, two years after the Beloozero principality had become a province of Muscovy. The only existing manuscript of this charter was given to P. M. Stroev's expedition in 1829 by a resident of Vologda. This excerpt suggests only part of the wealth of political, economic, and social data that can be gained from intensive study of such documents.
Reference: *PRP*, 3:170-74, as translated by Horace W. Dewey in "The White Lake Charter: A Mediaeval Russian Administrative Statute," *Speculum*, 32 (1957): 79-83 (with slight alterations by the editors of the present volume). See also Horace W. Dewey, comp., trans., and ed., *Muscovite Judicial Texts, 1488-1556*, Michigan Slavic Materials no. 7 (Ann Arbor: Department of Slavic Languages and Literature, University of Michigan, 1966), pp. 1-6.

I, Grand Prince Ivan Vasilievich of all Russia [Rus'], have granted to my subjects in Beloozero, townspeople and residents of the rural stany and volosti, all of Beloozero, that no matter which of our vicegerents [namestniki, i.e. "lieutenants" or governors] shall administer them, they shall proceed in accordance with this charter.

1. Whatever initial subsistence payments [*v"ezzhii korm*] shall be brought to our vicegerents when they first come [to administer], that [and only that] shall they take.

2. At Christmas our vicegerents shall be given subsistence payments from all tax units [sokhi] on princely lands, boyar lands, monasterial lands, black lands [i.e. state lands], and lands of charter grantees, and from all without exception. From [each] tax unit [the following shall be given]: in place of a half-carcass of meat, two *altyny*; in place of ten loaves of bread, ten dengi; in place of a barrel of oats, ten dengi; instead of a cartload of hay two altyny; and on Saint Peter's Day [June 29] our vicegerents shall be given subsistence payments

from all the same tax units, per tax unit [as follows]: in place of a ram, eight dengi; in place of ten loaves, ten dengi. And deputies [tiuny] [shall be given] subsistence payments at Christmas and on Saint Peter's Day [amounting to] half of that given the vicegerents. And court agents [dovodchiki] [shall be given] an assessment from all the tax units, per tax unit [as follows]: at Christmas, in place of a round loaf [kovriga], one denga; in place of a portion of meat, one denga; in place of a measure [zobnia] of oats two dengi; and on Saint Peter's Day they [shall be given] from all the [above-mentioned] tax units, in place of a round loaf, one denga; [and] in place of a cheese, one denga.

3. And our vicegerents shall maintain two deputies and ten court agents in the city and in the rural districts: in the rural districts eight court agents and two [court agents] in the city; and [the vicegerents shall] distribute the rural districts and villages among their court agents.

4. And the court agent shall ride in the rural district without an assistant and without extra horses, and he shall take no assessment in the rural district, [but shall] have his assessments from the hundredman [sotskii], in the city; and a court agent shall not ride from his district into another [in which he has no official duties to perform]; and where a court agent spends the night, there he is not to take his meal; and where he takes a meal, there he is not to spend the night. . . .

7. And vicegerents in the city of Beloozero shall have [the following] fees: goods duty from merchants who come from Moscow land, from Tver' and Novgorod lands, or from anywhere else by large vessel [amounting to] one grivna from the chief of the vessel [vataman], and one denga apiece from each person on the ship, regardless of how many there are; and whoever comes by small rowing vessels to Beloozero from Moscow or Novgorod lands, from the chief of the vessel and persons [on board], no matter how many there may be on the vessel, [there shall be taken] one denga apiece. And vicegerents shall maintain their own duty collectors at Slovenskii portage, and take goods duty in the same manner. . . .

9. And if a trial is held before the vicegerents or before [their] deputies over [a matter involving] one ruble, and [the litigants] desire to become reconciled, they shall give

one grivna to the vicegerents, with [their] deputies and court agents, as the entire fee. And if the vicegerents and deputies decree a judicial duel [to be fought] over [a matter involving] one ruble, and [the litigants] desire to become reconciled, they shall give a grivna to the vicegerents with [their] deputies and court agents, as the entire fee; and if it involves more or less than a ruble, the vicegerents shall take from them in the same proportion; and if they fight it out on the dueling field, the vicegerents shall order the amount in litigation to be taken from the loser, and for themselves shall order a *protiven* fee computed according to the litigated sum; and this [is to be paid] them with their deputies and agents as their entire fee.

10. And if evidence be brought against anyone of theft, or robbery or murder, the vicegerents shall order the damages taken from the guilty one, and that robber or murderer [shall be delivered] to the vicegerents for fine and punishment. . . .

14. And if a murder occurs in their city but the murderer is not found, the burghers shall pay a *vina* fine of four rubles; and if a murder occurs in any stan or any volost' and the murderer is not apprehended, then [the inhabitants] of the stan or volost' in which the murder took place shall pay a four-ruble vina fine. And if the murderer is apprehended and turned over to the vicegerents or their deputies, the peasants shall pay no *prodazha* fine. And if someone in their territory should be injured or killed by a tree in the forest, or be killed [falling] from a tree, or be devoured by a wild beast, or drowned in the water or be run over by a cart, or should commit suicide, and should be found accidentally, then in such matters there shall be no vina or prodazha fines. . . .

18. And if a person ploughs over or cuts down anyone's boundary strip, our vicegerents and [their] deputies shall take from the guilty person eight dengi in place of a ram.

19. And our vicegerents and their deputies shall not administer justice without hundredmen [sotskie] and without worthy citizens [dobrye liudi].

20. And deputies and servants of vicegerents shall not go uninvited to communal banquets and feasts; if anyone comes [thus] uninvited to a banquet or feast, they may send him away

with impunity. And if any one of them takes to drinking by force [i.e. forces his way into the banquet hall] and any loss occurs [thereby], he shall pay [for it] without trial, and [the offender] shall be punished by me, the grand prince. . . .

23. And whatever Beloozero townspeople, or inhabitants of a stan or volost' suffer offense from vicegerents [namestniki] or volost' chiefs [volosteli] or their deputies or agents, [the plaintiffs] shall themselves set a time of court appearance for the vicegerents and volost' chiefs and their agents.

And if anyone, in contravention of this, my charter, takes anything from them [unlawfully] or gives them offense in any way, that person shall be punished by me, the grand prince.

And [this] charter was issued in March 1488.

VI:7. THE SUDEBNIK OF 1497

One of the landmarks in Russian legal history is the law code or Sudebnik prepared under Ivan III, which sheds much light on the political and social conditions of the emerging Muscovite state. The sole manuscript of this code that has been discovered was found in 1817 by P. M. Stroev. The numbering of the articles was introduced later in the nineteenth century by the historian M. F. Vladimirskii-Budanov.

Reference: *PRP*, 3:346-57; English translation by Horace W. Dewey (slightly revised), as given in his doctoral dissertation, *The Sudebnik of 1497* (Ann Arbor: University Microfilms, 1955), 353 pp. and in Dewey, *Muscovite Judicial Texts*, pp. 7-21.

In the year 1497, in the month of September, Grand Prince of All Russia [Rus'] Ivan Vasilievich, with his children and boyars, issued a code of law on how boyars and okolnichie [in later Russian, okol'nichie] are to administer justice.

1. Boyars and okolnichie [together forming the Supreme Court] are to administer justice. And secretaries [d'iaki] shall be present at the court of boyars and okolnichie. And the boyars, okolnichie, and secretaries are not to receive bribes for judging or participation in deciding a case. Likewise no judge is to receive a bribe for judging. And no judge is to use the court for purposes of personal revenge or personal favors.

2. [The Boyar Court:] And if a plaintiff comes to a boyar [a member of the court], the boyar is not to dismiss the plaintiffs [sic], but shall give hearing in all matters to all plaintiffs for whom it is proper. [The Special Judge Court:] But whenever there is a plaintiff whom it is not proper for that boyar to hear, he shall inform the grand prince or send the plaintiff to [the special judge] to whom the administration of such people has been entrusted.

3. And the boyar and the secretary are to receive from the guilty party, whether plaintiff or defendant, out of a ruble case: the boyar, two altyny; the secretary, eight dengi. And if the case involves more than a ruble or less, the boyar shall be paid in the same proportion. . . .

8. Concerning theft: and if evidence is brought against a person of theft [tat'ba], or brigandage, or murder, or false accusation, or any other such evil deed, and [he] is a notorious criminal, then the boyar is to order him executed and the plaintiff's damages paid from his property, and whatever remains of this property shall be taken by the boyar and the secretary for themselves. . . .

9. And an insurgent [or "murderer of his master"] or a conspirator against the sovereign, a church thief, or murderer, or *podymshchik* [apparently a person who steals things left at the site of a fire, from *dym*—"smoke"], or arsonist, such a notorious evildoer shall not be allowed to live, but shall be put to death.

10. Concerning thieves: And if a thief [tat'] be caught for the first time with any stolen goods whatsoever, except [in the case of] church robbery and theft accompanied by murder, and there has been no previous accusation of other theft made against him, then he shall be punished in the marketplace, flogged with the knout and made to pay plaintiff's damages, and the judge shall impose a fine upon him. And if the thief has no property with which to pay damages, then, after flogging him with the knout, they shall give him over to the plaintiff [in slavery] to make good the plaintiff's loss [at the latter's discretion], and the judge shall receive nothing from him.

11. And if a thief is caught for the second

time with stolen goods, then he shall be executed and damages paid from his property, the remainder of his property going to the judge. . . .

38. And those boyars and deti boiarskie ["boyar sons" or petty nobles] to whom are granted offices with full jurisdiction shall administer justice, and at their court must be [present]: a steward [*dvorskii*], and elder [*starosta*] and outstanding citizens [*luchshie liudi*]. And without a steward and elder and outstanding citizens, the vicegerents [or lieutenants—namestniki] and volost' chiefs [volosteli] shall not hold court; and they are to receive no bribes for administering justice, nor shall their agents or assistants take bribes for their role in judging, either for their lord or for their deputy, and the fee collectors shall also not ask for bribes. . . .

43. Vicegerents and volost' chiefs who hold limited jurisdictional grants, and agents of the grand prince and of the boyars who hold full jurisdictional grants, shall not surrender [to the claimant] a male or female slave without report [to the grand prince or higher boyar] and shall not issue a release document; and shall not without report [to the higher authorities] release a thief or murderer, or fine, punish or release any other wrongdoer. . . .

54. And if a hired worker [*naimit*] does not serve out his period and goes away, he shall be deprived of his wages. . . .

56. And if a slave [*kholop*] is captured by Tatar enemy troops and escapes from captivity, he shall be free and no longer the slave of his former master.

57. Concerning leaving-time on the part of peasants: And peasants may leave a volost' [to go to another volost'] or go from village to village, once a year, during the week before and the week after the autumn Saint George's Day [November 26]. [Such] a peasant [having used a house and yard supplied by a landlord] shall [upon departure] pay one ruble for having used a house in the field area and half a ruble for one in the forest area. And if the peasant uses such a house for one year he shall upon leaving

pay one-fourth of the *pozhiloe* [departure payment]; if he stays two years he shall upon leaving pay one-half; if he stays three years he shall pay three-fourths; and if he stays four years he shall upon leaving pay the full amount of the pozhiloe. . . .

59. And a priest, a deacon, a monk [chernets], a nun [chernitsa], a watchman, and a widow, who are sustained by God's church, are to be judged by a bishop or his judge. And if a lay person [is in litigation] with a church person, then a mixed court shall decide the case. . . .

62. Concerning boundaries: And whoever ploughs up a boundary strip or cuts down markers, be he from the lands of the grand prince [and trespass on those of] a boyar or a monastery, or from boyar and monastery holdings [and trespass] on the lands of the grand prince, or from boyar and monastery lands [and trespass] on [lands of another] boyar, or from boyar lands [and trespass] on monastery land, whosoever has ploughed up a boundary strip or cut down markers shall be flogged with the knout, and the plaintiff shall take a ruble fine from him. And if peasants among themselves in a volost' or village plough across or mow beyond a boundary strip, then the volost' chief or the manager of the princely estate shall take from the guilty ones two altyny—the equivalent of a ram—and for bodily injury they shall fine according to the person, the injury, and the circumstances. . . .

66. Concerning full-slave documents: [One becomes] a slave by a full-slave document [i.e. one by which a person sells himself into slavery]. [One also becomes] a slave by accepting a position of [princely or boyar] agent or steward . . . both with one's wife and with one's children, provided they live under the same lord; and those children who have begun living under another lord, or by themselves, are not slaves, and by accepting a position of a city steward [one does not become] a slave. Whoever marries a female slave becomes himself a slave; a woman marrying a slave becomes herself a slave. Slaves may be passed on by donation or dowry and by will.

VI:8. A KORMLENIE *CHARTER OF IVAN III, 1462-1505*

The way in which local administrators were commonly paid in the fifteenth century (as well as a good deal later) is illustrated in this charter by which Ivan III allocated a kormlenie or "feeding." The right to administer justice, it should be understood, carried with it the right to collect fees for that service.

Reference: *PRP*, 3:156.

I, Grand Prince Ivan Vasil'evich of all Russia, have granted to Ivan son of Andrei Plemianni- kov [the villages of] Pushka and Osintsovo as a kormlenie with the right to administer justice [*pravda*] and to collect taxes on the purchase, sale, and branding of horses [*piatno*]. And you, all the people of this volost', honor him and obey him, and he will govern you and judge you and will conduct your affairs in every way as they were conducted heretofore.

[And on the back of the original is the signature: Grand Prince Ivan Vasil'evich. The original has a pendant seal in red wax.]

VI:9. THE LAST TESTAMENT OF IVAN III, 1504

The last will and testament of Ivan III reveals, among other things, how far the Muscovite grand principality had moved away from the ancient custom of providing sizable principalities for each son and toward the concentration of authority in the eldest.

Reference: *PRP*, 3:291-306. Also contained in Cherepnin and Valk, *Dukhovnye i dogovornye gramoty*, pp. 353-64. An annotated translation of the complete text has recently been published in Howes, *Testaments of the Grand Princes of Moscow*, pp. 268-98 (Russian text, pp. 143-54).

In the name of the holy and life-giving Trinity, the Father, the Son, and the Holy Ghost, and with the blessing of our father Simon, metro- politan of all Russia, I, the most sinful and un- worthy slave of God, Ivan, alive and in my right mind, am writing this testament. I give these directions to my sons—my son Vasilii and my younger children, Iurii, Dmitrii, Semen, and Andrei.

I entrust my younger children, Iurii and his brothers, to my son Vasilii, their eldest brother. And you, my children—Iurii, Dmitrii, Semen, and Andrei—shall hold my son Vasilii, your eldest brother, in the place occupied by me, your father, and obey him in all things. And you, my son Vasilii, shall deal with your younger brothers—Iurii and his brothers—honorably and shall not wrong them.

I bless my oldest son Vasilii with my patrimony, the grand principalities, with which my father blessed me and which God gave me. And I give him the city of Moscow with its volosti . . . and with its villages, and with all its town houses, and with its suburbs . . . and with its markets, and with its shops, and with its merchants' rows [*gostinye dvory*], and with all the tolls.

· · ·

[The will then enumerates many other towns with their surrounding areas that are to be given to Vasilii.] And also to him I give the city of Volodimir [Vladimir] with its volosti. . . . And the boyars and petty nobles [deti boiarskie] of Iaroslavl', with their patri- monial and purchased estates, may none of them forsake my son Vasilii to enter [the service of] anyone else, anywhere. And the lands of him who departs shall fall to my son. But as for those who serve him, he shall not interfere in their lands, nor in those of their wives, nor those of their children.

· · ·

As for the service princes in the land of Moscow and the land of Tver', they shall serve my son Vasilii, and they shall hold their hered- itary estates as they did in my time. But who- ever of these service princes leaves my son Vasilii to go over to my younger children, or to anybody else, his estates will fall to my son Vasilii.

· · ·

And what I have given to my younger children, Iurii, Dmitrii, Semen, and Andrei— the towns, the volosti, and the villages—over these they shall have authority as is written in this my testament, and beyond this they shall not interfere in any possession of my son Vasilii.

My son Iurii and his brothers may not coin money in their appanages in the lands of Moscow and Tver'; the money shall be coined by my son Vasilii in Moscow and in Tver', as was done in my time.

· · ·

My son Vasilii shall not buy lands, nor hold [lands], nor hold mortgagors [zakladni- people in pledge to a private person or a church institution; the exact meaning is disputed by such authorities as V. I. Sergeevich and N.P.

Pavlov-Sil'vanskii] in the appanages of my children, his brothers. And my children shall not buy lands, nor hold [lands], nor hold mortgagors under my son Vasilii in Moscow, nor in his whole grand principality. As for my villages which I have given to my boyars, princes, and deti boiarskie, granting them charters for the permanent possession of those villages by them and their children, or charters that I may have sold to anyone, neither my son Vasilii nor my other children shall interfere in these lands.

And my children, Iurii and his brothers, shall each from his appanage give to his brother Vasilii his [appropriate] share of [each] thousand rubles [needed by Vasilii] to discharge the payments [vykhod] to the

hordes, to the Crimea, to Astrakhan', to Kazan', and to the tsarevich's town [probably Kasimov, concerning which see Item VI:3 above], and to other tsars and tsarevichi [Tatar khans of various ranks] who will be in my son Vasilii's land, and to all the Tatar envoys who will come to Moscow . . . and for all the Tatar payments, whatever their amount. . . .

And he who violates this, my testament, may God be his judge, and may my blessing not be upon him.

I was witnessed [in signing] this testament by my spiritual father, Archimandrite Mitrofan. . . . Also present were my boyars [four names given]. . . .

And this my testament was written by my clerk Danilko Mamyrev.

B. OTHER DEVELOPMENTS OF THE PERIOD 1389-1505

VI:10. GRANTS TO RELIGIOUS INSTITUTIONS, CA. 1399-CA. 1473

An important fifteenth-century theme, the growth in wealth and power of the Russian church, is illustrated in these grants. They show some of the typical practices of the time.

Reference: Nikolai Kalachev, ed., *Akty otnosiashchiesia do iuridicheskogo byta drevnei Rossii*, 3 vols. (St. Petersburg, 1857-84), vol. 1, col. 442 [grant of 1399]; *PRP*, 3:51 [grant to Trinity Monastery]; *Akty sotsial'no-ekonomicheskoi istorii severovostochnoi Rusi*, 3 vols. (Moscow: AN SSSR, 1952-64), 1:63 [grant of ca. 1430]; Lev V. Cherepnin, ed., *Akty feodal'nogo zemlevladeniia i khoziaistva XIV-XVI vekov*, pt. 1 (Moscow: AN SSSR, 1951), p. 92 [grant of ca. 1448]; *PRP*, 3:48 [grant of ca. 1447-55]; *Akty feodal'nogo zemlevladeniia*, pt. 1, pp. 28-29 [grant of ca. 1464-73].

[A grant (*dannaia*) of January 1399:]

On the [date omitted] day of January in the year 6907 [1399], by the grace of God, I, Sava Dmietrievich Siuzev, have given to the Monastery [*dom*] of the Holy Savior and the Holy Annunciation [near Nizhnii-Novgorod], to Archimandrite Malafei and his brethren, the abandoned land of my patrimony [*votchinnaia pustosh'*] in the village of Spaskoe on the Kuliulserma River in the Kurmyshskii uezd, with all the land wherever the plow and scythe have gone and with the wild beehives that are found on that wasteland between the Urga and Uronga and Mukhina rivers. And when God has called for my soul, let Archimandrite Malafei and his brethren pray [*pominat'*] for my soul and the souls of my parents, and hold a commemorative feast [*korm staviti*] on Saint Sava's Day, on December 5. To this grant-deed I, Sava, have affixed my seal. The grant-deed was witnessed by my spiritual father the archpriest [*protopop*] of the Church of the

Holy Archangel, Fedor Fomin. And the grant-deed was drawn up by my bondman [*chelovek*] Ignat Moseev.

[This deed was granted to the famous Trinity Monastery of Saint Sergius, sometime between 1392 and 1427:]

I, Ivan Svatko, being in debt for the sum of ten rubles to my lord Abbot Nikon, give [to the monastery] for these ten rubles my abandoned land [pustosh'] of Stolbtsevskaia and Mikitkinskaia and Ivakinskaia, with their forests and whatever else belongs to them. And when I die, may [the monks] remember my soul [in their prayers].

[A grant of ca. 1430:]

I Boris Konstantinovich, and Fedor Vel'iaminovich, by order of Ivan Mikhailovich and according to his last will and testament, have given to the Holy Trinity Monastery of Saint Sergius in the village [selo] of Medenskoe with the money, movable property [zhivot], hamlets [*derevnia*], and everything that belongs to that village, to commemorate his parents and himself.

Witnessed by . . .

[A grant of ca. 1448:]

By the grace of God and his most pure [*prechistaia*] mother, and through the intercession [*molitvoiu*] of the holy miracle worker Peter, metropolitan of all Russia, I, Ignatii Vasil'evich [Minin], have given to the Cathedral of the Holy Mother of God in Moscow and to the holy miracle worker Peter, metropolitan of all Russia, and to my lord Bishop Jonah, nominated to the most holy Russian metropolitan see, or whomsoever shall be metropolitan after him, my patrimonial estate, the village of Aksin'inskoe in the Zvenigorod uezd, with the Church of Saint Nicholas, and with the hamlets that formerly belonged to that village, wherever my plow has gone, wherever the scythe has gone, and wherever the ax has gone, and with the meadows and plowland, and forest, and everything that as of old belonged to it. And let my lord keep this village in possession of the Cathedral of the Most Pure Mother of God, and not sell it, or give it to anyone, or exchange it with anyone. And I have given this village to commemorate my parents and myself and all my family.

Witnessed by . . .

[A grant of ca. 1447-55:]

I, Denis, son of Sava Klimentiev, have

given to the Monastery of the Life-Giving Trinity my hamlet of Kabanovskaia with its abandoned lands [pustoshi] and forest, and the empty villages [*selishche*] of Skorikovo, Vasil'evskoe, Bytyitsevo, with everything that as of old belonged to that hamlet and to those abandoned lands, wherever the ax, and the scythe, and the plow have gone. And I have given this to the Trinity Monastery of Saint Sergius, to Abbot Martinian and his brethren, to commemorate the souls of my parents and my own soul.

Witnessed by . . .

The deed [*gramota*] was written by Oleshko Galka.

[A grant of ca. 1464-73:]

I, Agrafena [Cheliadnina] wife [widow] of Fedor Mikhailovich, having consulted with my children Petr and Andrei, have given to the House of the Most Holy Mother of God [i.e. the Cathedral of the Dormition] and to our lord [*gospodin*] Philip, metropolitan of all Russia, our hamlet of Borisovskaia [in the Rostov uezd], which lies between the Karash hamlets belonging to the metropolitanate, to commemorate the soul of our lord [gospodin] [i.e. Agrafena's husband and Petr's and Andrei's father] Fedor Mikhailovich and the souls of all our kin. And we have given this hamlet together with all that as of old belonged to it, wherever the plow and scythe and ax have gone.

And I, Agrafena, have stamped this with the seal of my husband Fedor Mikhailovich.

VI:11. AN IMMUNITY CHARTER TO A MONASTERY, CA. 1432-1445

Immunity charters are a very important kind of primary source for the Muscovite period. They afford much of the earliest direct evidence we have on many aspects of life, especially on the governmental process, with its many economic and other ramifications. Through careful study of the immunities granted to certain persons or institutions, we can make deductions concerning the obligations of the rest of the subject population, and by comparing the kinds of immunities granted at various dates, we can attempt to trace the growth of the authority and functions of the central government. A few illustrative charters are presented in this chapter. This charter is a sample of a grant of tax and judicial immunity [zhalovannaia tarkhannaia i nesudimaia gramota]. Zinovii was abbot of the Trinity Monastery of Saint Sergius.

Reference: *Akty sotsial'no-ekonomicheskoi istorii severovostochnoi Rusi*, 1:67. Translation by Horace William Dewey, slightly revised. Cf. Dewey, *Muscovite Judicial Texts*, pp. 25-26.

For the sake of the life-giving Trinity, I, Grand Prince Vasilii Vasil'evich, have bestowed my favor upon Abbot Zinovii and his brethren, or whoever shall be abbot after him: that in their village of Prisetskoe there are three churches—

Saint Savior [Jesus Christ, the Redeemer], Saint Ilia, and Saint Nikola; and whoever shall sing [i.e. perform a service of worship] in those churches, [be he] abbot, or priest, or deacon, they need pay no tribute or taxes to me. And my tithe collectors of Bezhitskii Verkh and their deputies shall take no subsistence payments from them, nor send out their bailiffs after them in any matter, nor take taxes from them; they need likewise pay no Christmas, Easter, or Saint Peter's Day taxes, nor make payments to the tithe collectors when they are on tour, nor pay any other fees whatever. And if any person has litigation with the abbot or with a priest or deacon of those churches, then I, the grand prince, or my deputy boyar, shall try them.

And if anyone disobey this, my charter, he shall be punished by me.

And there is no other charter of mine that is in conflict with this one.

[On reverse:] the grand prince

VI:12. TOWARD SERFDOM: AN ORDER CURTAILING PEASANT MOVEMENT IN BELOOZERO, CA. 1450

This order helps to elucidate the complex process that gradually limited peasant movement and led eventually to serfdom.

Reference: *AAE*, 1:36 (see List of Abbreviations). Also in *Akty sotsial'no-ekonomicheskoi istorii severo-vostochnoi Rusi*, II:81-82. A translation of this document is included in the recently published work of Robert E. F. Smith, *The Enserfment of the Russian Peasantry* (Cambridge: At the University Press, 1968), pp. 68-69.

From Prince Mikhail Andreevich [of Beloozero] to my vicegerent in Beloozero, and to all the boyars and deti boiarskie and to my stewards [overseers of villages, *posel'skie*], to all without exception. My [spiritual] father Abbot Kas'ian of the Monastery of Saint Cyril has petitioned me, relating that you are furnishing discharge [*otkazyvat'*, i.e. paying the peasant's debt and thus enabling him to leave his master's land] to monastery peasants: debtors [*serebreniki*], share tenants [*polovniki*, those who cultivate the master's land and give him half the harvest or income in return], contract [*riadovye*] peasants, and Iuriev peasants [those who signed a contract for a year and were free to leave on Saint George's Day]; and you are furnishing them discharge not on Saint George's Day [November 26], but some on Christmas and some on Saint Peter's Day [June 29]. You should not furnish discharge thus to the debtors, share tenants, and the free [i.e. the "contract" and "Iuriev"] peasants but should furnish discharge to the debtors and share tenants on Saint George's Day [only], and they must [first] pay the debt; while after Saint George's Day a debtor must not be furnished discharge, and, if he pays the debt, then he may obtain discharge. I have ordered the abbot not to allow debtors to leave after Saint George's Day. If anyone disobeys this, my charter, he shall be punished by me.

VI:13. A DECREE CONCERNING SAINT GEORGE'S DAY, CA. 1454-1455

This excerpt from a decree of Prince Mikhail Andreevich of Beloozero, concerning indebted peasants (serebreniki) of a monastery on his land, illustrates the growing significance of Saint George's Day (November 26, according to the Julian calendar).

Reference: *RIB*, 32:22. For another recent translation with commentary, see Smith, *Enserfment of the Russian Peasantry*, pp. 65-67.

And I have granted to Abbot Ekim and the monk Martem'ian and to all the brethren that you [a steward of the prince's estates] should not take in debtor peasants from the monastery [during the year] from [one] Saint George's Day to the next, but should take them in only on Saint George's Day in the autumn. And if any monastery peasants come to your *put'* [area of jurisdiction] on Saint George's Day, they must pay the money [which they owe the monastery] then. . . . I have ordered the abbot and his brethren not to allow debtors to leave his hamlets from [one] Saint George's Day to the next and have ordered them to allow debtors to leave [only] during the two weeks before Saint George's Day and the week following. And those who shall come to your put' owing the monastery money must finish the work required by the debt and leave a surety for the debt, and when autumn comes they should repay the debt.

VI:14. TOWARD SERFDOM: A GRANT RETURNING PEASANTS TO A MONASTERY, CA. 1460

Here Vasilii II is seen supporting another part of the process that eventually bound the peasants to the land. The Trinity Monastery of Saint Sergius had very extensive holdings.

Reference: *AAE*, 1:48. A recent translation with commentary is in Smith, *Enserfment of the Russian Peasantry*, pp. 63-64.

I, Grand Prince Vasilii Vasil'evich, have granted [the following] to Abbot Vas'ian of the Trinity Monastery of Saint Sergius and his brethren with respect to their villages in the Uglich uezd: As for those peasants who have left their [the monastery's] villages this year to go into villages belonging to me, the grand prince or to my grand princess and into villages belonging to boyars . . . I, the grand prince, have shown favor to Abbot Vas'ian and his brethren and have ordered these peasants to be brought back again; and as for the peasants who live in their [the monastery's] villages at the present time, I, the grand prince, order that these peasants not be allowed to go elsewhere; and if the monastery steward [posel'skii] should need to have a constable [pristav], he shall obtain one of my constables from the Uglich vicegerent to [return] those peasants who have left their villages.

VI:15. A DECREE CONCERNING SAINT GEORGE'S DAY, CA. 1463-1468

Reference: *PRP*, 3:94. Also in *Akty sotsial'no-ekonomicheskoi istorii severovostochnoi Rusi*, 1:245. A recent translation is included in Smith, *Enserfment of the Russian Peasantry*, pp. 69-70.

From Grand Prince Ivan Vasil'evich to my boyar and vicegerent in Iaroslavl', Prince Ivan Vasil'evich, and to the volost' chiefs [volosteli] in the volosti, and to your deputies [tiuny] and your *zakazniki* [agents in charge of peasant transfers]. The abbot of the Trinity Monastery of Saint Sergius with his brethren has petitioned me that you are furnishing discharges for peasants to leave their [monastery] village of Fedorovskoe in Nerekhta and [its] hamlets to go to my patrimony [otchina] in Iaroslavl' between [one] Saint George's Day [and the next]. And I, the grand prince, have favored them [the monastery] and ordered that they should not allow peasants to leave their village of Fedorovskoe and [its] hamlets except on Saint George's Day. If someone should nonetheless obtain a discharge other than on Saint George's Day, I have ordered them to bring him back again. You should not furnish their peasants with discharges from them between [one] Saint George's Day [and the next]. To those who want to obtain discharges from them to go to my patrimony in Iaroslavl', you should furnish discharges on Saint George's Day, during the two weeks, the one preceding Saint George's Day and the one following. And you should not furnish anyone a discharge from them between [one] Saint George's Day [and the next], in accordance with this, my charter.

VI:16. AN IMMUNITY CHARTER, SEPTEMBER 11, 1464

This immunity charter (zhalovannaia gramota, tarkhanno-nesudimaia i l'gotnaia) was issued by a prince to an abbot.

Reference: Cherepnin, *Akty feodal'nogo zemlevladeniia*, pt. 1, p. 86.

I, Prince Iurii Vasil'evich [son of Vasilii II, and prince of Dmitrov] . . . have bestowed my favor upon the monastery villages of the Novinsk metropolitanate Monastery of the Holy Mother of God, on the Prisna River, and upon Abbot Evfimei and his brethren, or whomsoever shall be abbot after him. As for their villages in my patrimony [otchina] in the Dmitrov uezd . . . with the hamlets and unused lands [pustoshi] of those villages, and the longtime peasants [starozhil'tsy] who live in those villages and hamlets: these longtime peasants shall not be required to pay taxes of any kind to me for five years . . . or to feed my horses, or to mow my hay, or be under the jurisdiction of my local administrative agents [dvorskii and desiatskii] for any communal obligations [protory and rozmety], or be subject to any other kinds of duties [poshliny]. And whatever peasants Abbot Evfimii with his brethren brings in from other principalities [kniazhenie] and not from my patrimony, these newcomers [*prishlye liudi*] shall not be required to pay taxes to me for ten years. . . . And my Ramenskii volost' chiefs and their deputies shall not enter these villages and hamlets and the unused lands of these villages and hamlets, to either the long-settled peasants or the newcomers; nor send in [their agents] for any reason; nor take their subsistence payments [*korm*]; nor try them for anything except murder, brigandage, and thievery with material evidence [*tat'ba s polichnym*]; nor shall the constables [*pravedshiki*] or bailiffs [*dovodchiki*] collect any requisitions from them. . . . And if there should be a mixed [*smestnoi*] trial between the monastery peasants and the volost' peasants, then my Ramenskii volost' chiefs and their deputies shall sit in judgment, and Abbot Evfimei, or whoever he designates, shall sit in judgment with them. . . . And if anyone should lodge a complaint against Abbot Evfimei or against his steward [*prikazchik*], I myself, Prince Iur'i Vasil'evich, or my commissioned boyar [*boiarin vvedenoi*] shall sit in judgment. And let him not take in my own registered and tax-paying peasants [*pismenykh . . . moikh liudei i danskikh*]. And if anyone violates this, my charter, and seizes anything from them or in any way injures them, he shall be punished by me.

This charter was issued in Moscow in the year 6973 [1464] in the month of September, on the eleventh day.

VI:17. AN IMMUNITY CHARTER, MARCH 1504

Ivan III issued this grant of immunities (*zhalovannaia gramota*) to the metropolitan. (For sources on the controversy of ca. 1500 provoked in part by the material possessions of the church, see Section B of Chapter VII.)

Reference: Cherepnin, *Akty feodal'nogo zemlevladeniia*, pt. 1, p. 199.

I, Grand Prince of All Russia Ivan [III] Vasil'evich, in behalf of my [spiritual] father Simon, metropolitan of all Russia, have bestowed my favor upon the abbots, priests, and monks in the Vladimir uezd who live in the monasteries and churches of the Most Pure Mother of God and in the metropolitanate monasteries . . . and [upon the peasants] in the hamlets belonging to the metropolitanate in the Vladimir uezd. . . . Our vicegerents in Vladimir and the volost' chiefs and their deputies shall not judge the abbots, priests, and monks of those monasteries, or the metropolitanate or monastery peasants of all those villages and hamlets, for any crimes other than murder and brigandage with material evidence. Our father Simon, metropolitan of all Russia, or whoever he designates, shall himself administer and try these, his own people. And if there should be a mixed trial between his people and those from the town, volost', or stan, then our vicegerents in Vladimir and the volost' chiefs and their deputies shall sit in judgment over his people, while the metropolitanate steward [*prikazchik*] of our father Simon sits in judgment with them, and the court fees shall be divided in half. If anyone should lodge a complaint against the metropolitanate steward, then I myself, the grand prince, or my commissioned boyar [*boiarin vvedenoi*] shall sit in judgment. I have likewise granted to the people of those villages and hamlets that no one should come uninvited to the peasants of those villages and hamlets that belong to [the metropolitan], to drink at their feasts and holiday banquets [*bratchina*], whether it be the deputies or bailiffs [*dovodchiki*] or other agents of our vicegerents in Vladimir or of our volost' chiefs, or any peasants belonging to me, the grand prince, or bondmen and peasants belonging to a boyar or a monastery, or anyone else, whoever he might be. And if anyone arrives at one of their feasts or holiday banquets uninvited, he shall be ousted, but not fined. If anyone should forcibly attempt to drink and cause them any damage, he must pay twice the amount of the damage without trial or judgment [i.e. without recourse to the prince's court]. And our princes, boyars, military commanders [*ratnye voevody*], and messengers of any kind shall not quarter in these monasteries and villages and hamlets, nor take subsistence payments, or carts, or guides from them.

VI:18. THE VOSKRESENSK CHRONICLE CONCERNING THE COUNCIL OF FLORENCE AND ITS AFTERMATH, 1437-1441

The growing wealth of the church was accompanied by important developments in the sphere of religious politics. At the Council of Ferrara-Florence, Moscow's representative was its metropolitan, Isidor, who had been named to his post from Constantinople and who was an ardent advocate of the union of the churches. The Voskresensk Chronicle's account of what happened, while questionable in some of its details, provides an indication of the official Muscovite reaction to Isidor's endeavors.

Reference: *PSRL*, 8:100-01, 104-05, 108-09.

[A.D. 1437:] Metropolitan Isidor came from Tsar'grad [Constantinople] to Moscow . . . and a short time after his arrival began boldly to press for journeying to [participate in] a council; he declared that an eighth council was assembling in the Roman land because of turmoil and schism between the Greek faith and the Roman. . . . He concealed an evil intention in his heart, wishing to seduce God's people from the true path of the holy faith and to unite with the Latins, deeming that he alone was wiser than all the rest. . . . And thus Isidor came into the Roman region, into a city called Ferrara, where in the forty-seventh year [1438] the Roman pope Eugene had assembled the false-minded Eighth Council, repudiated by God. . . . Tsar John [Emperor John VIII] of Constantinople, and with him the ecumenical patriarch Joseph, and with him the metropolitan of the tsar of Trebizond, were also present there . . . and the metropolitans of many other lands were there, twenty in number . . . and the archbishops and bishops of the Latin lands, and Greeks, and ordinary monks, and a great number of all.

· · ·

The tsar [Emperor John] and the patriarch expressed their intention of holding the council in the Latin city of Florence . . . and they did thus, taking much gold, and the tsar and the patriarch, and Isidor in agreement with them, went to their city of Florence to carry out their evil treachery. . . . Then they held a great council with the pope, and came to an agreement among themselves, and certified it firmly in a document. And the tsar signed it, and Metropolitan Isidor with him. . . . [In August 1439] they dispersed, covered with the darkness of faithlessness. Alas for this pernicious deceit! Alas for the joining of abomination to Greek Orthodoxy! For the gloom of darkness had replaced the living light, and the faith of piety was surrendered to the Latins; the Orthodox tsar and patriarch

fell into the deceit of the Latin heresies; caught in nets of gold they perished through the lies of Isidor; having taken gold they turned away from God and joined with the Latins.

· · ·

[A.D. 1440:] Isidor came to the Russian land, into the God-protected city of Moscow [in March 1441], to the pious and Orthodox grand prince Vasilii [II] Vasilievich, concealing within himself the deceit of the Latin heresy. . . . And he ordered that the Latin cross be carried before him. . . . Then during the commemorative prayers of the holy service he mentioned first and lauded, instead of the holy ecumenical patriarchs, the Roman pope Eugene, to whom he had delivered the holy faith of Greek Orthodoxy for gold. Upon the conclusion of the holy service Isidor ascended the pulpit and ordered that the edict of the false-minded and apostate council be read in a loud voice. In it were written the Latin deceits, hateful and foreign to God: separating the Holy Trinity, saying that the Holy Ghost proceeds from the Son as well as from the Father, and joining to this their sophistry concerning unleavened bread, saying that it is proper for the body of Christ to be transformed both as fermented and unfermented bread; and concerning the dead it was written thus: those who have met death with humility, in the true faith and in penitence to God, but have not succeeded in performing the penance for their sins which their confessors have pronounced, such men will be purified after death by the purification of sins. But they did all this among themselves through sophistry, in order to deceive the true Orthodox faith and, having deceived it, to sever Christianity from the law of God.

· · ·

The grand prince, after hearing these things, and when he had seen the edict with the enactments of their false-minded council, and heard from [Isidor's] lips the name of the pope mentioned first, recognized the heresy of that rapacious wolf Isidor, did not accept the blessing from his hand, and called him a heretical Latin deceiver; and, quickly accusing him, he covered him with shame and called him a wolf rather than a shepherd and teacher; and he soon ordered that he be removed from his throne as metropolitan, as a mad deceiver and apostate from the faith, and ordered him to go into a monastery. . . . Isidor . . . left stealthily at night, the doors being open, took to flight with his pupil the monk Grigorii, and thus fled to Rome, whence he had come and brought the evil Latin heresies. The God-knowing worker of piety, the Orthodox grand prince Vasilii Vasilievich, did not send anyone after him to bring him back, not wishing to detain him, as someone bereft of reason and hateful to God.

VI:19. VASILII II'S LETTER TO THE BYZANTINE EMPEROR, 1448

After Metropolitan Isidor had been ejected for succumbing to the Latin "heresy," his see remained empty for several years. When in 1448 the Russian church finally proceeded to choose its own metropolitan, Vasilii II reported the event to the Byzantine emperor Constantine Paleologus in this fashion.

Reference: Arkheograficheskaia Komissiia, ed., *Akty istoricheskie*, 5 vols. (Saint Petersburg, 1841–42), 1:85.

And by the will of God, by the grace of the Holy Ghost, and by those divine sacred rules, having assembled the prelates [*Sviatiteli* and *Vladyki*] of our land and acting by means of our fathers these Russian prelates we have appointed our aforementioned father, Iona, bishop of Riazan', to the most holy Russian metropolitanate, to be metropolitan of Kiev and all Russia. But we have done this from great necessity, and not from haughtiness or insolence; and we ourselves observe piety in everything, in accordance with the ancient Orthodoxy bequeathed to us . . . in which we shall remain to the end of our earthly life, and to the end of the ages. And our Russian church of the most holy Russian metropolitanate asks and seeks the blessing of God's holy ecumenical Orthodox apostolic church of God's wisdom, Sancta Sophia in Tsar'grad [Constantinople], and shall obey it in everything in accordance with ancient piety.

VI:20. THE VOSKRESENSK CHRONICLE CONCERNING THE INDEPENDENCE OF THE RUSSIAN CHURCH, 1461

The transition of the Russian church to autocephalous status at the time of the Turkish conquest of Constantinople is recorded as follows, in the Voskresensk Chronicle.

Reference: *PSRL*, 8:149.

[A.D. 1461:] That same spring Iona, metropolitan of Kiev and all Russia, departed this life. . . . Iona had been appointed metropolitan in Moscow by the archbishops and bishops, with the blessing of the patriarch of Tsar'grad; Iona had gone to Tsar'grad and received the patriarch's blessing; and from that time they began to install metropolitans in Moscow without going to Tsar'grad; for the Turkish tsar ruled in Tsar'grad, and killed the [Greek] tsar. . . .

VI:21. THE VOSKRESENSK CHRONICLE ON THE TREATMENT OF NOVGORODIAN HERETICS, 1492

The Voskresensk Chronicle tells of the so-called Judaisers of Novgorod in terms that may lead the reader to recall the religious controversies and persecutions in western Europe in the age of the Reformation. (For subsequent religious developments see Section B of the next chapter.)

Reference: *PSRL*, 8:220.

The same autumn [1492], on the seventeenth day of October, by the order of the pious and Christ-loving grand prince Ivan [III] Vasilievich, sovereign and autocrat of all Russia, in the metropolitan's court assembled the most holy lord Metropolitan Zosima of all Russia, Archbishop Tikhon of Rostov, Bishops Nifont of Suzdal', Semion of Riazan', Vassian of Tver', Prokhor of Sarai [an office which by this time was located in the Moscow suburb of Krutitsy], and Filofei of Perm', and the archimandrites, the abbots [*igumeni*], the priests [*sviash-chennitsi*], the elder monks [*startsy*], and the whole holy council of the Russian metropolitanate to deal with the corrupters of the Christian faith: the Novgorodian archpriest Gavril; the monk Zakharii; the priest Denis, of the Church of the Archangel; the priest Maxim, of Saint Ivan's Church; the priest Vasilii, of the Pokrov church; the deacon Makar, of the church of Saint Nicholas; the sexton Gridia, of the church of Saints Boris and Gleb; Vasiuk, the son-in-law of Denis; Samukha, the sexton of the church of Saint Nicholas; and others of the same mind, intent on corrupting the true and immaculate faith in Christ our God, glorified in the Trinity, and on destroying Christ's flock, Orthodox Christendom. Yet this they could not do; they themselves were defeated and their wisdom was swallowed up. Thus they did not venerate the human image of Jesus Christ our Lord, the Son of God, painted on the icons, nor the image of the blessed Virgin, nor the images of the saints, but in a reviling and abusive way they said: "These are made by the hand of man; they have mouths but do not talk, and so on; those who made them and who set their hope on them shall become like them." And the divine service they performed in an unseemly manner, having eaten and drunk, and the body of Christ they set at naught, [regarding it] as plain bread, and the blood of Christ as plain wine and water; they committed many other heresies which cannot be recorded in writing and are contrary to the teachings of the holy apostles and the holy fathers; they have seduced many simple folk with their heresies. And in the council, before the grand prince, the metropolitan, the bishops, and the whole holy council they denied their heresies. But the pious and Christ-loving grand prince Ivan Vasilievich of all Russia, true defender of the Orthodox faith, like a second pious Tsar Constantine, together with his father the most holy metropolitan Zosima, and with the bishops, and with all the holy council of the Russian metropolitanate, after investigating their vile heresies, decided, on the ground of the authentic record of Archbishop Gennadii [of Novgorod] and the testimony collected in Moscow, and according to the teaching of the holy apostles and the holy fathers, to excommunicate those heretics, the Novgorodian archpriest Gavril, and the monk Zakharii, with their companions and followers, from the holy ecumenical and apostolic church, to expel them from the clerical order, to call down malediction on them, to exile and incarcerate them, and to reaffirm the true and immaculate Orthodox faith.

CHAPTER VII

Muscovy in the
Sixteenth Century

A. POLITICAL DEVELOPMENTS

VII:1. THE VOSKRESENSK CHRONICLE ON THE ANNEXATION OF SMOLENSK, 1514

As a result of the war of 1512-14 between Vasilii III and Sigismund I of Poland and Lithuania, Vasilii pushed the boundaries of Muscovy westward into territories formerly within the Kievan federation but more recently part of Lithuania (see Chapter V). The authors of the Voskresensk Chronicle told it as follows. (Concerning Vasilii's annexation of Pskov in 1510, see Chapter IV, Section C.)
Reference: *PSRL*, 8:255-56.

And in the month of July the grand prince himself and his retinue came up to Smolensk with a large force and a mighty array of cannon and harquebuses; and having set up the big cannon and harquebuses near the city, he gave the order to bombard the city from all sides. . . . The citizens were stricken with great fear, and they began wailing and calling out to the great sovereign that he have pity, and restrain his sword, and order the battle stopped, and they would be willing to do homage to the sovereign and to surrender the city; and the grand prince forthwith gave the order to stop the battle. The archbishop [*vladyka*] of Smolensk, Varsonofei, and the princes, boyars, burghers [*meshchane*], and all the citizens went forth from the city to petition the great sovereign that he spare his patrimony inherited from his forefathers [*dedina*], and withdraw from them his disfavor and his wrath, and let them behold the light of his eyes, and order them into his service. And the great sovereign did spare his patrimony, and he withdrew his disfavor and his wrath from the archbishop of Smolensk, Varsonofei, and from the princes, boyars, burghers, and all the citizens, and he let them behold the light of his eyes, and he ordered them to serve him. And on the thirty-first day of July the princes and boyars of Smolensk opened the city and went forth to the tents to do homage to the great sovereign and to behold the light of his eyes; there they pledged themselves to him and took the oath to him on the cross; and the grand prince

showed them favor, and talked to them graciously, and asked them to eat with him.
. . .

. . . And the princes of Smolensk, and the boyars, and the burghers, and all the citizens hailed the grand prince; and they, and the boyars and voevody [military commanders] and men of the grand prince, began hailing and kissing one another, rejoicing with great love, like brethren of the same faith jubilating together; and likewise the women among themselves, and the children, rejoiced, uttering shouts of thanks to the victorious cross and to the faithful Orthodox grand prince; rescued and liberated from the evil Latin delusions and outrages, they all gloried in their true shepherd and mentor, the Orthodox great sovereign, and they kissed one another. . . . And the grand prince summoned the princes, boyars, and burghers of Smolensk and addressed to them a speech [setting forth the relationship of Smolensk to his rule—*ustavnaia rech'*], declaring his complete favor, and he gave them his boyar Prince Vasilii Vasilievich Shuiskii as voevoda and vicegerent [or governor—*namestnik*], and he invited them to eat with him. They ate with the grand prince; and afterward he bestowed gifts on them: sable garments, velvets, damask, silks, golden satins, and money gifts, to each according to his standing; and he also made gifts to the deti boiarskie, the service men, and the burghers, to each as befitted him; and also to the hetmans of the mercenary soldiery and to the soldiers [*zholnyri*] themselves.

VII:2. AN ADMINISTRATIVE CHARTER OF JUNE 4, 1536

Various kinds of "feeding" arrangements (see Item VI:8, above) are illustrated in this administrative charter (ustavnaia gramota) issued in the name of Ivan IV (who was then a mere boy of six).
Reference: *AAE*, 1:152-53.

I, Grand Prince of All Russia Ivan Vasil'evich, grant my bounty to my people of Onega [i.e. tha basin of the Onega River] . . . to the elders and to all the people of the land of Onega: whoever be our vicegerent [namestnik] in their region, he shall observe this, our charter. Upon his arrival, let him take the entrance *korm* ["feeding" or subsistence payments], as much as the people may bring. On the three feast days—Christmas, Easter, and Saint Peter's Day—our vicegerent shall receive korm from all the *sokhi* [land units of taxation] . . . at Christmas our vicegerent shall receive from each ten sokhi a carcass of meat, ten loaves of bread, a measure of oats, and a cartload of hay; and at Easter, a carcass of meat and ten loaves; and on Saint Peter's Day, a sheep and ten loaves; and if the vicegerent is not pleased with the korm, let him have instead eight dengi [small silver coins] for the carcass, six dengi for the sheep, one for the bread, six for the measure of oats, and eight dengi for the cartload of hay. And his deputy [tiun] [shall receive], on the same feast days, one half of the vicegerent's korm, and the constable [*dovodchik*] [shall be given] revenue from three sokhi: at Christmas one loaf of bread, one cut of meat, and one small measure [*zobnia*—"cropful" or "crawful"] of oats, and at Easter a loaf and a cut of meat, and on Saint Peter's Day one loaf and a cheese; if the constable is not pleased with the revenue, let him have instead one denga for the loaf, one for the cut of meat, one for the cheese, and two for the small measure of oats. . . . In administering justice our vicegerent [and his deputy] shall observe this, our charter.

·   ·   ·

Our vicegerent and his deputy shall not sit in court without the elders and the best men. Neither the deputy nor other agents of the vicegerent shall attend feasts and communal celebrations [*bratchina*] uninvited. . . . And my princes and boyars and all kinds of messengers, if they happen to quarter themselves with the people of the stany and volosti of Onega, shall not take food for themselves or for their horses from them without pay, but they shall buy their own and their horses' food from them.

VII:3. THE NIKONIAN CHRONICLE ON BOYAR RULE DURING THE CHILDHOOD OF IVAN IV, CA. 1539-1543

The conditions around the throne during the boyhood of Ivan IV, as described here in the Nikonian Chronicle, may help to explain why Ivan did not handle his nobles gently.
Reference: *PSRL,* vol. 13, pt. 1, pp. 126, 127, 140, 141, 145.

On the murder of Feodor Mishurin. That same autumn [1539], at the prompting of the Devil, there arose enmity among the boyars of the grand prince: Princes Vasilii and Ivan Shuiskii were feuding with Prince Ivan Feodorovich Bel'skii and Prince Iurii Golitsin-Bulgakov, and with Ivan Khabarov and the grand prince's secretary, Feodor Mishurin, on the grounds that Prince Ivan Bel'skii had counseled the grand prince to grant the rank of boyar to Prince Iurii Golitsin and the rank of okolnichi to Ivan Khabarov. There was much strife among them over personal gain and over their kin, each looking after his own interests and not those of the state or of the land. And Princes Vasilii and Ivan Shuiskii had not been present at that council, wherefore they were seized with great hatred and wrath against Metropolitan Danil, Prince Ivan Bel'skii, and Feodor Mishurin. By reason of that hatred they seized Prince Ivan Bel'skii and put him under guard in Prince Feodor Mstislavskii's court, and they deported his advisers to the villages, and they put the secretary Mishurin to death by beheading him near the prison, without the sovereign's order. There was at that time much rioting and disorder in the Christian land, on account of our sins, the sovereign being young, and the boyars given to corruption without restraint; and they stirred up much bloodshed among themselves, and they dispensed justice wrongfully, and their deeds were not godly; and God suffered this, but the Fiend acted. . . .

That same winter [1539] . . . Metropolitan Danil was removed from his metropolitanate through the enmity of the grand prince's boyars, Prince Ivan Shuiskii and others, for having been in agreement with Prince Ivan Bel'skii; and the metropolitan was exiled from Moscow . . . to the Josephite monastery [at Volokolamsk].

· · ·

On the capture of Prince Ivan Bel'skii.
That same winter [1542], on the second day of January, the grand prince's boyar Prince Ivan Feodorovich Bel'skii was seized by [other] boyars, without the knowledge of the grand prince, on the grounds that the sovereign grand prince kept him close to himself, among his chief counselors, together with Metropolitan Iosaf. The boyars therefore became resentful against Prince Ivan and the metropolitan and began plotting evil with their advisers. . . . And on the advice of their followers they seized Prince Ivan Bel'skii in his home and detained him at the treasury house until morning. . . . The next day, Monday, they banished Prince Ivan Bel'skii to Beloozero to be imprisoned. And the advisers [*sovetniki*—also "companions"] of Prince Ivan Bel'skii were seized and exiled to other towns: Prince Petr Mikhailovich Shcheniatev to Iaroslavl', and Ivan Khabarov to Tver'. And on Metropolitan Iosaf they cast great dishonor and shame. Metropolitan Iosaf, unable to endure this, left his house and moved to the [Moscow] hostel [*podvorie*] of the Troitskii Monastery. And the boyars sent provincial deti boiarskie to the Troitskii hostel, to abuse him with unseemly words. They reviled him ignominiously, and they nearly killed him; the Troitskii abbot Aleksei, invok-

ing the name of Sergii the Miracle Worker, barely kept them from murder. And there was much turmoil in Moscow at that time. They struck fear into the sovereign, and they exiled the metropolitan to the Kirilov Monastery. And the boyars dispatched to Beloozero Petrok, son of Iarets Zaitsov, and Mit'ka, son of Ivan Klobukov, and Ivashka, son of Elizar Sergeev, to kill Prince Ivan Bel'skii in the prison. They journeyed secretly, without the knowledge of the grand prince, and killed Prince Ivan Bel'skii by the boyars' willful order.

· · ·

On the twenty-ninth day of December [1543], Grand Prince Ivan Vasilievich of all Russia could no longer tolerate the boyars' unruly and willful doings, in that they had committed many murders without the grand prince's orders, of their own free will and on the advice of their friends, and had committed many iniquities in the land while the sovereign was young. The great sovereign ordered that their leader, Prince Andrei Shuiskii, be seized and delivered to the dog-keepers, and the dog-keepers took him and killed him, while dragging him to the prison, in front of the Rizpolozhenskii Gate, inside the city [Kremlin]; and [the tsar] banished [Shuiskii's] friends; and from that time the boyars began to fear the sovereign.

VII:4. THE NIKONIAN CHRONICLE ON THE CORONATION OF IVAN IV, JANUARY 16, 1547

The earliest recorded ceremony of a tsar's coronation is that of Dmitrii Ivanovich, grandson of Ivan III, in 1498. At that time Ivan III wanted to ensure that Dmitrii, his grandson by his eldest son, would be his heir rather than his second son, Vasilii. Four years later, however, owing to court and political intrigues, Dmitrii was arrested and Vasilii proclaimed Ivan's co-ruler and heir. The features of the ceremony of 1498 were repeated in the coronation of Ivan IV, January 16, 1547—a noteworthy event in the development of the Muscovite State. The author of the Nikonian Chronicle here describes the occasion, bringing in the legend of Vladimir Monomakh along with such significant details as the text of the prayer describing the tsar's responsibilities.
Reference: *PSRL*, vol. 13, pt. 1, pp. 150-51. The ceremony of 1498 is in *PSRL*, 8:234-36.

That same winter [1547], on Sunday, the sixteenth of January, the pious grand prince Ivan Vasil'evich of all Russia was crowned tsar of Russia by the most holy Makarii, metropolitan of all Russia, and the archbishops and bishops, and the archimandrites, and the entire holy council of the Russian metropolitanate, as had been crowned his ancestor the great tsar Vladimir Monomakh, with the life-giving cross and the tsar's crown and necklet [*diadima*, evidently used here in the sense of

a collar or pallium, interchangeably with *barmy* (see below)]; as with the same life-giving cross and tsar's crown and necklet his ancestor Grand Prince Vladimir had been crowned Russian tsar in ancient times: invested with the regal purple, he had been given the name of Monomakh by the most holy metropolitan of Ephesus the lord Neophytus, with the blessing of the patriarch of Tsar'grad and upon the entreaty of the Greek tsar Constantine Monomachus. The coronation of Grand Prince Ivan Vasil'evich of all Russia as tsar, in accordance with ancient ancestral tradition, proceeded thus:

In the center of the Cathedral Church of the worthy and glorious Dormition of our most pure lady, the mother of God [and] queen of heaven, a large space was made ready for the prelates to stand, and two seats were set up in this place, one for the tsar, the other for the metropolitan. When the time came, Metropolitan Makarii arrayed himself in his priestly vestments, and all the archbishops, bishops, and archimandrites and the entire holy council arrayed themselves in their sacred robes, and the metropolitan ordered the lectern to be placed in the middle of the church; upon the lectern were placed the life-giving cross on a golden tray and the crown and collar [barmy; Herberstein describes this as a broad collar made of black silk overlaid with gold and jewels] of Tsar Constantine Monomachus, wherewith Grand Prince Vladimir Monomakh had been crowned as tsar of Russia. And when Grand Prince Ivan Vasil'-evich of all Russia entered the cathedral church, the metropolitan with the entire holy council began a thanksgiving service [moleben, Te Deum] to the life-giving cross and to the Virgin and to Saint Peter the Miracle Worker [a former metropolitan of Moscow]. . . . And the metropolitan took the life-giving cross from the golden tray and placed it upon the grand prince and uttered this prayer: ". . . Grant him, O Lord, a long life, and give into his right hand the scepter of tsardom, seat him on the throne of righteousness, protect him with all the weapons of the Holy Ghost, strengthen his sinews, bring all the barbarian peoples under his power, put thy fear into his heart, let him look with mercy upon those who obey him, maintain his faith uncorrupted, show him as a careful guardian of the commandments of thy holy catholic church, that he may judge thy people equitably, and that his judgment may rescue thy poor and the sons of the needy, and that he may inherit thy heavenly kingdom." And after the prayer

the metropolitan ordered . . . the necklet, that is, the collar, to be brought from the lectern, and, after making the sign of the cross over Grand Prince Ivan Vasil'evich, the metropolitan laid the collar upon him. . . . After the amen the metropolitan ordered the cap to be brought from the holy table . . . and the metropolitan took the cap, that is, the crown, and made the sign of the cross over the grand prince, saying: "In the name of the Father, and of the Son, and of the Holy Ghost," and placed the cap upon his head. . . . After the prayer the tsar sat down upon his seat, and the metropolitan upon his, and an archdeacon ascended the pulpit and intoned in a loud voice a prayer for the long life [mnogo-letie] of Ivan Vasil'evich, the Russian tsar, and the entire holy council of the Russian metropolitanate [chanted] the prayer for a long life, and all the deacons chanted the prayer for a long life. And after the prayer for a long life the metropolitan hailed the great tsar: "Rejoice and prosper for many years, O Orthodox tsar Ivan, by the grace of God autocrat of all Russia!" And the metropolitan bowed down before the tsar. Then the archbishops and bishops and the entire [holy] council bowed down and hailed the great tsar; and the boyars hailed the great tsar, and all the people likewise hailed the great autocrat. And the metropolitan performed the benediction, and then began the liturgy. After the liturgy was over the great tsar Ivan Vasil'evich, autocrat of great Russia, left the [Cathedral of the] Dormition, and all along the way from the church to his palace [cloths of] velvet and damask were spread wherever the great autocrat went. And as the great tsar left his seat, he was showered with gold coins at the doors of the church by his brother Prince Iurii Vasil'evich, and a golden vessel with gold coins was carried behind him by the great tsar's boyar and equerry [koniu-shei] Prince Mikhail Vasil'evich Glinskii; and in front of the [Church of the] Archangel they showered him [with coins], and on the middle stairway they showered him again.

VII:5. THE SUDEBNIK OF 1550

The Sudebnik or Code of Law of 1550 is one of the landmarks of Russian legal history. Among its many interesting features, illustrated by the excerpts below, is its treatment of the old problem of central as opposed to local control, as expressed in its provisions governing such traditional, locally chosen officials as the elders, the sworn assistants (tseloval'niki or "kissers," because they kissed the cross), and the public clerks.

Reference: *PRP*, 4:233, 248–60. The meanings of the terms *golovnoi tat'* and *podmetchik* in article 61 are discussed in ibid., 3:381–83. The various interpretations of *sud boiarskii* are discussed in ibid., 4:303–04. In connection with the present translation the editors wish to express gratitude for the expert assistance of Professor Horace William Dewey. See also, for a translation of all 100 articles, Dewey's *Muscovite Judicial Texts, 1488-1556,* Michigan Slavic Materials no. 7 (Ann Arbor: Department of Slavic Languages and Literature, University of Michigan, 1966), pp. 45-74.

In the year 7058 [1550], in the month of June, Tsar and Grand Prince of All Russia Ivan Vasil'evich, with his kinsmen and boyars, issued this Code of Law on how boyars, and okol'nichie, and majordomos [*dvoretskie*], and treasurers [*kaznachei*], and secretaries [*d'iaki*], and all prikaz officials [*prikaznye liudi*], and vicegerents in the towns, and volost' chiefs [volosteli] in the volosti, and [their] deputies and all [other] judges are to administer justice.

1. The justice of the tsar and grand prince is to be administered by boyars, okol'nichie, majordomos, treasurers, and secretaries. No one [of these] is to use the court for purposes of personal favor or revenge, or to accept bribes in administering justice; in like manner, no judge whatsoever is to accept bribes in administering justice. . . .

60. . . . If someone is brought [to court] for brigandage, or evidence is brought against someone of being a notorious brigand, such persons shall be handed over by the vicegerents to the *gubnye starosty* [elected heads of local criminal justice]. The gubnye starosty, except [in the case of] notorious brigands, shall not intervene in the jurisdiction of the vicegerents in any matter. And they shall judge thieves according to the [local] criminal statutes [gubnye gramoty] of the tsar and grand prince, as it is written in them.

61. The insurgent against the sovereign [or "murderer of his master"], and he who surrenders a fortress [to the enemy], and the rebel, and the church thief, and the *golovnoi tat'* [most likely a kidnapper of serfs, but perhaps one who commits murder in the act of robbery], and the *podmetchik* [perhaps one who plants stolen goods so as to accuse someone of theft or robbery, but possibly a traitor or spy], and the arsonist, and the notorious evildoer—their lives shall not be spared but they shall be put to death. . . .

62. Boyars and deti boiarskie who hold *kormleniia* with the right of boyar court [*sud boiarskii:* probably full jurisdiction over all

serious criminal offenses; perhaps (according to V. O. Kliuchevskii) the specific right to decide legal cases involving bondmen (*kholopy*)] shall administer justice; and at trials held by them or by their deputies there shall be present: the prince's steward [*dvorskoi,* in charge of estates belonging to the prince] where there is one, and a [peasant] elder, and worthy men as sworn assistants. Cases [tried] in the courts of the vicegerents and their deputies shall be recorded by the public clerk [*zemskii d'iak,* appointed by the elected authorities of the rural or urban community]; and the prince's steward, and the elder, and the sworn assistants shall sign [the records of] those cases. Copies of those legal cases shall be made, word for word, by the vicegerents' secretaries, and the vicegerents shall affix their seals to those copies. The vicegerents shall keep for themselves the [original] document of those legal cases recorded by the public clerk, with the signatures of the prince's steward, and of the elder, and of the sworn assistants; and the vicegerents shall give copies of those cases [recorded] by their secretaries, with seals, to the prince's steward, and to the elder and to the sworn assistants; and whichever elders or sworn assistants are unable to read and write, as well as those who can read and write, those elders and sworn assistants shall sign [or make their sign on] the court report of the public clerk; and a copy of those cases signed by the vicegerent's secretary shall be [given] to the elders and to the sworn assistants who are unable to read and write, and they shall keep it in case of dispute. The vicegerents and their deputies shall not hold trials without the prince's steward and the elder and the sworn assistants; and in those areas where there has been no steward of the prince heretofore, and where there is none now, the [local] elder and sworn assistants shall be present at trials held by vicegerents and their deputies; no trials shall be held without elders and sworn assistants. . . .

63. As for the right of boyar court: whatever vicegerent is given the right of boyar court

shall [have the right to] issue deeds of full
bondage [*polnye* and *dokladnye gramoty;* the
polnaia gramota was the document by which
a man sold himself into full bondage (polnoe
kholopstvo); the dokladnaia gramota was a
document of this sort brought before the
prince's vicegerent for confirmation]; and he
shall issue written court decisions [*pravaia
gramota*] [in cases involving bondmen], and
documents concerning runaway bondmen
[*beglaia gramota*] [only] by referring them
[to the central government for confirmation];
and without referring them [to the central
government] he shall not issue written court
decisions or documents concerning runaway
bondmen.

64. And the vicegerents in all the towns
shall [have jurisdiction to] try deti boiarskie
in accordance with the regional immunity
charters [*zhalovannye vopchie gramoty,* issued
for all the landowners in an uezd rather than
to individuals] of the sovereign tsar that are
now in force. . . .

68. If a vicegerent is given a town with its
volosti as a kormlenie, or if he is given volosti
as a kormlenie, and if in these volosti there have
not been any elders and sworn assistants heretofore, henceforth there are to be elders and
sworn assistants in all these volosti. And if anyone in those volosti should be a plaintiff or a
defendant before the vicegerent or his deputy,
elders and sworn assistants of the volosti from
which the plaintiffs or defendants come shall
be present at the trial held by the vicegerent
or volost' chief or their deputies. Legal cases
shall be recorded by the public clerk of that
same volost'. And without [the presence of]
elders and sworn assistants, the vicegerents and
volost' chiefs, whether or not they hold
kormleniia with the right of boyar court, shall
not hold trials, nor shall their deputies. Vicegerents and volost' chiefs and their deputies
shall not accept bribes in legal cases. . . .

70. As for those whom agents of the vicegerent or volost' chief shall order to obtain bail,
before or after the trial, but who cannot obtain
bail, the agents of the vicegerent shall present
these persons in a town to the town judges
[*gorodovoi prikazchik*], and to the prince's
steward, and to the elder and the sworn assistants; and in a volost' they shall present [these
persons] to the elders and sworn assistants who
participate in trials held by the vicegerents and
volost' chiefs and their deputies; and without

[first] presenting [in this manner] those persons who have no bail, the agents of the vicegerent and volost' chief shall not take them
into custody and shall not put them in chains.
As for those whom the agents of the vicegerent or volost' chief take into custody and
put in chains, without [first] presenting them
to the [town] judges, and prince's steward,
and the elder and the sworn assistants, if any
kinsmen and clansmen of those [unlawfully
imprisoned] persons should come [with com-
plaint] against the agents of the vicegerent or
volost' chief to the [town] judges and the
prince's steward and the elder and the sworn
assistants, to make petition and representa-
tion regarding this matter, then the [town]
judges, and the prince's steward, and the elder,
and sworn assistants shall take those persons
from [the custody of] the agents of the vicegerent and volost' chief; and if anyone whom
they take from [the custody of] the agents of
the vicegerent and volost' chief is in chains,
and has not been presented to them, then
recompense for injured honor [*bezchestie*]
shall be taken from the agent of the vicegerent
or volost' chief, [the amount] depending on
the person [wronged]; and for whatever
damages that [wronged] person sues the
agent of the vicegerent or volost' chief, double
that sum shall be taken from him [the offend-
ing agent]. . . .

75. And if anyone sends a bailiff [*pristav*]
after a vicegerent, a boyar or a *syn boiarskii,*
or after a volost' chief, or after their deputies,
or after an agent of the tsar and grand prince,
or after [local] constables [dovodchiki], then
the vicegerent, volost' chief, their deputies,
the agents of the grand prince, and the [local]
constables shall come [to court] on the trial
date. . . .

76. Concerning justice for bondmen
[kholopy]. [One becomes] a bondman
through a deed of full bondage [polnaia gra-
mota]. [By being] a village steward [on a
landowner's estate], provided a deed of bondage is presented [to the prince's administrative
agent], [one becomes] a bondman together
with one's wife and with [those] children who
are living with him in the service of the same
master on the basis of the same document,
and who were born in bondage; but those of
his children who were born before he became
a bondman and who live with another master,
or by themselves, are not bondmen. And [by

being] a steward in town one does not become a bondman. [By marrying] a bond-woman, [a man becomes] a bondman; by [marrying] a bondman, [a woman becomes] a bondwoman. [One may be] a bondman by last will and testament [i.e. bondmen can be bequeathed]. . . .

77. Documents of manumission [otpusknye] are to be referred up to the boyars [for confirmation]; and the boyars are to affix their seal to those documents of manumission, and the secretaries shall sign them. Documents of manumission are to be presented in Moscow to the boyars and secretaries, and in Novgorod the Great and Pskov documents of manumission are to be presented to the vicegerents and secretaries. . . . And except in Moscow and Novgorod the Great and Pskov, in no other town shall documents of manumission be confirmed. . . .

81. Deti boiarskie who are in service and their children who have not served the state shall not be taken by anyone as bondmen, except for those [deti boiarskie] whom the sovereign shall dismiss from service. . . .

83. If a hired laborer [naimit] does not serve his master the full term but goes away, he shall be deprived of his wages. But if a master refuses to give the hired laborer his wages, and is convicted of this, he shall be made to pay the hired laborer twice the sum of his wages. . . .

87. If someone from the lands of the tsar and grand prince plows over a boundary strip or cuts down a marker on land belonging to a boyar or a monastery [or if a boyar's or monastery's man does this on the tsar's land] or if a boyar's man does this on a monastery's land, or a monastery's man on a boyar's land, he who plowed over the boundary strip or chopped down a marker shall be flogged with the knout and the plaintiff shall take one ruble from him; and if among the peasants in one volost' or village one [peasant] plows over or mows across another's boundary strip, then the volost' chief or prince's rural agent

[posel'skii] shall take from him two altyny in place of a sheep.

88. Peasants may move from volost' to volost' or from village to village once a year: during the week before and the week after Saint George's Day in the fall [November 26]. For a homestead in the fields they shall [upon leaving] pay one ruble and two altyny as a pozhiloe [departure payment], and for a homestead in the forest area, where it is [no more than] ten versty to a forest where wood for building may be obtained, [they shall pay] one poltina and two altyny. If a peasant lives [with a master] for a year he shall upon leaving pay one quarter of the pozhiloe; if he lives two years, he shall pay half; if he lives three years, he shall pay three quarters; and if he lives four years he shall pay the full pozhiloe, one ruble and two altyny. . . . A [village] priest shall not pay pozhiloe and shall be free to leave whenever he pleases. If a plowland peasant sells himself into full bondage to someone, he may leave at any time and shall not pay pozhiloe. . . .

91. And priests, deacons, monks, nuns, and old widows who are supported by God's church shall be under the jurisdiction of a prelate or his judges; and if a layman [has litigation] with a man [under the jurisdiction] of the church, then [the case shall be tried by] a joint court; but if a widow is not supported by God's church and lives in her own home, she shall not be under the jurisdiction of a prelate. And urban trading men shall not live in monastery households in the towns. Trading men who live in monasteries shall be removed from the monasteries and shall be under the jurisdiction of the vicegerents. And indigents who are supported by God's church are permitted to live in the monasteries. . . .

98. When new cases, not provided for in this Code of Laws, arise, as soon as these cases are decided by presentation to the sovereign and by the verdict of all the boyars, these cases shall be added to this Code of Laws.

VII:6. AN EDICT ON MESTNICHESTVO, CA. 1550

The system of mestnichestvo, or genealogical ranking applied to governmental and military service, was an important factor in the development of the Muscovite state. This 1550 edict reveals some of the complications of mestnichestvo and also illustrates how they could be circumvented. Not until 1682 was mestnichestvo officially discarded.

Reference: Arkheograficheskaia Komissiia, ed., Akty istoricheskie, 5 vols. (St. Petersburg, 1841-42), 1:251. Also in PSRL, vol. 13, pt. 1, p. 267.

Sovereign's edict. In the summer of 7058 [1550] the lord tsar decided in consultation with the metropolitan and with all the boyars: In the fighting units [*polki*] the princes and deti boiarskie are to serve together with the voevody without [regard to their] position [in the tables of precedence] and are to go on all sorts of missions together with all voevody so as to provide places for [all capable] people. In so doing they shall incur no prejudice to their ancestral claims; in the future, the selection of boyars and voevody shall be made according to each one's ancestral claim. *Concerning voevody:* As for the voevody in the fighting units [polki]: The [voevody in command of the] main body [*bol'shoi polk*], the right detachment

[*pravaia ruka*], and the left detachment shall be [selected] on the basis of position [in the tables of precedence], while the [voevody in command of the] advance detachment [*peredovoi polk*] and rear detachment [*storozhevoi polk*] shall be of lesser [genealogical] rank than the one principal voevoda in command of the main body, but shall be [selected] without regard to the [genealogical] position of the [voevody of the] right and left flank detachments and the other [i.e. the second] voevoda in the main body. He who is sent to serve under the [chief] voevoda of any unit is to be of lesser [genealogical] rank than [the chief], and the sovereign is to select the voevody taking into account the ancestral claims of each and his capability for military service.

VII:7. IVAN IV'S CHARTER TO VOLOSTI IN THE DVINA UEZD, FEBRUARY 25, 1552

This charter (*ustavnaia zemskaia gramota*), issued by Ivan IV to certain volosti of the Dvina uezd, sheds light on the conditions of the time as well as on the character of Ivan's reforms of local and regional administration.

Reference: *PRP*, 4:188-92, 195-96. A recent translation of this document in its entirety is in Horace W. Dewey, comp., trans., and ed., *Muscovite Judicial Texts 1488-1556* (Michigan Slavic Materials, no. 7; Ann Arbor: Dept. of Slavic Languages and Literatures, 1966), pp. 75-82.

1. I, Tsar and Grand Prince of All Russia Ivan Vasil'evich, have granted my favor to the men of Malaia Penezhka, and of the volost' of Vyia, and of Sura Poganaia, in the Dvina uezd —to Mishka Peneg of Penezhka, to Ermolka Klement'ev of Vyia, [and] to Stepanok Dement'ev of Sura, in behalf of all the peasants of those volosti.

2. [These peasants] have petitioned us, saying that in their parts, in Penezhka, Vyia, and Sura, many villages have been deserted because of our former volost' chiefs [volosteli] and their deputies [tiuny], constables [dovodchiki], and investigators [*obysknye liudi*], and because of evildoers, thieves, and robbers; and henceforth, they say, the people of Penezhka will be unable to provide korm [subsistence payments] to the volost' chiefs and their tax officials; and because of them and their abuses and exactions, the peasants, they say, have left Penezhka, Vyia, and Sura for other volosti and for monastery lands, permanently and without legal discharge. And [although] other peasants have wandered off one by one for unknown destinations, our Penezhka volost' chiefs and their deputies, they say, exact their korm, and the constables

and bailiffs their revenues, from the remaining peasants in full; and the remaining peasants, they say, henceforth will be unable to furnish in full all the exactions and various duties to our volost' chiefs and their tax officials.

3. And they have asked us to grant our favor to the people of Penezhka . . . and to remove the volost' chief of Penezhka, Vyia, and Sura and his deputy.

4. We have ordered, in response to their petition, that in Penezhka, Vyia, and Sura the best men shall be elected from among the volost' peasants, whomever all the peasants of Penezhka, Vyia, and Sura desire . . . to administer justice among them, the volost' peasants of Penezhka, Vyia, and Sura Poganaia, in cases of murder, and robbery with material evidence, and in all kinds of cases subject to local authority, in accordance with our Code of Laws. And they shall have jurisdiction over cases of robbery, and try them, and hold investigations, and punish the guilty upon investigation, and give redress to plaintiffs against robbers, without delay, in accordance with our Code of Laws. . . .

8. And I, Tsar and Grand Prince of All Russia Ivan Vasil'evich, have granted my

favor to all the peasants of Penezhka, Vyia, and Sura Poganaia . . . [and] have removed the Penezhka volost' chief from Penezhka, Vyia, and Sura, and have ordered that henceforth there shall be no volost' chief [there]; and I have ordered, in response to their petition, that there shall be elected heads [*izliublennye golovy*] in Penezhka, Vyia, and Sura, whomever the volost' peasants of Penezhka, Vyia, and Sura shall choose for themselves, . . . who shall administer justice among them in all cases under local authority. And I have imposed a tax in money [obrok] upon Penezhka, Vyia, and Sura, according to their petition. The peasants of Penezhka, Vyia, and Sura Poganaia shall give . . . one hundred rubles a year, in place of the korm to the volost' chief and his deputy, and the court fees [*prisud*], and the tax on the branding of horses [*piatno*], and the revenues to the bailiffs [*pravedchiki*] and the constables [dovodchiki], and the duty on goods paid by trading men from other regions [*gostinaia iavka*], and all the subsistence payments to the volost' chief, and all the exactions of the tax officials, and all other duties. . . .

10. The people of Penezhka, Vyia, and Sura shall be administered and judged by their elected heads—Elizarei Iakovlev, Semen Ivanov, and Timofei Antsyforov, and their assistants, ten men in all, chosen by the people of those volosti; and they will dispense justice among them, in accordance with our Code of Laws and the oath they have sworn on the cross, without any guile.

11. Should there be cases that the elected heads of those volosti are unable to settle, then the elected heads, Elizarei Iakovlev of Penezhka, Semen Ivanov of Vyia, and Timofei Antsyforov of Sura, with their assistants, ten men in all, shall meet at Vyia, to try in court all cases subject to local authority and to administer justice all together.

12. All the volost' peasants of Penezhka, Vyia, and Sura shall elect a public clerk [zemskii d'iak], whomever they desire, to keep written records of all matters for them;

and they shall administer the oath [upon the cross] to him. . . .

25. And should there be any cases the elected heads cannot settle without our knowledge, the elected heads, Elizarei Iakovlev, Semen Ivanov, and Timofei Antsyforov, and their assistants, ten men in all, shall send the written records of their court proceedings and investigations in all such cases to Moscow, to our treasurers, Ivan Petrovich Golovin and Feodor Ivanovich Sukin, and to our secretary Istoma Novgorodov, or to some other secretary; and I, the tsar and grand prince, shall give orders that our treasurers and our secretary report on these cases to me, the tsar and grand prince, and I shall issue my orders accordingly. . . .

28. Should the elected heads themselves begin to oppress and harm any of the people of the volosti, and impose excessive court fines [*prodazha*] upon them, and accept bribes and gifts in any lawsuit, they shall be put to death by me, the tsar and grand prince, and their possessions [and] property shall be seized and given to those people who have incurred losses and damages through them.

29. The court proceedings and investigations and all the affairs conducted by the elected heads shall be recorded in writing by the public clerk, chosen and elected by all three volosti as clerk; and the written records and all matters shall be supervised by the elected heads, Elizarei Iakovlev, Semen Ivanov, and Timofei Antsyforov, with their assistants, ten men in all, and along with them by the best men from among the volost' peasants; they shall have all matters recorded in their presence; and the written records shall be kept under seal. . . .

31. As for the deserted hamlets and villages in Penezhka, Vyia, and Sura, [new] peasants should be called in, and the former tiaglo-bearing peasants [i.e. bearers of tax and other obligations] should be brought back from other volosti and from monastery lands to their old villages, permanently and without any payment [to any former master], each to the village where he had lived before.

VII:8. IVAN IV'S CHARTER TO VOLOSTI IN THE USTIUG UEZD, OCTOBER 15, 1555

Some of the many variations within the same general framework of reform are illustrated in this charter (ustavnaia gramota) issued to part of the Ustiug uezd, in the basin of the Sukhona River.

Reference: *AAE*, 1:264-67. For an extensively annotated translation of a similar charter issued to the town of Toropets 35 years later, see the recently published work of Richard Hellie, ed. and trans., *Readings for Introduction to Russian Civilization: Muscovite Society* (Chicago: University of Chicago Syllabus Division, 1967), pp. 33-47.

I, Tsar and Grand Prince of All Russia Ivan Vasil'evich, bestow my favor upon the volost' peasants along the rivers Us'ia and Zaech'ia, in the Ustiug uezd:

... Inasmuch as heretofore we bestowed our favor upon our boyars and princes and deti boiarskie, by granting them towns and volosti as kormleniia, so now we have numerous petitions and ceaseless complaints from the peasants that our vicegerents and volost' chiefs and bailiffs [pravedchiki] and their tax officials are causing them much damage and loss, above the prescribed revenues we granted them; and from the vicegerents, volost' chiefs, bailiffs, and tax officials we have received many complaints and petitions that the posad men and volost' peasants avoid trial and surety [bail, poruka], and fail to pay them their korm, and beat them; therefore there is much false accusation and litigation among them; and because of this many peasant homesteads in the posady and many hamlets and homesteads in the uezd have been deserted, and our tribute and taxes are not received in full. And we, bestowing our favor upon the peasantry, because of that great damage and loss, have removed the vicegerents, volost' chiefs, and bailiffs from the towns and volosti; in place of the revenues to the vicegerents and volost' chiefs and constables, and the court fees, and the duties collected by the tax officials, we have ordered that a tax [obrok] in money shall be imposed upon the peasants in the posady and volosti, so that the peasantry may no longer suffer such damage and loss, and so that we may no longer have petitions and complaints from them about the vicegerents, volost' chiefs, and bailiffs, and from the vicegerents, volost' chiefs, and bailiffs about the posad men and volost' peasants, and so that the posady and volosti may not therefore be deserted. We have ordered that, in all the towns, stany, and volosti, elected elders [izliublennye starosty] be instituted to administer justice among the peasants, and to collect the revenues [formerly] due to the vicegerents and volost' chiefs and bailiffs and deliver them to us on the assigned date; [these are to be] men whom the peasants will choose among themselves and elect all together, and from whom they will suffer no extortions, no losses, and no injury, and who will be able to dispense justice among them fairly, without bribery and without delay, and who will be

able to collect the obrok, in place of the vicegerent's revenue, and to deliver it to our treasury on the assigned date, without arrears. And the volost' peasants along the Us'ia and Zaech'ia rivers, the best and the middle and the lesser men, and all the peasants together, have chosen among themselves their elected elders, from among the best men of the volost' peasants along the Us'ia and Zaech'ia rivers, who shall administer justice among them and collect the volost' chief's revenues and deliver them to us at the prescribed time.... And we ordered their elected judges and had them swear upon the cross to hold trials and to administer justice to the volost' peasants along the Us'ia and Zaech'ia rivers in accordance with the Code of Laws and with [this] administrative charter, observing the rules we have set forth for the administration of justice throughout the land, investigating [all cases] fairly, according to the oath sworn before us upon the cross, without bribery and without delay.... If they find it impossible to settle a case, they shall send the records of their court proceedings and both litigants to Moscow, to report to our treasurers.... In case of robbery the volost' peasants shall be tried and administered by the criminal judges [gubnye starosty, elected heads of local criminal justice] in accordance with the criminal administrative charters [gubnye ustavnye gramoty] and the written instructions. The sworn assistants [tseloval'niki] who sit with them in court and are sent on assignments for them, and the public clerks [zemskie d'iaki] who keep written records of the court proceedings for them, and the men who replace the constables [dovodchiki] to take charge of those out on surety and to bring the accused into court shall be elected by the elders ... and by all the volost' peasants of the Us'ia and Zaech'ia rivers the best and the middle and the lesser men, in their own volosti along the Us'ia and Zaech'ia rivers, whomever all the volost' peasants choose among themselves, from among the volost' peasants, who are able to sit in court with the elected elders: two sworn assistants from each volost', and one public clerk, and one man to replace the constable to take charge of those out on surety; and they shall be brought to take the oath upon the cross in their volost', according to the written regulations that have been issued to them.... And they [the elected elders] shall collect the yearly obrok from their entire [judicial] district [prisud], from the volosti along the Us'ia and Zaech'ia rivers, assessed on the basis of property and occupation, just as they apportion other taxes [tiaglo] among themselves. In apportioning the obrok no village shall be excessively taxed on any account. And should those elected elders and sworn assistants render justice dishonestly, and favor their friends in court and take revenge on their enemies, and accept bribes and gifts, and no longer be heedful of our tsarist concerns and local public [zemskie] concerns, and no longer observe our decrees, as they have sworn upon the cross to us, and should any evil result from their wiles or their neglect, and should they be denounced and there be evidence against them, such judges and sworn assistants shall be put to death.

VII:9. DECREES ON MILITARY SERVICE, 1556

In 1556 Ivan IV issued decrees regulating the service of those who held kormleniia or "feedings" and those who held service and hereditary estates. The following account of these decrees is from the Nikonian Chronicle. (For a foreigner's view of the military forces at this time, see Item VII:38, below.)

Reference: *PSRL*, vol. 13, pt. 1, pp. 267-69.

In the year 7064 [1556] Tsar and Grand Prince Ivan Vasil'evich of All Russia, with his kinsmen and with the boyars, issued a decree on kormleniia and service, as to how everyone should do service henceforth. Hitherto the boyars and princes and deti boiarskie had resided in the kormleniia in the towns and volosti, to dispense justice to the people and administer the lands in every way and to derive satisfaction and subsistence from service themselves. And there were vicegerents [namestniki] and volost' chiefs [volosteli] in various towns and volosti who dispensed justice and maintained order in those towns and volosti and averted all evil from them, turning it into good; and they themselves were satisfied with the payments [obroki] and the prescribed dues [*poshliny*] which the sovereign had assigned to them. But then the news reached the pious tsar that many towns and volosti had been despoiled by the vicegerents and volost' chiefs, who for many years, disdaining the wrath of God and the sovereign's regulations, had committed many evil deeds against [the people]; instead of being their shepherds and mentors, they became their persecutors and despoilers. Also the peasants of these towns and volosti would perpetrate much villainy and violence upon their agents; and when the holders of the kormleniia left [their posts], the peasants would file many complaints [against them]; thus there was much bloodshed and much corruption of souls, unbefitting even to mention in a land of Christian faith; and many vicegerents and volost' chiefs were deprived even of their property, their possessions and patrimonial estates. . . .

The tsar's decision. And the tsar ordered elders [starosty], *sotskie, piatidesiatskie,* and *desiatskie* [literally, heads of one hundred, fifty, and ten, respectively] to be installed in the towns and volosti and enjoined them, under frightful and awesome threat [of punishment], to sit in judgment in cases of robbery and theft and all kinds of [legal] affairs, on no account permitting any enmity, or iniquitous bribe, or false witness; and if they find any evildoers in their midst, [the tsar] ordered them to impose punishment; and obroki shall be imposed upon the towns and volosti according to occupation and land, and these taxes shall be collected for the tsar's treasury by their own [local] clerks [d'iaki]. And [the tsar] provided the boyars and magnates and all the warriors with revenues [kormleniia, here used in a general sense], with equitable emoluments, to each according to his descent and birth; and to those in the towns [the provincial service men] he assigned a monetary wage [to be paid] every fourth year, and to some every third year.

The tsar's ruling. Thereupon the tsar also made this ruling: as for those great lords and warriors who possess much land while reducing their service, so that their service no longer conforms to the sovereign's grants and their patrimonies [*votchiny*], the sovereign equalized their status: he had a land survey carried out for their pomest'ia [estates granted on condition of military service] and arranged for each to receive what he deserves, with the surplus to be divided among those who have little; and he imposed a fixed service quota upon the pomest'ia: from each hundred *chetverti* of good arable land [100 chetverti would be about 135 acres, and in this case probably three fields, each of that size, are implied], one man with a horse and full armor, and with two horses for a distant campaign; and the tsar will bestow his bounty upon those who fulfill their service [obligations] in accordance with the [amount of] land [they possess] and will give them monetary wages for the prescribed number of men [to be furnished for campaigns]; and those who hold land but do not pay for it in service will have to furnish money themselves for the men; and those who send men to serve in excess of [the quota for] their land will be given a large bounty by the tsar, and their men will be given two and a half times the prescribed [amount of] money. And the sovereign arranged everything so that the organization of the army and of the tsar's service may truly be without fraud and without sin. And the originals of the service registers [razriady] were given to the tsar's commanders and prikaz officials.

VII:10. TOWARD SIBERIA: THE GRANT TO THE STROGANOVS, APRIL 4, 1558

An early stage of Russia's Siberian expansion was foreshadowed by this charter from Tsar Ivan IV to Grigorii Stroganov.

Reference: G. F. Miller [Mueller], Istoriia Sibiri, 2 vols. (Moscow: AN SSSR, 1937-41), 1: 333.

I, Tsar and Grand Prince of All Russia Ivan Vasil'evich, have bestowed my favor upon Grigorii, son of Anika Stroganov, [and] have allowed him to found a settlement [gorodok] in that uninhabited region eighty-eight versty below Perm' the Great along the Kama River . . . on the state forest land downstream on both banks of the Kama to the Chusovaia River, wherever there is a strong and safe place; and I have ordered him to place cannon and harquebuses in the settlement, and to install cannoneers, harquebusiers, and gate sentries [vorotniki] for protection against the Nagai and against other hordes, and to cut down the forest near that settlement along the rivers and around the lakes and up to the sources [of the rivers], and to plow the plowland around that settlement, and to establish homesteads, and to invite into that settlement such men as are not listed in the registry books [nepismennye] and who do not bear the tiaglo. . . . And if any men should come to that settlement from our state or from other lands with money or with goods, to buy salt or fish or other goods, these men shall be free to sell their goods here and to buy from them without any imposts. And if any men should come from Perm' to live, Grigorii [Stroganov] shall receive [only] those men who have been discharged [from their community] and are not listed in the registry books and do not bear the tiaglo. And if any salt deposits should be found in this region, he shall establish salterns there and boil salt. And they may catch fish in the rivers and lakes of this region without paying a tax. And if silver or copper or lead deposits should be found anywhere, Grigorii shall straightway report to our treasurers about these deposits, and he shall not work these deposits himself without our knowledge. . . . And I have granted him [these] privileges for twenty years.

VII:11. THE NIKONIAN CHRONICLE ON THE ESTABLISHMENT OF THE OPRICHNINA, 1564-1565

The Nikonian Chronicle gives the following account of the beginning of the oprichnina and of the eight years of terror associated with this institution.

Reference: PSRL, vol. 13, pt. 2, pp. 391-95.

The great journey of the sovereign tsar and grand prince of all Russia Ivan Vasil'evich. That same winter [1564], on the third day of December, a Sunday, the tsar and grand prince of all Russia Ivan Vasil'evich, with his tsaritsa and grand princess Maria and with his children, the tsarevich Ivan and the tsarevich Feodor, set forth from Moscow to the village of Kolomenskoe and celebrated the feast of Saint Nicholas the Miracle Worker at Kolomenskoe. His departure was not such as heretofore, when he would journey to monasteries to pray, or travel around the countryside to attend to his pleasures: for he took with him the sacred objects, icons and crosses adorned with gold and precious stones, and gold and silver vessels, and all the chests with all kinds of gold and silver plate, and robes, and money; and he ordered his entire treasury to be taken with him. And his closest [*blizhnie*] boyars and dvoriane, and the officials [*prikaznye liudi*] whom he ordered to go with him, were ordered to take their wives and children with them; and the provincial dvoriane and deti boiarskie whom the sovereign had selected to accompany him were ordered to accompany him with men and with horses, and with all their service equipment. . . . And in Moscow . . . all were perplexed and dismayed at such a grand and unusual departure of the sovereign, and no one knew the route of his journey, nor where he was going. And on the third day of January [1565] the tsar and grand prince sent a letter from the [Aleksandrovskaia] sloboda to his father the pious Afanasii, metropolitan of all Russia, . . . and therein were written down all the treasonable deeds of the boyars and voevody and various officials, the treasonable deeds they had committed and the harm they had brought to his realm before he, the sovereign, came of age after [the death of] his father of blessed memory, the great sovereign tsar and grand prince of all Russia Vasilii Ivanovich. And the tsar and grand prince laid his wrath upon those who pray for him, the archbishops and bishops, and the archimandrites and abbots . . . and he cast his disfavor upon his boyars . . . and secretaries and deti boiarskie and all his officials, inasmuch as during his reign, after [the death of] his father of blessed memory, the great sovereign Vasilii, while he, the sovereign, was not yet of age, the boyars and all the officials had brought much harm to the people of his realm and had depleted the sovereign's treasury, without adding any revenues to his sovereign treasury; and his boyars and voevody had also seized the sovereign's lands for their friends and their kin; and the boyars and voevody, holding large pomest'ia and patrimonies [votchiny], and in possession of kormleniia granted to them by the sovereign, had amassed great wealth but would not exert themselves for the sovereign and his realm and all Orthodox Christendom, and would not defend Christendom against its enemies, the Crimean [Tatars], the Lithuanians, and the Germans, but rather

would do violence to Christians; and they began to evade service themselves and would not stand firm for the Orthodox Christians against the Moslems and against the Latins [Catholics] and Germans; and whenever the sovereign wished to investigate and punish his boyars and officials, and likewise the service princes and deti boiarskie, for their misdeeds, the archbishops and bishops, and the archimandrites and abbots, joining forces with the boyars, dvoriane, secretaries, and all the officials, would begin to shield them from the sovereign tsar and grand prince. And the tsar and grand prince, from the great sorrow of his heart, not wishing to suffer their many treacherous deeds, forsook his realm and set forth, to reside wherever God might instruct him. And to the gosti [leading merchants] and merchants and all the Orthodox Christians of the city of Moscow the tsar and grand prince sent a letter . . . and ordered this letter to be read before the gosti and all the people . . . and in his letter to them he wrote them not to be of doubtful mind, for there was no wrath upon them and no disfavor. And when the most eminent Afanasii, metropolitan of all Russia, and the archbishops and bishops and the entire holy council heard what had happened because of their sins, that the sovereign had forsaken his realm, they were sorely grieved therefrom and much perplexed. And the boyars, okol'nichie, deti boiarskie, and all the officials, and the priests and monks, and a multitude of people . . . wept and spoke thus: "Alas! Woe! How we have sinned before God and angered our sovereign with many offenses against him, and turned his great mercy into wrath and fury! To whom shall we turn now, and who will have mercy on us, and who will deliver us from the onslaught of foreigners? How can sheep be without a shepherd? When the wolves behold sheep without a shepherd, the wolves ravish the sheep, and who will escape them? And we, likewise, how shall we be without a sovereign?" And they spoke many other similar words to Afanasii, metropolitan of all Russia, and to the entire holy council; and they not only said these things but also implored him with loud voices and much weeping to perform a noble deed, together with the archbishops and bishops and the holy council, and quench their weeping and wailing, and beseech the pious sovereign and tsar to have mercy, so that the sovereign tsar and grand prince would avert his wrath, show his mercy, and withdraw his displeasure, and not forsake his realm, but possess and rule his dominions at his sovereign pleasure; and as for the sovereign's evildoers who committed treasonable deeds, they are under the authority of God and the sovereign, and the sovereign shall will them life or death. . . . Likewise, the gosti, the merchants, and all the townspeople of the city of Moscow similarly petitioned Afanasii, metropolitan of all Russia, and the entire holy council, to petition the sovereign and entreat him to show them his mercy, and not to forsake his realm, and not to surrender them to be ravished by wolves, and, above all, to deliver them from the hands of the strong; and as for the sovereign's evildoers and traitors, they did not defend such men and would themselves destroy them. . . . On that same day, the third day of January, the metropolitan Afanasii sent Pimen, archbishop of Novgorod the Great and Pskov, and also Levkii, archimandrite of the [monastery dedicated to] the miracle of Saint Michael the Archangel [Chudov Monastery in Moscow], to the pious tsar and grand prince at the Aleksandrovskaia sloboda, to implore and petition the tsar and grand prince . . . to show his mercy and avert his wrath . . . and retain his sovereignty and possess and rule his dominions as he, the sovereign, pleases; and as for those who betray or do evil to him, the sovereign, and to his realm, he, the sovereign, shall will them life or death. . . . And all the boyars and okol'nichie, and the treasurers and dvoriane and many officials . . . and likewise the gosti and merchants and many of the common people, with much lamentation and weeping, set forth from the city of Moscow behind the archbishops and bishops, to petition and implore the tsar and grand prince for mercy. . . . And the tsar and grand prince was gracious to them and let them look upon him. And they petitioned him first about themselves, that the sovereign show them his mercy and avert his wrath from them. . . . They pleaded with him with many tears and supplications for all the Christian people. . . . And the tsar and grand prince yielded to the petition of the archbishops and bishops on these terms: that he would cast into disgrace those traitors who had betrayed him, the sovereign, or had disobeyed him, the sovereign, in any matter,

and would punish others and seize their possessions and property; and he would establish in his realm an oprichnina, and establish a separate court [dvor] for himself and for his entire household. And he ordered instituted for himself a separate group of boyars and okol'nichie and a majordomo [dvoretskii] and treasurers and secretaries and various officials, and dvoriane and deti boiarskie . . . and various court servants [dvorovye liudi] for all his household needs, and also a corps of musketeers [strel'tsy]. And for the expenses of his own household, and the households of his children, Tsarevich Ivan and Tsarevich Feodor, the tsar and grand prince ordered [the following] towns and volosti [to be included in the oprichnina]. . . . [Note: Over forty towns and volosti are enumerated, mainly in the central and northern regions of the state.] And for certain other volosti the sovereign instituted a tax in place of the former korm, so as to take all the revenues from these volosti for his sovereign household, and to bestow his bounty upon the boyars and dvoriane and all the sovereign's court servants who would be with him in the oprichnina; and if the revenues from these volosti and towns should not suffice for the sovereign household, other towns and volosti would be taken [into the oprichnina]. The sovereign would establish with him in the oprichnina princes, dvoriane, and court and provincial deti boiarskie [dvorovye i gorodovye], one thousand men in all, and give them pomest'ia in those towns [regions] that he had taken into the oprichnina; and he ordered those holders of pomest'ia and patrimonies who were not to be in the oprichnina to be removed from those towns [regions] and given lands in other towns [regions] instead, inasmuch as he had ordered the oprichnina to be set apart for himself. . . . As for the streets and slobody [in Moscow] that the sovereign took into the oprichnina, he ordered the boyars and dvoriane and all the officials whom he had taken into the oprichnina to dwell in those streets; and those whom he had not ordered to be in the oprichnina he ordered to be removed to other streets of the city. And he directed that his Muscovite state, and the army, the courts of law, the administration of justice, and all kinds of public [zemskie] matters, be governed and administered by those boyars whom he ordered to be in the *zemshchina:* Prince Ivan Dmitrievich Bel'skii and Prince Ivan Feodorovich Mstislavskii, and all the boyars; and the equerry [*koniushii*], the majordomo, the treasurers, secretaries, and all the officials were ordered to remain in their prikazy and to manage affairs as of old, and in important matters to consult the boyars; and should there be any news of war or important public matters, the boyars were to come with such matters to the sovereign, and the sovereign would order the disposition of these affairs together with the boyars. And for the expenses of his journey, the tsar and grand prince ordered one hundred thousand rubles to be taken from the zemshchina; and as for those boyars and voevody and officials who for their great treachery to the sovereign had incurred the death penalty, or had incurred disfavor, the sovereign would take their possessions and property for himself. And the archbishops, bishops, archimandrites, abbots, the entire holy council, the boyars, and the officials left all these matters to the tsar's will.

VII:12. THE PISKAREV CHRONICLE ON THE OPRICHNINA, 1564-1565

Another view of the inauguration of the oprichnina is given in the account of the so-called Piskarevskii letopisets, written about 1621-25 by a Muscovite whose name has not come down to us. Although evidently only a boy himself in the 1560s, he later had abundant access to highly placed participants in the events of those years.

Reference: *Materialy po istorii SSSR,* vol. 2 (Moscow: AN SSSR, 1955), p. 76. On the chronicler, see ibid., pp. 13-14 ff.

Concerning the oprichnina. That same year [1564], because of our sins, God allowed the tsar and grand prince of all Russia Ivan [IV] Vasil'evich to be seized with fury at all Orthodox Christians upon the advice of evil men: Vasilii Mikhailov Iur'ev and Aleksei Basmanov and others like them; and they established the oprichnina, dividing the land and the towns. They took some boyars, dvoriane, and deti boiarskie into the oprichnina, and ordered others to be in the zemshchina. They likewise divided the towns and removed many people from the towns, whom he [Ivan] took into the oprichnina, and from their patrimonies and pomest'ia of long standing. The tsar himself lived beyond the Neglinnaia [River] on Petrovka, and all the oprichniki walked and rode in black, with brooms in their quivers. And in the land there was hatred for the tsar among all the people, and they petitioned him and presented a signed petition concerning the oprichnina, [saying] that it ought not exist. And here evil men who hate what is good came to the fore: they began to tell slanderous tales to the grand prince against all those people, and some perished as a result of these words. They began to incline toward Prince Vladimir Andreevich [Staritskii, i.e. of Staritsa, a cousin of Ivan IV]. And then there was great woe.

VII:13. IVAN TIMOFEEV ON THE OPRICHNINA OF THE 1560s

Shortly after the end of the Time of Troubles, the government official (d'iak) Ivan Timofeev looked back half a century and rendered a verdict, of which this excerpt gives the flavor, concerning Ivan's oprichnina.

Reference: V. P. Adrianova-Peretts, ed., *Vremennik Ivana Timofeeva* (Moscow: AN SSSR, 1951), pp. 11-12.

Conceiving a plan [filled with] exceeding fury against his slaves, he [Ivan IV] came to hate all the towns of his land; and in his wrath he divided a single people into two halves and subjected them to a kind of double allegiance, making some his own and estranging others, repulsing them like aliens [so that] many towns henceforth dared not even call themselves tsar's towns, because of his prohibition; and he split all the land of his realm into two halves, as with an ax. Thus he created consternation among all the people; and for a time he set up in his stead and in his presence, passing over the son of his blood [Tsarevich Ivan], another faithful tsar [Simeon Bekbulatovich] from among the Ishmaelites [Tatars]; and he humbled himself servilely and retained for himself a small part of his possessions, but soon he took everything back, thus making sport of God's people. He killed many loyal magnates of his realm, and he banished others into lands of foreign faith, away from his person, and in their stead he bestowed his favors upon newcomers from neighboring countries, showering them with costly gifts and admitting some of them into his secret thoughts.

VII:14. THE ALEKSANDR NEVSKII MONASTERY CHRONICLE ON THE ZEMSKII SOBOR OF 1566

In 1566 Ivan assembled a zemskii sobor—the first whose approximate composition is known—to decide whether or not to call a halt to the Livonian War. A manuscript of the 1600s belonging to the Aleksandr Nevskii Monastery tells the story.
Reference: *RIB*, vol. 3, cols. 277-278.

That same year [1566], on the twenty-eighth day of the month of June, the tsar and grand prince of all Russia Ivan Vasil'evich spoke with [his cousin] Prince Vladimir Andreevich [Staritskii]; and with those who pray for him [*bogomol'tsy*], the archbishops and bishops . . . the archimandrites and abbots, and the entire holy council; and with all his boyars and government officials [prikaznye liudi]; and also with the princes, deti boiarskie, and service men; and also with the gosti [merchants of the highest rank], and merchants [*kuptsy*], and all the trading men: [saying] that the Lithuanian envoys . . . do not wish to conclude an armistice without [deciding on] the Livonian lands and want [a settlement of] the Livonian lands to be written into the armistice agreement [as follows]: the towns [now] held by the tsar and grand prince shall be assigned to the tsar and grand prince, and the German [Livonian] towns held by the [Polish] king shall be assigned to the king. But if these German towns shall be assigned to the king by the armistice agreement, how can these towns be claimed in the future? Should we make claim to them now? Prince Vladimir Andreevich, the archbishops and bishops, and all the tsar and grand prince's boyars and officials, princes, deti boiarskie, gòsti, merchants, and trading men jointly resolved that the tsar and grand prince should not yield the Livonian towns to the Polish king but should take a firm stand upon this; and the archbishops and bishops, and the archimandrites and abbots put their signatures to the written resolution.

And the boyars, officials, princes, deti boiarskie, gosti, and merchants swore an oath upon the cross before the sovereign to what they had said.

VII:15. A STATEMENT OF THE ZEMSKII SOBOR, JULY 2, 1566

Another document concerning the sobor of 1566 is a "Statement of clergymen, boyars, okol'nichie, d'iaki, dvoriane, deti boiarskie, gosti, and merchants, made at the bidding of the sovereign tsar Ioann Vasilievich . . ." This statement, dated July 2, 1566, was signed by thirty clerics and twenty-seven lay members of the sobor.
Reference: Iu. V. Got'e, ed., *Akty otnosiashchiesia k istorii zemskikh soborov, Pamiatniki russkoi istorii*, vol. 3 (Moscow: N. N. Klochkov, 1909), pp. 4, 6-7.

Upon learning this day about the envoys' speeches, all the sovereign's boyars, okol'nichie, and officials spoke thus: "God disposes and so does our sovereign, as God instructs him; but as we deem it, how can the sovereign conclude an armistice with the [Polish] king and cede the German [Livonian] towns to the king, [thereby] placing Polotsk under threat of siege which it would be unable to withstand? And if the lands across the river [Dvina] from Polotsk are given up, then the suburbs [posady] of Polotsk on the other bank of the river will fall to the king; and on this side of the Dvina the Polotsk district [*povet*] is a poor one, and all the best lands of the Polotsk district are on the other side of the Dvina. Moreover, during the armistice years the Lithuanians will erect a stronghold beyond the Dvina, and when the armistice comes to an end, then Polotsk perforce will be unable to hold out. And in the Livonian towns the king will find large reinforcements, and then even Pskov will be in peril, let alone Iur'ev and its companion towns. Instead of allowing the king to reinforce his army, our sovereign should refuse to make peace with him, because of his boundless arrogance, and should pray for God's mercy. . . . In view of all these sovereign matters, and the sovereign's rightful cause, and all his intentions for the good of Christendom, and the [Polish] king's arrogance, we deem it unfitting to deal with the king; and all of us are ready to lay down our lives for the sovereign, seeing the king's arrogance, and to place our trust in God. God does not love the haughty; and all this is in the hands of God and our sovereign tsar and grand prince; but this is as we see it, and we express our thoughts to our sovereign."

. . .

[The dvoriane of the first rank spoke thus:] "We have conferred, and this is our thought: God disposes and so does our sovereign; whatever pleases the sovereign, so be it for us his slaves. But this is as we see it: if the king will not yield to our sovereign the Polotsk districts [povety] on the other bank of the Dvina, and if only fifteen versty up the Dvina River from Polotsk are retained, and five versty down the Dvina River, there can be no armistice. . . . God disposes and so does our sovereign. But this is as we, his slaves, see it: it behooves our sovereign to stand firm for all this; and we, his slaves, have the duty to serve

the sovereign and his rightful cause to the death."

[And the dvoriane and deti boiarskie of the second rank spoke thus:] "We have conferred on the Lithuanian affair at the sovereign's instruction, and this is our thought: God disposes and so does our sovereign; he performs his sovereign task at his sovereign will and pleasure, and as he thinks fit; and we, the service men, are the sovereign's slaves, and we are ready to do as he commands us. Through the sovereign's efforts God has entrusted the Lithuanian town of Polotsk to him; and thereafter God also entrusted Ozerishche to our sovereign; and how can these towns be [held] without their districts [uezdy]? And we, his slaves, are ready to lay down our lives for the sovereign's cause, and we are ready to die for the sovereign and for his children, for our lords the tsarevichi, and for their patrimonies. And our sovereign tsar and grand prince is in the right before the [Polish] king."

VII:16. HEINRICH VON STADEN ON MUSCOVY, 1566-1576

Heinrich von Staden (b. ca. 1545), an adventurer from Westphalia, lived for nearly twelve years (1564-76) in the Muscovite state. In the late 1560s and early 1570s he was one of Ivan's middle-rank oprichniki. Here are some excerpts from his colorful memoirs. Staden apparently exaggerates the importance of the role he played, but his report has exceptional value for historians because, unlike other accounts, it gives a participant's view of the oprichnina. When his work was finally discovered and published in the early decades of this century, it helped to stimulate a reinterpretation of Ivan's policies. (For other foreigner's reports on the sixteenth century, see Section B, below.)

Reference: Heinrich von Staden, *Aufzeichnungen ueber den Moskauer Staat,* ed. Fritz Epstein (Hamburg: Friederichsen, de Gruyter, 1930), pp. 22, 43, 77, 103-05, 189, 195-96, 202-03. Recently the whole of Staden's account has been translated into English: Heinrich von Staden, *The Land and Government of Muscovy, a 16th-century Account,* trans. and ed. Thomas Esper (Stanford: Stanford University Press, 1967).

The grand prince sent an order into the zemshchina: "Sudite pravedno, nashi vinovaty ne byli by," which means, "Judge fairly, so that our men should not be guilty." And the men of the zemshchina lost heart because of this order. For now anyone from the oprichnina could accuse any zemshchina man of owing him a certain sum of money. And even if the oprichnik had never before known or seen the zemshchina man accused by him, the latter would have to make payment forthwith, or else he would be beaten daily in the marketplace with clubs and cudgels until he paid. No one here was spared, neither cleric nor layman. The oprichniki

used all kinds of machinations, impossible even to describe, against the men of the zemshchina, all in order to obtain money and goods from them.

. . .

According to their oath the oprichniki could not exchange a word with those in the zemshchina, nor intermarry with them. And if any oprichnik had a father or mother in the zemshchina, he was never allowed to visit them.

The grand prince divided the city of Moscow into two parts: he took a trifling part for himself, and left the town and the castle [the Kremlin] to the zemshchina. And whenever the grand prince would take any town or district of the land into the oprichnina, he would also take over one or two streets in the slobody surrounding [Moscow] into his oprichnina. In this way the men of the zemshchina, both boyars and common folk, decreased in number, and the grand prince gained strength in the oprichnina and became more powerful.

· · ·

[Soon after the raid of the Crimean khan Devlet-Girei and his burning of Moscow in 1571:]

This brought the oprichnina to an end, and no one was allowed to say a single word about the oprichnina, under threat of the following punishment: the culprit would be stripped naked to the waist and lashed with whips in the marketplace. All those in the oprichnina had to restore to the zemshchina men their patrimonial estates; and all the zemshchina men who were still alive got back their patrimonial estates, which had been plundered and laid waste by the oprichniki.

· · ·

When anyone arrives at the Russian border, whoever he be, unless he be a Jew, he is forthwith questioned about his purpose in coming. If he then says that he wishes to serve the Russian grand prince, he is questioned again about various matters. Notes are secretly taken about his words and statements, and are sealed; and he himself is forthwith dispatched to Moscow on post horses, escorted by a nobleman, to arrive there within six or seven days. In Moscow he is again secretly and most thoroughly questioned on all matters. The better his answers accord with what he had said at the border, the more he is trusted and favored. No heed is given to his person, his clothes, or his noble birth; but the closest attention is given to all that he says. On the very day of his arrival at the border, he is given money for provisions until [he reaches] Moscow.

On the day of his arrival in Moscow he is given a *kormovaia pamiat'*, a voucher for a food allowance. . . . He is further given a voucher to present at the Office of Landed Estates [i.e. the Pomestnyi Prikaz], showing that the grand prince has granted him one, two, three, or four hundred chetverti as a pomest'e. Then the foreigner must himself look about the country or make inquiries to

find out where any nobleman has died without heirs or has been killed in battle. In such cases their women [widows] receive something for their subsistence. Thereupon the foreigner's allotment is entered in the books according to his voucher. . . . He is also given a sum of money to start with, and also clothing, sheets, silken garments, a number of gold coins, [and] long coats lined with miniver or sable. . . .

Before Moscow burned down, the grand prince used to give the foreigner a house in Moscow. At present he receives a site forty *sazheni* [one sazhen' equals seven feet] in length and width in the Bolvanovka [sloboda] outside the town, provided he is a mounted German soldier; foot soldiers are deemed of no account. A fence around the site is erected for him. Thereafter the foreigner may build upon it as he pleases. If he then petitions the grand prince [for assistance] in building a house, he will be given something. In that house he is free to keep a tavern. This is forbidden to [the grand prince's] own people, who consider it very shameful. In addition he also receives an annual wage. And he is exempt from customs duties throughout the land, and so are all his servants.

· · ·

Now it is a great joy to the noble lords in Moscow whenever a foreigner lets himself be baptized and embraces their faith. They zealously assist him in this, inasmuch as they regard themselves as the holiest Christians on earth. They personally serve as godfathers, give [the newly baptized foreigner] christening gifts and gold coins from the treasury, and promote him in every way.

· · ·

I rode forth with the grand prince, myself and two others, with a single horse; I came back with 49, of which 22 were pulling sleighs filled with goods. When the grand prince came to the town of Staritsa a muster was held so that he might see who had held out and remained with him. Then the grand prince said to me: "Henceforth you shall be called Andrei Vladimirovich." The particle "vich" signifies princely and noble rank. Henceforth I was treated as an equal of the princes and boyars; with these words the grand prince made clear to me that this meant knighthood. In this country a foreigner occupies the best position, provided he knows how to conduct himself in accordance with the customs of the land for a certain length of time.

The grand prince betook himself to the Aleksandrovskaia sloboda, and here he had a church built. I did not go with him but returned to Moscow. By this time all the princes and boyars who dwelt in the oprichnina courts had lost heart. Each of them feared for himself, knowing his own treachery.

· · ·

When the game was over, all the patrimonial estates were given back to the men of the zemshchina, on the ground that they had offered resistance to the Crimean tsar [khan].

Also the grand prince could no longer dispense with them. Those in the oprichnina were to receive other pomest'ia in their stead. In this way I was deprived of my patrimonies and pomest'ia and was no longer listed in the register of the princes and boyars, the reason being that all the Germans were entered together in a single register. The Germans thought that I was still on the register of the princes and boyars of the oprichnina. The princes and boyars thought that I was registered with the other Germans. In this way I was forgotten in the registers.

VII:17. THE THIRD NOVGORODIAN CHRONICLE ON IVAN IV'S RAVAGE OF NOVGOROD, 1570

One of Ivan's more striking aberrations was recorded as follows by an understandably partisan source.

Reference: Arkheograficheskaia Komissiia, ed., *Novgorodskie letopisi (Novgorodskaia vtoraia i Novgorodskaia tret'ia letopisi)* (St. Petersburg, 1879), pp. 338, 339, 342-43.

On the coming of the tsar and grand prince Ivan Vasil'evich, autocrat of all Russia; how he punished Novgorod the Great, through what is called the oprichnina and through devastation.

. . . At the prompting of evil-minded apostates and wicked men, malicious, spiteful, and treacherous tales were poured into the mind and ears of the tsar about Pimen, the archbishop of Novgorod, and his episcopal boyars, and the best men and the most notable among the townspeople: that they intended to surrender Novgorod to the foreigners; and because of these false tales the tsar's heart was embittered with wrath and fury against his patrimony of Novgorod the Great, and against all the people dwelling in Novgorod the Great and in the neighborhood of Novgorod.

. . . The sovereign tsar and grand prince of all Russia Ivan Vasil'evich came to Novgorod the Great, and with him [came] his son Ivan Ivanovich, and a large army of princes, boyars, and deti boiarskie, and a great many other soldiers; and 1,500 strel'tsy from Moscow were also with the sovereign. . . . And [the tsar] commanded [the Novgorodians] to be tortured before him cruelly and fiercely and inhumanly, with many kinds of tortures; and after many unspeakably cruel torments, the tsar ordered their bodies to be scorched, tortured by a fire made from some compound; and he ordered his deti boiarskie to tie those

tortured people by their hands, feet, and head to the rear of horse-drawn sleighs, one man to each, and to have them swiftly dragged behind those sleighs to the great Volkhov bridge; and he ordered them to be hurled from the bridge into the river Volkhov. And the sovereign ordered their wives and their children of all ages, male and female, even suckling infants, to be brought to the Volkhov bridge and taken up to a tower built for that purpose, with their hands and feet tied behind them, and the infants tied to their mothers; and the tsar ordered them to be hurled from the great height into the river Volkhov. Meanwhile other deti boiarskie and soldiers were cruising on the Volkhov in small boats, armed with weapons, pitchforks, lances, axes, and hooks; and whenever anyone came up to the surface of the water, they would seize him with the hooks, and pierce him with their lances and pitchforks, and hack at him with their axes, and plunge him down into the depths without mercy, delivering him to a cruel death. Such were the distress and suffering that resulted from the tsar's indomitable fury, and still more from the wrath of God, because of our sins; inasmuch as for five weeks and more, day after day, up to 1,000 people of all ages were thrown into the water daily, and on some days up to 1,500, and it was a fortunate day when [only] 500 or 600 people were hurled into the river. When it was over, the sovereign with his soldiers began to visit the monasteries in the neighborhood of Novgorod the Great, and [the tsar] gave orders to plunder the treasuries of the churches and monasteries, and the [monastic] cells, the service buildings, and the storehouses of every kind; he ordered the unthreshed grain gathered in the barns or stacked in the fields to be burned; and he ordered all the livestock, horses, and cows to be slaughtered. Then he returned to the city with a large army, and gave orders to loot the merchandise in the shops of the tradespeople in all the market-places, and to tear down the shops and raze them to the ground. Then the sovereign with all his soldiers rode all around the city and its posady [suburbs], and he gave orders to loot the possessions of all the townspeople, in their houses, in church basements [in Novgorod church basements were often used for storing merchants' goods], and in their chambers; and he ordered the men and women themselves to be beaten without mercy and without respite, and their households to be plundered, and the windows and doors of their houses to be smashed.

VII:18. IVAN IV AND ENGLAND: A LETTER TO KING EDWARD VI, FEBRUARY 1554

In response to Richard Chancellor's visit (see Section B, below), Ivan IV sent this letter to the king of England. In reproducing the English translation, Samuel Purchas adds: "This Letter was written in the Moscovian Tongue, in Letter much like to the Greeke Letters, very faire written in Paper, with a broad Seale hanging at the same, sealed in Paper upon Waxe. This Seale was much like the Broad Seale of England, having on the one side the Image of a man on Horse-backe in complete Harnesse fighting with a Dragon. Under this Letter was another Paper written in the Dutch Tongue, which was the Interpretation of the other written in the Moscovian Letters." Since, unbeknownst to Ivan, Edward VI had already died, the letter was in fact received by Mary Tudor.

    Reference: Samuel Purchas, ed., *Hakluytus Posthumus or Purchas His Pilgrimes,* vol. 11 (Glasgow: J. MacLehose and Sons, 1906), pp. 621-23.

The Almightie power of God, and the incomprehensible holy Trinitie, rightfull Christian Beliefe, &c. We great Duke Ivan Vasilivich, by the Grace of God great Lord and Emperour of all Russia, great Duke of Volodemer, Mosco, and Novograd, King of Kazan, King of Astracan, Lord of Plesko, and great Duke of Smolensko, of Twerria, Joughoria, Permia, Vadska, Bulghoria, and others, Lord and great Duke of Novograd in the Low Countrey, of Chernigo, Rezan, Polotskoy, Rostove, Yaruslaveley, Bealozera, Liefland, Oudoria, Obdoria, and Condensa, Commander of all Siberia, and of the North parts, and Lord of many other Countries, greeting. Before all, right, great and worthy of honour Edward King of England, &c. according to our most heartie and good zeale, with good intent and friendly desire, and according to our holy Christian Faith, and great Governance, and being in the light of great understanding, our Answere by this our Honourable Writing unto your Kingly Governance, at the request of your faithfull Servant Richard Chancelour, with his company, as they shall let you wisely know is this. In the strength of the twentieth yeare of our Governance, be it knowne, that at our Sea-coasts arrived a ship, with one Richard, and his company, and said, that he was desirous to come into our Dominions, and according to his request, hath seene our Majestie, and our eyes: and hath declared unto us your Majesties desire, as that wee should grant unto your Subjects, to goe and come, and in our Dominions, and among our Subjects, to frequent free Marts, with all sorts of Merchandizes, and upon the same to have wares for their returne. And they have also delivered us your Letters which declare the same request. And hereupon wee have given order, that wheresoever your faithfull Servant Hugh Willoughbie, land or touch in our Dominions, to be well entertayned, who as yet is not arrived as your Servant Richard can declare.

    And we with Christian beliefe and faithfulnesse, and according to your Honourable request, and my Honourable commandement will not leave it undone: and are furthermore willing that you send unto us your ships and Vessels, when and as often as they may have passage, with good assurance on our part to see them harmlesse. And if you send one of your Majesties counsell to treat with us whereby your Countrey Merchants may with all kindes of Wares, and where they will make their Market in our Dominions, they shall have their free Mart with all free Liberties through my whole Dominions, with all kinde of Wares, to come and goe at their pleasure, without any let, damage, or impediment, according to this our Letter, our Word and our Seale which wee have commanded to be under sealed. Written in our Dominion, in our Citie and our Palace in the Castle of Mosco, in the yeare 7060 [evidently a copyist's error; should be 7062, i.e. 1554] the second Moneth of Februarie.

VII:19. IVAN IV'S LETTER TO QUEEN ELIZABETH, OCTOBER 24, 1570

From the visit of Richard Chancellor in 1553 until the end of his life, Ivan IV negotiated frequently with the English crown. His correspondence (which has been assembled in a sizable tome) reveals him at times uncomprehending and abusive toward the British, as in this excerpt from a letter he sent to Queen Elizabeth on October 24, 1570. This excerpt also reflects a basic difference in their aims—Ivan IV wanted to conclude with England not only a commercial treaty but a political alliance as well, while the English interest in Russia was essentially commercial.

Reference: Iurii Tolstoi, ed., *Pervye sorok let snoshenii mezhdu Rossiei i Angliei 1553-1593* (St. Petersburg, 1875), p. 114.

You have sent us our ambassadour backe, but you have not sent your ambassadour to us, and you have not ended our affaires accordinge as your ambassadour did agree uppon, and your letters be not thereto agreeable, for such weightie affaires be not ended without *some golde* [mistranslated: the original means "without confirmation by oath"] or without ambassadours, but you have set aside those great affaires, and your councell doth deale with our ambassadour about marchants affaires; and your marchants sir W-m Garrard and sir W-m Chester did rule all busines. And wee had thought that you had been ruler over your lande and had sought honor to your self and profitt to your country, and therefore wee did pretend those weightie affaires betweene you and us; But now wee perceive that there be other men that doe rule, and not men but bowers and merchaunts the which seeke not the wealth and honour of our maiesties, but they seeke there owne profitt of marchauntdize: and you flowe in your maydenlie estate like a [common] maide.

VII:20. IVAN IV'S INSTRUCTIONS TO PISEMSKII, 1582

In addition to seeking an arrangement that would provide him with asylum in England, Ivan in his early fifties (and after at least five wives) had other adventurous notions, as illustrated in this excerpt from his instructions to Fedor Andreevich Pisemskii, whom he sent to speak with the British queen in 1582. After some delay, Elizabeth tactfully sent word back through Sir Jerome Bowes that the lady in question "is fallen into such an indisposition of health as that there is small hope she ever will recover such strength as is requisite . . ." and told Bowes to "use all the best perswasions you can to disswade him from that purpose . . ."

Reference: *SIRIO*, 38:5-6. For Elizabeth's reply, see Tolstoi, *Pervye sorok let*, p. 204.

And if the queen should send her counselors to Fedor [Pisemskii] or order [him] to speak before her with only a few counselors present, then Fedor shall say this, and speak these words:

"The great sovereign tsar and grand prince has ordered [me] to tell this to you, his beloved sister, Elizabeth the queen: We have questioned Doctor Roman, who came from your land, whether in your land there is a royal daughter, or a royal widow, or any woman or maiden of royal descent, and Doctor Roman told us that the appanage prince [*udel'nyi kniaz'*] [Lord] Huntington has a daughter, Mary Hastings, who is your niece, Elizabeth the queen. And you, our beloved sister Elizabeth the queen, should order that your niece be shown to our envoy Fedor and should have her portrait made and sent to us on canvas and frame, so that [we can see] whether she is suitable for our sovereign rank; and we shall arrange this matter with you, O Queen, as is fitting. . . ."

And when Queen Elizabeth orders that girl to be shown to Fedor, Fedor shall examine her thoroughly—what her height is, how tall, and what her complexion is, fair or swarthy—and after drawing her portrait and image on canvas and frame they shall give it to Fedor; and Fedor shall take from them her portrait and image on canvas and frame and bring it to the sovereign. And Fedor shall ask the counselors these things about her: what appanage prince is her father, and how old she is, and how she is related to Elizabeth the queen; and he shall determine in writing from Queen Elizabeth or from her counselors how she is related to her, and whose daughter she is, of what appanage prince, and how old she is, and whether she has any brothers or sisters. After obtaining this [information] in writing [Fedor] shall in addition make secret inquiries about her himself; and Fedor shall write down in his own hand whatever he learns.

And if Queen Elizabeth or her counselors should say to Fedor: "Why has the sovereign ordered you to look at this girl and ordered her portrait to be drawn and sent to him?" Fedor shall say: "Our sovereign has sent me

that I might see this girl and has ordered me to obtain her portrait and image from you and bring it to him; and after seeing whether she is suitable for the sovereign, the sovereign wishes to marry her."

. . .

And if they say this to Fedor: "You speak of such a great matter, but your sovereign is married, so how can such a thing take place?" Fedor shall say: "Our sovereign sent [envoys] to many states to find a bride of equal rank for himself, the great sovereign, but such a thing did not come to pass; and the sovereign took to himself a boyar's daughter from his own state, who was not of equal rank. And if the queen's niece shall be well-born and worthy of this great matter, then our sovereign tsar and grand prince shall put his [wife] away and betroth the queen's niece."

VII:21. SIBERIA: THE ESIPOV CHRONICLE ON THE ORIGIN OF ERMAK'S EXPEDITION, 1581

The Esipov Chronicle was compiled in 1636 in the Siberian town of Tobol'sk. It is designated by the name of its compiler, Savva Esipov, a clerk of the archbishop of Tobol'sk. Esipov's story of the conquest of Siberia, based on previous records, emphasizes the importance of the spread of Christianity there. The following excerpt deals with the first part of the story. (See also the grant to the Stroganoys, earlier in this section.)

Reference: Arkheograficheskaia Komissiia, ed., *Sibirskie letopisi* (St. Petersburg: I. N. Skorokhodov, 1907), p. 263.

In the reign of the tsar, sovereign, and grand prince of all Russia Ivan Vasil'evich there were many Cossacks on the Volga River and on the Don, and by command of the tsar they were greatly oppressed and driven from the Don and from the Volga; when captured they were cast into dungeons, while others were put to death; and because of this the Cossacks—the Volga ataman Ermak, son of Timofei, and

his 9 ataman companions, together with 540 Cossacks—came to Siberia in the year 7089 [1581]. Other chroniclers relate that the Stroganovs summoned them from the Volga and gave them possessions and fine clothing and weapons, firearms and field cannon, and gave them 300 of their own men, Germans and Lithuanians, and thus they went to Siberia.

VII:22. THE STROGANOV CHRONICLE ON ERMAK'S CONQUEST OF SIBERIA, 1581-1583

Ermak's expedition is described as follows by the Stroganov Chronicle, compiled in Perm' sometime in the 1600s. Since under the old church calendar the Russians began their new year on September 1, the date in the first line is still in the year 1581. (For subsequent developments in Siberia, see Chapter VIII.)

Reference: Arkheograficheskaia Komissiia, *Sibirskie letopisi*, pp. 10, 16-17, 31.

On the first day of September in the year 7090 [1581] . . . Semen, Maksim, and Nikita Stroganov sent the Volga atamans and Cossacks, Ermak Timofeev and his companions, into Siberia against the Siberian sultan, and with them assembled their soldiers from the forts, Lithuanians, Germans, Tatars, and Russians, 300 good and brave and warlike soldiers, and

[the Stroganovs] dispatched them together with the Volga atamans and Cossacks, forming a company of 840 brave and warlike men.

. . .

The soldiers fearlessly entered that land of Siberia and seized many Tatar forts and settlements [*ulus*] downstream along the Tura [River], and reached the Tavda River in their hardihood, and captured Tatars at the mouth of that river. . . . And . . . Tsar Kuchum heard of the coming of Russian soldiers and of their hardihood and bravery; and he was further informed [by a Tatar prisoner released by the Russians] how strong the Russian soldiers were: when they shoot from their bows [said the Tatar] flames burst out, and much smoke belches forth with a loud roar, like thunder in the heavens, and the arrows that emerge from them cannot be seen; they sting us [the Tatars] with wounds and strike deadly blows, and we cannot defend ourselves against them with any of our battle equipment; our wooden mail and armor plate and coats of mail and breastplates do not hold; they penetrate everything all the way through. Tsar Kuchum was grieved at this, and very much saddened, and was again in great perplexity.

· · ·

In the second summer after the taking of the Siberian land the sovereign tsar and grand prince of all Russia Ivan Vasil'evich sent the voevody Prince Semen Bolkhovskii and Ivan Glukhov from Moscow to Siberia with a great number of soldiers; the atamans and Cossacks met them with great honor; the sovereign's voevody declared that the sovereign had bestowed his favor upon them in accordance with the sovereign's list [*rospis'*], and [the voevody] came to the city of Sibir' and gave them [the tsar's gifts]; they, the atamans and Cossacks, gave the sovereign's voevody costly sables, foxes, and various furs as gifts, each one [giving] as much as he could, and they were filled with joy and rejoiced, thanking God, seeing that the sovereign's favor had been granted them, that the sovereign had bestowed his favor upon them for their service as atamans and Cossacks.

VII:23. THE ELECTORAL CHARTER OF TSAR BORIS GODUNOV, 1598

The zemskii sobor that endorsed Boris Godunov for the vacant throne in 1598 also approved an electoral charter, perhaps written by Patriarch Job, designed to cope with the unusual situation.
Reference: Got'e, *Akty . . . zemskikh soborov*, pp. 12-15.

Our sovereign, the tsar and grand prince Ivan [IV] Vasil'evich of all Russia . . . blessed his son to be tsar and entrusted him, the sovereign tsar and grand prince Feodor Ivanovich, autocrat of all Russia, to the kinsman by marriage of the tsar's family, the close friend, servant, and equerry boyar [*koniushii boiarin*] Boris Feodorovich [Godunov], who from the very first had been chosen, cherished, and foreordained by God many years before, and said: "To you I entrust in God's name this my son; look after his welfare to the end of his days; and upon his demise I bequeath this tsardom to thee." Likewise the pious great sovereign tsar and grand prince Feodor Ivanovich of all Russia . . . at the command of his father and by virtue of his own friendship, entrusted his realm to that same Boris Feodorovich, our great sovereign. And so by God's favor, by the providence of the Almighty God, the joint blessing of both tsars rests upon this, our great sovereign, Boris Feodorovich. . . . The patriarch . . . summoned to him his sons, the most holy metropolitans, the archbishops, the bishops, the entire holy council, the boyars and dvoriane, all the Christ-loving host [i.e. the army], and all Orthodox Christians; and he conferred with them about the election

of a sovereign tsar; and likewise he submitted to them the passages he had selected from the Holy Scriptures [concerning the election of a ruler]. And they all, as with a single voice, clamored loudly and at great length: "We want Boris Feodorovich to be tsar; there is no one save him; God himself has selected him; for upon him rests the blessing of two tsars, for the tsar's heart is in God's hands. . . ." And upon hearing this unalterable unanimous accord of the entire holy council, the boyars, the dvoriane, and all the multitude of the people, the most holy patriarch rejoiced in his soul and said: "Blessed be God who willed this! As it pleases the Lord, so it shall be; for the voice of the people is the voice of God." And together with them all he laid down a firm resolution that "unanimously, with God's help, we have elected a sovereign and autocrat of the tsardom and grand principality of Moscow and of all the dominions of the Russian realm, the brother-in-law, servant and equerry boyar of the great sovereign tsar and grand prince Feodor Ivanovich of all Russia, the guardian of the great tsardoms of Kazan' and Astrakhan', the firm, just, and merciful regent Boris Feodorovich, kinsman by marriage of the tsar's line, and the conqueror of the proud, boastful, and violently invading Crimean tsar [khan], . . . whose supremely victorious arm is feared by the Latin [Catholic] peoples and by all the Moslem tribes. . . . And in accordance with this election we shall serve him, our sovereign, the tsar and grand prince Boris Feodorovich, autocrat of all Russia, faithfully and honestly, without any deceit, and [likewise] his tsaritsa, the grand princess Maria Grigor'evna, and their sovereign children, Tsarevich Feodor Borisovich and Tsarevna Aksin'ia Borisovna, and whatever [children] God may grant them, the sovereigns, in the future; and we shall be obedient to their sovereign will in everything, and wish well to them, our sovereigns, with honesty, and be ready to lay down our lives for them, the sovereigns, against their enemies, and not desire, or seek, or consider, or conceive of any other sovereign in place of them, our sovereigns, in any manner or with any deceit; and to this we pledge our souls to them, our sovereigns, and swear upon the cross, all of us, great and small. And therefore all of us, the patriarch, the metropolitans, the archbishops, the bishops, and the entire holy council, and the boyars and okol'nichie, and all the tsar's council [sinklit], and the voevody, dvoriane, deti boiarskie, and the entire land have convened and, by the grace given to us from the Holy Ghost, have installed the worthy tsar and grand prince Boris Feodorovich, autocrat of all Russia, sovereign of the Russian land. . . ."

And those who lovingly read the Holy Scriptures will find among the kings holding the royal scepter and invested with the purple of sovereignty many who were not of royal lineage, but were commoners and not highborn, and yet ruled their kingdoms according to God's will, honorably and justly. God does not consider the noble birth of those who love him but selects those who maintain the true faith and observe the divine commandments; he esteems a pious soul, he accepts the worthy and casts forth the unworthy. . . .

Let no one say: "We must withdraw from them, for they have installed a tsar themselves." Let this not be so, let them not withdraw; for he who utters such words is foolish and accursed.

B. OTHER DEVELOPMENTS

VII:24. JOSEPH OF VOLOKOLAMSK ON CHURCH PROPERTY, CA. 1503

Joseph Sanin (b. ca. 1440, d. 1515), prior of the monastery at Volokolamsk, was an influential figure during the last years under Ivan III and the first decade under Vasilii III. These short excerpts from one of his treatises convey the gist of Joseph's stand on church property as opposed to the position of the "nonpossessors," such as Nil Maikov of the Sora Hermitage or Vassian Patrikeev, who attacked monastic wealth and participation in secular affairs (see also Chapter VI, Section B).

Reference: Vasilii N. Malinin, *Starets Eleazarova monastyria Filofei i ego poslaniia* (Kiev: Tipografiia Kievo-Pecherskoi Uspenskoi Lavry, 1901), app., pp. 128–29.

God's holy churches and monasteries must not suffer injury or violence, and their lands and belongings must not be taken away. . . . For all church and monastery [property], as well as the fruits of the monks' labor, are dedicated to God and are spent only on the poor, the wanderers, on the [ransom of] prisoners, and so on, and on the most essential needs of the churches, the monasteries, and the monks.

. . . He who spends church property otherwise than on the poor, the beggars, and the prisoners or on essential monastery needs is a sacrilegious person, and he who wants to take away anything that belongs to a monastery is an offender, and the holy regulations curse him.

VII:25. A PETITION OF JOSEPH OF VOLOKOLAMSK ON HERESY, CA. 1510

This is a portion of one of Joseph's eloquent and generally successful demands that the secular power help suppress the "heretics," especially the Judaisers, who bore some resemblance to the Protestants of western Europe.

Reference: N. A. Kazakova and Ia. S. Lur'e, *Antifeodal'nye ereticheskie dvizheniia na Rusi XIV-nachala XVI veka* (Moscow: AN SSSR, 1955), app., pp. 519-20. See also I. P. Eremin, ed., *Poslaniia Iosifa Volotskogo* (Moscow: AN SSSR, 1959).

Your supplicant, the sinful monk Iosif, together with the priests and with the brethren [monks] jointly, all tearfully petition the sovereign Vasilii Ivanovich, grand prince of all Russia.

For the love of God and the Virgin Mother, vouchsafe to look after and protect the divine churches and the Orthodox Christian faith and us, your wretched supplicants; for you, Sire, have been elevated by the almighty right hand of God to be autocrat and sovereign of all Russia. For Almighty God has spoken through the prophet: "Truly have I elevated you, tsar, and taken you by the hand and strengthened you." Hear, therefore, tsars and princes, and know that your power is given to you from God. For God has chosen you to take his place on earth, has raised you upon his throne, has seated you, and has given you power of life and death. It befits you, Orthodox sovereigns, tsars, and princes,

who have been granted dominion over the human race by God's command, to be solicitous not only of your own [family] and to order not only your own life but also to protect all that you possess from storms and to keep his flock unharmed by wolves; you should fear the sickle of heaven and not give free rein to evildoers who, I say, are foul and impious heretics, destroying the soul together with the body.

. . .

And now if you, Sire, do not exert yourself and make efforts on this account, if you do not overcome the foul heretics [and] their dark heretical teachings—then, Sire, all Orthodox Christianity shall perish from these heretical teachings, as perished many former realms: the great Ethiopian realm, and the Armenian, and the Roman [realm], which lived for many years in the Orthodox Christian faith [and yet] perished in this manner.

VII:26. JOSEPH OF VOLOKOLAMSK ON OBEDIENCE TO SECULAR RULERS, CA. 1515

Less well-known than Joseph's views on church property (see above) are his teachings concerning obedience to secular rulers. These excerpts are from a work he composed in stages during the period ca. 1493-1515, attacking the heresy of the Judaisers. After his death the work came to be known as "The Enlightener" (Prosvetitel').

Reference: Iosif Sanin (Volotskii), *Prosvetitel' ili oblichenie eresi zhidovstvuiushchikh* (Kazan', 1855), pp. 323, 324-25.

It is fitting to respect and to obey the tsar, the prince, or other [secular] rulers, because it is God's will that we should obey and submit to the rulers; for they are concerned about us and take care of us. . . . [But] it is fitting to serve the [secular] rulers with [our] body, not with [our] soul, and to render them royal honors, but not divine ones, as the Lord says: "Render therefore unto Caesar the things that are Caesar's, and unto God the things that are God's" (Matthew 22:21). If you respect and obey [the secular ruler] in such a way, it will not do any harm to your

soul, because in such a manner you will learn to fear God; for the tsar is God's servant when he benefits the people or punishes [the guilty]. But if the tsar dominates the people and if he himself is dominated by wicked passions and sins—avariciousness, anger, falsity, arrogance, fury, and, the worst of all, unbelief and blasphemy—such a tsar is not a servant of God but a servant of the Devil—not a tsar, but a tyrant [*muchitel'*]. . . . And you must not obey such a tsar or a prince who inclines you to unbelief and falsity, even if he torments you and threatens you with death.

VII:27. FILOFEI ON MOSCOW AS THE THIRD ROME, CA. 1510

One of the devices employed to glorify the newly independent Muscovite state in the time of Ivan III and Vasilii III was the portrayal of Moscow as the Third Rome, here stated in its most celebrated form by the monk Filofei (or Philotheus) in a letter to Vasilii III.

Reference: Malinin, *Starets Eleazarova monastyria Filofei i ego poslaniia*, app., pp. 50, 55.

To the Orthodox Christian tsar and ruler over all, who holds the reins over the holy divine altars of the holy ecumenical catholic [*sobornaia*] apostolic church . . . which shines in place of [the churches of] Rome and Constantinople. For the churches of ancient Rome fell because of the falsehood of the Apollinarian heresy; [as for] the churches of Constantinople, the second Rome, their doors have been cleft by the axes and halberds of the Mohammedans; but now the holy catholic apostolic church of your mighty realm, the third new Rome, shines to the ends of the earth in its Orthodox Christian faith brighter than the sun throughout the world. And may your rule, pious Tsar, know that all the realms of the Orthodox Christian faith have converged into your single realm. You are the only Christian tsar in all the world; it befits you, the tsar, to rule in fear of God.

. . .

Perceive, pious Tsar, how all the Christian realms have converged into yours alone. Two Romes have fallen, and the third stands, and a fourth there shall not be. Your Christian realm shall not pass under the rule of another.

VII:28. HERBERSTEIN ON MUSCOVY UNDER VASILII III, CA. 1517-1526

Sigismund von Herberstein's *Rerum Moscoviticarum Commentarii* (Commentaries on Muscovite affairs) was first published in Latin in 1549, then shortly after in Italian and German. For a long time thereafter it was perhaps the most important single source of information on Russia used in western Europe. Its author, who lived from 1486 to 1566, visited Moscow twice on diplomatic missions, in 1517 and 1526, staying about half a year each time. Since he already knew the Slovene and Czech languages from his youth in the Habsburg lands, he easily learned Russian. His commentaries are based not only on his own observations but also, apparently, on rather extensive reading; they provide a broad though not always infallible survey of Russian history, geography, politics, religion, and customs. Space permits only a few illustrative excerpts. (For other foreigners' accounts in the sixteenth century, see Item VII:16, above, and Chancellor, Jenkinson, and Fletcher below.)

    Reference: Sigismund von Herberstein, *Commentaries on Muscovite Affairs*, ed. and trans. Oswald P. Backus III (Lawrence: University of Kansas Bookstore, 1956), pp. 2, 16-19, 49-50, 54, 55-56, 64, 73-74. A translation of the author's own German version has recently appeared: Sigmund von Herberstein, *Description of Moscow and Muscovy 1557*, ed. Bertold Picard, trans. J. B. C. Grundy (London: J. M. Dent and Sons, 1969).

First among the princes who now rule over Russia is the Grand Duke of Moscow, who holds the largest part of it; the second, the Grand Duke of Lithuania; the third is the King of Poland, who is now in control of Poland and Lithuania.

. . .

    In the control which he [Grand Duke Vasilii Ivanovich] exercises over his people, he easily surpasses all the rulers of the entire world. . . . He obliges all people to do hard service, to such an extent that whomever he orders to be with him in court, or to go to war, or to go on any mission is forced to undertake whatever it may be at his own expense. The younger sons of the boyars are excepted, that is, of the nobles of lesser fortune. It is customary to send for them every year, and because they are oppressed by poverty, to support them with a fixed but inadequate salary. Those to whom he pays six pieces of gold per year stop getting wages in the third year. Those who are paid 12 pieces of gold in a given year are obliged to be ready and equipped to undertake any task at their own expense and with their own horses To the more important who undertake an embassy or more serious duties, either administrative office, or residences, or properties are granted, account being taken of their rank and service, but from them they pay to the prince specified annual taxes. They get no more than the fines which they extort from the poor people who happen in some way to be in the wrong and certain other things. The use in this manner of these possessions, he generally allows for a year and a half. If he looks upon someone with unusual favor or good will, he adds a few months, but when that time has passed all privilege comes to an end and you are obliged immediately thereafter to serve free for a full six year period. . . . He uses his authority as much in spiritual as lay affairs and freely decrees according to his own will concerning the life and properties of all people.

Of the counselors whom he had, there is no one of such authority that he would dare to disagree or to resist him in anything. They publicly declare that the will of the Prince is the will of God, and that whatever the Prince does is done by the will of God. Because of that, in addition, they call him the keykeeper and chamberlain of God, and consequently, believe him the executor of divine will. Thus, if at any time petitions are made on behalf of any captive, or concerning any other serious matter, the Prince himself is accustomed to answer, "When God orders, he shall be freed." But likewise if someone questions about something uncertain or doubtful, they are accustomed to answer, "Both God and the Great Prince know." It is uncertain whether such brutality of the people has made the Prince a tyrant, or whether because the Prince is a tyrant, the people has been rendered inhuman, hard, and cruel.

From the time of Riurik to this present ruler, the princes have used no other title than that of Grand Dukes of Vladimir, or Moscow, or Novgorod, etc. except Ivan Vasilievich who called himself lord of all Russia and Grand Duke of Vladimir, etc., but this Vasilii Ivanovich takes to himself both a royal title and name in this manner: the Great Lord Vasilii, by the grace of God, King and Lord of all Russia, and Grand Duke of Vladimir, Moscow, Novgorod, Pskov, Smolensk, Tver, Iugria, Perm, Viatka, Bulgaria, etc., Lord and Grand Duke of Nizhni-Novgorod, and Chernigov, Riazan, Vologda, Rzhov, Bielyi, Rostov, Iaroslavl, Bieloozero, Udora, Obdorsk, Kondina, etc." Furthermore since all now call him emperor, it seems necessary to explain the title and the cause for this error. In the Russian language, Tsar means King. That is because in the common Slavonic tongue in use among Poles, Bohemians, and all others, through a certain similarity in sound, by the last syllable which is stressed emperor or caesar is understood as tsar. . . . There are those who call the ruler of Moscow, "White King." I have diligently sought some reason why he should be called "White King," since no one of the previous princes of Moscow has used that title. Indeed, when the occasion arose, I have said openly to the counselors themselves that we do not recognize him as King but as Grandduke. However,

many have thought the reason for his name of King to be that he has kings under his control, but certainly they have no reason for white.

. . .

The Muscovites glory that they alone are truly Christian. They damn us as deserters from the primitive church and the old Holy constitutions.

. . .

Love is lukewarm among most married people, especially among the nobility and the princes because they marry a girl not seen before, and occupied by services of the prince, they are forced to desert them, contaminating themselves in the meantime with base lust for another.

The condition of women is very miserable, for no woman is thought to be modest unless she lives locked in her home, and unless she is so guarded that she never goes out. They believe, as I have said, a woman is almost totally immodest if she is seen by foreigners or people outdoors. Locked in the house, women spin and sew. Legal and business matters are absolutely never discussed in the home. All household duties are performed by serfs. . . . But the wives of the poor perform the household tasks and cook.

. . . Nevertheless on certain feast days they [the men] allow their wives and daughters to come together in very pleasant fields, where sitting as though on a wheel of fortune they are moved alternately up and down, or they hang a rope from something, sitting on which they are borne thence by a shove and move, or finally they amuse themselves by certain little songs, while they clap their hands. They do not perform any choruses.

. . .

After selection is had every other year or every third year throughout the provinces, the prince conscripts the children of the boyars, that he may know the number of them and how many horses and servants each one has. Finally he proposes a stipend to each one as was said above, but those who can because of the circumstances of their family affairs, fight without pay. Quiet rarely is given them, for he wages war either against the Lithuanians, the Livonians, or the Swedes, or the Tatars of Kazan. Or if he wages no war he is accustomed to place as a guard 20,000 men every year in spots near the Don and Oka Rivers to put a stop to the attacks and looting of the Perekop Tatars. He also is accustomed to call someone from his provinces each year who fill for him all necessary Muscovite offices. But in time of war, they are not forced to serve their annual posts in the normal order of rotation, but each and every one is forced to go to war like stipendiaries awaiting the favor of the ruler.

· · ·

The ruler has postal routes in all parts of his dominion, with an adequate number of horses, in different places, thus, when a courier is sent anywhere, he gets a horse on demand without delay, but the courier is free to choose any horse he might wish. When I travelled quickly from Novgorod the Great to Muscovy, the master of the post, who is called in their language *iamshchnik* [*iamshchik*] took care to have led to me sometimes thirty, at other times forty or fifty horses at sunrise, but I did not have need of more than twelve. Each one of our men therefore, took a horse which looked suitable to him. Then whenever the horses were tired we arrived at another post which they call iama [*iam*], we immediately changed horses but kept the saddle blanket and bit.

· · ·

The city [Moscow] itself is of wood and adequately large. From afar it appears larger than it is in fact, for the gardens and the spacious grounds around every house result in a large addition to the city, which is further greatly increased by the houses of smiths and other artisans who use fire, houses which are stretched out in a long row at the edge of the city and between which are meadows and fields. . . .

Not far from the city are several monasteries, which alone seem to be one city to spectators from afar. The great size of the city results in the fact that it is marked off by no definite limits, nor is it protected conveniently by a wall, a moat, or by ramparts. . . . With the exception of a few stone houses, churches and monasteries, it is mainly wooden. They say that there is a fairly comfortable number of houses in that city. In the year before our coming to Moscow, on the order of the ruler there was a census of the houses, and their number surpassed 41,500. . . . There is a citadel in it, constructed of brick which the Moskva River laps on one side, and the Neglinaia on the other. . . . But the citadel is of such magnitude, that in addition to the very broad and magnificently constructed home of the ruler, the metropolitan, bishop, likewise the brother of the ruler, nobles and others in great number have spacious wooden homes. In addition, there are many churches in it, so that they seem by the way in which they are dispersed to take the form of a city. . . . The fortress of this citadel and the house of the prince were constructed of brick in the Italian custom, by Italians, whom the ruler summoned from Italy, after great profits had been suggested. But, as I have said, there are many churches in it, almost all wooden; nevertheless excepting the two outstanding ones, which are constructed of stone, one of which is to the Blessed Virgin and the other to St. Mikhail. In the church of the Blessed Virgin are buried the bodies of two archbishops who got the rulers to transfer the seat of the empire and to establish the capital there. Mainly because of that, they are counted among the number of the saints. In another church, the rulers who have died are buried. Other churches were being built of stone when we were present.

VII:29. LEGENDS ABOUT THE ORIGINS OF THE MOSCOW DYNASTY, CA. 1523-1533

Strong and truly independent by the early 1500s, the Muscovite state needed an appropriate genealogy. The research methods of the time were adequate to the task. Using sources that remain obscure, the scholars of the church produced not one but several similar accounts, the earliest of which appeared sometime between 1523 and 1533. In subsequent years Muscovite chroniclers incorporated these accounts into their works, so that, for example, the story of Vladimir Monomakh and the Byzantine emperor Constantine Monomachus appears in the Voskresensk Chronicle under the year 1113, the year when Vladimir became prince of Kiev. The fact that the emperor in question actually died more than half a century earlier than that, at a time when Vladimir was an infant (he was born about 1053), was apparently not well enough known to present any difficulty.

The following passages are from the version that a Soviet scholar has judged to be the earliest (ca. 1523-33), and which was contained in a manuscript found in the monastery of Volokolamsk

Reference: R. P. Dmitrieva, *Skazanie o kniaziakh vladimirskikh* (Moscow: AN SSSR, 1955), pp. 174–77. See also, for example, *PSRL,* 7:231.

Augustus, the Roman caesar . . . began to impose tribute upon the whole world. . . . And he established . . . Prus, his kinsman, on the banks of the river Vistula . . . up to the river called Nieman, which flows into the sea. Prus lived for many years, until the fourth generation; and thenceforth and to this day it is called the Prussian land.

At that time a certain voevoda of Novgorod, Gostomysl by name, was nearing the end of his life; and he called to him all the rulers of Novgorod and said to them: "Oh men of Novgorod, this is my counsel to you: that you send wise men to the Prussian land and invite a ruler for yourselves from among the [princely] lines that are there." And they went to the Prussian land and found there a certain prince, Riurik by name, who was of the lineage of the Roman caesar Augustus. And the envoys from all the people of Novgorod besought Prince Riurik to come and rule over them. And Prince Riurik came to Novgorod, bringing with him his two brothers, one Truvor by name and the other Sineus, and a third person, his nephew Oleg. And thenceforth it was called Novgorod the Great; and the grand prince Riurik was the first to rule there.

The fourth generation from Prince Riurik was the grand prince Vladimir, he who illumined the Russian land through holy baptism in the year 6496 [988]. And the fourth generation from Prince Vladimir was the grand prince Vladimir Vsevolodovich Monomakh, his great-grandson. When he reigned in Kiev as grand prince . . . he gathered a host of many thousands, and he sent them to Thrace, a province of Tsar'grad [Byzantium], and they took many captives and returned with great wealth.

And the pious tsar Constantine Monomachus then reigned in Tsar'grad; at that time he was waging war against the Persians and the Latins. And he reached a wise and regal decision, and dispatched envoys to the grand prince Vladimir Vsevolodovich: Neophytus, metropolitan of Ephesus, and with him two bishops . . . and some of his nobles. And from his neck he took the life-giving cross made of the very life-giving wood upon which the Lord Jesus had been crucified. Likewise he took the tsar's crown from his head and placed it upon a golden tray; and he ordered brought to him . . . the necklet he wore on his shoulders, and a chain wrought from Arabian gold, and many other princely gifts. And he gave them to the metropolitan Neophytus and the bishops and his noble envoys, and he sent them to the grand prince Vladimir Vsevolodovich, entreating him and speaking thus: "Accept from us, O God-loving faithful Prince, these worthy gifts which since the immemorial beginnings of your lineage and descent have been the tsar's lot, for glory and for honor, and for your crowning as a free and autocratic tsar. And our envoys shall entreat you that we ask Your Grace for peace and friendship, so that God's churches may be undisturbed, and all Orthodoxy may live in peace under the present power of our empire and under your free autocratic rule over great Russia. And may you be known henceforth as the God-crowned tsar, crowned with this tsar's crown by the hand of the most holy metropolitan Lord Neophytus and the bishops."

And from that time on the grand prince Vladimir Vsevolodovich was called Monomakh, tsar of great Russia. And afterward in the years that followed he lived in peace and friendship with Tsar Constantine. Thenceforth and to this day the grand princes of Vladimir have been crowned with that crown of the tsars.

VII:30. THE MUSCOVITE RESPONSE TO THE FALL OF CONSTANTINOPLE, AS REVISED BY THE VOSKRESENSK CHRONICLE CA. 1533-1541

Byzantine legends mentioned certain "russet-haired people" who, toward the end of time, would help retake Constantinople. After these legends had been incorporated into the Russian chronicles, the copyists of the Voskresensk Chronicle (ca. 1533–41), influenced by the spirit of the era of Ivan IV, changed *rusyi* ("russet-haired") to *ruskii* ("Russian") and thus destined this passage to escape oblivion.

Reference: *PSRL,* 8:143–44.

[A.D. 1453:] ... Since it was so, and since [the fall of Constantinople] had happened thus, because of our sins, the lawless Mohammed seated himself on the tsar's throne, the noblest of all [thrones] on earth, and they ruled the rulers of the two halves of the earth, and conquered the conquerors of the proud Artaxerxes ... and destroyed the destroyers of most marvelous Troy, defended by seventy and four kings. But understand, o accursed ones! If all the signs concerning this city that were foretold by Methodius of Patara and Leo the Wise have come to pass, the last shall not be avoided but shall likewise come to pass; for it is written: "The Russian race with the former founders [i.e. the Greeks] shall conquer all the Mohammedans and shall receive the City of the Seven Hills with its former lawful masters [the Greeks] and shall reign in it."

VII:31. MEASURES AGAINST CRIME: A CHARTER OF OCTOBER 23, 1539

The charters issued by the Muscovite state to the local judicial districts, like the one issued to Beloozero excerpted here, give us a picture of crime and punishment in the sixteenth century.
    Reference: PRP, 4:176-77. A recent translation of this document is in Dewey, *Muscovite Judicial Texts,* pp. 33-34, along with translations and commentary on this and other similar documents, pp. 31-43.

1. From Grand Prince Ivan Vasilievich of all Russia to the Beloozero uezd: to the princes and the petty nobles [deti boiarskie], to the owners of hereditary estates [otchinniki], the pomeshchiki [holders of service estates], and all military service men; to the village elders [starosty] and sotskie and desiatskie [village officials, centurions and decurions], and to all the peasants—those belonging to me, the grand prince, and to the metropolitan, the bishops, the princes, the boyars, the pomeshchiki, and the monasteries; and to the state peasants; and to the dog-keepers, the beaters [for hunting], the birdcatchers, the beekeepers, the fishermen, the beaver-trappers, and the renters [of state land]; to all without exception, to whomever they may belong.

2. Complaints have reached us that in your volosti robbers plunder many villages and hamlets and loot your possessions and burn down the villages and hamlets and rob and beat many people on the highways and do many people to death, and that many other people in your volosti harbor the robbers in their homes, and that to some the robbers come back from their raids and bring them the loot of their robberies. We have sent to you in Beloozero our investigators [oby-shchiki], but our investigators, you say, cause you great expense. And you are not able with our investigators to capture those evil men because, you say, the procedural delays are too much for you; yet you say you dare not seek out and capture the bandits yourselves, without our knowledge.

3. You should agree among yourselves, all together, and choose some petty nobles to head your volosti, three or four men for every volost', who know how to read and write and are fit for the task; and with them five or six peasants, from among the elders and the desiatskie and the best men; and then you should seek out the evildoers and bandits all by yourselves, in the stany [subdistricts of the uezd] and volosti, after taking the oath to us upon the cross to act truly and without guile; and when you find such robbers, or the people who harbor them, or those who receive their loot, you shall seize such known robbers yourselves and shall make an inquest; and having found evidence against them, you shall interrogate them strictly; and if you obtain confessions of their robberies from them, such robbers should be beaten with knouts and put to death.

VII:32. MEASURES AGAINST CRIME AS RECOUNTED IN THE FIRST CHRONICLE OF PSKOV, 1541

The popular reaction to a charter like the preceding one is indicated in this chronicler's account.
    Reference: Pskovskie letopisi (Moscow: AN SSSR, 1941), 1:110.

The same summer [1541], by the sufferance of the Lord, on account of our many sins, the vicegerents [namestniki] of Pskov were fierce as lions, and their men were like wild beasts toward the peasants and began to slander good people with false accusations, and the good people fled to other towns. ... That same winter our sovereign, Grand Prince Ivan Vasilie vich of all Russia, granted his favor to the Russian land, he being young in years, eleven years of age, but old in wisdom: merciful to his patrimony, he showed his favor by granting charters to all the large towns, and to all the dependent towns and the volosti, that the peasants themselves might, under oath to the tsar, seek out evildoers and put them to death, without taking the evil men, robbers and thieves, to the vicegerents and their judges [tivuny]. And the resentment of the governors in the towns against the peasants was great. The people of Pskov received such a charter; and their sworn assistants [tseloval'niki] and the village sotskie [hundredmen] began trying evildoers in the prince's mansion, in the courtroom [sudnitsa] above the river Velikaia, and they punished them with death. . . . And there was a vicegerent in Pskov, Prince Vasilei Repnin Obolenskoi, and his enmity to the people of Pskov was great, inasmuch as the sovereign's charter was like a shield to them. To the peasants it was a joy and a great relief from the evildoers, and the slanderers, and the vicegerents with their bailiffs [nedel'shchiki] and their agents riding from volost' to volost'; and the people of Pskov offered prayers for the sovereign to God and to the Virgin Mother of God and to the holy miracle workers, on account of his having shown favor to his patrimony and mercy to his orphans.

VII:33. MEASURES AGAINST CRIME: INSTRUCTIONS OF AUGUST 25, 1555

The extension of such reliance on local initiative is illustrated in these instructions issued for the judicial district of Medyn', southwest of Moscow.
     Reference: PRP, 4:179-81. A recent translation of this document is in Dewey, *Muscovite Judicial Texts*, pp. 36-40.

The tsar . . . has granted his favor to all military service men . . . and to all peasants of Medyn' and the uezd of Medyn'. . . .
     We have received a complaint: They say that in their township of Medyn' and the uezd of Medyn', in the stany and volosti, great robberies and thieveries are being committed—villages and hamlets are being plundered, goods are being stolen, and on the highways many people are being beaten and robbed and done to death; and that there are many other people who harbor the robbers in their homes, where the robbers return from their raids and bring back the loot of their robberies, and from where they set forth on their raids. We have sent to them our investigators and bailiffs [nedel'shchiki—also "constables" or "policemen"] to inquire into the robberies, but they say that our investigators and bailiffs cause them great expense.
     1. And I, Tsar and Grand Prince Ivan Vasilievich of all Russia, in response to their complaint, grant them my favor. At the township of Medyn' and in the stany and volosti of the uezd of Medyn', Fedor, son of Vasilii Danilov, and Fedor, son of Mikhail Zasetskii, are to be district elders for criminal justice [gubnye starosty], in charge of cases of banditry and thievery, assisted by sworn district assistants [gubnye tseloval'niki] and

clerks; and the elders Fedor Danilov and Fedor Zasetskii with the sworn assistants shall come together in one place and deal with cases of banditry and thievery according to this instruction. They shall summon to their meeting men from the whole judicial district [guba] —princes, petty nobles, and their stewards [prikazchiki], and abbots, priests, and deacons; and peasants, those of the tsar and grand prince from the crown villages [dvorovye sela] and the state lands, and those belonging to the metropolitan, and the bishops, the princes, and the monasteries . . . one man from each vyt' [a plot of taxable land]. As soon as they have foregathered with the elders, the elders shall begin an inquest. . . . And if at the inquest they hear who are the evil men, the thieves and robbers, and who are those who shelter the robbers and receive their loot, and from whose houses the robbers set forth on their raids, and to whom the loot of the robberies is sold as such, and who has been beaten and who has been robbed, the elders shall order the local clerk [zemskii d'iachok] to write down truly in the records all that has been said. . . .
     2. If at the inquest some are said to be evildoers, but there are no plaintiffs against them, then the elders shall send for them, and shall order them seized and brought before them, and their goods and possessions shall be listed,

sealed, and guarded until the case is decided. When they come before the elders, the elders shall question these people about the robberies. . . . And those who confess their rob-beries shall be put to death, and about their possessions a report shall be written to the boyars of the Office for Criminal Affairs [Razboinaia Izba] in Moscow.

VII:34. A POMEST'E GRANT, JANUARY 12, 1546

This charter, granting a pomest'e or estate on service tenure (fief) to one Grisha Zhedrinskii, illustrates the system by which government servants (especially military men) were recompensed.

Reference: Nikolai Kalachev, ed., *Akty otnosiashchiesia do iuridicheskogo byta drevnei Rossii*, 3 vols. (St. Petersburg, 1857-84), 1:139-40.

I, Ivan Vasil'evich, grand prince of all Russia, grant to Grisha, son of Ivan Zhedrinskii, of Nizhnii-Novgorod, a third portion of the village of Frolovskoe in the Berezopolskii stan [administrative subdivision of the uezd] of the Nizhnii-Novgorod uezd, which formerly belonged to Eremei, son of Matfei Pagozskii; and also the obrok-paying hamlet of Kuchino in Strelitsa, which belonged to Rodia Kuchin. Since — [omission in original] this *syn boiarskii* died leaving behind no wife or children, and his land was not given as a pomest'e to anyone, thus I, the grand prince, grant it as a pomest'e with everything that belonged to this third of the village and to the hamlet as of old. As for the peasants who shall live on his land, in that third of the village and in the hamlet, our vicegerents in Nizhnii-Novgorod and the volost' chiefs [volosteli] and their deputies [tiuny] shall not sit in judg-ment over them for anything except murder and robbery with material evidence; Grisha himself or whoever he designates shall administer and judge his own peasants. And if there should be a mixed trial between his peasants and the inhabitants of the town or volost', then our Nizhnii-Novgorod vicegerents and volost' chiefs and their deputies shall sit in judgment over his peasants together with Grisha or his manager; and the court fees shall be equally divided between them. If anyone lodges a complaint against Grisha or his manager, then I myself, the grand prince, or my commissioned boyar [*boiarin vvedenoi*] shall sit in judgment. And the obrok from his obrok-paying hamlet shall be paid according to the books [*po knigam*] to [my] steward [*kliuchnik*] in Novgorod. Written in Moscow, on the twelfth day of January in the year 7054 [1546].

VII:35. IVAN PERESVETOV'S RECOMMENDATIONS, CA. 1547

Ivan Semenovich Peresvetov was a lesser nobleman who entered the Muscovite service in the late 1530s after long years in the service of Lithuanian, Moldavian, and other rulers of east central Europe. In the years 1547-49, just after Ivan IV had been crowned tsar, Peresvetov undertook to give advice to his young master. His advice took the form of tales presented to the tsar as "petitions" (chelobitnaia). Among them were tales of the Sultan Mohammed and of Peter, the voivode or ruler (later called the hospodar) of Moldavia (here misleadingly termed *voloskii* voivode, from the word for "Wallachian").

Reference: *CIOIDRMU*, 1908, bk. 1, pp. 62-65, 75-77. Recently there has appeared Peresve-tov's "Tale of the Sultan Mohammed," in Russian with abundant English annotations and a glossary, in John Fennell and Dimitri Obolensky, *A Historical Russian Reader* (Oxford: At the Clarendon Press, 1969), pp. 126-35, 198-200. See also D. S. Likhachev and A. A. Zimin, eds., *Sochineniia I. Peresvetova* (Moscow: AN SSSR, 1956).

Thus speaks the voivode of Moldavia [voloskii voevoda] of the Russian tsardom: "The great lords of the Russian tsar enrich themselves and grow lazy, but impoverish his realm; they are called his servants because they ride forth to his service in pomp, with many horses and men, but they do not stand firm for the Christian faith, nor do they play the fierce game of death with the enemy; and thus they are false to God and to the sovereign." And thus speaks the voivode of Moldavia: "It matters little that they are many, if they are faint of heart, and fear death, and are unwilling to die for the Christian faith, and always try to avoid death. The rich think not of war, but of a tranquil life; and even a valiant knight [bogatyr'] in waxing rich grows lazy." Thus speaks the voivode of Moldavia: "A warrior should be tended like a falcon, and his heart should be gladdened always, and all sorrow should be kept away from him." And thus speaks the voivode of Moldavia: "It befits such a mighty sovereign to collect revenues from the whole realm into his treasury, and out of his treasury to gladden the hearts of his warriors; then his treasury will never be exhausted, and his realm will not be impoverished. A warrior who fiercely plays the game of death with his sovereign's foe and steadfastly defends the Christian faith should be elevated and kept in good cheer, and his salary should be increased from the tsar's treasury; and [the tsar] should lift up the hearts of his other warriors, and draw them close to his person, and trust them in all things, and listen to all their complaints, and love them as a father loves his children, and be generous to them: a generous hand never grows empty but gathers glory for the tsar; in the tsar's generosity toward his warriors lies his wisdom. . . ."

. . . With great tears the voivode of Moldavia speaks of the Christian faith of the Russian tsardom, and he always prays to God that the Christian faith may be furthered by the eastern tsardom, by the faithful Russian tsar and grand prince of all Russia Ivan Vasil'evich. All those of the Greek faith now take pride in the Russian tsardom and hope that by the great mercy of God and with divine help they will be liberated by the Russian tsar from the tyranny of the alien Turkish tsar. And thus speaks the voivode of Moldavia: "This great realm, mighty and glorious and rich in all things, this Muscovite tsardom: is there any justice in that realm?" And he had in his service a Muscovite, Vaska Mertsalov, and he inquired of him: "You have much knowledge of the Muscovite tsardom, answer me truly." And he began to tell Peter, the voivode of Moldavia: "The Christian faith, Sire, is strong there, and is rich in everything, and the beauty of the churches is great, but there is no justice." And at this Peter the voivode wept and spoke thus: "Where there is no justice, there is nothing. . . ."

From earliest times the wise philosophers have disapproved of those men of high rank who find favor with the tsar neither for their services in war nor by virtue of their wisdom. The wise philosophers speak about them thus:

"These are sorcerers and heretics, who take away the tsar's happiness and wisdom, and cast a spell upon the tsar's heart by means of sorcery and heresy, and enfeeble the warriors." And the voivode of Moldavia speaks thus: "Such as these should be burned by fire or consigned to some other cruel death, so that the evil may not multiply. . . . For the tsar cannot exist without his warriors. . . . In his warriors lies the tsar's strength and glory. The tsar should rule his realm by the grace of God and with great wisdom; and he should be generous to his warriors, as a father to his children. In the tsar's generosity toward his warriors lies his wisdom; a generous hand will never be empty and it gathers great glory for itself."

[From the Tale of the Sultan Mahmet, or Mohammed:]
Thus spoke the Sultan Mahmet [Mohammed]: In a kingdom where the people are enslaved, they will not be brave and will lack the courage to battle against the foe, for the man who is enslaved does not fear disgrace and does not seek honor, whether he be strong or weak, saying thus: "I am a slave in any case, and will never have another name." And in Constantine's realm, under Tsar Constantine, his great lords held the best people in bondage, and they did not stand firm against the enemy; the great lords were a colorful sight in their armor, upon their horses; but their troops would not fight the enemy staunchly and would flee from the battlefield. . . .

And if a tsar's man stands firm against the enemy, and plays the game of death, and shatters the troops of the enemy, and serves faithfully, then the tsar should elevate him to high honor, even if he be of lesser lineage, and should give him a great name and reward him with a higher salary, and lift up the hearts of his warriors.

· · ·

And the Greeks had become weak in all respects, and had lost their righteousness, and had incurred the boundless wrath of God; and they let the Christian faith be desecrated by the heathen. And now the Greeks take pride in the sovereign realm of the Orthodox Russian tsar, ever since the conquest by Mahmet [Mohammed II, in 1453] and to this day. There exists no other free Christian realm of the Greek faith; and therefore they place their trust in God and in the Russian realm of the faithful Russian tsar; and they boast of the free sovereign tsar whenever, in a dispute with the Latins, the doctors of the Latin faith argue against the Greeks: "You Greeks have incurred the boundless wrath of the Lord, like the Jews, and he has delivered you into bondage to the Turkish tsar for your pride and your iniquity. . . ." This they deny, and they boast: "We have a free tsardom and a free tsar, the Orthodox sovereign Grand Prince Ivan Vasil'evich of all Russia, and in that tsardom the mercy of God is great."

VII:36. THE DOMOSTROI, CA. 1550

The Domostroi is a collection of rules of daily life from the early and middle 1500s. It is attributed in part to the priest Silvester, who in the years 1547-53 was a close adviser to Tsar Ivan IV, but much of it evidently antedates him and is the work of many hands. These short excerpts give merely a hint of the richness of the Domostroi as a source for social history.

Reference: *CIOIDRMU*, 1881, bk. 2, pp. 11, 16-17, 31, 60, 85, 88, 100-01, 108. Another edition has recently been reprinted: *Domostroi po Konshinskomu spisku i podobnym,* ed. A. S. Orlov, 2 vols. (Moscow: Sinodal'naia Tipografiia, 1908-10; reprinted The Hague: Mouton, 1967). Some additional excerpts are translated in Leo Wiener, ed., *Anthology of Russian Literature,* 2 vols. (N.Y.: G. P. Putnam's Sons, 1902), 1:126-30.

Instructions from a father to his son:
. . . In instructing your wife and punishing your domestics, do not use force or blows or heavy labor, [but] treat them as your children, keeping them in all tranquillity, fed and clothed, and in a warm dwelling, with everything well ordered.

· · ·

Fear the tsar and serve him faithfully, and always pray to God for him, and speak no falsehood before him on any account, but answer him truthfully [and] with submission, as God himself, and obey him in everything. As you serve truthfully the earthly tsar and fear him, thus shall you learn to fear the heavenly tsar. . . . Pay honor to your elders and bow before them. Respect your equals as brothers. Welcome the weak and the unfortunate lovingly. Love your subordinates as your children. Do no evil to any of God's creatures; do not seek earthly glory in anything, but ask God for eternal blessings.

· · ·

Visit those who are in monasteries and hospitals and hermitages and confined in prisons, and bring them as charity all the necessary things that they seek, whatever is possible; and seeing their misfortune, and affliction, and need of every kind, help them as much as is possible. Do not despise anyone who is afflicted, needy, poor, or indigent, but bring him into your house, furnish him with food and drink, make him warm, [and] clothe him with all charity and with a clear conscience.

· · ·

How to educate children and save [their souls] through fear:
Punish your son when he is young, and he will give you rest in your old age and will bring contentment to your soul. Do not weaken in beating the lad; for if you beat him with a stick he will not die, but will rather be healthier, since by beating his body you save his soul from death.

· · ·

It befits a husband to instruct his wife lovingly and with judicious punishment. A wife must consult her husband on all questions of conduct: how to save her soul, how to please God and her husband, and how to manage the household properly. She must obey her husband in all matters: whatever he orders she must accept and carry out with love and with fear, in accordance with his orders and with this epistle.

· · ·

And the mistress herself should never be idle for any reason except sickness, or her husband's wishes, lest the servants take bad example from looking at her. Whenever her husband comes in, or the usual guests come in, she should always be sitting at her needlework. Then honor and respect will go to her, and praise to her husband. And the servants should never awaken the mistress, but rather the mistress should herself awaken the servants and should go to bed straight from her needlework, after prayers, and should teach her servants to do likewise.

· · ·

A wife should consult with her husband every day, and seek his advice in all household matters, and remind him of what is needed. And as for paying visits, or inviting guests, she shall refer to her husband for permission.

. . .

If a wife or son or daughter does not follow, or heed, or obey, or fear admonitions and instructions, and does not do what the husband, or father and mother teach, such a person shall be beaten with a lash in accordance with the guilt, in private rather than in the presence of others; and after being instructed, he shall be reprimanded and forgiven, and there shall be no anger between them.

VII:37. THE STOGLAV, 1551

The Church Council of 1551 dealt with a long series of questions presented to it by the young Ivan IV and Metropolitan Macarius. The council's pronouncements numbered one hundred; hence the name Stoglav, or "Hundred Chapters." Some of the articles quoted below were later appealed to by the Old Believers as statements of unalterable dogmas of the Orthodox church. Other quotations give vivid descriptions of departures from the Orthodox ideal.

Reference: *Stoglav: Tsarskie voprosy i sobornye otvety* (Moscow, 1890), pp. 51, 66, 124–25, 127, 135–36, 163, 184, 191, 204–05, 329, 334, 339. Cf. E. Duchesne, ed., *Le Stoglav, ou les Cent Chapitres* (Paris: E. Champion, 1920).

CHAPTER 5. QUESTION 8. Concerning monasteries and monks: And in the monasteries monks and priests take the vows for the salvation of their souls. But some take the vows for the sake of bodily comfort, so that they might constantly indulge in drunkenness and ride to the [monastery] villages to take their leisure. Concerning archimandrites and abbots: Some archimandrites and abbots obtain their position through bribery, and know not the divine services and the refectory table and the brotherhood, and take their repose in their cells with guests. . . .

QUES. 25. [Concerning] those who shave their heads and beards: Through our sins, weakness and indifference and negligence have come into the world. At the present time men who call themselves Christians and are thirty years of age and older shave their heads, beards, and whiskers, and wear clothing and costumes taken from lands of dissident faith; how then can a Christian be recognized? . . .

CHAP. 26. Concerning schools of learning in all the towns: And in accordance with the tsar's advice we have jointly decreed that in the ruling city of Moscow and in all the towns these same archpriests and senior priests, together with all the priests and deacons, each in his own town, shall select, with the blessing of their bishop, worthy, pious priests and deacons and married sextons and pious men, with the fear of God in their hearts, who can be of use to others and who know their letters and reading and writing, and shall establish schools in the houses of these priests, deacons, and sextons, so that priests and deacons and all Orthodox Christians in each town would send them their children to learn reading and writing and church singing. . . .

CHAP. 27. . . . And whatever sacred books, gospels, epistles, psalters, and other books in each church are found to be written incorrectly and in error, you should jointly correct all these sacred books from good manuscripts. . . .

CHAP. 31. The sign of the cross must be made according to the rules, in the form of a cross; and the right hand, that is, the dextral hand, must be used in crossing oneself, with the thumb and the two lower fingers joined together, and the extended index finger joined to the middle finger, slightly bent; thus should prelates [and] priests give their blessing and thus should men cross themselves. . . . It befits all Orthodox Christians to hold their hand thus, and to make the sign of the cross upon their face with two fingers, and to bow, as we said before. If anyone should fail to give his blessing with two fingers, as Christ did, or should fail to make the sign of the cross with two fingers, may he be accursed. . . .

CHAP. 40. Concerning the sacred rules on the shaving of beards: The sacred rules likewise forbid all Orthodox Christians to shave their beards and to cut their whiskers. For such is not an Orthodox but a Latin and heretical tradition . . . and the rules of the apostles and [church] fathers strictly forbid and denounce this. . . .

CHAP. 41. QUES. 19. And jongleurs [*sko-morokhi*] wander through faraway lands, gathered together in large bands of up to sixty and seventy and a hundred men, and eat and drink much in the villages at the peasants' expense, and steal their goods from the larders, and rob men on the roads. . . .

QUES. 24. [Concerning] the festivities [*rusal'i*] on the eve of Saint John's and Christmas and the Epiphany: Men and women and girls gather at night for revelry, indecorous speech, devilish singing and dancing, and acts hateful to God; and youths are polluted and girls defiled. When the night comes to an end, then they go off to the river with great shouting, like devils, [and] wash themselves in the water; and when the bells begin to ring for matins they go to their houses and fall as if dead from the great clamor. . . .

CHAP. 42. Reply concerning the triple alleluia: that in Pskov, and in many monasteries and churches in the land of Pskov, and in many places in the land of Novgorod, triple alleluias are said to this day. . . . Henceforth Orthodox Christians must say "alleluia" twice, and the third time say "glory to thee, O Lord," as is held and taught by the holy catholic apostolic church, rather than say "alleluia" three times and the fourth time say "glory to thee, O Lord," as was formerly said in Pskov and in many [other] places. This is not an Orthodox tradition, but a Latin heresy, that they glorify the Trinity not three but four times. . . .

CHAP. 72. The reply of the council concerning the ransoming of prisoners: Whatever [prisoners] are ransomed by the tsar's envoys in the hordes, in Tsar'grad, in the Crimea, in Kazan', in Astrakhan', or in Kaffa [in the Crimea], or who ransom themselves: all these prisoners shall be ransomed out of the tsar's treasury. And if Greeks, Turks, Armenians, and other foreign merchants should ransom prisoners and bring them, Orthodox Christians, [to Moscow] and after being in Moscow should wish to take them back with them, they shall not do so; and this shall be firmly observed. And they shall be ransomed from the tsar's treasury, and whatever sum is expended from the tsar's treasury each year for ransoming prisoners, this shall be apportioned among the *sokhi* [agricultural tax units] throughout the land, upon everyone's land equally, since such ransoming is called an act of general charity, and the pious tsar and all Orthodox Christians shall be rewarded for this by God. . . .

CHAP. 75. Whatever patrimonial and purchased villages men have given to the holy churches for the commemoration of their souls and for the commemoration of their parents, without the right of repurchase, so as to inherit eternal blessings, and other church [and] monastery land, and other immovable property shall not be given away or sold, but firmly preserved, in accordance with the sacred and divine rules of the Holy Seventh Ecumenical Council and of other holy fathers [of the church]. . . .

CHAP. 76. Reply concerning [lending] the money of the prelates and monasteries without interest and grain without compensation [*nasop*—"pouring in" more grain than was lent]: And [as for the fact] that money belonging to the prelates is lent for interest and grain for compensation, and that likewise money belonging to the monasteries is lent for interest and grain for compensation, the divine Scriptures and sacred rules not only forbid this to bishops, presbyters, deacons, and all priests and monks but also prohibit ordinary men from taking interest and practicing usury. Thus henceforth, in accordance with the sacred rules, prelates and all monasteries shall lend money to the peasants in their villages without interest and grain without compensation, so that their peasants may live with them and so that their villages may not be empty.

VII:38. RICHARD CHANCELLOR ON MUSCOVY, 1553

Richard Chancellor (d. 1556), a sea captain, traveled via the White Sea to Moscow in 1553 and inaugurated Anglo-Russian diplomatic and trade relations. His famous letter to his uncle, in which he describes his "discoverie of Moscovia," is a significant document for both English and Russian culture of that time. (Concerning Russia and England, see also Section A, above.)

Reference: Purchas, *Hakluytus Posthumus*, 11:601–04, 606–13. For a somewhat different version done by Clement Adams in collaboration with Chancellor, see Lloyd E. Berry and Robert

O. Crummey, eds., *Rude and Barbarous Kingdom. Russia in the Accounts of Sixteenth-Century English Voyagers* (Madison: University of Wisconsin Press, 1968), pp. 9-41.

Russia is very plentifull both of Land and People, and also wealthie for such commodities as they have. They be very great fishers for Salmons and small Cods: they have much Oyle which wee call Trane Oyle, the most whereof is made by a River called Duina. They make it in other places, but not so much as there. They have also a great trade in seething of salt water. To the North part of that Countrey are the places where they have their Furres, as Sables, Marterns, greesse Bevers, Foxes white, blacke, and red, Minkes, Ermines, Miniver, and Harts. There are also a fishes teeth, which fish is called a Morsse. The takers thereof dwell in a place called Postesora, which bring them upon Harts to Lampas to sell, and from Lampas carrie them to a place called Colmogro, where the high Market is holden on Saint Nicolas day. To the West of Colmogro there is a place called Gratanove, in our language Novogorode, where much fine Flaxe and Hempe groweth, and also much Waxe and Honie. The Dutch Merchants have a Staplehouse there. There is also great store of Hides, and at a place called Plesco: and thereabout is great store of Flaxe, Hempe, Waxe, Honie.

. . .

The Mosco is from Jeraslave two hundred miles. The Countrey betwixt them is very well replenished with small Villages, which are so well filled with people, that it is wonder to see them: the ground is well stored with Corne, which they carrie to the Citie of Mosco in such abundance that it is wonder to see it. You shall meet in a morning seven or eight hundred Sleds comming or going thither, that carrie Corne, and some carrie fish. You shall have some that carrie Corne to the Mosco, and some that fetch Corne from thence, that at the least dwell a thousand miles off: and all their carriage is on Sleds. Those which come so farre dwell in the North parts of the Dukes Dominions, where the cold will suffer no Corne to grow, it is so extreme. They bring thither Fishes, Furres, and Beasts skinnes. In those parts they have but small store of Cattell.

The Mosco it selfe is great: I take the whole Towne to be greater then London with the Suburbes: but it is very rude, and standeth without all order. Their houses are all of timber very dangerous for fire. There is a faire Castle, the walls whereof are of bricke, and very high. . . .

The Emperours or Dukes house neither in building nor in the outward shew, nor yet within the house is so sumptuous as I have seene. It is very lowe built in eight square, much like the old building of England, with small windowes, and so in other points.

Now to declare my comming before his Majestie: After I had remayned twelve dayes, the Secretarie which hath the hearing of strangers did send for mee, advertising me that the Dukes pleasure was to have me to come before his Majestie, with the King my Masters Letters: whereof I was right glad, and so I gave mine attendance. And when the Duke was in his place appointed, the Interpreter came for mee into the outer Chamber, where sate one hundred or more Gentlemen, all in cloth of Gold very sumptuous, and from thence I came into the Counsell-chamber, where sate the Duke himselfe, with his Nobles, which were a faire companie: they sate round about the Chamber on high, yet so that he himselfe sate much higher than any of his Nobles, in a Chaire gilt, and in a long garment of beaten Gold, with an Imperiall Crowne upon his head, and a Staffe of Crystall and Gold in his right hand, and his other hand halfe leaning on his Chaire. The Chancellour stood up with the Secretarie before the Duke. After my dutie done, and my Letter delivered, he bade me welcome, and enquired of mee the health of the King my Master, and I answered that he was in good health at my departure from his Court, and that my trust was, that he was now in the same. Upon the which he bade me to dinner.

. . .

This Duke is Lord and Emperour of many Countries, and his power is marvellous great. For hee is able to bring into the field two or three hundred thousand men: he never goeth into the field himselfe with under two hundred thousand men: And when hee goeth himselfe, hee furnisheth his Borders all with men of Warre, which are no small number. He leaveth on the Borders of Liefland fortie thousand men, and upon the borders of Letto, sixtie thousand men, and toward the Nagayan Tarters sixtie thousand, which is wonder to

heare of: yet doth hee never take to his
Warres neither Husbandman nor Merchant.
All his men are Horse-men: hee useth no
Foot-men, but such as goe with the Ordnance and Labourers, which are thirtie
thousand. The Horse-men are all Archers,
with such Bowes as the Turkes have, and
they ride short as doe the Turkes. Their
Armour is a Coate of Plate, with a skull on
their heads. Some of their Coates are covered with Velvet or Cloth of Gold: their
desire is to be sumptuous in the field, and
especially the Nobles and Gentlemen: as I
have heard their trimming is very costly, and
partly I have seene it, or else I would scarcely
have believed it: but the Duke himselfe is
richly attyred above all measure: his Pavilion
is covered eyther with Cloth of Gold or Silver,
and so set with stones that it is wonderfull
to see it. I have seene the Kings Majesties of
England and the French Kings Pavilions,
which are faire, yet not like unto his. . . .
And now to the effect of their Warres: They
are men without all order in the field. For
they run hurling on heaps, and for the most
part they never give battayle to their Enemies: but that which they do, they do it all
by stealth. But I beleeve they be such men
for hard living as are not under the Sunne:
for no cold will hurt them. Yea, and though
they lye in the field two moneths, at such
time as it shall freeze more than a yard thicke,
the common Souldier hath neither Tent nor
any thing else over his head: the most defence
they have against the weather is a Felt, which
is set against the wind, and weather, and when
Snow commeth he doth cast it off, and
maketh him a fire, and layeth him downe
thereby. Thus doe the most of all his men,
except they be Gentlemen which have other
provisions of their owne. Their lying in the
field is not so strange as is their hardnesse:
for every man must carrie and make provision
for himselfe, and his Horse for a moneth or
two, which is very wonderfull. For hee himselfe shall live upon water and Oatemeale
mingled together cold, and drinke water
thereto: his Horse shall eate greene wood,
and such like baggage, and shall stand open
in the cold field without covert, and yet will
hee labour and serve him right well. I pray
you amongst all our boasting Warriours how
many should we find to endure the field with
them but one moneth. I know no such Region

about us that beareth that name for man and
beast. Now what might bee made of these
men if they were trayned and broken to order
and knowledge of Civill Warres: if this Prince
had within his Countries such men as could
make them to understand the things aforesaid, I doe beleeve that two of the best or
greatest Princes in Christendome were not
well able to match with him, considering the
greatnesse of his power and the hardnesse of
his people, and straight living both of people
and Horse, and the small charges which his
Wars stand him in; for he giveth no wages, except to strangers. They have a yearely stipend
and not much. As for his owne Countreymen,
every one serveth of his owne proper costs
and charges, saving that hee giveth to his
Harquebusiers certayne allowance for Powder
and shot: or else no man in all his Countrey
hath one penie wages. But if any man hath
done very good service, he giveth him a Ferme,
or a piece of Land; for the which he is bound
at all times to be readie with so many men as
the Duke shall appoint: who considereth in
his minde, what that Land or Ferme is well
able to find: and so many shall he be bound
to furnish at all and every such time as Warres
are holden in any of the Dukes Dominions.
For there is no man of living, but he is bound
likewise, whether the Duke call for eyther
Souldier or Labourer, to furnish them with
all such necessaries as to them belong.

    . . . Men may say, that these men are in
wonderfull great awe, and obedience, that
thus one must give and grant his goods which
he hath beene scraping and scratching for all
his life to be at his Princes pleasure and commandement. Oh, that our sturdie Rebels were
had in the like subjection to know their dutie
toward their Princes. . . . And whom he
sendeth most to the Warres hee thinketh he
is most in his favour. . . . If they knew their
strength, no man were able to make match
with them: for they that dwell neere them
should have any rest of them. But I thinke it
is not gods will: For I may compare them to
a young Horse that knoweth not his strength,
whom a little Child ruleth and guideth with a
bridle, for all his great strength: for if he did,
neither Child nor man could rule him. Their
Warres are holden against the Crimme Tar-
tarians, and the Nagayans.

    . . . Every Gentleman hath Rule and Justic
upon his owne Tenants. . . .

Their order in one point is commendable. They have no man of Law to plead their Causes in any Court: but every man pleadeth his owne Cause, and giveth Bill and Answere in writing: contrary to the order in England. The Complaint is in manner of a Supplication, and made to the Dukes Grace, and delivered him into his owne hand, requiring to have Justice as in his Complaint is alleaged. The Duke giveth sentence himselfe upon all matters in the Law. Which is very commendable, that such a Prince will take paines to see ministration of Justice. Yet notwithstanding it is wonderfully abused: and thereby the Duke is much deceived.

There is also another order in the Law, that the plaintiffe may sweare in some causes of debt. And if the partie defendant bee poore, hee shall be set under the Crucifixe, and the partie plaintiffe must sweare over his head, and when hee hath taken his oath, the Duke taketh the partie defendant home to his house, and useth him as his bond-man, and putteth him to labour, or letteth him for hire to any such as neede him, untill such time as his friends make provision for his redemption: or else hee remayneth in bondage all the dayes of his life. Againe, there are many that will sell themselves to Gentlemen or Merchants, to bee their bond-men, to have during their life, meate, drinke and cloath, and at their comming to have a piece of money; yea, and some will sell their wives and children to be bawds and drudges to the buyer. Also they have a Law for Fellons and pickers contrary to the Lawes of England. For by the Law they can hang no man for his first offence; but may keepe him long in Prison, and oftentimes beate him with whips and other punishment; and there hee shall remaine untill his friends bee able to bayle him. If hee be a picker or a cut-purse, as there bee very many, the second time he is taken, hee hath a piece of his Nose cut off, and is burned in the forehead, and kept in prison till he finde sureties for his good behaviour. And if hee be taken the third time,

he is hanged. And at the first time hee is extreamely punished and not released, except he have very good friends, or that some Gentlemen require to have him to the warres: And in so doing, hee shall enter into great bonds for him: by which meanes the Countrey is brought into good quietnesse. But they bee naturally given to great deceit, except extreame beating did bridle them. They bee naturally given to hard living as well in fare as in lodging. . . . The poor is very innumerable, and live most miserably. . . . In mine opinion there bee no such people under the Sunne for their hardnesse of living. . . .

They doe observe the Law of the Greekes with such excesse of superstition, as the like hath not beene heard of. They have no graven Images in their Churches, but all painted, to the intent they will not breake the Commandement: but to their painted Images they use such Idolatrie, that the like was never heard of in England. They will neither worship nor honour any Image that is made foorth of their owne Countrey. For their own Images (say they) have Pictures to declare what they bee, and how they be of God, and so be not ours: They say, looke how the Painter or Carver hath made them, so wee doe worship them, and they worship none before they bee Christened. They say wee be but halfe Christians: because we observe not part of the old Law with the Turkes. Therefore they call themselves more holy then us. They have none other learning but their mother tongue, nor will suffer no other in their Countrey among them. All their service in Churches is in their mother tongue. They have the old and new Testament, which are daily read among them: and yet their superstition is no lesse. For when the Priests doe reade, they have such trickes in their reading, that no man can understand them, nor no man giveth eare to them. For all the while the Priest readeth, the people sit downe and one talke with another. But when the Priest is at service no man sitteth, but gaggle and ducke like so many Geese.

VII:39. ANTHONY JENKINSON ON RUSSIA, 1557

Anthony Jenkinson's first trip to Russia was in 1557, as a merchant escorting Ivan IV's ambassador, Osip Nepeia, from London back to Moscow. Jenkinson made three later trips to Russia and was in the service of the Russia Company from 1557 to 1572, but unfortunately he did not leave any detailed account other than that embodying his first impressions of 1557.

Reference: Purchas, *Hakluytus Posthumus*, 11:628-30, 634-35. A recent republication with commentary is in Berry and Crummey, *Rude and Barbarous Kingdom*, pp. 43-58.

The Russian Ambassadour and his companie
with great joy got to shoare, and our ships
heere forthwith discharged themselves: and
being laden againe, and having a faire winde,
departed toward England the first of August.
The third of the said moneth I with other of
my companie came unto the Citie of Colmogro. . . . I tarried at the said Colmogro untill
the fifteenth day: and then I departed in a
little Boat up the River of Duina, which
runneth very swiftly. . . . And thus proceed-
ing forward, . . . I came to a place called
Ustiug, an ancient Citie, the last day of
Auguste. . . . Thus departing from Ustiug,
and passing by the River Sucana, we came to
a Towne called Totma. About this place the
water is very shallow, and stonie, and trouble-
some for Barkes and Boats of that Countrey,
which they call Nassades, and Dosneckes, to
passe that way: wherein merchandise are
transported from the aforesaid Colmogro
to the Citie of Vologda. These vessels called
Nassades, are very long builded, broad made,
and close above, flat bottomed, and draw not
above foure foot water, and will carrie two
hundred tunnes: they have no Iron ap-
pertayning to them, but all of Timber, and
when the winde serveth they are made to
sayle. Otherwise they have many men, some
to hale and draw by the neckes with long
small ropes made fast to the said Boats, and
some set with long poles. There are many of
these Barkes upon the River of Duina: And
the most part of them belongeth unto the
Citie of Vologda: for there dwell many
Merchants, and they occupie the said Boats
with carrying of Salt from the Sea side, unto
the said Vologda. The twentieth of September I came unto Vologda, which is a great
Citie, and the River passeth through the
midst of the same. The houses are builded
with wood of Firre trees, joyned one with
another, and round without: the houses are
foure square without any Iron or stone worke,
covered with Birch barkes, and wood over the
same: Their Churches are all of wood, two
for every Parish, one to be heated for Winter,
and the other for Summer. On the tops of
their houses they lay much earth, for feare
of burning: for they are sore plagued with
fire. This Vologda . . . is from Colmogro, one
thousand verstes.

All the way I never came in house, but
lodged in the Wildernesse, by the Rivers side,
and carried provisions for the way. And he
that will travell those wayes, must carrie with
him an Hatchet, a Tinder boxe, and a Kettle,
to make fire and seethe meat, when he hath it:
for there is small succour in those parts, unlesse
it be in Townes.

The first day of December, I departed from
Vologda in poste in a Sled, as the manner is in
Winter. . . . I arrived [in Moscow] the sixt day
of December.

· · ·

They have many sorts of meats and drinks,
when they banket and delight in eating of
grosse meates, and stinking fish. Before they
drinke they use to blow in the Cup: their
greatest friendship is in drinking: they are
great Talkers and Lyars, without any faith or
trust in their words, Flatterers and Dissemblers.
The Women be there very obedient to their
Husbands, and are kept straightly from going
abroad, but at some seasons.

· · ·

The [upper-class] Russe is apparelled in
this manner: His upper garment is of cloth of
gold, silke, or cloth, long, downe to the foot,
and buttoned with great buttons of silver, or
else laces of silke, set on with Brooches, the
sleeves thereof very long, which he weareth
on his arme, ruffed up. Under that he hath another long garment, buttoned with silke buttons, with a high coller standing up of some
colour, and that garment is made straight.
Then his shirt is very fine, and wrought with
red silke, or some gold, with a coller of pearle.
Under his shirt he hath linnen breeches, upon
his legs, a paire of hose without feet, and his
bootes of red or yellow leather. On his head
hee weareth a white Colepeck, with buttons
of silver, gold, pearle, or stone, and under it
a black Foxe cap, turned up very broad. When
he rideth on horse-back to the warres, or any
journey, he hath a sword of the Turkish
fashion, and his Bowe and Arrowes of the
same manner. In the Towne he weareth no
weapon, but onely two or three paire of
knives, having the hafts of the tooth of a Fish,
called the Morse.

In the Winter time, the people travell with
Sleds, in Towne and Countrey, the way being
hard, and smooth with snow: the waters and
Rivers are all frozen, and one horse with a
Sled, will draw a man upon it foure hundred
miles in three dayes: but in the Summer time,
the way is deep with myre, and travelling is
very ill.

VII:40. THE CHARTER OF THE PATRIARCH OF CONSTANTINOPLE, 1561

In 1561 Iosaf, patriarch of Constantinople, sent to Moscow this charter or official letter recognizing Ivan IV's right to the title of tsar. In his effort to please Moscow, Iosaf embraced the legend about the crowning of Vladimir Monomakh as tsar.

Reference: *RIB*, vol. 22, cols. 68–69.

Iosaf, by the grace of God archbishop of Constantinople, the New Rome, and ecumenical patriarch. Our Beatitude [*nashe smirenie,* literally "our humbleness"] has truly learned and determined, not only through the tales of many men worthy of credence, but also through writings, and through the accounts of chroniclers, that the present reigning tsar of Moscow and Novgorod, Astrakhan', Kazan', Nagai, and all Great Russia, the lord Ivan, is descended in lineage and royal blood from that ever-memorable tsaritsa and sovereign, Lady Anna, sister of the autocrat and tsar Monomachus, of the lineage of the pious tsar Constantine [the Great] and born to the purple . . . [who] together with the patriarch and with the consecrated archbishops of the Cathedral of Constantinople [Hagia Sophia] sent the most eminent metropolitan of Ephesus and Andiokhiiskii [Antioch?], a most prominent eparch, to crown the pious grand prince Vladimir as tsar and give him a royal crown [to place] upon his head, and a necklet [*diadima*] decorated with jewels, and other kingly regalia and gifts. Likewise did the most eminent metropolitan of Moscow and all Great Russia Lord Makarii apprehend this and lawfully crown the pious prince [Ivan IV] as tsar. . . . [We recognize] that [Ivan IV] is and should be called tsar, legitimately and piously crowned, and for the benefit of all pious and Christ-loving men we jointly [bestow upon him] our own and our church's enlightenment and blessing, since he is of royal lineage and blood, as we have said.

VII:41. TWO PRINTER'S NOTES ON THE BEGINNING OF PRINTING IN RUSSIA, 1553-1564

The printing of books in Moscow was begun in 1553 under the sponsorship of Metropolitan Makarii but at first proceeded slowly. A regular printing office was established ten years later by the deacon Ivan Fedorov and his assistant. The first book printed by them was an "Apostle," or book containing the acts and epistles of the apostles, completed on March 1, 1564. Its printers were soon obliged to flee to Lithuania (it was the time of the oprichnina), and they continued their publishing in L'vov and Ostrog. Fedorov died in L'vov in 1583. Meanwhile printing in Moscow became a state monopoly. The two excerpts below are from the printer's notes contained in the "afterword" of the *Apostle* printed in Moscow by Fedorov in 1563-64, and the "afterword" of the *Apostle* printed in L'vov (Lemberg) by Fedorov in 1573-74.

Reference: Pavel M. Stroev, ed., *Obstoiatel'noe opisanie staropechatnykh knig slavianskikh i rossiiskikh, khraniashchikhsia v biblioteke grafa F. A. Tolstova* (Moscow, 1829), pp. 27-28, 32-33. Cf. R. Jakobson, "Ivan Fedorov's Primer of 1574," in *Harvard Library Bulletin* 9, no. 1 (winter 1955): 5-45; M. N. Tikhomirov, ed., *U istokov russkogo knigopechataniia* (Moscow: AN SSSR, 1959); for more see L. A. Vezirova, comp., and A. D. Eikhengol'ts, ed., *Khrestomatiia po istorii russkoi knigi 1564-1917* (Moscow: Izd. "Kniga," 1965).

[From the volume of 1563-64:]

Afterword: . . . By command of the pious tsar and grand prince of all Russia Ivan [IV] Vasil'evich, and with the blessing of His Eminence Metropolitan [of Moscow] Makarii, they began to study the art of printing books, in the year 7061 [1553]. And in the thirtieth year of [Ivan IV's] reign [1563], the pious tsar ordered that a house be furnished by his royal treasury, where the work of printing could be done, and gave unsparingly from his royal wealth to the workers, the deacon Ivan Fedorov of [the Church of] Saint Nicholas the Miracle Worker of Gostun [in the Kremlin] and Petr Timofeev Mstislavets, for carrying on the work of printing and for their lodging, until their work should reach completion. And they began at first to print these sacred books, the Acts of the Apostles and the General Epistles and the Epistles of the apostle Saint Paul, on April 19 in the year 7071 [1563]. . . . And they were finished on the first day of March in the year 7072 [1564].

[From the volume of 1573-74:]

Afterword: . . . Through the will of the

Father and the help of the Son and the consummation of the Holy Ghost, by command of the pious tsar and grand prince of all Russia Ivan Vasil'evich, and with the blessing of His Eminence Makarii, metropolitan of all Russia, this print shop was opened in the ruling city of Moscow, in the year 7071 [1563], in the thirtieth year of [Ivan IV's] reign. I have begun to relate these things to you purposely, because of the exceeding persecution which we often encountered, not from the sovereign himself, but from many officials, church authorities, and preceptors who out of envy slanderously accused us of many heresies, wishing to turn good into evil and utterly to destroy God's work; for this often happens among immoral, ignorant, and unwise men who are neither skilled in the art of letters nor filled with spiritual wisdom, but who spread evil words without reason or purpose. . . . For they drove us from our country and our native land and our people, and removed us to other lands unknown.

VII:42. IVAN IV'S CORRESPONDENCE WITH PRINCE KURBSKII, 1564-1579

Prince Andrei Mikhailovich Kurbskii (1528-83) was a boyar, military commander, and close collaborator of Ivan's during the early years of his reign, but their relationship deteriorated, and in the spring of 1564 Kurbskii left Muscovy and entered the service of the grand duke of Lithuania. According to various seventeenth-century manuscripts, there ensued a correspondence between Kurbskii and the tsar in which are expressed both Ivan's views of his own role and the grievances that certain elements of Muscovite society nursed against him.

Reference: J. L. I. Fennell, ed. and trans., *The Correspondence between Prince A. M. Kurbsky and Tsar Ivan IV of Russia, 1564-1579* (Cambridge: At the University Press, 1955), pp. 3-5 [Kurbskii's letter of 1564]; 13-15, 27, 45-47, 67-69, 105, 153 [Ivan, 1564]; 189-95 [Ivan, 1577] 237 [Kurbskii, Sept. 3, 1579]; 243-45 [Kurbskii, Sept. 25, 1579]. Professor Fennell's translation has been used with only minor typographical changes. For the original Russian, see *RIB*, vol. 31, cols. 1-2 [Kurbskii, 1564]; cols. 9, 11, 25, 49, and pp. 56, 68, 104 [Ivan, 1564]; cols. 119-22 [Ivan, 1577]; col. 151 [Kurbskii, Sept. 3, 1579]; cols. 155-56 [Kurbskii, Sept. 25, 1579]. See also Fennell and Obolensky, *Historical Russian Reader*, pp. 136-146, 201-206. For more, see V. P. Adrianova-Peretts, ed., *Poslaniia Ivana Groznogo* (Moscow: AN SSSR, 1951).

[From Kurbskii's first epistle to Ivan, 1564:]

Wherefore, O Tsar, have you destroyed the strong in Israel [i.e. Muscovy, "the New Israel"] and subjected to various forms of death the voevody given to you by God? And wherefore have you spilt their victorious, holy blood in the churches of God during sacerdotal ceremonies, and stained the thresholds of the churches with their blood of martyrs? And why have you conceived against your well-wishers and against those who lay down their lives for you unheard-of torments and persecutions and death, falsely accusing the Orthodox of treachery and magic and other abuses, and endeavoring with zeal to turn light into darkness and to call sweet bitter? What guilt did they commit before you, O Tsar, and in what way did they, the champions of Christianity, anger you? Have they not destroyed proud kingdoms and by their heroic bravery made subject to you in all things those in whose servitude our forefathers formerly were? Was it not through the keenness of their understanding that the strong German towns were given to you by God? Thus have you remunerated us, [your] poor [servants], destroying us by whole families? Think you yourself immortal, O Tsar? Or have you been enticed into unheard-of heresy, as one no longer wishing to stand before the impartial judge, Jesus, begotten of God, who will judge according to justice the universe and especially the vainglorious tormentors?

[From the epistle of the tsar to all his Russian kingdom against Prince Kurbskii and his comrades, July 5, 1564:]

And as the words of God encircled the whole world like an eagle in flight, so a spark of piety reached even the Russian kingdom. The autocracy of this Russian kingdom, by the will of God, [has its] beginning from the great tsar Vladimir, who enlightened the whole Russian land with holy baptism, and [was maintained by] the great tsar Vladimir Monomakh, who received the supreme honor from the Greeks, and the brave and great sovereign, Aleksandr Nevskii, who won a victory

over the godless Germans, and the great and
praiseworthy sovereign Dmitrii, who beyond
the Don won a mighty victory over the godless sons of Hagar [and autocracy was handed
down] even to the avenger of evils, our grandfather, Grand Prince Ivan, and to the acquirer
of immemorially hereditary lands, our father
of blessed memory, the great sovereign,
Vasilii—and [autocracy] has come down even
to us, the humble scepter-bearer of the Russian kingdom. And we praise [God] for his
great mercy bestowed upon us, in that he has
not hitherto allowed our right hand to become stained with the blood of our own race;
for we have not seized the kingdom from
anyone, but, by the grace of God and with
the blessing of our forefathers and fathers, as
we were born to rule, so have we grown up
and ascended the throne by the bidding of
God, and with the blessing of our parents
have we taken what is our own, and we have
not seized what belongs to others.

· · ·

But as for the Russian autocracy, they
themselves [i.e. the autocrats] from the beginning have ruled all the[ir] dominions, and
not the boyars and not the grandees. And this
you have not been able to appreciate in your
wickedness, calling it "piety" when the autocracy is under the power of a certain priest
[Sylvester] and at the mercy of your impious
commands [literally "commands of impiety"].
While this, according to your understanding,
is evil—namely, that we ourselves rule[d]
[with] the power given us by God and had no
desire to be at the mercy of the priest and of
your wicked designs!

· · ·

Or do you consider this to be "light," for
a priest and overweening, cunning servants to
rule, and the tsar to be held in honor only by
virtue of his presidency and for the sake of
the renown of the kingdom, while in power
he is in no way better than a servant? And is
this "darkness," for the tsar to rule [literally
"to hold"] his kingdom and govern, and for
his servants submissively to fulfill his orders?
How, pray, can a man be called autocrat if he
himself does not govern [literally "build"]?

· · ·

We do not stain the thresholds with any
blood; and at the present time we have no
martyrs for the faith [i.e. genuine martyrs].
As for our well-wishers and those who lay

down their lives for us truly and not with
deceit . . . when we find one such man who is
free from all these evils and who serves us
with integrity [literally "performs his straight-
forward duty to us"] and forgets not . . .
the duties that are entrusted to him—such
a man do we reward with all kinds of great
rewards. And he who is found to be the opposite [of such a man]—as we said above—
then, according to his guilt will he receive his
punishment as well. And in other lands you
yourself will see how evil befalls the evil man;
there it is not the same as [it was] here! [i.e.
during the "rule of the traitors"]. For in your
devilish manner you decreed that traitors be
loved—but in foreign lands they love not
traitors; they punish them so that by this
[their country] may be strengthened.

"Torments and persecutions and various
forms of death" we have not conceived
against anyone. And as for your mentioning
"treachery and magic"—well, such dogs are
executed in all countries.

· · ·

But always one and the same thing have
you written in your calumnious document,
praising the rule of servants over the heads of
their masters. But I endeavor with zeal to
guide people to the truth and to the light in
order that they may know the one true God,
who is glorified in the Trinity, and the sovereign given to them by God; and in order that
they may cease from internecine strife and a
froward life, which things cause kingdoms to
crumble. Is this then bitterness and darkness—
to cease from evil deeds and to do good deeds?
Nay, this is sweetness and light! If a tsar's subjects do not obey him, then never will they
cease from internecine strife.

· · ·

Against the Christian race we do not devise
vessels of torture, but rather do we desire to
suffer for them in the face of all their enemies, not only to blood, but even to death.
As for our subjects, we recompense the good
with good, and to the evil are meted out evil
punishments, not because we wish it, not because we desire it, but of necessity, because of
their evil crime is there punishment.

[From Ivan's epistle sent from Wolmar, near
Riga, 1577:]
You have written that I am "corrupt in
understanding to a degree unparalleled even

among the [godless] peoples." And yet I will again place you as judge over myself; are you corrupt or am I, in that I wished to rule you and you did not wish to be under my power, and that for this I inflicted disgrace upon you? Or are you corrupt, in that not only did you [not] wish to be obedient and subordinate to me, but you even ruled over me, and took all my power from me, and ruled yourselves as you wanted and took all the sovereign authority from me: in word I was sovereign, but in fact I ruled nothing. How many evils I received from you, how many insults, how many injuries and rebukes! And for what? What was my guilt before you in the first place? Whom did I offend [and] in what?

. . .

If only you had not stood up against me with the priest [Sylvester]! Then none of this would have happened; all this took place because of your self-willedness. And why did you want to place Prince Vladimir [Staritskii] on the [throne of the] kingdom and to remove me and my children? Did I ascend the throne by robbery or armed force of blood-[shed]? I was born to rule by the grace of God. . . . And I could not endure such vexations; I stood up for myself. And you began still more to revolt against me and to betray [me]; and I therefore began to stand up against you still more harshly. . . . But you, like the Devil, with the priest Sylvester and Aleksei Adashev . . . did . . . think that the whole Russian land would be under your feet.

[From Kurbskii's fourth epistle to Ivan, September 3, 1579:]

Having gathered around you all your army and having rushed into the woods like a coward and a runaway, you tremble and hide, though no one chases—only your conscience

cries out within against you, exposing you for your foul deeds and limitless shedding of blood. It remains for you only perhaps to quarrel like a drunken servant girl; and as for what is verily befitting and worthy of royal dignity, namely just judgment and defence, this has already as good as disappeared, thanks to the prayer[s] and counsel of Vassian Toporkov of that cunning Josephian band [i.e. stemming from Joseph of Volokolamsk],—who whispered in your ear and advised you not to keep at your side counselors wiser [than yourself]—and of other such most cunning counselors of yours, both monks and laymen.

[From Kurbskii's fifth epistle to Ivan, September 25, 1579:]

The Devil . . . has brought to your side most foul parasites and maniacs; instead of strong generals and commanders—the Bel'skiis, most foul in deed and abhorrent to God, with their comrades; and instead of a brave army—the children of darkness or bloodthirsty oprichniki, hundreds and thousands of times worse than hangmen; instead of divinely inspired books and holy prayers, which your immortal soul [once] enjoyed and by which your royal ears were sanctified—buffoons with all sorts of pipes and devilish songs hateful to God, which defile and close the ears for the approach to theology; and instead of that blessed priest, who formerly reconciled you to God by means of pure penitence, and other spiritual advisers, who often conversed with you—you gather (so they tell us here; I know not if it is true) magicians and wizards from far distant lands, questioning them for days of fortune, as did Saul, foul and abhorrent to God. . . . But what happened to him in the end? This you yourself know well: destruction for him and his royal house.

VII:43. THE TSAR'S DECREE ON CHURCH LANDS, JANUARY 15, 1581

This decree illustrates one of the ways Ivan IV tried to deal with the problem of the vast church lands.

Reference: *AAE*, 1:373.

Together with the most pious tsar and grand prince of all Russia Ivan [IV] Vasil'evich . . . we, Our Eminence [*preosviashchennyi*] Antonii, metropolitan of all Russia, with the holy council and the Tsar's council [*sinklit*, i.e. the boyar duma], in order that the temples

of God and church property may be free from turmoil, and so that the military forces [*voinskii chin*] may be armed more strongly to fight against the enemies of the cross of Christ, hereby decree and arrange as follows: that the land and its productive resources [*ugod'ia*] and immovable objects, such as villages, hamlets, meadows, and hayfields . . . belonging to the metropolitanate and the bishoprics and the monasteries shall not be transferred, shall not pass from the possession of the metropolitanate and the bishoprics and the monasteries through any trial or litigation, and shall not be taken over or bought as patrimonial estates [*votchiny*] from the metropolitan or the bishops or the monasteries. . . . And from this day forward, the fifteenth day of January [1581], owners of patrimonial estates shall not bequeath them in commemoration of their souls, but shall give the monastery money instead, as much as that village is worth; and the village itself shall remain a patrimonial estate, even if it becomes necessary to bequeath it to a distant relative. If there is not even a distant relative in the family, then the patrimonial estate shall pass to the sovereign, and money for it shall be paid from the treasury. The metropolitan or bishops or monasteries shall not buy lands or hold them in mortgage; if anyone [of the clergy] should buy land after the issuance of this decree, or take it over in mortgage, such land shall also pass to the sovereign.

VII:44. AN ANONYMOUS ACCOUNT OF THE ESTABLISHMENT OF THE PATRIARCHATE IN MOSCOW, 1589

A manuscript of the late 1500s, copied in 1619, gives this general explanation of how the head of the Muscovite church became patriarch of Moscow and all Russia.
    Reference: *DAI*, 2:189-92 (see List of Abbreviations).

All these lands, cities, and regions [of Great Russia] accepted divine baptism in the year 6499 from the creation of the world [A.D. 991], under the guidance of the great and blessed sovereign of the realm, Vladimir, coequal with the apostles [*ravnoapostol'nyi*], who sprang from the line of Augustus, caesar of Rome, ruler over all the world. Vladimir then ruled over all the Slavs and over other peoples, of whom some afterward accepted holy baptism, but all were under the sovereignty of the Russian realm. . . . But as much as piety declined in ancient Rome and in other countries, so much and more did grace shine in the most glorious and reigning city of Moscow; and in the lands of the Russian metropolitanate many metropolitans and archbishops and bishops shone as does the sun amidst the stars, and [their] miracles caressed the earth. . . .
    . . . Thus many metropolitans and archbishops and bishops came to this pious tsar from the holy city of Jerusalem, and from Tsar'grad, and from other places . . . [and] declared to the pious tsar that in the Greek land the holy churches and monasteries of God were suffering from much destruction and plunder through the rule of the pagans.
    . . . Therefore, having heard these things, the true defender of piety, the pious tsar Feodor Ivanovich . . . being inflamed by divine zeal, convoked a council of piety [*Sovet blago-chestiia*] in the ruling city of Moscow, with the primate [*pervoprestol'nik*] of the holy church in the Russian land, and with the archbishops and bishops, and with other churchmen [*sviashchennye muzhi*], and with the magnates [*velmozhi*]: [and the tsar said:] "I desire, if it be pleasing to God and if the divine Scriptures do not oppose it, that there be erected a most exalted patriarchal throne in the ruling city of Moscow. . . ." Hearing these words, the most eminent metropolitan, and the other prelates [*sviatiteli*], and the noble boyars praised the counsel of the pious tsar . . . but said, however: "Pious Tsar! If it pleases your pious sovereignty, may this be made known to the four ecumenical patriarchs through an epistle . . . lest it be imagined, O pious Tsar, by other peoples . . . that a patriarchal throne was erected in the ruling city of Moscow solely through the power of the tsar alone." The pious tsar, hearing these things, readily agreed, even though he could have erected a most exalted patriarchal throne by his power as tsar and autocrat; but he thought it proper to bear obedience to the will of God and the counsel of the prelates, all the more since he was in every way an obedient son of the holy church: and straightway he ordered the word to be made deed, and thus an epistle from the tsar and the prelates was soon dispatched to the four patriarchs and to many metropolitans with such an inquiry. The envoys went eagerly on their way, and, by the grace of God, the [reply]

sought was received. After a certain time had passed, the envoys came into the ruling city of Moscow, to the pious tsar, bearing with them the counsel and statement of the four patriarchs and the metropolitans concerning the patriarchate, and bringing an epistle from the patriarchs and metropolitans and other bishops for even stronger confirmation. . . . In the third year after the envoys [had returned] there came to the ruling city of Moscow Jeremiah, by the grace of God archbishop of Constantinople and ecumenical patriarch, and with him the metropolitan of Monembasia [in the Peloponnesus], Erofei [Dorotheus?], and the archbishop of Elassonia [in Thessaly], Arsenius, and many other archimandrites and abbots from the worthy monasteries, bearing

with them blessings upon the pious tsar, the primate, the noble boyars, and all the people, and counsel and confirmation to the Russian metropolitanate concerning the patriarchate; the pious tsar ordered them to be greeted with due honor and summoned them to dine at the tsar's table, arranging it well. And thus in a few days, through a council of the tsar and patriarch and other prelates of the Greek and Russian lands, in the year 7097 [1589] from the creation of the world, in the sixth year of the reign of the pious tsar Feodor Ivanovich, Metropolitan Job of the ruling city of Moscow and all Great Russia was chosen and elevated to the most exalted patriarchal throne in the Russian metropolitanate.

VII:45. PATRIARCH JEREMIAH'S ADDRESS, 1589

Before establishing a patriarchate in Moscow, Patriarch Jeremiah of Constantinople addressed Tsar Fedor Ivanovich as follows, according to the account contained in the 1653 edition of the *Kormchaia kniga* or collection of church laws.
    Reference: *Kormchaia kniga* (Moscow, 1787; republished from the edition of 1653), pt. 1, p. 15.

You wish to honor and to adorn the great and holy church [of Russia] . . . with the lofty throne of the patriarchate, and with that great deed to glorify and enhance all the more the reigning city, Moscow, and all your great Russian tsardom. . . . For the ancient Rome has fallen through the Apollinarian heresy. The second Rome, which is Constantinople, is held by the Ishmaelites—the godless Turks. And the third Rome—your great Russian tsardom, O pious Tsar—has surpassed them

all in piety, and all pious people have been united in your tsardom. And you alone on earth are called a Christian tsar everywhere and among all Christians. And by God's providence and the grace of the most pure Virgin, and thanks to the prayers of the new miracle workers of the great Russian tsardom—Peter and Alexis and Jonah—and through your Church's request to God, and in accordance with your royal purpose, this great deed will be accomplished.

VII:46. AN ANONYMOUS ACCOUNT OF THE INSTALLATION OF THE MOSCOW PATRIARCH, JANUARY 26-28, 1589

This excerpt from an account of the installation of Patriarch Job is from a collection of manuscripts dating from the seventeenth century and kept by the Archeographical Commission.
    Reference: *RIB*, vol. 2, cols. 317-20.

And as the patriarch [of Constantinople] Jeremiah came into the vestibule [*seni*], the patriarch Job came out of the chamber [*palata*] and met him on the porch [*primost*] before the doors, and . . . Patriarch Jeremiah asked the blessing of Job, the newly elevated patriarch of Moscow.
    And the patriarch Job spoke to him thus: "You are for me the great lord and elder of elders and father: from you I have received the patriarchal blessing and elevation to the great throne in the Cathedral of the Honored

and Glorious Dormition of the Most Pure Mother of God and the Holy Moscow Miracle Workers Peter and Alexis and Jonah, and it is now fitting for you to give us your blessing."
    And in answer to this the patriarch Jeremiah spoke: "In all the world there is [now] but one pious tsar, while the future shall be as God may grant; it is here that the ecumenical patriarch should be, while in old Tsar'grad the Christian faith is being driven out by the infidel Turks for our sins."
    And after saying these things, the ecumen-

ical patriarch Jeremiah gave his blessing to the patriarch Job, and after receiving the blessing of the patriarch Jeremiah, the patriarch Job likewise gave his blessing, and they kissed each other in the name of Christ.

. . . And when they [the choir] began to sing "Long life to the Lord" [*Is Polla Eti Despota*] [meaning, the consecrated prelate, i.e. Job] the patriarch Jeremiah seated the patriarch Job in the place that had been prepared, paying him great honor and saluting him. . . . And the patriarchs seated themselves for a short time; and after the chanters had finished singing, the ecumenical patriarch Jeremiah arose, joyfully summoned in a loud voice the holy council [*osviashchennyi sobor—* the council consisting of the higher clergy] and all the Christian people to gather around him, and spoke to them thus: "Almighty God has shed his grace upon the Russian realm for its pure way of life, and for its supplications, and for its great charity, and for the prayers of the pious sovereign, tsar, and grand prince Feodor Ivanovich, autocrat of all Russia, to elevate a patriarch in the Apostolic Cathedral of the Honored and Glorious Dormition of the Most Pure Mother of God and of the Holy Russian Miracle Workers Peter and Alexis and Jonah, since in all the world there is but one pious tsar."

VII:47. GILES FLETCHER ON RUSSIA, 1588

In 1588 Giles Fletcher (1546-1611) was sent by Queen Elizabeth to conclude a commercial treaty with Tsar Fedor Ivanovich. Fletcher in his late twenties and early thirties had been at King's College, Cambridge, as a lecturer in Greek and then briefly as dean of arts, while at the same time earning his Doctor of Civil Laws degree (1581). In his late thirties he served a term in Parliament and then became an official of the City of London. In 1585-87 he journeyed to Hamburg and Stade for trade negotiations as a special agent of the queen, and it was apparently his success in that mission that led to his being sent soon thereafter to Russia. He remained there from the summer of 1588 to the summer of 1589, and in the autumn of that same year wrote his famous account *The Russe Commonwealth.* After revisions it was first published in London in 1591. Fletcher has been characterized as a "typical man of the Renaissance—a statesman by profession and a man of letters by avocation" (Berry). The scope and value of his observations on Russia are suggested by these excerpts.

Reference: Lloyd E. Berry, ed., *The English Works of Giles Fletcher, the Elder* (Madison: University of Wisconsin Press, 1964), pp. 179-83, 194, 200-01, 224-25, 233-36, 239, 241-42, 268-69, 274-76, 286-87. Berry's critical edition is fully annotated and contains further details on Fletcher's career. Some minor changes in capitalization, italicization, and spelling have been made in the present text in order to facilitate comprehension while preserving the flavor of Fletcher's own language, as done in an earlier but less definitive edition of Fletcher: Edward A. Bond, ed., *Russia at the Close of the Sixteenth Century, Comprising the Treatise "Of the Russe Common Wealth," by Dr. Giles Fletcher and "The Travels of Jerome Horsey, Knt."* (London, 1856). Students who would like to see what the original edition of 1591 looked like may refer to Giles Fletcher, *Of the Russe Commonwealth; Facsimile Edition with Variants,* with an introduction by Richard Pipes and a glossary-index by John V. A. Fine, Jr. (Cambridge, Mass.: Harvard University Press, 1966). Another edition which contains explanatory notes (as do those of both Berry and Fine) is Giles Fletcher, *Of the Rus Commonwealth,* ed. Albert J. Schmidt (Ithaca: Cornell University Press, 1966).

The native commodities of the countrie (wherewith they serve both their owne turnes, and sende much abroad to the great enriching of the emperour and his people) are many and substantiall. First, furres of all sortes.

. . .

The second commoditie is of wax. . . .
The third is their hony. . . .
Fourthly, of tallow they afoord a great waight for transportation. . . .

An other principall commoditie is their losh [elk] and cowe hide. . . .

An other very great and principall commoditie is their trane oyle, drawen out of the seal fish. . . .

. . .

Likewise of ickary or cavery, a great quantitie is made upon the river of Volgha, out of the fish called bellougina, the sturgeon, the severiga, and the sterledey. Wherof the most part is shipped by French and Netherlandish marchants for Italy and Spaine, some by English marchants.

The next is of flaxe and hempe. . . .

The countrey besides maketh great store of salt. . . .

Likewise of tarre they make a great quantity out of their firre trees in the countrey of Dvyna and Smolensko, whereof much is sent abroad. . . . [Also] the fishe tooth. . . .

In the province of Corelia, and about the river Dvyna towardes the North Sea, there groweth a soft rocke which they call slude [*sliuda*–mica]. This they cut into pieces, and so teare it into thin flakes, which naturally it is apt for, and so use it for glasse-lanthorns and such like. . . . Saltpeter they make in many places. . . . Their iron is somewhat brittle, but a great weight of it is made in Corelia, Cargapolia, and Ustug Thelesna. Other myne they have none growing within the realme.

· · ·

The manner of their government is much after the Turkish fashion: which they seeme to imitate. . . .

The state and forme of their government is plaine tyrannicall, as applying all to the behoofe of the prince, and that after a most open and barbarous manner: as may appeare by the *sophismata* or secretes of their government afterwards set downe, aswell for the keeping of the nobilitie and commons in an under proportion, and far uneven balance in their severall degrees, as also in their impositions and exactions, wherein they exceede all just measure without any regard of nobilitie or people: farther then it giveth the nobilitie a kinde of injust and unmeasured libertie; to commaund and exact upon the commons and baser sort of people in all partes of the realme where so ever they come, specially in the place where their landes lye, or where they are appoynted by the emperour to gouerne under him.

· · ·

[In the period of Ivan IV's oprichnina] this libertie of the one part to spoyle and kill the other, without anie helpe of magistrat or lawe (that continued seven yeeres), enriched that side and the emperours treasurie, and wrought that withall which hee intended by this practise, viz. to take out of the way such of the nobilitie as himselfe misliked: whereof

were slayne within one weeke to the number of three hundred within the citie of Mosko. This tyrannicall practise of making a generall schisme and publike division among the subjects of his whole realme, proceeded (as should seeme) from an extreame doubt and desperate feare which hee had conceived of most of his nobilitie and gentlemen of his realme, in his warres with the Polonian and Chrim Tartar. What time hee grewe into a vehement suspition (conceived of the ill successe of his affayres) that they practised treason with the Polonian and Chrim. Whereupon he executed some, and devised this way to be ridde of the rest.

And this wicked pollicy and tyrannous practise (though now it be ceassed) hath so troubled that countrey, and filled it so full of grudge and mortall hatred ever since, that it wil not be quenched (as it seemeth now) till it burne againe into a civill flame.

· · ·

Besides the taxes, customes, seazures, and other publique exactions done upon them by the emperour, they are so racked and pulled by the nobles, officers, and messengers sent abroad by the emperour in his publique affaires, specially in the yammes (as they call them) and thorough faire townes, that you shall have many villages and townes of halfe a mile and a mile long, stande all unhabited: the people being fled all into other places, by reason of the extreame usage and exactions done upon them. So that in the way towards Mosko, betwixt Vologda and Yaruslaveley (which is two nineties after their reckoning, little more then an hundreth miles English) there are in sigt fiftie darievnes or villages at the least, some halfe a mile, some a mile long, that stand vacant and desolate without any inhabitant. The like is in all other places of the realme, as is said by those that have better travelled the countrie then my selfe had time or occasion to doo.

· · ·

The souldiers of Russia are called sina-boiarskey [deti boiarskie], or the sons of gentlemen: because they are all of that degree, by vertue of their military profession. For every souldier in Russia is a gentleman, and none are gentlemen but only the souldiers, that take it by discent from their ancestors: so that the sonne of a gentleman (which is borne a souldier) is ever a gentleman and souldier withal, and professeth nothing els but militarie matters. . . . First, he hath of his *dworaney* [dvoriane], that is, pensioners or gard of his person, to the number of 15,000 horsemen, with their captaines and other officers, that are alwaies in a readines.

. . .

Besides these 15,000 horsemen . . . [there are] 65,000 horsemen, with all necessaries meet for the warres after the Russe manner. . . . And these 65,000 are to repaire to the field every yeere on the borders towards the Chrim Tartar (except they bee appoynted for some other service) whether there be warres with the Tartars or not.

. . .

Of footmen that are in continuall pay, he hath to the number of 12,000, all gunners, called *strelsey*. . . . Of mercenarie souldiers that are strangers (whom they call *nimschoy*), they have at this time 4,300 of Polonians: of Chirchasses (that are under the Polonians) about 4 thousand, whereof 3,500 are abroad in his garrisons: of Doutches and Scots, about 150: of Greekes, Turks, Danes, and Sweadens, all in one band, an 100 or thereabouts. But these they use onely upon the Tartar side, and against the Siberians: as they doe the Tartar souldiers (whom they hire sometimes, but onely for the present) on the other side against the Polonian and Sweaden: thinking it best pollicie so to use their service upon the contrary border.

. . .

If the Russe souldier were as hardy to execute an enterprise as he is hard to beare out toyle and travaile, or were otherwise as apt and wel trained for the warres as he is indifferent for his lodging and dyet, hee would farre excell the souldiours of our partes. Whereas now he is farre meaner of courage and execution in any warlike service. Which commeth partly of his servile condition, that will not suffer any great courage or valure to growe in him. Partly for lacke of due honour and reward, which he hath no great hope of, whatsoever service or execution he doe.

. . .

It is thought that no prince of Christendome hath better stoare of munition then the Russe emperour. And it may partly appeare by the artillerie house at Mosko, where are of all sortes of great ordnance, all brasse pieces, very faire, to an exceeding great number.

The Russe souldier is thought to be better at his defence within some castle or town, then hee is abroad at a set pitched field. Which is ever noted in the practise of his warres, and namely, at the siege of Vobsko [Pskov], about eight yeares since: where hee repulsed the Polonian King Stepan Batore with his whole armie of 100,000 men, and forced him in the ende to give over his siege, with the losse of many of his best captaines and souldiers. But in a set field the Russe is noted to have ever the worse of the Polonian and Sweden.

. . .

The election and appointing of the bishops and the rest, perteyneth wholy to the emperour himselfe. They are chosen ever out of the monasteries: so that there is no bishop, archbishop, nor metropolite, but hath bene a monke or frier before. . . .

As for preaching the worde of God, or any teaching or exhorting such as are under them, they neyther use it nor have any skill of it: the whole cleargie beyng utterlie unlearned bothe for other knowledge and in the word of God.

. . .

They have certeyne Eremites (whome they call Holy men). . . . They use to go starke naked, save a clout about their middle, with their haire hanging long, and wildely about their shoulders, and many of them with an iron coller, or chaine about their neckes, or middes, even in the very extremity of winter. These they take as prophets, and men of great holines, giving them a liberty to speak what they list, without any controulment, thogh it be of the very highest himselfe. . . .

Of this kinde there are not many, because it is a very harde and colde profession, to goe naked in Russia, specially in Winter. Among other at this time, they have one at Mosko, that walketh naked about the streets, and inveyeth commonly against the state, and government, especially against the Godonoes, that are thought at this time to bee great oppressours of that common wealth. An other there was, that dyed not many yeeres agoe (whome they called Basileo) that would take upon him to reproove the olde emperour for all his crueltie and oppressions done toward his people. His body they have translated of late into a sumptuous church neere the emperours house in Mosko, and have canonized him for a saint. . . . There was another of great account at Plesko (called Nichôla of Plesko), that did much good when this emperours father came to sacke the towne, upon suspition of their revolting and rebellion against him. The emperour, after hee had saluted the eremite at his lodging, sent him a reward. And the holy man, to requite the emperour, sent him a piece of rawe fleshe, beyng then their Lent time. Which the emperour seeing, bid one to tell him that he marvelled that the holy man woulde offer him flesh to eat in the Lent, when it was forbidden by order of holie Church. And doth Evasko (which is as much to saye, as Jacke) thinke (quoth Nicôla) that it is unlawful to eate a piece of beasts

flesh in Lent, and not to eate up so much mans flesh as hee hathe done already? So threatning the emperour with a prophecy of some hard adventure to come upon him, except hee left murdering of his people, and departed the towne, he saved a great many mens lives at that time.

. . .

The manner of making and solemnizing their marriages is different from the manner of other countries. The man (though he never saw the woman before) is not permitted to have any sight of hir al the time of his woing: which he doth not by himself, but by his mother or some other ancient woman of his kin or acquaintance.

VII:48. FEDOR'S DECREE ON RUNAWAYS, NOVEMBER 24, 1597

Tsar Fedor's decree of 1597, initiated by Boris Godunov, actual administrator of Muscovy under Fedor, offers one of our main clues concerning the conditions of the peasantry at that time. The paucity of background information has led to controversy over the decree's exact implications. Some suggest that it implies the issuance of a previous decree banning peasant movement altogether; others insist that the "fugitive peasants" covered by the decree are merely those who had left in violation of such long-standing rules as those about Saint George's Day and about paying one's debts.

Reference: Arkheograficheskaia Komissiia, *Akty istoricheskie*, 1:420-21. A full translation is included in the recently published Smith, *Enserfment of the Russian Peasantry*, pp. 98-101. A convenient collection of other documents on the 1500s and 1600s, in addition to those collections cited in this chapter and the next, is V. A. Aleksandrov and V. I. Koretskii, comps., A. A. Zimin, ed., *Khrestomatiia po istorii SSSR XVI-XVII vv.* (Moscow: Izd. Sotsial'no-Ekonomichesko Literatury, 1962). To supplement the other works in English mentioned in the reference notes of this chapter, the student may turn to Marthe Blinoff, ed. and trans., *Life and Thought in Old Russia* (State College, Pa.: Pennsylvania University Press, 1961). It contains short excerpts translated from several documents of the 1500s and later, grouped under topical headings.

On the twenty-fourth day of November in the year 7106 [1597] the tsar and grand prince of all Russia Fedor Ivanovich decreed, and the boyars resolved:

Whatever peasants have fled from boyars and nobles [dvoriane] and government officials [prikaznye liudi] and deti boiarskie and all manner of people, from pomest'ia and patrimonial estates . . . and monastery estates during the five years preceding the current year of [7]106, those fugitive peasants in their flight, and those owners of pomest'ia and patrimonies with whom, having fled, they live, [and] those landowners from whom they have fled . . . are to be brought before a court, and a diligent and thorough investigation is to be made, and upon trial and investigation

those fugitive peasants with their wives and with their children and with all their possessions are to be brought back, each to where he [originally] lived.

But regarding peasants who have fled six and seven and ten or more years previous to the current year of [7]106, [and] those owner of pomest'ia and patrimonies from whom they fled . . . who have not petitioned the sovereign tsar, the sovereign decreed and the boyars resolved that those fugitive peasants in their flight, and those owners of pomest'ia [and] patrimonies with whom, having fled, they live, are not to be brought before a court, and [the fugitives] are not to be brought back each to where he [originally] lived.

CHAPTER VIII

Muscovite Russia in the Seventeenth Century

Note: Some seventeenth-century sources are also contained in Chapter IX.

A. THE TIME OF TROUBLES, 1605-1613

VIII:1. THE "NEW CHRONICLE" CONCERNING EVENTS OF 1605-11

One valuable comprehensive narrative of the confused and tragic years preceding the establishment of the Romanov dynasty is the work of the so-called New Chronicler (*Novyi Letopisets*). This portion of his account evidently dates from the time of Tsar Michael, perhaps about 1630, though other portions were added later. He evidently had access to many official documents, charters, and diplomatic communications. His use of the year-to-year form characteristic of a chronicle reflects the style of the time. The short sample presented here picks up the story in the spring of 1605, when the first pseudo-Dmitrii, referred to here as Grishka Otrep'ev, sent his messengers, Naum Pleshcheev and Gavrila Puskin, to Moscow with "a letter to all the people."

Reference: Obshchestvo Istorii i Drevnostei Rossiiskikh, *Vremennik Imperatorskogo Moskovskogo Obshchestva Istorii i Drevnostei Rossiiskikh*, 25 vols. (Moscow, 1849-57), 17:68, 78, 138. A newer edition of a different version of the New Chronicle is in the *PSRL*, vol. 14, pt. 1; the corresponding, but not identical, excerpts are on pp. 65, 71, 112. This portion of the *PSRL* was recently reproduced photographically under the title *Novyi letopisets* (Ann Arbor: Xerox Co., 1967).

A multitude of people foregathered and came to the place that is called Lobnoe [Lobnoe Mesto, an elevated and enclosed area in Red Square next to the Kremlin, used for official proclamations and gatherings], and the assembly of people was joined by service men, some of their own will and others out of mortal fear. And the boyars, beholding the agitation of the people, hastened to Patriarch Job, making known to him what had occurred; and he tried in every way to quench the turmoil, threatening them with God's judgment and [eternal] torment, and admonishing them with kind words, but to no avail. And a great multitude, entering the Kremlin, forcibly led the boyars to the Lobnoe Mesto, to the assembly of all the people, and after bringing [the boyars] they made them stand there, and began to read out the message sent by this Grishka, proclaiming to all that he was the real son of the tsar. When they had read it for everyone to hear, all the people cried out in one voice, hailing him as the tsar; then they rushed to the palace and seized Tsar Feodor and his mother and sister, and they led them away and shut them up in the old house of Tsar Boris and placed them under guard; and they seized their kinsmen the Godunovs, Saburovs, [and] Vel'iaminovs and placed them under guard in their houses; and in the houses they not only looted their possessions but wrecked the buildings themselves; and they did likewise in their patrimonial

estates; and Naum and Gavrilo were sent with this news to Grishka; and he, hearing this, rejoiced.

Then Grishka Otrep'ev made his preparations and marched toward Tula. And in Moscow all the people kissed the cross to him as the rightful tsar.

[After the accession of Tsar Vasilii Shuiskii:]
In the summer of the year 7115 [1607] a great many bondmen [liudi] and peasants gathered, and they were joined by townspeople [*posadskie*] from the Ukrainian towns [region along the upper Oka, Seim, and Upa rivers]; and they began to jail the voevody [governors] in the towns and to plunder the houses of their masters; each did to his master all the evil he could devise; and they looted their property; and they took their wives and virgin daughters as wives for themselves, and slaughtered the males, and committed great evil and unspeakable outrages; and they elected among themselves a leader, surpassing all others in wickedness, a bondman of Prince Andrei Andreevich Teliatevskii, Ivashka Bolotnikov by name.

[After the formation of the First National Host, 1611:]
Among the commanders who stood before Moscow the hatred increased, and they outdid cne another in pride, each wanting to be esteemed by all the others and seeking honor

not in accordance with his ancestral standing [*otchestvo*]; and the most arrogant in his excessive pride was Prokofii Liapunov, who abused and insulted worthy people and treated even the boyars with disdain; and men would come to him to pay their respects and would stand at the door without being admitted into his presence; and he treated the Cossacks with great cruelty, wherefore he became hated most of all. And Zarutskii, having the Cossacks under his command, seized many towns and volosti for himself and gave the Cossacks great license, and the Cossacks committed great robberies everywhere, in the towns and on the highways. And the other soldiers who stood before Moscow were perishing from hunger. And Trubetskoi was not held in any regard at all among them. Seeing this, the soldiers again conferred and together with the Cossacks submitted a petition to all the commanders, wherein they wrote that the boyars and the commanders should take a stand before Moscow, and would they please stand united; also, that they should reward the soldiers according to merit and not by arbitrary choice, and that they should take for themselves, according to their deserts, the patrimonial estates and pomest'ia [estates granted on condition of service] of those boyars who had committed treason and remained in Moscow [with the Poles]; and all the rest should be taken into the treasury to feed and reward the soldiers.

VIII:2. WIELEWICKI ON THE FIRST PSEUDO-DMITRII, CA. 1606

The Jesuit priest Jan Wielewicki, who went to Moscow with the Polish delegation accompanying Marina Mniszek in 1606, later wrote an account of the events of that time. In the first part of the following excerpt, Wielewicki quotes from a letter dated April 10, 1606, sent from Pope Paul V via a Jesuit messenger to the short-lived tsar.

Reference: Pavel A. Mukhanov, ed., *Zapiski getmana Zholkevskogo o Moskovskoi voine*, 2d ed. (St. Petersburg, 1871), cols. 147-49, 171-72.

The letter to Dmitrii was as follows: "The most holy father, Pope Paul V, sends peace and his apostolic blessing to his most beloved son Dmitrii. . . . Now, with God's help, you reign in tranquillity; your power rests on a firm foundation. . . . You have a vast field in which you can plant, sow, and reap; in which you can instill everywhere the sources of Christian godliness; in which you can erect edifices whose roofs shall touch the heavens. And so, make use of the advantages of this place and, like a second Constantine, be the first therein to strengthen the young with the light of knowledge, and show them the true duties of a Christian through your own example; be the first to comprehend the duty, reserved to you by God, of enlightening your realm, and be the first to carry it out. There is but a single Catholic faith; let there be but a single Catholic unanimity over the entire face of the earth; may this unanimity draw us closer together and bind us with the closest ties of love, even though an immeasurable expanse of land should separate us. . . ."

. . .

[As of the spring of 1606] Dmitrii was much changed, and no longer resembled the Dmitrii who had been in Poland. He thought little of the Catholic faith and religion, despite so many promises. He now spoke disrespectfully and even contemptuously of the pope, to whom, in the letters he had sent from Poland, he had dedicated both himself and his subjects. According to the words of trustworthy witnesses, he was addicted to sins of the flesh and, it was said, had various dealings with magicians. All the heretics [i.e. the Orthodox] had access to him, and in the main he followed their advice and suggestions. He grew so proud that he not only compared himself to all the Christian monarchs but even considered himself above them, and said that he, like a second Hercules, would be the glorious leader of all Christendom against the Turks. Of his own accord he adopted the title of emperor, and demanded that not only his own subjects, but even foreign sovereigns should address him thus.

VIII:3. SHUISKII'S INSTRUCTIONS FOR THE DISCREDITING OF THE FIRST PSEUDO-DMITRII, MAY 1606

In May 1606, shortly after the boyars led by Vasilii Shuiskii had murdered Tsar Dmitrii (the first pseudo-Dmitrii), Shuiskii faced the task of justifying his own usurpatory actions and destroying the legend he had earlier endorsed that had brought his predecessor to the throne. Not having modern means of mass communication at his disposal, Shuiskii sent out messengers like Gavrila Shipov, bearing instructions like those preserved here.

Reference: A. M. Gnevushev, comp. and ed., *Akty vremeni pravleniia tsaria Vasiliia Shuiskogo (19 maia 1606 g.-17 iiulia 1610 g.)* (Moscow: Izd. Imperatorskogo Obshchestva Istorii i Drevnostei pri Moskovskom Universitete, 1914), pp. 1-3.

Instructions to Gavrila Shipov: He shall go to Putivl' [about three hundred miles south of Moscow, not far west of Kursk], since he bears a message sent to Putivl' from the sovereign tsar and grand prince of all Russia Vasilii Ivanovich [Shuiskii], to the voevoda Prince Andrei Bakhteiarov and his associates, and to the dvoriane and deti boiarskie, and strel'tsy captains [*sotniki* – hundredmen], and strel'tsy, and Cossacks, and trading men, and to all the people. And when Gavrila arrives in Putivl', he shall go to the cathedral and straightway order the voevoda Prince Andrei Bakhteiarov and his associates, and the strel'tsy colonels [*golovy*] and captains and strel'tsy and Cossacks and all the service men and the common people from the entire town of Putivl', to assemble in the church. And when they assemble, Gavrila shall say aloud to all the people: "The great sovereign tsar and grand prince Vasilii Ivanovich, autocrat of all Russia, and the metropolitans and archbishops and bishops and all the holy council, and the boyars and dvoriane and deti boiarskie, and the leading merchants [gosti] and the trading men, and the service men and common people of the Muscovite state have ordered [me] to tell you [the following]. By God's rightful judgment, and for the sins of all Orthodox Christendom, the lowly peasant, notorious rogue, and apostate Grishka, son of Bogdan Otrep'ev, having renounced God and taken counsel from the Devil and from evil men who always wish to bring ruin and bloodshed upon the Muscovite state, called himself the son of Tsar and Grand Prince Ivan [IV] Vasil'evich – Prince Dmitrii Ivanovich of Uglich. And in Poland and Lithuania he deceived the king and many nobles and service men by means of witchcraft and black magic; and not only in Poland and Lithuania but even in the Muscovite state he deceived many people, who fancied him to be Tsarevich Dmitrii. And that same apostate, rogue, and defrocked monk, Grishka Otrep'ev, following his own diabolical design and the advice of the Polish king and Council of Lords, brought great turmoil and

ruin upon the Muscovite state, and desecrated God's churches, and put to death many Orthodox Christians who recognized his villainy and denounced it. And he took to himself the daughter of the voevoda of Sandomierz [Marina Mniszek], of the Latin faith, and, without baptizing her, he married her in the Cathedral of the Dormition [in Moscow] and admitted her to communion; and he brought many Poles and Lithuanians to Moscow, to the ruin of Christians; and he reviled God's churches and the holy icons, and committed many outrages and bloody deeds against Orthodox Christians. And lastly, after taking counsel with the Poles and Lithuanians, he treacherously intended to kill the boyars, dvoriane, prikaz officials, leading merchants [gosti], and various prominent men [*luchshie liudi*], and to destroy the Muscovite state. But our merciful God, glorified in the Trinity, spared us Orthodox Christians in his infinite mercy, and revealed their wicked design to all the people. And hearing of this, the sovereign tsar and grand prince of all Russia Vasilii Ivanovich, and the metropolitans, archbishops, bishops, and the entire holy council, and the boyars, dvoriane, deti boiarskie, leading merchants [gosti], various service men, and the common people implored Almighty God with tears and with lamentation, that in his infinite mercy he avert from us his righteous wrath and deliver not the holy churches and the Orthodox faith to destruction, nor Orthodox Christians to spoliation and bondage, and that he send retribution upon him [the pseudo-Dmitrii] for his bloody and avaricious deeds. And after praying to God for his mercy, and taking counsel about this with all the Orthodox Christians, and questioning truly the mother of Tsarevich Dmitrii, the tsaritsa and grand princess, the nun Marfa, as well as Mikhail and Grigorii Nagoi and their kin, who knew Tsarevich Dmitrii and witnessed his death, we seized the apostate Grishka Otrep'ev and his advisers; and the apostate himself avowed, for all the people of the Muscovite state to hear, that he was indeed the rogue Grishka Otrep'ev and that he had made himself sovereign in Moscow by renouncing God and summoning evil spirits. And God sent him retribution for his evildoing: he died an evil death. . . ." And after saying this, Gavrila shall give the tsar's message to the voevody and to all the people and shall order it read aloud to all the people in the cathedral and in the square and in conspicuous places where travelers foregather, so that the tsar's letter should be made known to all. . . .

VIII:4. SHUISKII'S CHARTER TO PERM', MAY 20, 1606

These excerpts from Vasilii Shuiskii's charter to the city and region of Perm' the Great illustrate further how Vasilii, having come to the throne neither by inheritance nor by election, strove both to legitimize his reign and to win popular support. (Concerning the various ranks mentioned in this and subsequent documents, see the *Dictionary of Russian Historical Terms* and also Item VIII:22, at the beginning of Section B in this chapter.)

Reference: A. I. Iakovlev, ed., *Pamiatniki istorii Smutnogo vremeni, Pamiatniki russkoi istorii,* vol. 4 (Moscow: N. N. Klochkov, 1909), pp. 17–19. For part of this translation the editors wish to express their gratitude to Professors Alexander Baltzly and Samuel Kucherov.

The metropolitans, archbishops, bishops, and the entire holy council [*osviashchennyi sobor*— the council consisting of the higher clergy], the boyars, *okol'nichie,* dvoriane, prikaz officials, stol'niki, and *striapchie,* and the deti boiarskie, gosti, trading men, and sundry men of the Muscovite state have petitioned us to be sovereign, tsar, and grand prince of the Muscovite state, in accordance with the rank held by our ancestors; for God granted [this state] to the great sovereign Riurik who was descended from the Roman caesar, and then [to his descendants] for many years up to the time of our ancestor the great sovereign Aleksandr Iaroslavich Nevskii, from whom our ancestors received the appanage of Suzdal' as their share by kinship. And we, the great sovereign, tsar, and grand prince of all Russia, Vasilii Ivanovich, by the grace of God and by the entreaty of our pious metropolitans, archbishops, bishops, and the entire holy council, and by the petition of the boyars, okol'nichie, dvoriane, and sundry men of the Muscovite state, and by our own descent, have established ourselves in the Muscovite state as sovereign, tsar, and grand prince of all Russia; and with God's help we wish to maintain the Muscovite state as did our ancestors the great sovereigns [and] tsars of Russia; and we wish to bestow our favor upon all of you and love you more than ever and in accordance with the service you perform; to all of which I, the tsar and grand prince of all Russia, Vasilii Ivanovich, in the Cathedral of the [Dormition of the] Holy Virgin, before all the people, have sworn an oath upon the life-giving cross to all the men of the Muscovite state; and our boyars, dvoriane, deti boiarskie, and gosti have sworn an oath to us in accordance with this document; and we have sent to you [to Perm' the Great] [copies of] those documents upon which I, the tsar and grand prince, have sworn and upon which the boyars and the entire land have sworn. . . .

We, Vasilii Ivanovich, by the grace of God great sovereign, tsar, and grand prince of all Russia, have become tsar and grand prince of the Russian state, the patrimony of our ancestors, through the generosity and mercy of the glorified God, the prayers of the entire Russian holy council, and the petitions and entreaties of all Orthodox Christianity. God granted this state to our ancestor Riurik, who was descended from the Roman caesar; and then for many years, up to the time of our ancestor Grand Prince Aleksandr Iaroslavich Nevskii, my ancestors sat on the throne of this Russian state, after which they received the appanage of Suzdal' as their share, not through seizure or force, but through kinship, as it was the custom for highborn men to sit in high places.

Now we, the great sovereign, sitting on the throne of the Russian tsardom, wish that Orthodox Christianity remain under our benevolent rule in peace, tranquillity, and prosperity; and I, Vasilii Ivanovich, tsar and grand prince of all Russia, wish to swear upon the cross that I, the great sovereign, will not without holding a regular trial with my boyars execute any man, nor take away the patrimonial estates, homesteads, or possessions of his brothers, wives, or children, unless they were his accomplices; likewise if a gost', a merchant, or any one of the chernye liudi ["black" or tiaglo-bearing people] is executed upon trial and investigation, his homestead, shops, and possessions are not to be taken from his wife and children, unless they also are guilty of the offense. I, the great sovereign, will not listen to false denunciations but will conduct strict investigations and confront [the accuser with the defendant], so that no Orthodox Christian shall perish without just cause. If anyone speak falsehood about another man, the liar shall be punished after investigation, just as if he had committed the act of which he falsely accused the other.

To all that is written down in this document, I, Vasilii Ivanovich, tsar and grand prince of all Russia, swear upon the cross to all Orthodox Christians that, in bestowing my favor upon them, I will hold true [and] just trials, and will not turn my wrath against anyone without just cause, and will not deliver anyone unjustly to his enemy, and will protect men from acts of violence.

VIII:5. AN ENGLISH ACCOUNT OF BOLOTNIKOV'S UPRISING, 1606-1607

This account of Bolotnikov's rebellion was evidently written in the spring of 1607 by an Englishman then in Russia, perhaps John Merrick, who was in Moscow at this time to discuss Anglo-Russian trade with the government of Vasilii Shuiskii. The writer's sometimes ambiguous punctuation has been left as it was reproduced by Smirnov, and the reader will need to supply his own. Abbreviations, however, have been expanded.

Reference: Ivan I. Smirnov, *Vosstanie Bolotnikova 1606-1607* (Moscow: AN SSSR, 1951), pp. 553-55 (app. 4). For more, see also A. I. Kopanev and A. G. Man'kov, comps., *Vosstanie I. Bolotnikova: Dokumenty i materialy* (Moscow: Sotsekgiz, 1959).

They [the people of Putivl'] gave out that Demetrie was yett liveinge and had solicited them to reestablishe him in the Kingdome. Which Rumore meetinge which [meaning "with"?] discontented and factious persons tooke soe succesfull effectes, that most the Townes in those partes revoulted from their Alleageance to the present Emperour, and tooke an newe oathe to the supposed liveinge Demetrie, this made the Empereur to gather forces and raise an Army with [meaning "which"?] the rebells understandinge drewe all the Malecontents in those Quarters into their Partie and in shorte tyme grewe to such a heade they marched 60,000 men and made their approache within three Englishe myles of the Mosco: the presence of such an Army togeather with the report that Demetrius was alive did soe distracte the people of the Countrie that they stoode doubtefull what to doe expecting the sacke and spoyle of the Mosco beinge more then halfe beseiged the other parte of the Towne, I Knowe not througt what blindenes left open to take in forces and Victuals untill it was too late that they went aboute to blocke it upp but were twice beaten off with greate losse. Notwithstandinge they continued the Seige and Writt letres to the Slaves with in the Towne, to take Armes against their Masters and to possesse themselves of their Goodes and substance, the feare of whome was almost as greate, as it was of the Enemie abroad and the rather in regard of the Comon sorte of people whoe lately infected with robbinge and spoyleinge of the Poales were very unconsent and readie to Mutine uppon every reporte, as hopeinge to share with Rebells in the spoyle of the Cittie—the Nobles and better sorte stoode as doubtefull as they rest, uppon the reporte made by the Rebells which were taken. Whereof one of them was sett uppon a Stake and at his death did constantly affirm that the late Emperour Demetrie did live and was at Poteemoe [Putivl']. In the ende the Rebells writte letres into the Towne requireinge by name divers Noble men and some principall Citizens to be delivered unto them as cheefe Actors in murtheringe the late Emperour. Their Nobles and better sorte of Citizens perceaveinge in what extremitie they were, imployed all their Creditt and means to supporte and assist the emperour, perswaded him that there was noe means to free himselfe of this danger but to hazard a Battell which beinge resolved uppon it happened that there fell a dissention betweene two principall Commander of the Rebells Campe, the one of them beinge an olde Robber or Borderer of the Volga called Bolotincke [Bolotnikov] the other called Pasca [Pashkov] in soe much that this Pasca forsooke the partie and came and submitted himselfe to the Emperour with 500 followers: By him the Emperour understoode of the State of the Enimys Campe and that the Rumor of Demetrius liveinge was but a forged conceipte. The Enymie beinge abashed at the departure of one of their cheefe Leaders, and with all devided emongst themselves, the Emperour sett uppon them and in the ende putt them to flight. Bolotincke fled with such of his men as escaped to a Towne called Calloog [Kaluga] some 100 Myles or more from the Mosco where he fortified himselfe and hath indured three Monethes Seige beinge favored by the fruitfullest parte of that Countrie lyinge betweene the Rivers Tanais [Don] and Baristenes [Dnieper].

The event whereof is uncertaine.

VIII:6. THE CHRONICLE OF IVAN TIMOFEEV CONCERNING VASILII SHUISKII'S REIGN, 1606-1610

An important source concerning the late sixteenth and early seventeenth centuries is Ivan Timofeev's Chronicle (*Vremennik*). Timofeev was a *d'iak* or secretary—one of the relatively well educated bureaucrats who served the Muscovite state. He was already fairly prominent in Moscow by 1598, and he continued to serve there till 1607, when he was assigned to Novgorod. It was there, during the years from about 1610 to about 1617, that most of his account was written—partly under the difficult conditions of the Swedish occupation, but favored by the patronage of Metropolitan Isidor of Novgorod. In the 1620s he served in various other towns. His death came not long after 1629.

Reference: V. P. Adrianova Peretts, ed., *Vremennik Ivana Timofeeva* (Moscow: AN SSSR, 1951), pp. 101-02, 153, 162.

The aforementioned Vasilii, without the consent of the people of the entire land, by chance and hurriedly, to the extent that haste was possible in such a matter, was first acclaimed in his own courtyard and was then installed as tsar of all great Russia, solely by the people who were present here in the ruling city [Moscow], and without any resistance on his part. He even failed to make his acclamation known to the primate [of the Russian church], lest there be any objection from the people, thereby treating the primate as one of the common herd; only afterward did he make this known to him. He was able to act so shamelessly toward [the primate] only because no one dared to oppose him or to contradict him in this great matter. Yet even more hurried and doubly dishonorable was the downfall of that "self-crowned tsar" from his lofty throne. . . . The entire land of Russia was stirred up with hatred toward him, because he had made himself tsar without the consent of all the towns.

. . .

Quickly without delay, and hastily without deliberation, he ascended to the highest place [the tsar's throne]; unlike the usurpers who preceded him, he did not try to win the lesser people over to him. As a result he was hated by the people, and the entire land was unwilling that he should possess and rule it for long, and it rose up against him in violent war, coming with an army up to the very capital of the realm, in which they shut him up by siege with all his family and isolated him like a bird in a cage. Because of him the fire of hatred flared up in the entire land, and many towns under his perfidious rule renounced his name and his authority; and in many places, in separate towns, infamous false tsars began to spring up from among the most insignificant and obscure people, and especially from among the lowliest laborers; and they were raised high by the populace of the towns amid noisy clamor, to the dismay of legitimate tsars. And people throughout the land became demoralized at the spectacle of the usurpers who appeared before them.

. . .

Such was the sickness that took hold of us because of the weakness of fear and of our discord and dissensions, lacking in brotherly love: as two towns or two localities are many versts away from each other, so are we far away from a loving union with each other; we turn our backs to each other, some looking eastward and some westward. But this discord of ours has given great strength to our enemies. . . . And until we are united in brotherly love, as it behooves us to be according to the Scriptures, our enemies will not cease to harm us as before and to prevail against us.

VIII:7. ABRAHAM PALITSYN ON THE TIME OF TROUBLES, 1608-1612

Averkii Ivanovich Palitsyn, a nobleman, began his government service under Ivan the Terrible. In 1588, during the regency of Boris Godunov, he was obliged to become a monk, taking the name of Avraamii or Abraham. From 1608 to 1619 he served as steward in charge of supplies in the famous Trinity Monastery of Saint Sergius and participated actively in many of the events of the Time of Troubles. His account of that period, of which a few excerpts are given here, was widely read in the seventeenth century.

Reference: Lev V. Cherepnin, ed., *Skazanie Avraamiia Palitsyna* (Moscow: AN SSSR, 1955), pp. 117, 119, 120-22, 202-03, 212, 213, 218-19, 226-27.

[During the struggle between Tsar Vasilii Shuiskii and the "Rogue of Tushino," the second pseudo-Dmitrii:]

The enemies [the followers of the second pseudo-Dmitrii] overcame the Orthodox Christians and, with nothing to hinder them, came [in 1608] to the ruling city of Moscow and besieged it, intending to capture it. Who can describe the misery that prevailed at this time throughout Russia? Sitting at the same table, feasting in the ruling city, after such gaiety some returned to the tsar's apartments and some deserted to the Tushino camp. And all the people divided themselves into two groups, all thinking cunningly: "If Moscow is taken, our fathers and brothers and relatives and friends are there [in Tushino], and they will save us. If we [the followers of Tsar Vasilii Shuiskii] win, then we shall likewise protect them." The Poles and the Lithuanians and the rogues and the Cossacks had no confidence whatever in these "fly-overs" [*pereletÿ*]—this was what they called them at that time—and they toyed with them as wolves do with dogs. . . . The armed Poles and Lithuanians stood idly by, laughing at their madness and quarreling. And if it happened in battle that the Poles or Lithuanians took a good soldier prisoner, who stood for truth, they were merciful to him and did not kill him. But if on the other hand it happened that the Russian traitors [the Tushino people] took a prisoner, then they attacked him with weapons as if he were a wild beast and tore him limb from limb. The Poles and Lithuanians, seeing such tortures and cruelties inflicted by one compatriot upon another and on people of the same faith, stood back astonished at the enemy's damnable cruelties and shuddered in their hearts . . . saying to one another: "Notice, brothers, what these Russians are doing to one another. What will they do to us?" And [the Poles and Lithu-

anians] called them more evil than devils. And [the Tushino people] called the merciful Poles and Lithuanians weaklings and women.

· · ·

[In Moscow] each began to elevate himself above his station: the slaves desiring to be masters and the bondmen escaping to freedom. They disregarded reasonable men altogether, and no one dared to say a word against them. With the tsar [Vasilii Shuiskii] they played as with a big child, and each wanted a greater recompense than his due. Many of them, who came to be called "sly ones," first kissed God's cross [to Tsar Vasilii] and then joined the enemy; and after being in Tushino and kissing God's cross and receiving recompense from God's enemies, they would return to the ruling city [Moscow] and receive still greater honors and riches and gifts from Tsar Vasilii, and then again go over to the enemy. Many of them, throwing the entire Russian state into confusion, moved back and forth between Moscow and Tushino twice and even five and ten times. As for any lack in Tushino of the necessities of life, or food or weapons of warfare, and various medicinal herbs and salts, traitors from the ruling city of Moscow, falling into crooked ways, secretly filled the traitors' camp at Tushino with all these things. And the accursed ones rejoiced at the acquisition of much silver, not realizing what the final outcome would be.

. . . And crowds gathered on the squares of the ruling city and preached false things with unbridled speech. But if these devils heard anything that was not to their advantage, they would lower their gaze and stand mute, unable to lift their eyes to the sky, and then would disperse with fiendish sighs. Others, incited by the audacity of the Antichrist [the second pseudo-Dmitrii] and the anticipation of eternal torment, called sweet bitter and bitter sweet, and light darkness and darkness light. And so the people were enticed away from hearing and believing the truth. And in this confusion many who really knew of various schemes, and of the departure of traitors to [join] the rogue [the pseudo-Dmitrii] and the Poles, did not report them to the tsar or to the magnates; and those who did report them were called calumniators and slanderers.

· · ·

At that time the holy churches of God were destroyed by the true believers themselves [the Tushino people], just as the great Vladimir had once destroyed the heathen temples, in that case for the glory of God but now for the amusement of devils and Lutherans. What we and our brothers, their descendants, have done is a greater evil. . . .

. . . And none of the Russian people were spared those misfortunes. The monks and priests were not put to death at once, but first were cruelly tortured in various ways and burned by fire, so that they would reveal [the hiding-places of] their treasures, and then were put to death. And they took the monks who did not move from place to place but lived in the same spot, and those they put to work; they [the monks] stood guard for them, and brewed wine and beer for them, and likewise prepared food for them and for their horses, and tended their herds. Likewise [the Tushino people] worked the priests to death at the mills and as carters and as woodcutters, and [the priests] cared for the harlots, and did work for them, and carried water for them, and washed their dirty clothes, and did all the work that was ordered for their horses. Old and saintly men groveled at their feet like slaves, and [the Tushino people] insulted them, ordering them to sing obscene songs and jump and clap; and those who did not obey them were put to death.

. . . At that time men hid in thickets and in dense dark forests, in unknown caves and in the water among the bushes, resting and imploring their Creator that night might come and allow them to rest at least a while on dry land. But neither night nor day afforded the fugitives any rest, or a hiding-place, and instead of the moon many fires lit up the fields and the forests at night, and no one dared move from his place: [the Tushino people] waited for men to come out of the forests as for wild beasts. And the evildoers ceased to hunt animals but pursued their own brothers instead, tracking them down with dogs, like wild beasts. The real beasts devoured the fugitives, and those who had turned into beasts [the Tushino people] devoured them also, not physically but by their actions; the [real] beasts subjected them to only one death, but the others devoured them both body and soul. . . . The peasant farmers and all those who fled had nowhere to hide their supplies of grain; everywhere the beasts dug them out of the pits [where the seeds were buried] and ate them. Other beasts simply scattered them far and wide in the woods and in the mud. In the same way the Cossacks and the traitors, wherever some seeds were left, poured them into the water and into the mud and trampled them with their horses. And when they did not burn the houses or could not take the household goods [with them], they smashed everything into bits and threw it into the water, breaking the doors and the bolts so that no one would be able to live there.

· · ·

This monastery [the Trinity Monastery of Saint Sergius] shone all over Russia like the sun or the moon amidst the stars. After the great Tsar Feodor Ivanovich, the heir to his realm was Boris Feodorovich [Godunov], and he had a strong faith in the Monastery of the Holy Trinity. I do not know what came over him: he was the first to borrow from the treasury of [the Monastery of] Saint Sergius— 15,400 rubles for his soldiers. After Boris, by the will of God [and] because of our sins, his realm was usurped by the heretical unfrocked monk Grigorii [Grishka] Otrep'ev. And he, through his evil, heretical nature, took from the treasury of Saint Sergius 30,000 rubles. God's judgment soon overtook him and he died an evil death. After that Tsar Vasilii Ivanovich Shuiskii first took 18,355 rubles from the monastery; and a second time, during the siege of Moscow, he took 1,000 rubles from the steward [of the monastery estates], the monk Avraamii Palitsyn; and again a third time [he took] 900 rubles during the siege of Moscow. And in all, during the reigns of Tsar Boris, the unfrocked monk, and Tsar Vasilii, 65,655 rubles in money were taken from the treasury of Saint Sergius the Miracle Worker. And because of that a shortage of money was felt in the monastery for the first time.

· · ·

[When Moscow was attacked by the Poles in 1611:]

And [Moscow] was protected not only by strong and high walls but also by many stalwart bearers of arms, warriors, and wise men. This ruling city of Moscow, which I call the New Rome, bloomed with holy churches and miraculous relics of saints, and was sustained through their prayers by the Almighty, and grew and towered and was honored by many states, and was famed and marveled at for its riches and glory, its multitude of inhabitants and great size, not only in Russia but in many states near and far. Yet wondrous though it was, it fell in a single hour, consumed by fire and sword.

· · ·

In that same year of 7119 [1611], on the nineteenth day of March, on Tuesday of Holy Week, Mikhailo Saltykov and the Polish voevody Gosiewski and Strus with all the Poles and foreigners began to slaughter all the Orthodox Christians in the ruling city of Moscow. First of all they barricaded Kitai-gorod [an inner quarter of Moscow]. There they slaughtered a great many of the Orthodox and looted the marketplaces. After this they set fire to all the dwelling houses in the great Belyi-gorod and in Dereviannyi-gorod [outer quarters of Moscow], and men of all ages and buildings of every kind in the ruling city of Moscow—alas!—were given over to fire and sword. Dereviannyi-gorod was entirely destroyed by fire. The churches, monasteries, and various holy objects were profaned and desecrated. The new martyr, the most holy Hermogen, patriarch of Moscow and all Russia, they [the Poles] ignominiously cast from his throne and imprisoned in a desolate place; and there the new martyr departed this earth, having reached the end of his life's course.

· · ·

[Concerning the Second National Host, 1612:]

After missives from the Monastery of the Life-Giving Trinity had reached all the cities of the Russian state, they again began to be of one mind. Particularly in Nizhnii-Novgorod did they take up these writings, and a great many men listened to them for many days. One day they gathered together in accord . . . and elected a leader for all the soldiery, the stol'nik and voevoda Prince Dmitrii Mikhailo-

vich Pozharskii, and with him the posad man Kuz'ma Minin, to gather a treasury of the land. And so their intention and undertaking was good and was realized. News of this spread throughout Russia, and dvoriane and deti boiarskie and various service men from all the towns came together in Nizhnii-Novgorod to the stol'nik and voevoda Prince Dmitrii Pozharskii. And he gave to each, according to his dignity, monetary wages and provisions, and set up mess tables for them, and supplied them with arms, to be ready for battle. And all those of military ranks, and the destitute who had been made rich, were supplied with horses and arms, and so a large army was formed.

· · ·

Again the Devil created great unrest in the army: all the Cossacks rose up against the dvoriane and deti boiarskie in the host of Prince Dmitrii Pozharskii, saying that they were enriching themselves with much wealth, while [the Cossacks] were naked and hungry; and they wanted to separate from the Muscovite state, while others wanted to kill the dvoriane and plunder their wealth. And there was great disagreement among them. When they heard this in the Monastery of Saint Sergius the Miracle Worker, the archimandrite and the steward and the senior monks called a council: at that time there was a great shortage of money in the treasury of [the Monastery of] Saint Sergius, and they did not know what to send the Cossacks, and what honors to bestow on them, and how to persuade them not to separate from the Muscovite state without taking vengeance on the enemies who had shed Christian blood [the Poles]. After pondering thus, they sent them church treasures: chasubles and surplices and stoles worth more than a thousand rubles, and they also wrote to them with many prayers from the Holy Scriptures that they should bring to fulfillment the heroism of their ordeals and not separate from the Muscovite state and so forth. And [the Cossacks], after receiving the writings and reading them before the entire army, and hearing the words of praise for their service and their suffering, came to their senses and into the fear of God, and returned to the Monastery of the Life-Giving Trinity the chasubles that had been sent to them [and sent] two of their atamans with missives to the archimandrite and to the steward and to all the brethren, that everything would be done as they had beseeched. Even if countless misfortunes and sorrows should come, [the Cossacks] would endure them all and would not leave without capturing Moscow and taking revenge upon the enemies who had shed Christian blood.

VIII:8. CORRESPONDENCE BETWEEN RUSSIAN CITIES, 1608-1609

A precious source of material on the Time of Troubles is contemporary correspondence between the cities of Muscovy. The letters excerpted here and further on illustrate various aspects of Russian public life in a succession of crises. The first group deals with the years 1608 and 1609. When the second pseudo-Dmitrii in Tushino was challenging the Moscow regime of Vasilii Shuiskii, much of Shuiskii's support came from the towns of northern Russia. How they mobilized their forces is suggested in letters like these. The first is from the authorities of Ustiug to those of Sol'vychegodsk (both towns are in the basin of the Northern Dvina, about four hundred miles northeast of Moscow).

Reference: *AAE*, 2:179-81 [Nov. 27, 1608], 230-31 [June 1609]; Arkheograficheskaia Komissiia, ed., *Akty istoricheskie* 5 vols. (St. Petersburg, 1841-42), 2:144 [Dec. 15, 1608].

[From Ustiug to Sol'vychegodsk, November 27, 1608:]

To Lord Pospel Eliseevich [the local voevoda] and all the people of Usol'e [the region around Sol'vychegodsk], to the volost' peasants and elders and tseloval'niki [sworn men performing various functions] and to all the people: Ivan Streshnev and the clerk [*pod'iachii*] Shestoi Kopnin and all the people of the community of Ustiug, the townspeople [posad people] and elders and tseloval'niki and volost' peasants send greetings. . . . We, sir, have conferred with the townspeople and volost' peasants of Ustiug. . . . And the people of Ustiug, sir, the townspeople and the volost' peasants, have assured us firmly that they would not kiss the cross to him who calls himself Tsar Dmitrii [i.e. the second pseudo-Dmitrii] and that they wish to take a firm stand and to recruit men forthwith from the entire Ustiug uezd, from each household. As for the Muscovite state, they and other people have reported that the Muscovite state, with God's help, stands sound as of old. And you, Lord Pospel Eliseevich, should take counsel at Sol'vychegodsk with the Stroganovs, Maksim and Nikita, and with the entire land of Usol'e, [to learn] what they think: do they wish to be steadfast on that matter with us and with the people of Ustiug, and to take steadfast counsel with us on that matter? If your thought is the same as ours, then you, sir, after conferring with the Stroganovs and with the entire land of Usol'e . . . should quickly come with five or six or ten of the best men from the towns [posady] and from the volost' to take counsel with us in Ustiug. And this is our thought: if you come to us, and wish to take your stand with us, then we should kiss the cross among ourselves, and you should likewise kiss the cross, that we shall live and die together with you, and you with us.

[From Perm' to Sol'vychegodsk, December 15, 1608:]

We have read your letter . . . before all the people of Perm' the Great; and the elders of Perm' the Great, and the tseloval'niki, and the best and the middle townspeople, and the volost' peasants, having listened to your letter and to the entire message, declared with one accord that they, all the Orthodox Christians of the land of Perm', would gladly stand up for the sovereign tsar and grand prince of all Russia, Vasilii Ivanovich [Shuiskii].

[From Ustiug to Sol'vychegodsk, June 1609:]

To the townspeople of Sol'vychegodsk and to the volost' elders and tseloval'niki and all the inhabitants of the entire Usol'e uezd: Ivan Streshnev and the *prigovornye liudi* [elected members of a temporary local council] from the towns [posady] and volosti of the entire Usol'e uezd, and the judges of the land, and the elders and tseloval'niki, and all the inhabitants send greetings. . . . And we, sirs, here in Ustiug . . . have resolved by the whole community, and have put the resolution in writing with our signatures, that we should take three hundred rubles in money from the sovereign's treasury, from the customs office, to save time until the amount can be collected from the *sokhi* [land measure used as unit of taxation]; and with this money it was decided to recruit volunteers from among the free Cossacks, and to give each man one ruble in money for weapons, and to send them to the sovereign's voevody in Iaroslavl', to serve the sovereign. . . . And you, sirs, should write us your thoughts on this matter forthwith. We on our part have sent the same message to Viatka, and to the Vaga region, and to Kholmogory, and to the Ust'ianskie volosti [situated along the Ust'ia River, a tributary of the Vaga]: that, mindful of God and of their souls, they should help Iaroslavl' in every way, recruiting soldiers and dispatching them straightway to Iaroslavl'. And you should write about this matter to Perm' the Great and to the Vychegda and Vym and Sysola regions, that they too should recruit soldiers and send them straightway to Iaroslavl', before the rogues [followers of the second pseudo-Dmitrii] gather strength; and you should likewise recruit soldiers and dispatch them to Iaroslavl' with artillery and ammunition for the cannon.

VIII:9. SIGISMUND'S AGREEMENT WITH THE BOYARS, FEBRUARY 4, 1610

Disillusioned with the rogue (the second pseudo-Dmitrii), a group of his followers at Tushino—boyars, d'iaki, and merchants—proposed to King Sigismund III that his son Wladyslaw be accepted as tsar. An agreement between the two parties was concluded in Sigismund's camp before Smolensk on February 4, 1610. In these excerpts the reader may observe to what extent the agreement was intended to protect the interests of elements other than the boyars.

Reference: Iakovlev, *Pamiatniki istorii Smutnogo vremeni*, pp. 47-49.

2. The holy Orthodox Greek faith and the holy apostolic church shall preserve its integrity and beauty as heretofore . . . and shall not be violated in any way; and the preceptors of the Roman and Lutheran and other faiths shall cause no rift within the church. . . . To this His Royal Grace [King Sigismund] has deigned to give his approval. Yet the people of the Roman faith need a Roman church, as has already been discussed with Boris [Godunov], and Polish chaplains or priests in this church; and [the king] will negotiate with the patriarch and with the entire state and with the Duma boyars about this, so that there may be at least one church for Catholics in the capital city of Moscow, where the Poles and Lithuanians might worship. . . . Neither His Grace the king nor His Royal Grace's son [Wladyslaw] shall order anyone to turn away from the Greek faith to the Roman or to any other faith; inasmuch as faith is a divine gift, and it is not right to turn anyone away from his faith by force or coercion; and Russians shall be free to practice the Russian faith, and Poles and Lithuanians the Polish faith. . . .

8. Justice shall be dispensed and administered according to custom and the Sudebnik [law code of Ivan IV]; and should changes be desired in order to strengthen justice in the courts, this shall be done at the discretion of the boyars and of the entire land; and His Grace the sovereign shall deign to allow changes in the courts, whatever is needed for the sake of sacred justice. . . .

11. If anyone, of whatever rank, should commit an offence and deserve punishment, in matters concerning the sovereign and the land, His Grace the sovereign shall punish him according to his guilt and his transgression, after first holding a fair trial with the boyars and [other] Duma members; but wives, children, [and] brothers who had not assisted in the act nor had any knowledge of it nor given leave to do it shall not be punished and shall in any case be left in possession of their patrimonies [*votchiny*] and pomest'ia. And without evidence of guilt and without trial in court by the boyars, no one shall be punished, nor deprived of honor, nor imprisoned, nor deprived of pomest'ia and patrimonies. Men of high rank shall not be reduced in rank without guilt; and those of lower rank shall be elevated according to merit. Patrimonies and possessions shall not be taken away from anyone. . . . And His Grace the sovereign shall do all things after consultation and discussion with the Duma boyars, and without consultation and discussion with the boyars, His Grace the sovereign shall deign not to do anything.
. . .

16. His Grace the king shall not allow peasant men to transfer from Russia to Lithuania, nor from Lithuania to Russia, nor within Russia between people of various ranks.

17. His Royal Grace shall keep slaves in bondage to boyars in accordance with ancient custom, so that they may serve the boyars and nobles as heretofore; and His Grace the sovereign shall not grant them freedom.

VIII:10. THE AGREEMENT BETWEEN ZOLKIEWSKI AND THE MOSCOW BOYARS, AUGUST 1610

In August of 1610 the boyar government in Moscow concluded an agreement with Hetman Stanislaw Zolkiewski, commander of the invading Polish army, on the basis of the agreement of February 4, 1610, considerably modified. The following excerpts from the agreement make understandable not only the boyars' preference for Wladyslaw rather than the pseudo-Dmitrii from Tushino, but also King Sigismund's lack of enthusiasm for the arrangement.

Reference: Iakovlev, *Pamiatniki istorii Smutnogo vremeni*, pp. 52-57.

With the blessing and counsel of the most holy Hermogen, patriarch of Moscow and all Russia, and the metropolitans, archbishops, bishops, archimandrites, abbots, and the entire holy council, and with the approval of the boyars and okol'nichie . . . and every rank of service men and inhabitants of the great Muscovite state, we, the boyars Prince Fedor Ivanovich Mstislavskii, Prince Vasilii Vasil'e-vich Golitsyn, and Fedor Ivanovich Shere-metev . . . met with Stanislaw Zolkiewski of Zolkiew, the voevoda of Kiev, the hetman of the Polish crown, of the great sovereign Sigismund, king of Poland and grand duke of Lithuania . . . and spoke and took counsel concerning the election of a sovereign to the tsardoms of Vladimir and Moscow and all the great tsardoms of the Russian state, and decided: that the most holy Hermogen, patriarch of Moscow and all Russia . . . and the entire holy council . . . and every rank of service men and inhabitants of the Muscovite state should make petition to the great sovereign Sigismund, king of Poland and grand duke of Lithuania, and to his son the *krolewicz* ["prince" in the sense of king's son and heir] Wladyslaw Sigismundovich, that the great sovereign King Sigismund deign to grant them his son the krolewicz Wladyslaw as tsar of Vladimir and Moscow and all the great tsardoms of the Russian state. . . . And we, all the boyars, and okol'nichie, and dvoriane . . . and every rank of service men and in-habitants of the Muscovite state swear upon the holy life-giving cross of God to the great sovereign, the krolewicz Wladyslaw Sigis-mundovich: that we shall serve him, the sov-ereign, and his children forevermore, and wish them well in everything, as we did the former great sovereign [and] tsars by native right . . . and not desire anyone from the Muscovite state or from other states [as sovereign] in the Muscovite state, except the sovereign krolewicz Wladyslaw. . . . And the sovereign krolewicz Wladyslaw Sigismundovich, as soon as he comes to the ruling city of Moscow,

shall be crowned sovereign of the state of Vladimir and Moscow and all the great and glorious tsardoms of the Russian state with the tsar's crown and diadem, by the most holy Hermogen, patriarch of Moscow and all Russia, and by the entire holy council of the Greek faith, in accordance with the traditional ceremonies and dignities, as former great sov-ereigns [and] tsars of Moscow were crowned. And when the krolewicz Wladyslaw Sigis-mundovich is sovereign of the Russian state, he shall honor and adorn God's churches in Moscow and in all the towns and villages of the Muscovite state and in the entire Russian tsardom, as has been the custom heretofore, and preserve them from any destruction, and worship and revere the holy icons of God and the Holy Virgin, and all the holy and miracu-lous relics; and the prelates and priests and all Orthodox Christians shall remain in the Ortho-dox Christian faith of the Greek law as before; and no churches of the Roman faith and various other faiths, or houses of prayer of any other faith shall be erected anywhere in Moscow or in [other] towns and villages; and as to what the hetman said upon the instruc-tions of the king, that there should be at least one Roman church in the ruling city of Mos-cow for the Poles and Lithuanians who will live at the court of the sovereign krolewicz, the sovereign krolewicz shall confer with the patriarch and with all the clergy and with the boyars and with all the members of the Duma concerning this; and our Orthodox Christian faith of the Greek law shall not be violated or dishonored in any way, and no other faiths shall be brought in, so that our holy Ortho-dox faith of the Greek law should preserve its integrity and beauty; and Orthodox Chris-tians of the Russian state shall not be led away from the Greek faith into the Roman or any other faith by force or compulsion or any other means; and Jews shall not enter any part of the Russian state for trade or for any other reason. . . . The Poles and Lithuanians in Moscow shall not be appointed to any judicial posts of the land, and shall not be voevody or prikaz officials in the towns; and Poles and Lithuanians shall not be made vicegerents or elders [starosty] in the towns. . . . In the Muscovite state, the sovereign krolewicz shall maintain the boyars, okol'nichie, [Duma] dvoriane, Duma secretaries, stol'niki, dvoriane, striapchie, secretaries, zhil'tsy, dvoriane from the towns, strel'tsy commanders, prikaz officials, deti boiarskie, gosti, trading men, strel'tsy, Cossacks, cannoneers [*pushkari*], and every rank of service men and inhabitants of the Russian state, in dignity, honor, bounty, and favor, as under former sovereigns [and] tsars of Moscow; and he shall not alter the former customs and ranks which existed in the Muscovite state; and he shall not injure or lessen the birthright and honor of Muscovite princely and boyar families by [elevating] newly arrived foreigners. And monetary wages, revenues [obrok], pomest'ia, and patrimonial estates shall remain as before, whatever each previously received; and no one shall be deprived of his parental patrimonial estates, and in the future every man in the Russian state shall be rewarded according to his service and merits. The various foreigners who left their various states [to serve] the Muscovite sovereigns shall be rewarded as before, and they shall not be deprived of their revenues and pomest'ia and patrimonial estates. . . . In Moscow and in the towns trials shall be held and decided according to former custom and the code of laws of the Russian state; and if it is desired to supplement it in any way to improve justice, the sovereign shall allow this with the consent of the Boyar Duma and the entire land, so that justice may be done. . . . And if anyone, whatever his rank, is guilty of a crime against the sovereign or the land, and deserves punishment, he shall be punished according to his guilt after first being tried by the boyars and [other] members of the Duma; but his wife, children, [and] brothers, if they did not participate in the crime and did not know of it and did not desire it, shall not be punished, and shall remain as before in every way, and shall not be deprived of their patrimonial estates, pomest'ia, possessions, and homesteads; and without an investigation of guilt and a court trial by all the boyars, no one shall be punished, dishonored, cast into prison, or deprived of his pomest'ia and patrimonial estates and homesteads. . . . Trading or plowing peasants shall not shift to Lithuania from Russia, or from Lithuania to Russia; likewise in Russia peasants shall not shift [from owner to owner]. Boyars and dvoriane and men of every rank shall keep serfs as was previously the custom, in accordance with the deeds of bondage. As to the need for Cossacks on the Volga, the Don, the Iaik [Ural], and the Terek [rivers], the sovereign krolewicz shall discuss this with the boyars and [other] Duma members, when he becomes sovereign. . . . And as for baptism, the sovereign krolewicz Wladyslaw Sigismundovich shall vouchsafe to be baptised in our Orthodox Christian faith of the Greek law, and to adhere to our Greek Orthodox Christian faith.

VIII:11. THE MEMOIRS OF HETMAN ZOLKIEWSKI CONCERNING EVENTS OF 1610-1611

Zolkiewski fortunately left a personal record of his occupation of Moscow. In his account he refers to himself impersonally as "the hetman." He was already a mature statesman of sixty-three at this time, and by no means a mere tool of the king. Zolkiewski pursued his career until 1620, when, at the age of seventy-three, he lost his life in a war against the Turks.

Reference: Translated from Mukhanov, *Zapiski getmana Zholkevskogo o Moskovskoi voine*, pp. 71-72, 78-79, 81, 85, 89-90, 95, 113-14, 121-24, and subsequently amended on the basis of M. W. Stephen's translation from the Polish, in Stanislas Zolkiewski, *Expedition to Moscow: A Memoir by Hetman Stanislas Zolkiewski*, Polonica Series no. 1 (London: Polonica Publications, 1959), pp. 88-89, 93, 95, 98, 100-01, 104, 118, 123, 125.

[In the summer of 1610] the hetman [Zolkiewski], upon receiving news of the deposition of Shuiskii, and being aware that the pretender [the second pseudo-Dmitrii], who had been awaiting a favorable opportunity, was hurrying toward Moscow, wrote a letter to the Duma boyars. In it he praised them for having deposed Shuiskii; he informed them that the pretender was approaching the capital and that by order of His Majesty the king [Sigismund III] he was willing to help them against the impostor and to defend them against all

Ivanovich Mstislavskii and his associates, and the dvoriane and various people of every rank of the Muscovite state had previously written to us from Moscow: that the Lithuanian hetman Stanislas Zolkiewski and his colonels and cavalry captains, while encamped outside Moscow, concluded an agreement with the boyars and [other] Duma members of the entire Muscovite state, [to the effect] that Sigismund, king of Poland and grand duke of Lithuania, would give his son the krolewicz Wladyslaw to become sovereign of the Muscovite state; and that the king himself would yield Smolensk; and that his son the krolewicz Wladyslaw would be baptized in the Orthodox Christian faith, and be sovereign of the Muscovite state, and withdraw all the Polish and Lithuanian soldiers from Moscow and all the Muscovite towns, and not violate our Orthodox Christian faith of the Greek creed in any way. But King Sigismund did not carry out his oath, in accordance with the agreement concluded with the hetman and the Poles and Lithuanians, which they had sworn to; and he did not give his son Wladyslaw to become sovereign of the Muscovite state. And the Poles and Lithuanians whom the king had sent from outside Smolensk with Hetman Zolkiewski to join [the king's supporters] in Moscow were admitted into the city of Moscow through the treason of Mikhailo Saltykov and Fed'ka [Fedor] Andronov with their associates and advisers; and they made themselves masters of Moscow and devastated many towns and uezdy by their heavy taxes and extortions, monetary levies, forcible requisitions of food for themselves and their horses, and every kind of damage; and they utterly ruined and impoverished merchants and peasants; and they carried away the entire treasury of the former Muscovite sovereigns to Lithuania, leaving nothing behind; and the remainder [sic] the Lithuanians divided among themselves; and on the nineteenth day of March they burned Moscow to the ground; and they destroyed God's holy churches and monasteries; and they desecrated the miraculous icons and the oft-healing holy relics; and they demolished the shrines of the saints; and they cruelly put to death the boyar Prince Andrei Vasil'evich Golitsyn and other boyars and dvoriane and men of various ranks and a great multitude of Christians, men and women and

even suckling infants; and they imprisoned the most holy Hermogen, patriarch of Moscow and all Russia; they plundered the riches of the tsars, acquired by former great sovereigns in ages past, and the entire treasury of the tsars, and the countless wealth of all the men of the Muscovite state; and they laid waste the ruling city, the mother of all cities. And beholding such a wicked and fierce assault and such devastation of the Muscovite state and of all Orthodox Christians, the boyars, voevody, dvoriane, deti boiarskie, atamans, Cossacks, strel'tsy, and various service men from the towns of the Ukraine and of Seversk and of the Plain [Pole, the southern frontier of the Muscovite state, including the towns of Kursk, Voronezh, and Belgorod] and beyond the Moskva River [Zamoskov'e, the old core of Muscovy north and east of Moscow in the region of the Upper and Middle Volga] and of Novgorod and of the Lower Volga and of the Littoral [Pomor'e, the broad northern strip from Onega along the White and Barents seas to the Ural Mountains], and various men from all the towns of the Russian state, joined together and swore an oath among themselves on the life-giving cross of the Lord, to die together, one and all, for the Cathedral of the Dormition [in Moscow] and the great Miracle Workers of Moscow and our true Orthodox Christian faith and the Muscovite state; and to make a stand against our ferocious enemies, the Poles and Lithuanians, and their adherents, the heretics and apostates Mikhailo Saltykov and Fed'ka Andronov and their companions, and to fight them to the death. And having made their preparations, they, the boyars and voevody with all the soldiers from all the towns of the Muscovite state, came up to the ruling city of Moscow and took up positions at the gates of the tsar's Kamennyi-gorod ["Stone Town"—an outer quarter of Moscow also known as Belyi-gorod or "White Town"]; and they laid siege to the Poles and Lithuanians in Kitai-gorod ["Chinese Town"—a quarter of the inner city] and in the Kremlin.
. . .

And we should kiss the cross ourselves, and bring all the service men and inhabitants to kiss the cross, and bring the Tatars and Ostiaks to take the Moslem oath of allegiance [shert'], so that we should all be in agreement and in common accord, and make common cause with them for our true incorruptible Orthodox danger. He reiterated that His Majesty the king had been moved to come solely out of Christian compassion, having heard about the great turmoil in this land, and wishing to restrain and halt the bloodshed and to restore peace and tranquillity in the realm. . . .

When the Duma boyars saw that on one side the imposter was advancing along the Serpukhov road, and that on the other side the hetman's troops were approaching from Mozhaisk, they dispatched two deti boiarskie to the hetman [Zolkiewski], to ask him whether he was coming as a friend or as a foe. The hetman replied, in accordance with what he had written in his letter, that he had no thought of undertaking any hostile action and that, on the contrary, if they should be disposed, as some had informed him, to accept the king's son Wladyslaw as their sovereign, he would help them against the pretender. After regaling the deti boiarskie and loading them with gifts, he dismissed them.

· · ·

[On August 29 (N.S., 1610] . . . a certain Fedor Andronov, of Moscow, came from Smolensk bringing the hetman a letter from His Majesty the king, which instructed the hetman to assume power not in the name of the king's son [Wladyslaw] but in the name of the king himself. A few days later the starosta [royal vicegerent] of Wieliz [Gosiewski] arrived with [another] letter and instruction from the king, of the same contents. But inasmuch as the matter [the election of Wladyslaw] was already settled, the hetman did not wish to disclose this; and the starosta of Wieliz himself, although he had brought this instruction, did not advise [that the king's order be followed], realizing, as a man well informed about Muscovite affairs, that these things were impossible.

· · ·

Prince Mstislavskii came to the hetman with the most eminent of the boyars . . . [and] hailed him as regent.

· · ·

Almost all the towns, as soon as they heard that Moscow had taken an oath of allegiance to the king's son [Wladyslaw], took the oath with as much zeal as in the capital city.

· · ·

The hetman . . . now had to consider how, with the troops at his disposal, to occupy the capital without danger. . . . It seemed to the hetman that if he led his army away from the capital, the Muscovite populace, always inclined to rioting, might start an uprising, summon the imposter, and upset everything. He observed that the more farsighted boyars entertained the same misgivings. . . . The boyars . . . wished to be safe from the fury of the people, under the protection of the troops of His Majesty the king. The patriarch and the populace, who were opposed to the entry of these troops, were got around by various means. At length matters were so arranged that the troops entered the city. The hetman chose quarters for them suitable for any contingency. The regiments and detachments were disposed among separate mansions in such a way as to be able to help one another in any emergency. . . .

The hetman ordered that the greatest care be taken lest our men [the Poles] start quarreling with the people of Moscow; he installed judges from among both our people and the people of Moscow to settle any disputes; our men lived so quietly that the boyars and the populace, knowing the willfulness of our people, marveled and praised us for living so peacefully, without causing the least injury to anyone. . . . Thus we lived there in orderly fashion and in great comfort. There was no lack of anything. For a price provisions and all necessities were obtained; for we opened the main roads from Vologda and Iaroslavl' and in other directions. From Kolomna ships loaded with grain and various commodities came up the Moskva River.

· · ·

His Majesty the king, both in writing and through the starosta of Wieliz, made known his desire to obtain the Muscovite sovereignty not for his son Wladyslaw but for himself. The hetman had explored the wishes of the Muscovites enough to know that they would never agree to this. . . . He foresaw that great confusion and difficulties would necessarily arise as soon as His Majesty the king's intentions were disclosed.

· · ·

Meanwhile, the news that His Majesty the king was unwilling to let his son become the Muscovite tsar spread farther and farther throughout the Muscovite land, as a result of which riots and treasonable acts occurred in many places, intensified chiefly because of a certain Prokofii Liapunov.

. . .

[As Liapunov's troops approached Moscow in March 1611,] our people [the Poles] decided among themselves to burn down Dereviannyi-gorod and Belyi-gorod [quarters of Moscow], to shut themselves up in the Kremlin and in Kitai-gorod, and to attack the strel'tsy and anyone else they met. On the Wednesday before Easter, they did so. Drawing up and marching out the troops, they suddenly set fire to Dereviannyi-gorod and Belyi-gorod. . . .

Thus the Muscovite capital was burned down, with great bloodshed and incalculable damage. This city, which covered a vast area, had been affluent and wealthy; those who have traveled in foreign lands report that neither Rome nor Paris nor Lisbon equals this city in its circumference. The Kremlin remained intact, but Kitai-gorod was looted and plundered by the mob and the teamsters during the confusion; not even the churches were spared.

VIII:12. CORRESPONDENCE BETWEEN CITIES, FEBRUARY-JUNE 1611

These excerpts are from three of the many letters that tell us how in the spring of 1611 near Moscow the heterogeneous force (*opolchenie*) often referred to as the First National Host was formed.

Reference: *AAE*, 2:305 [February letter], 321 [June]; S. K. Bogoiavlenskii and I. S. Riabinin, eds., *Akty vremeni mezhdutsarstviia (1610-1613)* (Moscow: Izd. Imperatorskogo Obshchestva Istorii i Drevnostei pri Moskovskom Universitete, 1915), pp. 6-7 [March letter].

[From Iaroslavl' to Vologda, February 1611:]

In Moscow, sirs, the people of the city have suffered much oppression and outrage from the Lithuanians; and from Moscow, sirs, the most holy Hermogen, patriarch of Moscow and of all Russia, and the men of Moscow, have written to Prokofii Liapunov in Riazan', and to all the towns of the Ukraine [i.e. the basin of the upper Oka and Upa rivers] and of the Lower Volga [Ponizov'e—the region encompassing the former Tatar khanates of Kazan' and Astrakhan'], urging them to join with the neighboring towns and with those on the [Middle] Volga, and to march on Moscow against the Poles and Lithuanians, and to bring help to the Muscovite state quickly, before Lithuania should take possession of Moscow and of the neighboring towns. And from Riazan', sirs, Prokofii Liapunov has written to Nizhnii [-Novgorod], and from Nizhnii they have written to us in Iaroslavl', that in the towns of Riazan' [i.e. the territory of the former principality of Riazan'] and Seversk [i.e. the region along the Desna and lower Seim rivers] many soldiers are assembled; and that from the towns of the Lower Volga, from Kazan' and from Nizhnii, many soldiers have set forth to join them on the march to Moscow against the Poles and Lithuanians. . . . And you, sirs . . . should stand firm, one and all, in the Orthodox Christian faith, and should not betray the Orthodox Christian faith for the Latin faith, lest you destroy your souls . . . and you, sirs, should in any case go to join us forthwith and send your soldiers without delay, on horseback or on skis, while the season for skis lasts; and we shall wait for you in Iaroslavl'; and we have written to other neighboring towns that they should set forth themselves, and send the soldiers whom they have recruited, to join us.

[From Sol'vychegodsk to Perm', not long after March 4, 1611:]

To the lords Ivan Ivanovich and Piatyi Filat'evich [the voevody], and to all the elders and tseloval'niki [sworn men] of the land of Perm' the Great, and to all the townspeople [*posadskie liudi*] and inhabitants, and to all the volost' peasants of the uezd: Nikifor Zasetskii and the townspeople of Sol'vychegodsk, and the elders, tseloval'niki, townspeople, inhabitants, and volost' peasants of the entire Usol'e uezd send greetings. In the current year of 119 [1611], sirs, on the twenty-eighth day of February, [the voevody] Ivan Ivanovich Volynskii and Ivan Ozeretskii, and the dvoriane, deti boiarskie, town [posad] elders, tseloval'niki and all the inhabitants wrote to us from Iaroslavl'; and they sent the *syn boiarskii* [petty nobleman] Ivan Dmitrievich Zhokhov and the posad man of Iaroslavl', the tanner Tikhon Kashintsov; and with them they sent us copies of messages [from other towns] regarding common action and the [recruiting of] soldiers and urging all us

Orthodox Christians to make common cause
for God's holy churches and for the Orthodox
Christian faith and for the Muscovite state,
and to recruit soldiers and dispatch them to
Iaroslavl' and to other towns forthwith, to
join the voevody and march on Moscow to
succor the Muscovite state and to clear it of
the Poles and Lithuanians, and to free the
Orthodox Christians from the Latin faith.
And in response to these messages, sirs, praying for God's grace and mindful of our former
oath, we have hired soldiers in Sol'vychegodsk
and in the Usol'e uezd, with all their battle
equipment, three men from each small sokha
[land measure used as unit of taxation], and
have dispatched them to Iaroslavl' and to other
towns, as required, to join the voevody, and
to join the soldiers from all the Muscovite
towns before Moscow. And you too, sirs,
mindful of God and of the Holy Virgin and of
the Miracle Workers of Moscow [the canonized Moscow metropolitans Peter, Alexis, and
Jonah], and of your former sworn oath,
should make common cause with us and with
all the Muscovite towns together, for the
Orthodox Christian faith and God's holy
churches, and should recruit soldiers forthwith
with all their battle equipment, and send them
to Iaroslavl' and to the other towns and to
Moscow, to join the voevody and soldiers, in
order to bring speedy help to the Muscovite
state, to clear Moscow of the Poles and Lithuanians, and to deliver the Orthodox Christians
from the Latin faith, so that God in his mercy
may likewise free us from our enemies, the
Poles and Lithuanians, and from the Latin
faith, and not deliver us into captivity to our
enemies.

[From Iaroslavl' to Kazan', early June, 1611:]

We write to you not on behalf of Iaroslavl'
alone, and we make known to your entire
community what is going on here. You know
yourselves how the Lithuanians deceived the
Muscovites for their sins: they pretended to be
willing to give the king's son [to be tsar], and
they kissed the cross to this outside Moscow;

and the Muscovites likewise kissed the cross
and confirmed it in writing; and they, the
impious, godless villains, having used the oath
to deceive, took possession of Moscow and
[other] towns. The people of Moscow had
placed their greatest trust in the villains and
heretics, the betrayers of the Christian faith,
[who are] worse than infidels—Mikhailo
Saltykov and his son Ivan, and Fed'ka [Fedor]
Andronov, and their followers; [the people
of Moscow] had trusted in them, in their
oaths sworn in God's name and upon the
cross. . . . And their betrayal and desecration
of the Orthodox faith cannot be described:
they intended that Moscow and all the towns
should kiss the cross to the [Polish] king,
and they considered father and son [Sigis-
mund and Wladyslaw] to be inseparable; and
the king wanted to come to Moscow with all
his men; and the boyars were seduced by [the
promise of] appanages, and some were moved
by fear; they sent all the service men away
from Moscow; and we poor Orthodox Christians were all in despair, with no one to defend
or to help us, either by word or by deed. But
the Lord was not yet utterly wroth with us,
and the unhoped-for came to pass: the father
of fathers, the most holy God-loving great
lord, the most holy patriarch Hermogen of
Moscow and all Russia stood up for the Orthodox faith unwaveringly, without fear of death.
When he heard these things from the heretics,
from Mikhailo Glebov and his followers and
the Lithuanians, he summoned all the Orthodox Christians and talked to them and en-
couraged them, and he bade them stand and
die for the Orthodox faith, and he denounced
the heretics before all the people. And if God
had not sent him, and if the patriarch had not
done this most marvelous deed, who would
have taken this stand? . . . The patriarch also
sent messages to the towns, bidding them to
defend the Orthodox faith and [declaring that]
those who died would become new holy
martyrs; and hearing all these things from the
patriarch, and seeing them with their own eyes,
the towns exchanged messages and [their men]
marched toward Moscow.

VIII:13. THE PROCLAMATION OF THE FIRST NATIONAL HOST, JUNE 30, 1611

After much discussion, Liapunov and the other leaders of the First National Host issued on June
30, 1611, a proclamation designed to lay the basis for a new government. The extracts below
reflect the attitudes of those leaders on the problems that faced them and help to explain why
this host, despite Liapunov's promise, earlier that spring, of freedom to "boyars' bondmen," did

not retain mass support. It may be noted that the word "land" (*zemlia*) is used in this document not only in the sense of nation and region but also to refer to the assembly of representatives of the whole country.

Reference: Iakovlev, *Pamiatniki istorii Smutnogo vremeni,* pp. 65–70.

In the year 7119 [1611], on the thirtieth day of June, the tsarevichi [Tatar princes serving the Muscovite state] of the various lands of the Muscovite state, and the boyars . . . and dvoriane from the towns, and deti boiarskie from all the towns, and atamans, and Cossacks and various service men [*sluzhilye liudi i dvorovye*], who, encamped before Moscow, stand up for the Cathedral of the Dormition and the Orthodox Christian faith against the destroyers of the Christian faith, the Poles and the Lithuanians, have resolved and have chosen by the entire land the boyars and voevody Prince Dmitrii Timofeevich Trubetskoi and Ivan Martynovich Zarutskii and the Duma dvorianin and voevoda Prokofii Petrovich Liapunov, so that they, as a government, should take charge of the affairs of the land and of the host and administer justice among all the people equitably; and the soldiers and all the men of the land shall obey these boyars in all matters of the land and of the host. . . .

And those . . . service men of every kind who are now serving with the troops outside Moscow and who stand up for the Orthodox Christian faith together with the land, without absenting themselves, and who possess no pomest'ia, or whose pomest'ia have been laid waste, or who are not in possession of their pomest'ia because of devastation by the Lithuanians: all these, because of their poverty and ruin, shall receive pomest'ia out of those pomest'ia which, by the present resolution of the boyars and of all the land, shall be expropriated from the boyars and dvoriane and deti boiarskie who are now in Moscow.

. . .

And as for those dvoriane and deti boiarskie who by the twenty-fifth day of May had not appeared outside Moscow to serve the land, it was ordered, in accordance with a previous resolution of the boyars and of all the land, to expropriate their pomest'ia and distribute them [to others], irrevocably; and since the time of that resolution many have appeared to serve, and they petition the boyars and all the land that they did not come hitherto because of poverty and ruin; and an investigation of these men shall be made in their towns, and the reports shall be signed by dvoriane. If

investigation shows that some failed to come because of poverty and ruin, rather than laziness and knavery, these shall have their pomest'ia returned in accordance with their petitions, in consideration of their poverty and ruin. As for those who did not come by the twenty-ninth of June and do not appear soon to serve, and if the dvoriane report upon investigation of them that they failed to come because of laziness and knavery rather than poverty; and as for those who were in service but left without permission from the boyars, although they were able to serve: their pomest'ia shall be expropriated and distributed irrevocably among those who serve. . . . And a dvorianin of high rank [i.e. a Moscow dvorianin], together with secretaries, shall be chosen by the entire land and placed in the Pomestnyi Prikaz to take charge of matters concerning pomest'ia; and they shall be ordered to provide with pomest'ia first of all those dvoriane and deti boiarskie who are poor and ruined, who have small pomest'ia or no pomest'ia at all, or who are not in possession of their pomest'ia because of devastation by the Lithuanians. . . .

As for those atamans and Cossacks who have served for a long time and now wish to be recompensed with pomest'ia and monetary wages and to serve with the towns [with the local landowning service men], they shall be recompensed for their service with pomest'ia and monetary wages according to their ancestry and service; and as for those atamans and Cossacks who do not desire to be recompensed [thus], those atamans and Cossacks and strel'tsy shall receive a food allowance [*khlebnyi korm*] from the [Prikaz Bol'shogo] Dvortsa [the bureau having jurisdiction over villages and towns belonging to the crown and over the service men in them] and money from the [Prikaz] Bol'shogo Prikhoda [the central financial organ of the state] and from the chetverti [territorial financial organs], in all regiments equally. And the atamans and Cossacks shall be relieved of bailiff's duties [*pristavstvo*] in the towns and crown villages and *chernye* volosti [inhabited by tiaglo-bearing state peasants]; and they shall not be permitted to commit any violence in the towns and the countryside, or any robbery and murder on the highways; and worthy dvoriane shall be sent for their sustenance [korm] into the towns and volosti, together with deti boiarskie and Cossacks and strel'tsy for various assignments; and sustenance [korm] shall be collected in accordance with instructions, as the boyars shall decree and instruct, and beyond this nothing shall be done to oppress and impoverish Christians. And if any deti boiarskie or Cossacks or strel'tsy or boyars' slaves, or any other people in the host in Moscow and outside Moscow, or in the towns and volosti, or on the highways, should begin to steal, rob, plunder, and commit murder, thorough investigations shall be made, and every kind of lawlessness shall be suppressed, and punishments and the death penalty shall be meted out; and for this purpose a Razboinyi Prikaz [central department in charge of criminal affairs] and a Zemskii Prikaz [central department for the maintenance of public order and tranquillity] shall be established, as was in Moscow heretofore. And the boyars who have been chosen by the entire land [i.e. Trubetskoi, Zarutskii, and Liapunov] shall set the land in order and take care of all the affairs of the land and of the host, in accordance with this resolution of the entire land. And without the verdict of the entire land the boyars shall not impose an undeserved death penalty or deport people to various towns; and no one shall form gangs or conspiracies to injure another, or take vengeance on anyone out of enmity. If anyone has a claim against another, let him petition the boyars and the entire land for justice. If anyone goes to join a gang and to form conspiracies, and if anyone kills another out

of enmity, and if anyone accuses another of some traitorous act against the land, the matter shall be investigated fairly, and upon investigation [and] depending on the guilt, punishment or the death penalty shall be meted out by the boyars after consultation with the entire land. And they shall not put anyone to death or deport anyone to various towns without informing the entire land; and whoever puts another to death without the verdict of the land shall himself be punished by death. . . .

As for those peasants and bondmen [liudi] whom in the present time of troubles and devastation the dvoriane and deti boiarskie carried away from their fellow dvoriane and deti boiarskie [by paying off the peasants' indebtedness to their former masters], or who have fled from them and live in the towns in the posady, these shall be sought out in accordance with their [former masters'] petition, and upon investigation the peasants and bondmen shall be returned to their former pomest'e owners.

And if the boyars now chosen by the entire land to administer the affairs of the land and of the host should fail to look after the affairs of the land zealously, to dispense justice equitably, and to administer the affairs of the land and of the host in accordance with the present resolution of the entire land; and if on their account the affairs of the land should come to a standstill; and if the voevody should fail to obey the [governing] boyars in all matters: then we shall be free to replace the boyars and the voevody by all the land and to choose in their place, after conferring with the entire land, others who will be better suited for affairs of the host and of the land.

VIII:14. NOVGOROD'S TREATY WITH SWEDEN, JULY 11, 1611

Metropolitan Isidore and the voevoda Ivan Nikitich Odoevskii, in concluding this treaty with the invading Swedes under Jakob de la Gardie, seemed to be resurrecting an earlier Novgorodian tradition.

Reference: Iakovlev, *Pamiatniki istorii Smutnogo vremeni*, pp. 74-76.

1. We, the people of Novgorod, desire to maintain sincere friendship and eternal peace with the most august king and with the Kingdom of Sweden, on the strength of the oath sworn at Teusin [Treaty of Teusin (Tiavzin) in 1595 between Russia and Sweden] and of the agreements concluded between Sweden and Russia in the reign of Tsar Vasilii Shuiskii;

we shall not accept the Polish king, nor his male heirs, nor any of the Poles and Lithuanians, and we intend to resist them as our enemies in every way, since they have violated their promises and their oath. And instead of the Polish king, we accept as protector and defender against our foes the most august king of Sweden, as well as his male heirs and successors and the Kingdom of Sweden; and we promise to repulse the enemy [the Polish king] with our united forces, loyally and courageously, and not to conclude any alliance or peace with him without the knowledge and assent of the above-named king and the Kingdom of Sweden. . . .

2. Moreover, we, the people of Novgorod, choose and invite either of the sons of the most august king [Charles IX], their Serene Highnesses Prince Gustavus Adolphus or Prince Charles Philip, and his male heirs, to become tsar and grand prince of Vladimir and Moscow; and we confirm this election with our oath of allegiance, by virtue of which the Muscovite state and the principality of Vladimir shall acknowledge the most august king as their protector, and the son of His Royal Majesty as their tsar and grand

prince, to the exclusion of all others.

· · ·

4. . . . I, Jakob de la Gardie, . . . irrevocably promise . . . not to hinder or to persecute their religious faith and worship, not to coerce them to embrace another faith, but to maintain the free observance of the ancient Greek faith as it was heretofore; neither to destroy nor to plunder their temples, monasteries, sacred vessels, and images; not to inflict any injury upon the priesthood, namely: the metropolitan, archbishops, archimandrites, abbots, and all the clergy; to treat them not with contempt for their faith but with respect; and finally, not to deprive them of their hereditary estates and church revenues.

· · ·

6. . . . The ancient rights and laws shall be maintained.

VIII:15. KING SIGISMUND'S MESSAGE TO THE POPE, SEPTEMBER 22, 1611

Pope Paul V on August 20, 1611, sent a letter to King Sigismund congratulating him on his "most glorious victory over the Muscovites" (the taking of Smolensk, in June). In response, Sigismund on September 22, 1611, instructed Pawel Wolucki, the bishop of Luck, to convey a message to the pope. These passages from the instructions show how Sigismund depicted his invasion of Muscovy and how he envisioned the future.

Reference: Bogoiavlenskii and Riabinin, *Akty vremeni mezhdutsarstviia*, pp. 179-80 (Latin), 187-89 (Russian).

The magnitude of [King Sigismund's] zeal for the propagation of Christianity is clearly attested by this very war, conducted, as it were, before the eyes of Your Holiness and of this holy see and exposed to the view of the entire world; a war that he has been waging in Muscovy for several years at great cost and expense, with great detriment to his affairs and to his other dominions. He undertook it, not so much with the intention of expanding his own and his kingdom's domains, as in order to maintain and to strengthen the Christian cause against the barbarians and to return Muscovy itself from schism to this holy apostolic see. With regard, then, to his personal interests and those of his kingdom, he may consider that he has done enough for the restoration of his rights and for the glory of his kingdom by regaining Smolensk and the vast Duchy of Seversk [the region along the Desna and lower Seim rivers], torn away and excluded from the Polish kingdom nearly a century ago by the perfidy of the Muscovites; and he considers the labors and dangers he is now incurring in this campaign to be necessary,

not so much for his own benefit, glory, or interests, as for the whole of Christendom, and in particular for this holy apostolic see. When, with the extinction of the line of Ivan Vasil'evich [Ivan IV], there appeared to be a similar opportunity, his predecessor, King Stephen [Bathory] of blessed memory, likewise conceived the plan of subjecting Muscovy. By gaining dominion over Muscovy, which for a great distance borders on the Turkish Empire and through which the road is open into Persia, a possible ally which might provide forces against the Turks, [he hoped] above all to put fetters, as it were, upon Turkish power, long a formidable threat to Christendom, and to return Muscovy itself from error and schism to obedience to the holy apostolic see. This plan was not only approved by the predecessor of Your Holiness, Sixtus V of blessed memory, but was taken up by him as a personal concern and task, so that he even assigned very considerable subsidies and aid for this war. Subsequently [the project] was either interrupted or abandoned upon the death of King

Stephen and of Pope Sixtus V, and also as a result of changes within the Muscovite state. Since that time it has been revived by my most serene king [Sigismund], upon another occasion which one may say was sent from above; all the more ardently since in addition to all the other enormous benefits that would accrue to all of Christendom from the subjugation of Moscow, he anticipates that it would enable him in part to return his Kingdom of Sweden to his own control and authority and to that of this holy apostolic see. . . . Thus far not only Smolensk and the vast Duchy of Seversk have been brought back under his control, with great effort and after two years of siege, but also a great many towns and fortresses in the rest of Muscovy and even the very capital of that immense empire. The grand prince himself [Vasilii Shuiskii], a striking example of human fortune, as well as military commanders and other men of high birth and rank, have been carried away into Poland. Because of all this, [the king] entertains the strong hope that, particularly if the favor and blessing of Your Holiness be granted him, this immense northern world, hitherto almost unknown because of its vast expanse, may with God's help be easily joined to his own realm as well as to the holy apostolic see, to the great benefit and increase of all Christendom.

VIII:16. LETTERS FROM KAZAN' AND TOBOL'SK, SEPTEMBER-OCTOBER 1611

The September letter both records the failure of the First National Host and sounds the keynote of the Second. The October letter summarizes the events of the year 1611 as they were transmitted from the Siberian administrative center of Tobol'sk to the small town of Narym, several hundred miles further east.

Reference: Iakovlev, *Pamiatniki istorii Smutnogo vremeni,* pp. 79-80; Bogoiavlenskii and Riabinin, *Akty vremeni mezhdutsartsviia,* pp. 44-46.

[A letter from Kazan' to Perm', September 1611:]

We, sirs, are glad to be united with you in amity and concord and are ready to make common cause with you for the true Christian faith, against the destroyers of our Christian faith, the Poles and the Lithuanians, and against the Russian rogues. And outside Moscow, sirs, the protector and defender of Christ's faith, who stood up for the Orthodox Christian faith and for the Cathedral of the Dormition [in Moscow] and for the Muscovite state against the Poles and the Lithuanians and the Russian rogues, Prokofii Petrovich Liapunov, has been murdered by the Cossacks, in violation of their oath. . . . And the metropolitan, and we, and people of every rank of the state of Kazan', and the [Tatar] princes, and the murzas [Tatar nobles], the Tatars, the Chuvash, the Cheremis, and the Votiaks, have exchanged messages with Nizhnii-Novgorod, with all the towns on both banks of the Volga, with the Tatars on both banks of the Volga, and with the Tatars and Cheremis of the meadow [left or eastern] bank, vowing to live together in concord and unity, and to stand up for the states of Moscow and Kazan', and not to fight one another, and not to pillage, and not to do evil to anyone; and he who commits an offence should be punished in accordance with his sentence, depending on his guilt. . . . And the sovereign of the Muscovite state should be chosen by the entire land of the Russian realm; and should the Cossacks choose a sovereign for the Muscovite state arbitrarily, by themselves, without consultation with the entire land, we shall not want such a sovereign for the state. And whatever be your thought, sirs, and whatever news you may receive from Novgorod the Great, or from Vologda, or from Ustiug, or from any other town, you should not keep us uninformed but should write to us often about such news; and if any news reaches us about the Muscovite state, we shall likewise write to you about it.

[A letter from Tobol'sk to Narym, ca. October 1611:]

[Prince] Ivan Katyrev-Rostovskii sends greetings to Lord Miron Timofeevich. In the current year of 120 [1611], on the first day of October, the boyars and voevody Prince Dmitrii Trubetskoi and Ivan Zarutskii and the Duma nobleman [*dumnyi dvorianin*] and voevoda Prokofii Liapunov . . . and all the service men and inhabitants of the entire Muscovite state wrote to us from Moscow the same thing that the boyars Prince Fedor

Christian faith and for the Cathedral of the Dormition and for the Miracle Workers of Moscow, against the enemies and destroyers of our Christian faith, against the Poles and the Lithuanians. . . . And we, sir, here in Tobol'sk, have read that message from the boyars aloud before all the people; and you should likewise order this message to be read aloud in the fortified settlement [ostrog] of Narym before all the people.

VIII:17. AN APPEAL OF ARCHIMANDRITE DIONYSIUS, OCTOBER 6, 1611

After Patriarch Hermogen, who assailed both Poles and Cossacks, was incarcerated, the struggle to arouse the people against the Polish army of occupation was carried on by the Trinity Monastery of Saint Sergius, near Moscow. These excerpts from the monastery's circular letter of October 6, 1611, to various Russian towns from the archimandrite Dionysius and the steward (*kelar'*) Avraamii Palitsyn, show the position taken by Dionysius toward the Cossack troops of Trubetskoi. (See also Item VIII:7, above.)

Reference: Iakovlev, *Pamiatniki istorii Smutnogo vremeni*, pp. 80–82.

By God's rightful judgment, for the manifold sins of all Orthodox Christendom, in recent years there has been intestine strife in the Muscovite state, not merely among people sharing the Christian faith but even severing the natural ties of kinship: father rose against son, and son against father, and brother against brother; blood of the same stock was shed in intestine strife. And beholding such intestine strife in the Muscovite state, and heeding the enemy's prompting, those betrayers of Christianity Mikhailo Saltykov and Fed'ka [Fedor] Andronov [collaborators with the Poles in the Kremlin], with their advisers, forsook our true Orthodox Christian faith and went over to the accursed Latins [Catholics], to the Poles and Lithuanians, from time immemorial the eternal foes of Christianity; and they caused this alien people to destroy God's sacred churches, and to desecrate the holy images, and to bring ruin on our true Orthodox Christian faith. . . . And in the past year of 119 [1611], on the nineteenth day of March, those same betrayers of Christianity, Mikhailo Saltykov and Fed'ka Andronov with their advisers, instigated an evil and horrible deed: together with the Poles and Lithuanians they burned Moscow to the ground, and slaughtered the people, and utterly destroyed and desecrated God's sacred churches and images, and ignominiously deposed from his see the firm adamant and unshakable pillar, whom one may regard as a new confessor of the faith, the most holy Hermogen, patriarch of Moscow and all Russia, and exiled and imprisoned him, and shed Christian blood without measure; but we still regard him as our pastor and mentor, irremovable from his primatial see, and we never cease to address entreaties and prayers for him to God. And beholding such a wicked and horrible deed, all remaining Orthodox Christians, the boyars and voevody of the Muscovite state, Prince Dmitrii Timofeevich Trubetskoi, and Ivan Martynovich Zarutskii with many voevody, together with dvoriane, deti boiarskie, strel'tsy colonels, atamans, Cossacks, strel'tsy, and various service men, placing their trust in Almighty God and the Holy Virgin, arrived before Moscow from many towns and uezdy, to rescue our true Orthodox Christian faith, lest our Orthodox Christian faith be utterly destroyed by the betrayers of Christianity; and they are encamped before Moscow in the tsar's great Kammenyi-gorod [outer quarter of Moscow], and the traitors and apostates and betrayers of the Christian faith, Mikhailo Saltykov and Fed'ka Andronov with their followers, and the Poles and Lithuanians, are besieged in Kitai-gorod and in the Kremlin. . . .

And you, sirs, fathers and brothers and all Orthodox Christians, all the Christian people of the land of Perm' the Great [other towns had already been named], with its uezdy and dependent towns [*prigorody*] (inasmuch as we were all born of Christian parents and were marked with the seal of the King of Heaven through holy baptism, and have vowed to believe in the holy, life-giving, and indivisible Trinity, the true living God): you should now pray to Almighty God for his grace, and place your trust in the power of the life-giving cross of the Lord, and make common cause with us against the betrayers of Christianity and the apostates Mikhailo Saltykov and Fed'ka Andronov with their advisers, and against the eternal enemies of Christ's cross, the Poles and the Lithuanians.

VIII:18. A LETTER FROM NIZHNII-NOVGOROD TO VOLOGDA, 1612

This letter, written sometime in 1612, describes how the Second National Host was formed.
Reference: *AAE,* 2:348-50.

As you yourselves know, because of the common sins of all of us Orthodox Christians, intestine strife broke out in the Russian state . . . and beholding such discord among us, those ravishers of our salvation, the Poles and Lithuanians, purposed to destroy the Muscovite state and to convert our radiant and immaculate Christian faith into their Lithuanian faith, abominable to God. . . . They utterly destroyed the ruling and illustrious city of Moscow through deceit and perfidy; and they delivered countless Christians, from the highest to the lowest in rank, to the all-destroying sword; they deposed from his ecumenical see the invincible and firm adamant, the most holy Hermogen, patriarch of Moscow and all Russia; and they brought countless calamities and ruin upon our Christian race. And beholding such iniquity, all the towns of the Muscovite state exchanged messages and affirmed by kissing the cross that all we Orthodox Christians should live in amity and concord, and avoid the former intestine strife, and strive relentlessly, as long as we live, to clear the Muscovite state of our enemies, the Poles and Lithuanians; and that we should not under any circumstances pillage and oppress the Orthodox Christians; and that we should not choose a sovereign for the Muscovite state arbitrarily, without consultation with the entire land. . . . And now we, all the people of Nizhnii-Novgorod, having exchanged messages with Kazan' and with all the towns of the Lower Volga and of the [Middle] Volga, and having recruited many soldiers, [and] seeing the utter ruin of Moscow and the towns of the Upper Volga by the Poles and Lithuanians, and praying to God for his grace, are all setting forth ourselves to succor the Muscovite state. . . .

And you should yourselves write to all the towns of the [northern] Littoral about the decision and the agreement, that no one in any town should abandon our agreement, and that their soldiers should come here soon and join us against the Poles and the Lithuanians and be of one accord with us. . . . And from Kazan', and from Sviazhsk, and from Cheboksary, and from all the towns of the Lower Volga, they have written to us that they are setting forth themselves to serve with the host, and that from Kazan' they have sent a vanguard and strel'tsy with their colonel to us, and that they will be with us soon. And once all the towns of the Lower Volga and the Upper Volga have joined forces, we shall all choose together a sovereign for the Muscovite state, as God may grant. And as for whatever news may reach you at Vologda, and whatever decision all of your people may reach regarding the campaign and regarding the place where you should join forces with us, you should make haste to write to us truly about all these things, so that we may know about your decision and about the departure of your soldiers. Your soldiers should in any case join the others together with us, and should not abandon our agreement. And with us here in Nizhnii [-Novgorod] are soldiers from many different towns, and dvoriane, deti boiarskie, strel'tsy, and Cossacks; and they are marching on Moscow in a great assemblage, to liberate the Muscovite state.

VIII:19. POZHARSKII'S APPEAL TO SOL'VYCHEGODSK, APRIL 7, 1612

From their headquarters in Iaroslavl' during the spring and summer of 1612, Pozharskii and the other leaders of the Second National Host called on other towns and regions for help. This message of April 7, 1612, from Prince Pozharskii and his troops to the people of Sol'vychegodsk shows how recent events were depicted in support of the cause.
Reference: Iakovlev, *Pamiatniki istorii Smutnogo vremeni,* pp. 93-95.

The Devil . . . created pernicious disunity among Orthodox Christians: many were seduced into joining a corrupt and iniquitous company, and rogues of every rank banded together and brought about intestine strife and bloodshed in the Muscovite state through their evil designs; and son rose against father, father against son, and brother against brother, and everyone drew his sword against his kinsman, and there was much shedding of Christian blood. And all this rabble gathered together and, led by Ivashka [Ivan] Bolotnikov,

came up to the ruling city [Moscow], intending in their malice to plunder the ruling city
and to slaughter the boyars and people of
every rank, and gosti and trading men; but
merciful God in his mercy prevailed over
them and rescued the Muscovite state from
their evil design. But the remaining rogues
reassembled in the Ukrainian towns [here
meaning the region along the upper Oka and
Upa rivers] and, according to their knavish
custom, chose among themselves a rogue and
again gave him the name of Tsar Dmitrii; and
the Lithuanian king joined their impious assembly . . . and sent Poles and Lithuanians
with that rogue; and joining forces with those
rogues the Poles and Lithuanians laid waste
to many towns, and destroyed the great
sacred monasteries, and reviled the incorruptible bodies of the saints, and put countless Orthodox Christians to the sword. And
much enmity broke out, and incalculable
perfidy poured forth, and many of the pil-
lagers and insatiable shedders of blood called
themselves tsars: Petrushka, and Avgust, and
Lavrushka, and Fed'ka, and many others;
and much blood was spilled by them, and
countless worthy men were put to death by
the sword. . . .

And the impious Poles and Lithuanians,
who had entered the ruling city by deceit,
now began to commit much violence against
Orthodox Christians, and erected Roman
Churches inside the ruling city, and, after
taking counsel with the betrayers of the
Christian faith and the enemies of the Muscovite state, Mikhailo Saltykov and Fed'ka
Andronov, they burned Moscow to the ground,
destroyed God's churches and monasteries,
spilled Christian blood beyond measure,
looted the treasures of the tsars, gathered in
the course of many years. And in the region
of Riazan', the Duma dvorianin and voevoda
Prokofii Petrovich Liapunov, beholding the
utter ruination of the Muscovite state and
the violation of the Orthodox Christian faith
by the Poles and Lithuanians, exchanged messages with all the towns of the Muscovite state
and came up to the ruling city, together with
boyars and voevody and stol'niki and striapchie
and dvoriane of high rank [*dvoriane moskovskie,* or "Moscow dvoriane," as opposed to
dvoriane gorodovye, or "provincial dvoriane"]
and dvoriane and deti boiarskie from all the
towns, and service men of every kind; and

they took counsel together and kissed the
cross to stand up for the image of the Holy
Virgin and the icon of Vladimir, and for the
miraculous relics of the great Miracle Workers
[the Moscow metropolitans Peter, Alexis, and
Jonah], and for the ruling city of Moscow,
and for all the towns of the Muscovite state,
against the Polish and Lithuanian enemies;
and [they vowed] to fight them to the death;
and they set siege to the Lithuanians in Moscow and pressed hard upon them. And the
former instigators of great evil, the atamans
and Cossacks who had served the false tsar
[the second pseudo-Dmitrii] at Tushino,
knavishly plotted with their commander Ivan
Zarutskii, desiring to weaken the Poles and
Lithuanians so as to become masters themselves, in their own knavish manner; and they
killed Prokofii Liapunov and began to commit every kind of villainy according to their
knavish Cossack custom; and they began
looting and murdering in the camp and on
the highways, and subjected dvoriane and
deti boiarskie to shameful deaths. . . . And
the stol'niki and striapchie and dvoriane and
deti boiarskie from all the towns, beholding
[the Cossacks'] iniquitous undertaking, dispersed from [their encampment] outside
Moscow to the towns and began to take counsel with all the towns, so that all Orthodox
Christians would be in agreement and unity
and would elect a sovereign by the entire land.
. . . And the atamans and Cossacks . . . kissed
the cross to the rogue Sidorka [the last pseudo-
Dmitrii, established in Ivangorod and Pskov in
1611-12], giving him the name of their former
tsar. . . .

And now, sirs, we Orthodox Christians, having exchanged messages with the entire land,
have vowed to God by common agreement
and have pledged our souls not to serve their
knavish tsar Sidorka, or Marina [Mniszek] and
her son, but to stand firmly and immovably
against the enemies and depredators of the
Christian faith, the Poles and Lithuanians.
And you, sirs, should take counsel together
with all the people, mindful of God and of
our faith, lest we remain without a sovereign
in these times of utter ruin, so that by counsel
of the entire state we may choose a sovereign
by common agreement, whomever God may
grant us in his righteous love of mankind, lest
the Muscovite state be utterly destroyed by
such calamities. You know yourselves, sirs:

how can we defend ourselves now, without a sovereign, against our common enemies, the Poles and Lithuanians, and Germans [Swedes], and the Russian rogues who are renewing bloody strife in the state? How can we, without a sovereign, negotiate with neighboring sovereigns about great matters of the state and of the land? And how can our realm stand firm and unshakable henceforth? You should dispatch to us in Iaroslavl', by common counsel, two men from every rank, together with your written decision, bearing your signatures.

VIII:20. A LETTER FROM THE SECOND NATIONAL HOST TO PUTIVL' AND OTHER TOWNS, JUNE 1612

This circular letter, sent from the leaders of the Second National Host in Iaroslavl' to Putivl' and other towns, not only reviews some recent history but also illustrates the nature of the appeal made by the host and some of its ideas concerning the future.
Reference: Iakovlev, *Pamiatniki istorii Smutnogo vremeni,* pp. 98-101.

The boyars and voevody of the Muscovite state, and Prince Dmitrii Pozharskii, the stol'nik and voevoda in charge of the affairs of the army and of the land, elected by people of every rank, with his associates, . . . send greetings.

. . .

[After the failure of the First National Host:] And in Nizhnii-Novgorod the gosti and the posad men and the elected deputy Kuz'ma Minin, concerned for the general good and unsparing of their possessions, began to provide the soldiers with monetary wages; and they repeatedly sent for me, Prince Dmitrii [Pozharskii], from Nizhnii [-Novgorod], [urging] that I go to Nizhnii to take counsel with the land; and at their request I went to them in Nizhnii; and in Nizhnii boyars and voevody and stol'niki and striapchie and dvoriane of high rank [Moscow dvoriane] and [other] dvoriane and deti boiarskie began to come to me from Viaz'ma, Dorogobuzh, Smolensk, and various other towns; and I, praying for God's grace, began to confer with them all and with the elected deputy Kuz'ma Minin and the posad men, that we might all make common cause for the Muscovite state against the enemies and destroyers of the Christian faith, the Poles and Lithuanians, and not serve the rogue who is in Pskov [Sidorka] or Marina [Mniszek] and her son, and oppose them and those who would serve them, and choose a sovereign by all the land, whomever the merciful God may grant. And having so resolved, we pledged our souls to God on this, and gave monetary wages to all the soldiers without stint.

Upon hearing of our decision, all the people of the Kazan' state joined us unanimously, and the towns beyond the Volga, and the towns of the [northern] Littoral, and the towns beyond the Moskva River, joined us in united and firm agreement; and many dvoriane and deti boiarskie from many towns of the Ukraine [i.e. the region of the upper Oka, upper Seim, and Upa rivers], hearing of our agreement, came to us. And I, Prince Dmitrii, assembled all the soldiers and marched to Iaroslavl'; and from Iaroslavl' we intended to march with all the men toward Moscow. . . .

And you, sirs, mindful of God and of your souls and of the Orthodox Christian faith and of your fatherland, should repudiate that notorious rogue [Sidorka] as well as Marina [Mniszek] and her son and be in concord and unity with us and with the entire land; and we should choose a sovereign by all the land, whomever the merciful God may grant us. . . . And we implore you, sirs, and tearfully beseech you, brothers of our own blood, Orthodox Christians, to have mercy on yourselves and on your souls, to abandon that pernicious undertaking, to repudiate the rogue and Marina and her son, and to unite with us and with the entire land, lest the Poles and Lithuanians utterly destroy both you and us through our disunity. And from Novgorod the Great the metropolitan of Novgorod, Isidor, and the boyar Prince Ivan Nikitich Odoevskii and people of various ranks have written to us and have sent us letters bearing their signatures, [declaring] that in their city of Novgorod the Great the Orthodox Christian faith has suffered no harm and the Orthodox Christians no ruin from the Germans [Swedes], and that all the Orthodox Christians live in Novgorod without any affliction; and that the Swedish king Charles [IX] has passed away, and after him his son Gustavus Adolphus ascended the throne, and

his other son Charles Philip will soon come to
Novgorod as sovereign, and he is willing to
submit wholly to the will of the people of the
Novgorod state and to be baptized into our
Orthodox Christian faith of the Greek creed.
Of all this we write to you truly, in keeping
with our vow as Christians, just as [the people
of Novgorod] wrote to us. And you, sirs,
should know about this; and you should send
us two or three men from every rank to hold
a common council of the land; and in response
to this letter you should send us your written
judgment, with your signatures, [as to] how
we should stand up against our common enemies, the Poles and the Lithuanians, and how
we are to live without a sovereign in these
evil times; and we should choose a sovereign
by all the land, whomever God in his righteous
love of mankind may grant.

And if you, sirs, should fail to send us [your
men] soon to take counsel, and fail to repudiate
the rogue and Marina and her son, and fail to
unite with us and with the entire land and to
choose a sovereign for the Muscovite state by
common counsel with us, then we shall have
to part with you, with heartfelt tears; and we
shall choose a sovereign by common counsel
with the towns of the Littoral and of the
Lower Volga [i.e. the middle and lower regions,
from Kazan' to Astrakhan'] and beyond the
Moskva River, whomever God may grant us,
lest we be without a sovereign in these evil
times, and lest the Muscovite state and all the
towns of the Muscovite state be utterly ruined
without a sovereign.

And this we make known to you: on the
sixth day of June the boyars and voevody

Prince Dmitrii Trubetskoi and Ivan Zarutskii,
and the voevody, dvoriane, deti boiarskie,
atamans, Cossacks, and various service men
and inhabitants, who are now encamped with
the host before Moscow, wrote to us from
outside Moscow . . . and sent us a letter with
their signatures, confessing their guilt; and in
this letter they write in great contrition that
they had acted like rogues and had kissed the
cross to the rogue who is now at Pskov, giving
him the title of tsar; and now they have found
out that the one in Pskov is indeed a rogue,
not the same as the one who was in Tushino
and Kaluga [the second pseudo-Dmitrii]; and
now they have repudiated him and have kissed
the cross among themselves not to serve that
rogue and henceforth not to contrive any
other rogue and to put to death anyone who
would do so, and to join us all in common
counsel and union, and to stand against our
enemies, the Poles and Lithuanians, and to
clear the Muscovite state of the Lithuanians,
and to reject Marina and her son for the Muscovite state. . . .

And you, sirs, should repudiate that rogue
[Sidorka] and Marina and her son, and join
us and the entire land and the towns of the
Lower Volga and the Littoral and beyond the
Moskva River in common counsel as before,
steadfast in truth and union, to deliver the
Muscovite state from the Poles and Lithuanians, and reject Marina and her son for the
Muscovite state, and choose a sovereign for
the Muscovite state by common counsel of
the entire Muscovite state, whomever the
merciful God may grant us. And you, sirs,
should write us your judgment soon.

VIII:21. AN INVITATION TO JOIN IN THE ZEMSKII SOBOR, NOVEMBER 19, 1612

After the Second National Host had liberated Moscow from the Polish occupiers, its leaders sent
messages to the towns and regions of Russia inviting them to choose and send representatives to
a zemskii sobor empowered to elect a tsar. A sample of such a message is this letter from Moscow
to the voevoda and secretary in Beloozero. (For the official account of the action of the sobor,
see the next item.)

Reference: *CIOIDRMU*, 1911, bk. 4, p. 99.

To the voevoda Stepan Nikiforovich Chepchiu-
gov and to the secretary Bogdan Il'in in Beloozero, the boyar and voevoda Dmitrii Trubetskoi
and the stol'nik and voevoda Dmitrii Pozharskii
send greetings.

By the grace of Almighty God glorified in
the Trinity, and through the supplications and
help of the Holy Virgin, and the prayers of all
the saints, and the endeavors and steadfast

service of the boyars and voevody and stol'niki
and dvoriane and all the soldiers, the Cathedral
of the Dormition [in Moscow] and the oft-
healing relics of the Muscovite Miracle Workers
[the canonized Moscow metropolitans Peter,
Alexis, and Jonah] in the ruling city of Moscow
have been delivered from the Poles and Lithuanians; and praying for God's grace, the boyars
and people of all ranks are firmly established

in Moscow: in Great Tsar'-gorod [another name for Kamennyi- or Belyi-gorod], in Kitai-gorod, and in the Kremlin. And boyars . . . and dvoriane from the towns and men of various ranks came to us, Dmitrii Trubetskoi and Dmitrii Pozharskii, and they conferred with us and resolved that we should all send messages to all the towns, to you, the voevody, and to all the people, great and small, so that we may restore a sovereign tsar and grand prince to the states of Moscow and Vladimir and to all the great states of the Russian tsardom. And from the posady in the towns and from the uezd of Beloozero you should choose ten worthy men for the worthy assembly that is to elect [a sovereign]; and the appointed date [for the arrival of the delegates] shall be Saint Nicholas's Day [December 6] in the autumn of the current year.

And you, sirs, having chosen ten of the best, wisest, and most steadfast men from among the abbots and the archpriests and the people of the posady and the uezd, and from the crown villages and *chernye* volosti [of tiaglo-bearing state peasants], should send

them to us in Moscow to confer about the great affairs of God and of the land. And you shall give them complete and firm and adequate instructions, that they might speak out freely and fearlessly about the great matter of the state, on behalf of all the people of Beloozero and of the uezd; and you should instruct them—[omission in original] well, with great emphasis, to act honestly without any guile. And you yourselves, sirs, should set aside all other matters forthwith and proceed to elect at Beloozero ten men from among the clergy and the posad men and the [peasants of the] chernye volosti of the uezd, and order them to make haste to join us in Moscow, for the sake of the great affairs of God and of the land, by the appointed date of Saint Nicholas's Day in the current year of 121 [1612], so that there be no delay in such a great undertaking. We make this known to you, although you know it yourselves: that if the Muscovite state does not have a sovereign soon, we shall not be able to live without a sovereign. There is no land anywhere where the state exists without a sovereign.

B. POLITICAL DEVELOPMENTS UNDER THE EARLY ROMANOVS

VIII:22. THE ELECTORAL CHARTER OF TSAR MICHAEL, FEBRUARY 1613

The election of Michael Fedorovich Romanov to the tsardom of Muscovy in February 1613 was confirmed by a charter (*utverzhdennaia gramota*) signed on its reverse by persons present at the Sobor. Here are some excerpts.

In connection with this and other documents, a word of explanation may be in order concerning the various ranks of *sluzhilye liudi* or service men. By the seventeenth century, these ranks had crystallized into three broad categories: (1) those who sat in the Duma: (a) boyars, (b) okol'nichie, (c) dumnye liudi or dumnye dvoriane, (d) dumnye d'iaki; (2) those who served in Moscow: (a) stol'niki, (b) striapchie, (c) dvoriane moskovskie, (d) zhil'tsy; (3) those who served in the provinces: (a) dvoriane gorodovye, (b) deti boiarskie dvorovye, (c) deti boiarskie gorodovye. Falling outside the above "table of ranks," although sometimes listed alongside them in documents, were titles held by officials of the tsar's household: dvoretskii (majordomo), koniushei (equerry), chashnik (cupbearer), spal'nik (gentleman of the chamber), kaznachei (treasurer), and so on. Normally, persons occupying these offices also held one of the ranks mentioned above. For further details, consult the *Dictionary of Russian Historical Terms*.

Reference: *CIOIDRMU*, 1906, bk. 3, pp. 23-26, 42-46, 74. For the text in the old script see *Kniga ob izbranii na tsarstvo . . . Mikhaila Fedorovicha . . .* (Moscow: Sinodal'naia Tipografiia, 1856).

The line of the great sovereigns, the Russian tsars, issued from the most exalted throne of the caesars and from the flourishing and illustrious line of Augustus Caesar, who was master over the entire world.

The first grand prince, Riurik, held the scepter of the great Russian realm in Novgorod the Great. . . .

After Sviatoslav a shining star arose, the great sovereign, his son, Grand Prince Vladimir Sviatoslavich, who illumined the darkness of unbelief and banished the seducements of idolatry, and illumined the whole Russian land through holy baptism, wherefore he was called the equal of the apostles, and for expanding his dominions was given the title of autocrat, and to this day he is revered and glorified by all. . . . Grand Prince Vladimir Vsevolodovich . . . received the supreme honor of a tsar's crown and necklet [*diadima*] from the Greek tsar Constantine Monomachus, wherefore he was called Monomakh; and after him all the great Russian sovereigns were crowned tsars with this crown. . . .

After the great sovereign Aleksandr Nevskii, his son, Grand Prince Daniil Aleksandrovich, removed from Vladimir to Moscow, and established there the scepter of the tsardom, and installed there the most exalted throne of the tsardom, which to this day is protected and guarded by God.

· · ·

[Under Tsar Fedor Ivanovich] the reigning city of Moscow waxed strong and expanded and flourished in possession of all the blessings of the world, above all the great empires. And the name of the great sovereign tsar and grand prince Fedor Ivanovich, autocrat of all Russia, was famed throughout the world.

· · ·

[After the narrative has been brought up to 1612:]

The boyars and voevody of the Muscovite state, and the entire Christ-loving host [i.e. the soldiers] . . . having delivered themselves from all their misfortunes and vanquished the enemies of their faith . . . wrote to all the towns of the Muscovite state . . . that from all the towns of the entire Russian tsardom the metropolitans and archbishops and archimandrites and abbots should come to join the boyars in Moscow; and that the best, most steadfast, and wisest men should be chosen from among the dvoriane and deti boiarskie, and gosti, and trading men, and posad men, and peasants, as many as is fitting, and should be sent to Moscow for a council of the land [*zemskii sovet*] and for the election of a sovereign; and that by a decision of the land a sovereign tsar and grand prince of all Russia should be chosen, of Muscovite Russian lineage, whomever God may grant, for the sovereignties of Vladimir and Moscow, and the tsardoms of Kazan' and Astrakhan' and Siberia, and all the great dominions of the Russian realm. . . . And at the sobor, men from all the towns of the Russian tsardom spoke their mind plainly for many days and made known the common decision of all the people, old and young, of all the towns: "that

. . . Mikhail Fedorovich Romanov-Iur'ev should be tsar and grand prince and autocrat of all Russia; and that neither the kings and princes of Poland, Lithuania, Sweden, or any other kingdom, nor any men of Muscovite family, nor any of the foreigners serving in the Muscovite state, should ever become sovereign, save only for Mikhail Fedorovich Romanov-Iur'ev, inasmuch as he, the great sovereign . . . is the son of Fedor Nikitich Romanov-Iur'ev, first cousin of the great sovereign tsar and grand prince Fedor Ivanovich, autocrat of all Russia." . . . And the [church] authorities, and all the clergy, and the boyars, okol'nichie, cupbearers, stol'niki, and the entire Christ-loving host, and the gosti and trading men, and the posad men, and all kinds of men from among the common people of the entire Russian realm, left the matter to the will of God; and to give [the decision] greater force, they postponed [the final election] from the seventh of February to the twenty-first of February, for two weeks. . . . [Meanwhile] loyal and God-fearing men were sent secretly to all the towns of the Russian realm, except the most distant, to find out what various people thought about the election of a sovereign [and] who was desired in all the towns as sovereign tsar of the Muscovite state. And in all the towns and uezdy all the people, old and young, had the same thought: that Mikhail Fedorovich Romanov should be the sovereign tsar of the Muscovite state; and they wanted no one but him, the great sovereign, for the Muscovite sovereignty.

. . . Those in the Muscovite state who pray for the sovereign, the metropolitans, archbishops, bishops, archimandrites, abbots, and the entire holy council, and the tsars and tsarevichi [Tatar princes] from various lands who serve in the Muscovite state, and the boyars, okol'nichie, cupbearers, stol'niki, striapchie, dvoriane of high rank [*bol'shie dvoriane*, i.e. Moscow dvoriane, as opposed to the provincial dvoriane], and the dvoriane and secretaries in the Duma, and the provincial dvoriane, and secretaries, zhil'tsy, and all kinds of government officials, and deti boiarskie, and military commanders [*golovy*], captains [*sotniki*], atamans, Cossacks, and strel'tsy, and gosti, trading men, and posad men, and all the people of every rank in the Muscovite state, a countless multitude of all the people, all the Orthodox Christians, people of every age, both old and young, chose as sovereign tsar and grand prince and autocrat of all Russia, of the sovereignties of Vladimir and Moscow and Novgorod, and the tsardoms of Kazan' and Astrakhan' and Siberia, and all the great [and] glorious dominions of the Russian realm, the flourishing offspring of the noble tsarist line of the former great, noble, pious, and God-ordained Russian sovereign tsars,

Mikhail Fedorovich Romanov-Iur'ev.

. . .

And at the sobor were present . . . service men and inhabitants of every rank in the Muscovite state and from all the towns of the Russian tsardom, and likewise elected deputies from all the towns of the Russian tsardom, who had been sent with certificates of election signed by all the people for the election of a sovereign.

VIII:23. A MESSAGE FROM THE ZEMSKII SOBOR TO BOLKHOV, FEBRUARY 27, 1613

This message from the Zemskii Sobor of 1613 to the voevoda in Bolkhov (some 160 miles south of Moscow) illustrates one of the ways in which the sobor assumed governmental authority.
    Reference: *CIOIDRMU*, 1911, bk. 4, p. 129.

To the voevoda Lord Iurii Zakhar'evich Bogdanov in Bolkhov: Kirill, metropolitan of Rostov and Iaroslavl', and the archbishops and bishops and the entire holy council, and the boyars and okol'nichie and people of every rank of the Muscovite state send greetings.
    Many letters have heretofore been sent to you in response to petitions from dvoriane and deti boiarskie and various people, with orders to pay them monetary wages in Bolkhov out of various revenues. But now we, Kirill, metropolitan of Rostov and Iaroslavl', and the archbishops and bishops and the entire

holy council, and the boyars and okol'nichie and people of every rank of the Muscovite state, have resolved that no wages shall be paid to anyone for any expenses on the strength of all those letters, without a decision of the entire [zemskii] sobor and of the boyars.
    And you, sir, should collect all kinds of revenue for the chetverti [territorial financial organs, same as cheti; see next item] and the tavern taxes, and send them to Moscow to the sovereign tsar and grand prince of all Russia Mikhail Fedorovich.

VIII:24. CHARTERS FOR LOCAL ADMINISTRATION, 1615 AND 1622

These charters granted by Tsar Michael suggest some of the problems of local administration, both urban and rural, in the early seventeenth century. The charter of 1615 was granted to the posad men of Shuia (about 150 miles east and north of Moscow). The term "posad men" (*posadskie liudi*) refers in general to those people—mostly artisans and traders, but also others, including some peasants—who were enrolled in an urban or suburban community (posad) and paid tiaglo. The charter of 1622, granted to the Ust'ia volosti, deals with the administration of the free peasantry. The Ust'ia River is a tributary of the Vaga, which in turn runs into the Northern Dvina. (See the *Dictionary* for more on the special terms used in these items.)
    Reference: Nikolai Kalachev, ed., *Akty otnosiashchiesia do iuridicheskogo byta drevnei Rossii*, 3 vols. (St. Petersburg, 1857-84), 1:144-45; *AAE*, 3:176-77.

[From the charter to Shuia, August 20, 1615:]
    From the tsar and grand prince of all Russia Mikhail Feodorovich to Shuia, to the posad elders [posadskie starosty] and sworn assistants [tseloval'niki] and all the posad men. You have complained to us that our voevody administer justice to you in all cases, and that the voevody inflict great losses and injuries upon you; and yet by the charter we had granted you, you were ordered to administer justice among yourselves, electing sworn assistants every year; and [you have petitioned] that we bestow our favor upon you [and]

order you to administer justice among yourselves, according to the previous charter, and forbid the voevody to judge you. . . . And we have bestowed our favor upon you, the posad men of Shuia, and have forbidden the voevody to judge you, and have ordered you to administer justice among yourselves, electing sworn assistants every year. When this, our charter, reaches you, you shall elect among yourselves two or three sworn assessors from among the best men of the posad, to act as judges; and after electing them you shall make them take an oath that they will judge you fairly, according to their oath to us upon the cross, and that they will collect the duties [*poshlina*] and bring them to us in Moscow each year together with the obrok money. They shall administer justice in all cases according to the previous charter; and those cases they cannot settle they shall send on to Moscow to be reported to us; and in Moscow they shall submit them to our secretary Semen Golovin at the Galich Chet'. [Note: The cheti were financial organs of the central government, each having jurisdiction over the tiaglo-bearing inhabitants of a particular region in matters of justice and taxation. There were five cheti in the seventeenth century: Novgorod, Kostroma, Galich, Ustiug, and Vladimir.]

[From the charter to the Ust'ia volosti, September 8, 1622:]

We bestow our favor upon the peasants of the volosti along the Usia and Zaechia rivers, to Pianok Agafonov, and to Ievok Durakov, and to Senka Karpov, and to all the Ust'ia volost' peasants, the best and the middle and the lesser men; for they have petitioned us and said that in years past, before the devastation of Moscow [i.e. the Time of Troubles], there were no government officials [*prikaznye liudi*] in their Ust'ia volosti, and they were tried by judges elected by the village communities [*mirskie vybornye sudeiki*]; but after the devastation of Moscow, they said, officials [*prikazchiki*] were sent to them, and because of these officials they suffered exactions, losses, and great expenses through bribes and *korm* [subsistence payments]; and because of those exactions, abuses, and bribes of the officials they, the peasants, have become impoverished and have nothing left wherewith to pay taxes to us; and they wish to wander away; and they ask us to grant them our favor and give orders that henceforth there be no more officials in the Ust'ia volosti, and that there be judges elected by the village communities as before; and that an obrok be laid upon them in addition to the old obrok, at our discretion, lest they be utterly ruined by the abuses and the bribes and the exactions of the officials, and wander away. And we, bestowing our favor upon the peasantry, on account of those great exactions and losses, have dismissed the officials in the towns and the volosti; and in place of the revenues [paid] to the officials as court fees [*prisud*], and the duties collected by their tax officials, we have ordered that an obrok in money be imposed upon the peasants of the posady and volosti, so that the peasantry may not suffer from exactions and losses, and the posady and volosti may not be deserted therefrom; and we have ordered elected elders to be instituted in all the towns and stany and volosti to administer justice among the peasants, and to collect all our revenues, and to deliver them to us at the prescribed time; [these are to be] men whom the peasants will choose among themselves and elect all together, who will not inflict exactions and losses and injuries upon them but will administer justice to them fairly, without bribery and without delay; and who will be able to collect our obrok and to deliver it to our treasury at the prescribed time, without arrears. . . . And in criminal cases the volost' peasants shall be tried and administered by the criminal judges [*gubnye starosty*], according to their criminal charters [*gubnye gramoty*] and the written instructions. And the sworn assistants [tseloval'niki] who shall sit with them in court and be sent on assignments for them, and the public clerks [zemskie d'iaki] who shall write the records of the court proceedings, and the men who shall replace the constables [*dovodchiki*] to take charge of those out on bail and bring the accused into court shall be elected in their volosti by all the peasants of the Ust'ia volosti, the best and the middle and the lesser men, whomever all the volost' peasants choose among themselves, [and] who would be able to sit in court with the elected elders of those volosti: two sworn assistants from each volost', and one public clerk, and one man in place of the constable to take charge of those out on bail.

VIII:25: A CALL TO THE ZEMSKII SOBOR, JULY 5, 1619

This is a portion of a letter sent from the tsar's office to Novgorod with instructions for the sending of elected deputies from Novgorod to Moscow for the Zemskii Sobor of 1619. The message was addressed to Novgorod the Great, to the voevody Prince I. A. Khovanskii and M. A. Vel'iaminov and the secretary (d'iak) Tret'iak Kopnin.

Reference: Iu. V. Got'e, ed., *Akty otnosiashchiesia k istorii zemskikh soborov,* Pamiatniki russkoi istorii, vol. 3 (Moscow: N. N. Klochkov, 1909), pp. 21-22.

[The letter begins by mentioning an earlier sobor in Moscow.]

We, the great sovereign tsar and grand prince of all Russia Mikhail Fedorovich, with our pious father the most holy patriarch Filaret Nikitich of Moscow and all Russia, and the metropolitans and archbishops and bishops and the entire holy council, and with the boyars and okol'nichie and [other] Duma members and all the people of the Muscovite state, have come together and discussed all matters, how to put things right and set the land in order. ... We have directed that men elected from every town be brought to Moscow, to furnish information and to set the land in order: one man from the clergy of each town, two good and sensible men from the dvoriane and deti boiarskie, and two from the posad men, who would be able to tell of their wrongs and grievances and impoverishment, and [to tell] how to increase the wealth of the Muscovite state, wherewith to recompense the soldiers, and how to organize the Muscovite state so as to put everything in proper order. When this our letter reaches you, you should summon to the Cathedral of [Sancta] Sophia—the Divine Wisdom—the archimandrites and abbots and the entire holy council, and the dvoriane and deti boiarskie, and the gosti, and the posad men and peasants, and all the people of the Novgorodian state; and when they come together, you should have this, our message, read to all the people aloud; and after reading this, our message, you should direct the clergy and dvoriane and deti boiarskie and posad men and all the people to choose good and sensible men from all the ranks: one or two from the clergy, two from the dvoriane and deti boiarskie of every province [*piatina*], and two from the gosti and posad men, and give them written and signed certificates of election, and send them to us in Moscow, so that we and our father ... may learn of all their needs and afflictions and impoverishment, and of various deficiencies. And we, the great sovereign, shall confer with our pious father, the most holy Filaret Nikitich, patriarch of Moscow and all Russia, in accordance with their petitions; and praying for God's grace, we shall concern ourselves with the Muscovite state, so as to improve all things in the best possible way.

VIII:26. THE TSAR'S DIRECTIVE ON ELDERS OF JUDICIAL DISTRICTS, JANUARY 23, 1627

This letter from Tsar Michael to his voevoda in the Torzhok area, northwest of Moscow not far from Tver', sets forth the procedure for selecting a new elder or top official in a judicial district.

Reference: *AAE*, 3:253-54.

From Tsar and Grand Prince Mikhail Fedorovich of all Russia, to Torzhok, to our voevoda Prince Voin Mikhailovich Kropotkin and to the clerk [*pod'iachii*] Bogdan Ondreev.

We have directed that judicial district elders [gubnye starosty] be established in all towns—worthy noblemen, from the lists of the best people, men of upright character and of substantial means, who can read and write, who can be trusted in all our affairs, and who will be suited to the tasks of the judicial district [*guba*]. Henceforth detectives [syshchiki] shall not be sent out to the towns to inquire into cases of thievery, robbery, and murder. The investigation [and trial] of cases of thievery, robbery, and murder, and other affairs of the judicial district, shall be held·in the towns by the judicial district elders and then reported to us in Moscow. As soon as this letter reaches you, you shall send many bailiffs to the judicial district of Novotorzhok, and you shall summon to a conference with you [the following persons]: the archimandrites and abbots, the archpriests and priests and deacons; the nobles [dvoriane] and petty nobles [deti boiarskie]; the township elders [posadskie starosty] and the townspeople; also the elders and stewards of our crown villages and state [chernye] volosti ... and of the episcopal and monastic estates, and of the pomest'ia and patrimonies [*votchiny*] and villages and hamlets of the boyars, nobles, and petty nobles; and sworn assistants [tseloval'niki], and peasants, and all kinds of inhabitants [zhiletskie liudi]. ... And when they come together from the whole judicial district of Novotorzhok to the conference with you, then you shall direct them to choose, from the list of the best people, in place of the former judicial district elder, Druzhina Vil'iashev, a new judicial district elder who is a worthy nobleman, of upright character and a man of means, able to read and write, who can be trusted in all our affairs, and who is suited to the tasks of the judicial district. . . . And when the nobles and petty nobles and people of all kinds have chosen a new judicial district elder by name, you shall order them to put their votes for the new elder in writing . . . and the electors shall put their signatures to the votes; and if any of the electors do not know how to write, you shall direct their confessors to sign in their stead. . . . And when they have chosen the elder and given you their votes for him, you shall write a report about it; you shall send to us in Moscow the report and the certificate of election and the judicial district elder himself, to take the oath to us on the cross and to receive our instructions; and you shall direct the judicial district elder to present himself at the Razboinyi Prikaz [the central department in charge of criminal affairs] and to submit the report and the certificate of election.

VIII:27. CERTIFICATES OF ELECTION FROM THE NORTHERN PROVINCES, 1627-1652

In the seventeenth century, while in the center and south the spread of serfdom was enhancing the power of the estate owner and the bureaucratization of the government was enlarging the role of the voevoda, the common people of the northern provinces retained some tradition of local self-government. The following excerpts from certificates of election illustrate various aspects of this tradition. They serve also to suggest the abundance of detail this type of document may provide on living conditions in general. Space permits only a very few samples.

Reference: *CIOIDRMU*, 1910, bk. 1, app. pp. 84-85 [document of Jan. 2, 1643], 86-88 [Jan. 18, 1652], 98-99 [Sept. 29, 1627], 99-100 [ca. summer of 1632].

[From the Cherevkovskaia volost' of the Ustiug uezd, September 29, 1627:]

September 29, 7136 [1627]. I, Loban Gavrilov Go — novo, elected public judge of the Cherevkovskaia volost', and Zamiatnia Kharitonov, former public sworn assistant, and the [following] peasants . . . [twenty names], representing all the peasants of the Cherevkovskaia volost', have elected and chosen for the said volost' Tomil, son of Ananii Dmitrov, a man of good repute, upright and prosperous, to be sworn public tax assessor [*zemskii dannyi razrubnyi tseloval'nik*] from Saint Simeon's Day [September 1] of the current year of [7]136 to Saint Simeon's Day of the year 137. And he, the tax assessor, is to apportion the sovereign's tax at the table in the refectory of the church, reducing the impositions of the heavily burdened and increasing those of the lightly burdened, according to their possessions and occupation, and giving equality to the peasants [i.e. apportioning the taxes among them fairly]; and we, the peasants, are to provide the tax assessor with appraisers [*zasadchiki*] from the *sokhi*, with whose help he is to apportion the tax and furnish assessment lists [*rozmety*] to the collectors in the sokhi, and receive the monies from the collectors, and give receipts for such monies to the public clerks [zemskie d'iaki] who are to be provided by the mir [commune].

Upon receipt of the sovereign's tax from the collectors, he is to give it to the judge; and [the tax assessor] is to carry to Velikii Ustiug and pay to the elders [the chief elders for the entire uezd] the post tax [*iamskie den'gi*] and the tax for the maintenance of the clergy [*ruzhnye den'gi*]; and he, the tax assessor, is to go to Velikii Ustiug on the sovereign's or the mir's business, and he is to go to the houses of the boyars [i.e. the voevoda and government officials] and bring them the mir's offerings. And if priests or people from the mir are needed in Velikii Ustiug to attend to the sovereign's or the mir's business, or if the tax assessor needs messengers, the tax assessor may hire — [them; omission in text] after consulting the mir. And all year long the tax assessor is to be present at the departure of boyars [i.e. government officials] or messengers or Ustiug strel'tsy or bailiffs [*pristavy*], and he is to assist their departure in accordance with their travel orders, furnishing our communal food supplies and transport. And whatever money is needed for the sovereign's or the mir's urgent business, he, the tax assessor, is to borrow such money after consulting the mir, and give out promissory notes [*kabaly*], and promise to pay interest, as may be required; and we, the peasants of the Cherevkovskaia volost', are to assume from him such promissory notes and interest. And the mir has agreed that the tax assessor's salary is to be six rubles in money for the entire year, and he, the tax assessor, is to take his own salary, and give the clerk and constable [their salaries], out of our communal money. And when the tax assessor's year is up, we, the peasants, are to assume from him the promissory notes [and] interest contracted in connection with loans obtained for the expenses of the mir, and we, the peasants, are not to cause him to suffer any losses from his service as a tax assessor. And he, the tax assessor, is to settle his account with us, the peasants, faithfully, according to his income and expenditure books and certificates of receipt, [and] in accordance with his oath to the sovereign. . . . To this effect the tax assessor has been given the mir's certificate of election. The public [clerk] Iakunka Karamzin wrote the original certificate of election by order of the mir.

[From the posad of Velikii Ustiug, ca. summer of 1632:]

We, the public judges [zemskie sud'i] of Velikii Ustiug, Pavel Semenov Kabakov, Petr Nikitin, and Bazhen Klement'ev Shapochnik, and the court elder [sudetskii starosta] Fedor Zhilin, and the tax assessors [razrubnye tseloval'niki] . . . and all the posad men, the best, the middle, and the lesser, have, in accordance with the sovereign's decree, chosen for the posad of Velikii Ustiug, as public judges for the year 141 [September 1, 1632-August 31, 1633], the posad men Ivan Moiseev Zavalin and Grigorii, son of Iurii Gubin, and Iakov Ivanov Kozhevnik, and as court elder, Bogdan Rostovets. Ivan and his associates are to be public judges in the posad of Velikii Ustiug from the first day of September 141 [1632], to the first day of September 142 [1633]. They are to administer justice to us, the posad men, in lawsuits involving loan obligations [kabaly], complaints, and various written documents [zapisi] and deeds [kreposti], honestly and justly, according to their oath to the sovereign, and they are not to favor or prejudice anyone in any way. The judges are to have full jurisdiction throughout the land in all matters concerning the mir. And we, the posad men, are to obey the judges, Ivan and his associates, in all matters concerning the mir, and are to consult with them, the judges, on matters concerning the mir, and are to recognize their jurisdiction. And should

we, the posad men, fail to come for consultation, in that event the judges are to act even without the men of the mir in all matters concerning the mir: complaints, sentences, elections, investigations, and any other matter concerning the mir. And we, the posad men, are to assent to such actions. And if in the course of the year any government officials should come to Ustiug on order of the sovereign, and ask the judges for sworn assistants from among the posad men for the sovereign's business, then the judges, Ivan and his associates, are to select sworn assistants from among us, the posad men, and are to furnish certificates of election signed by them on behalf of all the posad men. Should it be necessary to elect men to travel on the sovereign's business, they, the judges, are to dispatch [such men] and give [them] corresponding certificates of election; and they are to write resolutions and petitions concerning the mir's needs, and all documents pertaining to the mir, on behalf of all the posad men. And should the judges have to go to Moscow on public business [zemskie dela], the mir is to give them a monetary subsidy. And the judges, Ivan and his associates, are to collect from us, the posad men, according to the tax units [pobelochno: the belka, or "squirrel skin," was the unit of taxation, with eighty rubles of capital equaling one belka], the sovereign's taxes [dannye den'gi] and rents [obrochnye den'gi] for the year 141, according to the tax register [sotnaia kniga] and the sovereign's charter, without arrears, and including the cost of carrying [the taxes to Moscow]; defaulters are to be dealt with mercilessly, jailed for their debt, and brought to court with immunity to the prosecutors. And if any [defaulters] should abscond, the sovereign's money is to be recovered from their wives and children, with immunity to the prosecutors. After collecting the sovereign's taxes and rents, the judges are to take these monies to Moscow and to bring back to their mir a certificate of receipt in full. And the judges, Ivan and his associates, and the tax assessors are to verify truly, in accordance with their oath to the sovereign, the income and expenses of the public judges for the previous year, 140 [1631-32], Pavel Kabakov and his associates, and the sworn assistants, Stepan Kopylov and his associates. If any money is found to be due from these judges and sworn assistants, such money is to be collected from them by the new tax assessors and used for the mir's expenses. And in accordance with the mir's certificate of election, the mir is to pay any promissory notes and losses the judges and sworn assistants may have assumed on the mir's account. . . . And we, the people of the mir, are to support the judges against the defaulters. As for any losses the judges may incur in transacting the mir's business, or in connection with administrative delays in Moscow, and any expenses arising from the mir's business, they shall truthfully enter [them] in the books and submit an account to the mir. And we are to verify these losses and expenses and make good the losses incurred during their tenure of office. The judges are to select three apparitors [nedel'-shchiki] from among the posad men, for the period of one year, and are to administer the oath to them. And any monetary fines the judges may collect from litigations are to be used for the maintenance of the mir's churches and for the affairs of the mir, as need be. . . . And the judges were elected and took the oath, and the certificate of election was given to them. The certificate of election was written by the public court clerk [zemskii sudetskii d'iachok].

[From the Chushevitskaia volost', along the upper reaches of the Vaga River, January 2, 1643:]

I, Piatoi, son of Avtomon, the former elected public judge [zemskii sud'ia] of the Chushevitskaia volost', and the church elder [tserkovnyi starosta] and former sworn assistant [tseloval'nik] Vishniak, son of Mikhei, . . . and all the peasants of the Chushevitskaia volost', of the parish of the [Church of the] Intercession [of the Virgin Mary: Pokrov], have chosen and elected, for one year, in our Chushevitskaia volost', as public judge of the Chushevitskaia volost', the good and upright peasant Konan, son of Luka Kolosov. . . . To assist him we have chosen Ivan, son of Parfen, as sworn court assistant [sudetskii tseloval'nik], and to assist them we have chosen Pozdei, son of Falalei Kalapyshin, as sotskii [police officer]. And we, the mir [commune], have elected them to act as public judge and sworn court assistant with the judge, and they are to administer justice to us, the peasants of the Chushevitskaia volost', and to enforce judgment on us peasants equitably, true to the

oath they swear to the sovereign, without favoring their friends or taking vengeance upon their enemies. And the sworn assistant is to sit in court with the judge and receive complaints from the peasants and, when petitioned to do so, is to go to the peasants and investigate disputes relating to land boundaries and to field damage caused by cattle, and is to draw up the official reports. He is to collect from us, the peasants of the Chushevitskaia volost', the sovereign tsar's monies, the revenues paid into the [Ustiug] chetvert' [financial office, in Moscow but serving much of northern Russia], the taxes [dannye den'gi] and rents [obrochnye den'gi] for the year 152 [September 1, 1643, to August 31, 1644], as was done in the past year, 151 [1642–43], and he is to prosecute defaulters and hand [the money] over to the judge for account. And the judge is to carry the sovereign's money to Moscow, and in Moscow he is to pay it to the sovereign's secretary in the Ustiug chetvert', and bring back from Moscow a certificate of payment, and hand it over to the peasant mir of the Chushevitskaia volost'. And the judge and sworn assistant and sotskii are to exercise the greatest diligence to ensure that no thieves or robbers come on foot or on horse to the peasants of the Chushevitskaia volost', and that no beer is brewed for sale and no spirits are distilled, and that no one admits to his house anybody with liquor for sale. . . . And the peasants are not to play dice and are not to do anything unlawful. To this effect the mir has given to the judge, the sworn assistant, and the sotskii the mir's certificate of election [vybor]. The certificate of election was written by Vaska, son of Kirill, the public [and] church clerk [zemskii tserkovnyi d'iachok, who served the church as psalmist and clerk and served the volost' in the latter capacity] of the Chushevitskaia volost'. The second day of January 7151 [1643].

To this certificate of election the priest Emel'ian — [omission in text] of the Chushevitskaia volost' has affixed his signature by order of the mir.

[From the Chadromskaia volost', in the Vaga River region, January 18, 1652:]

I, Antip, son of Ivan Kulakov, former elected public judge of the Chadromskaia volost'; and the public sworn assistant [zemskii tseloval'nik] Fedor, son of Andrei Puliaev; and I, Fedor, son of Selivan Kiselev, elected sotskii; and I, Nikita, son of Elistratii Kharlov, *piatidesiatnik* [i.e. *piatidesiatskii*]; and I, Ivan, son of Timofei Kholzakov, church elder; and the [following] peasants of the Chadromskaia volost' . . . [fifty-four names]; and all the peasants of the parish of Saint Nicholas in the Chadromskaia volost', have chosen and elected in Chadromskaia volost' Sidor, son of Grigorii Priezhzhikov, as elected public judge; and Grigorii, son of Ivan Nikonov, as public sworn assistant; and Iakov, son of Bogdan Istomin, as sotskii; and Kalistrat, son of Petr Kashin, as piatidesiatskii to attend to the affairs of the sovereign tsar for one year. . . . And the judge and his associates are to administer justice to us peasants and enforce judgment in accordance with their oath to the sovereign in all affairs of the sovereign and of the land, in accordance with the sovereign's decree, and the code of laws, and the administrative charters the sovereign has granted to all the peasants of the volosti of Ustiug, and the written instructions [of the central government: *nakaznye spiski*]. They shall collect from us peasants the taxes and rents and all the sovereign's monetary revenues paid into the chetvert' for the year 161 [1653] and bring them to the sovereign in Moscow. And the public judge Sidor Grigor'ev, together with his associates, is to investigate cases of brigandage and theft, according to the sovereign's edict, and the code of laws, and the administrative charters granted by the sovereign, and the book of new enactments [issued since the last sudebnik: *stateinyi spisok*], and the written instructions, and he is to administer justice in all instances according to the sovereign's edict and to enforce judgment in accordance with the sovereign's administrative charters and the book of new enactments on criminal cases. And the sworn assistant, the sotskii, and the piati-

desiatskii are to act together with the elected judge Sidor Grigor'ev in matters concerning the sovereign and the land, and in investigating cases of theft and brigandage, and in apprehending the criminals in cases of theft and brigandage, and in examining and torturing [criminals]. And we, the peasants, together with the elected judge Sidor Grigor'ev and his associates, are to conduct searches for thieves and brigands, and go out in pursuit of them, and catch [them]. . . . And we, the peasants, are to furnish the elected judge Sidor Grigor'ev and his associates with sworn prison assistants, guards, and watchmen for those who are confined in prison. And when thieves, brigands, and any kind of criminals are to be tortured, we, the mir, are to furnish a qualified person to torture the thieves and brigands. Whatever thieves, or brigands, or any criminals are found, we, the peasants, are to provide sotniki, piatidesiatniki, and desiatniki, and these sotniki, piatidesiatniki, and desiatniki, and all the peasants are to obey the public judge Sidor Grigor'ev and his associates in everything and are to go out to fight the criminals and the brigands in full military array, with bows, harquebuses, and lances. They are not to abandon the elected judge Sidor Grigor'ev and his associates in such fighting but are to go out in pursuit of the criminals, the brigands. And if anywhere in the volost', in the district of any sotnik, piatidesiatnik, or desiatnik, thieves or brigands or criminals are reported by the sotniki, piatidesiatniki, desiatniki, or peasants, such sotniki, piatidesiatniki, desiatniki, and peasants are to catch those criminals, thieves, and brigands and bring them to the elected public judge Sidor Grigor'ev and his associates. And he has been given a certificate of election to this effect. Konanko Petrov Ponomarev wrote the certificate of election by order of the mir of the Chadromskaia volost'. The eighteenth day of January 160 [1652].

VIII:28. AN ENACTMENT OF THE ZEMSKII SOBOR, JANUARY-FEBRUARY 1634

This is an excerpt from the record of the enactments of the Zemskii Sobor of 1634, when war with Poland-Lithuania was straining Moscow's resources.
Reference: *AAE,* 3:366, 370.

In the year 142 [1634], on the 28th day of January, the sovereign tsar and grand prince Mikhail Fedorovich, autocrat of all Russia, ordered that the sobor be attended, in his sovereign presence, by the metropolitans and

archbishops and bishops, and the archimandrites and abbots, and the entire holy council, and by the boyars and okol'nichie and [other] Duma members, and the stol'niki, striapchie, and dvoriane, and the gosti and trading men of every rank in the Muscovite state. And the sobor convened in the Banquet Hall [Stolovaia Izba—in the Kremlin] on the twenty-ninth day of January.

At the sobor, in the sovereign's presence, this speech was delivered to the [church] authorities and boyars and people of every rank:

"In the previous year, 141 [1633], the sovereign tsar and grand prince of all Russia Mikhail Fedorovich, after taking counsel with his father of blessed memory, the great sovereign, the most holy patriarch Filaret Nikitich of Moscow and all Russia, made known to you at the first sobor the many iniquities of the former Polish king Sigismund [III] and his son Wladyslaw and the Poles and Lithuanians."

· · ·

And at the sobor the [church] authorities,

the metropolitans and archbishops, the archimandrites and abbots, and the entire holy council, and the boyars and okol'nichie and [other] Duma members, and stol'niki, and dvoriane, and officials [prikaznye liudi], and gosti and all kinds of trading men, all declared that to help the soldiers and to rescue the Orthodox Christian faith from the Polish and Lithuanian king and the Poles and Lithuanians they would give money, each according to his means, as much as he could give, to pay the wages of the soldiers at present engaged in the sovereign's service with the boyars and voevody under Prince Dmitrii Mastriukovich Cherkasskii.

And on the fourth day of February, the sovereign tsar and grand prince Mikhail Fedorovich of all Russia directed that this extraordinary levy [zaprosnye i piatinnye dengi] be collected from all the people.

VIII:29. THE RECORD OF THE ZEMSKII SOBOR OF 1642

The following passages are from the official record of the Zemskii Sobor of 1642, which, in the course of its discussions of the Azov affair, touched upon many questions of government policy. Significant here are both the composition of the sobor and the tone and content of the criticisms it voiced. (For more on the Cossacks and Azov, see Section F of this chapter.)

Reference: Got'e, *Akty zemskikh soborov*, pp. 37-39, 50-57.

On the third day of January [1642], the sovereign tsar and grand prince of all Russia Mikhail Feodorovich ordered that a sobor be called and that the sobor be attended by . . . the entire holy council, and by the boyars . . . and secretaries, and dvoriane . . . and provincial deti boiarskie, and gosti, and trading men of the *gostinaia sotnia, sukonnaia sotnia,* and *chernye sotni,* and by the service men and inhabitants of every rank; and [the tsar ordered] that the people of all ranks be told that a Turkish envoy is on his way to see the tsar and that written messages have been received saying that the envoy is coming to discuss the Azov matter. And [the tsar ordered] that they should choose good and wise men from every rank, from among the best, the middle, and the lesser people, to discuss this matter; and those who are chosen should bring certificates of election.

And by the tsar's order, the sobor came together in the banquet hall; and at the sobor were assembled, in the presence of the sovereign tsar and grand prince of all Russia Mikhail Feodorovich: the metropolitan of Krutitsa, Serapion; and archimandrites and abbots, and archpriests, and the entire holy council; and

boyars and okol'nichie and [other] Duma members; and stol'niki and striapchie and Moscow dvoriane, and secretaries, and [military] commanders [golovy] and captains [sotniki]; and provincial deti boiarskie, and gosti, and trading men of the gostinaia sotnia, sukonnaia sotnia, and chernye sotni, and service men and inhabitants of every rank. And the keeper of the seal [pechatnik] and Duma secretary Fedor Fedorovich Likhachev addressed the sobor, and said:

"The sovereign tsar and grand prince of all Russia Mikhail Feodorovich ordered that a sobor be called, inasmuch as a Turkish envoy is coming to see the sovereign; and we have been informed through many written messages that he is coming to discuss Azov; and the messages indicate that in the spring the Turkish sultan intends to wage war against the Muscovite state, laying siege to Azov.

· · ·

"And should the sovereign tsar and grand prince of all Russia Mikhail Feodorovich break off relations with the Turkish and Crimean tsars because of Azov, and should he receive Azov from the atamans and Cossacks of the Don? And if he receives Azov and breaks off relations with the Turkish and Crimean [tsars], then a great many soldiers will be needed, to be sent to Azov and to the border towns and to the towns of the Plain [Pol'skie] and on the Volga; and a great deal of money will be needed to fortify Azov and to pay the soldiers' wages; and grain and ordnance supplies of every kind will be needed for more than one year, inasmuch as wars with the Turks last more than a year; and where will such great amounts of money and supplies for those years be found? And the stol'niki and Moscow dvoriane and secretaries, and commanders and captains, and provincial dvoriane and deti boiarskie, and gosti and tradesmen of the gostinaia sotnia, sukonnaia sotnia, and chernye sotni, and service men and inhabitants of every rank should think hard about this, and make their thoughts known in writing to the sovereign tsar and grand prince of all Russia Mikhail Feodorovich, that he be informed about all these matters."

After this message was read aloud to all the men, separate copies of this message were given, by order of the sovereign, to each [group] of elected deputies of various rank, in the boyars' presence, that they be informed truly; and a similar copy was sent to the metropolitan of Krutitsa, Serapion, so that he should assemble the archimandrites, abbots, and archpriests and the entire holy council, discuss the matter with them, put his opinion in writing, and make it known to the tsar.

· : ·

And the dvoriane and deti boiarskie of the various provinces said: . . . "Pious Sovereign Tsar and Grand Prince of All Russia Mikhail Feodorovich! You should pray to Almighty God for his mercy, and order Azov to be received from the atamans and Cossacks of the Don, and break off relations with the Turkish and Crimean tsars, because of their many iniquities against you, the sovereign. . . . For if you refuse to receive Azov from the Don Cossacks, Azov shall be left to the heathen. . . . Do not bring down the wrath of the Lord, Sire, upon the entire Russian state. . . . Your sovereign boyars and closest advisers [blizhnie liudi] who are now with you, Sire, have been favored with your sovereign bounty, with many pomest'ia and patrimonial estates, according to their rank and their service to you, the sovereign; and now, Sire, in view of this

onslaught of the heathen, let mounted and foot soldiers be taken from the patrimonial estates of your boyars and closest advisers, as many as you, the sovereign, shall decree. And your secretaries and clerks, Sire, have been favored with your sovereign bounty, with money and with pomest'ia and with patrimonial estates; and in attending ceaselessly to your affairs, Sire, they have enriched themselves and have gathered great wealth through their iniquitous extortions, and they have bought many patrimonial estates and have built many houses for themselves, mansions of stone, wondrous beyond words, such as in the days of former sovereigns of blessed memory were not owned even by highborn people for whom it would have been fitting to live in such houses. Give orders, Sire, for mounted and foot soldiers to be taken from their pomest'ia and patrimonial estates; and order a monetary levy to be imposed upon them in accordance with their property and means; and order money to be taken from them, as much as you, Sire, shall decree, to pay the wages of your soldiers. . . . And order, Sire, recruits [datochnye liudi] on horse and on foot to be taken from the estates belonging to the patriarch, the metropolitans, the archbishops, the bishops, the monasteries, and all the clergy: as many peasants as you, the sovereign, shall decree. . . . And we, your slaves, shall gladly work heart and soul for the Cathedral of the [Dormition of the] Holy Virgin [in Moscow], and for the Miracle Workers of Moscow [the canonized metropolitans of Moscow, Peter, Alexis, and Jonah], and for the veritable true Orthodox Christian faith, and for you, the pious sovereign tsar and grand prince of all Russia, Mikhail Feodorovich, and for the great mercy that you, Sire, have shown us, your slaves, against the invasion of the heathen into your land. And order that upon those of us, your poor slaves, who are impoverished and helpless and have no pomest'ia, or whose pomest'ia are uninhabited or small, there be bestowed your sovereign bounty in the form of pomest'ia and money, as much as God will instruct you to give, so that we shall have the means to serve you, the sovereign. . . . And if you, Sire, should soon require revenue in addition to your own treasury and the above levies, order that the treasury of the patriarch and the metropolitans, the archbishops and bishops, and likewise the household funds of the monasteries, be taken for your own pressing service needs. And from your gosti, Sire, and from the various trading men who carry on a big trade, and from your chernye liudi, order, Sire, that money be taken into your treasury from their transactions and trades, as much as God will instruct you, to pay the wages of your soldiers; and thus you will obtain a large treasury for yourself. And order, Sire, that the account books of your officials, secretaries, clerks, and customs officials be examined in Moscow and in your [other] towns, so that your treasury should not diminish without account and should be of use to you, the sovereign, to pay wages to your soldiers; and order your sovereign treasury to be collected by your gosti and the local public [zemskie] authorities. And as for the men, Sire, who at present are in charge of your sovereign affairs, [serving] under the voevody in various of your sovereign towns and in the prikazy, order them, Sire, to appear with a large retinue to serve the sovereign against the ungodly heathen; and thus your entire land will be ready to meet the invasion of the ungodly heathen."

. . .

And the dvoriane and deti boiarskie of the various provinces . . . having thought about the matter, said: "Relations should be broken off with the Turkish tsar and the Crimean tsar because of Azov, and Azov should be received from the atamans and Cossacks of the Don. To surrender Azov to the heathen would bring God's wrath upon the entire Russian state. . . . [And they also said:] Order, Sire, that a call be issued in Moscow and in all the towns for volunteers to go to Azov, from among the dvoriane and deti boiarskie, and the strel'tsy, Cossacks, cannoneers, and the chernye liudi, all except bondmen [kholopy] and serfs [krepostnye]; and order that wages be paid to all these soldiers and that supplies of various kinds be sent to Azov. . . . And order, Sire, that money and all kinds of supplies be collected from men of every rank, from each according to the number of peasant households he has. . . . And order that money and various supplies be collected, in accordance with your sovereign decree, from the [church] authorities and the monasteries and from all ranks of the clergy, and from the secretaries, clerks, and gosti and all the trading men of the land. . . . And we, your slaves, with our men and with all our humble equipment, are ready to serve you, the sovereign, against your enemies, wherever you, Sire, shall decree; but we, your slaves, have been reduced to poverty, not so much by the Turkish and Crimean infidels as by Muscovite procrastination and injustice, and by the iniquitous courts of law. And these are the thoughts and words of your slaves, the dvoriane and deti boiarskie of the various provinces."

. . .

And the humble gosti and the lowly trading men of the gostinaia sotnia and the sukonnaia sotnia said: . . . "We, your slaves, are humble gosti and lowly trading men of the gostinaia sotnia and the sukonnaia sotnia of various towns, and we make our living in those towns by our petty trades; and we have no pomest'ia or patrimonial estates at all; and we serve you, the sovereign, in Moscow and in the other towns, year after year without ceasing; and because of this ceaseless service and because of the fifth part of our income [piatinnye den'gi, an extraordinary tax, amounting to 20 percent of yearly income, levied upon all trading men and merchants] which we paid to you to aid the soldiers and all the service men in the Smolensk campaign [against the Poles, in 1632-34], many people have been reduced to poverty and are utterly destitute. And we, your slaves, in serving you, the sovereign, in Moscow and in the other towns, collecting [moneys] into your treasury under oath, bring you great profit: where in the reigns of former sovereigns and in previous years of your reign, Sire, the yield was five or six hundred [rubles], we, your slaves, now collect from ourselves and from all the land five or six thousand [rubles] or more. But our own business has become much worse than in former years, Sire, since much of our trade in Moscow and in the other towns has been taken away by foreigners, by Germans [Nemtsy, i.e. foreigners from central and western Europe] and Persians, who come to Moscow and to other towns with much capital and carry on trade in every kind of goods. In the towns many people have become destitute and reduced to utter poverty by your voevody, Sire; and the trading men who travel from town to town to trade have lost their business through being detained and ill-used by your voevody along the way. In the time of former sovereigns the criminal judges [*gubnye starosty,* elected elders who administered local criminal justice] had jurisdiction in the towns, and the posad men administered justice among themselves, and there were no voevody in the towns. And according to the former orders of the sovereigns, voevody were sent with soldiers only to the border towns, for protection against those same Turkish and Crimean and Nogai Tatars, lest they devastate the land. And we, your slaves and orphans, entreat you, Great Sovereign Tsar and Grand Prince of All Russia Mikhail Feodorovich, to be merciful so that you may bestow your favor upon your patrimony and heed our poverty."

. . .

And the sotskie and elders [starosty; sotskie here are the elected heads of sotni, starosty—of slobody] and all the tiaglo-bearing men of the chernye sotni and slobody said: "Sovereign Tsar and Grand Prince of All Russia Mikhail Feodorovich! Do as you please and as God will instruct you about the Azov fortress and about the soldiers. . . . And we, your orphans, the sotskie and elders and all the tiaglo-bearing men of the chernye sotni and slobody, have now for our sins been made impoverished and destitute by the great fires, and by the tax of a fifth part of our income, and by the levy of recruits, and by the

[requisition of] horses and carts which we, your orphans, supplied for the Smolensk campaign, and by the house tax [*povorotnye den'gi*], and by building earthwork fortifications, and by all your heavy taxes, Sire, and by the many services of various kinds that we perform for you, the sovereign, in Moscow under oath. . . . For there are some 145 sworn assistants [tseloval'niki] from amongst us, your orphans, serving in your various prikazy, Sire, each year; and there are 75 of us, your orphans, who are on duty continuously and without leave in the police headquarters [*zemskii dvor*] as constables [*iaryzhnye*] and cart drivers, for the evil season of fires. And to those sworn assistants and constables and drivers we pay a large subsidy every month. And because of their great poverty many tiaglo-bearing men have wandered away from their sotni and slobody and have abandoned their homesteads. And as for the fortress of Azov, if it be your will, Sire, to receive Azov in order to rescue Orthodox Christians, this is a matter that concerns all the Orthodox Christians of your land. And whatever you, Sire, may decree concerning service to you, the sovereign, and concerning the soldiers, let [the obligations] be imposed on the entire land and on people of all ranks, so that no one in the land of your patrimony, Sire, shall be exempt; and let it be done as God shall instruct you."

VIII:30. THE "NEW CHRONICLER" CONCERNING THE REBELLION IN MOSCOW, JUNE 1648

The so-called New Chronicler, apparently writing soon after the event, reported in these words the outbreak of violence in Moscow in the summer of 1648, over the salt tax and other grievances.

Reference: Obshchestvo Istorii i Drevnostei Rossiiskikh, *Vremennik Imperatorskogo Moskovskogo Obshchestva Istorii i Drevnostei Rossiiskikh,* 17:193-94.

In the year 7156 [1648], on the first day of June, a Friday, the Moscow populace [chernye liudi] looted the house of the boyar Boris Ivanovich Morozov, the house of the okol'nichii Petr, son of Tikhon Trakhaniotov, the house of the secretary of the Duma and the Ambassadorial Prikaz, Nazarii Chistyi, killing Nazarii himself, and the house of the chief of police [*zemskii sud'ia*], Leontii Pleshcheev. And on the third day of June, a Saturday [sic], there was great turmoil; a mob of posad men and various common folk invaded the palace with great rudeness, and they complained bitterly to the sovereign against Leontii

Pleshcheev and the many outrages and unjust exactions that they, the common people, had suffered from him, and they asked that he be put to death. And by order of the sovereign, Leontii Pleshcheev was delivered to them bodily; they took him to the Lobnoe Mesto [elevated and enclosed area in Red Square where the tsar made official appearances before the people and where public proclamations were read] on Red Square, and they all stoned and beat him to death; afterward they looted many more houses of boyars, okol'nichie, dvoriane, and gosti. . . . A few days later the okol'nichii Petr Trakhaniotov was put to death, being beheaded on Red Square, likewise in response to the petition of the populace. And on the twelfth day of June, just before dawn, by decree of the sovereign, likewise in response to the petition of the populace, the boyar Boris Ivanovich Morozov was exiled to the Monastery of Saint Cyril in Beloozero.

VIII:31. THE SUMMONS TO THE ZEMSKII SOBOR, JULY 16, 1648

One of the most important zemskii sobors was that of 1648–49, summoned to discuss a new ulozhenie or code of laws in place of the incomplete and outdated Sudebnik of 1550. The instructions of July 16, 1648, from the boyar Prince Nikita Ivanovich Odoevskii and his associates to the Novgorod chetvert' or administrative department, concerning the designation of representatives to a zemskii sobor, contain information on the circumstances that produced this sobor and on its composition.

Reference: *CIOIDRMU*, 1913, bk. 4, pp. 6–7. For other related documents, see Vasilii Latkin, ed., *Materialy dlia istorii zemskikh soborov XVII stoletiia* (St. Petersburg, 1884).

In the current year, 156 [1648], on the tenth day of June, the Moscow dvoriane and *zhil'tsy*, and the provincial dvoriane and deti boiarskie, and foreigners [in Russian service], and gosti, and trading men of the gostinaia sotnia and sukonnaia sotnia and various other sotni and slobody petitioned the sovereign tsar and grand prince of all Russia Aleksei Mikhailovich that the sovereign bestow his favor upon them and order a sobor to be convoked; and that the sobor be attended by the patriarch and the [church] authorities [*vlasti*] and the boyars and [other] Duma members [*dumnye liudi*]; and that the sovereign direct that the sobor be attended by elected deputies, the best men from among the stol'niki and Moscow dvoriane and zhil'tsy, and the provincial dvoriane and deti boiarskie. At the sobor they would petition the sovereign about their various affairs.

And by order of the sovereign tsar and grand prince Aleksei Mikhailovich, the sobor assembled in the Banquet Hall [Stolovaia Izba], in the sovereign's presence; and at the sobor were present the sovereign's [spiritual] father, who prays for him, the most holy Joseph, patriarch of Moscow and all Russia, and the [church] authorities, and the boyars and okol'nichie and [other] Duma members; and at the sobor were also present the stol'niki and Moscow dvoriane and zhil'tsy, and [provincial] dvoriane and deti boiarskie . . . and gosti, and the best men from the gostinaia sotnia and sukonnaia sotnia and from various other sotni and slobody.

And the Moscow dvoriane and zhil'tsy, and the provincial dvoriane and deti boiarskie, and the foreigners, and the gosti and trading men of various ranks petitioned the sovereign tsar and grand prince of all Russia Aleksei Mikhailovich about their various affairs; and they petitioned the sovereign to order that a code of laws [sudebnik] and a book of statutes [ulozhennaia kniga] be written, to cover all kinds of legal cases, so that in the future all matters would be conducted and decided in accordance with that book of statutes.

And the sovereign tsar and grand prince of all Russia Aleksei Mikhailovich, after taking counsel with his [spiritual] father who prays for him, Joseph, patriarch of Moscow and all Russia, and with the entire holy council and all the clergy, and after conferring with the boyars and okol'nichie and [other] Duma members, ordered the boyars Prince Nikita Ivanovich Odoevskii and Prince Semen Vasil'evich Prozorovskii, and the okol'nichii Prince Fedor Fedorovich Volkonskii, and the secretaries Gavrila Levont'ev [Leont'ev] and Fedor Griboedov to take charge of this matter and to draw up a book of statutes on the model of the codes of law [sudebnik] and statute books of former sovereigns. . . .

For that great undertaking of the state and of the land, the sovereign decreed, after taking counsel with his [spiritual] father [the patriarch] who prays for him, and the boyars resolved to choose from among the stol'niki and striapchie, and from among the Moscow dvoriane and zhil'tsy, two men from each rank; and likewise from among the dvoriane and deti boiarskie of all the provinces [literally, "towns"] except Novgorod [which would send more], two men from each greater province ["town"] and one from each lesser province ["town"]; and three men from among the gosti, and two men from the gostinaia sotnia and the sukonnaia sotnia, and one man from [each] chernaia sotnia and sloboda, and from [each] town.

And the sovereign directed that messages to this effect should be sent from him, the sovereign, to the voevody in every town, and he ordered that they be told his sovereign decree, so that the dvoriane and deti boiarskie and trading men might know of this and, for this great undertaking of the state and of the land—drawing up a statute book for various matters—choose good and sensible men from among the dvoriane and deti boiarskie and trading men of each town, who are accustomed to [dealing with] such affairs of the state and of the land, so that with the help of all the elected deputies this great royal affair

of the state and of the land might be confirmed and arranged, and so that all these great acts, in accordance with his present sovereign decree and the statutes of the sobor, might henceforth remain inviolate. And the sovereign ordered that a date be set for the elected deputies: to arrive in Moscow by Saint Simeon's Day [September 1] in the year 157 [1648].

And to those whom the dvoriane and deti boiarskie and trading men in the towns shall choose for this great undertaking of the state and of the land, to those elected deputies the dvoriane and deti boiarskie shall give signed certificates of election; and the trading men likewise shall give signed certificates of election to their own brethren.

VIII:32. THE ULOZHENIE OF 1649

The lengthy Ulozhenie of 1649, of which 1,200 copies were printed, begins with an introductory section explaining how this code of laws came to be drawn up. In the code proper, the passages excerpted here contain provisions on certain important questions of the relations of individuals to each other and to the state and illustrate the requirements of the state from various categories of the population.

Reference: Gosudarstvennaia Tipografiia, *Ulozhenie gosudaria tsaria i velikogo kniazia Alekseia Mikhailovicha* (St. Petersburg: 1913), pp. xvii-xx, 15, 17-18, 23, 31, 124-26, 129-30, 136, 139, 173-74, 197, 221-22, 223, 225-28, 233, 234, 243, 247, 248, 254, 261, 277, 280-81. See also *PRP*, vol. 6; M. N. Tikhomirov and P. P. Epifanov, *Sobornoe Ulozhenie 1649 goda* (Moscow: Izd. Moskovskogo Universiteta, 1961). Excerpts different from those we chose were recently translated in Dmytryshyn, *Medieval Russia*, pp. 261-68.

[From the Introduction:]

In the year 7156 [1648], on the sixteenth day of July, the sovereign tsar and grand prince Aleksei Mikhailovich . . . took counsel with his [spiritual] father who prays for him, the most holy Joseph, patriarch of Moscow and all Russia . . . and with the entire holy council, and decided together with his boyars and okol'-nichie and [other] Duma members [dumnye liudi]: that any articles written in the rules of the holy apostles and the holy fathers and in the civil laws of the Greek tsars [Byzantine emperors] pertaining to affairs of state and of the land should be copied out; and that the decrees of the former great sovereigns, tsars, and grand princes of Russia and the boyar resolutions [*prigovory*] . . . regarding various affairs of state and of the land should be compiled; and that these sovereign decrees and boyar resolutions should be compared with the old codes of law [sudebniki, referring to the sudebniki of 1497 and 1550, and perhaps also to the draft code of 1589]. And

as for matters that were not previously covered in the codes of law, by the decrees of former sovereigns, and on which there have been no boyar resolutions, articles [on these matters] should likewise be written down and presented for common discussion, in accordance with his sovereign decree, so that the dispensation of justice in the Muscovite state shall in all cases be equal for men of every rank, from the highest rank to the lowest. And the sovereign ordered . . . the boyars Prince Nikita Ivanovich Odoevskii and Prince Semen Vasil'evich Prozorovskii, and the okol'nichii Prince Fedor Fedorovich Volkonskii, and the secretaries [*d'iaki*] Gavrila Levont'ev [Leont'ev] and Fedor Griboedov, to compile everything and to submit it in written form.

And for this great sovereign act of state and of the land, the sovereign ordered, upon taking counsel with the patriarch of Moscow and all Russia, and the boyars resolved, that from among the stol'niki and striapchie and Moscow dvoriane and zhil'tsy, two men shall be chosen from each rank; likewise that from among the dvoriane and deti boiarskie of all the provinces [gorod; but here used to mean the entire territory of which the town was the administrative center], two men shall be taken from each greater province, except Novgorod; and from Novgorod, one man from each fifth [*piatina,* one of the five territorial divisions]; and from the lesser provinces, one man each; and from among the gosti, three men; and from the gostinaia and sukonnaia sotni [in Moscow], two men each; and from the chernye sotni and slobody [in Moscow], and from the posad in each town, one man each: good and sensible men, so as to confirm and arrange, with all these elected deputies, this sovereign act of state and of the land, so that henceforth all these great acts, in accordance with his present sovereign decree and the statutes of the sobor, shall remain inviolate.

. . .

In accordance with the sovereign's . . . decree, the boyars Prince Nikita Ivanovich Odoevskii and his associates, having copied out [articles] from the rules of the holy apostles and the holy fathers, from the civil laws of the Greek tsars, and from the old codes of law of former great sovereigns, and from the decrees . . . of the tsar and grand prince of all Russia Mikhail Feodorovich, and from the boyar resolutions, and articles [on matters] that were not included in the former codes of law and in decrees of former sovereigns and in boyar resolutions, wrote down [all] these articles anew and brought them before the sovereign.

And in the current year, 157 [still 1648, since the year 7157 began on September 1], on the third day of October, the tsar . . . with his father who prays for him, the most holy Joseph, patriarch of Moscow and all Russia, and with the metropolitans, and with the archbishops and with the bishops, and likewise with the sovereign's boyars, and with the okol'nichie, and with the [other] Duma members, listened to this compilation; and it was read to the elected deputies who had been chosen in Moscow and from the towns to this general sobor, so that this entire ulozhenie should henceforth be permanent and immutable. And the sovereign ordered that a transcript [spisok] of this entire ulozhenie be drawn up and that this transcript be ratified by the most holy Joseph, patriarch

of Moscow . . . and by the entire holy council, and by the sovereign's boyars and okol'nichie and [other] Duma members, and by the elected deputies from the dvoriane, deti boiarskie, gosti, and trading and posad men of the Muscovite state and of all the towns of the Russian tsardom. After the ulozhenie had been ratified by the signatures [of those persons], the sovereign ordered that it be copied into a book, and that this book be certified by the signatures of the secretaries Gavrila Levont'ev and Fedor Griboedov; and that many copies of this book be printed for use in all the prikazy in Moscow, and in the towns, and that all affairs be conducted in accordance with this ulozhenie.

And in accordance with the decree of the sovereign tsar and grand prince of all Russia Aleksei Mikhailovich, a transcript of this ulozhenie was drawn up. The most holy Joseph, patriarch of Moscow and all Russia . . . and the entire holy council, and likewise the boyars and okol'nichie and [other] Duma members, and the elected dvoriane, deti boiarskie, gosti, and trading [and] posad men, affixed their signatures to the transcript of this ulozhenie. . . .

[Sections from the Ulozhenie proper:]
CHAPTER VII.

8. Whoever of the sovereign's soldiers [*ratnye liudi*] of any rank are in the sovereign's service in the regiments, and who, having been examined [*po razboru*], are [found] capable of serving the sovereign but who desert the sovereign's service without waiting for discharge, to them shall be applied the rule for desertion: whoever deserts a first time shall be beaten with the knout; if he deserts a second time, he shall again be beaten with the knout, and his emolument in pomest'e land [*pomestnyi oklad*] shall be reduced . . . and if he deserts a third time, he shall again be beaten with the knout, and his pomest'e shall be taken away and given for distribution [to others]. . . .

17. If any service men [*sluzhilye liudi*] petition the sovereign that they are incapable of serving the sovereign because of age, or injuries, or sickness . . . these petitioners shall be examined in Moscow and in the towns. And if the examination shows that these service men are truly incapable of serving the sovereign because of age, or injuries, or sickness

those service men shall be ordered to send in their place to serve the sovereign, with all their retinue [*sluzhba*] and equipment [*zapasy*], those of their children, brothers, nephews, and grandsons who have no pomest'ia and who, being eighteen years of age, are old enough to serve the sovereign but are not in the sovereign's service and are not enrolled in any rank; but they shall send no one to serve in their place who is under eighteen years of age. And if they have no such children or brothers or nephews or grandsons, and if they themselves are incapable of serving the sovereign in any way, because of sickness or age: from them recruits [*datochnye liudi*] or money shall be taken for the sovereign's service, in proportion to [the size of] their pomest'ia and patrimonies and to their means [*prozhitok*]. . . .
CHAP. VIII.

1. For ransoming captives [most of whom were seized by the Tatars in their perennial raids], money shall be collected yearly from the towns of the entire Muscovite state: from the posad households and from the post riders [*iamshchiki*], and from all the inhabitants [*zhiletskie liudi*] who live in the towns in posady . . . and from the peasants and *bobyli* [peasants without plowland, or with small holdings, and thus not bearing tiaglo] on monastery estates—eight den'gi [den'ga—a small silver coin worth half a copeck] from each household; and from peasants living in the sovereign's crown villages [*gosudarevy dvortsovye sela*], and in the chernye volosti [inhabited by tiaglo-bearing peasants], and on pomest'ia and patrimonial estates—four den'gi from each household; and from the service men, from the strel'tsy, cannoneers [*pushkari*], stockade tenders [*zatinshchiki*], and gate guards [*vorotniki*] and from the state [*kazennye*] carpenters and blacksmiths, and from sundry service men—two den'gi from each household. This money shall be paid yearly into the Ambassadorial [Posol'skii] Prikaz . . . so that no one should be exempt from this monetary levy, since such ransoming is called an act of common charity. . . .
CHAP. X.

1. The judicial authority [*sud*] of the sovereign tsar and grand prince of all Russia Aleksei Mikhailovich shall be exercised by the boyars and okol'nichie and [other] Duma members and secretaries, and by the various government officials [prikaznye liudi] and

judges [sud'ia]; and justice shall be dispensed equitably to all men of the Muscovite state, from the highest rank to the lowest. . . .

2. Lawsuits that for any reason cannot be decided in the prikazy shall be taken out of the prikazy and submitted to the sovereign tsar and grand prince of all Russia Aleksei Mikhailovich, and to his, the sovereign's, boyars and okol'nichie and [other] Duma members. And the boyars and okol'nichie and [other] Duma members shall sit in the chamber and, in accordance with the sovereign's decree, shall decide such cases jointly. . . .
CHAP. XI.

1. Peasants and bobyli of the sovereign's crown villages and chernye volosti who have fled from the sovereign's crown villages and from the chernye volosti, and who live with the patriarch [i.e. on his land] . . . or with the monasteries, or with boyars . . . or with various owners of patrimonies and pomest'ia, and who themselves, or whose fathers, are registered as the sovereign's in the registry books [*pistsovye knigi*] with the registrars [*pistsy*] have submitted to the Pomestnyi Prikaz and other prikazy since the Moscow fire of the year 7134 [1626]: these, the sovereign's fugitive peasants and bobyli, shall be found and returned, with their wives and children and with all their peasant possessions, to the sovereign's crown villages and to the chernye volosti, to their old plots [of land—*zhereb'i*], in accordance with the registry books, without time limit [*bez urochnykh let*].

2. Likewise, if any owner of a patrimony or pomest'e petitions the sovereign concerning his fugitive peasants and bobyli . . . these peasants and bobyli shall be returned upon investigation, in accordance with the registry books. . . . And fugitive peasants and bobyli shall be returned from flight to men [their owners] of every rank, in accordance with the registry books, without time limit.

3. And whomever it falls upon to return fugitive peasants and bobyli, upon court decision and investigation, shall return these peasants with their wives and children and with all their possessions, and with their harvested and unharvested grain. . . .

9. And whatever peasants and bobyli are listed with anyone [a landowner] in the census books [*perepisnaia kniga*] of the previous years of 154 and 155 [1646 and 1647],

and who subsequent to [the compilation of] these census books have fled, or shall henceforth flee, from those men with whom they are listed in the census books: those fugitive peasants and bobyli, and their brothers, children, nephews, and grandchildren with their wives and with their children and with all their possessions, and with their harvested and unharvested grain, shall be returned from flight to those men from whom they fled, in accordance with the census books, without time limit; and henceforth under no circumstances should anyone receive peasants who are not his and keep them with him.

10. And if anyone, subsequent to [the promulgation of] this sovereign ulozhenie, should receive fugitive peasants and bobyli, and their children and brothers and nephews, and keep them with him, and if the pomest'e and patrimony owners discover these, their fugitive peasants, with him, . . . that person shall pay ten rubles for each peasant for every year, as restitution for the sovereign's taxes and the pomest'e-owner's income; and he shall give [this money] to the plaintiff who owns these peasants and bobyli. . . .

30. And the pomest'e and patrimony owners with whom peasants and bobyli . . . are registered on their pomest'e and patrimonial land separately shall not remove their peasants from their pomest'e land to their patrimonial land and thereby depopulate their pomest'ia. . . .

CHAP. XIII.

1. Prior to [the promulgation of] the present sovereign ulozhenie, lawsuits involving metropolitans . . . and abbots . . . and church servitors [prichet] were in every case conducted in the prikaz of the Great Palace [Bol'shogo Dvortsa, primarily in charge of the tsar's household].

But now the sovereign, tsar, and grand prince of all Russia Aleksei Mikhailovich, upon the petition of the stol'niki, and striapchie, and Moscow dvoriane, and provincial dvoriane and deti boiarskie, and gosti, and the gostinaia and sukonnaia and various other sotni and slobody, and the trading and posad men of the towns, has decreed that there be a separate Monastery Prikaz, and that all lawsuits brought by plaintiffs against metropolitans . . . and monasteries . . . and priests, and church servitors shall be tried in the Monastery Prikaz. . . .

[Article 61 of chapter XVI established that aged and disabled dvoriane and deti boiarskie who were childless could hold their pomest'ia in lifetime tenure and send recruits (datochnye liudi) to serve in their place.]

CHAP. XVII.

42. . . . The sovereign tsar . . . has ordered and the sobor has decreed that after the promulgation of the present ulozhenie the patriarch, metropolitans, archbishops, bishops, and monasteries shall not buy ancestral, or service-earned, or purchased patrimonies from anyone, or take them in mortgage, or hold them in possession, or under any circumstances take them for the eternal commemoration of souls; . . . and no patrimony owner shall give his patrimony to a monastery. . . .

CHAP. XIX.

1. Whatever slobody in Moscow belong to the patriarch and the metropolitans and bishops and monasteries, and boyars and okol'nichie and [other] Duma members and closest advisers [blizhnie liudi], and men of every rank, and are inhabited by tradesmen and artisans who are engaged in various trades and keep shops but do not pay taxes to the sovereign and are not in [his] service, all these slobody, with all the men who live in these slobody, except for contractual bondmen [kabal'nye liudi], shall all be made to bear tiaglo to the sovereign and to serve him eternally and immutably. . . .

5. And whatever slobody near Moscow belong to the patriarch and prelates and monasteries, and boyars and [other] Duma members and men of every rank, these slobody with all their men who are engaged in various trades, except for contractual bondmen, shall likewise be taken for the sovereign upon investigation. As for plowland peasants [pashennye], if any of them are found upon questioning to be old-time peasants of pomest'ia and patrimonies, who have been brought to these lands [the slobody], those men from whom these slobody are taken shall be ordered to remove [the peasants] from these slobody to their patrimonies and pomest'ia. And if these plowland peasants keep shops, cellars, and salterns in Moscow and in the towns, they shall sell these shops, cellars, and salterns to men who bear the sovereign's tiaglo, and henceforth no one who does not bear the sovereign's tiaglo shall keep shops, cellars, and salterns. . . .

11. And whatever strel'tsy, Cossacks, and dragoons engage in various trading enterprises and keep shops in the towns, these strel'tsy, Cossacks, and dragoons shall pay customs duties on their trading enterprises, and obrok on their shops, but shall not pay tiaglo with the posad men or be subject to tiaglo service. . . .

13. As for those tiaglo-bearing posad men in Moscow and in the towns who themselves, or whose fathers, formerly lived in the posady and slobody of Moscow or in the towns, and were obliged to pay and did pay tiaglo, or who lived in posady and slobody as shop clerks or hired hands of tiaglo-bearing men, but who at present live in pledge [v zakladchikakh] to the patriarch, the metropolitans, the archbishops, the bishops, the monasteries, the boyars . . . and to men of every rank in Moscow and in the towns, on their homesteads and on patrimonies, and on pomest'ia and on church land: they shall all be sought out and returned, permanently and irrevocably, to their old posad places, wherever each one formerly lived. And henceforth no men who are taken for the sovereign shall enroll themselves in pledge to anyone or call themselves anyone's peasants or bondmen [liudi]. If henceforth they should pledge themselves to anyone, or call themselves anyone's peasants or bondmen, for this they shall be severely punished, beaten with the knout in the marketplace, and banished to Siberia to live on the Lena River. And those men who henceforth receive them in pledge shall likewise be in the sovereign's great disfavor, and the lands where such men should henceforth come to live in pledge to them shall be taken for the sovereign. . . .

15. And whatever bondmen and peasants of boyars and men of other ranks, in Moscow and in the towns, have bought or taken in mortgage tiaglo-bearing homesteads [tiaglye dvory], shops, storehouses, stone cellars, and salterns, and who trade in various goods, these bondmen and peasants of boyars and men of other ranks shall sell these tiaglo-bearing homesteads, shops, cellars, storehouses, and salterns to tiaglo-bearing trading and posad men; and henceforth they shall not own tiaglo-bearing homesteads, shops, cellars, storehouses, or salterns; and henceforth no one's bondmen or peasants, but only the sovereign's trading posad men, shall buy tiaglo-

bearing homesteads, shops, cellars, storehouses, or salterns from anyone. . . .

17. And whatever peasants come to Moscow and to the towns from the country [uezd] with various goods, they shall sell these goods in the market square from carts and barges, freely and without payment [of impost]; but they shall not buy or rent shops in the market rows. . . .

39. . . . Tiaglo-bearing men [chernye liudi] belonging to chernye sotni and to slobody of tiaglo-bearing homesteads shall not mortgage or sell their homesteads to men who do not bear tiaglo. If anyone sells or mortgages a tiaglo-bearing homestead to "white" men [who do not bear tiaglo], these homesteads shall be taken and returned to the sotnia without recompense. . . . And if any tiaglo-bearing men sell or mortgage their homesteads, these tiaglo-bearing men shall be beaten with the knout for their offense.

40. And whatever homesteads belong to Russian men of every rank in Moscow, in Kitai- or Belyi- or Zemlianoi-gorod [and] in suburban slobody, these homesteads and homestead plots shall not be bought or taken in mortgage from Russian men by foreigners [nemtsy] or foreign widows. . . . And as for the foreign churches [kirk] that have been erected on foreign homesteads, these churches shall be torn down, and henceforth no churches shall stand on foreign homesteads in Kitai- or Belyi- or Zemlianoi-gorod, but they shall stand beyond the city, beyond Zemlianoi-gorod, far away from the [Orthodox] churches of God.

CHAP. XX. . . .

2. Henceforth no one shall take deti boiarskie as bondmen [v kholopi] whether they have been classified for service or not [verstanyi i neverstanyi]. . . .

31. And whoever is registered in bondage by a title-deed [krepost'], these people shall transmit their bondage from wife to husband, and from husband to wife. . . .

34. And if anyone's bondman is taken captive into some other land, and afterward this bondman leaves captivity, he shall no longer be the bondman of his former master [boiarin], and his wife and children shall be returned to him for his sufferings as a captive. . . .

52. And whatever men keep bondmen in accordance with their father's contracts

[*kabala*], after their fathers have died, they shall set their father's men free; and these men shall be the bondmen of him to whom they give, of their free will, a contract of servitude [*sluzhilaia kabala*] upon themselves. . . .

70. And unbaptized [non-Orthodox] foreigners in Moscow and in the towns may keep foreigners of various and sundry faiths to work in their households; but Russian men shall not be in bondage to unbaptized foreigners, whether by title-deeds or of their own will. . . .

113. . . . In accordance with the sovereign's decree, it is forbidden for anyone to take contracts [of servitude] from his peasants or his peasants' children. . . .

CHAP. XXI. . . .

3. The criminal judges [*gubnye starosty*] and sworn assistants [*tseloval'niki*] shall have jurisdiction in the towns over cases of robbery, murder, and theft, in accordance with instructions from the Criminal [Razboinyi] Prikaz, and the voevody shall have no jurisdiction over such matters in towns. But where there are no criminal judges, in those towns the voevody and government officials shall have jurisdiction over criminal cases.

4. The criminal judges for such matters in the towns should be good and prosperous dvoriane, who have been discharged from service because of age or wounds, or whose children or nephews serve in their place, and who can read and write; but those who cannot read and write should not be chosen as criminal judges. As for towns where there are no dvoriane, in those towns deti boiarskie who are likewise good and prosperous men shall be chosen as criminal judges. . . . And the criminal judges in the towns shall be chosen by the dvoriane, deti boiarskie, posad men, town inhabitants [*zhiletskie liudi*] of every rank, and district cadastral peasants [*uezdnye soshnye liudi*]; and the dvoriane, deti boiarskie, posad men, town inhabitants of every rank, and district peasants shall certify the election of these criminal judges with their signatures . . . and the criminal judges in the towns shall have sworn assistants and clerks with them for cases of robbery and theft, and the prisons shall have prison guards; they shall likewise be chosen by the cadastral peasants and shall take an oath upon the cross [*krestnoe tselovanie*].

VIII:33. KOTOSHIKHIN ON RUSSIA, CA. 1660

Grigorii Karpovich Kotoshikhin, a Russian born about 1630, had risen by 1658 to the post of an undersecretary (*pod'iachii*) in the Posol'skii Prikaz or Foreign Office of the Muscovite government. In the early 1660s he was involved in Russia's negotiations with Poland and Sweden, in the course of which he gave information to the Swedes in return for money. In 1664, perhaps fearing arrest, he fled to Poland. From there he moved early in 1666 to Stockholm, where he adopted Protestantism and entered the service of the Swedish government. His service was short, for he inflicted mortal injuries on his landlord in a scuffle, was convicted of murder, and was executed in November 1667. Fortunately for future historians, his months in the Swedish service were largely devoted to composing for his new masters a description of their Muscovite rivals. Although a Swedish translation was made in 1669, his original Russian manuscript dropped out of sight, not to be discovered until the 1830s. Kotoshikhin's work, while understandably colored somewhat by his emotions, is nevertheless an exceedingly valuable historical document. It presents systematically a wide range of political, social, and economic data and is especially helpful concerning the organization and functions of the various parts of the Muscovite government. Unfortunately no more than a few samples can be given here.

Reference: Grigorii Karpovich Kotoshikhin, *O Rossii v tsarstvovanie Alekseia Mikhailovicha*, 3d ed. (St. Petersburg, 1884), pp. 26-27, 31, 58-59, 63, 106-07, 125-26, 131, 145, 151-52, 157-58, 160-61, 164, 178-79. The fourth edition, published in St. Petersburg by the Tip. Glavnogo Upravleniia Udelov in 1906, was reprinted in The Hague by Mouton in 1969. (In that edition the excerpts are on pp. 24, 28-29, 52-53, 57, 95, 111-12, 117, 129, 135, 139, 141-42, 145, and 157-58.) The translation of the present excerpts has been checked and amended on the basis of Benjamin P. Uroff, "Grigorii Karpovich Kotoshikhin, *On Russia in the Reign of Alexis Mikhailovich:* An Annotated Translation" (Ph.D. dissertation, Columbia University, 1970), vol. 1, pp. 61, 74, 111-13, 119, 180, 208-10, 218, 238, 246-47, 254-55, 258-59, 263-64, 283-84.

[From chapter 2:] When the tsar sits in the Duma with those boyars and the [other] Duma members [to discuss matters] concerning foreign affairs and the affairs of his own state, the boyars and okol'nichie and Duma dvoriane then seat themselves on benches, with [each member's] distance from the tsar depending upon his rank. Each boyar [sits] below those boyars to whom he is inferior in lineage, regardless of whether he is higher or senior in rank; in the same way, below the boyars [sit] the okol'nichie; below the okol'nichie [sit] the Duma dvoriane, likewise according to lineage rather than service; and the Duma secretaries [d'iaki] stand, although sometimes the tsar permits them to sit; and they consider whatever [matters] must be considered together with the tsar, as is also the custom in other states. And when the tsar speaks his mind on some matter, having spoken he orders them, the boyars and the [other] Duma members, to ponder and suggest the means for [carrying out] this matter; and those boyars who are more eminent and more intelligent, or even those who are less eminent, declare their opinion as to the means; while other boyars hold their beards rigid and do not answer, since in many cases the tsar confers boyar rank not for intelligence but for exalted lineage, and many of them are unlettered and uneducated; although, such men aside, other boyars of higher or lower degree can be found who give intelligent answers. And the tsar and the boyars order the Duma secretaries to make note of whatever [action] they resolve [prigovoriat] in any matter, and to write down that resolution.

· · ·

And noble status [dvorianstvo] is not granted to any posad men, or to sons of priests or peasants, or to bondmen; but if any posad man or peasant or anyone should release his son to serve as a foot soldier, or as a cavalryman, or as a clerk [pod'iachii] or other official of the tsar in a prikaz, and if these children should rise through service from low dignity to high, and obtain pomest'ia and patrimonial estates for their service, then he and his descendants shall be noblemen.

[From chapter 4:] The men of the Russian state are arrogant by nature and untrained in all things, because they do not and cannot receive a good education in their country. . . . They do not send their children to foreign lands for education and study, being afraid that a knowledge of the beliefs and customs of foreign lands and the blessed freedom of those lands will change their children's beliefs, and that upon their return the children will have no care and thought for their own homes and kinsfolk. It is forbidden for Muscovites to travel abroad on any occasion, except for those who are sent by order of the tsar or are given travel permits for trading purposes. Although merchants do go abroad for trade, they must produce written pledges from well-born and eminent men, guaranteeing that they will not remain in foreign lands with their goods and possessions but will return home with everything. If a prince, or a boyar, or anyone else, should go abroad himself, or send his son or his brother abroad for whatever purpose without informing and petitioning the tsar, he would be charged with treason, and his patrimonial estates and pomest'ia and possessions would be confiscated by the tsar.

· · ·

In the Muscovite state those of the female sex are unlettered, such being the custom, and are by nature simple in mind and foolish and bashful in speech: since from childhood until marriage they live in their father's house in private apartments, and no one but the closest relatives can see them or be seen by them; and from this one can deduce how little chance there is for them to be very intelligent or bold. And even when they are married, men see little of them.

[From chapter 7:] If any boyar or okol'nichii . . . or [man of any] other service rank earns a pomest'e through service, this pomest'e . . . is granted to him . . . for life, and to his wife and children and grandchildren after him; and upon his death it is given to the survivors—wife or children and brothers and nephews—and is divided as decreed: to the widow and unmarried daughters for their subsistence and to the sons in perpetuity; and whatever remains from the distribution is given to petitioners from other families. And if a pomest'e has been given to someone for service, and after him to his wife and children or to someone else, none of them may sell that pomest'e or mortgage it or bequeath it to a monastery or church for the commemoration of his soul. But if two men should wish to exchange one pomest'e for another, or a pomest'e for a patrimonial estate, they are permitted, upon petition, to make the exchange with one another, whether it be inhabited land for uninhabited, or uninhabited land for inhabited, or the same kind; and that exchange shall be recorded in the books for future reference and in case of dispute.

. . .

The Little Russian Prikaz: . . . This prikaz has had jurisdiction over Little Russia, the Zaporozhian Cossack host, and the districts of Kiev and Chernigov with other towns, since the time when they separated from the Polish king and became subjects of the tsar. And no revenue comes from Little Russia, because when the tsar received them under his rule as subjects, he promised them and took an oath that he would let them remain eternally as subjects under his rule with the same liberties and privileges they enjoyed as subjects of the Polish king, without altering anything or depriving them of any liberties. And the [Zaporozhian] host has been ordered to have 60,000 men ready at all times [to fight] against the enemies of the tsar, and to defend these districts; and the wages for that host are collected from the local urban inhabitants in the posady and from the rural inhabitants. And envoys are sent from Little Russia for various matters: the hetmans send colonels, and the colonels send captains [*sotniki*] and lieutenants [*esauly*], twenty or thirty or fifty or one hundred men at a time, and in Moscow they are given food and drink and fodder for their horses each day at the tsar's expense. . . . And when they are dismissed they are granted a bounty. . . . Likewise, stol'niki are dispatched to the hetmans and to the colonel and to the commanders with gifts for their service: cloth, damask, taffeta, and sables in great quantity. And with them come monks and priests and various men from these districts, to make petition concerning patrimonial estates and windmills and meadows and the erection or repair of churches, and they are given new or confirming grant charters for this [and] money for building churches and for church vestments; and they too are given food and drink and bounties, depending on the person; and they are given bounties and daily subsistence so that, having only recently taken

an oath of allegiance [to the tsar], they might thereby be more firmly drawn to eternal allegiance; but once they have grown old in their allegiance, then their honors and bounties will be reduced.

. . .

Altogether there are forty-two prikazy in Moscow, in addition to the local and church offices and the customhouses; and in these prikazy and with the voevody in the towns there are about one hundred secretaries and about one thousand clerks [pod'iachie].

[From chapter 8:] In the Muscovite state there are about twenty stone-walled towns or a few more, not counting the monasteries, while the rest all have wooden walls.

[Chapter 9, Section 7:] The Don Cossacks: These Don Cossacks are taken from the Don [region] for military duties, to be sent on patrol, or to reconnoiter and to carry off enemy guards; and they are given the same wages as the other Cossacks. And there are about 20,000 of these Cossacks on the Don, who are charged with the protection of the regions of the Lower Volga [Ponizovye] from the approach of Turks, Tatars, Nagai, and Kalmyks. And by origin they are from Moscow and other towns, and newly baptized Tatars, and Zaporozhian Cossacks, and Poles; many of them are trading men and peasants of Muscovite masters who were sentenced to be punished for brigandage and theft and other offenses, and who, after robbing and stealing from their masters, went to the Don; and after being on the Don even for a week, or a month, if they should for any reason happen to come to Moscow, no one may henceforth take any action against them for any offense, no matter what their crime, since the Don frees them from all harm. And they have been granted [permission] to live on the Don as they please, and they choose their own leaders atamans and others, from among their own number, and they administer justice in all matters according to their own will, and not according to the tsar's decree. . . . And when they come to Moscow, they are given the same honors as eminent foreigners; and if they did not have their freedom they would refuse to serve on the Don and remain in obedience; and were it not for these Don Cossacks the tsardoms of Kazan' and Astrakhan' with their towns and lands would not have long ago become consolidated and subject to the Muscovite tsar as his possessions.

[From chapter 10:] Gosti are drawn from the ranks of trading men, the gostinaia and sukonnaia sotni, and from the posad men. They receive this title of gost' for serving the tsar as trusted heads [*vernye golovy*] or sworn assistants [tseloval'niki] in the sable treasury, in customhouses, and in liquor shops. They carry on their own trade and engage in various enterprises. They are permitted to keep liquor in their homes for their own use, and to brew [beer] and distill [vodka] the whole year round; and they have the right to buy patrimonial estates, to keep them, and to take them in mortgage. And once they have become gosti they continue to serve the tsar, taking turns as heads and secretaries of the sable treasury and in collecting monetary levies [from the posad population]. There are about thirty gosti. . . .

The gostinaia and sukonnaia sotni have been organized in this way: [their members] serve as sworn assistants, associates of gosti in the collection of the tsar's revenues in Moscow and in the provinces, and they likewise carry on their own trade and engage in various enterprises, and they are allowed freely to keep various kinds of liquor in their homes; but they are forbidden to buy or keep peasants. And there are about two hundred of these men.

The trading men of Moscow are organized in sotni and slobody; in all [other] towns the posad men are likewise organized in slobody. Some among them are chosen each year to serve the tsar in customhouses, taverns, and other enterprises as trusted heads and sworn assistants.

[From chapter 11:] Legal jurisdiction over peasants of the tsar's crown [dvortsovye] villages and volosti belongs to the palace [dvorets, i.e. the Prikaz Bol'shogo Dvortsa] in Moscow, and in the villages and volosti to the stewards, according to [the tsar's] charters, in all cases except murder, robbery, theft, and arson. In some of the tsar's chernye volosti [inhabited by state peasants], where there are no stewards, there are ten or so elected judges, peasants of these same volosti, who administer justice in all matters except

cases of murder and robbery, according to the tsar's charters or even without them. The peasants collect from among themselves taxes in money and in kind, as much as each ought to pay, depending on his occupation, his means, and his land: how much land each has and how much grain he sows and how much hay he mows.

. . .

Boyars and [other] Duma members, and closest advisers [blizhnie liudi], and men of all ranks who own pomest'ia and patrimonial estates administer and judge their peasants in all peasant matters except brigandage and robbery. They direct the [peasant] elders and their own men to collect the tsar's taxes from the peasants and to pay them into the tsar's treasury, according to the tsar's decrees. As for their own exactions, they impose them upon the peasants themselves, [deciding] how much to take from each.

When boyars and persons of other ranks mentioned above are granted a pomest'e or a patrimonial estate, it is written in the grant charter that they must protect and defend their peasants from all kinds of harm and extortions from outsiders and must impose obligations on their peasants according to their capacity [to pay], as much as each can afford to give and not above the limit of their capacity, so as not to drive them away from their pomest'ia and patrimonial estates and make beggars of them; and they may not forcibly seize their cattle or other animals, nor their grain or [other] possessions; they must not transfer them from pomest'e villages to live in patrimonial villages, thereby depopulating the one to enrich the other.

[From chapter 12:] In the town of Archangel [Muscovite government agents] trade in grain, hemp, potash, tar [*smolchiuga, smol'chiuga*— resin, pitch, or tar], raw silk, and rhubarb. And they gather that grain in the towns of the Littoral [Pomorskie gorody] and of the lower and middle Volga, from the peasants of the chernye slobody in the uezdy, and they buy this grain and hemp in many towns, with money from the tsar's treasury, from the Prikaz Bol'shogo Prikhoda [the central financial organ of the state]; and they exchange it with visiting foreigners for various goods, and sell it for money. Potash and tar works: these have been established in the tsar's wild forests, in the borderland; likewise boyars and okol'nichie and [other] Duma members and closest advisers and gosti and trading men have established [such enterprises] on lease in the same forests or in others belonging to the tsar; and in addition to the payment for the lease every tenth barrel of potash and tar is taken for the tsar. And these goods—grain, hemp, potash, and tar—are brought to the town of Archangel by the tsar's post transport, and by hired [transport]. Rhubarb is sent from Siberia, where it is collected from the local inhabitants.

On the lower Volga they trade in fish caught by means of weirs, whatever remains after the needs of the palace [are supplied]; likewise they quarry and boil and transport salt up the Volga River to Kazan' and to Nizhnii [-Novgorod] and to Moscow. And whatever fish and salt remain from the tsar's own use are sold in Moscow and in the provinces to men of various rank.

[From chapter 13:] The boyars and [other] Duma members and closest advisers keep 100 or 200 or 300 or 500 or 1,000 men and women in their homes, depending upon their dignity and wealth; and they pay these people [as follows:] to those who are married, a yearly wage of two or three or five or ten rubles each, depending on the person and on his duties, and likewise whatever clothing is appropriate, and a monthly supply of grain and various provisions; and they live in their own chambers in the same household with the master or separately. And they, the boyars, send their dependable married bondmen, for a year at a time in turn, to their patrimonial estates, to their villages and hamlets, as stewards, and order them to collect their wages and various requisitions from the peasants, as much as they need to live on. And bachelors of the upper category are given a small monetary wage, but those of the lower category are given no wages; these bachelors are given all their clothing, and headgear, and shirts, and boots. Those bachelors of the upper category live in the farther chambers downstairs, while those of the lower category live in the upstairs chambers, and they eat and drink out of the boyar's kitchen; and on feast days each one is given two cups of vodka.

VIII:34. DR. SAMUEL COLLINS CONCERNING TSAR ALEXIS, CA. 1668

Dr. Samuel Collins, employed during most of the 1660s in the service of the tsar, wrote up his experiences in a long letter to a fellow-doctor in London. This letter was rearranged topically and published in 1671, shortly after Collins's death, under the title *The Present State of Russia.* Dr. Collins describes many aspects of Russian life—social, religious, legal, economic—and also individuals like Ordin-Nashchokin and, in the excerpts below, Alexis himself. Judging from the context, this description dates from the late 1660s, after 1667.

Reference: Samuel Collins, *The Present State of Russia* (London, 1671), pp. 110-11, 121-25. Excerpts were chosen from among those originally selected by Messrs. Baltzly and Kucherov, to whom the editors are indebted.

I shall now give you a further description of the Czar. He is a goodly person, about six foot high, well set, inclin'd to fat, of a clear complexion, lightish hair, somewhat a low forehead, of a stern countenance, severe in his chastisements, but very careful of his Subjects love. Being urged by a Stranger to make it death for any man to desert his Colours; he answer'd, it was a hard case to do that, for God has not given courage to all men alike. He never appears to the people but in magnificence, and on Festivals with wonderful splendour of Jewels and Attendants. He never went to any Subjects house but his Governours when he was thought past all recovery. His Centinels and Guards placed round about his Court, stand like silent and immoveable Statues. No noise is heard in his Pallace, no more than if uninhabited. None but his Domesticks are suffer'd to approach the inward Court, except the Lords that are in Office. He never dines publickly but on Festivals, and then his Nobility dine in his presence. At *Easter* all the Nobility and Gentry, and Courtiers kiss the Emperours hand, and receive Eggs. Every meal he sends dishes of meat to his Favourites from his own Table. His stores of Corn, and dry'd flesh are very considerable, with these he pays his *Strelsies* or *Janzaries,* giving them some cloth, but very little money; for they have all Trades, and great Priviledges.

· · ·

As to the *Czars* Religion, he is of the Greek Faith, and very strict in the observation thereof. He never misses divine Service, if he be well he goes to it, if sick it comes to him in his chamber. On Fast-dayes he frequents midnight prayers (the old vigils of the Church) standing four, five or six hours together, and prostrating himself to the ground sometimes a thousand times, and on great Festivals fifteen hundred. In the great Fast he eats but three meals a week, *viz.* on *Thursday, Saturday, Sunday;* for the rest he takes a piece of brown bread and salt, a pickled Mushroom or Cucumber, and drinks a cup of small beer. He eats Fish but twice in the great Lent, and observes it seven weeks together, besides *Maslinets* (or cleansing) week, wherein they eat milk and eggs. Out of the Fast he observes *Mondays, Wednesdays* and *Fridays* and will not then eat any thing that comes of flesh. In fine, no Monk is more observant of Canonical hours, then he is of Fasts. We may reckon he fasts almost eight months in twelve, with the six weeks fast before *Christmas,* and two other small fasts.

Those that ínstituted so many Fasts advanced fish to spare flesh, which else would be destroy'd, because they are forc'd to house their Cattle all the winter, sometimes five months space. The *Czar* does not disdain to assist at the Processions bare-headed, and on foot if it be not rainy. He is great Patron of the Church, yet restrains the profuse bounty of dying men to the Clergy. None can found a Monastery without his licence. He makes bold with the Church Treasury upon loan in time of war, and pays it again *ad Graecas Calendas* [literally "at the Greek calends," a way of saying "never"]. For indeed should he not do so his contribution would fall short, seeing the Church holds almost two third parts of the *Czardom.* In his Pallace he has an Hospital of very old men, 120 years old, with whom he often discourses, and delights to hear them tell what pass'd in his Ancestors time. Once a year, *viz,* upon good *Friday,* he visits all the prisons in the night, and taking personal cognizance of all the Prisoners, buys out some that are in debt, and releases others that are criminal, as he thinks fit: He pays great sums for such as he is inform'd are really necessitated. His *Czaritza* buys out Women. He disposes of all Ecclesiastical preferments, but has left the election of the Patriarch to lot, having (as he thinks) had ill luck in using his Prerogative for the late Patriarch *Nicon.* To conclude this Chapter, without doubt this present Emperour of *Russia* is as pious, conscientious, clement, merciful and good a Prince as any in the world. As for his People and Ministers of State, they are like other Nations, ready to act any thing for Bribes or Money, and to deceive as many as they can.

VIII:35. THE TSAR'S EDICT CONCERNING STEPAN RAZIN, AUGUST 1, 1670

In his edict of August 1, 1670, calling upon his service men to proceed against Stepan (Stenka, "Steve") Razin, Tsar Alexis described the disconcertingly rapid spread of Razin's rebellion.

Reference: *DAI,* 6:57-58. Cf. *Krest'ianskaia voina pod predvoditel'stvom Stepana Razina: Sbornik dokumentov,* 3 vols. (Moscow: Gospolitizdat, 1954-62).

And that rebel Stenka, forgetting Almighty God . . . and the holy Orthodox Christian faith, forsook the holy Catholic [*sobornaia*] church and spoke blasphemous and violent words about our savior Jesus Christ, such as an Orthodox Christian should not even think of, and forbade the erection of God's churches on the Don and [church] services, and drove the priests away from the Don, and committed treason against us, the great sovereign, and against the entire Muscovite state, and took Satan as his helper, and, gathering together rebels like himself, treasonably marched to the Don to the town of Cherkask . . . and killed and drowned many of the old Cossacks of the Don who had served us, the great sovereign, and went to the Volga for his treasonable purposes, marching as before past Tsaritsyn; and the service men of Tsaritsyn, entering into an agreement with that rebel, betrayed us, the great sovereign, and surrendered the town of Tsaritsyn, and killed the voevoda Timofei Turgenev, and turned over to Stenka Razin those deti boiarskie and various service men of Tsaritsyn and other local towns who had refused to join and had fought the rebels; and together with Stenka Razin they killed them and threw them into the water. . . .

From Tsaritsyn he went to the Volga, plundering, beating to death, and throwing into the water our, the great sovereign's, service men of all ranks, and government officials [prikaznye liudi], and merchants, not only good men of high birth, but also strel'tsy, and soldiers, and bondmen belonging to [various] masters [boiarskie liudi]; and they committed all manner of evil, treasonable abominations. ... And those of our, the great sovereign's, service men who were sent from Astrakhan' with the voevoda Prince Semen L'vov against the rebel Stenka, those service men of Astrakhan' betrayed us, the great sovereign, and joined him, the rebel, and surrendered the voevoda Prince Semen L'vov to the rebel, and killed and threw into the water their commanders and the Moscow strel'tsy; and

[Razin] came with the Astrakhan' traitors to [the town of] Astrakhan' to persuade the Astrakhan' strel'tsy to let him into the city treasonably and secretly, and to turn over to him the boyar and voevoda and all the commanders, and the Moscow strel'tsy, and to side with him. And the Astrakhan' strel'tsy betrayed us, the great sovereign, let the rebel Stenka into the city, and handed over to the rebels the boyar and voevoda and the commanders and the Moscow strel'tsy; and the rebel Stenka Razin ordered that the boyar and voevoda Prince Ivan Semenovich Prozorovskii be thrown down from the embankment, and his associates and the commanders and the deti boiarskie, and the Moscow strel'tsy who did not join the rebels were killed.

VIII:36. A REPORT OF RAZIN'S CAPTURE, MAY 15, 1671

Razin's capture was reported as follows in the tsar's dispatch of May 15, 1671, to the voevoda of Vologda, calling for the vigorous pursuit of other rebels still at large.
 Reference: *AAE*, 4:234.

From Tsar and Grand Prince Aleksei Mikhailovich, autocrat of all Great and Little and White Russia, to Vologda, to our voevoda Konstantin Ustinovich Nashchokin and to our secretary [d'iak] Sidor Skvortsov. On the tenth day of May of the current year of 179 [1671], the ataman Kornei Iakovlev and his Cossack companions and the entire host of the Don wrote from the Don to us, the great sovereign ... that they, the Cossacks of all the settlements, had united in common accord and, to serve us, the great sovereign, had made an expedition from the town of Cherkask to Kagal'nik [both not far east of modern Rostov], for

the purpose of catching the rebels and traitors Stenka Razin and his companions, and ... that they, the Cossacks of the Don, ataman Kornei Iakovlev and the entire host of the Don, had killed many rebels near Kagal'nik, and had taken the rebel and traitor Stenka Razin and his accomplices ... and brought Stenka to Cherkask, and put him in irons, and placed him under close guard, and killed and hanged all his companions and accomplices, and sent the rebel Stenka to us, the great sovereign, under the guard of the ataman Kornei Iakovlev and his companions.

VIII:37. DEPOSITIONS OF 1672 CONCERNING THE REBELS IN ASTRAKHAN' IN 1670

The Muscovite government, in attempting to learn the nature and extent of the rebellion that had shaken the state, collected depositions from eyewitnesses. The excerpts below are taken from those recorded in 1672.
 Reference: Arkheograficheskaia Komissiia, *Akty istoricheskie*, 4:432-33, 484, 487-89. Cf. *Krest'ianskaia voina*, 3:213-20, 243-50.

The parish priests ... said upon interrogation that in the previous year, 179 [1670], the Cossack rebels ataman Vaska Us and his companions came to Astrakhan' (but Stenka Razin and Fedka Sheludiak did not come to Astrakhan'; they sailed up the river, they [the parish priests] did not know where), and these rebels, Vaska Us and his companions, wrote a seditious proclamation; and they, the

priests, had assembled to conduct funeral services for Metropolitan Iosif [of Astrakhan'] and to place his coffin into the sepulcher; and the Cossack rebels came from their circle [*krug*, assembly or meeting] with sabers, and took [the priests] forcibly from the cathedral to the circle, and ordered their rebel clerk Ianka Efremov to read that seditious proclamation aloud in the circle; and their proclamation read as follows: "The atamans and all the Cossacks of the Don and Astrakhan' and Terek and Grebni [in the northern Caucasus], and the cannoneers and stockade tenders and the posad men, and the trading people of the marketplace [*gostinyi dvor*] have written an agreement among themselves to live here in Astrakhan' in amity and concord, and not to kill anyone in Astrakhan', and to stand wholeheartedly for one another, and they [the Cossacks] are to sail up the river to kill and exterminate the traitorous boyars." No other declaration was read to [the priests], and they were ordered to affix their signatures to that declaration, and those refusing to sign were threatened to be beaten to death; and the priests, fearing death, signed on behalf of their spiritual children and parishioners, as ordered; and that written agreement remained in the circle with the Cossacks, and they heard a rumor that the Cossacks had taken it to the Trinity Monastery.

. . .

On the eleventh day of July of the current year, 180 [1672], the cathedral priests Kirill Eliseev and Petr Ivanov said, upon interrogation: . . . "On the eleventh day of May, during the offertory [*proskomidiia,* the office preceding the introit], the rebel and apostate Cossacks came from their diabolical assembly, the circle, to the apostolic cathedral church, to get the great lord, the most reverend Iosif, metropolitan of Astrakhan' and of the Terek, and summoned him, with great rudeness, to their circle. . . . And the metropolitan, vested in his robes, ordered the ringing of the big churchbell for the priests to assemble and accompany him to the circle. And the prelate went to the circle with an archpriest and the priests of the cathedral. . . . And upon arriving at the circle, he, the great lord, began to speak to the rebel ataman Vaska Us: 'Why have you summoned me, you rebels and perjurers?' And the ataman Vaska Us said to [the Cossack esaul or captain] Kochenovskii: 'Why do you stand silent? Explain why you have come from the host, and speak first.' And Kochenovskii began to speak to the great prelate: 'I am sent from the host with accusations that you are in treasonable correspondence with the Terek and the Don and that on account of your correspondence the Terek and Don have defected from us.' And he, the great lord, said to the rebels: 'I have

not corresponded with them, and even if I had, it is not like corresponding with the Crimea or Lithuania. Besides, I tell you yourselves that you should stop your rebellion and ask mercy of the great sovereign.' And many rebels in the circle shouted: 'Why is he covering up his treason, saying that he has not corresponded? What kind of righteous man is he? Why has he come to the circle with a cross? We are Christians ourselves, and you come to us as if we were heathen.' And the rebels started to come forward out of the circle to disrobe the metropolitan; and out of the midst of the rebel Cossacks a certain Cossack of the Don, named Miron, came forward and began to speak to the rebels: 'How is it, brothers, that you want to lay your hands on such a high dignitary? We must not even touch such a high dignitary.' And the Cossack Aleshka Gruzinkin dashed forward and seized Miron by the hair, with many Cossacks following suit; and before the prelate's eyes they began stabbing and slashing and beating Miron in dead earnest, and they dragged him away from the circle and killed him. Soon afterward the rebels turned to the archpriest and the priests and started to push them and abuse them with unseemly words, saying: 'Strip the metropolitan of his rank. Didn't he strip Patriarch Nikon of his rank?' And he, the great lord, seeing what the rebels had in mind, passed the cross from his own episcopal hands to the priest of the archbishop's chapel Efrem, and himself took off his miter and his panagia [image of the Virgin worn around the neck by prelates]. . . . And the archdeacon took off his omophorion and saccos and all his vestments, and he handed them to the priests; and the great prelate was left with only his black velvet cassock. . . . And the Cossacks pushed all of us [other priests] out of the circle, saying: 'This does not concern you'; and they led the prelate to the powder magazine to be tortured. And Larka, the executioner, stripped him of his two cassocks and bound him hand and foot, and, inserting a log [between his arms and legs], pushed him down into the fire, clothed only in a black woolen tunic; and that tunic caught fire, and [the executioner] tore the tunic to shreds, and burned [the prelate] naked on the fire, and, placing his foot on the latter's belly, questioned him: 'Tell me, Metropolitan, about your treason, about your correspondence'; and the great prelate gave him no answer, but prayed while lying on the fire, and cursed Larka. . . . And they led the prelate from the torture to an embankment; and he was limping as he went, for they had hurt his leg during the torture. And as the prelate passed the corpse of Miron, the Cossack who had been killed, he blessed the corpse and bowed to it. . . . And the rebels . . . laid him on his side on the edge of the embankment, and pushed him to roll down. . . . And as he, the great lord, fell to the ground, there was a great noise and fright; and all the rebels in the circle became frightened and were quiet for a long time. For a third of an hour they stood in amazement, their heads bowed, saying nothing to each other."

VIII:38. JOHN STRUYS ON STEPAN RAZIN, 1669

John Struys, a Dutchman in the service of the tsar, wrote about Stepan Razin in Astrakhan' in 1669. Whether or not Struys had unimpeachable sources for the story that closes this excerpt, he rendered a service to Russian balladry.

Reference: John Struys, *The Voiages and Travels of John Struys,* trans. John Morrison (London, 1684), pp. 186-87. Excerpt selected from among those chosen earlier by Messrs. Baltzly and Kucherov. For other foreigners' accounts see A. G. Man'kov, ed., *Zapiski inostrantsev o vosstanii Stepana Razina* (Leningrad: AN SSSR, 1968).

I have seen him [Razin] several times upon the *Stroegs* [vessels] and in the City; he is a brave man as to his person, and well proportioned in his limbs, tall and streight of Body, pock-pitted, but only so as did rather become than disfigure him, of good conduct, but withall severe and cruel. . . . The *Cosacks* who were his Followers came dayly into *Astrachan* where they sold their Booty which was very rich and costly. The Silk they sold for a 3rd of the current value, which was bought up by the *Persian* and *Armenian* Merchants. I bought a Gold-chain of one of them which was almost a fathom long, and in joynts like a Bracelet, between each piece were precious stones: the price I gave for it was not fully 7 pound *sterl.* Shortly after their Arrival Captain *Butler* went to visit him, taking 2 bottles of Brandy along with him, which he thought might be an acceptable present, since they had been so long at Sea, and presented them to him and his Minion, whom the *Russians* called *Devils-Whisker* by a Nick-name. When we came to his Tent; and desired admittance, he sent to know who we were; Answer was returned him that we were *Dutch,* and imployed in the service of the Czaar, upon a Ship in the *Caspian* sea. He forthwith gave order to a Gentleman to conduct us into his Tent where himself and some of his Council sat, and caused us to sit down, took our present in good part, and drank the Emperours health. Another time we went through the Camp where we saw him going aboard a Yacht to divertise himself upon the Water, with some of his officers: he had with him a *Persian* Princes which he had taken, together with her Brother. The Brother he presented to the *Waywod* [voevoda] of *Astrachan,* but the Sister he kept for his Concubine. Being now in the heighth of his Cups, and full of Frolicks, bragged of the many presents he had given and received, since his being restored to the Emperours favour, and on a sudden brake out into those extravagant terms, speaking to the *Wolga: Well, said he, thou art a noble River, and out of thee have I had so much Gold, Silver and many things of Value. Thou art the sole Father and Mother of my Fortune and advancement: but, unthankful man that I am; I have never offered thee any thing: well now, I am resolved to manifest my gratitude.* With those words he took her into his Arms and threw her into the *Wolga,* with all her rich Habit and Ornaments; her attire was of rich Cloth of Gold, richly set out with Pearls, Diamonds and other precious Stones. The Lady was of an angelical Countenance and amiable, of a stately carriage and Body, and withall excellently well qualified as to her Parts, being of a singular wit, and always pleasing in her demeanour toward him, when he was in the heat of fury, and yet at last became the instance of his Cruelty.

VIII:39. THE CORONATION PROCEDURE OF JUNE 18, 1676

The record of the coronation of the fifteen-year-old Theodore (Fedor or Feodor) III (ruled 1676-82), son of Alexis, comes down to us through texts preserved in the *Polnoe Sobranie*

Zakonov Rossiiskoi Imperii (Complete collection of the laws of the Russian Empire), published in the 1830s on the basis of government archives. In this detailed account are seen the preservation of the ancient legends as well as some variations on the ceremony of 1547.

Reference: *PSZRI*, 1st ser., 2:42–43, 52–53, 57, 59–60, 64 (see List of Abbreviations).

Petition was made to the great sovereign, tsar, and grand prince Feodor Alekseevich, autocrat of Great and Little and White Russia, by the great lord, the most holy lord Joachim, patriarch of Moscow and of all Russia, with the metropolitans, the archbishops and bishops, the archimandrites and the abbots; and likewise the tsarevichi [Tatar princes] of Siberia and of Kasimov; and the boyars, okol'nichie, [other] Duma members [*dumnye liudi*], stol'niki, striapchie, Moscow dvoriane, secretaries, zhil'tsy, provincial dvoriane, and deti boiarskie, and gosti, and service men and trading men of various rank; and they said . . . "And now the time has come for you, the great sovereign, tsar, and grand prince Feodor Alekseevich, autocrat of Great and Little and White Russia, to be crowned tsar and grand prince of Moscow, Kiev, Vladimir, and Novgorod, and tsar of Kazan', Astrakhan', and Siberia, and of all the great and glorious realms of the Russian tsardom, with the tsarist crown and necklet [*diadima*], which is the same as the sacred collar [*barmy*], and to be anointed with holy oil, according to your ancient tsarist ritual; and this coronation of Your Tsarist Majesty with the tsarist crown will bring joy to all Orthodox Christians of the Russian realm, of every rank and nation, and will increase its glory in all neighboring Christian realms, while making the heathen fear and tremble."

. . .

[From the Tsar's speech at the Cathedral of the Dormition, in the Moscow Kremlin:]

"By the grace and will of Almighty God, glorified in the Trinity, the great sovereigns, tsars, and grand princes of all great Russia have sat for many years on this tsarist throne, since the time of Grand Prince Riurik, and the pious Grand Prince Vladimir Sviatoslavich, coequal with the apostles, who illumined the entire Russian land through holy baptism, and the pious grand prince Vladimir Vsevolodovich Monomakh, who received the greatest honors and a tsarist crown and necklet from the Greek tsar Constantine Monomachus, wherefore he took the name of Monomakh; and after him all the great sovereigns have been crowned with a tsarist crown. . . .

And the most holy patriarch questioned the great sovereign thus: "Great Sovereign, Tsar, and Grand Prince Feodor Alekseevich! What is your creed and how do you profess your faith in the Father, the Son, and the Holy Ghost?" And the pious sovereign replied: "This is my creed: I believe in one God, the Father Almighty, and so forth" [the Nicene Creed].

And after the [tsar's] confession of faith, the most holy patriarch spoke thus: "May the grace of the Holy Spirit be with Thee. . . . By the will of the Almighty Creator, God the Father, and by the grace of his only-begotten Son, our lord and savior Jesus Christ, and with the furtherance of the most holy and life-giving Spirit, by the will and desire of the omnipotent, holy, and consubstantial Trinity, there has emerged the race of the great sovereigns, the Russian tsars, who have ruled great Russia as autocrats, from the time of the most highly exalted first grand prince Riurik, [descended] from Augustus Caesar who ruled over the whole world, and of the pious grand prince Vladimir Sviatoslavich, coequal with the apostles, who illumined the Russian land through holy baptism, and of Grand Prince Vladimir Vsevolodovich Monomakh who received the greatest honors, [and] a tsar's crown and necklet from the Greek tsar Constantine Monomachus, wherefore he took the name of Monomakh; and after him all the great autocrats of the Russian tsardom have been crowned with a crown."

. . .

And the most holy patriarch Joachim, having made the sign of the cross over the tsarist crown, kissed it, and blessed the tsar and grand prince with the tsarist crown, saying: "In the name of the Father, and of the Son, and of the Holy Ghost," and, having enjoined the tsar to kiss it, he placed the tsarist crown upon the tsar's head.

. . .

And the most holy patriarch took up the tsarist scepter and orb, and, having made the sign of the cross over them, he gave them to the great sovereign, tsar and grand prince Feodor Alekseevich, autocrat of all Great and Little and White Russia, placing the scepter in his right hand and the orb of dominion in his left hand, and he spoke to him thus:

"Crowned by God, endowed by God, adorned by God, O pious Great Sovereign, Tsar and Grand Prince Feodor Alekseevich, autocrat of all Great and Little and White Russia! Receive from the Lord what has been given to you: the scepter and the orb of dominion, for the Lord God has entrusted to you the banners [khorugvi] of the great Russian tsardom; guard it and preserve it with all your strength, and with God's help." And the tsar and grand prince received the scepter and the orb and bowed before the patriarch, without removing the tsarist crown from his head.

. . .

Then Patriarch Joachim blessed the tsar crowned by God and, taking him by the right hand, seated him on his tsarist seat.

. . .

And after this the most holy Joachim, patriarch of Moscow and all Russia, addressed an exhortation to the sovereign tsar. . . .

". . . And you, Sire, my son whom God has crowned, Orthodox Tsar and Grand Prince Feodor Alekseevich! Have the fear of God in your heart; preserve our true Orthodox faith of the Greek law uncorrupted and inviolate; maintain your tsardom in righteousness and in purity as it has been given to you this day by God; and love truth and mercy and justice; be merciful to those who obey you; and hold the holy Cathedral of the Dormition, and all the holy churches, in faith and the fear of God, and render them honor. . . . And to ourselves, and to all the clergy, who pray for you in the Holy Spirit, [you owe] spiritual obedience . . . for if honor is paid a prelate, that honor ascends to Christ himself. . . .

"To your boyars and magnates be bountiful, and care for them in accordance with their ancestral rank and service and with justice. And to the princes, and princelings [kniazhata], and deti boiarskie, and all the Christ-loving warriors, be accessible and merciful and affable, as befits your rank and dignity. Protect and bestow your bounty upon all Orthodox Christians, and care for them with all your heart. Defend with authority and manliness those who are wronged; do not permit or allow anyone to be wronged; and act lawfully and justly in all things. For you, O Tsar, have received from God the scepter of sovereignty, the sacred banners of the great Russian tsardom, so that you may judge and rule your people justly, and protect and guard them watchfully against the fierce wolves intent on their destruction, lest the flocks of Christ's sheep whom God has committed to you should melt away; carry the scepter entrusted to you in accordance with God's sacred will and your immemorial and ancestral tsarist destiny as sovereign of the great Russian realm. . . ."

. . .

And the most holy patriarch Joachim stood at the holy altar near the Royal Doors [the main entrance to the sanctuary], while Metropolitan Kornilii held the holy oil in a precious vessel upon a golden tray. Then the patriarch took the holy oil from the precious vessel and anointed the tsar with the oil, in front of the Royal Doors, on the forehead, on both ears, and on the mouth, on the chest, on the neck, on the shoulder, on both arms, and on the palms, and on the hands, saying with each anointment: "The seal and gift of the Holy Ghost, Amen."

VIII:40. A CLAIM UNDER MESTNICHESTVO, MID-SEVENTEENTH CENTURY

The following excerpt is from a mid-seventeenth century statement designed to bolster a claim under the system of mestnichestvo—the system of appointments on the basis of the positions held by one's ancestors. Even in this brief a sample, the drawbacks of the system become obvious.
Reference: RIB, vol. 22, cols. 64-65.

In the year [70]85 [1577], Prince Timofei Romanovich Trubetskoi and the third voevoda [in command], Mikhail, son of Ivan Golovin, were sent with the main body [of the army] into the German land.

With the vanguard were another voevoda, my great-grandfather Astafei Mikhailovich Pushkin, and Mikhail Andreevich Beznin. With the rear guard was another great-grandfather of mine, Ivan Mikhailovich Pushkin. And according to this precedent [sluchai] my great-grandfathers Astafei and Ivan Mikhailovich Pushkin were higher [in rank] than Mikhail, son of Ivan Golovin. In the year

[70]91 [1583], Roman Alfer'ev sought his ancestral position over Petr Golovin, and that matter was not decided, and therefore Roman Alfer'ev was equal in ancestral rank [mestnik] to Petr Golovin. And Roman Alfer'ev was an assistant [tovarishch] of my great-grandfather Astafei Mikhailovich.

VIII:41. THE DECISION TO ABOLISH MESTNICHESTVO, JANUARY 12, 1682

This decision constituted an important step in the gradual bureaucratization of the Muscovite state. Here are passages from the official proceedings of the Boyar Duma, January 12, 1682.
Reference: PSZRI, 1st ser., 2:374-76.

The great sovereign . . . vouchsafed to say to the sovereign's boyars that they too should make a sincere report concerning this [mestnichestvo] to him, the great sovereign, each speaking his mind without any constraint.

And the boyars and okol'nichie and [other] Duma members and closest advisers [blizhnie liudi] and everyone declared zealously to him, the great sovereign and tsar . . . that he, the great sovereign, should decree in accordance with the petition of the most holy patriarch and the bishops, that they all must occupy the various ranks without reference to genealogical seniority [mesto], for this reason: that in past years in many of the sovereign's military and diplomatic affairs of every kind these precedents [sluchai] had given rise to great evil and discord and ruin, had brought joy to the enemy, and had resulted in deeds odious to God, hatred, and great and prolonged animosity among them.

. . .

And the great sovereign tsar . . . vouchsafed to say to the most holy patriarch and the [church] authorities [vlasti] and to the sovereign's boyars . . . in accordance with this honorable common intention which God has granted: "We, the great sovereign, order by our tsarist command that these precedents and positions based on genealogical seniority be completely eradicated; and for their complete eradication and eternal oblivion we desire the requests concerning precedents and the registers [zapiski] of genealogical seniority to be consigned to the flames, so that this rancor and hatred should perish completely and never be recalled in the future, and so that there would be no temptation or hindrance for anyone. . . . And from this day forward we command that there shall be no claims of genealogical seniority among our boyars and okol'nichie and [other] Duma members and closest advisers and people of sundry ranks [who are] in military service with the regiments, or serving in the prikazy in Moscow in judicial or diplomatic posts, or anywhere in any post; and that in the future no one shall consider himself above another through any previous precedent, or reproach anyone; and that no one shall be elevated above another through any previous [i.e. ancestral] superiority [nakhod]. . . ."

And having heard this with benevolence, the most holy patriarch with the entire holy council and the sovereign's entire Sinklit [Boyar Duma] all gave thanks to God with great zeal, and joyfully received this, his sovereign benevolence, and confirmed it willingly, saying: "May this mestnichestvo, hateful to God, productive of enmity, incompatible with brotherhood, and destructive of love, perish in flames, and may it never be recalled in the future!"

And on that same day those books were consigned to the flames.

VIII:42. THE DECREE ABOLISHING MESTNICHESTVO, JANUARY 12, 1682

Among the Muscovite records (razriadnye zapiski) has been found this account of the decree which, while modernizing the state, frustrated unborn generations of archive-loving historians. Fortunately many of the appointment records survived.
Reference: DAI, 9:186.

On the twelfth day of January in the year 7190 [1682], the great sovereign, tsar, and grand prince Feodor Alekseevich, autocrat of all Great and Little and White Russia, decreed that all ranks should occupy the various offices without regard to genealogical seniority [bez mest] and that in the future there should be no claims based on genealogical seniority [otecheskikh del ne vchinat'] under any circumstances, and that if anyone should attempt [to make such claims] he should be put to death and be accursed. And the [church] authorities burned the service registers and books of precedents [*rozriadnye i sluchnye knigi*] in an oven in the front entrance hall [of the tsar's palace], and people of various lineages were chosen as captains [*rotmistry*] and senior and junior lieutenants [*porutchiki starshie i ne starshie*], and from that day forward everything began to be done without regard to genealogical seniority.

VIII:43. AN OFFICIAL ACCOUNT OF THE MUTINY OF THE STREL'TSY, MAY 15-19, 1682

This account of the mutiny that ushered in the regency of Sofia is taken from one of the official records of the time (*razriadnye zapiski*). The impact of these events on the ten-year-old Peter may help explain some of his subsequent actions.

Reference: *DAI*, 10:23-24.

On the fifteenth day of May in the year 7190 [1682] there was turmoil in Moscow. The Kremlin was entered by soldiers of the regiment [commanded by] Matvei Krapkov and strel'tsy from all the regiments with pikes and halberds and muskets, and cannoneers with their cannon; and entering the Kremlin they fired their muskets and killed many boyar servants and horses and wounded others.

And coming to the Red [or Beautiful] Portico [*Krasnoe kryl'tso*, at the head of the staircases at the main entrance to the tsar's palace], they assembled in full force.

And by order of the great sovereign [Petr Alekseevich], the boyar Prince Ivan Andreevich Khovanskii came out to them and asked them: "Why have you come here thus?" And they all said to the boyar: "We have heard that the boyars are betraying the great sovereign," and [they demanded] that the sovereign, tsarevich, and grand prince Ioann [Ivan] Alekseevich be shown to them.

And the boyar informed the great sovereign of what they had said. And the great sovereign and the sovereign tsaritsa and the sovereign tsarevich and the most holy patriarch came out to them, onto the Red Portico. . . . And [the strel'tsy] petitioned the great sovereign and informed the boyars that the great sovereign should order to hand over to them the [following] boyars: Prince Iurii Alekseevich Dolgorukov, Prince Grigorii Grigor'evich Romodanovskii, Prince Mikhailo Iur'evich Dolgorukov, Kirill Poluekhtovich Naryshkin, Artemon Sergeevich Matveev, [and] Ivan Maksimovich Iazykov; and the boyar and armsbearer [*oruzheinichii*] Ivan Kirillovich Naryshkin, the chamberlain [*postel'nichii*] Aleksei Timofeevich Likhachev, the treasurer [*kaznachei*] Mikhailo Timofeevich Likhachev, the cupbearer [*chashnik*] Semen Ivanovich Iazykov; the Duma secretaries [*d'iaki*]: Larion Ivanov, Danilo Polianskii, Grigorii Bogdanov, Averkii Kirilov; and the gentlemen of the chamber [*spal'niki*]: Afanasii, Lev, Martem'ian, Fedor, Vasilii, [and] Petr Naryshkin.

And the great sovereign ordered them to be told that none of these [boyars] were upstairs in the palace of the great sovereign. And they all went upstairs with muskets into the palace of the great sovereign and to the sovereign tsaritsa and to the sovereign tsarevich and to the sovereign tsarevny, and searched in the palace and everywhere, and seized the [following] boyars: Artemon Sergeevich Matveev they threw from the Red Portico onto the pikes; and Prince Grigorii Grigor'evich Romodanovskii they seized in the patriarch's quarters and killed; and Prince Mikhailo Iur'evich Dolgorukov they threw from above onto the pikes; and Ivan Maksimovich Iazykov they caught on Nikitskaia [Square], brought before the [Church of the] Archangel, and cut to pieces; and Prince Iurii Alekseevich Dolgorukov they found ill in his house, threw from the great staircase, quartered, and left on the square in front of his house; and Larion Ivanov and his son Vasilii and Colonel Andrei Dokhturov and Grigorii Goriushkin they cut to pieces; and Afanasii Naryshkin they discovered upstairs under the altar in the Church of the Savior, [the house chapel] of the sovereign tsaritsa, and threw onto the pikes; and they carried out the bodies of all of them through the Spaskie Gates to Red Square to the Lobnoe Mesto, and there mocked them shamefully, and leaving the palace they pillaged the Sudnoi [Judicial] and Kholopii [Bondman] Prikazy, brought outside various documents, and tore them to pieces.

. . .

On the following day, the sixteenth day of May, they likewise came to the Bedchamber Portico [*Postel'noe kryl'tso,* which looked down on the inner courtyard and was at an entrance to the tsar's living quarters]; and the sovereign tsarevny came out to speak to them, [saying] that they should remember the oath they had sworn upon the cross, and not enter the sovereign's palace thus rudely.

And they petitioned as they had petitioned before, that the doctors Stepan Zhid and Ian be handed over to them.

And the great sovereign ordered to be handed over to them: the Duma secretary Averkii Kirilov, the doctor Ian, and the son of Stepan, and they killed them; and they forgave all those about whom they had petitioned the great sovereign. . . .

On the seventeenth day of May they came again to the Bedchamber Portico. Again the sovereign tsarevny came out to them and vouchsafed to say to them that they should forgive the boyar Kirill Poluekhtovich Naryshkin and the doctor Stepan for the continued welfare of the sovereigns. And they forgave the boyar Kirill Poluekhtovich

but [demanded] that he take monastic vows and that the others be handed over, and they were ready to go upstairs. And the great sovereign ordered them to be handed over: and they seized them, Ivan Naryshkin and the doctor Stepan, and led them into the torture chamber in the Konstantin Tower and tortured them, and after torturing them cut them to pieces and impaled the skull of Ivan Naryshkin upon a pike.

And on the eighteenth day of May, chosen representatives [*vybornye liudi*] came from all the regiments without arms and petitioned the great sovereign and the sovereign tsarevny that the great sovereign should order the boyar Kirill Poluekhtovich Naryshkin to take monastic vows.

And the great sovereign ordered him to take monastic vows in the Chudov Monastery. . . .

During those three days, when they came fully armed, [and] when they killed the boyars, the tocsin was rung and drums were beaten. And some plundered the houses of the slain people and of people of various rank, but they [the others] seized and executed them, and decided among themselves that no one's house should be plundered.

C. SOCIAL AND ECONOMIC CONDITIONS

Note: Material on social and economic conditions is also contained in many of the documents in other sections of this chapter.

VIII:44. PLEDGES OF INDENTURED SERVICE, 1606-1693

These pledges of individual lifelong service (*kabal'nye zapisi* or *sluzhilye kabaly*) from the seventeenth century illustrate the evolution, begun in the late sixteenth century, of a special and intermediate category of unfree persons.

Reference: Arkheograficheskaia Komissiia, *Akty iuridecheskogo byta,* 2:24-25 [contract of 1606]; 1:592-93 [1635, 1674]; 2:32 [1683], 37 [1689]; 1:601 [1693]. For translations of other similar documents see the recent work by Hellie, *Readings,* especially pp. 233-301. Among the collections of documents dealing with the peasantry in pre-Petrine Russia, in addition to collections cited elsewhere in this and preceding chapters, see especially V. V. Mavrodin, E. M. Androsenkov, and N. N. Kononov, eds., *Materialy po istorii krest'ian v Rossii XI-XVII vv. (sbornik dokumentov)* (Leningrad: Izd. Leningradskogo Universiteta, 1958).

[A contract of 1606:]

I, Prokofii, son of Stepan, with my wife Varvara, daughter of Grigorii, and with my step-daughter Mar'ia, daughter of Ovsei, have borrowed from our master [*gosudar'*] Ivan, son of Mikhail Pustoshkin, three rubles in Moscow currency on the twentieth day of February and until the same day of the following year, the twentieth day of February; and for interest we shall serve in the house-

hold of our master Ivan Pustoshkin unceasingly, and if the money is not repaid on the date due we shall similarly serve in the household of our master Ivan unceasingly. And this has been witnessed by . . .

[A contract of 1635:]

I, Iakim, son of Grigorii, surnamed Krasovskoi, a native of Pereiaslavl' Zalesskii, have borrowed from Grigorii, son of Fedor Besednyi, two rubles in Moscow currency on the eleventh day of September for a year to the day; and for interest I, Iakimka, surnamed Krasovskoi, shall live and serve in the household of Grigorii Fedorovich Besednyi; and if the money is not repaid on the date due I, Iakimka, surnamed Krasovskoi, shall for interest similarly live and serve in the household of my master Grigorii Fedorovich Besednyi unceasingly. Witnessed by: Vasilii, son of Aleksandr Kodovin, and Ivan, son of Pavel. And the contract [kabala] was drawn up by the posad man of the Vologodskaia Square, Merkut Markov, in the year 7144 [1635].

[A contract of 1674:]

I, Maksim, son of Mikhei Omel'ianov, have borrowed from Vasilii Andreianovich Suvorov three rubles in Moscow currency in actual money [priamye bez pripisi, i.e. without counting the interest] on the twenty-eighth day of July and until the twenty-eighth day of July in the following year; and for interest on this money I shall serve in the household of my master Vasilii Andreianovich unceasingly and perform every kind of work; and if the money is not repaid on the date due I shall similarly serve in the household of my master Vasilii Andreianovich unceasingly. Witnessed by: Ivan Andreev, Lev Dobrynin. And the contract was drawn up by Grishka Dobrynin, in the year 7182 [1674].

[A contract of 1683:]

I, Afanasii Vasil'ev, have petitioned Prince Boris Andreevich Kozlovskii to take me into bondage [v kholopstvo], and of my own free will I give him a service contract [sluzhilaia

kabala] upon myself; and I, Afanasii, shall serve in the household of my master Prince Boris Andreevich as long as he lives. . . . And the service contract was drawn up by the clerk of the Ivanovskaia Square Senka Kozmin, on the seventeenth day of December in the year 7192 [1683].

[A contract of 1689:]

I, Mikita, son of Afanasii Paduchev, on the nineteenth day of November in the current year, [7]198 [1689], have petitioned Vasilii Andreianovich Suvorov to take me, a free man, into bondage; and I, Mitka, give of my own free will to him, Vasilii Andreianovich, a service contract; and I, Mitka, shall serve in the household of my master Vasilii Andreiano- vich as long as he lives. This contract was wit- nessed by Fedor Grishenin. And the service contract was drawn up by the clerk of Kashin- skaia Square, Vaska Dobrynin, on the nine- teenth day of November in the year 7198 [1689].

[A contract of 1693:]

I, Ivan, son of Stepan Zhilka, on the twelfth day of January in the current year, [7]201 [1693], petition the lieutenant of cavalry Ivan Grigor'evich Kacheev to take me into bondage, and I give him of my own free will a service contract upon myself; and I shall serve him, my master, in his household as long as he lives. This service contract was witnessed by Grigorei Titov. And the service contract was drawn up by the clerk of the Ivanovskaia Square, Ivashko Troitskov, on the twelfth day of January in the year 7201 [1693].

VIII:45. PEASANT AGREEMENTS WITH LANDLORDS, 1628-1687

The following excerpts from seventeenth-century agreements between peasants and landlords (for the most part pomeshchiki or holders of pomest'ia, i.e. estates on service tenure) illustrate various aspects of the gradual process by which the farming population became enserfed. (See also the relevant provision of the Ulozhenie of 1649, in the preceding section.)

Reference: Mikhail A. D'iakonov, ed., Akty otnosiashchiesia k istorii tiaglogo naseleniia v Moskovskom gosudarstve, 2 vols. (St. Petersburg, 1895-97), 1:9 [agreement of 1628], 21-22 [1636], 53 [1650], 62 [1672], 63-64 [1676], 66 [1682]; Arkheograficheskaia Komissiia, Akty iuridicheskogo byta, 3:428 [agreement of 1687].

[An agreement of 1628:]

Before the voevoda . . . and before the secre- taries . . . the Pskov pomeshchik Lavrentii Goriainov presented a peasant contract-deed [poriadnaia zapis'], and brought with the deed the peasant Vaska, son of Ignatii, and said that

this Vaska had contracted with him, Lavrentii, to be his peasant; and the peasant Vaska Ignat'ev said that he had contracted with Lavrentii Goriainov to be his peasant and had given a contract-deed upon himself to that effect, and in the deed is written: I, Vasilii, son of Ignatii, a free man [*vol'nyi chelovek,* i.e. one who neither serves the sovereign nor bears tiaglo], have given a deed upon myself to the Pskov pomeshchik Lavrentii, son of Ivan Goriainov, to the effect that I, Vasilii, have contracted with him, Lavrentii, to be his peasant in the Pskov region, in the Voronatskii uezd, in the Zaklinskaia *guba,* on half [of the land] of the hamlet of Borisko Lbov, on the Shesta River; and I, Vasilii, shall come on the due date, Saint Philip's day, the day before the [Christmas] fast [Advent—November 14], in the current year of [7]137 [1628], and having arrived shall build a peasant's living quarters, and plow the plowland, and enclose the fields, and clear the hayfields, and pay revenue to the pomeshchik yearly, and live in that half-hamlet quietly and peacefully; [and I shall] not keep taverns and brothels, and not allow any criminal to enter, and not flee from him, Lavrentii, nor contract with anyone else as a peasant or *bobyl'* [landless peasant].

[An agreement of 1636:]

I, Ivan, son of Pavel, surnamed Selivankov, a free plowman, with my children . . . have contracted to be peasants of the Pustorzhevsk pomeshchik Afanasii, son of Ivan Dubrovskii, in the Pustorzhevsk uezd . . . in the hamlet of Mutovuzovo, in the existing house, with tax exemption [*l'gota*] for three years from the current year of 144 [1636]. And while we live as peasants of Afanasii in that hamlet of Mutovuzovo, I, Ivashka, and my children shall during these tax-exempt years build up [our] peasant homestead [*dvor*], plow the fallow plowland, build fences, and clear the hayfields. And I, Ivan, and my children have taken from him, our master Afanasii Ivanovich Dubrovskii, as aid, five quarters [*chet'*] of rye grain, five quarters of various spring grains for seed, and two horses, one a seven-year-old bay gelding worth five rubles, the other an eight-year-old fallow bay mare worth six rubles, and a brown cow worth two rubles, two sheep worth four grivna, and two hogs worth a ruble. And I, Ivan, and my children shall live as peasants of Afanasii, according to this contract-deed, quietly and peacefully, and when the tax-exempt years expire we shall pay taxes to the state and revenue of various kinds to the pomeshchik, and perform every kind of work with his peasants

for him, the pomeshchik, and shall not leave him, Afanasii, to be peasants of another pomeshchik, or of the crown, or of a monastery, or of a church, nor shall we mortgage ourselves to anyone. And if I, Ivan, and my children . . . leave him, Afanasii, and go elsewhere as peasants, or do not perform all the work described in this contract-deed, then he, Afanasii, shall take from me, Ivashka, and from my children . . . according to this, my contract-deed, the full amount of the aid, and he, Afanasii, shall take from me, Ivashka, and from my children a forfeit in money of five rubles. And thenceforth I, Ivan, with my children, according to this contract-deed, shall be permanently bound to him, Afanasii, as peasants.

[An agreement of 1650:]

We have given—I, Savelii, with my wife, my son, and my grandson—a loan note [*ssudnaia zapis'*] from ourselves to Afanasii Mikhailovich Tolbuzin, and we have taken from our master Afanasii Mikhailovich a loan of five rubles in money for various purchases, and in return for that loan we shall live as peasants of Afanasii Mikhailovich in the Solovskii uezd, in the P'sovskii stan, on his pomest'e, in the hamlet of Krutitsa, and plow the plowland for him, and perform every kind of work, and pay taxes to the state and to him, the pomeshchik, and we shall not flee from Afanasii Mikhailovich and make off with his loan.

[An agreement of 1672:]

I, Kipriian Volodimerov, a free man of the city of Kolomna, with my wife and children, give upon ourselves this deed to the superior [*stroitel'*] of the Monastery of Saint Theodore, Iskhirion, and his brethren, that we will live as peasants of this Monastery of Saint Theodore in the village of Tseputinkovo; and I, Kipreianko, with my wife and children, have taken from him, the superior, Iskhirion, and his brethren, fifty rubles in money as a loan for various peasant household goods; and whoever shall be superior with the brethren after him, we shall likewise live in return for this money as peasants . . . at the Monastery of Saint Theodore eternally, and shall perform all manner of work for the monastery, and shall pay yearly the obrok which the superior of the Monastery of Saint Theodore and his brethren, or whosoever shall be superior after him, shall impose upon me.

[An agreement of 1676:]

I, Maksimko, son of Ivan Gorlov, with my wife, Aksinitsa, with my children . . . have taken from our master, the stol'nik Petr Savich Khitrovo, a loan of ten rubles in money for grain to be used for seeds and for our own consumption [*na siemena i na iemena*], for horses and for cows, and for household structures, and for various peasant household goods. And in return for this loan we shall live as peasants of our master Petr Savich in his pomest'e in the village of Muravlevo in the Karachovskii uezd, or wherever he orders us; and while we live as peasants of our master we shall plow the plowland for him, our master, and mow hay, and perform various work for the master, and pay taxes and obrok on an equal basis with my brethren the peasants, and not flee from him, my master, and not make off with that loan, and not mortgage [*zalozhit'sia*] myself to other owners of pomest'ia or patrimonies. And if we . . . flee from him, our master, with the loan, and mortgage ourselves to another owner of a pomest'e or patrimony, and if he, our master, discovers us after we have run away, then he, our master, shall take from us the full amount of the loan he has given us, and we shall thenceforth continue to be his peasants.

[An agreement of 1682:]

I, Fedor Ivanov, a free man [*guliashchii chelovek*], give upon myself this deed to the archimandrite Pitirim and the brethren of the Viaz'ma Monastery of Saint John the Baptist, which stands in the town [posad] of Viaz'ma,

to the effect that I, Fedka Ivanov, with my wife and children, shall live eternally as peasants of the Monastery of Saint John the Baptist. And I, Fedka, have taken with my wife and children . . . from the treasurer, the elder monk [*starets*] Sergei, a loan of ten rubles in money for horses, grain, and plowshares, scythes, and various peasant household goods. And henceforth, I, Fedka, with my wife and children, shall live eternally as peasants of the Monastery of Saint John the Baptist and shall not flee anywhere from the monastery and not make off with the loan. And while living as a peasant of the monastery I shall pay the various taxes to the state and to the monastery and perform various work for the monastery together with my brethren [peasants].

[An agreement of 1687:]

I, Semen, son of Ivan, have taken . . . from the widow Mar'ia Fedorovna a loan of ten rubles in money for various peasant household goods, and in return for that loan I shall live as a peasant of my mistress Mar'ia Fedorovna in her pomest'e in the village of Drachevo in the Berezopol'skii stan of the Nizhnii-Novgorod uezd, and while living there I shall plow the plowland and perform various work for my mistress, pay taxes to the great sovereign and tiaglo to the landowner on an equal basis with my brethren [peasants], [and I shall] not run away anywhere nor mortgage myself to anyone else; and if I flee and make off with that loan and mortgage myself to someone else, then she, my mistress, shall take from me the full amount of her loan, and I shall continue to be her peasant thenceforth. To which have witnessed . . .

VIII:46. MICHAEL'S DECREE ON RUNAWAYS, 1641

Tsar Michael's decree (apparently issued in 1641) concerning fugitive peasants is commonly considered to be one of the important steps in the development of serfdom.
   Reference: *AAE*, 3:496.

And the sovereign, tsar, and grand prince of all Russia Mikhail Fedorovich decreed and the boyars resolved that [fugitive peasants] of the sovereign, tsar, and grand prince of all Russia Mikhail Fedorovich [who have fled] during [the past] ten years are to be brought back into his sovereign crown villages [*dvortsovye sela*] and into the volosti inhabited by state

peasants [*chernye*], upon trial and investigation and according to the title-deeds . . . and that fugitive peasants and bobyli [who have fled] from Moscow [service] men of every rank [*chiny moskovskikh liudei*], and from provincial [*gorodovye*] dvoriane and deti boiarskie . . . during the same ten years are to be seized and brought back, to whomever they may belong.

VIII:47. AN ESTATE OWNER'S INSTRUCTIONS TO HIS STEWARD, JUNE 1649

Under the system of serfdom, the estate owner became in most respects the final authority for his peasants in judicial as well as other matters, and it was up to him to delegate appropriate responsibility, as he saw fit, to the steward (*prikazchik*) of each of his landed estates. Here is an excerpt from the orders given by the prominent boyar B. I. Morozov in June 1649 to one Liubim Osanov, the steward of one of his patrimonial estates in the Nizhnii-Novgorod uezd. Among other things, the orders show something of the continuing role of the peasant community.

Reference: A. I. Iakovlev, ed., *Akty khoziaistva boiarina B. I. Morozova*, 2 pts. (Moscow: AN SSSR, 1940–45), pt. 1, pp. 150-51. For other similar documents, see also, among other works, A. A. Novosel'skii, *Votchinnik i ego khoziaistvo v XVII v.* (Moscow: Gosizdat., 1929; reprinted The Hague, Mouton, 1968).

He, Liubim, shall supervise my peasants and bobyli in the newly settled hamlet of Sergach with its hamlets and new clearings [*pochinok*], and shall hold trials over them and administer justice among them without procrastination, without taking bribes, and without personal profit; and he shall hold trials together with the elder and with the sworn assistants [tseloval'niki] and with the elected peasant deputies [vybornye]. And [Liubim] shall order the peasants throughout my entire patrimonial estate to choose ten men for managing all my affairs, whomever they, the peasants, shall choose, good and sensible and honest peasants who shall manage my affairs together with Liubim; and [Liubim] shall obtain from all the peasants a certificate of election [vybor] of these peasant deputies, signed by the priest. And he, Liubim, shall hold trials over the peasants and bobyli justly, without holding an innocent man guilty or a guilty man innocent. And whenever he should go to [survey] the land or measure it [in the event of a dispute], he shall go together with the elder and with a sworn assistant and with the elected peasant deputies and see that justice is done, without favoritism and without taking bribes, not favoring anyone. . . . And if any peasants or bobyli should engage in thievery, and should receive thieves or them-selves begin to steal, Liubim—together with the elder, the sworn assistant, and the elected peasant deputies—shall punish such peasants at the assembly in front of all the peasants, so that all the peasants should know and see this. The first offense shall be overlooked, depending on the offense: if it is a minor offense, [the offender] shall be verbally reprimanded and shall obtain surety [i.e. one or more persons who assume liability for his future conduct]; if he should steal a second time, he shall be beaten with rods; and if anyone should steal a third time, such a man shall be beaten with the knout and shall obtain a firm written surety; as for those without surety who are known to be thieves, he, Liubim, shall put them in jail until they can obtain a firm surety and shall report this to Moscow [to the owner of the estate]. . . . And if anyone should begin selling tobacco, or buying it from another, or should begin to drink, he shall be beaten with rods without mercy and shall obtain surety; and if he should continue, he shall be beaten with the knout. . . . And Liubim shall give strict instructions to the peasants that the peasants and bobyli shall not travel anywhere without reporting it; if anyone should happen to travel anywhere, he shall [first] report to him, Liubim, and to the elder, and to the elected peasant deputies.

VIII:48. A DECREE PUNISHING A NOBLE, JUNE 7, 1669

The Muscovite government, having bound the serfs to the estate owners without regulating their reciprocal relations, did not, however, shrink from punishing the estate owners on occasion for abusing their privileges. One illustration is provided by this decree of June 7, 1669, here reproduced in its entirety.

Reference: *PSZRI*, 1st ser., 1:792.

The great sovereign has ordered that the stol'nik Prince Grigorii, son of Venedikt Obolenskii, be cast into prison because on June 6, Sunday of All Saints' Week, his bondmen [liudi] and peasants did common labor [*chernaia rabota*] on his homestead, and he, Prince Grigorii, used foul language.

VIII:49. A PETITION FROM MUSCOVITE MERCHANTS TO THE TSAR, 1646

Some of the problems of another class of the population may be seen in these passages from a petition submitted by the merchants of several Muscovite towns to the young Tsar Alexis.
Reference: *AAE*, 4:14-16.

To the tsar and grand prince of all Russia Aleksei Mikhailovich, your slaves and orphans, Sire, the humble gosti and the lowly trading men of the *gostinaia sotnia*, the *sukonnaia sotnia*, and the *chernye sotni* make petition. . . . Our complaint, Sire, is against the foreigners, the English and the Dutch merchants and those of Brabant and of Hamburg, who come to Moscow to trade.

. . .

The English merchants now come to the Muscovite state in parties of sixty or seventy or more; and they have built and bought for themselves many yards and warehouses in the town of Archangel and in Kholmogory, in Vologda, in Iaroslavl', in Moscow, and in other towns; and they have built mansions and cellars of stone; and now they remain in the Muscovite state without leaving, just as in their own country; and they no longer sell their wares to Russians or barter them for Russian wares in the town of Archangel but take their various wares to Moscow and to other towns themselves; and as soon as certain goods become expensive, they begin to sell those goods; but as for goods that are cheaper and not in demand, they keep those goods in their warehouses for two or three years, and when the price of those goods goes up, then they start selling them. And the Russian wares in the Muscovite state, which we, your slaves and orphans, used to exchange for their wares, they are now buying up themselves, conspiring among each other; and they send [Russian men] to make purchases in the towns and in the countryside, having concluded loan agreements and made debtors out of many poor and indebted Russians; and the Russians buy those goods and bring them to [the foreigners], and they take them out to their country without paying customs duties . . . and they cheat you out of your customs duties, Sire; and all the trade that we, your slaves and orphans, have carried on from time immemorial has been seized by the English foreigners; and as a result of this we, your slaves and orphans, have been deprived of our ancient trading pursuits, carried on from time immemorial, and we no longer journey to Archangel. And not only, Sire, have those foreigners left us, your slaves and orphans, without a livelihood, but they have reduced the entire Muscovite state to starvation, buying up meat and grain and all kinds of provisions in Moscow and other towns, Sire, and taking them out of the Muscovite state to their own country.

VIII:50. THE DECREE CONCERNING RESTRICTIONS ON ENGLISH MERCHANTS, JUNE 1, 1649

Reference: *PSZRI*, 1st ser., 1:163.

The sovereign tsar and grand prince Aleksei Mikhailovich of all Russia has decreed, and the boyars have resolved, that you Englishmen [must] betake yourselves beyond the seas with all your possessions; and that, to trade in all kinds of goods with the trading men of the Muscovite state, you may come from beyond the seas to the town of Archangel, but that you may not journey to Moscow and to other towns, either with or without merchandise.

. . . And you Englishmen are being prohibited from remaining in the Muscovite state for this reason: heretofore you carried on your trade in the Muscovite state on the strength of the sovereign's charters, which had been granted to you at the request of your sovereign, the English king Charles [I], out of brotherly friendship and love. But now it has become known to our great sovereign, His Majesty the tsar, that the entire English nation has committed a most evil deed, putting to death their sovereign, King Charles; and on account of that evil deed you have been prohibited from remaining in the Muscovite state.

And you Englishmen should heed the decree of His Majesty the tsar and should betake yourselves from the Muscovite state beyond the seas, with all your possessions.

VIII:51. THE NEW TRADE STATUTE OF APRIL 22, 1667

The New Trade Statute (Novotorgovyi Ustav) of 1667, as the following excerpts show, tried to provide means to counter the impact of Dutch, English, and other foreign merchants.
Reference: *PSZRI,* 1st ser., 1:651-53, 659-61.

The great sovereign tsar ... has ordered ... upon the petition of the gosti, the gostinaia sotnia, and the trading men of the *chernye slobody* in the Muscovite state, who have been greatly injured in trade with visiting foreigners ... that the trading men of the Muscovite state and the border towns of Great Russia shall carry on free trade, as is fitting; for in all neighboring states free and profitable trade is among the most important matters of state [and] is given every protection and maintained in freedom, for the collection of customs duties and the general prosperity of the entire nation. ...

1. In the town of Archangel on the [Northern] Dvina, a gost' shall sit with his associates in the customhouse during the fair; and the voevoda shall have no jurisdiction over the gost' and his associates in any matters involving customs duties and trade, lest the treasury of the great sovereign should incur losses in the collection [of customs duties].

2. All disputes in commercial matters between Russians and foreigners in the town of Archangel shall be settled in their entirety by the gost' and his associates in the customhouse. ...

12. As for the various goods that Russian men have to sell for money or to exchange: the gost' and his associates shall collect a customs tax of ten den'gi on each ruble of the actual selling price from all goods sold by weight [*veschii tovar*], and eight den'gi on each ruble from all goods not sold by weight. ...

56. If any foreigners should want to transport their goods from the town [of Archangel] to Moscow and to other towns, they shall pay in Archangel, in gold and *efimki* [foreign talers used as currency in Russia during the sixteenth and seventeenth centuries for want of a native coin of large denomination], a transport tax of one grivna on each ruble for all imported goods, since Russians and foreigners in Moscow pay fifths and tithes and various taxes, and perform services, while foreigners [in Archangel] pay nothing. ...

63. It shall be strictly forbidden for a foreigner to trade or sell or exchange any goods with [another] foreigner, since [thereby] in the customhouses the great sovereign suffers great loss in collecting [taxes] for his treasury, while Russian men suffer difficulties and impoverishment in their trade; and if foreigners should begin to trade among themselves, and this is discovered for certain, these goods shall be taken for the great sovereign. ...

83. In Moscow and in the towns no foreigners from any lands shall sell any imported goods in retail, nor shall they travel to fairs in any town themselves, nor send any salesmen, with their goods and money.

84. And if they, the foreigners, should begin selling their goods in retail, or begin traveling to fairs with their goods and money, those goods and [that] money shall be taken for the great sovereign.

VIII:52. A DECREE ON FOREIGN STYLES, AUGUST 6, 1675

This decree is one of many indications of the penetration of western European ways before Peter the Great.
Reference: *PSZRI,* 1st ser., 1:967.

The great sovereign has ordered that the stol'niki, and striapchie, and Moscow dvoriane and zhil'tsy be told of his, the sovereign's decree, that they may not imitate the customs of Germans and other foreigners, cut the hair on their heads, [and] likewise wear costumes, coats, and hats of foreign model, or allow their servants to wear similar [clothing]. And if in the future anyone should cut his hair and wear costumes on the foreign model, or if his servants are found wearing such costumes, he shall suffer the wrath of the great sovereign, and from higher rank shall be demoted to lower rank.

VIII:53. THE CHARTER OF THE MOSCOW ACADEMY, 1682

The Moscow (Slavonic-Greek-Latin) Academy received its founding charter from Tsar Fedor Alekseevich in 1682 but did not actually begin operating until 1685, when two Greek scholars, the brothers Ioannikii and Sofronii Likhud, arrived. Along with the regulations included in the following excerpts, the charter (in articles 13-15) also prescribed that those guilty of heretical teachings or blasphemy against Orthodoxy were liable to be burned.

Reference: Nikolai I. Novikov, ed., *Drevniaia rossiiskaia vivliofika*, 2d ed., 12 vols (Moscow, 1788-91), 6:402, 405-07, 408, 411-12.

An academy shall be founded; and in it we wish to implant the seeds of wisdom, that is, the civil and spiritual sciences, beginning with grammar, poetics, rhetoric, dialectic, rational, natural, and moral philosophy, and embracing even theology, which teaches of divine things and moral purification.

Thus the academy in its entirety, that is, in all its schools, shall include the teaching of canon and civil law and all the other liberal arts. And in it all the officers [i.e. members] of the academy shall be registered, and shall be recognized, installed, and confirmed upon our tsarist discretion, upon counsel with our pious father the most holy patriarch; and [the officers] shall be held inviolate in their entirety. The rector [*bliustitel'*] of this [academy] and its teachers shall institute appropriate regulations enjoining all who search for wisdom to come hither, and eat the bread of the divine word, and drink the wine of wisdom, gratuitously and without any payment.

And therefore, to secure and confirm for all time to come this, our praiseworthy tsarist act, and to safeguard our Eastern Orthodox faith from all heretics and heresies, by this our tsarist word [and] with God's help, we institute inalterably and confirm eternally [the following regulations].

In our academy there shall be a rector and teachers, pious and of pious parentage, who have been raised in the Eastern Orthodox Greek faith of the Russian and Greek nations.

. . .

And if learned men come into our realm from the Lithuanian land and from Little Russia and from other lands, wishing to become rectors and teachers here in our schools, and describing themselves as being pious and of pious parentage and raised in the Eastern Orthodox faith: without obtaining authentic information about them, and without the testimony of trustworthy pious men, their word shall not be trusted and they shall not be appointed rectors or teachers.

. . .

This school which we, the great sovereign, have established shall be free and open to men of every rank, station, and age, without any discrimination, as long as they come to study the Eastern Orthodox Christian faith; and all the pious arts the church has blessed shall be [taught] in it.

. . .

If any industrious youths should seek to extract diligently this most precious treasure, that is, wisdom [philosophy], grammar, and other liberal arts, like gold from the bowels of the earth, out of writings in various dialects and particularly in Slavonic, Helleno-Greek, Polish, and Latin: they shall receive a worthy reward for their diligence in study from us, the great sovereign, upon the attestation of the rector and teachers of the schools. And upon completion of the [study of the] liberal arts they shall be graciously granted a rank appropriate to their intellect and shall be granted our special bountiful tsarist favor as wise men. And children of men of sundry rank who have not learned the liberal arts, unless they are of noble birth, shall not be permitted [to hold] our, the sovereign's, ranks as stol'niki, or striapchie, or other ranks that we, the great sovereign, confer upon nobles, for any attainments except learning, and likewise military deeds and other acts of state which augment our sovereign possessions and enlarge the state.

VIII:54. OLEARIUS IN MUSCOVY, 1633-1639

Adam Olearius (ca. 1599-1671), secretary of the missions sent by Holstein to Muscovy in 1633, 1636, and 1639, left an account that was first published in Schleswig in 1647. It quickly achieved wide popularity. Olearius did an expanded second edition in 1656, and in the ensuing decades of the seventeenth century his work appeared in more than a dozen editions in German, French, Dutch, and Italian. His role in forming European impressions of Russia was great. The following excerpts show something of the scope and nature of his descriptions. They also suggest why his work, although translated into Russian in the late 1600s, remained unpublished in that language until 1861.

Reference: Adam Olearius, *Der Welt-beruehmten Adami Olearii Reise-Beschreibungen . . . nach Musskau und Persien,* 4th ed. (Hamburg, 1696), pp. 93, 98, 100, 102-03, 105-07, 111-13, 143, 158-59, 166. Since the preparation of these excerpts there has appeared a new English translation: *The Travels of Olearius in Seventeenth-Century Russia,* trans. and ed. by Samuel H. Baron (Stanford: Stanford University Press, 1967).

There lives in Moscow a prince, Nikita Ivanovich Romanov by name, the highest born and richest after the tsar, whose close kinsman he is, a merry nobleman and a friend of German music. He has a great fondness for all foreigners, especially the Germans, and even for their attire; so that he had Polish and German clothes made . . . which he would wear sometimes himself, for pleasure, when riding forth on a hunt, regardless of what the patriarch would say. And even in matters of religion, when the patriarch disapproved of anything he did, he would give him curt and willful answers. . . .

If the Russians be considered in respect to their character, customs, and way of life, they are justly to be counted among the barbarians.

. . .

The vice of drunkenness is so common in this nation, among people of every station, clergy and laity, high and low, men and women, old and young, that when they are seen now and then lying about in the streets, wallowing in the mud, no attention is paid to it, as something habitual. If a cart driver comes upon such a drunken pig whom he happens to know, he shoves him onto his cart and drives him home, where he is paid his fare. No one ever refuses an opportunity to drink and to get drunk, at any time and in any place, and usually it is done with vodka.

. . .

The Russians being naturally tough and born, as it were, for slavery, they must be kept under a harsh and strict yoke and must be driven to do their work with clubs and whips, which they suffer without impatience, because such is their station, and they are accustomed to it. Young and half-grown fellows sometimes come together on certain days and train themselves in fisticuffs, to accustom themselves to receiving blows, and, since habit is second nature, this makes blows given

as punishment easier to bear. Each and all, they are slaves and serfs.

. . .

Because of slavery and their rough and hard life, the Russians accept war readily and are well suited to it. On certain occasions, if need be, they reveal themselves as courageous and daring soldiers.

. . .

Although the Russians, especially the common populace, living as slaves under a harsh yoke, can bear and endure a great deal out of love for their masters, yet if the pressure is beyond measure, then it can be said of them: Patientia saepe laesa fit tandem furor [Patience, often wounded, finally turned into fury]. A dangerous indignation results, turned not so much against their sovereign as against the lower authorities, especially if the people have been much oppressed by them and by their supporters and have not been protected by the higher authorities. And once they are aroused and enraged, it is not easy to appease them. Then, disregarding all dangers that may ensue, they resort to every kind of violence and behave like madmen.

. . .

They own little; most of them have no feather beds; they lie on cushions, straw, mats, or their clothes; they sleep on benches and, in winter, like the non-Germans [i.e. natives] in Livonia, upon the oven, which serves them for cooking and is flat on the top; here husband, wife, children, servants, and maids huddle together. In some houses in the countryside we saw chickens and pigs under the benches and the ovens.

Russians are not used to delicate food and dainties; their daily food consists of porridge, turnips, cabbage, and cucumbers, fresh and pickled, and in Moscow mostly of big salt fish which stink badly, because of the thrifty use of salt, yet are eaten with relish. Their fish-market therefore can be smelled long before it is seen or set foot upon. Because of splendid pastures they have good meat—mutton, beef, and pork; but since on account of their religion they have nearly as many fasts as days when they eat meat, they are used to coarse and bad food, which is also less expensive. Yet they know how to prepare such a variety of dishes from fish, pastry, and vegetables that one can well do without meat.

· · ·

The artisans, who need little for their simple life, are commonly able to earn enough, by their handicrafts, for food and a cup of vodka, and can support themselves and their families. They are eager to learn, and what they have seen of German crafts they imitate well, and in the course of a few years they have learned from them a great many things they had not known before. Therefore they are now selling wares of better workmanship and at higher prices than ever before. In particular I was surprised by the goldsmiths, who are now able to chase silver vessels with raised work, and rather well shaped, as skillfully as any German craftsman.

· · ·

The Russians can endure extreme heat. In the bathhouse they stretch out on benches and let themselves be beaten and rubbed with bunches of birch twigs and wisps of bast (which I could not stand); and when they are hot and red all over and so exhausted that they can bear it no longer in the bathhouse, men and women rush outdoors naked and pour cold water over their bodies; in winter they even wallow in the snow and rub their skin with it as if it were soap; then they go back into the hot bathhouse. And since bathhouses are usually near rivers and brooks, they can throw themselves straight from the hot into the cold bath.

· · ·

Such a way of bathing we observed not only in Russia but also in Livonia and Ingria, where the common folk, in particular the Finns, in the fiercest cold of winter rush out of the bath-house into the streets to rub their bodies with snow and then rush back into the hot bath; and the sudden change from hot to cold does not harm them, since their constitution has been used to it since childhood. Therefore the Finns and the Letts, like the Russians, are tough, strong, and hardy people who can well endure both cold and heat.

· · ·

Generally people in Russia are healthy and reach old age; they are rarely ill, and if one of the common people is bedridden, be it with burning fever, the best cure for him is vodka and garlic; yet the highborn are beginning to seek the advice of German doctors and to use proper drugs.

· · ·

Generally noble families, even the small nobility, rear their daughters in secluded chambers, keeping them hidden from out-siders; and a bridegroom is not allowed to have a look at his bride until he receives her in the bridal chamber. Therefore some happen to be deceived, being given a misshapen and sickly one instead of a fair one, and some-times a kinswoman or even a maidservant in-stead of a daughter; of which there have been examples even among the highborn. No wonder therefore that often they live together like cats and dogs and that wife-beating is so common among Russians.

· · ·

As for the government of the Russians, it is a monarchia dominica et despotica (as the political theorists call it), where the sovereign, that is, the tsar or the grand prince who has obtained the crown by right of succession, rules the entire land alone, and all the people are his subjects, and where the nobles and princes no less than the common folk—towns-people and peasants—are his serfs and slaves, whom he rules and treats as a master treats his servants.

· · ·

As for the present grand prince, while he has the same power as former tyrants to use force against his subjects and their property, he does not do so; although some still write as if he did, perhaps on the authority of old writers, such as Herberstein, Jovius, Guagnino, and others, who wrote about the miserable condition of the Russians as it existed once under the iron rule of the tyrant [Ivan IV]. Much is being written about the Russians that is no longer true today, doubtless because of the general change in the times, the govern-ment, and the people themselves. The present ruling grand prince is a God-fearing man who, like his father, would not let any of his peas-ants sink into poverty.

· · ·

Inasmuch as the Russians in their schools learn to read and to write solely in their own language and at best in Slavonic, no Russian, whether priest or layman, highborn or lowborn, understands a single word of Greek or Latin.

But now they are planning, at the insistence of the patriarch and the grand prince, to make their youth learn Greek and Latin—which is rather surprising; and they have already established a Greek and Latin school close to the patriarch's court; it is supervised and directed by a Greek named Arsenius.

. . .

In the Kremlin and in the city there are a great many churches, chapels, and monasteries, both within and without the city walls, over two thousand in all. This is so because every nobleman who has some fortune has a chapel built for himself, and most of them are of stone. The stone churches are round and vaulted inside.

. . .

They allow neither organs nor any other musical instruments in their churches, saying: Instruments that have neither souls nor life cannot praise God.

. . .

In their churches there hang many bells, sometimes five or six, the largest not over two hundredweights. They ring these bells to summon people to church, and also when the priest during mass raises the chalice. In Moscow, because of the multitude of churches and chapels, there are several thousand bells, which during the divine service create such a clang and din that one unaccustomed to it listens in amazement.

. . .

The Muscovites tolerate and get on well with all kinds of nationalities and religions, such as Lutherans, Calvinists, Armenians, Tatars, Persians, and Turks. But they do not wish to have anything to do with Papists and Jews; and there is no greater insult to a Russian than to be called a Jew, although many among the merchantry rather resemble Jews. Lutherans and Calvinists have been well received so far, not only here and there all over the country but also in Moscow at court, on account of their vast trade and dealings with the Russians, and also because of their services to His Majesty the tsar, who employs them both at home and in the field; and there are now about a thousand of them living in Moscow. Everyone is allowed to worship openly in his church according to his own rite.

VIII:55. KRIZANIC ON RUSSIA IN THE 1660s

Juraj (Iurii or George) Krizhanich (Krizanic, 1617-82) was a Croatian Catholic priest and missionary who went to the Ukraine in 1659 and thence to Moscow in 1661 with the aim of promoting the union of Moscow and Rome. Before long he was sent "on state service" to Tobol'sk, where he remained in what amounted to exile until 1676. Shortly thereafter he succeeded in leaving the country. While in Siberia Krizhanich wrote, among other things, a description of the Russian state in the middle of the seventeenth century. Some of his ideas are indicated in the following passages. His often recurring "we" usually means the Slavs in general.
Reference: Iurii Krizhanich, *Russkoe gosudarstvo v polovine XVII veka*, ed. P. Bezsonov (Moscow, 1859), pp. 167-68, 169, 179, 181, 207, 215, 295, 345, 374, 375. See also Iurii Krizhanich, *Politika (tekst i perevody)*, comp. V. V. Zelenin, trans. and commentary A. D. Gol'dberg, ed. M. N. Tikhomirov (Moscow: Nauka, 1965).

A reply to the barking of foreigners. . . . All those who write anything about the Russians, or any other Slavic people, seem to write foolish, caustic tales rather than the truth. They exaggerate our defects, imperfections, and innate failings and make them seem ten times greater than they actually are; and where there are no evils at all, they invent them and lie. And they write shameful lying tales about us too. Here is one: It would seem, allegedly, that the great sovereigns of Russia were obliged by compulsion and by treaty to greet on foot the Crimean envoy [of the khan of the Crimean Tatars] riding on a horse, and to serve him mare's milk with their own hands as a token of honor; and while drinking, the envoy would purposely spill milk on his horse's mane, and the great sovereign was allegedly obliged to lick the milk from the mane with his tongue. These fine writers cite and report such fables not as a joke, but as a true story.

. . .

You [foreigners] scorn our temperate,

modest way of life, and consider this to be mere coarseness, barbarism, and slovenliness. But as for your own excesses and luxury and effeminate life, you regard this as if it all came from heaven, and as if there were nothing wrong with it. But if we indulged in your excesses and concern for the body and softness, if we sunk ourselves into feather beds, if we slept until noon, and if we ate viands with a thousand different sauces, then you would scorn us prodigiously for being immoderate and dissipated.

. . .

Our great national misfortune is our intemperate use of power. Our people do not know how to observe moderation in anything, nor do they know how to follow the golden mean; always they indulge in extremes and in excess. With us power is sometimes boundlessly dissolute, arbitrary, disorderly; at other times it is boundlessly strict, harsh, and cruel. . . .

Another of our grievous misfortunes is that other peoples, Greeks, Italians, Germans, Tatars, involve us in [the affairs of] their countries, involve us in their quarrels, and sow disharmony in our midst. And we in our foolishness allow them to lead us astray, and we fight for others, and make foreign wars our own, and come to hate each other, and fight [each other] to the death, and brother drives out brother without any need or reason. We trust the foreigners in everything, and keep friendship and faith with them; but we are ashamed of ourselves and of our own people, and turn away from them.

. . .

That which the Greeks call xenomania, and we call the foreign craze [chuzhebesie], is a senseless love for foreign things and peoples: an unwarranted, senseless trust in foreigners. This deadly sickness (or infectious disease) has infected our entire nation. It brings untold harm and shame, from which our entire nation (on either side of the Danube) has suffered and continues to suffer as a result of the foreign craze. That is, we trust foreigners too much and make friends and intermarry with them; and we let them do what they please in our land. Truly all the evils we endure flow from that source: that we mix too much with foreigners and trust them too much.

. . .

Under the guise of commerce, the foreigners reduce us to extreme impoverishment. . . . Here in Russia (except for the tsar's treasury) one cannot see or hear of any riches anywhere; instead there is wretched, empty-handed poverty everywhere. All the wealth of this realm and all the fat and sweetness of this land are carried away by foreign tradesmen or thieves, or are consumed by them as we look on passively.

Under the pretext of being experts and of serving us, [foreigners] likewise draw out all our possessions: for they work as doctors, own mines, [and] make glass, weapons, powder, and other things. And these experts will never teach our own natives, so that they may continue to reap all the profit themselves.

. . .

And what is the situation here in Russia? Foreign tradesmen, Germans, Greeks, and Bokharans, rake in all the wealth and products of this realm for themselves. Everywhere they own warehouses and act as tax farmers and engage in various trades and transactions. They travel freely throughout the land and buy our goods at the lowest prices; while they bring in to us many useless [but] expensive wares: beads, precious stones, and Venetian glass. . . . And finally, being sly, they cheat our tradesmen out of large sums of money.

. . .

The Russian people have acquired a bad reputation among some peoples, who write that the Russians are descended from cattle and donkeys and that they can do nothing worthwhile unless driven with sticks and cudgels, like donkeys. Thus writes Olearius. But this is an outright lie. . . . And as for the fact that at present many of the Russians act not for the sake of honor but for fear of punishment, this is caused by the despotic rule which makes not only honor but life itself hateful to them. The truth is evident: If the German people or anyone else lived under such a despotic rule, they would have morals similar to ours or even worse.

. . .

It is a foolish and flagrant lie that Tsar Ivan, or Vladimir the Great, was born of the race of Augustus. For at the time of Vladimir's ancestor [Riurik], that is, around the year A.D. 800, there were neither Romans, nor Electors [Kurfürsten], nor any sort of Germans at all in Prussia.

In the first place, Prussia was never a Roman province, nor were the neighboring lands even closer [to Rome], that is, Pomerania and Silesia

In the second place, the line of Augustus soon died out even in Rome—properly speaking, with Augustus himself. For Augustus did not have a son of his own, but only a stepson, Tiberius, who ruled after him. . . . Nero died without progeny, and after Nero no one on earth could call himself the kinsman of Augustus—save for Tsar Ivan alone, fifteen hundred years after Nero.

. . .

At the present time this glorious realm suffers from two great and exceeding national evils or injuries, at the hands of two peoples, the Crimean [Tatars] and the Germans. Somehow they have both subjected Russia to their power and make us pay tribute and extortions, the Crimeans by force, the Germans by cunning. And they have reduced our sovereign, the most powerful and glorious tsar, to such a state that he sits between them in such a fashion as if he were a collector of revenues for them. All the

best that this land produces goes in part to the Crimea, in part to the German land. And the greed of these peoples knows no bounds; as a result this realm has perforce turned into a savage tyranny, and into a merciless, inhuman extortion. Which of these two evils causes greater harm to the sovereign tsar and to the entire nation, I cannot judge. But this I do avow: that the injury caused by the Germans is more shameful and disgraceful than that caused by the Crimeans.

. . .

And [the Germans] themselves have a saying that I have heard many times from these same Germans, in which they boast and avow: "Whoever wants to get his bread for nothing should come to Moscow." And so, in accordance with their saying, they keep coming to visit and feast here; and those of our people who happen to be with them they simply call dogs and pigs and the names of various cattle, and frequently beat them besides.

D. RELIGIOUS AFFAIRS

VIII:56. DOCUMENTS ON CHURCH SELF-GOVERNMENT IN NORTHERN RUSSIA, 1657-1697

The following documents illustrate some of the ways in which various local church affairs were handled in northern Russia in the seventeenth century.

Reference: *RIB*, vol. 14, cols. 420-21 [Nov. 6, 1657, document]; Arkheograficheskaia Komissiia, *Akty iuridicheskogo byta*, vol. 1, cols. 11-12 [1684]; *RIB*, vol. 12, cols. 711-12 [Feb. 4, 1686], 1070-71 [Dec. 25, 1692], 1285-87 [1696-97].

[A mir's certificate of election of a priest, November 6, 1657:]

I, the church elder of the [Church of the] Archangels in Shenkursk Fort [*ostrog*] . . . and the peasants of the Archangels' parish . . . the peasants of the Epiphany parish . . . the peasants of the Transfiguration parish . . . [and] the peasants of Saint Nicholas's parish . . . have chosen and elected for the Cathedral Church of the Archangels Michael and Gabriel, and others in Shenkursk Fort, and for the [Church of the] Annunciation of the Holy Virgin, and [the Church of] the Miracle Worker Blessed Father Sergei of Radonezh, and for the territory of our former priest Mark Vlas'ev, elected by the mir to the Cathedral Church of the Archangels, his son, the priest Kirill Markov of [the Church of] the Transfiguration. And in accordance with this, the mir's certificate of election, the priest Kirill is to be the priest of these churches of God . . . in place of his father, and he is to

officiate his weeks in full [he had shared his duties with another priest] in the churches of God, and to visit the sick and the women in childbirth throughout the mir, his parish, and to come [to his parishioners] with prayers, without refusing, and to devote himself to the services and to everything connected with God's churches; and he is to have . . . the plowland and meadowland . . . of the Chernobaevskaia hamlet of the Church of the Archangels . . . and all the church income his father, the priest Mark Vlas'ev, had, and he is to receive the same salary [*ruga*] as heretofore. . . . And the priest Kirill Markov has been given a certificate of election to this effect. The certificate of election was written by the clerk-psalmist [*d'iachok*] of the Church of the Archangels, Gerasimko Onsiforov, in the year 166 [1657], on the sixth day of November.

[A certificate of election of a parish priest, 1684:]

We, the parishioners of the village of Kozmo-

dem'iansk, the . . . crown peasants of the
great sovereign in the volost' of Kozmodem'iansk in the Poshekhonsk uezd . . . and
all the parishioners of the parish of the Church
of Saints Cosmas and Damian . . . in the village
of Kozmodem'iansk. By the will of God, our
spiritual father the priest Nester Vasil'ev has
become a widower; his wife has departed this
life, and he has left for the Monastery of
Saint Nicholas in Vykksin'ia; and we, the
parishioners, taking counsel among ourselves
at the communal assembly, have chosen the
priest Samson Mikhailov for the church of the
uncovetous doctors [besrebreniki] and
miracle workers Cosmas and Damian . . . and
we, the parishioners, have all chosen him, the
priest Samson Mikhailov, because he is a good
and gentle man, does not engage in any
knavery, is not a drunkard, [and] shuns any
evil doing; and we, the people of the commune [mirskie liudi], have made him, the
priest Samson Mikhailov, our choice. And the
election [document] was written in accordance
with the will of the parishioners, by the church
clerk-psalmist.

[Agreement between church elders and a
priest, February 4, 1686:]
    In the year [7]194, on the fourth day of
February, Averkii Semenov Krotov and
Dmitrii Emel'ianov Slobotskikh, the church
elders of the Church of the Holy Prophet
Elijah, of the Kotovalskaia volost', of the
Sukhonskii taxpaying [chernyi] stan, have
resolved [to appoint] Matfei, son of Ivan
Shergin, to that church. And he is to be with
us in that church, and to labor and officiate,
and he is not to fail to hold services in the
church. And we have agreed upon a salary for
the priest Matfei of half a chetverik [one-
eighth of a chetvert'] of rye and the same
amount of oats, and each year he is to mow
himself the lower hayfields on the Striga
River from the meadow set aside for the
church. . . . And he is to visit the parish sick
with every appropriate ministration, without
laziness. And he, Matfei, is to live in the
church enclosure; and we have resolved to
erect a new dwelling [for him]. To this effect
we, the elders and parishioners, have given
him a certificate of election [izliub]. Written
by Senka Romanov Gogolev, clerk of the said
church, by order of the elders and parishioners.

[A certificate of election of church elders,
December 25, 1692:]
    In the year 7201 [1692], on the twenty-
fifth day of December, by order of the most
reverend Aleksandr, archbishop of Velikii
Ustiug and Tot'ma. . . . The parishioners of
the Church of the Transfiguration of the
Savior, of the Shchekinskii pogost . . . and all
the peasants of that parish, the entire mir
being consulted, have chosen and elected
Vanka Petrov Permitinovykh [and] Kuzemka
Avramov Tokmakovykh, peasants of good
repute, prosperous, and not drunkards, as
church elders for the Church of the Savior in
their parish. In accordance with this, our communal certificate of election, the church elders
are to administer the church treasury of the
church of God, and to supervise the church of
God, and to work zealously for its welfare, and
to enter in the books all income and expenditure, specifically by item, faithfully, in keeping with the commandments of the Gospel.
To this effect the elders have been given this
certificate of election. The certificate of election was written by Mitka Ivanov D'iakonov,
church clerk, by order of the people of the
mir.
    [On the reverse:] In the year 7201 [1693],
on the third day of January, the most reverend
archbishop, having heard this certificate of
election, directed that his decree [confirming
the appointment] be given them and that the
certificate of election be registered.

[Excerpts from a lawsuit concerning complaints against an archbishop, 1697. The dispute
was between Aleksandr, archbishop of Velikii
Ustiug, and the chief public elders of the uezd
(vseuezdnye zemskie starosty) of Velikii Ustiug,
regarding the complaints made to the tsar against
the archbishop by the mir of Velikii Ustiug.]
    On the eleventh day of August [1697], acting
on the petition of the archbishop described abov
dated August 2, Fedka Betiukov, elder for the
previous year, was questioned a second time. At
the examination, Fedka repeated what he had
said at the first examination, namely, that in the
previous year, 204 [1696], during Fedka's
tenure of office, while he was a chief elder of
the uezd, the elected best men of the volosti,
with the general consent of the mir and acting
upon information from the peasants of the
volosti, wrote to the great sovereign a petition
of grievances against the most reverend Aleksand

archbishop of Velikii Ustiug and Tot'ma, and affixed their signatures to it; and he, Fedka, affixed his signature to that petition upon the resolution of the people of the mir, and he could not refuse to affix his signature to that petition and disobey the people of the mir; and they wrote the petition at an assembly, according to what each one had said, and the petition was not written in haste, for the people of the mir never put anything into a petition from the mir without first making an investigation and establishing the truth. And which wrongs and grievances were mentioned in the petition, and where, when, and against whom the archbishop and his men did perpetrate offenses, he cannot remember definitely without the people of the mir; this is known exactly to the people of the mir in those volosti in which such wrongs and extortions took place. . . . And in the uezd administration building [*uezdnaia izba*] they write all kinds of papers, in addition to drawing up formal documents; and any one of the literate people of the mir who happens to be in the uezd administration building—Grishka Mylnikov for one, if he happens to be in the administration building—writes regarding the needs of the mir at the request of the people of the mir, but does not compose anything on his own; and of the best people of the mir there is none more experienced than Grishka, with whom one could consult regarding the affairs of the mir, because he, Grishka, lives not far from the administration building and the people of the mir often call him, and that is why Grishka knows the affairs of the mir; and in the mir it is altogether impossible for Grishka or for the public elder, or for anybody to write or do anything without the endorsement of the people of the mir; and the clerk Iakushko Drushkov was not elected, but hired, and he too writes all kinds of papers and petitions by order of the mir, and not on his own responsibility.

VIII:57. TSAR ALEXIS'S LETTER TO NIKON, MAY 1652

Patriarch Joseph having died in April 1652, Tsar Alexis favored Nikon, then metropolitan of Novgorod and Velikie Luki, as his successor in the patriarchal see. The tsar's sentiments at that time are reflected in these words he wrote to Nikon in May.

Reference: *AAE*, 4:76-77.

To the excellent and steadfast shepherd and preceptor of our souls and bodies, the merciful, gentle, kindhearted, [and] meek lover and confidant of Christ, and zealous leader of the spiritual flock. O stout fighter and toiler of the Heavenly King! O holy prelate, my beloved companion and friend! Pray for me, sinner that I am, and may your holy prayers keep me from sinking into the mire of my sins. I put my faith in your blameless, meek, and saintly life, and I write to you, who shine brightly as a prelate—for, as the sun shines upon the entire universe, so do you shine upon our entire realm, because of your worthy life and good works—to our great lord who prays for us, the most holy and most illustrious metropolitan Nikon of Novgorod and Velikie Luki, our own friend both spiritual and worldly. We want to know of your episcopal welfare and how God protects you, light of our soul; and if you wish to know of us, we, through the grace of God and your episcopal blessing, are indeed called the true Christian tsar; although because of my evil [and] hateful deeds, I am unworthy to be a dog, let alone a tsar; and though a sinner, I call myself the servant of the Light that created me. Through your holy prayers, to this day . . . God has granted good health to all of us, to ourselves, and our tsaritsa, and our sisters, and our daughter, and our entire state. . . . And now, great lord, hear my entreaty. For the sake of the Lord, hasten to return to us so that there may be elected to the patriarchate a man known to God [*Theognost*: the tsar is referring to Nikon himself, not wishing to name him directly], for without you we shall not undertake anything at all. I ask your blessing and your forgiveness [for myself] and for the entire state, and I send you my warmest greetings. . . . I have signed this with my own hand, God's servant Tsar Aleksei of all Russia.

VIII:58. THE KORMCHAIA KNIGA ON CHURCH AND STATE, 1653

The *Kormchaia kniga* is a translation into Slavic of a variant of the Byzantine Nomocanon or digest of church canons and civil laws. The *Kormchaia* circulated in manuscripts in Russia from the thirteenth century onward. It was printed in Moscow in 1650 under Patriarch Joseph and then revised and printed anew under Patriarch Nikon in 1653. (The Old Believers recognize only the 1650 edition as valid.) This excerpt, included also in earlier versions of the *Kormchaia,* is from the preface to Emperor Justinian's Sixth Novel. The concept set forth here was one of the foundations of Nikon's ideas on the "symphony" of church and state.

Reference: *Kormchaia kniga* (Moscow, 1787; republished from the edition of 1653), pt. 1, p. 7.

Of all God's gifts to man, given to him from on high through God's love for mankind, the greatest are the priesthood and the tsardom: the one serving the divine, the other ruling and caring for the human: both proceed from one and the same source in enhancing human life; and therefore, nothing brings greater benefit to a realm than the honor paid a prelate.

VIII:59. NIKON CONCERNING THE POWERS OF THE CHURCH, CA. 1663

Nikon's views on the relationship between the state and the church were set forth in a lengthy statement he wrote sometime after August 15, 1662, entitled "A Refutation or Demolishment by the Most Humble Nikon, Patriarch by the Grace of God, of the Questions Which the Boyar Simeon Streshnev Addressed to Paisius Ligarid, Metropolitan of Gaza, and Paisius's Answers." These brief excerpts convey something of his argument.

Reference: Nikolai F. Kapterev, *Patriarkh Nikon i Tsar' Aleksei Mikhailovich,* 2 vols. (Sergiev Posad: Tip. Sviato-Troitskoi Sergievoi Lavry, 1909-12), 2:128-29, 181, 183. There is a full translation of Nikon's "Refutation" in W. Palmer, *The Patriarch and the Tsar,* 6 vols. (London, 1871-76), vol. 1.

[Replying to the question whether the spiritual power is higher than the secular] Nikon says, "As opinions are divided, we shall first take the view of those learned in the canon law, who assert that the tsar's authority must be subordinate to episcopal authority, to which Almighty God has entrusted the keys of the kingdom of heaven and given, on earth, the power to bind and to loose; moreover, episcopal authority is spiritual, while that given to the tsar is of this world; and matters of heavenly, that is, spiritual, authority stand far above those of this world or of temporal [authority]. Hence, it is very clear that the tsar must be lower than the prelate and obedient to him, for I also say that the clergy are chosen people and are anointed by the Holy Ghost. And if all Christians owe obedience to the prelates, such obedience is owed still more by him who with his sword forces the insubordinate to obey the prelates. ... When the Lord God Almighty created heaven and earth, he ordered the two luminaries, the sun and the moon, which move across [heaven], to shine upon the earth. The sun represents episcopal authority, while the moon represents the authority of the tsar; for the sun illuminates the day, as the prelate enlightens the soul, while the lesser luminary illuminates the night, which is the body. As the moon receives its light from the sun ... so it is with the tsar. He is consecrated, anointed, and crowned by a prelate, from whom he must thereupon receive his perfect light, to wit, his most rightful power and authority. Throughout Christendom the difference between these two persons is like unto that between the sun and the moon; for the authority of the prelate is over the day, that is, over souls, while the authority of the tsar is over the things of this world; and that authority lies in this: the tsar's sword must be ready against the enemies of the Orthodox faith; if the prelates and all the clergy demand that he defend them from all unrighteousness and violence, then the civil [authority] must obey the spiritual [authority]. ... In spiritual matters which are of concern to all, the supreme bishop [i.e. the patriarch] is higher than the tsar, and all the Orthodox owe obedience to the bishop because he is our father in the Orthodox faith, and the Orthodox church is entrusted to him.

· · ·

The clergy is a more honored and higher authority than the state itself. ... The throne of the clergy has been erected in heaven. Who says this? The Heavenly King Himself: "Whatsoever you shall bind on earth shall be bound in heaven. ..." Thus it is the tsars who are anointed by the priests and not the priests by the tsars.

· · ·

In ancient as in modern times, the priesthood does not come from men, nor is it created by men, but [comes] from God himself, and not from tsars; for the tsar's authority was and still is derived from the priesthood, as the rites of the tsar's coronation testify. The priesthood is everywhere honored above the tsardom. . . . Priestly authority excels civil power as heaven excels earth, yea, and much more so. For our [priestly] abode is in heaven, and our life is hid there in spirit with God. . . . Therefore, those who have this authority are honored above princes, local [rulers], and even those who have been invested with regal insignia. . . . As a drop of rain is to a big cloud, such is the dimension of earth as compared with the heavens, and even so does the tsardom diminish when compared with the priesthood.

VIII:60. THE RUSSIAN CHURCH COUNCIL ON AVVAKUM, MAY 13, 1666

In the spring of 1666 a Russian Church Council dealt with the question of the reforms instituted under Nikon and the conservative response of Archpriest Avvakum (1620 or 1621 to 1682; see below) and others.
Reference: *DAI*, 5:448.

[Proceedings, May 13, 1666:]

There appeared [before the council] the mendacious Avvakum, former archpriest of Iurevets on the Volga, who in past years had been sentenced to imprisonment in Siberia for schism, sedition, and false teachings, was released from there by the mercy of the scepter bearer [the tsar], but persisted in propagating his evil designs and false doctrines orally and in writing, thus leading simple folk astray and tearing them away from the one holy Eastern Orthodox Catholic church. He condemned in writing the correction of the holy creed, the joining of the first three fingers for making the sign of the cross, the correction as well as the correctors of [ecclesiastical] books, [and] the coordination of church singing [i.e. between the choir and the priest]; he also calumniated the Moscow priests, saying that they do not believe in the incarnation and resurrection of Christ . . . and without fearing God, he wrote many similar falsehoods and calumnies, to which we may finally add his seditious words in forbidding Orthodox Christians to take communion from priests who officiate according to the newly corrected books. On all the foregoing [matters] he was admonished by the holy council and did not submit; on the contrary, calumniator and slanderer that he is, he added hatred to hatred by rebuking the entire holy council to its face, for not being Orthodox; thus the council judged rightfully in depriving him of his sacerdotal dignity and pronouncing anathema upon him. . . . Later he was again urged to repent, but all efforts and hopes proved futile, and he was sentenced by a secular court [*gradskii sud*] to confinement in the fortress of Pustozersk.

VIII:61. THE CHURCH COUNCIL'S DECISION ON NIKON, DECEMBER 12, 1666

In the autumn of 1666 began the famous Church Council of 1666–67, attended not only by Russian but also by Greek prelates, including two patriarchs—Paisius, patriarch of Alexandria, and Macarius, patriarch of Antioch. On one of the matters before it, the question of Nikon, the council issued a decision dated December 12, 1666, and worded in part as follows.
Reference: *PSZRI,* 1st ser., 1:629, 631.

In the name of the Father and of the Son and of the Holy Ghost, amen. Whereas Nikon, the former patriarch of Moscow, did offend our long-time tsar, sovereign, and grand prince, Aleksei Mikhailovich, autocrat of all Great, Little, and White Russia, did plunge his entire Orthodox realm into turmoil, and did involve himself in matters unbecoming the patriarchal authority and dignity, our God-crowned tsar communicated these matters and informed us, the four ecumenical patriarchs, [asking] whether we consider it proper and warranted for a patriarch to act thus. . . . [Nikon] finally left the [patriarchal] throne, and yet he did not leave it, for he slyly would not allow another patriarch [to be chosen]. Though cognizant of such deceitfulness and such wrongdoing and of Nikon's slyness, guile, impudence, sacrilege, and insatiability, yet our most clement [*tishaishii*] monarch, the most holy prelates, and the entire illustrious council [*sinklit*, Boyar Duma] did not dare raise another patriarch to the illustrious Muscovite see, lest people say that there are two patriarchs at the same time, one outside and the other within [the city], and a double authority. Therefore, our sovereign tsar desired that the ecumenical patriarchs should come in person to the ruling city of Moscow, so that they might see and convince themselves with their own eyes as to what had happened, that the most clement ruling power of the tsar's realm be free from any blame, that any future censure by the common people be avoided, and that Nikon not be deposed from the patriarchal see through human passion. . . . Whereas we have now learned that Nikon lived tyrannically, and not meekly as befits a prelate, and that he was given to iniquity, rapacity, and tyranny, we debar him, in accordance with the divine and sacred canons of the evangelizing apostles and of the ecumenical and local Orthodox councils, from every sacerdotal function, so that henceforth he shall have no power to perform any episcopal act; and we truly [and] entirely depose him, [stripping him] of the omophorion and epitrachelion [episcopal and priestly insignia], and we decree with the entire local church council that henceforth he be known as a common monk called Nikon, and not as patriarch of Moscow; he will be assigned a place to dwell to the very end of his days, and may it be some old and suitable monastery, where he can lament his sins in great silence.

VIII:62. THE CHURCH COUNCIL'S CONDEMNATION OF THE SCHISM, MAY 13, 1667

On the broad question of the recent reforms and the conservative opposition to them, the Church Council of 1666–67 arrived at a statement recorded in the official proceedings of the council under the date of May 13, 1667.
    Reference: *DAI*, 5:483–84, 486–88.

For our sins, with God's sufferance and with the help of the Devil, that enemy and hater of Orthodox Christendom, many ignorant men, not only common people but priests and monks as well—some through great ignorance of Holy Scripture and corruption of mind; some under guise of reverence and virtuous life, appearing abstinent and virtuous, yet full of all kinds of stupidity and presumptuous sophistry, who deeming themselves wise have instead turned into fools; some thinking themselves zealous and indeed having such zeal, but unwisely—have stirred many weak souls, in word and in writing, speaking and writing under Satan's inspiration. They have called heretical and corrupt the printed books newly corrected and translated under Nikon, the former patriarch; they have calumniated the clergy who did the correcting in conformity with the Greek and old Russian texts, falsely calling them by abusive names and disparaging their episcopal rank and dignity; they have disturbed the people with their violent acts, saying that the church is not the church, the prelates are not prelates, the priests are not priests, and other similar lies. And because of their diabolically inspired false discourse, the priests have lost their zeal for keeping the church in good order and care. . . . And because of the clergy's great ignorance and neglect of Christ's fold entrusted to them, their lack of zeal and concern for keeping the church in good order, and their indecorous life, many Christians have abandoned church attendance and prayer and have deprived themselves of confessing and doing penance for their sins and of receiving the precious body and blood of Christ. Those who could, began to keep widowed priests in their homes, without episcopal benediction and certification. Many of these priests, though under interdiction and unfrocked by their own prelates, officiated in homes for the satisfaction of those insubordinate to the holy Eastern church who did not want to hear the singing in churches, where it is performed according to the corrected printed books, in conformity with the customs of the holy Eastern church. Consequently, many people formed the opinion that the churches and the church offices, sacraments, and rituals are defiled by many heresies and by the filth of the Antichrist. They also questioned the correction of the holy creed, the triple alleluia, the sign of the precious and life-giving cross, the joining of the first three fingers, the form of addressing Jesus in prayer [i.e. whether his name should be spelled with one "I" or two], and so forth. In view of these faults, we, all the prelates, metropolitans, archbishops, bishops, and notables from other church ranks, archimandrites, abbots, and archpriests of the great Russian state, have assembled in the patriarch's Hall of the Cross [Krestovaia Palata, in the Kremlin], and have examined at length and in great detail the newly corrected and newly translated printed books and the old Slavonic-Russian parchment manuscripts in connection with the above-mentioned and other matters, and have found nothing perverse, corrupt, or contrary to our Orthodox faith in the newly corrected and newly translated printed books, but [found] everything to be in accordance with the old Slavonic-Russian parchment books. . . . For this reason Nikon, the former patriarch, ordered the books to be corrected and translated from the Greek and old Slavonic-Russian parchment books, not on his own account but by order of our most pious sovereign tsar and grand prince Aleksei Mikhailovich, autocrat of all Great, Little, and White Russia, with the benediction, advice, and consent of the most holy ecumenical patriarchs, and the agreement of the prelates of the entire Russian realm and of the entire holy council. . . .

The archimandrites and the abbots are to instruct their brethren in the monasteries; while the archpriests, priests' elders [*starosty popovskie*, senior parish priests with supervisory duties over all the parishes in a given district], and priests . . . and all members of the clergy are to instruct all their spiritual children [*deti dukhovnye*], men and women and youths, and instruct them often, in all the churches as well as in private, so that everyone may, without misgiving, conform in everything to the holy Eastern church; and the books, the *sluzhebniki* [containing the regular church services: mass, matins, and vespers] and *trebniki* [for special service: weddings, baptisms, and so forth] and others, which by order of the Orthodox great sovereign tsar and grand prince Aleksei Mikhailovich, autocrat of all Great, Little, and White Russia, and with the benediction and counsel of our brethren, the most holy ecumenical patriarchs, were corrected, translated, and printed under Nikon, the former patriarch, and after his retirement, with the benediction of the holy council, are to be accepted, since they have been rightfully corrected; and you are to command that all church services be performed in conformity with [these books],

decorously, without disturbance, and harmoniously. . . .

. . . If anyone disobeys our commands and does not submit to the holy Eastern church and to this holy council, or begins to contradict or oppose us, we shall, by the power given to us from the all holy and life-giving Spirit, deal with such a recalcitrant: if he be a member of the clergy, we shall excommunicate him, and deprive him of all priestly functions and grace, and place a curse upon him; if he be a member of the laity, we shall excommunicate him, and alienate him from the Father, the Son, and the Holy Ghost, and curse and anathematize him as a heretic and rebel, and cut him off from the Orthodox community and fold, and from the church of God, as a rotten and useless limb, until he gains understanding and returns to the truth through penance. . . .

Regarding the [church] council that was held [in 1551, the Stoglav] in the reign of the pious great sovereign tsar and grand prince Ivan [IV] Vasil'evich, autocrat of all Russia, under Makarii, metropolitan of Moscow, and what was written about the sign of the precious cross, that is, about joining two fingers, and about the double alleluia, and about other matters, which through simplicity and ignorance were inadvisedly written into the Stoglav book, and regarding the anathema that was unrighteously and inadvisedly pronounced [upon those who failed to follow the decisions of the council]: we, the Orthodox patriarchs, Paisius, pope [*papa*] and patriarch of Alexandria and ecumenical judge, and Macarius, patriarch of Antioch and of all the Orient, and Joasaph, patriarch of Moscow and all Russia, and the entire holy council do annul and abrogate this unrighteous and inadvised anathema pronounced by Makarii and that council, and regard that council and that anathema as not having taken place, since Makarii and those with him, in their ignorance, reasoned inadvisedly, willfully, without either referring to the Greek and old Slavonic parchment books or consulting the most holy ecumenical patriarchs and discussing these matters with them.

VIII:63. AN ACCOUNT OF THE PUNISHMENT OF AVVAKUM, APRIL 4, 1670

An eyewitness left the following account of the punishment of Avvakum and others in Pustozersk on April 4, 1670. Pustozersk was a remote settlement on the Arctic Ocean in the estuary of the Pechora, beyond the Arctic Circle, where Avvakum had been exiled at the end of 1667 and was destined to spend the rest of his life. He remained the leader of the Old Believers until he was burned at the stake in 1681.

Reference: Vasilii G. Druzhinin, ed., *Pamiatniki pervykh let russkogo staroobriadchestva,* vol. 3, *Pustozerskii Sbornik* (St. Petersburg: M. A. Aleksandrov, 1914), p. 17.

On the fourteenth day of April in the year [7]178 [1670], on Thursday of Easter week, in the fortress of Pustozersk, in accordance with the tsar's decree, the *polugolova* [lieutenant colonel] Ivan Elagin led the archpriest Avvakum, the priest Lazar', the deacon Fedor, and the monk Epifanii from the prison, and they went to the designated place for punishment, where the block stands; all the instruments of torture were ready, and the executioner was preparing to carry out the sentence. They [the condemned men] were not the least downcast, but jointly blessed the people and said their farewells with bright and cheerful countenances; they stood unshaken in their piety and accepted death for the sake of their ancestral traditions, saying to the people: "Do not be seduced by Nikon's teaching! We suffer and die for the truth." First Avvakum blessed the block: "Here stands our throne." Then

they blessed each other and kissed each other for the last time, expecting to be beheaded. And then they were brought forth, and a message from the tsar was read to them: instead of being put to death, Avvakum was ordered to be cast into an earthen prison covered with earth, with a small window above, and to be fed bread and water or kvass in small amounts. Upon hearing this the archpriest was greatly offended, and he spat and said: "I spit upon his bread, and I will die without eating it rather than betray piety." Ivan [Elagin] returned him to the prison. He [Avvakum] began to weep and to cry at being separated from his brothers.

And it was ordered to cut out the tongues of the priest Lazar' and the deacon Fedor and the monk Epifanii for their words, and to cut off their hands for the way they made the sign of the cross.

VIII:64. AVVAKUM'S OWN STORY, CA. 1672-1676

Avvakum justified his doctrinal position in his autobiography ("Life"), written in his place of exile, Pustozersk, between 1672 and 1676, as well as in his epistles. His writings, unlike most literature of his day, retained the force and vigor of the spoken language. The first three passages below are from his "Life"; the rest are from his epistles.

Reference: *RIB*, vol. 39, cols. 52, 58, 66, 292, 320, 412, 414-15, 475-76, 532, 567-68, 571, 825. The translation of cols. 52, 58, and 66 is based in part on Avvakum, *The Life of Archpriest Avvakum, by Himself,* trans. Jane Harrison and Hope Mirrlees (London: L. and V. Woolf at the Hogarth Press, 1924), pp. 111-12, 120-21, 132, considerably revised. See also Nikolai K. Gudzii, ed., *Zhitie protopopa Avvakuma* (Moscow: Goslitizdat, 1960). Excerpts from the "Life" have recently been translated in Dmytryshyn, *Medieval Russia,* pp. 280-89.

When they took me . . . to the Chudov monastery . . . in Moscow, they brought me before the ecumenical patriarchs, and all our [Nikonian churchmen] sat there like so many foxes. I spoke of many things in Holy Scripture with the patriarchs. God opened my sinful mouth and Christ put them to shame. The last word they spoke to me was this: "Why," said they, "do you remain stubborn? All our Christian lands, the Serbs and Albanians and Wallachians and Romans and Poles, all cross themselves with three fingers; you alone remain obstinate and cross yourself with five fingers [i.e. two fingers, but because of their position it was sometimes considered that all five fingers were employed]; it is not seemly." And I

answered them for Christ this way: "O you teachers of Christendom! Rome fell long ago and lies prostrate, and the Poles perished with it, being enemies of Christians to the end. And your own Orthodoxy has been tainted by the violence of the Turkish [sultan] Mohammed; and no wonder, for you have become impotent. And from now on it is you who should come to us to learn; for by the grace of God we are an autocratic [independent] realm. Before the time of Nikon, the apostate, in our Russia under our pious princes and tsars the Orthodox faith was pure and undefiled, and the church was free from turmoil. Nikon the wolf, together with the Devil, ordained that men should cross themselves with three fingers, but our first shepherds made the sign of the cross and blessed men with five fingers, according to the tradition of our holy fathers."

. . .

In the [patriarch's] Hall of the Cross [in the Kremlin] the [church] authorities held disputation with me. They led me to the cathedral church, and after the Elevation of the Host they unfrocked me and the deacon Feodor, and then they cursed us and I cursed them back. And there was much turmoil during that mass. . . . Satan has succeeded in obtaining from God our bright, shining Russia, and may he purple it with martyr's blood. You have conceived a clever plan, O Devil, and it is sweet for us to suffer for our dear Lord.

. . .

God will bless you: suffer tortures for the way you place your fingers, do not reason too much! And I am ready to die with you for this and for Christ. Even if I am a foolish man and without learning, yet this I know, that all the traditions of the church, handed down to us by the holy fathers, are holy and incorrupt. I will maintain them even unto death, as I received them. I will not alter the eternal rules that were laid down before our time; may they remain so unto ages of ages.

. . .

I know all your evil cunning, dogs, whores, metropolitans, archbishops, Nikonians, thieves, renegades, foreigners in Russian garb. You have changed the images of the saints and all the church canons and rituals: and a bitter thing it is for good Christians!

. . .

Alas and alack! These apostates have now extinguished the last great light, the great Russian church of old, which worked for the enlightenment of souls, shining throughout the world.

. . .

Oh you dogs! What do you have against the olden ways? Impious ones, thieves, sons of whores. . . . It does not befit us, the faithful, to speak much to you pagans. . . . And that you curse us with your devil: we laugh at that. Even a child would burst into laughter at your madness. If you curse us for [maintaining] the holy olden ways: then also should you curse your fathers and mothers, who died in our faith.

. . .

[Addressed by Avvakum to Tsar Aleksei Mikhailovich:] Take a good, old-fashioned breath, as in Stefan's time [Stefan Vonifat'ev, formerly court priest to Tsar Aleksei, later exiled for his opposition to Nikon], and say in the Russian tongue: "Lord, forgive me, a sinner!" And be done with *Kyrie eleison;* this is what the Hellenes say; spit on them! For you are a Russian, [Aleksei] Mikhailovich, not a Greek. Speak in your native tongue; do not degrade it in church, or at home, or in sayings. It befits us to talk as Christ taught us. God loves us no less than the Greeks; he taught us to read and write in our tongue, through the holy Cyril and his brother [Methodius]. What better can we want? . . . Stop tormenting us! Seize those heretics who destroy your soul, and burn them all, the filthy dogs, Latins and Jews; but release us, your countrymen. Truly, it will be good.

. . .

We, the true believers, follow the Sacred Scriptures and hold steadfastly to what the old printed books teach us about the Deity and about other dogmas; we seek integrity of mind in the old books printed in Moscow [in the reign] of former pious tsars.

. . .

And thenceforth for twenty-three years . . . to this day they burn and hang the confessors of Christ without ceasing. The Russians . . . poor dears—one may think them stupid, but they rejoice that the tormentor has come at last—brave the fire in hosts, for the love of Christ, the Son of God's Light. The Greeks, those sons of whores, are cunning; [their] patriarchs eat delicate viands from the same dish with the Turkish barbarians. Not so our dear Russians—they throw themselves into the fire, rather than betray the true faith! In Kazan' the Nikonians burned thirty men, in Siberia the same number, in Vladimir six, in Borovsk fourteen men; while in Nizhnii [-Novgorod] a most glorious thing took place: some were being burned by the heretics, while others, consumed with love and weeping for the true faith, did not wait to be condemned by the heretics, but themselves braved the fire, so that they might keep the true faith intact and pure; and having burned their bodies and committed their souls into God's hands, they rejoice with Christ unto ages of ages, martyrs by choice, slaves of Christ. May their memory live forever unto ages of ages! Theirs was a noble deed.

. . .

The fire here need only be endured for a short time—in the twinkling of an eye the soul departs [from the body]. Doesn't this sound reasonable to you? Do you fear that furnàce? Be bold, spit on it, fear not! The furnace inspires fear beforehand; but once you enter it, all is forgotten. When it is lit, then you will see Christ, and with him the angelic hosts who take the soul from the body and bring it before Christ.

E. SIBERIA

Note: The documents in this section illustrate various parts of the process by which Russia in the seventeenth century swept eastward across fur-rich Siberia and consolidated its control over a vast territory between the Urals and the Pacific. The process bears comparison with the settlement of the United States and Canada. The documents deal with such problems as (1) exploration and conquest, (2) the importing of settlers, (3) relations with the natives, (4) the collection of tribute, and (5) the exercise of government control over the administrators as well as the administered. However, since often more than one topic is touched on in a single excerpt, the items have not been grouped by topics but are simply presented in chronological order. For earlier documents relating to Siberia, see Items VII:10, 21, and 22. For convenient collections of documents other than those cited with the excerpts in this section, see also A. V. Efimov, ed., and N. S. Orlova, comp., *Otkrytiia russkikh zemleprokhodtsev i poliarnykh morekhodov XVII v. na severo-vostoke Azii. Sbornik dokumentov* (Moscow: Gos. Izdat. Geograficheskoi Literatury, 1951); and M. I. Belov, ed., *Russkie arkticheskie ekspeditsii XVII-XX vv. Voprosy istorii izucheniia i osvoeniia Arktiki. Sbornik* (Leningrad: Gidrometeorologicheskoe Izdatel'stvo, 1964).

VIII:65. INSTRUCTIONS TO FRONTIER SETTLEMENTS, 1600-1604

The early fur traders were soon followed by the apparatus of government, as illustrated by these excerpts from three instructions issued under Tsar Boris Fedorovich Godunov. The first two show some of the many attempts to check excesses on the part of the adventurous men of the frontier. The third excerpt is from one of the many orders that led to the founding of a Siberian town—in this case, Tomsk. Verkhotur'e, an important port of entry for seventeenth-century Siberia, lies east of Perm' and beyond the Urals, on the upper reaches of the Tura River. Turinsk and Tiumen' are further east and downstream on the Tura.

Reference: *RIB*, 2:69 [instructions of 1600], 78 [1604]; G. F. Miller [Mueller], *Istoriia Sibiri*, 2 vols. (Moscow: AN SSSR, 1937-41), 2:169-70 [1601]. In selecting these and other sources for this section, the editors were much aided by the late George V. Lantzeff's pioneering monograph, *Siberia in the Seventeenth Century: A Study of the Colonial Administration* (Berkeley: University of California Press, 1943).

[From the instructions to the commander in Tiumen', Fedor Ivanov, January 30, 1600:]

And when the plowland is ready [for cultivation], you shall distribute it to the peasants and to the volunteer post riders [*iamskie okhotniki*], finding [suitable] places around the forts; but you shall not give the Tatar plowland, whatever land is plowed by the Tatars, to the peasants and to the volunteer post riders; and you shall order them to plow the plowland for us and for themselves in accordance with local conditions, so that our treasury should derive the greatest possible profit and the peasants should plow as much land as they need to feed themselves; and you shall distribute grain for seeds to the peasants and volunteer post riders from our grain stores which are brought from Verkhotur'e.

[From the instructions to the commander of Turinsk, August 30, 1601:]

From the tsar and grand prince of all Russia Boris Fedorovich to Siberia, to the new fortress on the Tura [River], to the commander Fedor Konstantinovich Fofanov. In accordance with our decree, the voevody and *golovy* in all the Siberian towns are ordered to see to it strictly that the tribute- [*iasak-*] paying inhabitants of the Siberian land suffer no oppression, injury, or losses from anyone and that tribute not be collected from them in excess or increased again arbitrarily; and we order [the voevody] to grant [the Siberians] all possible exemptions. We order them to collect the regular tribute for us, as much as each [Siberian] is able to pay, depending on his patrimony and occupation. And if a burdensome tiibute should be imposed upon anyone, which is beyond his means, and if in the future he is unable to pay that tribute, we order that this be investigated; and if the tribute was imposed improperly and is burdensome to him, we order that he pay a reduced tribute. It is forbidden to collect tribute from poor people who are unable to pay tribute.

[From a letter to Tiumen', March 30, 1604:]

From the tsar and grand prince of all Russia Boris Fedorovich to Siberia, to the town of Tiumen', to the commander Aleksei Ivanovich Bezobrazov. In accordance with our decree, we have ordered a town to be built in the basin of the upper Ob' [River] in the Surgut uezd, on the Tom River [a tributary of the Ob'], in the Tomsk volost'; and for building [this] town we have ordered Gavrila Pisemskii to be sent from Surgut and Vasilii Tyrkov [to be sent] from Tobol'sk, and additional service men [to be sent] from Tiumen' along with them, the service men from Tobol'sk, Surgut, and Berezov.

VIII:66. A LETTER ON ENCOURAGING SETTLERS, AUGUST 6, 1609

This letter from Tsar Vasilii Shuiskii to the voevody of Pelym explains some of the means by which settlers were persuaded to move east across the Urals. The now almost forgotten settlement of Pelym is about one hundred miles northeast of the port of entry at Verkhotur'e.
   Reference: Miller, *Istoriia Sibiri*, 2:213.

As soon as this, our letter, reaches you, you should . . . order volunteers to be gathered to [settle on] plowland in Taborinsk [volost'], in accordance with our previous decree: from fifty to a hundred men who are not enrolled in a tiaglo: a father's son, and a brother's brother, and an uncle's nephews, and neighbors' neighbors, but not men from a tiaglo. And you should order town criers [birichi] to proclaim this repeatedly in the marketplaces and in the little marketplaces in Perm' and in Sol'vychegodsk and in the countryside, and to tell them: those who wish to go to Taborinsk as peasants shall be allowed, in accordance with our decree, to settle on plowland in Taborinsk as agreed upon, upon whatever plot each

may want to occupy; and we order that they be given plowland and various other resources [ugod'ia] and money from our treasury as assistance [and] for horses and for farm buildings, and that they, like the Tiumen' peasants, shall plow our plowland by plots, as agreed upon, whatever [plot] each may occupy; and we order that they be given exemptions [from taxes] for a year or two or more, depending on the type of land. . . . And for the peasants' travel, to enable them to travel up to Pelym, you should order that in Perm' and in Sol'vychegodsk they be given one or two rubles apiece, depending on the man and his family . . . while the remaining money that was agreed upon shall be given to them in Verkhotur'e.

VIII:67. INSTRUCTIONS TO THE VOEVODA OF KUZNETSK, 1625

These instructions from the central government to the voevoda of Kuznetsk, Fedor Golenishchev-Kutuzov, deal with two important problems of the day. The "measured plowland" (desiatinnaia pashnia) mentioned in this selection and later was that land, measured out in desiatinas, which the peasants were obliged to cultivate for the state, as contrasted with the land they could cultivate for their own use and profit. Concerning the mention of importing grain into Siberia from European Russia, it may be noted that not till the 1680s did the government decree such imports to be no longer necessary.
   Reference: Arkheograficheskaia Komissiia, *Akty istoricheskie*, 3:218-19, 222. Concerning the situation in the 1680s, see ibid., 5:199.

First of all you are to order that the tributary Tatars and Ostiaks of the tributary [iasachnye] volosti send into town one or two men from each volost'; and at this time you are to be in the voevoda's office yourself in full dress, and

you are to order the service men to be in full dress and armed. And when the tributary men are assembled, you are to proclaim to the tributary men of Kuznetsk the favor of the sovereign tsar and grand prince Mikhail

Fedorovich, autocrat of all Russia: that heretofore at the Kuznetsk fort, the voevody and
Cossacks and their own newly baptized Tatar
and Ostiak brethren—those who do them
violence—treated [the tributary natives]
without consideration and subjected them to
impositions and great extortions in their
payment of tribute; they took excessive
tribute from them, against the sovereign's
orders and for personal gain; and the voevody
did not look after this, and did not administer
justice to them impartially, but themselves
subjected them to extortions and losses, and
took many bribes and presents from them,
and collected double tribute from them,
without orders from the sovereign; and the
voevody sent interpreters and Cossacks to
their volosti for tribute, and the interpreters
and Cossacks subjected them to extortions,
taking bribes and presents and collecting
double tribute from them; and the sovereign
tsar and grand prince of all Russia Mikhail
Fedorovich has granted them his bounty in
all matters; he has ordered that the people
who have wronged them, or subjected them
to any extortions, or taken bribes and
presents from them, be brought before an
impartial court, that thorough investigations
be conducted, that justice be rendered, and
that [the tributary natives] be protected
from all Russian men; and he has ordered that
they be treated with every consideration, that
no one should subject them to violence, losses,
and extortions, that no excessive tribute be

collected, and that tribute not be increased
arbitrarily; and he has ordered that the regular
tribute be collected from them according to
each one's ability to pay, depending on his
land and occupation. . . . And he has given
orders not to collect tribute from the poor
people who are unable to pay tribute.

. . .

The sovereign's plowland has been instituted at the Kuznetsk fort in Siberia, and the
plowing is done by the sovereign's plowland
peasants. On arriving at the Kuznetsk fort,
Fedor [Golenishchev-Kutuzov] is to look
over the plowland peasants, make thorough
investigations, and see for himself how much
measured plowland each [peasant] can plow
and how much hay he can mow for the sovereign; and wherever possible the sovereign's
measured plowland is to be increased, and
additional plowlands and hayfields are to be
assigned to these peasants and entered in the
tax registers, on the basis of investigations
and personal judgment, depending on the
individual and his family, and how much plowland each man can plow and how much hay he
can mow, in order to increase the sovereign's
revenue without overburdening the peasants,
so that no one at all should be left unregistered
as a taxpayer, and so that the Kuznetsk plowland should grow sufficient grain to provide
the service men of Kuznetsk and other Siberian
towns . . . with their yearly compensation in
grain, [according to] their wage scales, without
sending [additional grain] from Moscow.

VIII:68. THE TSAR'S LETTER TO VERKHOTUR'E, OCTOBER 31, 1632

Some of the eastward movement of settlers was traceable to letters like the following from the
tsar to the voevoda of Verkhotur'e, Fedor Boiashev.

Reference: Archeograficheskaia Komissiia, *Akty istoricheskie*, 3:314-15.

In accordance with our decree, you are ordered
to send from Verkhotur'e to Tomsk and to the
forts of the Tomsk region [*razriad*] for settlement, the best of the good, prosperous, and
affluent plowland peasants with large families,
from Verkhotur'e: men from the smaller plots,
who plow no more than one desiatina of our
plowland; you shall select a hundred men,
give them our bounty as aid . . . ten rubles to
each man, [and] send them without delay to
Tobol'sk with their wives and children and
all their peasant possessions, along with whatever service men are available in Verkhotur'e

to act as guides; and in their place we order
you to settle new peasants on their plots, on
our measured [desiatinnaia] plowland, summoning them from among the itinerant men
[*guliashchie i vol'nye liudi*, i.e. those who do
not bear tiaglo], and to give them aid similar
to that given the other plowland peasants of
Verkhotur'e; and according to the assessment
books [*okladnye knigi*] of Verkhotur'e, there
are a total of 477 peasants, old settlers and
newcomers, in the vicinity of the town of
Verkhotur'e and in the villages; and they plow
387 desiatinas of our measured plowland.

VIII:69. THE TSAR'S DISPATCH TO THE VOEVODA OF CHERDYN', 1634

A likely sequel to such orders is revealed in these lines from the tsar's dispatch of 1634 to Il'ia Streshnev, the voevoda of Cherdyn', in the upper basin of the Kama north of Perm', just west of the Urals.

Reference: Arkheograficheskaia Komissiia, *Akty istoricheskie*, 3:325-26.

In the current year, 142 [1634], the voevoda Danilo Miloslavskii and the clerk Vtoroi Shestakov wrote to us [Tsar Mikhail Fedorovich] from Verkhotur'e in Siberia that, in accordance with our decree, eighty plowland peasants, with their wives and children and all their farm possessions, have been moved in the course of the past year, 141 [1633], from Verkhotur'e to Tomsk and the forts of the Tomsk razriad; and [the voevoda and secretary] have given orders to summon volunteer freemen to these [vacated] plots to plow our plowland; but there are no volunteer freemen in Verkhotur'e to summon to take the place of the peasants who were moved. . . . And as soon as you receive this, our dispatch, you shall order criers in the town and uezd of Cherdyn' in [the region of] Perm' the Great to proclaim publicly for many days that volunteer itinerant freemen who do not bear tiaglo and are not obliged to plow [for the sovereign], or do not bear tiaglo and are not registered with the cadastral [*soshnye*] peasants in the cadastral books, should enroll themselves in the uezd of Verkhotur'e as plowland peasants; but under no circumstances should you permit tiaglo-bearing posad men or peasants to be enrolled and moved from their tiaglo and plowland [to Verkhotur'e]. . . . And you should tell those volunteer freemen that in Verkhotur'e they will receive our bounty, loans and subsidies, as do other such plowland peasants, and they will be given ready homesteads and cleared land to plow for themselves and for us, the plots of the peasants formerly settled there whom they have been summoned to replace; and, in accordance with our decree, they will be treated in all matters with kindness, gentleness, and consideration.

VIII:70. INSTRUCTIONS TO A CUSTOMS INSPECTOR AT VERKHOTUR'E, MARCH 1635

Some of the measures employed to maintain the profitable state fur monopoly are seen in this dispatch from the tsar to Danilo Miloslavskii, voevoda of Verkhotur'e, on rendering assistance to Danilo Obros'ev, the customs and frontier tollhouse head (*tamozhennyi i zastavnyi golova*) at Verkhotur'e. Subsequent orders to the customs heads not only repeated the details on searching for furs but also limited the amounts of money that travelers could take back from Siberia.

Reference: Arkheograficheskaia Komissiia, *Akty istoricheskie*, 3:337. See also ibid., 5:43-44.

When any Siberian voevody or secretaries or *pismennye golovy* [military officers serving as assistants to the voevody, with primarily secretarial duties], or any trading men or *promyshlenniki* [private traders or hunters] or service men [on their way back to Russia] arrive at the frontier tollhouse [*zastava*], Danilo is ordered to search such voevody, secretaries, and pismennye golovy, and their children, brothers, nephews, and attendants, and all the trading men, promyshlenniki, and service men for sables and foxes, and sable and fox fur coats, and martens and beavers, and any kind of furs in the carriages, trunks, boxes, bags, valises, clothing, bedding, pillows, wine barrels, and among supplies of every kind, and among baked loaves of bread, using every possible means to detect [concealed articles], and [to search] the wives of the Siberian voevody, secretaries, and pismennye golovy; whenever any voevody, secretaries, and pismennye golovy may be sending their wives, children, brothers, nephews, and attendants from Siberia to Russia ahead of them, these also are to be carefully searched for sables and foxes, and sable and fox and marten fur coats, and martens and beavers, and any kind of furs in the sleighs, carriages, bags, valises, boxes, clothing, pillows, bedding, barrels, loaves of baked bread, and the upholstery and runners of sleighs; and their female servants also are to be carefully searched; and when they begin to search, the wives of the voevody, secretaries, and pismennye golovy shall be ordered to step out of the sleighs and carriages and coaches, and the [customs] head himself, together with the sworn assistants, is to inspect the furs in such carriages, sleighs, and coaches; and the voevody, secretaries, and [pismennye] golovy, and their children, nephews, and attendants, male and female, and the trading men, promyshlenniki, and service men are also to be searched carefully, without any apprehension or fear of anybody or anything, so that no furs whatsoever may be carried across [the border] under coats, in the pants, or sewn into the clothing; and if any furs, sables, and fur coats of sable, and black-brown or brown fox, and caps of black or black-brown fox, and beavers, and any Siberian furs are found on the voevody, the secretaries, the pismennye golovy, and their wives, children, nephews, and attendants,

and the trading men, promyshlenniki, and service men, all such furs, . . . fur coats . . . and all furs, except for two or three fur coats of red fox or marten or squirrel which a voevoda may have just purchased for the trip, are to be confiscated on our behalf and entered item by item in special books in the customhouse [tamozhennaia izba]. And when the trading men and promyshlenniki leaving Siberia arrive at the frontier tollhouse, he [the customs head] is ordered to take the travel papers by which they are allowed to leave the Siberian towns where they had traded, and check the furs they carry against those listed in the travel papers, and verify that the furs bear our Siberian stamps. (A copy of the description of the stamps of our Siberian towns, with which trading men are required to stamp their merchandise, has by our order been sent to the customs head Danilo.)

VIII:71. INSTRUCTIONS TO THE VOEVODY OF THE LENA, FEBRUARY 10, 1644

These instructions from the central government to the voevody of the Lena (at Iakutsk), Vasilii Pushkin and Kirill Suponev, and to the secretary Petr Stenshin, suggest some of the rich variety of information that can be gained from the study of such documents.
Reference: *DAI*, 2:265-70, 272-74.

By order of the sovereign tsar and grand prince of all Russia Mikhail Fedorovich, in the previous year, 146 [1638], there were sent to the great river Lena the stol'niki and voevody Petr Golovin and Matvei Glebov and the secretary Evfimii Filatov; and with them were sent from Moscow 2 pismennye golovy, Vasilii Poiarkov and Enalei Bakhteiarov, and service men from Kazan', 5 deti boiarskie, and foot Cossacks and strel'tsy from the Siberian towns, 245 men from Tobol'sk, 50 men from Berezov, [and] 100 men from the Eniseisk fort, altogether 395 men with firearms, to build forts and to find and subject new lands of nontributary people, and to collect tribute, and to attend to all the sovereign's affairs; and 2 men, good smiths, versed in the armorer's trade and every kind of smith's work, [were sent] to repair weapons and do every kind of smith's work for the sovereign. . . . And the following food supplies were sent with them from Tobol'sk to the Lena to feed the tributary people, for the discovery and subjection of new lands: fifty *chetverti* [one chetvert' was about one hundred eighty pounds] of rye flour, twenty chetverti of oat flour, twenty chetverti of

rye malt, ten chetverti of groats and oatmeal, fifty poods of salt, one hundred vedros of spirits, twenty poods of honey, and, in the event that enemy soldiers should threaten and approach the forts, two small, one-pound cannons, ten one-pound field harquebuses [*pishchali polkovye*], and, as ammunition for all these cannon and harquebuses, twenty-six poods of gunpowder and one hundred rounds of balls and of leaden bullets for each harquebus and for the 395 service men, thirty poods of powder and a similar amount of lead, as advance supply for the Lena fort. . . . And Petr and his companions have been ordered to proceed, in the service of the sovereign tsar and grand prince of all Russia Mikhail Fedorovich, from the Eniseisk fort to the great river Lena, to the small forts erected by the Eniseisk service men, and [they are] to verify carefully whether these small forts are built in the proper locations, what fortifications these forts possess, whether these forts can hold out against enemy soldiers, whether there is arable land in the area or in other places nearby, whether there is much plowland and of what quality, and how many people can be settled on that land, and where. And if the small forts have been built

in the proper locations and can hold out
against enemy soldiers, then [Petr and his
companions] are to strengthen these small
forts, and dig moats around these small forts,
and erect palisades, and fortify them thoroughly with all manner of fortifications, and place
the guns in each small fort to the best advantage, and place and arrange the sovereign's
money and grain stores and all other supplies
in storehouses, and protect them securely
from damage and loss, and build and consecrate a church and provide it with books and
various church articles which will be sent to
them from Moscow and Tobol'sk; and if, on
inspection and on questioning various people,
they find that the old small forts on the Lena
River are not situated in the best locations
and that better locations for forts are available, Petr and his companions are ordered to
replace the old small forts with one new fort,
where it seems most advisable, so that the new
fort will be in a suitable location, and, having
erected the fort, to fortify it with all kinds of
fortifications, so that men can live in that
fort without fear of enemy soldiers; and when
the new fort has been erected and fortified
with all kinds of fortifications, they are to
move from the old small forts into the new
fort and place all the sovereign's stores and
guns in that fort, and they are to send [their
men] from the new fort to the Lena and
other rivers, to the tributary people [iasachnye
liudi] in the new lands who have submitted
to the exalted arm of the sovereign tsar, and
to instruct the best men from among the
tributary people in the new lands to come to
them to the fort. . . .

And upon arriving at the Iakutsk fort [the
voevody] are to summon to the voevoda's
office [s"ezzhaia izba] the deti boiarskie,
Cossacks, strel'tsy, cannoneers, stockade
tenders and all the inhabitants of the Lena
and proclaim to them the bounty of the sovereign tsar and grand prince Mikhail Fedorovich, autocrat of all Russia: that the sovereign
tsar and grand prince of all Russia Mikhail
Fedorovich has granted them his bounty; he
has ordered that the sovereign's emolument
to them be given in full, in accordance with
their wage scales [oklady], and he has ordered
that the service men and inhabitants be
treated with consideration, that no one should
subject them to privation, oppression, injury,
and impositions. . . . And after the Russian

people [come], they are to convoke the tributary people from the volosti, the princelings
and the best men of the ulusy [native settle-
ments], as many men as seems advisable, and
they, [the voevody] Vasilii and Kirill and the
secretary Petr, are to be present at that time
in the voevoda's office in full dress, and the
Russian service men are, for the occasion, to
be in full dress and armed; and they are to
proclaim to the tributary princelings and the
tributary people of the Lena the bounty of the
sovereign tsar and grand prince Mikhail Fedorovich, autocrat of all Russia, that heretofore
the voevody, [pismennye] golovy, government officials, deti boiarskie, atamans, strel'tsy,
Cossacks and their brethren, and other people
of various callings have treated them without
consideration and subjected them to impositions and great extortions when they paid
their tribute, and have taken excessive tribute
from them, against the sovereign's orders and
for personal gain; and the voevody did not
look after this and did not administer justice
to them impartially; and the voevody sent
deti boiarskie, interpreters, and Cossacks into
their volosti to collect the tribute, and these
deti boiarskie, interpreters, and Cossacks
came to them and inflicted extortions upon
them, taking bribes and presents from them;
and the sovereign tsar and grand prince of all
Russia Mikhail Fedorovich has granted them
his favor in all matters; he has ordered that
those men who have wronged them in any
manner or taken bribes and presents from
them be brought to court, and that an impartial investigation be conducted and justice
rendered; he has ordered that they be protected from the Russians and from all people;
and he has ordered that they always be
treated with consideration, and suffer no
violence, losses, extortions, or impositions,
and that they, the tributary people of the new
lands, should live in the tsar's bounty in peace
and quiet without any fear, and pursue their
occupations, and faithfully serve the sovereign
tsar and grand prince Mikhail Fedorovich,
autocrat of all Russia, and wish him well in all
things, in accordance with the oath they took
to the great sovereign. . . . And after dismissing
the tributary people [the voevody] should send
to their lands and ulusy for the collection of
tribute the best service men from Tobol'sk,
Eniseisk, and Berezov, and with each man, one
or two sworn assistants [tseloval'niki], worthy

men from among the trading men and promyshlenniki who may be found on the Lena now
or in the future, and who shall take an oath
to the sovereign; and service men should be
sent to other new lands along the great river
Lena, and along the Aldan, the Chaia, and
the Viliui, and along other rivers to reconnoiter, explore, and subject [these lands].
. . . And the service men are to be ordered to
summon the nontributary men of the new
lands, to bring them under the exalted arm
of the sovereign tsar, and to collect tribute
from them with great diligence, in various
ways, [but always] with kindness and not
with violence, in order to bring the people of
these new lands under the exalted arm of the
sovereign tsar. . . . And to ensure the [pay-
ment of] tribute, as many hostages [amanaty]
as necessary should be taken from among the
best men of these lands and kept in the fort.
. . . And without fail the voevody and the
secretary are to look diligently for arable land
along the Lena River and along other rivers
near the Lena, so as to organize the cultiva-
tion of land on the Lena River, near that fort
where the voevody and the secretary are going to live with the service men, and to settle
peasants to plow these lands, and to provide
grain on the Lena for the service men and
ecclesiastics and men under contract to the
government, and for various local needs, thus
making it unnecessary henceforth to supply
the Lena with grain from Tobol'sk and
Eniseisk; and a call is to be issued for free
peasants, for various itinerant men [gulia-
shchie liudi], to plow the land, offering
them subsidies and temporary tax exemption;
loans and subsidies are to be given in accordance with the previous decree of the sovereign and as local circumstances may warrant.
. . . [Tribute collectors] should not engage in
thievery, as was formerly done by the Eniseisk
service men ataman Ivan Galkin and his companions, who, when going from the Eniseisk
fort to the Lena River to collect tribute for
the sovereign, used to take with them many
wares of their own, and for these wares, as
well as for money, would buy and barter
from the tributary men in the tributary
volosti, ulusy, and lands, a great many furs,
the best sables, foxes, and beavers, and would
bring [these furs] with them from the Lena
to the Eniseisk fort, and would bring only a
little tribute for the sovereign; and the voevody

in the Eniseisk fort, befriending them, and
for the sake of personal fraudulent gain,
would not confiscate their illegal sable furs
on behalf of the sovereign but would merely
levy the sovereign's 10 percent duty [desiataia
poshlina] on these furs; and through the
thievery of these Eniseisk service men and the
connivance and illicit greed of the voevody,
the sovereign's treasury incurred great losses,
and the tributary people [suffered] oppression
and injury.

. . .

And the service men whom they will send
to subject new lands and to collect tribute
along the Lena, Aldan, and other rivers are to
be under strict orders while collecting tribute
not to inflict unnecessary injury or impositions upon any of the tributary people in any
manner whatsoever [but] to collect the sovereign's tribute from them with gentleness and
kindness, and not with harshness and violence,
so that the sovereign's tribute may be collected
with profit, without harsh treatment of the
natives, according to their ability [to pay],
and only once a year, not two or three times
a year. . . . Should any people of the new
lands become unruly, and it be altogether impossible to bring them under the exalted arm
of the sovereign tsar by gentle means, . . .
against such people Russian service men are
to be sent from the small fort in whatever number appears advisable, with orders first to try
every possible gentle means to persuade [the
natives] with gentleness and kindness to take
the oath that they will be under the exalted
arm of the sovereign tsar and will pay tribute;
and if it is absolutely impossible to persuade
these insubordinates, and if they are likely to
cause trouble in the future, such insubordinates
are to be pacified by war, by devastating some
of their lands . . . and once they are brought
under the exalted arm of the sovereign tsar,
as many of the princelings and best men among
the tributary people as seems advisable are to
be taken from them and are to take their turn
as hostages held at the Lena fort, and through
the holding of these hostages as surety the
sovereign's tribute is to be collected from the
people of these new lands as well, depending
on the individual, and in the same manner as
from the other tributary men; and the sovereign's stores are to be used to feed the hostages
held in the fort, and the hostages are to be
under strong guard. . . . And Vasilii and Kirill

and the secretary Petr and the clerks and the service men are not to have in their households any native men or wives or children, and are not to buy any natives from anybody through a third party, and are not to baptize them, and are not to carry them off to Moscow themselves or send them off with anybody else, and are to forbid service men or any other people to baptize the natives, so that the Lena land of Siberia may prosper and not become depopulated. If any of the tributary people should freely choose to be baptized, such people are to be baptized, after carefully investigating whether it is actually of their own free will that they wish to be baptized; and after baptism they are to be taken into the sovereign's service to fill the vacancies left by Russian service men, and they are to be assigned the sovereign's compensation in money and grain, depending on the individual and the position for which he is suited; if any of the female sex, married women or maidens, should wish to be baptized, such married women and maidens are to be baptized and married to newly baptized [natives] or to Russian service men. And Vasilii and Kirill and the secretary Petr are on no account to have any natives in their households, and they shall not permit service men or any other people to keep any natives with them or to force any Russians or natives, baptized or unbaptized, to perform any compulsory labor for them in their households. . . . And while on the sovereign's service on the Lena River, whether on expeditions or in the fort, the voevody and the secretary are not to inflict any injury, violence, or oppression upon the sovereign's service men and tributary people, and are not to find fault with anybody without good reason, and are to treat the service men and all the ecclesiastics with kindness, gentleness, and consideration; they are not to defraud the sovereign's treasury of money, sables, or anything else, and they are not to bring goods with them from Russia to Siberia, or from the Siberian towns to the Lena River, except for the sovereign's and their own stipulated supplies; they are not to carry on any trade with the tributary men, trading men, and promyshlenniki; and they are not to send any of their money, goods, clothes, spirits, or tobacco with the tribute collectors to be traded or bartered for furs in the tributary volosti and the new lands; they are to watch carefully that the service men sent with them from Tobol'sk to the Lena River do not bring and transport any spirits, tobacco, or any kind of goods, or exchange them for furs, or carry on any trade with the tributary men, whether in the small forts on the Lena River or while collecting tribute; and should tobacco or any goods be found in the possession of any service men on the Lena River, such tobacco and goods are to be confiscated on behalf of the sovereign, and those from whom the tobacco and goods have been taken are to be punished, beaten with the knout, and made to provide surety, in accordance with the sovereign's decree, so that none of the service men should bring with him from the Siberian towns to the Lena River any spirits, tobacco, or goods, or do any trading with the tributary natives on the Lena River or anywhere else, lest they diminish the tribute collected for the sovereign thereby.

VIII:72. A REPORT ON POIARKOV'S VOYAGE, 1646

This is an excerpt from the record of the complaint lodged in 1646 by the group ("mir") of men who managed to return from Poiarkov's expedition to the Sea of Okhotsk in 1643-45. The specific charges may well have been exaggerated, as such petitions often were, but the document at least serves as a reminder of the extremes to which men could sometimes be driven by the rigors of the frontier, whether in Siberia or North America.

Reference: *DAI*, 3:58-59.

The mir's petition against the voevoda Petr Golovin reads as follows: In the past year, 151 [1643], he, Petr, inducted into service ninety-six new men from among the promyshlenniki and the itinerant men, and sixteen more from among the old service men, and he sent them with his adviser Vasilii Poiarkov to the Pegaia horde [an Ostiak clan]; and while in the sovereign's service Vasilii Poiarkov beat and tortured service men without cause, and took away their grain supplies, and threw them out of the fort, and ordered them to go and eat the slain natives; and these service men, to escape useless death, ate many dead natives and service men who had died from hunger, eating about fifty men; and Vasilii beat some [men] to death with his own hands, saying, "Service men come cheap. You can get a *desiatnik* [approximately, "corporal"] for ten den'gi and a rank-and-file man for two groshi." And Vasilii lost a total of about one hundred of the sovereign's service men; and when Vasilii, with the remainder of the service men, was sailing along the river Zeia, the local natives would not permit them to land and called them unclean cannibals. . . . And the pismennyi golova Vasilii Poiarkov

said upon interrogation that, when he was at the Pegaia horde with the service men and newly inducted men, he did not beat and torture any service men, nor take away their supplies, nor throw them out of the fort, and he did not order them to eat dead natives but they ate dead men of their own accord, and he did not beat anyone to death with his own hands, nor say that you can get a desiatnik for ten den'gi and a rank-and-file man for two groshi; and about eighty service men were lost, some being killed, and some dying.

VIII:73. DEZHNEV'S ACCOUNT OF EXPLORATIONS IN 1648-1651

The exploration of the remote northeastern tip of Siberia is dealt with in this report, written in 1655, from the service men Semen Dezhnev and Nikita Semenov to Ivan Akinfov, the voevoda of Iakutsk. A glance at the map will show why this account provides the basis for Dezhnev's distinction as leader of the first European party to pass through the Bering Strait.

Reference: *DAI*, 4:19, 25-26. See also A. V. Efimov, *Otkrytiia*, chap. 4; Belov, ed., *Russkie arkticheskie ekspeditsii*, pp. 127-143 ("Podlinnye dokumenty o plavanii S. I. Dezhneva," ed. T. D. Lavrentsov); and V. A. Samoilov, *Semen Dezhnev i ego vremia* (Moscow: Izdat. Glavsevmorputi, 1945).

[In January 1651] our companions, the promyshlenniki, left us on the lower reaches of the Anadyr' River . . . and went up the Anadyr' River to the winter quarters where tribute is collected, to the sovereign's hostage Chekcha and to our companions, Semen Motora and his companions, with food, clothing, and various household articles. Our companions, who were guarding the sovereign's treasury [the furs paid as tribute] and the hostage, were dying of hunger; they lived on cedar bark, saving their small store of fresh fish to feed the hostage, a little at a time, lest from privation he should get scurvy and die, and we should incur the sovereign's wrath and punishment.

. . .

In the previous year of 156 [1648], on the twentieth day of June, I, Semeika [Semen], was sent from the river Kolyma to the new river Anadyr' in search of new people who did not pay tribute. And in the previous year of 157, after the feast of the Intercession of the Holy Virgin [Pokrov Bogoroditsy, October 1, O.S., which would still be the year 1648 in the Western calendar], I, Semeika, was tossed helplessly hither and thither by the

sea and was cast ashore on a promontory beyond the river Anadyr'; there were twenty-five of us in the boat, and we all went uphill, without knowing where we were going, cold and hungry, naked and barefoot, and it took me, poor Semeika, and my companions exactly ten weeks to walk to the Anadyr' River; we came to the Anadyr' River at its lower reaches near the sea, and we could not get any fish; there was no wood, and out of hunger we unfortunates went in separate directions. Twelve men went upstream along the Anadyr', and they walked twenty days and saw neither people nor reindeer sleds nor native trails, and they turned back, and at three days' walk from camp they stopped for the night and started to dig holes in the snow. . . . [Most of these perished.] And out of the twenty-five there were only twelve of us left; the twelve of us sailed in boats up the Anadyr' River, and we came to the Anaul people [Iukagirs of the Anadyr' coast] and captured two men after a fight, and I was grievously wounded; we took tribute from them, and the tribute books list by name what was taken from whom, and what was taken as the sovereign's tribute.

VIII:74. A REPORT FROM THE PARTY SEEKING KHABAROV, JUNE 30, 1652

This passage is from a report from the service man Ivan Uvarov on the Tugir (evidently also called the Tugur) River, near the Sea of Okhotsk, to Dimitrii Frantsbekov, voevoda of Iakutsk.

Reference: *DAI*, 3:354-55.

In accordance with the sovereign's order and on instructions from the voevoda, we were sent . . . down the Amur River to search for the government official Erofei Pavlovich Khabarov . . . and thus we, the sovereign's slaves, sailed along the Amur River, and . . . sailed out into the Amur Bay. While sailing along the Amur River, we, the sovereign's slaves, did not find the government official Erofei Pavlovich and saw no trace of him anywhere. . . . While we were encamped, the Giliak men attacked us from many boats, and God helped us to sink one boat and kill the men in that boat, some forty of them; and from there we, the sovereign's slaves, went by sea, rowing, and we rowed out of the bay into the sea, and we, the sovereign's slaves, were tossed amidst the ice on the sea, and we were tossed amidst the ice for ten days and were carried ashore at an uninhabited place, and here the ice pushed us, the sovereign's slaves, against the shore ——. The boat was crushed and sank, and we, the sovereign's slaves, managed to get only our bodies and souls ashore; the bread, the lead, and the powder sank into the sea, and all the clothing sank into the sea, and we were left without anything. From there we, the sovereign's slaves, went on foot along the sea, and for five days we, the sovereign's slaves, walked on foot along the sea, and we lived on berries and herbs, and on the shore we found slaughtered elks, sea animals, seals, and walruses, and with these we defiled our souls, eating them because of our need. . . . And we, the sovereign's slaves, walked from the mouth of the Amur River to [another] river, [walking for] eight weeks and three days, and we lived on herbs, water, and those sea animals, the seals; and on that river we, the sovereign's slaves, spent the autumn; from that river we ascended the mountain range on sleds and crossed over to the slopes of the Lena, and we went on sleds for four weeks and one day. . . . On the third day of Christmas we found Tungus tents, and we took two Tungus men and kept them as hostages, and we took seventy-eight sables from them as tribute for the great sovereign, and we, the sovereign's slaves, took from these Tungus tents supplies for half a year, and now we, the sovereign's slaves, are living on these supplies. . . . And you, the sovereign's voevoda Dmitrii Andreevich and the secretary Osip Stepanov, should send us powder and lead, and a Tungus interpreter, and tools for building boats, drills, axes, and adzes, for we, Ivashko [Ivan] and my companions, here on the Tugir [Tugur] River, are naked and barefoot, and hungry and cold, and perishing utterly from privation, freezing to death from cold, because we have no axes.

VIII:75. A REPORT FROM KHABAROV, AUGUST 1652

These passages are from the report of August 1652, from service man Erofei Khabarov to the Iakutsk voevoda Dimitrii Frantsbekov, telling of the recent activities of Khabarov's "service men and free volunteers" in the land of the Daurs or Daurians on the Amur.

Reference: *DAI,* 3:360, 371.

We immediately laid siege to that [Daurian] town, and the Daurian men started to shoot arrows at us from the towers; and I, the government official, ordered the interpreters to tell [the besieged] of the sovereign's majesty, that our sovereign tsar and grand prince of all Russia Aleksei Mikhailovich is awesome and dread and holds all kingdoms under his sway, and no horde can withstand our sovereign tsar and grand prince of all Russia Aleksei Mikhailovich and stand against us in combat; and that [the native chieftans], Prince Goigudar, Prince Olgodii, and Prince Lotodii, should be obedient and submissive to our sovereign tsar and grand prince of all Russia Aleksei Mikhailovich, and should surrender without fighting, and should give tribute to our sovereign as [they] are able; and the sovereign will order that [they] be protected against other hordes who do violence to [them]. And Goigudar said: "We are paying tribute to Shamshakan, the Chinese tsar [presumably the Chinese emperor Shun Chih, 1644-61]; why should we give you tribute?" . . . And, asking God's grace and zealously serving the sovereign, we reconnoitred and made an armed attack; we erected breastworks around the heavy guns and the cannon and started to fire at the towers in the lower part of the town, and we fired at [the Daurians] in the towns from small arms, muskets, and harquebuses, and the Daurian men shot at us from the town; the arrows came flying at us incessantly from the Daurian men, from the town, and the arrows the Daurians shot at us from the town into the plain looked like wheat standing in the field; and we fought with the Daurians all night long till sunrise, and we breached the wall near a tower and . . . took that lower town.

. . .

We . . . do not know where we shall winter; with [so few] men we do not dare make camp in the Daurian land at the mouth of the Zeia or at the mouth of the Shingal, lest we bring harm to the sovereign's [fur] treasury and

lose the lives of Cossacks in vain; for the land of the Chinese is close by, and a large army is coming against us with firearms and cannon and small arms. During the summer we sail on the Amur River and summon the natives to submit to the sovereign's majesty, and we ravage those who do not obey and submit; and in winter we sail downstream; it is impossible to subjugate the people . . . of that land, because that land [downstream] is populous and they have firearms, and we dare not leave this land and the Amur River for other rivers without the sovereign's orders.

VIII:76. A FURTHER REPORT FROM THE AMUR, JULY 22, 1656

Like Khabarov's report (above), this report from government official Onufrii Stepanov to Mikhail Lodyzhenskii, voevoda of Iakutsk, illuminates the process that led by 1689 to the Treaty of Nerchinsk.
Reference: *DAI*, 4:80–83.

To the voevoda . . . and the secretary, . . . the government official of the new Daurian land on the great river Amur, Onofreiko [Onufrii] Stepanov, sends greetings. By the sovereign's decree and memorandum of instructions [*nakaznaia pamiat'*], I, Onofreiko, have been ordered to attend to the sovereign's affairs on the great river Amur, to supervise the collection of tribute in sables, and to administer justice to the service men. . . . All the service men and the volunteer Amur Cossacks are now cold and hungry and lacking in everything; no grain stores whatsoever are left among the troops, and there is no lead and no powder; everything has been used up. We do not know how we are to live and what we are to eat, and we, the sovereign's slaves, do not know how we are to attend to the [collection

of the] sovereign's tribute and to look after ourselves; and now everybody among the troops is hungry and destitute, and we are living on herbs and roots and awaiting the sovereign's orders, for we dare not move anywhere from the river Amur without the sovereign's orders. Chinese soldiers [*Bogdoiskie voinskie liudi*] are camped close by, and we have nothing left with which to oppose and fight the Chinese; there is no lead or powder left at all. And I, Onofreiko, have sent from the mouth of the Shingal River to the sovereign in Moscow the sovereign's sable tribute collected from the Daurians, and Diucherians, and Giliaks for the past year, 163 [1655], and the current year, 164 [1656], along with the reports and the tribute books.

VIII:77. ADMINISTRATIVE INSTRUCTIONS FOR WESTERN SIBERIA, 1664-1680

Meanwhile, as settlement increased in western Siberia, the government faced a variety of problems there. Some of these problems and the policies that were designed to cope with them are illustrated in these three excerpts.
Reference: *DAI*, 4:357–58; 6:111; 8:228.

[From instructions sent to Prince Aleksei Golitsyn, voevoda of Tobol'sk, February 19, 1664:]
And the voevody . . . are to inquire of the Siberian serving men, trading men, posad men, and plowland peasants of Tobol'sk, and are themselves to make careful investigations, regarding the possibilities of increasing the amount of the great sovereign's measured

plowland and his dues in grain and hay [*posopnyi khleb i seno*] in Tobol'sk and in the slobody of the Tobol'sk uezd. If this is found possible, the voevody are to order an increase in the former measured plowland and in dues in grain and hay, depending upon the individual and his family and means, so as to increase the sovereign's grain revenue without causing any hardship to the plowland peasants; and once again [the voevody] are to call for additional plowland peasants to settle on the sovereign's plowland, offering financial aid, temporary tax exemption, and loans to free volunteers from among the itinerant men, and to grant them such financial aid, temporary tax exemption, and loans, depending on local conditions and the individual and his family, against security and following the example of previous years in the way temporary tax exemption, loans, and financial aid have previously been given to other plowland peasants. . . . And the boyar and voevoda Aleksei Andreevich [Golitsyn] is to send orders to the Siberian towns to which plowland peasants are assigned [*pashennye goroda*] and to the forts of the Tobol'sk razriad . . . that plowlands be enlarged in those Siberian towns and forts, and that, wherever possible, the measured plowland of the old-time plowland peasants be increased, and that once again a call be issued for volunteer plowland peasants to settle on the sovereign's plowland, offering them financial aid and temporary tax exemption. . . . [Representatives from the various groups, selected by the voevoda] are to be ordered to collect from the Tobol'sk priests, deacons, clerks, trading men, all manner of nonservice men, and plowland peasants, who plow land for themselves and do not pay the great sovereign's obrok to the sovereign's treasury from their plowland, every fourth sheaf of good grain, every fifth sheaf of medium grain, and every sixth sheaf of poor grain; and they are to be ordered to record in a book, accurately and by individual, how many sheaves or hundred sheaves of grain have been collected from each person and are to have that grain threshed by those from whom it is collected.

[From the tsar's dispatch to Fedor Khrushchev, voevoda of Verkhotur'e, November 13, 1670:]

When this dispatch from us, the great sovereign, reaches you, you are to order that in Verkhotur'e and in the uezd of Verkhotur'e, strong frontier posts be erected where necessary, so that henceforth in no case should fugitive peasants from the Russian towns and uezdy be admitted into the Siberian towns, lest our, the great sovereign's, taxes in grain and money and all other taxes be reduced in the towns of the [northern] Littoral [Pomorskie goroda]; and we, the great sovereign,

have sent a decree to Tobol'sk, to our boyar and our voevody, to Prince Ivan Borisovich Repnin and his associates, regarding the deportation of fugitive peasants from Siberia to the towns of the Littoral.

[From instructions sent to Ivan Pogozhevo, voevoda of Turinsk, February 13, 1680:]

It has become known to us, the great sovereign, that in our sloboda and volosti of Turinsk the plowland peasants plow the sovereign's measured plowland, but many do not plow for themselves as they should in accordance with our, the great sovereign's, decree, and some do not plow at all, enjoying tax exemption [*l'gota*] through connivance with the government officials [*prikaznye liudi*], but allow newcomers to settle on their plots; and the metropolitan's deti boiarskie, officials, and church dignitaries, archimandrites and abbots, and deti boiarskie, and Russian service men of all ranks, and dragoons, post riders [*iamshchiki*], and foreigners [*inozemtsy*] have occupied much land, and built villages and hamlets, and settled newcomers to cultivate this land, and these settlements and vast landholdings occasion many disputes among the [Russians and] foreigners, to the detriment of our tributary people [*iasachnye liudi*, the Siberian natives]. . . . And now we, the great sovereign, have ordered that a register be made of all the cultivated and uncultivated lands and hayfields and all the *ugod'ia* in Siberia, in Tobol'sk, in the towns of the Tobol'sk razriad—Verkhotur'e, Pelym, Turinsk, Tiumen', [and] Tara—and in the countryside around those towns, and in our, the great sovereign's, villages and sloboda and hamlets, and in [lands held by] . . . the metropolitan of Siberia and Tobol'sk, monastery peasants, the church, deti boiarskie, all ranks of service men, dragoons, post riders, plowland peasants, obrok-paying peasants, posad men, and men of every status, [indicating] through which of our, the great sovereign's, decrees they hold [these] villages, lands, and ugod'ia. . . . The register shall indicate, with each person listed separately by name, how much of our, the great sovereign's, measured plowland each peasant plows, how much grain he pays as obrok, how much land he plows for himself, and where there are fisheries, meadows, forests, and ugod'ia of all kinds; and land over which a dispute arises shall be delimited between the

Russians and the tributary men; and the amount of our, the great sovereign's, measured plowland and obrok grain imposed upon the plowland and obrok-paying peasants shall be increased in accordance with the amount of plowland they cultivate for themselves and the amount of obrok grain [previously] paid, depending on individual and family circumstances; and whatever old-time *zavodnye* peasants [those brought to Siberia by the government, supplied with land and inventory, and obligated to plow the measured plowland for the sovereign], living in slobody, have settled itinerant men with their wives and children as taxpayers [*na tiaglo*] in their stead, and have themselves settled [elsewhere] with their former possessions, enjoying exemption from taxes and living unregistered [in the tax lists, *izbylye*] for many years: such old-time peasants, who have left [their former land] to be tax exempt, and who are newly settled in slobody and are living tax exempt or cultivating but little plowland [for the sovereign] and not paying any taxes, shall be made to cultivate plowland [for the sovereign].

VIII:78. A VERDICT OF THE IAKUTSK VOEVODA, AUGUST 4, 1681

In this sample of a voevoda's punitive verdict, one wonders which of the various misdeeds he recites were considered most grievous.
    Reference: *DAI*, 7:301–02.

On August 4, 189 [1681], after hearing previous reports, summary extracts from such reports, testimonies, and the petition of the Tungus from Okhotsk, and in accordance with the sovereign's decree and order, the stol'nik and voevoda Ivan Vasil'evich Priklonskii has sentenced the deti boiarskie Iurii Kryzhanovskii and Petr Iaryzhkin to be whipped without mercy on the bench [*na kozle*] and on their feet [*v provodku*] for their many misdeeds; and you [Iurii and Petr] are to be banished to the Daurian forts to serve as foot Cossacks, and your possessions and households are to be confiscated on behalf of the sovereign's treasury, inasmuch as in the previous year, 188[1680], while serving the sovereign [on the Sea of Okhotsk] at the Okhotsk fort [*ostrozhek*], you, Iurii, oppressed the Tungus natives and imposed great extortions on them, and made substitutions in the sovereign's [fur] treasury, [and] took for yourself out of the sovereign's tribute [*iasak*], before the furs for the sovereign had been selected, the good sables and the black foxes, and in place of those sables sent to the sovereign's treasury your own inferior sables; and because of your misdeeds against the sovereign's people the stol'nik Danilo Bibikov and the *piatidesiatskii* Ustin Panfilov and their companions were killed by the natives [*inozemtsy*].

F. THE DON COSSACKS

Note: In connection with these documents on the Don Cossacks, see also Items VIII:29 and 33, above.

VIII:79. THE TSAR'S MESSAGE TO THE DON COSSACKS, MARCH 18, 1614

The free community of Cossacks that firmly established itself in the Don region during the sixteenth century was, at the start of the seventeenth, not yet an integral part of the Muscovite state. Something of its role and position under the first Romanov tsar is conveyed by his message of March 18, 1614, to the Cossack Host of the Don.
    Reference: *RIB*, vol. 18, cols. 65, 69.

Henceforth we, the great sovereign, intend to bestow upon you, the atamans and Cossacks and your entire host, our gracious bounty and our care even more than heretofore. And as regards what you have written to us concerning our bounty, that we grant you our bounty and send our bounty to you—money and cloth and provisions, to feed and clothe you in these times, while you are at peace with the men [Tatars] of Azov—we, the great sovereign, in view of your fidelity to God and your services to us, the great sovereign, and your true zeal and obedience, have granted our bounty to you, the atamans and Cossacks and your entire host, and are sending you money, cloth, saltpeter, provisions, and spirits.

. . .

You have likewise written to us, through the ataman Ignatii Bedrishchev, [requesting] that we grant you our mark of favor and send you our banner, with which to withstand our enemies and attack them. And we have bestowed our favor upon you [and] sent to you, through the same ataman Ignatii Bedrishchev, our mark of favor, the tsar's banner; and may you with this banner withstand our enemies and attack them.

VIII:80. THE CAPTURE OF AZOV, IN A REPORT OF DECEMBER 3, 1637

The capture by the Don Cossacks of the strategically important Turkish fortress and base at Azov is related in this message from the Cossack Host of the Don to the tsar.

Reference: *RIB*, vol. 18, cols. 636-37.

We, your slaves, went forth against the fortress of Azov in great sorrow, mindful of our baptism, and the holy churches of God, and our true Orthodox Christian faith; inasmuch as from that fortress of Azov the wicked predatory wolves of the Mohammedan faith, the brood of Hagar, the foul pagan tribe, have inflicted much harm upon your patrimony, Great Sovereign Tsar, in the border towns and above all in the countryside, and have wrought destruction on God's holy churches, and have shed innocent Christian blood, and have carried away Orthodox Christians into captivity— our fathers and mothers, our brothers and sisters. From time immemorial they, the men of Azov, have desecrated our true Orthodox Christian faith, and have sold our fathers and brothers and sisters as galley slaves beyond the seas, loading their ships with Russian captives to be sent to the Turkish land. And to us your slaves, Sire, those pagan men of Azov have done great injury.

VIII:81. A REPORT ON THE DON COSSACKS, FEBRUARY 11, 1638

This excerpt from the report of one of the tsar's emissaries upon his return from the Don provides information on the structure of the host.

Reference: *RIB*, vol. 18, cols. 660-61.

When questioned, the *syn boiarskii* Trofim Mikhnev said . . . he arrived in Azov to meet the atamans and Cossacks one week after Christmas. And on the same day the atamans and Cossacks took him to their circle [*krug*], and when he came to the circle he gave them the sovereign's message, and they took the sovereign's message from him respectfully; and after taking the message they read it aloud in the circle to the atamans and Cossacks; and after reading the sovereign's message they said to him, Trofim, [that] it is written in the sovereign's message to them that they should dispatch from Azov to Moscow together with him, Trofim, the best men from among the atamans and Cossacks, as many as was fitting, to attend to various affairs of the sovereign. And they, so they said, had already sent their best men to Moscow, to the sovereign . . . the ataman Antip Ustinov with companions, ten men in all, and through them they had written truly to the sovereign in Moscow about the entire Azov affair. And the best men among them, so they said, are those whom the host chooses to send to the tsar; otherwise they have no best men on the Don, they said, all being equal among them.

VIII:82. A CALL FROM THE HOST AT AZOV TO COSSACK SETTLEMENTS, 1638

In the summer of 1638 the Don Cossack Host encamped at Azov sent this message to the Cossack settlements upstream.

Reference: *RIB*, vol. 18, col. 839.

From Azov, from the atamans and men of the Don, from Timofei Iakovlev and the entire great host of the Don: a petition to the atamans and men of the upstream settlements. . . . The Crimean [Tatar] prisoners, when questioned, made known to the host that the Crimean tsar [khan], by order of the Turkish tsar [sultan], is marching on Azov. . . . And you, the atamans and men, should come to Azov to the aid of the host, lest your Cossack glory be lost; [for] we risked our lives in the struggle for the fortress of Azov, and so now, praying to the merciful Savior, we shall stand together like brothers, lest our Cossack glory be lost, and lest we have to surrender this fortress of Azov. And you, the atamans and

men, should make haste to join the host at Azov; do not tarry, ride day and night. And this message from the host shall be carried by horsemen with the greatest speed, from settlement to settlement, throughout the Cossack territory.

VIII:83. THE RECORD OF THE TSAR'S BOUNTY TO THE DON COSSACKS, 1638-1645

This list, dated August 20, 1646, is from the Muscovite government's record of the subsidies (zhalovanie) sent to the Don Cossacks during the preceding eight years. The record was based upon and was meant to confirm the statement rendered by the Cossacks in connection with their petition for another subsidy.
Reference: RIB, vol. 26, cols. 195-97.

In the year 146 [1638] the sovereign's bounty was sent to the Don, to the atamans and Cossacks . . .: 200 cheti [or chetvert'—in the seventeenth century one chetvert' of rye varied from 5 to 8 poods; one pood is about 36 pounds] of rye flour, 50 cheti of groats, 50 cheti of oat flour, 150 pails of spirits, 100 poods of powder for firearms, 150 poods of cannon powder, 200 poods of lead, 500 rubles in money.

In the year 147 [1639] the sovereign's bounty was sent to the atamans and Cossacks of the Don . . .: 6,000 rubles in money, 1,000 cheti of rye flour, 500 cheti of rusks, 300 cheti of oat flour, [and] 200 cheti of groats: 2,000 cheti in all. [Also] 100 poods of cannon powder, 200 poods of powder for firearms, 200 poods of lead, and 350 iron cannonballs for the cannon, and 5 poods of fuses.

In the year 148 [1640] the sovereign's bounty was sent to the atamans and Cossacks, through their envoys, Ivan Katorzhnoi and his companions: 6,000 rubles.

In the year 149 [1641] the sovereign's bounty was sent to the atamans and Cossacks . . .: 8,000 rubles in money; 5,000 cheti of grain supplies were also ordered to be sent, but these supplies were not sent in that

year because the Turks attacked Azov.

In the year 150 [1642] . . . the sovereign's bounty was sent to the atamans and Cossacks: 5,000 rubles.

In the year 151 [1643], the sovereign's bounty was sent to the atamans and Cossacks: 2,000 rubles in money, 200 rolls of nastrofil [a kind of cloth] and English cloth; also 2,500 cheti of grain supplies, 200 pails of spirits, 250 poods of powder for firearms, 50 poods of cannon powder, 300 poods of lead.

In that same year . . . were sent to the atamans and Cossacks: 2,000 rubles in money, 23 rolls of cloth, 100 pails of spirits.

In the year 152 [1644] were sent . . .: 150 poods of powder for firearms, 50 poods of cannon powder, 150 poods of lead. In the same year, 152 . . . the sovereign's [bounty] was sent to the atamans and Cossacks: 5,000 rubles in money, 100 rolls of English cloth, 350 poods of powder for firearms, 60 poods of cannon powder, 350 poods of lead; also 3,000 cheti of grain supplies.

In the year 153 [1645] . . . were sent to the atamans and Cossacks: 2,000 rubles in money, 50 rolls of cloth, 200 poods of powder for firearms, 100 poods of cannon powder, 200 poods of lead.

VIII:84. MESSAGES FROM THE DON COSSACK HOST AT AZOV TO THE TSAR, 1640-1642

Reference: RIB, vol. 24, cols. 50, 53 [message of 1640], 177 [1641], 288 [1642].

[September 10, 1640:]
And we, your slaves, have taken the fortress of Azov by the grace of God . . . to be your sovereign patrimony. But now, Sire, we, your slaves, have no men left to hold your tsarist patrimony: all have wandered off their separate ways, being naked and barefoot, and hungry and cold.
. . .

And if we do not receive your favor and bounty, Sire, we, your slaves, shall have to go back from this fortress to our old yurts, and we shall not be able to hold this fortress; for we are not garrison soldiers: our men are unruly, and cannot be restrained from going where they please; and may Your Sovereign Majesty not be disgraced and reproached in foreign lands by infidel pagan tribes.

[Concluding portion of a message of May 8, 1641:]

And we, your slaves, Sire, have sent our Cossacks to the people of the town of Cherkask [on the Don] and to the people living along the Manych River [a left tributary of the Don], to come to our aid against your enemies, Sire, and to defend your, the sovereign's, patrimony, the fortress of Azov; and they replied to us: "We do not wish to die for the stones [of the fortress]. We shall die," they said, "for our own wooden chips [i.e. our own homes]," and they do not heed us at all, Sire, and do not come to our fortress. But those on the upper Don, Sire, are responding to the message from our host and are coming to our aid. And we, your slaves, Sire, are glad to die for the Church of John the Baptist [the Orthodox church built by the Cossacks in Azov] and for you, the righteous sovereign, and for your, the sovereign's, patrimony, the fortress of Azov.

[February 7, 1642—after a summer and fall of assaults by a large Turkish-Tatar army:]

And if, Sire, your voevoda does not come to us soon with his soldiers, then dire necessity will force us to abandon this place, for we, Sire, have no grain supplies whatever, nor lead, nor gunpowder, and we are utterly destitute and dying of starvation; and there is no one [i.e. no able-bodied defenders] left, Sire, and nowhere and no means to live: the entire fortress is destroyed and all the houses are wrecked; and many men, Sire, lie very sick from their wounds, and many others have lost their eyes or their arms or their legs. And others, Sire, while awaiting your decree, have wandered away from the fortress upstream in search of food, since there is nothing left to eat or drink in the fortress. But if, Sire, you will order your voevoda to join us here soon with his soldiers, then we, your slaves, shall be glad to serve you, Sire, together with your voevoda and soldiers, as long as merciful God gives us help, and we shall be ready to stand up against your enemies, Sire, and die together, and lay down our lives.

VIII:85. AN ORDER FROM THE TSAR TO THE DON COSSACK HOST, APRIL 30, 1642

This message sent in the name of the tsar to the Host of the Don signaled the end of a colorful episode in Cossack history.
    Reference: *RIB*, vol. 24, cols. 339–40.

And we, the great sovereign, dispatched to you, the atamans and Cossacks and the entire Host of the Don, our dvorianin Afanasii Zheliabuzhskii and the clerk [*pod"iachii*] Orefa Bashmakov with our sovereign bounty and our gracious address; and we ordered them to inspect the fortress of Azov. Their inspection showed that the fortress of Azov has been wrecked and destroyed to its foundations by the Turks and Crimeans, and there is no way of rebuilding that fortress in a short time, and there is no place [from which] to withstand the attack of [enemy] soldiers. . . . And now it has come to our certain knowledge that the [Turkish] sultan Ibrahim has a great many soldiers in readiness to attack Azov, Turks and Crimeans and men of other lands, more than heretofore; and that before long they will advance on Azov by land and by sea; and that after laying siege to Azov they intend to devastate our border towns. And it would not be expedient for us now to receive the fortress of Azov and to dispatch a voevoda and soldiers there; and it would be impossible for them to stay in such a devastated place. . . . Out of pity for you, the atamans and Cossacks, and all Orthodox Christians, [and] in order to stop the shedding of Christian blood, we, the great sovereign, have ordered you to abandon the fortress of Azov and to return to your former places where you lived before, lest the infidel Mohammedans come and destroy you. And in the future we, the great sovereign, shall favor you with our tsarist bounty as heretofore, as soon as you go back to live in your former places.

VIII:86. INSTRUCTIONS FOR RECRUITMENT FOR SERVICE ON THE DON, 1646

In order to replace the heavy losses suffered by the Don Cossacks in the Azov war of 1637–42, the Moscow government in 1646 sent the following instructions (among others) to the dvoriane Zhdan Kondyrev and Mikhail Shishkin. The "itinerant men" [*guliashchie liudi*] referred to were *vol'nye liudi*, literally "free" or "unattached" men, who bore neither tiaglo nor service obligations and were not enrolled in any urban or village community.

Reference: *RIB*, vol. 24, cols. 751-52.

And when Zhdan and Mikhail and the clerk Kirill arrive in the towns of the Plain [pol'skie goroda], and in Voronezh, they shall order town criers in those towns to summon, day after day, itinerant men to enlist: sons living with fathers, and brothers with brothers, and nephews with uncles [i.e. men who were not heads of households and were therefore free to leave]; and such men should be recruited from all the border towns. Wages should be paid to them according to this, the sovereign's decree, as written above: those who have their own harquebuses [*pishchali;* could also mean muskets] shall be given five and a half rubles each; and those who do not have their own harquebuses shall be given four rubles and a harquebus each; and to each man shall be given one pound of gunpowder and two pounds of lead when he leaves.

. . .

And when Zhdan and his companions have recruited 3,000 itinerant men in the towns of the Plain and in Voronezh, according to this, the sovereign's decree, . . . Zhdan shall collect grain supplies, spirits, gunpowder, lead, canvas, iron, and tar, and plenty of oakum, and ships, and boatsmen; and they shall load the money given by the sovereign, and the cloth, the grain supplies, the spirits, the powder, the lead, and everything else upon those ships and shall sail to the Don without delay, taking with them the itinerant men whom they will have recruited according to the sovereign's decree.

VIII:87. THE VOEVODA OF VORONEZH CONCERNING FUGITIVES AMONG THE COSSACKS, JUNE 22 AND 26, 1646

These reports to Tsar Alexis from the voevoda Andrei Buturlin in Voronezh concern a Cossack embassy (*stanitsa*) under Ataman Ivan Katorzhnoi which was on its way back from Moscow to the Don. The embassy had evidently attracted some fugitives.

Reference: *RIB*, vol. 24, cols. 883, 1106-07.

[Report of June 22, 1646:]

Your message, Sire . . . in answer to the petition of Roman Boborykin, has reached me. And this is written in your message: that Roman's bondmen [*kabal'nye liudi*] have run away from him . . . and that Roman Boborykin's runaway bondmen and many others, Sire, are known to be now in Voronezh with Ataman Katorzhnoi and his companions. And I, your slave, in response to the message from you, the sovereign tsar and grand prince of all Russia Aleksei Mikhailovich, sent commanders [*golovy*], captains [*sotniki*], dvoriane, deti boiarskie, strel'tsy, and Cossacks to Ataman Ivan Katorzhnoi and his companions, and I ordered them to seize Roman Boborykin's runaway bondmen and to bring them to the voevoda's office [*s"ezzhaia izba*]. And Ivan Katorzhnoi and his companions disobeyed your order, Sire, and refused to surrender the fugitives, and they said: "Should the voevoda himself come to seize the fugitives, we shall cut off his ears and send them to Moscow; for we have an oral order from the sovereign not to surrender men who have fled from their masters."

[Report of June 26, 1646:]

And in obedience to your decree, Sire, we, your slaves, ordered the ataman Ivan Katorzhnoi and his companions to appear at the voevoda's office. And on the sixteenth day of June, Ivan Katorzhnoi and his Cossacks did come to the voevoda's office. And we, your slaves, told them in accordance with your letter and instructions, Sire . . . that they should return the bondmen and peasants who had fled from their masters to the petitioners who had made petition concerning them, and should not take them to the Don with them. And the ataman and the Cossacks did not obey your order, Sire, and they answered us, your slaves, that they would not surrender the men who had fled from their masters [and] were now with them. They denounced your messages and instructions as being fraudulent. . . . And they also said that they had an oral order from you, the sovereign, not to surrender bondmen who had fled from their masters. . . . On the eighteenth day of June, Sire, in response to the petition of Roman Boborykin, we, your slaves, sent word once again to Ivan Katorzhnoi that he should come to the voevoda's office. And Ataman Katorzhnoi came to the voevoda's office with his entire embassy and with many men who had fled from their masters. And at the voevoda's office we, your slaves, ordered your sovereign decree to be read to Ivan and the Cossacks, and we spoke to them and told them, in accordance with your instructions, that they should return those men who had fled from their masters to the petitioners. And Ivan, in my presence and in the presence of the people of Voronezh, the commanders, the dvoriane, and the trading men, struck Danilo [Danilo Miasnoi, the dvorianin sent from Moscow to seize the fugitive bondmen and peasants who were leaving for the Don with the Cossacks] in the windpipe, and snatched from him, Danilo, your sovereign order which you had dispatched to him from the Ambassadorial [i.e. Foreign] Office [*Posol'skii Prikaz*], and thrust it into his boot-top and kept it there.

VIII:88. A COSSACK PETITION, JANUARY 12, 1659

When, in 1658, there was a delay in Moscow's subsidy, the Cossack Host of the Don petitioned the tsar as follows.

Reference: *RIB*, vol. 34, cols. 371-72. For records of the continuing subsidies for 1651-61, see ibid., cols. 775-77.

Deprived of your bounty, Sire, deprived of provisions, we, your slaves, are perishing; we are dying of hunger to no purpose, our entire host along the entire river [Don]; and lacking gunpowder, Sire, and lacking lead, we are delivered to your enemies, Sire, for naught. Because of this great and pressing hunger and nakedness, many of our brethren are ready to wander off their separate ways; and we know not, Sire, what is our offense against you, the great sovereign, that we have been deprived of your sovereign bounty—grain supplies and powder and lead. For we, your slaves, have served your father, the great sovereign tsar and grand prince of all Russia Mikhail Fedorovich of blessed memory; and we serve you, Great Sovereign, living off grass and water alone, and not off pomest'ia, Sire, nor off patrimonial estates. . . . And for you, the great sovereign, and for your sovereign Muscovite and Russian state we fight against your enemies, Sire, the Turks and the Tatars; we do not hesitate to sacrifice our lives, we sustain wounds and mutilations, and we endure captivity; and now we, your helpless slaves, suffer want and great hunger without provisions. . . . Merciful Sovereign Tsar . . . grant us your bounty . . . and for our services and for our blood and for the sufferings we have endured, reward us with your bounty, in money and grain supplies, and gunpowder, lead, and cloth, . . . lest we, your slaves, disperse our separate ways because of such great hunger and want, and leave deserted your, the sovereign's, patrimony, the river Don.

CHAPTER IX

The Ukraine, Poland-Lithuania, and Russia
in the
Late Sixteenth and Seventeenth Centuries

Note: Concerning earlier developments in the geographical regions treated here, see especially Chapter V.

Its military and economic strength sorely taxed from 1558 on by the Livonian War, the Grand Duchy of Lithuania sought help from Poland. The Poles in return sought to tighten the bonds between the Grand Duchy and the Kingdom of Poland. The parties discussed the issue in a diet at Lublin. From the "diary" or record of the Diet of Lublin one can see the arguments presented on each side, as illustrated in part by the following excerpts. The first is from the speech of the bishop of Cracow, Philip Podnewski, to the Lithuanian Senators (i.e. members of the Council of Lords) on February 12, 1569.

Reference: Arkheograficheskaia Komissiia, ed., *Dnevnik Liublinskogo seima 1569 g.* (St. Petersburg, 1869), pp. 62-63, 65-66, 69.

King Iagailo [Jagiello], being the true hereditary sovereign of the Grand Duchy of Lithuania . . . [and] wishing to carry out the obligations he had assumed in relation to the Kingdom of Poland at the time of his election as king of Poland, relinquished to the kingdom for all time to come the rights of succession and inheritance he enjoyed in the Grand Duchy of Lithuania and granted them to the Kingdom of Poland, or, more correctly, granted them to a single commonwealth [*rzeczpospolita*] composed of two nations. He united both these countries into a single whole and did this with the consent of the lords in council and men of every estate in Lithuania, who agreed to this voluntarily and subsequently themselves confirmed this in treaties concluded with us, saying that they wished to live in brotherly amity with the Poles for all time to come. . . .

Iagailo and Vitovt . . . joined the Grand Duchy of Lithuania to the Kingdom [of Poland] in such a way that from that time onward there would be not two federated nations but a single state, a single people, a single Council [of Lords], under a single sovereign.

. . .

And so, noble lords, your ancestors . . . always recognized this union. . . .

Therefore we beg you, our kind and dear lords and brothers, not to cast doubt upon the charters and the indubitable and weighty deeds of your ancestors. Renew and conclude with us such a union as would not deviate in any way from the previous agreements and would be honorable and profitable both for you and for us.

. . .

On the basis of their previous incorporation, out of the two above-mentioned nations the Kingdom of Poland and the Grand Duchy of Lithuania form a single identical, indivisible body, a single assembly, [and] a single nation, so that henceforth this single assembly of two nations, [this] unity, [this] indivisible nation, and [this] virtually uniform, homogeneous, identical, and indivisible body shall have a single head: not separate sovereigns but a single one—the Polish king, who shall be elected in Poland and nowhere else, in accordance with the old customs and privileges, by joint vote of the Poles and the Lithuanians.

The Lithuanian senators on February 15, 1569, presented a written reply containing a lengthy statement of their position (of which only a fragment is given here) followed by their own plan for union.

Reference: Arkheograficheskaia Komissiia, *Dnevnik Liublinskogo seima*, pp. 75, 83-85.

There have been Lithuanian grand dukes in Lithuania who were not at the same time kings of Poland; but this did not disrupt their brotherly love, because your ancestors did not aspire to enlarge their kingdom at the expense of Lithuania, but together with our own ancestors they preserved the integrity of both states; they loved each other and thereby inspired fear in their enemies.

For brotherly love must exist on the basis of equality; it must bring equal benefit to both nations. But if the Grand Duchy of

Lithuania is incorporated into the Kingdom [of Poland], there will not be any love, since in such a case the duchy would perforce be eclipsed and its people would perforce turn into a different people; and in this way there could not be any brotherhood, since one of the brothers, that is, the Lithuanian nation, would be lacking.

[The Lithuanian plan for union:]

This common sovereign, the Polish king, who shall at the same time be the grand duke of Lithuania, shall be obliged to go to the Grand Duchy of Lithuania within three months after his coronation to be enthroned in Vil'no [Vilna, Vilnius, Wilno]. Until he comes to the [Grand] Duchy of Lithuania, ascends the throne with all the traditional ceremonies, and takes an oath to maintain our rights and liberties, he shall have no authority to issue decrees in the Grand Duchy of Lithuania.

· · ·

These general diets shall be held alternately—first in Poland, then in Lithuania.

However, separate diets, convoked by the king of Poland or by him in his capacity as grand duke of Lithuania, may be held both in the Kingdom [of Poland] and in the Grand Duchy of Lithuania, to satisfy all the particular needs of these states that may arise.

· · ·

Dignities, offices, and likewise the standing of estates in the Grand Duchy of Lithuania shall remain inviolate for all time to come.

· · ·

Both Poles in Lithuania and Lithuanians in Poland shall be permitted to acquire residence and immovable property of every kind in any lawful way; but no spiritual or temporal dignities, or any land [*zemskie*, of the state administration], court, or legal offices shall be bestowed upon anyone who is not a native resident of the Grand Duchy of Lithuania.

IX:3. LUBLIN: THE MANIFESTO OF KING SIGISMUND AUGUSTUS CONCERNING VOLYNIA AND PODLIASH'E, MARCH 12, 1569

The Lithuanian senators having left the diet in a huff, King Sigismund Augustus was prevailed upon to issue on March 12, 1569, a "universal" or proclamation concerning Volynia and Podliash'e, which together with Kiev and Podolia constituted the vast southern part of the Lithuanian state. This is the crucial passage from that universal. A similar universal was issued concerning the Kiev region on June 6, 1569.

Reference: Arkheograficheskaia Komissiia, *Dnevnik Liublinskogo seima*, p. 189. For the proclamation on Kiev, see S. Kutrzeba and W. Semkowicz, *Akta unji Polski z Litwa, 1385-1791* (Krakow: Nakladem Polskiej Akademji Umiejetnosci i Towarzystwa Naukowego Warszawskiego, 1932), pp. 309-18.

We have restored to the Kingdom of Poland, and united to it for all time to come, our lands of Podliash'e and Volynia, which had indeed for some time remained under the Grand Duchy of Lithuania, not by any legal right, but on the pretext that we were the

sovereign of both these states; but [these lands] in the past had always belonged to the Kingdom [of Poland], and had always been under the rule and administration of the kings of Poland and of the commonwealth of the kingdom.

IX:4. LUBLIN: A LITHUANIAN RESPONSE, JUNE 27, 1569

Faced with the loss of their southern provinces, the Lithuanians rejoined the Diet of Lublin. The diary records that on June 27, 1569, the starosta of Samogitia [Zhmud', the old Lithuanian heartland in the north], Khodkevich [Chodkiewicz], spoke as follows.

Reference: Arkheograficheskaia Komissiia, *Dnevnik Liublinskogo seima*, p. 471.

"It would be most painful for us or for our grandchildren if in time it would be necessary to look upon these acts not with joy but with bitterness; or if we should come to reproach ourselves for not realizing our enslavement.

"We are now driven to such an extremity that we must kneel at the feet of Your Majesty with a humble petition."

Thereupon the Lithuanians fell to their knees with great outcries, and the starosta of Samogitia continued:

"We beseech you in God's name to remember our services, our loyalty to you, and the blood we have shed for your sovereign glory. Vouchsafe to arrange matters so that we might all depart with honor and not with derision or humiliation, so that our good name and your royal conscience may be preserved. In God's name we beseech you to recall what you have confirmed by your own royal oath."

Whereupon the Lithuanians arose weeping. And among us Poles there were but few who did not weep or who were not moved with pity, for many lords of the council were weeping.

IX:5. LUBLIN: THE ACT OF JULY 1, 1569

Finding their entreaties to be in vain, the Lithuanians on July 1, 1569, signed the act that is known as the Union of Lublin. Although all the provisions of the act were not immediately enforced, it initiated a new stage in the Polonization of the Lithuanian-Russian state, as the following passages suggest.

Reference: Arkheograficheskaia Komissiia, *Dnevnik Liublinskogo seima,* app. 83, pp. 725-28.

The Kingdom of Poland and the Grand Duchy of Lithuania shall henceforth form a single indivisible body and likewise a single joint commonwealth, in which the two states and the two nations have joined and merged into a single nation and a single state. This single nation must henceforth [and] for all time to come be ruled by a single head, a single sovereign, a single common king, who shall be elected by joint vote of the Poles and the Lithuanians (which election must take place in Poland) and shall then be seated on the royal throne and crowned in Cracow. This election, in accordance with the Charter of [King] Alexander, must not be prevented by the absence of one of the parties, because for this act the lords in council and all the other estates of the Kingdom of Poland and of the Grand Duchy of Lithuania must be summoned without fail and in legal form.

The election and coronation of the grand duke of Lithuania, which heretofore has taken place in Lithuania separately, must now come to an end, so that henceforth there should be no sign or semblance to show the existence of the coronation or anointment of a grand duke of Lithuania. But since the title and offices of the Grand Duchy of Lithuania remain, each new king, upon election and coronation, must be simultaneously proclaimed king of Poland and grand duke of Lithuania, Russia, Prussia, Masovia, Samogitia, Kiev, Volynia, Podliash'e, and Livonia.

· · ·

This double state must always have a common Council [of Lords] and Diet, headed by its sovereign, the king of Poland. The Lithuanian lords must sit in person amidst the Polish lords [at the Council], and the Lithuanian delegates [must sit] amidst the Polish delegates [at the Diet]; and they must discuss together their common needs, both in the Diet and outside it, in Poland and in Lithuania. So that one side would give the other advice and aid, the king must preserve inviolate and unbroken all the rights and privileges that belong to the lands and peoples of the Kingdom of Poland and the Grand Duchy of Lithuania.

· · ·

All the statutes and enactments of whatever kind which, against [the interests of] the Polish nation, were drawn up and approved in Lithuania concerning the acquisition and possession by Poles of estates in Lithuania ... must be declared invalid, as being contrary to justice, mutual brotherly love, and the common unity or union. Poles shall be permitted to acquire and possess estates in Lithuania, and likewise Lithuanians in Poland, by any means that correspond to the laws of the country in which the acquired estate is located.

· · ·

Henceforth the king shall not summon any separate diets for the estates of the kingdom and of Lithuania, but shall always convoke a common diet in Poland for both nations, since they already form a single body, in such a place as the king and the Polish and Lithuanian lords in council shall find most convenient.

IX:6. THE CHURCH UNION OF BREST: PRINCE CONSTANTINE OSTROZHSKII'S CIRCULAR, JUNE 25, 1595

The tightening of Polish political control over the eastern territories in the decades following the Union of Lublin was supplemented in the religious sphere by the Catholic Counter-Reformation, of which the Jesuits were the most active representatives. Several Orthodox bishops proved receptive to the idea of recognizing the authority of the Roman pope, provided the traditional Slavonic rituals were not changed. On June 1, 1595, three bishops signed the draft of the "Articles of the Union," which they sent to King Sigismund and the pope. When this became known to the prominent Orthodox leader Prince Constantine Ostrozhskii (1526-1608, founder of the famous press at Ostrog, about 150 miles west of Kiev, where many works of a religious character were published), he sent a circular letter of June 25, 1595, to the Orthodox clergy and laity to express his convictions on the proposed union.

    Reference: *AOIZR*, 4:100-01.

Outside the one true faith, implanted in Jerusalem and nourishing [Christians] as the source of the ever-flowing word of God, there is no other faith. . . . But . . . at the present time, through the devious wiles of the all-cunning Devil, [who is] the enemy and foe of the Christian race, the leading hierarchs of our true faith, seduced by the glories of this world and cast into darkness by love of pleasure, our pretended pastors, the metropolitan [of Kiev, Mikhail Ragoza] with his bishops, have turned into wolves and abandoned the one true faith of the holy Eastern church; they have renounced the most holy patriarchs, our pastors and ecumenical teachers, have adhered to the western [church authorities], have cloaked themselves in hypocrisy as in sheep's clothing, to conceal the wolf that lies hidden within, and do not reveal their intent, but have secretly agreed among themselves, as did Christ's betrayer, Judas, with the Jews, to lead astray surreptitiously all the pious Christians of this region and to cast them into perdition along with themselves, as is revealed by their pernicious and clandestine correspondence. . . . And if the faith of the Tatars, who know little of God, and of God's enemies the infidel Jews, and likewise of the Armenians and others [who live] in the state of His Royal Grace our sovereign, is protected inviolate, then should not we Christians of the true faith be protected all the more, if only we unite together and earnestly make common cause? As for myself, in fulfillment of my Christian duties, I have given my labors and my fortune all the days of my life and to this very day for the prospering of the immaculate law of the one true faith of the holy Eastern church, for the dissemination of the holy scriptures and books, and for other pious acts that praise God's holy name; I promise with God's help to serve with all my strength [and] to the best of my ability for the benefit of my kin [and] brethren, Orthodox Christians, to the very end; and I wish to stand in piety together with all of you Orthodox Christians, as long as my strength shall last.

IX:7. BREST: THE EDICT OF THE UNIATE METROPOLITAN MIKHAIL RAGOZA, OCTOBER 8, 1596

Ostrozhskii's protest did not stop the promoters of the religious union between the Roman Catholics and the Eastern Orthodox in the Polish-Lithuanian Commonwealth. The union was recognized by King Sigismund on September 24, 1595, and was praised in a papal bull later that year. In May 1596 King Sigismund authorized Metropolitan Mikhail Ragoza to convoke in Brest (-Litovsk) a council of the West Russian ("Ruthenian") church for the purpose of completing the union. The council met on October 6 and at once broke into two separate groups, the Uniate and the Orthodox. Each refused to recognize the other. Although the Orthodox group numbered over a hundred, the Polish government considered the Uniate council, headed by Ragoza, the only valid one. That council's decision was expressed in these words in the encyclical edict of October 8, 1596.

    Reference: *AOIZR*, 4:139-40. On pp. 77-78 of the same volume is Mikhail's edict of December 2, 1594, expressing his and his colleagues' desire to subordinate themselves to the pope of Rome.

We, the undersigned metropolitan and bishops of the Greek rite, by God's will assembled at a legitimate council in the Cathedral Church of Saint Nicholas in Brest, in the year of our Lord 1596, on the eighth day of October according to the old [Julian] calendar, make known for all time to come that, taking into consideration that the autocratic nature of God's church was founded and confirmed in the Gospel through the words of our Lord Jesus Christ, we [acknowledge] that the church of Christ, standing firmly upon Peter alone, as upon a rock, was governed and administered by him solely, so that the single head of a single body and the single master of a single house and the collector of God's tithes placed over mankind might look after the proper maintenance and general welfare of all. . . . In no lesser degree did the patriarchs of Tsar'grad [Constantinople], from whom this Russian land adopted the holy faith, recognize for a long time the supremacy of the Roman see of Saint Peter and subordinate themselves to it and receive their blessings from it; even though they apostatized from it many times, they always reunited with it and returned in obedience to it; finally at the Council of Florence in the year of our Lord 1438, through the patriarch Joseph and the caesar [emperor] of Tsar'grad John Paleologus, they returned in complete obedience, recognizing that the pope of Rome is the father and teacher and ruler of all Christendom and is the true vicar of Saint Peter. At the Council of Florence was likewise present our archbishop of Kiev and all Russia, the metropolitan Isidore, who brought home to Russia [the decision concerning] the union of the patriarchate of Constantinople and all the churches subordinate to it and confirmed this obedience to the church of Rome and its supremacy. . . . The patriarchs of Constantinople once again apostatized from this union of churches, and for this sin of apostasy and rupture of religious unity they fell into the power of the heathen Turks; this was followed

by many errors and evil deeds, and a lack of proper supervision in these Russian lands, and much open simony, so that heresy spread and took possession of all Russia, with churches desolated and the glory of God profaned. Not wishing to participate in such a great sin and in the pagan bondage that was the fate of the patriarchs of Constantinople, not wishing to support them in their schism and rupture of the unity of the holy church, seeking to protect churches from desolation and human souls from perdition through the heresies that have now appeared, and heedful of our own salvation and the salvation of the spiritual flock entrusted to us by God, we took counsel and last year dispatched envoys to the most holy father Clement VIII, the Roman pope . . . requesting that he receive us in obedience to him as supreme pastor of the ecumenical catholic church and deliver and absolve us from the supremacy of the patriarchs of Constantinople, while maintaining our rites and ceremonials of the Eastern Greek and Russian churches, not making any changes in our churches but allowing us to continue in the traditions of the holy Greek fathers for all time to come. This [the pope] has done, and he has sent [us] his charters and envoys to this effect, telling us to convoke a synod and make a confession of holy faith, and render obedience to the Roman see of Saint Peter, to Clement VIII and his successors. All this we have done today at this synod.

IX:8. BREST: THE EDICT OF THE ORTHODOX DIGNITARIES, OCTOBER 9, 1596

The Orthodox authorities at Brest issued their own encyclical edict whose burden was as follows.
    Reference: *AOIZR*, 4:141–42.

In addition to their other misdeeds, that apostate, the metropolitan of Kiev, Galicia, and all Russia, Mikhail Ragoza by name, together with the bishops who aided him in his evil intent, namely, Ipatii of Vladimir [-Volynsk], Kirill of Lutsk [Luck], German of Polotsk, Dionisii of Kholm [Chelm], [and] Iona of Pinsk, finally refused to heed our canonical invitation and accordingly appear at a synod before us, to answer for their godless

acts. . . . Outraged by [the actions of] these men, the divine holy Eastern church authorizes and definitively decrees through us at this council that the above-named Metropolitan Mikhail, along with the said bishops, shall be deposed and . . . stripped of all their episcopal vestments, and deprived of all [rights of] administration and authority, and even of the name of bishop . . . and cast out and excluded [from the church].

IX:9. BREST: A LETTER FROM A PARTICIPANT, 1596

A letter has survived, evidently written by one of the participants in the Brest council. Though his identity is not known, his description leaves no doubt as to his point of view.
    Reference: *AOIZR*, 4:146.

In October [15]96 . . . there was a great synod in Brest for the sake of [reaching] an agreement between the Greeks and the Romans [i.e. Orthodox and Catholics], at which the metropolitan [Mikhail] Ragoza [of Kiev] and the prelates, . . . having forsaken holy ecumenical Greek Orthodoxy, secretly and shamefully repaired to the communion of the Roman pope . . . for which they were all feted at the castle by the Romans, and were diverted like bears by buffoons' music and rattles; though in reality they were being laughed at [by the Catholics]. But [the prelates who joined the Catholic church] were not able to seize and draw after them a single sheep, but were alone in surrendering themselves to the wolf; while the entire flock, praise be to God, being safely protected by God himself [and] united in heart and word, remained to praise God in its ancient orthodoxy; but they [the prelates], being traitors and enemies, violators and transgressors of their oath to the sovereign king and of the freedoms and tranquillity of Christians, were removed from [the ranks of] the clergy and from all authority in the church, and deprived of their episcopal power, and transformed into laymen, through the [action] of the patriarchal legates and the other metropolitans, bishops, archimandrites, abbots, archpriests, and presbyters, one hundred and six in number, in addition to many princes, lords, and envoys from both states, the Kingdom of Poland and the Grand Duchy of Lithuania, and by all Orthodox Christians jointly.

IX:10. BREST: THE EDICT OF MIKHAIL RAGOZA, OCTOBER 10, 1596

The Uniate Council's final edict was issued by Metropolitan Ragoza on October 10, 1596. The import of this edict, including the last sentence of the excerpt quoted here, is to be understood in the light of King Sigismund's proclamation of five days later, recognizing the Uniate church as the only legal "Ruthenian" church in the Polish-Lithuanian Commonwealth.
    Reference: *AOIZR*, 4:148-49.

By the will and at the command of His Royal Grace [King Sigismund III of Poland], we assembled a council on the sixth day of October according to the old [Julian] calendar. . . . Having gathered here in Brest on the day appointed for the synod, the bishop of Peremyshl', Mikhail Kopystenskii, and the bishop of L'vov, Gedeon Balaban, and other confederates of theirs who are named below, refused to gather with me, their metropolitan and superior, in the church [designated as] the usual meeting-place for the synod; but in defiance of His Royal Grace's authority and mine, their elder pastor's, they held some kind of meeting in an unwonted and unseemly place, in a house where heretical meetings often took place and blasphemous sermons [were read]; and there, in that shameful house, they allowed masses to be said, and they gathered secretly with heretics and with persons who did not belong to the council. More than once did we remind them that they should stop these clandestine meetings and sit with me, their elder archbishop, and the other bishops in the usual place, in the cathedral church where councils were formerly held, and determine, discuss, and reach decisions concerning God's church. But since they have acted both against the authority of the sovereign and against our pastoral will, and have congregated with heretics in violation of our laws and canons, and have allowed masses to be celebrated in an alien diocese against regulations, we therefore, by virtue of the authority given to me by God and by my superior [the Roman pope], through the authority of the council, and with all my brethren, the reverend bishops who are with us here, deprive [the following men] of their ecclesiastical rank: Mikhail Kopystenskii, bishop of Peremyshl' and Sambor; Gedeon Balaban, bishop of L'vov and Kamenets [Kamieniec]; Nikifor Tur, nominated archimandrite of the Kiev Monastery of the Caves . . . and all the priests [*sviashchenniki*] who congregated with the heretics and held evil counsel in communion with them, having separated from our lawful and holy council; may a curse be upon them all, and we hereby depose and remove them from their episcopal sees and dignities forever, so that they should not dare to wear a stole around their neck, or to perform any holy offices of any kind, for all time to come and without any absolution by God the Father and the Son and the Holy Ghost. And if anyone should recognize those whom we have cursed as bishops or priests, may he himself and his house be accursed by the Father and the Son and the Holy Ghost. We have made these things known to His Royal Grace our sovereign, so that His Royal Grace, as our supreme lord, should vouchsafe to fill these bishoprics and abbacies and the churches of those archpriests and priests, which are now vacant, with other persons of His Royal Grace's own choosing.

IX:11. CHARTERS ESTABLISHING ORTHODOX BROTHERHOODS (BRATSTVA), 1582-1597

One of the responses of the Orthodox to the pressure from the Catholic church in the closing decades of the sixteenth century was the creation of *bratstva* or fraternities in cities that had significant Orthodox populations, such as Vil'no, Minsk, Mogilev, Kiev, L'vov, Lutsk, and Brest. These fraternities received moral and even some financial support from the Orthodox patriarchs of the Near East, who viewed them as outposts in enemy territory. Some of the privileges and functions of the fraternities are illustrated in the following excerpts from their charters.

Reference: *AOIZR*, 3:269-70 [charter of 1582]; 4:22-24 [1589], 53-54 [1592], 172 [1597].

[Statutory confirming charter of the king of Poland and grand duke of Lithuania Stephen (Batory), given to the Orthodox merchants of Vil'no, March 1582:]

Our subjects, the townspeople [*meshchane*] of our city of Vil'no, members of the merchant fraternity, have petitioned us, the sovereign, and have brought to our knowledge that their merchant fraternity has a brick house in our city of Vil'no, built a long time ago at their own expense, ... in which house the merchant fraternity of the Greek faith in our city of Vil'no gathers to discuss the needs of its churches and asylums; and, in accordance with their ancient customs, they buy mead for the great holy festivals with their own contributions, eight times a year, ... and they come together for three days and drink that mead; and they allot and use the wax from the honey for church candles, and the profit from the mead for church needs and repairs and servitors, and for charitable gifts to the asylum of the Holy Virgin and others, and for alms to the poor. ... And in response to their petition, we, the sovereign, have ordered the regulations [drawn up for their fraternity] to be inscribed in this, our charter, beginning as follows ... "The elders elected each year by the senior and junior brethren of the merchants' fraternity from their midst will be entrusted with the administration and disposition of the fraternity funds and of all its affairs and property, in consultation with the brethren. These elders shall appoint stewards [*kliuchniki*] each year to serve the fraternity. And these elders, chosen for a year, shall watch diligently over all the property of the fraternity so that it may suffer no loss but rather that it be in-creased; and when they reach the end of their term of office, they shall render an account to the senior and junior brethren and submit a financial statement. ... If an elder be guilty of any action detrimental to the fraternity, the senior and junior brethren shall be entitled to punish him. ..."

[Statutory charter granted by King and Grand Duke Sigismund III to the Orthodox citizens of Vil'no, for a religious fraternity attached to the Trinity Monastery of that city, July 21, 1589:]

In response to the petition of many and sundry reputable townspeople of our capital city of Vil'no, men of Russian nationality and Greek faith, we have graciously given our approval to the rules and regulations concerning church affairs which the aforesaid estates and above-mentioned community of the Russian faith, the townspeople of Vil'no, of the Church of the Holy Trinity, have placed before us, the sovereign, for the greater glory of God and the increase of church services and Christian actions, almsgiving, piety, and other deeds befitting men of the Greek faith; which [rules and regulations], long observed in the churches of God and existing in printed form, those [the townspeople] calling themselves "the fraternity of the Trinity Church," have adopted for themselves to realize these purposes. ...

First, whoever wishes to join the religious fraternity and to become an enrolled brother shall give to the common fraternal treasury as much as he wishes, according to his desire and ability. Moreover, every enrolled brother is bound each Sunday, after attending the early divine service, to go to the religious fraternity

and give as much as he can and wishes to the
fraternity fund for charitable purposes. . . .
And for the support of the asylums, and
prisoners, and street beggars, they shall voluntarily give alms two times a year, namely, at
Christmas and Easter. Should any enrolled
brother, by God's will or through mischance,
lose his fortune, then he shall be given every
possible brotherly aid from the fraternal
treasury as a Christian duty; and likewise in
case of sickness, a needy enrolled brother
shall be given every possible brotherly aid in
his hour of distress, both to restore his health
and for his subsistence; and he shall be supplied
with all kinds of necessities. And should it be
the will of the Lord God to inflict death upon
a needy enrolled brother and there be no
means to bury his body, then the brethren of
the religious fraternity shall provide for his
burial from the fraternal treasury, according
to Christian custom, as their wishes and piety
may dictate. In the fraternity school, the
children of the enrolled brethren as well as
poor orphans shall be taught without charge
to read and write in Russian, Greek, Latin,
and Polish, at the expense of the fraternity,
according to its statutes. And they shall engage men of learning, clerical and secular, to
teach the school subjects and choir singing.
. . .

We likewise grant them these freedoms
and liberties: that they, in accordance with
the regulations described above and below in
this, our charter, may hold their meetings
and maintain their fraternity school attached
to the Monastery of the Holy Trinity in the
city of Vil'no, in the customary places where
they had them heretofore with the blessing
of their supreme shepherd and father, the
patriarch of Constantinople; and in their
religious fraternity they shall maintain and
observe the fraternity regulations as set down
in the patriarch's charter and issued in print
and shall voluntarily follow all their fraternity
rules. And to the records of their fraternity
affairs (whenever it may be necessary) they
shall affix a seal bearing the image of the
Holy Trinity, given them by the patriarch.
And we grant them permission: to found and
to improve churches; to maintain under their
authority clerical and secular men of learning,
to teach the school subjects as well as choir
singing; likewise to print various books, of the
Old and the New Testament, in Greek, Slavonic,

Russian, and Polish, for the needs of the
school and of the church. Furthermore: if
anyone has voluntarily given or bequeathed to
their religious fraternity any property, movable
or immovable, or should give or bequeath it
in the future, it shall remain the property of
their religious fraternity forevermore, for all
time to come. . . . And should anyone consider himself injured at the hands of the
religious fraternity, be it in religious matters
or in their other fraternal affairs, then no
other official shall judge them, but rather we,
the sovereign, alone, as the defender of all
spiritual values and of religious fraternities,
shall dispense justice.

[Charter given by King and Grand Duke
Sigismund III to the Orthodox townspeople
of Minsk, for their "cathedral church fraternity,
September 11, 1592:]

By this, our document [and] charter, we
grant permission to the townspeople of our
city of Minsk, to the religious fraternity they
maintain in our city of Minsk, to build a
wooden asylum on a suitable site, at their own
expense, according to their ability, to give
shelter there to all people afflicted by Almighty God with sickness or infirmity; likewise to build or to purchase a fraternity house,
there to hold meetings and to discuss the
needs of the asylum and the church; likewise
to buy mead at their own expense, four times
a year, . . . and to sell it, the profit to be
directed and used for the needs and decora-
tion of the church, as well as for the distribution of alms to the inmates of the asylum and
for other charitable purposes. . . . Furthermore, we grant permission to this same fraternity to maintain a school for young children,
and to retain a holder of a baccalaureate to
teach the children to read and write in Russian
and in Greek.

[Charter given by King and Grand Duke Sigismund III to the Orthodox townspeople of
Mogilev, permitting them to establish a religiou
fraternity and school affiliated with the Monastery of the Savior [Spasskii] in that city,
March 21, 1597:]

In this fraternity school the children of enrolled brethren as well as needy orphans will
be taught the Slavonic, Russian, Greek, Latin,
and Polish languages free of charge, at the expense of the brethren, according to the statute

of our fraternity; likewise we shall maintain under our jurisdiction scholars versed in letters, clerical and secular, to preach the word of God and to instruct the children in school subjects and choir singing.

IX:12. COURT AND OTHER REPORTS ON THE PEASANTRY IN THE UKRAINE, 1563-1630

The following excerpts from various types of reports and complaints have to do with the peasants of the western Ukraine in the late sixteenth and early seventeenth centuries. Both Lutsk (in the Pripet basin south of Pinsk) and Vladimir (a short distance to the west) were in the Polish-Lithuanian state.

Reference: *Arkhiv iugo-zapadnoi Rossii,* 8 pts. in 35 vols. (Kiev: Tip. G. T. Korchak-Novitskogo, 1859-1914), pt. 6, 1:46 [document of 1563], 149 [1585], 446 [1624], 471 [April 1630], 474-75 [May 1630].

[Report of the court agent (*vizh*) to his office in the Lutsk *povet* (district), July 7, 1563:]

Mistress [*pani*] Bogumila Ivanovna, the wife of Matvei Seniuta, has informed me, the court agent, that . . . on the night of May 28 the serfs rebelled, namely: the ataman [here a village elder, like starosta] of [the village of] Voinegovo with his son, and the peasants of Voinegovo . . . and the peasants of the village of Kashchinets, the ataman and his sons, and the ataman of Varivodinets with his sons. . . . They entered the manor with various weapons, broke into the house, and beat to death and murdered her husband, the master [pan] Matvei Seniuta; and that same night they fled with their wives, their children, and their belongings.

[From the list of peasants and their obligations on the Zhitany estate in the Vladimir povet, May 26, 1585:]

Tiaglo-bearing peasants: . . . These peasants are obligated: to work [for the master] five days each week; to ride with carts wherever ordered; [to pay] from each half-*lan* [the "large" lan was about twenty desiatinas, but this varied considerably from district to district] twenty Lithuanian *groshi,* two groshi as watchman's payment, two groshi as nut payment, and three *matsy* [variable unit of dry measure] of oats and three hens as rent from each half-lan.

[Report of the court investigator (*voznyi*) concerning the flight of "subjects" from the Okhmatkovo estate (Lutsk povet), July 3, 1624:]

[The local peasants] said that [ten serfs] had fled because of heavy labor, excessive taxes, the imposition of unbearable obligations, and unjust beatings. . . . They all left with their wives and children and belongings, while the horses, cattle, sheep, pigs, grain, and oxen that some left behind were appropriated by the deputy judge [*podsudok*] for his own benefit. I have myself seen this depopulation of that estate of Okhmatkovo, and witnesses from the gentry have confirmed it.

[Complaint of the landlord or master (pan) A. Firlei against the master A. Linevskii alleging oppression of peasants on the estates he had leased from Firlei in the Lutsk povet, April 17, 1630:]

As soon as he had taken over the above-mentioned estate, he began to burden his subjects with labor, rental payments, taxes, and obligations, including [the furnishing of] carts for transport, in excess of the inventory regulations [*inventar'*] and his contract [*zapis'*] . . . and he continues to burden them to this day and does great injustice to subjects [serfs] and boyars alike. [Note: In the Grand Duchy of Lithuania, boyars were a very mixed class of servitors, some belonging to the gentry (*boiare-szlachta*), and others differing from peasants only in possessing certain personal rights.] . . . He forces his tiaglo-bearing subjects . . . to work for him almost every day of the week, and after working for him all week long they are ordered on Saturday, on the eve of Sunday, to drive their carts to nearby fairs, wherever necessary.

[Complaint in the name of the landlord or master Balaban against the master Benevskii, concerning the latter's oppression of peasants on an estate leased from Balaban, in the village of Khorokhorino (Lutsk povet), May 25, 1630:]

Master Benevskii . . . is causing the plaintiff and his subjects much injustice and injury, oppressing in various ways the subjects whom he has leased, and depopulating the estate, that is: he forces his subjects to do excessive plowing and work; thus, according to the inventory regulations, those who hold half a *voloka* [land unit usually ranging from fifteen to twenty desiatinas] are required to plow in turn only four days one week, and three days the next, but his honor, the said Master Benevskii, orders and forces those who hold half a voloka to plow three days each week with oxen and then to work another three days with the same oxen or on foot. . . . Second: contrary to the inventory regulations, he forces his subjects to drive their carts to Lublin or to L'vov or even farther, and although they have been sent out with carts they are still required to do the usual work at home.

Third: he orders and forces them to work on Sundays and other holidays that are exempt by agreement, and even on Easter Day. Fourth: he makes his subjects or their wives spin spools of yarn larger than required by ancient custom and agreement, and what takes the oppressed [peasants] two days to spin is only accepted as one day's [work]. Fifth: church lands that in ancient times were granted to the church of God by the ancestors of the plaintiff and are not subject to lease have been seized illegally and are being exploited [by Benevskii]. . . . Ninth: by great and unbearable injustices and excessive work, and likewise by beating and tormenting his subjects, he has driven away in the current year several of his rented [peasants], who could not endure such injustice and were compelled to flee.

IX:13. THE COSSACKS, AS DESCRIBED IN THE DIARY OF LASSOTA, 1594

In 1594, Emperor Rudolf II of the Holy Roman Empire sent a party under Erich Lassota von Steblau to the region of the Zaporozhian Cossacks, near the rapids at the big bend in the lower Dnieper River. Although that region was then within the borders of the Polish-Lithuanian state, the Cossacks largely controlled their own affairs, and Lassota's mission was to obtain Cossack help for the emperor's war against the Turks. Lassota's diary of his trip contains one of the earliest eyewitness accounts of the Zaporozhian Cossacks, including their character, their customs, and their organization. Some passages of his diary, the reader will note, are written in the form of a report to the emperor.

Reference: Erich Lassota von Steblau, *Tagebuch des Erich Lassota von Steblau*, ed. Reinhold Schottin (Halle, 1866), pp. 208, 210-12, 214-15, 219-20, 223.

[June 3, 1594:] The Muscovite envoy Vassil Nikiporowicz arrived here with an escort of Cossacks after sailing down the Psël [a southward-flowing tributary of the Dnieper which originates not far south of Kursk]. He was sent by the grand dukes with gifts for the Zaporozhian troops, and he had a safe conduct from the Cossacks. After breakfast I met with this envoy. He told me that his master [Fedor I of Moscow; Boris Godunov was ruler in fact] was willing to aid [Your] Imperial Majesty when he realized the war would be continued. Further, he permitted the Zaporozhian Cossacks, whom he had kept in his service until now, to be used in the service of [Your] Imperial Majesty. The envoy informed me that his master wanted to bestow honor and gifts upon them. After the conference was over, we returned to the boat and stayed together until we were back in camp.

. . .

[June 9, 1594:] Arrived at the island of

Bazavluk. . . . About two miles from this place the Cossacks have for some time had their field camp. As we arrived, many shots were fired from the heavy cannon. The Cossacks, sent to meet us by some of their more noble comrades, received us in the name of the whole group. After we stepped off the boat, they accompanied us to the circle (Kolo, an assembly or council). Chieftain [*Haubtmann*, i.e. the koshevoi ataman or elected head of the Cossack Host] Bogdan Mikossinski, with fifty of his galleys and 1,300 men, had already put to sea several days before, namely, on May 31. We had it announced in the circle that we were exceedingly gratified to have found the knightly company together in good health. Since the chieftain was not present, and not all the troops were together, we did not think it proper at this time to conduct negotiations. Rather, we wanted to wait until the happy return of the chieftain with his men.

. . .

On June 20 we received an audience in the circle, and we delivered in writing the proposal with which we were charged.

Thereupon, they begged us to leave them, and our message was publicly read and each one was invited to express his opinion. After everyone had been completely silent despite repeated urgings from the chieftain, they separated (in accordance with their custom when they had something important to debate) and made two circles. In one were the commanders and in the other the troops or *czerna* [the common people] as they were called. When they conferred back and forth with one another, the troops, with their usual acclamations, finally agreed to enter the service of Your Imperial Majesty. As a sign of this a hat was thrown into the air, and forthwith they ran over to the commanders in the other circle and even threatened that, if any commander were against the decision, they would rush him to the water and drown him. The commanders consented immediately, for they did not dare to oppose the troops, who are strong and united and tolerate no contradictions when angry. The commanders merely requested that someone confer with us about the conditions. For this purpose twenty deputies were elected who formed, by sitting on the ground, a small circle in the middle of the larger one. After a long conference, we were required to reenter the circle and to come to them. As we sat in the midst of them, they said they were all willing to enlist themselves in the service of Your Imperial Majesty and to risk life and limb in this endeavor. In regard to serving in Wallachia or crossing the Danube and invading Turkish territory, they were not greatly opposed; however, there were many difficulties attached to such an action and accordingly they refused to undertake it.

. . .

As the *jassawuli* (similar to commanders or those who would like to be considered lieutenants) went over to the large circle to communicate with the others, the ordinary troops split off from the remainder again and made a special circle. After the conference was held once again, the decision was endorsed with solemn acclamations and a hat was thrown into the air. As we left the circle the army drums and trumpets were played, ten shots were fired out of the heavy cannon, and in the darkness many rockets were set off. However, in the night some restless souls, together with such people as poachers and those who have their own ships [*Czolne*] and who are daily well provisioned, found their way to the common soldiers. They ran from one hut to the other and convinced the troops of the length and the danger of the journey they were about to take. They warned that the men should reexamine their actions in order not to lead themselves astray. They said that only a small and poor compensation had been sent and that as a result it would not be possible for the men to start out and maintain themselves over such a long journey, particularly since there were even poorer comrades within their ranks. What did they intend to do with such money anyway? asked the restless ones. Should not one purchase one's daily bread first rather than a [war] horse? His Imperial Majesty might even scatter them deep in his own lands with poor reward when he did not need them any more, especially since they had no guarantee from him in the form either of a seal or of letters. With these and similar words, the common men were aroused. As the men formed the circle again early in the morning on the next day (June 21), they were of an entirely different mind. They said that on the basis of such uncertain knowledge they would not proceed any further. In addition, they questioned whether the money were available for them and who would forward the money to them, since they had received no written confirmation from His Imperial Majesty. They had also received no written confirmation about the presents and grants to be offered in the future. As a result, some [of the Cossacks] were sent to our lodgings to announce these things. . . . Since they continued to hold to their opinion, the chieftain [*Haubtmann*] became angry and gave up the rule over the circle and renounced his office. He announced that since so few of them aspired to honor, fame, and a good name, he could and would no longer be their chieftain.

After dinner the jassawuli called the whole company again to a circle, and partly drove them with beatings. Then [the assembled men] begged Mikossinski to assume again the office of chieftain, which he did. [Then the circle dispersed.]

. . .

On the twenty-fourth of June I consigned to them in the open circle, in the middle of which Your Imperial Majesty's flags fluttered, the 8,000 gold ducats. Some of them immediately spread out their Tatar capes or coats which they usually carry, poured the money onto them, and told several commanders to count [the money]. After this I left the circle for my hut of brushwood, but they remained together longer.

The next day the Cossacks again met earnestly in the circle and decided something different, namely that they did not want to send Chlopiczki [one of the subordinate atamans] to Your Imperial Majesty but rather to the grand duke in Moscow. In [Chlopiczki's] place they chose and empowered Sasko Pedrowicz and Nicipor to go jointly with me to Your Imperial Majesty. They were to conclude with you the conditions of their service and subsistence. In the meantime, Mr. Jacob Henkel was to stay behind with them in order that he might report to Your Imperial Majesty on the duties performed in service of Your Majesty.

. . .

After I had communicated with the Muscovite envoy [embassy], I sailed away from Bazavluk around noon on July 2 in a Turkish *sandal* [small boat]. With me were the Zaporozhian envoys Sasko Fedrowicz [sic] and Nicipor, who took about ten other Cossacks with them. As we pulled away from the shore, the troops fired some shots from the heavy cannon and played the army drums and trumpets.

IX:14. ROYAL MANIFESTOS CONCERNING COSSACK UPRISINGS IN THE WESTERN UKRAINE, 1596

These passages from manifestos of King Sigismund III of Poland bespeak a "Cossack problem" long before Khmel'nitskii.

Reference: *Arkhiv iugo-zapadnoi Rossii,* pt. 3, 1:85 [manifesto of Jan. 27, 1596], 131-32 [Sept. 1, 1596].

[Manifesto of the king inviting the gentry of Volynia to join the royal troops sent against the rebellious Cossacks, January 27, 1596:]

Because the unruly men of the Ukraine, not content with the crimes they have heretofore perpetrated in the Ukraine, have gathered and entered further into our domains, seizing, plundering, burning, and committing unspeakable acts of violence upon cities, towns, fortified points, and manor houses, [therefore] we, upon deliberating with those lords in council who were currently with us, and desiring to safeguard the commonwealth and protect our subjects from injury, have written our commanders [hetmans] to send troops and to act against them as against enemies of the crown. . . . Therefore we inform you of this, most noble lords, that you might make all haste to join our forces, not from obligation but from love of the fatherland and for your own safety, and after uniting with our forces might set out against those unruly men who defy the law and are enemies of your noble lords' common fatherland.

[Manifesto of the king to the inhabitants of the *voevodstva* of Volynia, Kiev, and Bratslav, September 1, 1596:]

We have received news that some unruly men from the recently dispersed unruly Cossack forces are still loitering around our castles, towns, and settlements, and in villages belonging to us, the sovereign, and to the gentry; and being without occupation they congregate again into groups, blustering and making threats. And, taking timely precautions, we, the sovereign, inform you, noble lords, of this, and order you to keep careful watch over them and to forbid them to congregate again; and most particularly, if such men who are without occupation should congregate even in small groups of five or six men, you should disperse them and quiet them down, putting some in jail, imprisoning them in our castles; as for other vagrants who are without occupation and present a danger, particularly if they create disorder, lead unruly lives, and perpetrate murders, violence, assaults, robberies, and threats, you should seize them and put them to death. . . . You should not allow Zaporozhian [Cossacks] to emerge from Zaporozhie into the Ukraine, as they wish; and you should set forth against them on horseback, fully equipped, as against enemies of the crown.

IX:15. A SERMON OF SKARGA, 1610

The condition of peasants under the Polish nobility around 1600 was eloquently criticized by the eminent Jesuit priest, preacher, and author Peter Skarga (Piotr Poweski, 1536-1612), as, for example, in this plea from the second version of his "seventh sermon," as published in 1610. In this sermon Skarga was discussing unjust laws, which he called "the fifth illness of the commonwealth."

Reference: Piotr Skarga, *Kazania sejmowe*, ed. Stanislaw Kot (Krakow: Nakladem Krakowskiej Spolki Wydawniczej, 1925), pp. 169, 179-80.

Let us touch on this evil law, according to which peasants [*kmiec*] and the little free people, Poles and faithful Christians, poor subjects, are made into slaves as if they were *mancipia*, bought or taken in a just war. And others do with them as they wish in respect to their possessions, health, and life, leaving them absolutely no defense and no court protection [*forum*] for their wrongs, sometimes intolerable, and putting on them a *supremum dominium* [supreme rule]. If it is honorable and if such law has any justice we might question the laws and customs of all the Christian world, secular and ecclesiastical. If those people are not bought nor war prisoners, if they are Poles of the same blood, not Turks or Tatars, if they are Christians, why do they moan in this slavery? Why do we not use them, not as slave laborers, but as hired laborers? If he settles on your soil and does not behave properly drive him away, but do not take his inborn and Christian freedom, and do not set yourself up as his supreme lord over his health and life without a judge! The early Christians who had slaves acquired by purchase used to give freedom to all of them as brothers in Christ when, through holy baptism, they freed themselves from slavery to the Devil; but we, faithful and blessed Christians, Poles of the same nation, who were never slaves, without any legal right make slaves by might; and like bought cattle, if, poor and wan, they flee elsewhere to look for food, we claim them back and ask for ransom, like the Turks for their prisoners. Nothing like that exists in Christian lands! Even though I know that not everybody does that, still, in accordance with an evil and savage custom and an unjust law, everybody could do it, God help them, for the damnation of their souls. How are we, having such laws, not ashamed before the whole Christian world? How may we stand before God's eyes with such tyrannical wrongdoing? How can we be not afraid that as God's vengeance some pagans will not gain such power and *absolutum dominium* over ourselves?

. . .

And that blood or sweat of living subjects and peasants, which runs all the time without stopping—what punishment does it prepare for all the kingdom? You yourself concede that there is not a land in which the subjects and soil-tillers are oppressed under such absolutum dominium, used over them by the nobility without any lawful hindrance. And we see ourselves the great oppressions not only of the little peasant under the nobility but also of those in royal possessions, from which no one can save and deliver them. An angry nobleman or royal administrator [starosta] not only can take away all that the poor man possesses but can even kill [him] whenever he wishes and however he wishes, and for that he does not suffer even a bad word.

In such a way has this kingdom provided for those poor wretches, thanks to whom we all live.

IX:16. A COSSACK PLEA TO THE SEIM, SEPTEMBER 6, 1632

This is part of the instructions the Zaporozhian Cossack host gave on September 6, 1632, to the envoys it was sending to the seim (*sejm*) or diet that was to elect a new king of Poland. The Orthodox church had been outlawed in the Polish-Lithuanian Commonwealth after the Union of Brest (see above). In 1620 the patriarch of Jerusalem, Theophanes, while passing through Kiev on his way from Moscow back to the Near East, had responded to the pleas of the local population and, under the protection of the Zaporozhian Cossacks, had restored the West Russian Orthodox hierarchy. After that the Orthodox kept pressing for recognition of their rights in the commonwealth. Under Cossack pressure, as exemplified in this request, the Diet of 1632 granted legal recognition to the Orthodox church. It did not, however, abolish the Uniate church.

Reference: *Arkhiv iugo-zapadnoi Rossii,* pt. 3, 1:340-41.

Now that there is a place and occasion for everyone to vote and to demand his privileges, we bring to the Convocation [general assembly preceding the election of a king, at which the rules and limitations binding the future sovereign were set forth], to the members of all the estates [stany], our pleas, tearfully asking of Your Graces the noble lords that our Russian nation [narod nasz Ruski] and our priests may no longer be subjected to evils and injuries from those new and strange Uniates. . . . And so at the present election for choosing His Grace a king as our most fortunate sovereign, we order our envoys to beg and beseech the commonwealth with tears that our Russian nation retain its rights and freedoms and that our ecclesiastics of the true faith remain in possession of their churches, under the jurisdiction of their worthy bishops, and retain the lands belonging to them, be free to perform their religious activities, and suffer no more evils and oppression at the hands of those disgraceful Uniates.

IX:17. LETTERS FROM KHMEL'NITSKII TO THE TSAR, JUNE 8, 1648, AND MAY 3, 1649

The first of these two letters from Bogdan Khmel'nitskii to Tsar Alexis came just after Bogdan's victories over the Poles in April and May 1648.

Reference: Arkheograficheskaia Komissiia, ed., *Akty otnosiashchiesia k istorii iuzhnoi i zapadnoi Rossii,* 15 vols. (St. Petersburg, 1863-92), 3:207-08, 309. For a convenient collection of documents on this period see also A. Z. Baraba and I. L. Butich, comps., *Dokumenty ob osvoboditel'noi voine ukrainskogo naroda, 1648-1654* (Kiev: Naukova Dumka, 1965).

[June 8, 1648:]

Our Creator and Savior Jesus Christ, moved to pity by the wrongs suffered by his lowly people and by the bitter tears of poor orphans, has looked down upon us with mercy and compassion . . . and has vouchsafed to rescue us. [The Poles] have themselves fallen into the pit they dug for us—Almighty God has helped us to prevail over their two armies with their supply trains and to capture three commanders alive. . . .

. . . It is our desire to have in our land such a sovereign autocrat as Your Tsarist Majesty, an Orthodox Christian tsar. May the ancient prophecy of Christ our Lord come true, that everything should rest in the hands of his holy grace. And we assure Your Tsarist Majesty of this: if it be God's will, and if Your Majesty acts promptly to attack that state [Poland] without delay, we are ready to serve Your Tsarist Majesty with the entire Zaporozhian Host. Zealously we offer to you our humble services for this purpose, namely: should it come to the knowledge of Your Tsarist Majesty that the Poles once again are preparing to attack us, may you then hasten to advance immediately against them on your side, and we, with God's help, shall move against them from here; and may God fulfill the prophecy uttered in ancient times! Entrusting ourselves to him, we humbly and submissively prostrate ourselves at the feet of Your Gracious Tsarist Majesty. Written at Cherkassy [on the Dnieper about one hundred miles southeast of Kiev], on the eighth day of June 1648.

The humble servants of Your Tsarist Majesty Hetman Bogdan Khmel'nitskii with the Zaporozhian Host of His Royal Grace [the king of Poland].

[May 3, 1649:]

We petition Your Tsarist Majesty: Do not banish us from your favor; and we pray to God that Your Tsarist Majesty, as a faithful Orthodox sovereign, may rule over us as tsar and autocrat. In such a unification of all the Orthodox lies our hope under God that any enemy will utterly perish. May Your Tsarist Majesty let our emissary depart in peace; and take under your mercy and protection us and all the Russians [vsiu Rus'] who, with God's help, are now uniting against the Poles.

IX:18. THE TSAR'S REPLY TO KHMEL'NITSKII, JUNE 13, 1649

Tsar Alexis on June 13, 1649, gave the hetman's emissary Fedor Veshniak, colonel of the Chigirin regiment, a letter containing this reply.

Reference: Arkheograficheskaia Komissiia, *Akty iuzhnoi i zapadnoi Rossii,* 3:320-21.

For the good will shown toward us, the great sovereign . . . by you, the hetman, and by the entire Zaporozhian Host, in that you aspire to Our Tsarist Majesty's favor and promise to serve us, the great sovereign, with the entire Zaporozhian Host, we most graciously praise you. And as for what you wrote to us, the great sovereign, that we should order our troops to advance against your enemies . . . we inform you that our father [in 1634] . . . and we, the great sovereign, concluded an eternal treaty with Wladyslaw, the king of Poland, and with his successors the kings of Poland and grand dukes of Lithuania, and with the Polish Kingdom and with the Grand Duchy of Lithuania, confirmed on both sides by the oaths of the sovereigns, as well as by charters and seals. And because of this eternal treaty we, the great sovereign, cannot wage war and send our troops against the Lithuanian land and violate the eternal treaty. But should His Royal Majesty set you and the entire Zaporozhian Host free without violating the eternal treaty, then we, the great sovereign, Our Tsarist Majesty, shall grant you our favor, and we shall receive you, the hetman, and the entire Zaporozhian Host under the exalted arm of Our Tsarist Majesty.

IX:19. A LETTER FROM A KIEVAN ABBOT TO THE TSAR, JULY 8, 1649

The ecclesiastical school founded in Kiev by Peter Mogila (or Mohyla, metropolitan of Kiev, 1632-46) soon established a mutually beneficial exchange with Moscow, for Tsar Alexis responded favorably to letters like the following, from Innokentii Gizel', the abbot of the Monastery of the Epiphany (Bogoiavlenskii) in Kiev.

Reference: Arkheograficheskaia Komissiia, *Akty iuzhnoi i zapadnoi Rossii*, 3:323-24.

Hitherto we had a wealthy benefactor, the late Petr Mogila of blessed memory, metropolitan of all Little Russia, who, with the blessing of the most holy patriarch of Jerusalem, the lord Theophanus, who had visited us here, established at his own expense religious schools attached to his church, founded for the instruction of devout youths and the strengthening of piety; he provided for and increased the most needful teaching of the Slavonic and Greek languages, and also of Latin since they live here among Latins [Catholics], so as to thwart the beguilements of those of alien faith; the most holy patriarch of Jerusalem, Lord Paisius, who is now visiting us, has confirmed these schools, bestowing his praise and patriarchal blessing in writing. And that same Petr Mogila, metropolitan of Kiev, chose us humble monks for the task of teaching, and he settled us to live in this holy monastery. But when God recalled our aforesaid shepherd from this life, the alms-giving hand of our benefactor was withdrawn from us and we were left orphans. For a time a few noble and pious men helped us with alms; but now, in the present internecine war, some of these have been slain, others have disappeared, and we, having spent all that was given us, have no help from any source. . . . Inasmuch as Your Tsarist Majesty has summoned teachers from our church to serve you in religious matters, we are sending, in response to Your Tsarist Majesty's request, these teachers whom we have chosen from among ourselves, the hieromonk Arsenii and the hieromonk Epifanii, to serve Your Tsarist Majesty in any way you direct, and may God help them in their task; and with them we send to you the hieromonk Feodosii, a teacher and preacher of God's word. . . . And humbly we entreat Your Tsarist Majesty to grant us, the beggarly monks, your charitable gifts, such as are usually bestowed upon others, out of your benevolence and generosity.

IX:20. KHMEL'NITSKII'S PROCLAMATION OF SEPTEMBER 20, 1650

Having concluded the Peace of Zborov with the Polish government in 1649 on conditions favorable for his Cossack Host, Khmel'nitskii helped to restore the "subjects" or peasants to their former state, as shown in this proclamation or universal of September 20, 1650.

Reference: *Arkhiv iugo-zapadnoi Rossii*, pt. 6, 1:573-74.

It has come to our knowledge that in this hour, when our troops have advanced as far as the Wallachian land, some willful people, subjects of their masters, instead of being obedient and devoted to them, have become their enemies and have drowned and beaten to death many of the gentry, their masters; and now, persisting in their intentions, they still threaten the lives of their masters, and refuse to obey, and are given to rioting and insubordination. We therefore, by our present proclamation, authorize the landlords, acting in concert with our regimental commanders of Belaia Tserkov' and Kiev, to punish severely with death whatever unruly people are still found who make attempts on the lives of their masters and refuse to obey them; and those who have shed innocent blood and caused unrest shall not escape capital punishment, just as we here have put many to death.

IX:21. THE DECISION OF THE ZEMSKII SOBOR, OCTOBER 1, 1653

Having been for some time an attentive observer of the course of affairs in the Polish-Lithuanian part of the Ukraine, Tsar Alexis in the fall of 1653 decided to act. He assembled in Moscow a zemskii sobor, with the following consequences as recorded in the sobor's official decision of October 1, 1653.

Reference: *PSZRI*, 1st ser., 1:284, 287-88, 291.

The great sovereign, tsar, and grand prince Aleksei Mikhailovich, autocrat of all Russia, ordered a sobor to be convoked to deal with these same Lithuanian and Cherkassian [*Cherkaskii*—from the town of Cherkasy on the Dnieper] affairs. . . . And the sovereign tsar . . . came to the sobor in the Hall of Facets [Granovitaia palata], and at the sobor were present the great sovereign, the most holy Nikon, patriarch of Moscow and of all Russia . . . archimandrites, and abbots, with the entire holy council, boyars, okol'nichie, [other] Duma members . . . and Moscow dvoriane . . . and provincial dvoriane and deti boiarskie, gosti, and trading men from the *gostinaia* and *sukonnaia sotnia* and the *chernye sotni* and palace [*dvortsovye*] slobody, and people of various other ranks, and strel'tsy. And by order of the sovereign, tsar, and grand prince of all Russia Aleksei Mikhailovich, [the following] was read aloud to all concerning the iniquity of Jan Casimir, king of Poland, and the Council of Lords [*pany rada*], and concerning the petition of Bogdan Khmel'nitskii and the entire Zaporozhian Host to become subjects of the sovereign: . . . In past years the Zaporozhian hetman, Bogdan Khmel'nitskii, and the entire Zaporozhian Host have sent their envoys to the sovereign, tsar, and grand prince of all Russia Aleksei Mikhailovich many times, [declaring] that the Council of Lords and the entire [Polish] commonwealth have risen up against the Orthodox Christian faith of the Greek creed and against the holy Eastern churches of God, and have engaged in great persecution; and they have begun to tear away the Zaporozhian Cossacks from the true Orthodox Christian faith in which they long have lived, and to force them into their Roman faith; and they have sealed up the churches of God, and in others established the Union, and have inflicted upon them all manner of persecution and insults and unchristian hatred. . . . And they, the Cossacks . . . began to defend the Orthodox Christian faith and the holy churches of God against them, and [now] ask the favor of His Tsarist Majesty, that he, the great Christian sovereign, out of compassion for the pious Orthodox Christian faith and the holy churches of God and the shedding of the innocent blood of Orthodox Christians, should take pity on them, order them to be received under the exalted arm of His Tsarist Majesty and extend them help against the Poles, who persecute the Christian faith and the holy churches of God, and send his army. . . . And the stol'niki, and striapchie, and Moscow dvoriane, and secretaries, and *zhil'tsy*, and provincial dvoriane and deti boiarskie, and strel'tsy commanders, and gosti, and the tiaglo-bearing men of the gostinaia and sukonnaia sotnia and the chernye sotni and the palace slobody, and the strel'tsy were all questioned separately according to rank, concerning the honor of the sovereign and concerning the reception of Hetman Bogdan Khmel'nitskii and the entire Zaporozhian Host. And they too said that the honor . . . of the tsar and grand prince of all Russia Aleksei Mikhailovich must be defended, and that war must be waged against the Lithuanian king. And they, the service men, [said that] they would fight the Lithuanian king for the honor of their sovereign without sparing their lives and that they were glad to die for the honor of their sovereign; and the trading men of various rank [said that] they would be glad to give assistance and to lay down their lives for the honor of their sovereign; and [they said that] the great sovereign, tsar, and grand prince of all Russia Aleksei Mikhailovich should grant his favor to Hetman Bogdan Khmel'nitskii in accordance with their petition, for the sake of the Orthodox Christian faith and the holy churches of God, [and] order them to be received under his exalted sovereign arm [i.e. as subjects].

IX:22. THE REPORT OF BUTURLIN'S EMBASSY CONCERNING THE PEREIASLAVL' RADA AND THE UNION OF THE UKRAINE WITH MOSCOW, JANUARY 8, 1654

In October 1653, Tsar Alexis sent an embassy headed by the boyar Vasilii Buturlin to notify Hetman Khmel'nitskii of the tsar's readiness to accept as subjects the Cossacks of the Ukraine. The embassy reached Pereiaslavl', about fifty miles southeast of Kiev, on December 31. On January 8, 1654, the general assembly or Rada of the Cossacks was convoked. The following three excerpts from the official report (*stateinyi spisok*) of Buturlin's embassy deal with three events of that momentous day: (1) the meeting of the Rada (as reported to Buturlin by the secretary of the Cossack host, Ivan Vygovskii); (2) Buturlin's speech to the hetman and other Cossack dignitaries (after the Rada); and (3) the ceremony of the investiture of the hetman (following the oath of allegiance of the Cossacks and of the whole people in the Pereiaslavl' cathedral).

Reference: *PSZRI*, 1st ser., 1:306-08. For a detailed description of Buturlin's embassy and the Rada, see Arkheograficheskaia Komissiia, *Akty iuzhnoi i zapadnoi Rossii*, 10:137-276. Cf. *Vossoedinenie Ukrainy s Rossiei: Dokumenty i materialy*, 3 vols. (Moscow: AN SSSR, 1954), 3:423-90, especially 460-61, 464, 466-67.

[From the report on the general assembly (Rada) held by the Zaporozhian Cossacks in Pereiaslavl':]

After a secret assembly which the hetman held with his colonels on the morning of that day [January 8, 1654], at one o'clock the drums were beaten for an hour to assemble all the people, in order to hear their counsel concerning the matter they wished to decide. And when a great multitude of people of every rank had gathered, a large circle was cleared for the hetman and for the colonels, and then the hetman himself came out under his staff of office [*bunchuk*], and with him were judges, *esauly* [assistants to the hetman], the secretary, and all the colonels; and the hetman stood up in the middle of the circle, and the chief esaul [*voiskovoi esaul*] ordered everyone to be silent; when all were silent the hetman began to speak to all the people with these words:

"Gentlemen Colonels, Esauly, Captains [*Sotniki*], and all the Zaporozhian Host and all Orthodox Christians! You all know how God delivered us from the hands of our enemies who persecute the church of God and revenge themselves upon all Christians of our Eastern Orthodox creed; [you know] that for six years we have been living without a sovereign in our land, in ceaseless conflict and bloodshed with our persecutors and enemies, who wish to extirpate the church of God so that the very name of Russia [*imia Russkoe*] would be forgotten in our land. This has greatly wearied us all, and we see that we can no longer live without a tsar. For this reason we have now called together a public assembly [Rada] of all the people, so that together with us you might choose a sovereign from among the four [possible choices], whomever you wish: the first is the Turkish tsar, who has repeatedly invited us through his envoys [to come] under his rule; the second is the Crimean khan; the third is the Polish king, who, if we should desire, can even now receive us in his favor as before; the fourth is the Orthodox Eastern tsar of Great Russia, whom for six years now we have been beseeching with ceaseless entreaties to be our tsar. Choose now whomever you wish. . . ."

In response to these words all the people cried out: "We wish to be under the mighty arm of the Orthodox Eastern tsar [and] to die in our pious faith, rather than to fall under the rule of a pagan, an enemy of Christ."

Then the colonel of the Pereiaslavl' [regiment], Teteria, going around to every side of the circle, asked aloud: "Do you all assent to this?" The people all said: "All unanimously." Then the hetman spoke in a loud voice: "If it be so, may almighty God strengthen us under his mighty tsarist arm." And the people all cried out after him with one accord: "May God sanction, may God strengthen us, to be all united for all time to come."

[The final section of Buturlin's speech:]
    "And our great sovereign, His Tsarist Majesty, seeing on the part of the king [of Poland] such illegal and provocative acts, violations of the eternal treaty, and persecution of the Orthodox Christian faith and of the holy churches of God, and not wishing to see you, our fellow Orthodox Christians, utterly destroyed and the pious churches laid waste and blasphemed by the Latins [Catholics], has ordered you, Hetman Bogdan Khmel'nitskii, and the entire Zaporozhian Host with [its] towns and lands, to be freed from allegiance to the king because of his oath-breaking and to be taken under his exalted arm, and he has ordered his, the sovereign's, soldiers to render aid to you against those who are false to their oath and against

those who wish to destroy the Christian faith. And you, Hetman Bogdan Khmel'nitskii and the entire Zaporozhian Host, seeing the favor and bounty granted to you by our great sovereign, His Tsarist Majesty, should serve him, the sovereign, and wish him well in everything, and depend upon the favor of His Tsarist Majesty; and our great sovereign, His Tsarist Majesty, shall hold you the hetman and the entire Zaporozhian Host in His Tsarist Majesty's favor, and shall defend and protect you from your enemies."

The ceremony confirming Hetman Bogdan Khmel'nitskii in his office:
    In accordance with the decree of the sovereign, tsar, and grand prince of all Russia Aleksei Mikhailovich, the boyar Vasilii Vasil'evich [Buturlin, the tsar's envoy] and his companions presented to him, the Hetman Bogdan Khmel'nitskii, [the tokens of] the sovereign's favor: a banner, a mace, a robe, a cap, and sables.

IX:23. THE TERMS OF MOSCOW'S ACCEPTANCE OF THE ZAPOROZHIAN HOST,
MARCH 21 AND 27, 1654

In March of 1654 the chief justice (*voiskovoi sud'ia*) of the host, Samoilo Bogdanovich Zarudnyi, and the colonel of the Pereiaslavl' regiment, Pavel Teteria, came to Moscow as emissaries from Bogdan Khmel'nitskii and the Cossack Host. After discussions they reached agreement (March 21) on a set of articles defining the terms by which the population of the area controlled by Khmel'nitskii would become subjects of the Muscovite state. On the basis of that agreement the tsar issued a charter on March 27 to the Zaporozhian Host. Here are some of the significant portions of the articles and the charter. It should be noted that although Khmel'nitskii and his successors continue to use the title "hetman of the Zaporozhian Host," the area they controlled was a large part of the Ukraine and included many Cossacks other than the Zaporozhians.
    Reference: *Vossoedinenie Ukrainy s Rossiei*, 3:560-65, 567-70; Arkheograficheskaia Komissiia *Akty iuzhnoi i zapadnoi Rossii*, vol. 10, cols. 477-84 [articles], 489-94 [charter]; also in *PSZRI*, 1st ser., 1:311-12, 314-15. (Note: In *PSZRI* the articles are incorrectly dated March 12, which was the date of the arrival of the Cossack embassy in Moscow.) Translations based on George Vernadsky *Bohdan, Hetman of Ukraine* (New Haven: Yale University Press, 1941), pp. 131-40, somewhat revised.

[Articles concluded between the Cossack envoys and the tsar:]
    To the great sovereign, tsar, and grand prince Aleksei Mikhailovich, autocrat of all Great and Little Russia, and sovereign and possessor of many states: His Tsarist Majesty's subjects Bogdan Khmel'nitskii, hetman of the Zaporozhian Host, and the entire Zaporozhian Host, and the entire Christian Russian world, make petition that His Tsarist Majesty grant them all that their envoys shall petition of him, and they shall serve His Tsarist Majesty

in all his sovereign wishes for all time to come.
    . . .
    1. [The Cossacks ask] that in [Ukrainian] towns the officeholders be chosen from among those natives who are worthy of this; they shall govern the subjects of His Tsarist Majesty and collect all the revenues for the tsarist treasury honestly. For if a voevoda of His Tsarist Majesty should come [to a Ukrainian town] and begin to violate their rights and make new ordinances it would be a great annoyance to them; but if their own people be officeholders, they will

govern in accordance with their rights.

[The tsar's resolution:] And His Tsarist Majesty has granted his favor to this article and ordered it to stand according to their petition; and there shall be [elected] office-holders in the towns—mayors [*voity*], burgo-masters [*burmistry*], counselors [*raitsy*], and court assessors [*lavniki*]—and they shall collect all the revenues in money and in grain for His Tsarist Majesty, and shall pass them over to his, the sovereign's, treasury, to those people whom His Tsarist Majesty will send.
. . .

5. [The Cossacks ask] that the hetman and the Zaporozhian Host be free to receive envoys who have long come to the Zaporozhian Host from foreign parts, so long as they mean well; and only in the event that there should be something inimical to His Tsarist Majesty must the host notify His Tsarist Majesty.

Concerning this article His Tsarist Majesty has ordered that [the host] receive and dismiss envoys who mean well, and write truly and immediately to His Tsarist Majesty [to inform him] on what business they came and with what [instructions] they were dismissed. As for envoys sent by someone on business detrimental to His Tsarist Majesty, such ambassadors and envoys should be detained by the host, and [the host] should immediately write about them to His Tsarist Majesty for his orders; and they should not be dismissed without His Tsarist Majesty's orders. There should be no exchange of envoys with the Turkish sultan or with the Polish king without orders from His Tsarist Majesty.

[The charter granted by the tsar to the Zaporozhian Host:]

By the grace of God, we, the great sovereign, tsar, and grand prince Aleksei Mikhailovich, autocrat of all Great and Little Russia, have bestowed our favor upon Our Tsarist Majesty's subjects Bogdan Khmel'nitskii, hetman of the Zaporozhian Host, and the secretary [*pisar'*] Ivan Vygovskii, and the justices of the host, and the colonels, and the esauly, and the captains [*sotniki*], and the entire Zaporozhian Host; for in this year of 162 [1654], by the grace of God, he, the hetman Bogdan Khmel'nitskii, and the entire Zaporozhian Host have come under our exalted sovereign arm and have sworn an oath of eternal allegiance to us, the great sovereign, and to our, the sovereign's, children and successors. . . .

And we, the great sovereign, Our Tsarist Majesty, have graciously commanded our subject Bogdan Khmel'nitskii, hetman of the Zaporozhian Host, and Our Tsarist Majesty's entire Zaporozhian Host, to be under the exalted arm of Our Tsarist Majesty, according to their former rights and privileges which have been granted to them by the kings of Poland and the grand dukes of Lithuania; and we have ordered that these, their rights and privileges, be not violated by any means and have commanded that they be tried by their elders in accordance with their former rights; and we have decreed that the quota of the Zaporozhian Host, according to their own petition, be set at 60,000 and always be filled. And in the event that, by God's judgment, the hetman should die, we, the great sovereign, will allow the Zaporozhian Host to elect a [new] hetman, according to their former customs, by themselves and among themselves, and to notify us, the great sovereign, as to who has been elected hetman; and the newly elected hetman shall swear his oath of loyalty and allegiance to us, the great sovereign, before [our deputy] whom we, the great sovereign, shall appoint. And we have forbidden [anyone] to deprive the Cossacks, their widows, and their children of their estates and lands which they use for their sustenance, and we [have decreed] that [such estates and lands] be [registered] with them, as before — And in accordance with Our Tsarist Majesty's favor, Our Tsarist Majesty's subjects, the hetman of the Zaporozhian Host Bogdan Khmel'nitskii and Our Tsarist Majesty's entire Zaporozhian Host shall be under the exalted arm of Our Tsarist Majesty, according to their former rights and privileges and all the articles that have been written above; and they shall serve us, the great sovereign, and our son, the sovereign tsarevich Aleksei Alekseevich, and our successors, and be loyal and wish us well in everything, and set forth against our enemies and fight them whenever this shall be our sovereign will, and be obedient to our sovereign will in everything for all time to come.

IX:24. THE TREATY OF GADIACH (HADZIACZ), SEPTEMBER 6, 1658

After Bogdan Khmel'nitskii's death (1657) dissension started among different groups of Cossack officers (*starshina*), as well as between the starshina and the common Cossacks. Under the new hetman, Ivan Vygovskii (Vyhovskyi), an influential group of starshina began secret negotiations with Poland, which resulted in the treaty between the Cossack host and Poland, signed in Gadiach (Hadziacz) on September 6 (16, N.S.), 1658. Excerpts from this treaty follow.

Reference: Arkheograficheskaia Komissiia, *Akty iuzhnoi i zapadnoi Rossii*, 7:252-53 (this is a Russian translation of a condensed Polish version of the treaty). For full texts see Michael S. Hrushevsky, *Istoriia Ukraini-Rusi*, 10 vols. in 11 pts. (New York: Knigospilka, 1954-58; facsimile reprint of original edition of 1905-36), 10:334-45.

1. Three conquered provinces [*voevodstva*]—Kiev, Bratslav, and Chernigov—[forming the] Russian principalities are to be united [with the Polish-Lithuanian Commonwealth] in the same manner as the [Grand] Principality of Lithuania is; they shall have their own dignitaries.

2. The metropolitan of Kiev shall have a seat in the Senate below His Grace the [Roman Catholic] archbishop of L'vov. . . .

5. The landed estates of the Orthodox, both of the laymen and of the monasteries, which have been given to the Roman Catholics, shall be returned [to the Orthodox].

6. The Orthodox burghers [*meshchane*] shall have the same liberties and rights as the Roman Catholics.

7. Taxes from the three above-mentioned provinces . . . shall be used for hiring foreign soldiers. That armed force shall be 10,000 strong . . . and shall be under the command of the present hetman of the Zaporozhian Host [i.e. Vygovskii]. After his death it will revert to the command of the [Polish] crown hetmans and will be quartered in the Ukraine permanently for the prevention of riots. . . .

10. For the election of a new hetman of the Zaporozhian Host [after Vygovskii's death] four candidates are to be nominated [by the Cossacks], and His Grace the king is to confirm one of them.

11. The contingent of the Zaporozhian Host is 60,000. However, it is to be reduced to 30,000. . . .

13. There shall be two [Orthodox] schools [of higher learning], one in Kiev and the other in the [Grand] Principality of Lithuania. . . .

17. One hundred Cossacks from each regiment, in accordance with the lists to be submitted by the hetman, will be ennobled.

IX:25. THE NEW ARTICLES GOVERNING THE ZAPOROZHIAN HOST, OCTOBER 1659

The Treaty of Gadiach proved unacceptable to a considerable number of the Cossack starshina, as well as to most of the common Cossacks. They revolted against Hetman Vygovskii, elected a new hetman, Iurii (George) Khmel'nitskii (son of Bogdan), and expressed their willingness to come back under the tsar's protection. A Cossack rada was convoked in Pereiaslavl' in October 1659, and the Muscovite representatives concluded a new treaty with the Cossacks. The articles of 1654 were confirmed with some modifications, and a number of new articles were agreed upon. Articles of agreement similar to these were subsequently concluded also with Iurii Khmel'nitskii's successors: Ivan Briukhovetskii (1664 and 1665), Dem'ian Mnogogreshnyi (1669), and Ivan Samoilovich (1672).

(Note: Concerning the Ukraine in around 1660, see also Item VIII:33, above.)

Reference: *PSZRI*, 1st ser., 1:475-79, 482.

1. [The Zaporozhian Host petitions] that His Tsarist Majesty grant his favor [and] vouchsafe to confirm the rights and liberties of the host, which have long existed in the Zaporozhian Host: that they be tried in accordance with their own laws and maintain their liberties as regards their possessions and in court affairs, that no boyar, or voevoda, or stol'nik should interfere in trials within the host, but that they shall be tried by the elders [*starshie*] of their brotherhood [*tovarishchestvo*]: where there are three Cossacks, two shall judge the third.

And concerning this article His Tsarist Majesty has granted his favor to Hetman Bogdan Khmel'nitskii and to the entire Zaporozhian Host [and] has ordered that the article stand as in their petition.

2. In the towns the officeholders [*uriadniki*]

should be chosen from among those of their number who are worthy, and they shall have to administer, or govern, the subjects of His Tsarist Majesty and truthfully turn over the appropriate revenues into the treasury of His Tsarist Majesty.

Concerning this article His Tsarist Majesty has granted his favor [and] has ordered that the article stand as in their petition; there shall be officeholders in the towns, mayors [voity], burgomasters [burmistry], counselors [raitsy], [and] assessors [lavniki], and they shall collect for His Tsarist Majesty sundry taxes in money and grain and turn them over into his, the sovereign's, treasury, to those people whom His Tsarist Majesty will send.

. . .

8. That His Tsarist Majesty should grant his favor [and] forbid any violation of the rights accorded both to ecclesiastics and laymen in past times by princes and kings.

His Tsarist Majesty has granted: that neither spiritual nor secular rights shall be violated in any way; and the metropolitan of Kiev, and likewise the other ecclesiastics of Little Russia, shall be under the blessing of the most holy patriarch of Moscow and of all Great and Little and White Russia; but the most holy patriarch shall not interfere with [their] spiritual rights.

9. The hetman shall not receive ambassadors and envoys and couriers from neighboring or any other states, and shall not himself send ambassadors and envoys and couriers to neighboring or other states in reply to those missives, which would result in monetary losses and sundry other expenses to the Zaporozhian Host, unless the great sovereign, His Most Serene Tsarist Majesty, allows him, the hetman, to send [an emissary] into some state concerning a particular matter; and if ambassadors and envoys and couriers come to him, the hetman, from neighboring states, they are to be told in reply: whatever their mission may be, they must go to the great sovereign, to His Tsarist Majesty, to Moscow.

· · ·

New articles. . . .

1. By order and command of His Tsarist Majesty, the great sovereign, tsar, and grand prince Aleksei Mikhailovich, autocrat of all Great and Little and White Russia, the hetman and his entire host are always to be ready to serve him, the sovereign, wherever his tsarist pleasure sends them.

And the hetman and colonels and all the elders [starshina] and common people [*chern'*] in the Rada [assembly], having heard this article, resolved: "Let this article stand as it is written."

2. Likewise, wherever the great sovereign orders several regiments to be sent on the sovereign's service, he, the hetman, is to send these regiments without any delay.

And the hetman, and colonels, and all the elders and common people in the Rada, having heard this article, resolved: "Let this article stand as it is written."

3. The hetman is to remain faithful and constant for all time to come and not be tempted by any Polish enticements, nor likewise give credence to any slander concerning the Muscovite state; and if anyone should engage in such slander [the hetman] shall punish such people by death and shall write to the great sovereign about slanderous matters of any kind. . . .

And the hetman and colonels and all the elders and common people in the Rada having heard this article, resolved: "Let this article stand as it is written."

4. Without the order and without the command of the great sovereign, His Tsarist Majesty, the hetman himself with the entire Zaporozhian Host shall not go to war anywhere, nor use large or small regiments of the Zaporozhian Host to assist any neighboring states, nor send people to help them, lest by such assistance the Zaporozhian Host should diminish; and if anyone goes to war willfully, without the hetman's knowledge, he shall be punished by death.

And the hetman and colonels and all the elders and the common people in the Rada, having heard this article, resolved: "Let this article stand as it is written."

5. The great sovereign, His Tsarist Majesty, has ordered voevody of his tsarist majesty to be [stationed] with soldiers, for defense against the enemy, in the [following] Cherkassian [Cherkaskie, here could be translated as "Ukrainian"] towns of His Tsarist Majesty: Pereiaslavl', Nezhin, Chernigov, Bratslavl', [and] Uman'; and these voevody are not to interfere in the rights and liberties of the [Cossack] Host. . . .

7. If any hetman, having become hetman of the host through the decree of His Tsarist Majesty and through election by the entire host, should subsequently commit any offense,

the host shall not itself replace the hetman without the decree of His Tsarist Majesty, [even] if the newly elected hetman has committed some offense, except for treason: and the great sovereign, His Tsarist Majesty, has ordered such matters to be investigated by the entire host and has ordered a decree to be issued upon investigation, as has long been the custom in the host; and they are not to replace the hetman themselves; likewise the hetman shall not appoint colonels or other commanders without the Rada and without the counsel of all the common people, and he shall appoint the colonels of the host at the Rada, whomever they choose among themselves, from their own regiments, and shall not choose as colonels persons from other regiments, and likewise the hetman must not dismiss these colonels without the Rada.

And the hetman, and colonels, and all the elders and common people, having heard this article at the Rada, resolved: "Let this article stand as it is written."

. . .

And I, the hetman Georgii [Iurii Khmel'nitskii], with the colonels, and captains [sotniki], and with the officers of various ranks [chinovnye liudi], and with the people of various ranks in the entire Zaporozhian Host, shall be constant under the mighty arm of His Tsarist Majesty for all time to come, and shall serve him, the great sovereign, and his, the sovereign's, son . . . and their successors faithfully, and defend them against any enemy of the sovereign, upon his sovereign command, without any treachery; and we shall not make alliances with the Polish, or Turkish, or Crimean, or any other sovereign.

IX:26. THE TREATY OF ANDRUSOVO, JANUARY 30, 1667

Here are some of the more important passages of the treaty concluded January 30, 1667, at Andrusovo, near Smolensk. The treaty followed thirteen years of conflict between Russia and the Polish-Lithuanian state and provided for an armistice of a specified length of thirteen and one-half years.
    Reference: *PSZRI,* 1st ser., 1:633-35.

3. The [following] cities and lands which were conquered during this last war from the Polish crown and the Grand Duchy of Lithuania shall remain in the possession and under the sovereignty of His Tsarist Majesty, namely: Smolensk and the entire land of Seversk, with their towns and rural districts [uezdy] . . . [including Chernigov] . . . shall remain under His Tsarist Majesty. . . . And the Cossacks on the lower Dnieper, the so-called Zaporozhians, in whatever forts, islands, and settlements of their own they may live, shall owe obedience to and shall be under the protection and exalted arm of both our great sovereigns, to serve them in common against any attacking— may God forbid—Moslem forces; however, all the inhabitants, of whatever rank they may be, who remain in the the territories provisionally ceded by this treaty to His Tsarist Majesty are to enjoy everywhere the free exercise of the holy Catholic faith, without any hindrance to the performance of their

devotions in their homes; and likewise all Russian people, of whatever rank they may be, who remain in the territories returned to His Royal Majesty by this treaty are to enjoy the free exercise of the Greek [Orthodox] faith, without any hindrance to the performance of the divine services. . . .
    6. Of the cities and lands conquered [by the Russians], the following are returned to His Royal Majesty: Polotsk, Vitebsk, Dinaburg [Duenaburg, Daugavpils, Dvinsk], Liutin, Rezhitsa, Mariengauzen, and all of southern Livonia, and all the rural districts belonging as of old to the above-mentioned cities. . . .
    7. As for the city of Kiev itself, with the Monastery of the Caves and the other environs of Kiev which remain [in Russian hands] . . . it shall be evacuated and returned to His Royal Majesty and the [Polish-Lithuanian] Commonwealth [Rzeczpospolita] . . . within two years from the date of the present treaty.

IX:27. THE PEACE TREATY WITH POLAND, APRIL 26, 1686

Although at Andrusovo in 1667 Russia had promised to cede Kiev to Poland within two years, she kept the city beyond the agreed term and continued parleys with the Poles about it. In 1678 a new treaty was negotiated for a thirteen-year armistice, under whose terms Poland left Kiev in

Russian hands in return for the towns of Nevel', Sebezh, and Velizh with their districts, plus 200,000 rubles in cash. A treaty of "eternal peace" between Russia and the Polish-Lithuanian state was concluded in Moscow on April 26 (May 6, N.S.), 1686. Some of its important provisions are given here.

Reference: *PSZRI,* 1st ser., 2:773-74, 776-78.

3. We have likewise agreed and resolved that all cities and lands conquered from the Polish crown and the Grand Duchy of Lithuania during the past war, that is, Smolensk with its cities and districts [uezdy] . . . Dorogobuzh, Belaia, [and] Krasnyi with their towns and districts and all that belongs to them, as they have existed up to this time according to the armistice agreement, shall be in the possession of Their Tsarist Majesties [Ivan and Peter]; while on the other side Roslavl' and the region around the Seversk cities, Chernigov, Starodub, Novgorod-Seversk, Pochep, and others, and likewise all of Little Russia on this side of the Dnieper, the cities of Nezhin, Pereiaslavl', Baturin, Poltava, Perevolochnaia, and all the cities, lands, and towns of that area of Little Russia . . . as they have been heretofore in the possession of Their Tsarist Majesties according to the armistice agreement, shall now remain in the possession of Their Tsarist Majesties for all time to come. . . . Kiev shall likewise remain in the possession of Their Tsarist Majesties. . . . The Cossacks beyond the Dnieper River [Zadneprie, i.e. on the right bank] in its lower reaches, which is called Zaporozhie, living in the Sech' and in Kadak and in other towns . . . shall according to this eternal treaty be in the possession and under the rule of the great sovereigns, Their Tsarist Majesties, in accordance with all the ancient liberties and together with the regions they possess. . . . The kings of Poland and grand dukes of Lithuania . . . shall have no access now and for all time to come in the future to any of the above-mentioned cities and regions or to Zaporozhie . . . and shall not send anyone for any reason to those Cossacks of the cities or the lower reaches, to the inhabitants of the above-mentioned cities on both sides of the Dnieper, which have been yielded by His Royal Majesty and by the commonwealth into the possession of Their Tsarist Majesties for all time to come. . . .

8. As for the conquered cities and lands which during the years of armistice, in anticipation of this eternal peace, have been yielded into the possession of His Royal Majesty—Polotsk, Vitebsk, Dinaburg, Nevel', Sebezh, Velizh, Liutin, Rezhitsa, [and] Mariengauzen, with all of southern Livonia and with all the provinces [voevodstva] and districts [povety] of these cities which have belonged to them as of old—these cities shall be in the possession of His Royal Majesty, likewise for all time to come, and the great sovereigns, Their Tsarist Majesties and the successors of Their Tsarist Majesties, shall not interfere with these above-mentioned cities and regions. . . .

9. . . . His Royal Majesty shall not order or allow any persecution of the churches of God and the dioceses . . . of the Greco-Russian faith and of all the people living under the Polish crown and in the Grand Duchy of Lithuania who remain in that faith, or any compulsion either toward the Roman faith or toward the Union [Uniate church], but shall observe all the various freedoms and liberties of the church according to its ancient rights. . . . And in return, the great sovereigns, Their Tsarist Majesties, shall not cause the subjects of Their Tsarist Majesties of the Roman faith [living] in the states of Their Tsarist Majesties, and particularly in the lands currently detached [from the commonwealth], any injustice in their faith, or employ any coercion toward another faith, [but] they shall all the more be entirely free to adhere to that faith. . . .

10. Mindful of the welfare of Christianity, and desiring to free the peoples groaning under the Moslem yoke from such heavy bondage, . . . seeing moreover the unreliability of any kind of agreement with pagans, since those common enemies of the holy cross and of all Christians, the Turkish sultan and the Crimean khan, in violation of the peace treaties concluded with the great sovereigns, Their Tsarist Majesties, have dispatched beys and other mirzas in military attacks upon Their Tsarist Majesties' cities and regions in the Ukraine with large armies from the Crimea and from Azov, which captured many prisoners and caused notable destruction, and likewise have made warlike attacks upon the state of

the great sovereign, His Royal Majesty, failing to keep the peace concluded with them: accordingly, after much negotiation, it has been agreed and resolved that the great sovereigns, Their Tsarist Majesties, in accordance with their brotherly friendship and love for the great sovereign, His Royal Majesty, and in accordance with the desire of His Majesty the [Holy] Roman Emperor and His Majesty the king of France and the Elector of Branden-

burg, and likewise the Commonwealth of Venice, shall vouchsafe, upon the commencement of the eternal peace [now] concluded, to tear asunder the temporary peace which heretofore has existed with the Turkish sultan and the Crimean khan, and to accept an eternal alliance with His Royal Majesty, defensive against the pagans and offensive while the war with the Moslems shall continue.

IX:28. THE LETTER FROM DIONYSIUS CONCERNING THE DIOCESE OF KIEV, MAY 1686

With the gradual tightening of Moscow's control of the Ukraine the Muscovite government succeeded in obtaining the agreement of Dionysius, patriarch of Constantinople, to the transfer of the diocese of Kiev from his jurisdiction. Dionysius's letter, addressed to tsars "Ivan, Petr, and Sofiia" (Tsarevna Sophia), read in part as follows.
    Reference: *PSZRI,* 1st ser., 2:792-93.

The most esteemed messages from your God-protected realm have been brought to us. . . . Your Most Orthodox Tsarist Sovereignty . . . has asked this diocese of Kiev to be subordinated to the most holy patriarchal see of Moscow, so that when the need arises to consecrate a worthy person [as metropolitan of Kiev], upon his election by the archbishops, archimandrites and abbots, priests, hieromonks, monks, boyars, and others under the jurisdiction of this metropolitanate, and upon the permission and notification of the then governing most glorious hetman, may the then govern-

ing most blessed patriarch of Moscow and all Russia be free to consecrate him in accordance with the traditions and regulations of the church, and ordain him as the true and just and legitimate metropolitan of Kiev. . . . May the most blessed patriarch of Moscow and of all Russia, the lord Joachim . . . be free to consecrate the person who has been chosen metropolitan of Kiev in accordance with the regulations of the church. . . . In the same manner may this metropolitanate of Kiev be under the jurisdiction of the most holy patriarchal see of Moscow.

BIBLIOGRAPHY

Note: This bibliography is limited to those works that were used in the preparation of the Source Book and does not include all of the collections mentioned in the reference notes as supplementary material. In general, the publisher is given only for works published since 1900.

Adrianova-Peretts, V. P., ed. *Vremennik Ivana Timofeeva.* Moscow: AN SSSR, 1951.
———, and D. S. Likhachev, eds. *Povest' vremennykh let.* Moscow: AN SSSR, 1950.
Aksakov, Ivan S. *Polnoe sobranie sochinenii I. S. Aksakova.* 7 vols. Moscow, 1886-87.
Aksakov, Konstantin S. *Polnoe sobranie sochinenii K. S. Aksakova.* Ed. I. S. Aksakov. 2 vols. Moscow, 1861-71.
———. *Zamechaniia na novoe administrativnoe ustroistvo krest'ian v Rossii.* Leipzig, 1861.
Akty sobrannye v bibliotekakh i arkhivakh Rossiiskoi Imperii arkheograficheskoiu ekspeditsieiu Imperatorskoi Akademii Nauk. 4 vols. St. Petersburg, 1836.
Akty sotsial'no-ekonomicheskoi istorii severovostochnoi Rusi. 3 vols. Ed. B. D. Grekov (vol. 1), L. V. Cherepnin (vols. 2 and 3). Moscow: AN SSSR, 1952-64.
Aleksandra Fedorovna: see *Letters of the Tsaritsa to the Tsar;* see also Tsentral'nyi Gosudarstvennyi Istoricheskii Arkhiv v Moskve, ed., *Perepiska . . .*
Annales Bertiniani. Ed. G. Waitz. Hanover, 1883.
Antonovich, Vladimir B. *Monografii po istorii zapadnoi i iugozapadnoi Rossii.* Vol. 1. Kiev, 1885.
Arkheograficheskaia Komissiia, ed. *Akty istoricheskie.* 5 vols. St. Petersburg, 1841-42.
———. *Akty otnosiashchiesia do iuridicheskogo byta drevnei Rossii.* Ed. Nikolai Kalachev. 3 vols. St. Petersburg, 1857, 1864, 1884.
———. *Akty otnosiashchiesia k istorii iuzhnoi i zapadnoi Rossii.* 15 vols. St. Petersburg, 1863-92.
———. *Akty otnosiashchiesia k istorii zapadnoi Rossii.* 5 vols. St. Petersburg, 1846-51.
———. *Dnevnik Liublinskogo seima 1569 g.* St. Petersburg, 1869.
———. *Dokumenty ob"iasniaiushchie istoriiu zapadno-russkogo kraia i ego otnosheniia k Rossii i Pol'she.* St. Petersburg, 1865.
———. *Dopolneniia k aktam istoricheskim.* 12 vols. St. Petersburg, 1846-72.
———. *Letopis' po Ipatskomu spisku.* St. Petersburg, 1871.
———. *Letopis' po Lavrent'evskomu spisku.* St. Petersburg, 1897.
———. *Novgorodskie letopisi (Novgorodskaia vtoraia i Novgorodskaia tret'ia letopisi).* St. Petersburg, 1879.
———. *Polnoe Sobranie Russkikh Letopisei.* 31 vols. St. Petersburg, 1841-1968.
———. *Russkaia istoricheskaia biblioteka.* 39 vols. St. Petersburg: Arkheograficheskaia Komissiia, 1872-1927.
———. *Sibirskie letopisi.* St. Petersburg: I. N. Skorokhodov, 1907.
Arkhiv iugo-zapadnoi Rossii. 35 vols. Kiev: Tip. G. T. Korchak-Novitskogo, 1859-1914.
Arkhiv russkoi revoliutsii. Ed. I. V. Gessen. 22 vols. Berlin: Slovo, 1921-27.
Avvakum, *The Life of Archpriest Avvakum, by Himself.* Trans. Jane Harrison and Hope Mirrlees. London: L. and V. Woolf at the Hogarth Press, 1924.

Bakunin, Mikhail A. *Izbrannye sochineniia.* 5 vols. Petrograd: Golos Truda, 1920-22. See also Maximoff.
Bartenev, Petr I., ed. *Deviatnadtsatyi vek.* 2 vols. Moscow, 1872. See also *Russkii arkhiv.*
Bazilevskii, B. [Vasilii Ia. Iakovlev], ed. *Literatura partii Narodnoi Voli.* Paris: Société nouvelle de librairie et d'édition, 1905.
———. *Revoliutsionnaia zhurnalistika semidesiatykh godov . . .* Paris [?], 1906.
Belinskii, Vissarion G. *Polnoe sobranie sochinenii.* 13 vols. Moscow: AN SSSR, 1953-59.
Belinsky, Vissarion G. *Selected Philosophical Works.* Moscow: Foreign Languages Publishing House, 1948.

Benedetto, L. F. *The Travels of Marco Polo.* Trans. Aldo Ricci. London: G. Routledge and Sons, 1931.

Berry, Lloyd E., and Robert O. Crummey, eds. *Rude and Barbarous Kingdom: Russia in the Accounts of Sixteenth-Century English Voyagers.* Madison: University of Wisconsin Press, 1968.

Bodemann, Eduard, ed. *Briefe der Kurfuerstin Sophie von Hannover an die Raugraefinnen und Raugrafen zu Pfalz.* Publicationen aus den K. Preussischen Staatsarchiven, vol. 37. Leipzig, 1888.

Bogoiavlenskii, S. K., and I. S. Riabinin, eds. *Akty vremeni mezhdutsarstviia (1610-1613),* Moscow: Izd. Imperatorskogo Obshchestva Istorii i Drevnostei Rossiiskikh pri Moskovskom Universitete, 1915.

Bogucharskii: See Iakovlev, V. Ia.

Bolotov, Andrei T. "Nakaz dlia derevenskogo upravitelia." In Vol'noe Ekonomicheskoe Obshchestv *Trudy Vol'nogo Ekonomicheskogo Obshchestva,* Vol. 16, pp. 69-230. St. Petersburg, 1770.

Borozdin, Aleksandr K., ed. *Iz pisem i pokazanii dekabristov.* St. Petersburg: M. V. Pirozhkov, 1906.

Browder, Robert Paul, and Alexander F. Kerensky, eds. *The Russian Provisional Government, 1917: Documents.* 3 vols. Stanford: Stanford University Press, 1961.

Bruce, Peter H. *Memoirs of Peter Henry Bruce, Esq.* Dublin, 1783. Reprint. New York: Da Capo, 1968.

Bubnoff: see *The Russian Co-operator.*

Buchanan, George W. *My Mission to Russia and Other Diplomatic Memories.* 2 vols. Boston: Little, Brown, 1923.

Burtsev, Vladimir L., comp. and ed. *Za sto let, 1800-1896: Sbornik po istorii politicheskikh i obshchestvennykh dvizhenii v Rossii.* London, 1897. Reprint. The Hague: Europe Printing, 1965.

Buryshkin, Pavel A. *Moskva kupecheskaia.* New York: Chekhov, 1954.

Burzhuaziia nakanune fevral'skoi revoliutsii: see Tsentral'nyi Gosudarstvennyi Istoricheskii Arkhiv v Moskve.

Butashevich-Petrashevskii, Mikhail V. *Delo Petrashevtsev.* 3 vols. Moscow: AN SSSR, 1937-51.

Carpini, Giovanni de Plano. *The Mongol Mission.* Ed. and intro. Christopher Dawson. New York: Sheed and Ward, 1955.

Catherine II. *Memoirs of Catherine the Great.* Trans. Katherine Anthony. New York: Knopf, 1927. See also Reddaway; Chechulin.

———. *The Memoirs of Catherine the Great.* Ed. Dominique Maroger, intro. G. P. Gooch, trans. Moura Budberg. New York: Macmillan [1955].

———. *Pis'ma Imperatritsy Ekateriny II k Grimmu. Sbornik Imperatorskogo Russkogo Istoricheskogo Obshchestva,* vol. 23. St. Petersburg, 1878.

Chaadaev, Petr Ia. *The Major Works of Peter Chaadaev.* Trans. and commentary Raymond T. McNally. Notre Dame, Ind.: University of Notre Dame Press, 1969.

———. *Peter Yakovlevich Chaadayev: Philosophical Letters and Apology of a Madman.* Trans. and intro. Mary-Barbara Zeldin. Knoxville: University of Tennessee Press, 1969.

———. *Sochineniia i pis'ma P. Ia. Chaadaeva.* Ed. M. O. Gershenzon. 2 vols. Moscow: A. I. Mamontov, 1913-14. *See also* Moskoff.

Chancellor, Richard. "A Letter of Richard Chancellor . . . Touching His Discoverie of Moscovia." In *Hakluytus Posthumus or Purchas His Pilgrimes,* ed. Samuel Purchas. Vol. 11. Glasgow: J. MacLehose and Sons, 1906.

Chechulin, Nikolai D., ed. *Nakaz Imperatritsy Ekateriny II, dannyi Komissii o sochinenii proekta novogo Ulozheniia.* St. Petersburg: Tip. Imperatorskoi Akademii Nauk, 1907.

Cherepnin, Lev V., ed. *Akty feodal'nogo zemlevladeniia i khoziaistva XIV-XVI vekov.* Pt. 1. Moscow: AN SSSR, 1951.

———. *Pamiatniki prava perioda obrazovaniia russkogo tsentralizovannogo gosudarstva. Pamiatniki russkogo prava,* vol. 3. Moscow: Gosiurizdat, 1955.

Cherepnin, Lev V., and S. V. Bakhrushin, eds. *Dukhovnye i dogovornye gramoty velikikh i udel'nykh kniazei XIV-XVI vv.* Moscow: AN SSSR, 1950.

Cherniavsky, Michael, ed. *Prologue to Revolution: Notes of A. N. Iakhontov on the Secret Meetings of the Council of Ministers, 1915.* Englewood Cliffs, N.J.: Prentice-Hall, 1967.

Chernov, Viktor M. *Konstruktivnyi sotsializm.* Prague: Volia Rossii, 1925.

[Chernov, Viktor M.] *Ocherednoi vopros revoliutsionnogo dela.* London: Agrarian Socialist League, 1900.

Chernyshevskii, Nikolai G. *Polnoe sobranie sochinenii N. G. Chernyshevskogo.* 10 vols. St. Petersburg: I. Kraig, 1905-06.

———. *Selected Philosophical Essays.* Moscow: Foreign Languages Publishing House, 1953.

Chertkov, Vladimir G., ed. *Studencheskoe dvizhenie 1899 goda.* Purleigh, Eng.: Svobodnoe slovo, 1900.

Chronicle of Novgorod: see Michell.

Chteniia v Imperatorskom Obshchestve Istorii i Drevnostei Rossiiskikh pri Moskovskom Universitete: see Obshchestvo Istorii i Drevnostei Rossiiskikh.

Collins, Samuel. *The Present State of Russia.* London, 1671.

Constantine Porphyrogenitus. *De administrando imperio.* Greek text ed. Gy. Moravcsik, Eng. trans. R. J. H. Jenkins. Budapest: Institute of Greek Philology of Peter Pazmany University, 1949.

Coxe, William. *Travels into Poland, Russia, Sweden, and Denmark.* 3 vols. London: T. Cadell, 1784-90.

Cross, Samuel H., and Olgerd P. Sherbowitz-Wetzor, eds. and trans. *The Russian Primary Chronicle. Laurentian Text.* Cambridge, Mass.: Mediaeval Academy of America, 1953.

Custine, Astolphe, Marquis de. *Journey for Our Time: The Journals of the Marquis de Custine.* Ed. and trans. Phyllis P. Kohler. New York: Pellegrini and Cudahy, 1951.

Czartoryski, Adam J. *Memoirs of Prince Adam Czartoryski and His Correspondence with Alexander I.* Ed. Adam Gielgud. 2d ed. 2 vols. London, 1888.

Desiatiletie Ministerstva Narodnogo Prosveshcheniia, 1833-1843, St. Petersburg, 1864.

Desnitskii, V., ed. *Delo petrashevtsev. Pamiatniki obshchestvennoi mysli,* vol. 1. Moscow: AN SSSR, 1937.

Dewey, Horace W., comp., trans., and ed. *Muscovite Judicial Texts, 1488-1556.* Michigan Slavic Materials No. 7. Ann Arbor: Department of Slavic Languages and Literatures, University of Michigan, 1966.

———. *The Sudebnik of 1497.* Ann Arbor: University Microfilms, 1955.

———. "The White Lake Charter: A Mediaeval Russian Administrative Statute." *Speculum,* 32 (1957): 74-84.

D'iakonov, Mikhail A., ed. *Akty otnosiashchiesia k istorii tiaglogo naseleniia v Moskovskom gosudarstve.* 2 vols. St. Petersburg, 1895-97.

Dmitrieva, R. P. *Skazanie o kniaziakh vladimirskikh.* Moscow: AN SSSR, 1955.

Dmytryshyn, Basil, ed. *Imperial Russia: A Source Book, 1700-1917.* New York: Holt, Rinehart and Winston, 1967.

———, ed. *Medieval Russia: A Source Book, 900-1700.* New York: Holt, Rinehart and Winston, 1967.

Documents diplomatiques français, 1871-1914. Ser. 1 (1871-1900), 16 vols. Paris: Imprimerie Nationale, Alfred Costes, L'Europe Nouvelle, 1929-56.

Domostroi, intro. I. E. Zabelin. In *Chteniia v Imperatorskom Obshchestve Istorii i Drevnostei Rossiiskikh pri Moskovskom Universitete.* Moscow, 1881, bk. 2.

Domostroi po Konshinskomu spisku i podobnym. Ed. A. S. Orlov. 2 vols. Moscow: Sinodal'naia Tipografiia, 1908-10. Reprint. The Hague: Mouton, 1967.

Dostoevskii, Fedor M. *The Diary of a Writer: F. M. Dostoevsky.* Trans. Boris Brasol. 2 vols. New York: Charles Scribner's Sons, 1949.

———. *Polnoe sobranie sochinenii F. M. Dostoevskogo.* 12 vols. St. Petersburg: A. F. Marks, 1894-95.

Dovnar-Zapol'skii, Mitrofan V., ed. *Akty Litovsko-Russkogo Gosudarstva, vypusk I (1390-1529 gg.).* In *Chteniia v Imperatorskom Obshchestve Istorii i Drevnostei Rossiiskikh pri Moskovskom Universitete,* vol. 191, Moscow, 1899, bk. 4.

——. "Materialy dlia istorii votchinnogo upravleniia v Rossii," *Kievskie Universitetskie Izvestiia* (Kiev), 1903, no. 12; 1904, no. 6; 1909, no. 7; 1910, no. 11.

Druzhinin, Vasilii G., ed. *Pamiatniki pervykh let russkogo staroobriadchestva.* 3 vols. St. Petersburg: M. A. Aleksandrov, 1912-14.

Dubel't, M. L. "Iz epokhi osvobozhdeniia krest'ian, rasskaz gen.-leit. M. L. Dubel'ta, 1861." *Russkaia starina,* 69 (February 1891): 469-74.

Dubiecki, Marjan, comp. *Powstanie styczniowe w swietle zrodel.* Teksty zrodlowe do nauki historji w szkole sredniej, pt. 54. Krakow: Nakladem Krakowskiej Spolki Wydawniczej, 1924.

Dubrovin, Nikolai F., comp. *Sbornik istoricheskikh materialov izvlechennykh iz arkhiva Pervogo Otdeleniia Sobstvennoi Ego Imperatorskogo Velichestva Kantselarii.* 16 vols. St. Petersburg: Pervoe Otd. S. E. I. V. Kantseliarii, 1876-1917.

Dukhovnye i dogovornye gramoty velikikh i udel'nykh kniazei XIV-XVI vv. Moscow: AN SSSR, 1950.

Duma: see Gosudarstvennaia Duma.

Dumont, Jean. *Corps universel diplomatique du droit des gens.* 8 vols. bound in 16. Amsterdam, 1726-31.

Durnovo, P. N. "Zapiska." *Krasnaia nov',* no. 10 (November-December 1922). pp. 178-99.

Dzhivelegov, A. K., S. P. Mel'gunov, and V. I. Picheta, eds. *Velikaia reforma.* 6 vols. Moscow: Sytin, 1911.

Edie, James M., James P. Scanlan, and Mary-Barbara Zeldin, eds.; collab. George L. Kline. *Russian Philosophy.* 2 vols. Chicago: Quadrangle Books, 1965.

Entsiklopedicheskii Slovar'. 41 vols. St. Petersburg: Brokgauz and Efron, 1890-1904.

Fennell, John L. I., ed. and trans. *The Correspondence between Prince A. M. Kurbsky and Tsar Ivan IV of Russia, 1564-1579.* Cambridge: At the University Press, 1955.

Fennell, John L. I., and Dimitri Obolensky, eds. *A Historical Russian Reader: A Selection of Texts from the Eleventh to the Sixteenth Centuries.* Oxford: Clarendon Press, 1969.

"Fevral'skaia revolutsiia 1917 goda." *Krasnyi arkhiv,* 21 (1927 no. 2): 3-78; 22 (1927 no. 3): 3-70.

Filipowicz, Tytus, ed. *Confidential Correspondence of the British Government respecting the Insurrection in Poland: 1863.* Paris: Soudier, 1914.

Fischer, George. *Russian Liberalism.* Cambridge: Harvard University Press, 1958.

Fletcher, Giles. *Of the Rus Commonwealth.* Ed. Albert J. Schmidt. Ithaca, N.Y.: Cornell University Press, 1966. See also Berry.

——. *Of the Russe Commonwealth: Facsimile Edition with Variants.* Ed. John V. A. Fine, Jr., intro. Richard Pipes. Cambridge: Harvard University Press, 1966.

——. *Russia at the Close of the Sixteenth Century, Comprising the Treatise "Of the Russe Common Wealth" by Dr. Giles Fletcher and "The Travels of Jerome Horsey, Knt."* Ed. Edward A. Bond. London: Hakluyt Society, 1856.

Fonvizin, Mikhail A. "Obozrenie proiavlenii politicheskoi zhizni v Rossii." In *Obshchestvennye dvizheniia v Rossii v pervuiu polovinu XIX veka,* comp. V. I. Semevskii, V. Bogucharskii, and P. E. Shchegolev, vol. 1, pp. 97-202. St. Petersburg: Tipo-litografiia Gerol'd, 1905.

Garkavi, Avraam Ia. *Skazaniia musul'manskikh pisatelei o slavianakh i russkikh (VII-X vv.).* St. Petersburg, 1870. Reprint. The Hague: Mouton, 1969.

Ger'e, Vladimir [Guerrier, W.], ed. *Sbornik pisem i memorialov Leibnitsa otnosiashchikhsia k Rossii i Petru Velikomu.* St. Petersburg: Tip. Imperatorskoi Akademii Nauk, 1873. See also Guerrier.

Gertsen, Aleksandr I. *Byloe i dumy.* Moscow: OGIZ, 1946.

——. *Izbrannye filosofskie proizvedeniia.* 2 vols. Moscow: OGIZ, 1946.

——. *My Past and Thoughts: The Memoirs of Alexander Herzen.* Trans. Constance Garnett. 6 vols. London: Chatto and Windus, 1924-27. Rev. ed. by Humphrey Higgens. 4 vols.

(London: Chatto and Windus, 1968).

———. *Polnoe sobranie sochinenii i pisem*. Ed. M. K. Lemke. 22 vols. Petrograd-Leningrad-Moscow: Gosizdat and others, 1917–25.

———. *Sochineniia A. I. Gertsena*. 7 vols. bound in 3. St. Petersburg: F. Pavlenkov, 1905.

Giovanni de Plano Carpini: see Carpini.

Glinskii, Boris B. *Revoliutsionnyi period russkoi istorii (1861–1881)*. 2 vols. St. Petersburg: A. S. Suvorin, 1913.

Gnevushev, A. M., comp. and ed. *Akty vremeni pravleniia tsaria Vasiliia Shuiskogo (19 maia 1606 g.-17 iiulia 1610 g.)*. Moscow: Izd. Imperatorskogo Obshchestva Istorii i Drevnostei Rossiiskikh pri Moskovskom Universitete, 1914.

Goetz, Leopold K. *Deutsch-Russische Handelsvertraege des Mittelalters*. Hamburg: L. Friederichsen, 1916.

Golder, Frank A., ed. *Documents of Russian History 1914–1917*. Trans. Emanuel Aronsberg. New York: Century, 1927. Reprint. Gloucester, Mass.: Peter Smith, 1964.

Golovin, Nikolai N. *The Russian Army in the World War*. New Haven: Yale University Press, 1931.

Gorbachevskii, Ivan I. *Zapiski i pis'ma dekabrista*. Ed. B. E. Syroechkovskii. Moscow: Gosizdat, 1925.

Gosudarstvennaia Duma. *Stenograficheskie otchety Gosudarstvennoi Dumy I, II, III, i IV sozyvov*. 36 vols. St. Petersburg: Gosudarstvennaia Tipografiia, 1906–17.

Gosudarstvennyi Sovet: see *Otchet po . . .*

Got'e, Iu. V., ed. *Akty otnosiashchiesia k istorii zemskikh soborov. Pamiatniki russkoi istorii*, vol. 3. Moscow: N. N. Klochkov, 1909.

Granovskii, Timofei N. *Sochineniia T. N. Granovskogo*. 3d ed. 2 vols. Moscow, 1892.

———. *T. N. Granovskii i ego perepiska*. 2 vols. Moscow, 1897.

Grekov, Boris D., ed. *Pravda Russkaia*. 2 vols. Moscow: AN SSSR, 1940–47.

Grushevskii: see Hrushevsky.

Gudzii, Nikolai K., ed., and L. B. Lekhtblau, comp. *Russkie satiricheskie zhurnaly XVIII veka*. Moscow: Uchpedgiz, 1940.

Guerrier, W. *Leibniz in seinen Beziehungen zu Russland und Peter dem Grossen*. Leipzig, 1873. See also Ger'e.

Gurko, Vladimir I. *Features and Figures of the Past: Government and Opinion in the Reign of Nicholas II*. Palo Alto: Stanford University Press, 1939.

Hansard's Parliamentary Debates. 3d ser., vol. 132. London, 1854.

Hanway, Jonas. *An Historical Account of the British Trade over the Caspian Sea, with a Journal of Travels from London through Russia into Persia and Back*. 2 vols. London, 1753.

Harkavy: see Garkavi.

Haxthausen, Baron August von. *The Russian Empire, Its People, Institutions, and Resources*. Trans. Robert Farie. 2 vols. London, 1856.

———. *Studien ueber die innern Zustaende, das Volksleben und insbesondere die laendlichen Einrichtungen Russlands*. 3 vols. Hanover, 1847–52.

Hellie, Richard, trans. and ed. *Readings for Introduction to Russian Civilization: Muscovite Society*. Chicago: University of Chicago Syllabus Division, 1967.

Herberstein, Sigismund von. *Commentaries on Muscovite Affairs*. Ed. and trans. Oswald P. Backus III. Lawrence: University of Kansas Bookstore, 1956.

———. *Description of Moscow and Muscovy 1557*. Ed. Bertold Picard, trans. J. B. C. Grundy. London: J. M. Dent, 1969.

Herrmann, Ernst, ed. *Russland unter Peter dem Grossen: Nach den handschriftlichen Berichten Johann Gotthilf Vockerodt's und Otto Pleyer's*. Leipzig, 1872. See also *Rossiia pri Petre . . .*

Hertslet, Edward, ed. *The Map of Europe by Treaty since the General Peace of 1814*. 4 vols. London, 1875–91.

Herzen: See Gertsen.

Howes, Robert C., trans. and ed. *The Testaments of the Grand Princes of Moscow.* Ithaca, N.Y.: Cornell University Press, 1967.

Hrushevsky, Michael S. *Istoriia Ukraini-Rusi.* 10 vols. in 11 pts. New York: Knigospilka, 1954-58 (facsimile reprint of original edition of 1905-36).

Iablonskis, K. I., ed. *Statut velikogo kniazhestva litovskogo 1529 goda.* Minsk: AN BSSR, 1960.

Iakhontov, A. N. "Tiazhelye dni." *Arkhiv russkoi revoliutsii,* 18 (Berlin: Slovo, 1926): 5-136.

Iakovlev, A. I., ed. *Akty khoziaistva boiarina B. I. Morozova.* 2 pts. Moscow: AN SSSR, 1940-45.

———. *Pamiatniki istorii Smutnogo vremeni. Pamiatniki russkoi istorii,* vol. 4. Moscow: N. N. Klochkov, 1909.

Iakovlev, Vasilii Ia. [pseudonyms: B. Bazilevskii, V. Bogucharskii], ed. *Gosudarstvennye prestupleniia v Rossii v XIX veke, sbornik izvlechennykh iz ofitsial'nykh izdanii pravitel'stvennykh soobshchenii.* 3 vols. St. Petersburg: Russkaia Skoropechatnia, 1906. See also Bazilevskii.

Intelligentsiia v Rossii: Sbornik statei. St. Petersburg: Knigoizdat. "Zemlia," 1910.

Iosif Volotskii: see Sanin.

Iswolsky [Izvol'skii], Alexander P. *The Memoirs of Alexander Iswolsky.* Ed. and trans. C. I. Seeger. London: Hutchinson, 1920.

Iushkov, Serafim V., ed. *Pamiatniki prava feodal'no-razdroblennoi Rusi XII-XV vv. Pamiatniki russkogo prava,* vol. 2. Moscow: Gosiurizdat, 1953.

———. *Pamiatniki prava Kievskogo gosudarstva. Pamiatniki russkogo prava,* vol. 1. Moscow: Gosiurizdat, 1952.

Iuzefovich, T., ed. *Dogovory Rossii s vostokom: politicheskie i torgovye.* St. Petersburg, 1869.

Izveshchenie o III s"ezde Rossiiskoi Sotsial'-demokraticheskoi Rabochei Partii. Geneva: Izd. RSDRP, 1905.

Izveshchenie o vtorom ocherednom s"ezde Rossiiskoi Sotsial'-demokraticheskoi Rabochei Partii. Geneva: Izd. RSDRP, 1903.

Izvol'skii: see Iswolsky.

"Iz zapisnoi knizhki arkhivista: Dva dokumenta iz istorii Zubatovshchiny." *Krasnyi arkhiv,* 19 (1926, no. 6): 210-11.

Jakobson, Roman. "Saint Constantine's Prologue to the Gospels." *Saint Vladimir's Seminary Quarterly,* vol. 7, N.S., 1963.

Jordanes. *The Gothic History.* Trans. C. C. Mierow. Princeton: Princeton University Press, 1915. Photographically reprinted, Cambridge, Eng., and New York, 1960.

Kalachev, Nikolai V., ed. *Doklady i prigovory v . . . Senate v tsarstvovanie Petra Velikogo.* 6 vols. St. Petersburg: Tip. Imperatorskoi Akademii Nauk, 1880-1901.

Kalinychev, F. I., comp. *Gosudarstvennaia Duma v Rossii v dokumentakh i materialakh.* Moscow: Gosiurizdat, 1957.

Kapterev, Nikolai F. *Patriarkh Nikon i Tsar' Aleksei Mikhailovich.* 2 vols. Sergiev Posad: Tip. Sviato-Troitskoi Sergievoi Lavry, 1909-12.

Karamzin, Nikolai M. *Zapiska o drevnei i novoi Rossii.* Ed. Richard Pipes. Cambridge: Harvard University Press, 1959. See also Pipes.

Katkov, Mikhail N. *Sobranie peredovykh statei "Moskovskikh Vedomostei" s 1863 po 1887 god.* 24 vols. Moscow, 1897-98.

Kennan, George. *Siberia and the Exile System.* 2 vols. New York, 1891.

Khomiakov, Aleksei S. *Izbrannye sochineniia.* New York: Chekhov, 1955.

———. *Polnoe sobranie sochinenii A. S. Khomiakova.* 8 vols. Moscow: Tip. Imperatorskogo Moskovskogo Universiteta, 1900-07.

Khrestomatiia po istorii SSSR. Moscow: Gosudarstvennoe Uchebno-Pedagogicheskoe Izdatel'stvo Ministerstva Prosveshcheniia RSFSR. Vol. 1, *S drevneishikh vremen do kontsa XVII veka.* Comp. V. I. Lebedev, M. N. Tikhomirov, V. E. Syroechkovskii. 4th ed., 1951. Vol. 2, *1682-1856.* Comp. S. S. Dmitriev and M. V. Nechkina. 3d ed., 1953. Vol. 3, *1857-1894.* Comp. S. S.

Dmitriev. 2d ed., 1952.

Kireevskii, Ivan V. *Polnoe sobranie sochinenii I. V. Kireevskogo.* Ed. M. O. Gershenzon. 2 vols. Moscow: Tip. Imperatorskogo Moskovskogo Universiteta, 1911.

"K istorii Loris-Melikovskoi 'Konstitutsii.'" *Krasnyi arkhiv* 8 (1925, no. 1): 132-50.

Knox, Alfred. *With the Russian Army 1914-1917: Being Chiefly Extracts from the Diary of a Military Attaché.* 2 vols. New York: E. P. Dutton, 1921.

Kohn, Hans, ed. *The Mind of Modern Russia: Historical and Political Thought of Russia's Great Age.* New Brunswick, N.J.: Rutgers University Press, 1955.

Kokovtsov, Vladimir N. *Iz moego proshlogo: Vospominaniia, 1903-1919.* 2 vols. Paris: Illiustrirovannaia Rossiia, 1933.

——. *The Memoirs of Count Kokovtsov: Out of My Past.* Ed. Harold H. Fisher, trans. Laura Matveev. Palo Alto: Stanford University Press, 1935.

Korb, Johann G. *Diarium itineris in Moscoviam* . . . Vienna, 1700 or 1701.

——. *Diary of an Austrian Secretary of Legation at the Court of Peter the Great.* Trans. and ed. Count Macdonnell. 2 vols. London, 1863. Reprint. New York: Da Capo, 1968.

——. *Dnevnik puteshestviia v Moscoviiu (1698-1699 gg.).* Trans. and commentary, A. I. Malein. St. Petersburg: A. S. Suvorin, 1906.

Kormchaia Kniga. Republished from the edition of 1653 (under Patriarch Nikon). 2 pts. Moscow, 1787.

Korobkov, Nikolai M., ed. *Fel'dmarshal Kutuzov, sbornik dokumentov i materialov.* Moscow: OGIZ, 1947.

Korsakov, Dimitri A. *Votsarenie Imperatritsy Anny Ioannovny.* Kazan', 1880.

Kotoshikhin, Grigorii. *O Rossii v tsarstvovanie Aleksiia Mikhailovicha.* 3d ed. St. Petersburg: Arkheograficheskaia Komissiia, 1884. See also Uroff.

Krachkovskii, Ignatii Iu., ed. *Puteshestvie Ibn-Fadlana na Volgu.* Moscow: AN SSSR, 1939.

Krasnyi arkhiv. 106 vols. bound in 35. Moscow, 1922-41.

Kravchinskii [Stepniak], Sergei M. *The Russian Peasantry: Their Agrarian Condition, Social Life, and Religion.* New York: Harper and Brothers, 1905.

Krizhanich, Iurii. *Russkoe gosudarstvo v polovine XVII veka.* ed. P. Bezsonov. Moscow, 1859.

Kropotkin, Peter. *Memoirs of a Revolutionist.* Boston: Houghton Mifflin, 1930.

——. *Modern Science and Anarchism.* 2d ed. London: Freedom Press, 1923.

——. *Mutual Aid: A Factor of Evolution.* New York: MacLure Phillips, 1902.

Kurakin: see Semevskii.

Kurbskii, Prince Andrei M. *Sochineniia kniazia Kurbskogo. Russkaia istoricheskaia biblioteka,* vol. 31. St. Petersburg: Arkheograficheskaia Komissiia, 1914.

Kutrzeba, Stanislaw, and W. Semikowicz, eds. *Akta unji Polski z Litwa, 1385-1791.* Krakow: Nakladem Polskiej Akademji Umiejetnosci i Towarzystwa Naukowego Warszawskiego, 1932.

Kutuzov: see Korobkov.

Lamzdorf [Lamsdorff], Vladimir N. *Dnevnik 1891-1892.* Moscow: AN SSSR, 1934.

Langer, William L. *The Franco-Russian Alliance 1890-1894.* Cambridge: Harvard University Press, 1929.

Lannoy, Ghillebert de. *Oeuvres de Ghillebert de Lannoy, voyageur, diplomate, et moraliste.* Louvain, 1878.

Lantzeff, George V. *Siberia in the Seventeenth Century: A Study of the Colonial Administration.* Berkeley: University of California Press, 1943.

Lassota von Steblau, Erich. *Tagebuch des Erich Lassota von Steblau.* Ed. Reinhold Schottin. Halle, 1866.

Laue, T. H. von: See Von Laue.

Lavrov, Petr L. ["Mirtov"]. *Historical Letters.* Ed. and trans. James P. Scanlan. Berkeley: University of California Press, 1967.

——. *Istoricheskie pis'ma.* St. Petersburg, 1870.

Lazarevskii, N. I., ed. *Zakonodatel'nye akty perekhodnogo vremeni 1904-1908.* St. Petersburg: Izd. Pravo, 1909.

Lemke, Mikhail K., ed. *Politicheskie protsessy v Rossii 1860-kh gg.* 2d ed. Moscow: Gosizdat, 1923. Reprint. The Hague: Mouton, 1969. See also Gertsen.

Lenin, Vladimir I. *The Essential of Lenin in Two Volumes.* London: Lawrence and Wishart, 1947.

———. *Sochineniia.* 2d ed. 30 vols. Moscow: Gosizdat, 1926-30.

———. *What Is to Be Done?* Trans. Sergei V. and Patricia Utechin. New York: Oxford University Press, 1963.

Letters of the Tsar to the Tsaritsa: see Vulliamy.

Letters of the Tsaritsa to the Tsar, 1914-1916. Intro. Bernard Pares. London: Duckworth, 1923.

Levshin, A. I. "Dostopamiatnye minuty v moei zhizni, zapiska A. I. Levshina." *Russkii arkhiv,* 1885, no. 8, pp. 475-557.

Lewicki, Tadeusz, ed. *Zrodla arabskie do dziejow slowianszczyzny.* Vol. 1. Wroclaw and Krakow: Wyd. Polskiej Akademii Nauk, 1956.

Liubavskii, Matvei K. *Ocherk istorii litovsko-russkogo gosudarstva.* 2d ed. Moscow: Moskovskaia Khudozhestvennaia Pechatnia, 1915.

Loubat, J. F. *Narrative of the Mission to Russia, in 1866, of the Honorable Gustavus Vasa Fox, Assistant-Secretary of the Navy, from the Journal and Notes of J. F. Loubat.* New York, 1874.

Loukomsky [Lukomskii], Alexander S. *Memoirs of the Russian Revolution.* London: T. F. Unwin, 1922.

———. *Vospominaniia Generala A. S. Lukomskogo.* 2 vols. Berlin: Otto Kirchner, 1922.

Macartney, Carlile A. *The Magyars in the Ninth Century.* Cambridge: At the University Press, 1930.

Maklakov, Vasilii A. *The First Duma: Contemporary Reminiscences.* Trans. Mary Belkin. Bloomington: Indiana University Press, 1964.

———. *Iz vospominanii.* New York: Chekhov, 1954.

———. *Pervaia Gosudarstvennaia Duma: Vospominaniia sovremennika.* Paris: Dom Knigi, 1939.

———. *Vlast' i obshchestvennost' na zakate staroi Rossii: Vospominaniia sovremennika.* Paris: Illiustrirovannaia Rossiia, 1939.

———. *Vtoraia Gosudarstvennaia Duma: Vospominaniia sovremennika.* Paris [1946].

Malinin, Vasilii N. *Starets Eleazarova monastyria Filofei i ego poslaniia.* Kiev: Tip. Kievo-Pecherskoi Uspenskoi Lavry, 1901.

Manifest Rossiiskoi Sotsial'-demokraticheskoi Rabochei Partii, 1898 g. Geneva: T. A. Kuklin, 1903.

Manstein, Christopher Hermann von. *Mémoires historiques, politiques et militaires sur la Russie depuis l'Année 1727 jusqu'à 1744, par le Général de Manstein.* 2 vols. Paris, 1860.

———. *Memoirs of Russia from the Year 1727 to 1744.* Ed. David Hume. London, 1770.

———. "Zapiski Manshteina o Rossii, 1727-1744." *Russkaia starina,* 1875, no. 12, suppl.

Martens, Fedor F. *Recueil des traités et conventions conclus par la Russie avec les puissances étrangères.* 15 vols. bound in 8. St. Petersburg: A. Böhnke, 1874-1909.

Materialy po istorii SSSR. Vol. 2. Moscow: AN SSSR, 1955.

Matlaw, Ralph E., ed. and intro. *Belinsky, Chernyshevsky, and Dobrolyubov: Selected Criticism.* New York: E. P. Dutton, 1962.

Maximoff, G. P., comp. and ed. *The Political Philosophy of Bakunin: Scientific Anarchism.* Glencoe, Ill.: Free Press, 1953.

Mazour, Anatole G. *The First Russian Revolution, 1825: The Decembrist Movement.* Berkeley: University of California Press, 1937.

Memoirs of Catherine . . .: see Catherine II, *Memoirs . . .*

Metternich, Prince Richard, ed. *Memoirs of Prince Metternich.* Arr. M. A. Klinkowström, trans. Mrs. Alexander Napier. 5 vols. New York, 1880-82.

Mezhdutsarstvie 1825 goda i vosstanie dekabristov v memuarakh i perepiske chlenov tsarskoi sem'i. Moscow: Gosizdat, 1926.

Michell, Robert, and Nevill Forbes, eds. and trans. *The Chronicle of Novgorod.* Intro. C. Raymond Beazley, commentary by A. A. Shakhmatov. London: Royal Historical Society, 1914 (Camden, 3d ser., vol. 25).

Mikhailovskii, Nikolai K. *Poslednie sochineniia N. K. Mikhailovskogo.* 2 vols. St. Petersburg: Russkoe Bogatstvo, 1905.
———. *Sochineniia N. K. Mikhailovskogo.* Vols. 1-3 (of 6), 4th ed. St. Petersburg: Russkoe Bogatstvo, 1906-09. Vols. 4-6, St. Petersburg: Russkoe Bogatstvo, 1897.
Miliukov, Pavel N. *God bor'by, 1905-06.* St. Petersburg: Obshchestvennaia Pol'za, 1907.
———. *Russia and Its Crisis.* London: T. F. Unwin, 1905.
———. *Vospominaniia 1859-1917.* 2 vols. New York: Chekhov, 1955.
Miliutin, Dmitrii A. *Dnevnik D. A. Miliutina, 1873-1882.* Ed. Petr A. Zaionchkovskii. 4 vols. Moscow [Bibl. Lenina], 1947-50.
Miliutina, Mariia A. "Iz zapisok Marii Aggeevny Miliutinoi." *Russkaia starina,* 98 (April 1899): 105-27.
Miller [Mueller], G. F. *Istoriia Sibiri.* 2 vols. Moscow: AN SSSR, 1937-41.
Mishulin, A. V. "Drevnie slaviane v otryvkakh greko-rimskikh i vizantiiskikh pisatelei po VII v. n. e." *Vestnik drevnei istorii,* 14 (1941, no. 1), suppl.
Monas, Sidney. *The Third Section: Police and Society in Russia under Nicholas I.* Cambridge: Harvard University Press, 1961.
Moskoff, Eugene A. *The Russian Philosopher Chaadayev: His Ideas and His Epoch.* New York: Colonial Printing and Publishing, 1937.
Mukhanov, Pavel A., ed. *Zapiski getmana Zholkevskogo o Moskovskoi voine.* 2d ed. St. Petersburg, 1871.

Naumov, Aleksandr N. *Iz utselevshikh vospominanii 1868-1917.* 2 vols. New York: A. K. Naumova and O. A. Kusevitskaia, 1954-55.
Nevskii, Vladimir I., comp. *1905: Sovetskaia pechat' i literatura o sovetakh: Materialy i dokumenty.* Vol. 3. Moscow: Gosizdat, 1925.
Nolde, Boris. *L'Alliance Franco-Russe.* Paris: Librarie Droz, 1936.
Nomad, Max. *Apostles of Revolution.* Boston: Little, Brown, 1939.
Novgorodskaia pervaia letopis'. Ed. A. N. Nasonov. Moscow: AN SSSR, 1950.
Novikov, Nikolai I., ed. *Drevniaia rossiiskaia vivliofika.* 2d ed. 12 vols. Moscow, 1788-91. Vol. 6, 1788.
———. *Satiricheskie zhurnaly N. I. Novikova.* Ed. P. N. Berkov. Moscow: AN SSSR, 1951.
Novosil'tsev, N. N. "N. N. Novosil'tsev's Project for a Constitutional Charter for the Russian Empire." Ed. David Urquhart. *The Portfolio,* 5 (1837): 512-22, 610-39; 6 (1837): 72-83.

Obshchestvo Istorii i Drevnostei Rossiiskikh. *Chteniia v Imperatorskom Obshchestve Istorii i Drevnostei Rossiiskikh pri Moskovskom Universitete.* 264 vols. Moscow: Universitetskaia Tipografiia, 1846-1918.
Obshchestvo Istorii i Drevnostei Rossiiskikh. *Vremennik Imperatorskogo Moskovskogo Obshchestva Istorii i Drevnostei Rossiiskikh.* 25 vols. Moscow, 1849-57.
Olearius, Adam. *Der Welt-beruehmten Adami Olearii Reise-Beschreibungen . . . nach Musskau und Persien.* 4th ed. Hamburg, 1696.
———. *The Travels of Olearius in Seventeenth-Century Russia.* Trans. and ed. Samuel H. Baron. Stanford: Stanford University Press, 1967.
Osvobozhdenie. Ed. and publ. P. B. Struve. Stuttgart, 1902-04; Paris, 1904-05.
Otchet po Gosudarstvennomu Sovetu za 1886 god. St. Petersburg, 1888.

Page, Stanley W., ed. *Russia in Revolution: Selected Readings in Russian Domestic History since 1855.* Princeton: Van Nostrand, 1965.
Paléologue, [Georges] Maurice. *An Ambassador's Memoirs.* Trans. F. A. Holt. 4th ed. 3 vols. New York: George H. Doran, 1924-25.
———. *La Russie des tsars pendant la grande guerre.* 6th ed. 3 vols. Paris: Plon-Nourrit, 1922.
Palitsyn, Avraamii. *Skazanie Avraamiia Palitsyna.* Commentary by O. A. Derzhavina and E. V. Kolosova, ed. L. V. Cherepnin. Moscow: AN SSSR, 1955.
Palmer, W. *The Patriarch and the Tsar.* 6 vols. London, 1871-76.

Pamiatniki russkogo prava. 8 vols. Moscow: Gosiurizdat, 1952-61. See also Cherepnin; Iushkov.

Pamiatniki russkoi istorii. Ed. members of the history faculty of Moscow University. 8 vols. Moscow: N. N. Klochkov, 1909-11. See also Got'e; Iakovlev; Pososhkov.

Pares, Bernard. *Day by Day with the Russian Army, 1914-15.* London: Constable, 1915.

———. *The Fall of the Russian Monarchy: A Study of the Evidence.* New York: Alfred A. Knopf, 1939.

Pawlowski, Bronislaw, comp. *Krolestwo kongresowe i powstanie listopadowe.* Teksty zrodlowe do nauki historji w szkole sredniej, pt. 49. Krakow: Nakladem Krakowskiej Spolki Wydawniczej, 1923.

Perepiska Nikolaia i Aleksandry Romanovykh 1914-1917: see Tsentral'nyi Gosudarstvennyi Istoricheskii Arkhiv v Moskve.

Peresvetov, Ivan. *Sochineniia I. Peresvetova.* Ed. A. A. Zimin and D. S. Likhachev. Moscow: AN SSSR, 1956.

———. *Sochineniia Ivana Peresvetova.* Ed. V. F. Rzhiga. In *Chteniia v Obshchestve Istorii i Drevnostei Rossiiskikh pri Moskovskom Universitete.* Moscow, 1908, no. I.

Perry, John. *The State of Russia under the Present Czar, By Captain John Perry.* London, 1716.

Pestel', Pavel I. *Russkaia Pravda.* Ed. and intro. P. Shchegolev. St. Petersburg: Izd. "Kul'tura," 1906.

"Petr Mikhailovich Bestuzhev-Riumin i ego pomest'e." *Russkii arkhiv.* vol. 42 (1904, no. 1), pp. 5-42.

Pipes, Richard. *Karamzin's Memoir on Ancient and Modern Russia: A Translation and Analysis.* Cambridge: Harvard University Press, 1959.

Pisarev, Dmitrii I. *Izbrannye sochineniia.* Vol. 1. Moscow: Gosudarstvennoe Izd. Khudozhest-vennoi Literatury, 1935.

———. *Selected Philosophical, Social, and Political Essays.* Moscow: Foreign Languages Publishing House, 1958.

———. *Sochineniia.* 4 vols. Moscow: Gosudarstvennoe Izd. Khudozhestvennoi Literatury, 1955-56.

Pis'ma i bumagi Imperatora Petra Velikogo. 11 vols. Vols. 1-7, St. Petersburg: Gosudarstvennaia Tipografiia, 1887-1918. Vols. 8-11, Moscow: AN SSSR, 1948-64.

Plekhanov, Georgii V. *Dnevnik sotsial-demokrata.* Vol. 1. Petrograd: M. V. Popov, 1916.

———. *Nashi raznoglasiia.* St. Petersburg: Novyi Mir, 1906.

———. *Selected Philosophical Works.* 2 vols. Moscow: Foreign Languages Publishing House, 1959.

———. *Sochineniia.* 24 vols. Moscow: Gosizdat, 1923-27.

Pobedonostsev, Konstantin P. *Moskovskii sbornik.* Moscow, 1896.

———. *Pis'ma Pobedonostseva k Aleksandru III.* 2 vols. Moscow: Novaia Moskva, 1925-26.

———. *Reflexions of a Russian Statesman.* Trans. Robert C. Long. London, 1898.

Pokrovskii, Mikhail N., et al., eds. *Vosstanie dekabristov.* 11 vols. Moscow: Gosizdat, 1925-54.

"Politicheskoe polozhenie Rossii nakanune fevral'skoi revoliutsii v zhandarmskom osveshchenii." *Krasnyi arkhiv,* 17 (1926, no. 4): 3-35.

Polner, Tikhon J. *Russian Local Government during the War and the Union of Zemstvos.* Russian Series, "Economic and Social History of the World War," no. 9. New Haven: Yale University Press, 1930.

Polnoe Sobranie Zakonov Rossiiskoi Imperii . . . 1649-1913. 134 vols. St. Petersburg, 1830-1916 (1st ser., 46 vols., containing laws of 1649-1825; 2d ser., 55 vols., covering 1825-81; 3d ser., 33 vols., covering 1881-1913).

Polnyi sbornik platform vsekh russkikh politicheskikh partii. 4th ed. St. Petersburg, 1907.

Polovtsev, Aleksandr A. "Dnevnik A. A. Polovtseva, 1901-1908." *Krasnyi arkhiv,* 3 (1923): 75-172; 4 (1923): 63-128.

Ponomarev, A. I. *Pamiatniki drevnerusskoi tserkovno-uchitel'noi literatury.* Pt. 1. St. Petersburg: Izd. zhurnala "Strannik," 1894.

Pososhkov, Ivan T. "Donesenie boiarinu F. A. Golovinu o ratnom povedenii." In *Pamiatniki russkoi istorii,* vol. 8. Moscow: N. N. Klochkov, 1911.

———. *Kniga o skudosti i bogatstve.* Moscow: AN SSSR, 1937.

Po voprosam programmy i taktiki: Sbornik statei iz "Revoliutsionnoi Rossii." [Paris:] Tip. Sotsialistov-Revoliutsionerov, 1903.

Pravitel'stvennyi vestnik. St. Petersburg, 1869-1917.

Pravo (weekly legal journal). 1898-1917.

Priselkov, Mikhail D. *Khanskie iarlyki russkim mitropolitam.* St. Petersburg: Nauchnoe Delo, 1916.

Procopius. *History of the Wars.* Trans. H. B. Dewing. Loeb Classical Library, vol. 4. Cambridge: Harvard University Press, 1924.

Programma i organizatsionnyi ustav Partii Sotsialistov-Revoliutsionerov. Paris: Izd. TsK PS-R, 1906.

Programma i ustav Rossiiskoi Sotsial'-Demokraticheskoi Rabochei Partii, Paris: *Sotsial'demokrat,* 1909.

Protokoly ob"edinitel'nogo s"ezda Rossiiskoi Sotsial'-demokraticheskoi Rabochei Partii, sostoiavshegosia v Stokgol'me v 1906 g. Moscow: TsK RSDRP, 1907.

Protokoly pervoi obshchepartiinoi konferentsii P.S-R. 1908 g. Paris: Izd. TsK PS-R, 1908.

Protokoly zasedanii soveshchaniia . . . po peresmotru osnovnykh gosudarstvennykh zakonov. St. Petersburg: Gosudarstvennaia Tipografiia, 1906.

Pskovskie letopisi. Ed. A. N. Nasonov. Moscow: AN SSSR, 1941.

Pugachevshchina: see Tsentral'nyi Gosudarstvennyi Istoricheskii Arkhiv v Moskve.

Purchas, Samuel: see Chancellor.

Putnam, Peter, ed. *Seven Britons in Imperial Russia.* Princeton: Princeton University Press, 1952.

Radishchev, Aleksandr N. *A Journey from St. Petersburg to Moscow, by A. N. Radishchev.* Ed. Roderick Page Thaler, trans. Leo Wiener. Cambridge: Harvard University Press, 1958.

———. *Puteshestvie iz Peterburga v Moskvu.* Moscow: AN SSSR, 1935 (reprint of ed. of 1790).

Raeff, Marc. *The Decembrist Movement.* Englewood Cliffs, N.J.: Prentice-Hall, 1966.

———. *Plans for Political Reform in Imperial Russia, 1730-1905.* Englewood Cliffs, N.J.: Prentice-Hall, 1966.

———, ed. *Russian Intellectual History, an Anthology.* New York: Harcourt, Brace and World, 1966.

Reddaway, W. F., ed. *Documents of Catherine the Great: The Correspondence with Voltaire and the Instructions of 1767.* Cambridge: At the University Press, 1931.

Riasanovsky, Nicholas V. *Nicholas I and Official Nationality in Russia, 1825-1855.* Berkeley: University of California Press, 1959.

Riha, Thomas, ed. *Readings in Russian Civilization.* 3 vols. Chicago: University of Chicago Press, 1964. 2d ed. 1969.

Rittikh, Aleksandr A., ed. *Krest'ianskoe zemlepol'zovanie.* St. Petersburg: V. F. Kirsbaum, 1903.

Rockhill, William W., ed. *Journey of William of Rubruck to the Eastern Parts of the World, 1253-1255, as Narrated by Himself.* London: Hakluyt Society, 1900.

Rodzianko, Mikhail V. "Ekonomicheskoe polozhenie Rossii pered revoliutsiei: Zapiska M. V. Rodzianki." *Krasnyi arkhiv,* 10 (1925, no. 3): 69-86.

———. "Gosudarstvennaia Duma i fevral'skaia 1917 g. revoliutsiia." *Arkhiv russkoi revoliutsii,* 6 (1922): 5-80.

———. "Krushenie Imperii." *Arkhiv russkoi revoliutsii,* 17 (1926): 1-169.

Rossiia pri Petre Velikom, po rukopisnomu izvestiiu I. G. Vokerodta i O. Pleiera. Trans. A. N. Shemiakin. *Chteniia v Imperatorskom Obshchestve Istorii i Drevnostei Rossiiskikh pri Moskovskom Universitete,* vol. 89, pt. 4. Moscow, 1874, bk. 2.

Rousset de Missy, Jean. *Recueil historique d'actes . . . et traitez de paix depuis la Paix d'Utrect.* 21 vols. The Hague, 1728-55.

Rozen, Andrei E. *Zapiski dekabrista.* St. Petersburg: Obshchestvennaia Pol'za, 1907.

The Russian Co-operator: A Journal of Co-operative Unity. Ed. J. V. Bubnoff and A. N. Balakshin. London, 1916-21.

Russian Primary Chronicle: See Cross.

Russkaia istoricheskaia biblioteka: see Arkheograficheskaia Komissiia.

Russkaia starina. Ed. M. I. Semevskii. St. Petersburg, 1870-1918.

Russkii arkhiv. Ed. P. Bartenev. Moscow, 1863-1917.

Rychkov, Petr I. "Nakaz dlia derevenskogo upravitelia . . ." *Trudy Vol'nogo Ekonomicheskogo Obshchestva,* 16: 9-68. St. Petersburg, 1770.

Sanin [Volotskii], Iosif. *Prosvetitel' ili oblichenie eresi zhidovstvuiushchikh.* Kazan', 1855.

Sazonov, Sergei D. *Fateful Years 1909-1916: The Reminiscences of Serge Sazonov.* London: J. Cape, 1928.

Sbornik dogovorov i diplomaticheskikh dokumentov po delam Dal'nego Vostoka 1895-1905 gg.. St. Petersburg: Ministerstvo Inostrannykh Del, 1906.

Sbornik Imperatorskogo Russkogo Istoricheskogo Obshchestva. 148 vols. St. Petersburg: Tip. Imperatorskogo Russkogo Istoricheskogo Obshchestva, 1867-1916.

Segel, Harold B., ed. and trans. *The Literature of Eighteenth-Century Russia.* 2 vols. New York: E. P. Dutton, 1967.

Semennikov, Vladimir P., ed. *Monarkhiia pered krusheniem, 1914-1917: Bumagi Nikolaia II i drugie dokumenty.* Moscow: Gosizdat, 1927.

——. *Politika Romanovykh nakanune revoliutsii.* Moscow: Gosizdat, 1926.

Semenov, Nikolai P. *Osvobozhdenie krest'ian v tsarstvovanie Imperatora Aleksandra II: Khronika deiatel'nosti komissii po krest'ianskomu delu.* 3 vols. St. Petersburg, 1889-92.

Semevskii, M. I., ed. *Arkhiv kniazia F. A. Kurakina.* Vol. 1. St. Petersburg, 1890. (Contains "Zhizn' kniazia Borisa Ivanovicha Kurakina.")

Senn, Alfred E., ed. *Readings in Russian Political and Diplomatic History.* 2 vols. Homewood, Ill.: Dorsey Press, 1966.

Sergeev, A. A. "Pervaia Gosudarstvennaia Duma v Vyborge." *Krasnyi arkhiv,* 4 (1923, no. 2): 85-99.

Sergeevskii, Nikolai D., ed. *Konstitutsionnaia khartiia 1815 g. i nekotorye drugie akty byvshego Tsarstva Pol'skogo (1814-1881). Biblioteka Okrain Rossii,* vol. 5. St. Petersburg: Izd. Sergeevskogo, 1907.

Shavel'skii, Georgii. *Vospominaniia poslednego protopresvitera russkoi armii i flota.* 2 vols. New York: Chekhov, 1954.

Shcherbatov, Mikhail M. *On the Corruption of Morals in Russia.* Ed. and trans. A. Lentin. Cambridge: At the University Press, 1969.

——. *Sochineniia Kniazia M. M. Shcherbatova.* Ed. I. P. Khrushchov and A. G. Voronov. St. Petersburg, 1898.

Shchipanov, I. Ia., ed. *Izbrannye sotsial'no-politicheskie i filosofskie proizvedeniia dekabristov.* 3 vols. Moscow: Gosudarstvennoe izdatel'stvo politicheskoi literatury, 1951.

Shil'der, N. K. *Imperator Aleksandr Pervyi, ego zhizn' i tsarstvovanie.* 4 vols. St. Petersburg: A. S. Suvorin, 1897-98.

Shilovskii, Petr P. *Akty otnosiashchiesia k politicheskomu polozheniiu Finliandii.* St. Petersburg: M. M. Stasiulevich, 1903.

Shul'gin, Vasilii V. *Dni.* Belgrade: Novoe Vremia, 1925.

Skarga, Piotr. *Kazania sejmowe.* Ed. Stanislaw Kot. Krakow: Nakladem Krakowskiej Spolki Wydawniczej, 1925.

Smirnov, Ivan I. *Vosstanie Bolotnikova 1606-1607.* Moscow: AN SSSR, 1951.

Smith, Robert E. F. *The Enserfment of the Russian Peasantry.* Cambridge: At the University Press, 1968.

Solov'ev, Ia. A. "Zapiski Senatora Ia. A. Solov'eva." *Russkaia starina,* 27 (1880): 319-62; 30 (1881): 211-46, 721-56, 903-05.

Solov'ev, Sergei M. "Istoriia padeniia Pol'shi." *Sobranie sochinenii S. M. Solov'eva.* St. Petersburg: Obshchestvennaia Pol'za, 1900.

Solov'ev [Solovyof], Vladimir S. *The Justification of the Good.* Trans. Nathalie A. Duddington, note by Stephen Graham. London: Constable, 1918.

——. *Opravdanie dobra: Nravstvennaia filosofiia Vladimira Solov'eva.* 2d ed. Moscow, 1899.
——. *Sobranie sochinenii Vladimira Sergeevicha Solov'eva.* 9 vols. St. Petersburg: Obsh-
chestvennaia Pol'za, [1901]-07.
Sovremennoe polozhenie i zadachi partii: Platforma, vyrabotannaia gruppoi Bol'shevikov. Paris:
Izd. Gruppy "Vpered," 1910.
Spector, Ivar and Marion, eds. *Readings in Russian History and Culture.* Palo Alto: Pacific Books,
1968.
Speranskii, Mikhail M. *Plan gosudarstvennogo preobrazovaniia, vvedenie k "Ulozheniiu Gosudarst-
vennykh Zakonov" 1809 g.* Moscow: Izd. Russkoi Mysli, 1905.
Staden, Heinrich von. *Aufzeichnungen ueber den Moskauer Staat.* Ed. Fritz Epstein. Hamburg:
Friederichsen, de Gruyter, 1930.
——. *The Land and Government of Muscovy: A Sixteenth-Century Account.* Trans. and ed.
Thomas Esper. Stanford: Stanford University Press, 1967.
Staehlin-Storcksburg, Jacob von. *Original Anecdotes of Peter the Great.* London, 1788.
Statut velikogo kniazhestva litovskogo 1529 goda. Ed. K. I. Iablonskis. Minsk: An BSSR, 1960.
Steblau: see Lassota.
Stoglav: Tsarskie voprosy i sobornye otvety. Moscow, 1890.
Stroev, Pavel M. *Obstoiatel'noe opisanie staropechatnykh knig slavianskikh i rossiiskikh,
khraniashchikhsia v biblioteke grafa F. A. Tolstova.* Moscow, 1829.
Struys, John. *The Voiages and Travels of John Struys.* Trans. John Morrison. London, 1684.
"Studencheskie volneniia v. 1901-1902 gg. Vvodnaia stat'ia A. Syromiatnikova." *Krasnyi
arkhiv,* 89-90 (1938, nos. 4-5): 258-308.
"Studencheskoe dvizhenie v 1901 g., s predisloviem V. Orlova." *Krasnyi arkhiv,* 75 (1936, no.
2): 83-112.
"Sudebnik 1497 g." *Pamiatniki russkogo prava,* 3: 346-57. Moscow: Gosizdat, 1955.
"Sudebnik 1550 g." *Pamiatniki russkogo prava,* 4: 233-61. Moscow: Gosizdat, 1956.
Sudebniki XV-XVI vekov. Ed. B. D. Grekov. Moscow: AN SSSR, 1952.
Svod Zakonov Rossiiskoi Imperii. 3d ed. 16 vols. St. Petersburg: Gosudarstvennaia Tipografiia,
1857-1916.

Tatishchev, Sergei S. *Imperator Aleksandr II.* 2 vols. St. Petersburg: A. S. Suvorin, 1911.
Tolstoi, Iurii K., ed. *Pervye sorok let snoshenii mezhdu Rossiei i Angliei 1553-1593.* St. Peters-
burg, 1875. Reprinted by Burt Franklin. New York: 1963.
Tolstoi, Lev N. *Polnoe sobranie sochinenii.* 90 vols. Moscow: Gosudarstvennoe Izd. Khudozhest-
vennoi Literatury, 1928-58.
——. *Sochineniia grafa L. N. Tolstogo.* 12th ed. 20 vols. Moscow: T. and I. N. Kushnerev, 1911.
——. *The Works of Leo Tolstoy: Tolstoy Centenary Edition.* 21 vols. London: Oxford Univer-
sity Press, 1928-37.
Tooke, William. *The Life of Catharine II, Empress of Russia.* 2d ed. 3 vols. London, 1800.
——. *View of the Russian Empire during the Reign of Catherine the Second and to the Close
of the Eighteenth Century.* 2d ed. 3 vols. London, 1800.
Traités et conventions entre L'Empire du Japon et les puissances étrangères. Tokyo: Z. P. Maruya,
1908.
Trudy Vol'nogo . . . : see Vol'noe Ekonomicheskoe Obshchestvo.
Tsentral'nyi Gosudarstvennyi Istoricheskii Arkhiv v Moskve, ed. *Burzhuaziia nakanune fevral'skoi
revolutsii.* Moscow: Gosizdat, 1927.
——. *Perepiska Nikolaia i Aleksandry Romanovykh 1914-1917.* Vols. 3-5. Moscow: Gosizdat,
1923.
——. *Pugachevshchina.* 2 vols. Moscow: Gosizdat, 1926-29.
Tsentral'nyi Statisticheskii Komitet. *Ezhegodnik Rossii 1906 g.* St. Petersburg: Ministerstvo
Vnutrennikh Del, 1907.
——. *Ezhegodnik Rossii 1910.* St. Petersburg: Ministerstvo Vnutrennikh Del, 1911.
——. *Statisticheskii Ezhegodnik Rossii 1914.* St. Petersburg: Ministerstvo Vnutrennikh Del,
1915.

Ulozhenie gosudaria tsaria i velikogo kniazia Alekseia Mikhailovicha. St. Petersburg: Gosudarst-vennaia Tipografiia, 1913.

Uroff, Benjamin Phillip. "Grigorii Karpovich Kotoshikhin, *On Russia in the Reign of Alexis Mikhailovich:* An Annotated Translation." 2 vols. Ph.D. dissertation, Columbia University, 1970.

Urusov [Urussov], Sergei D. *Memoirs of a Russian Governor, Prince S. D. Urussov.* Trans. Hermann Rosenthal. New York: Harper and Brothers, 1908.

Ustrialov, Nikolai G. *Istoriia tsarstvovaniia Petra Velikogo.* 5 vols. (nos. 1-4, 6) St. Petersburg, 1858-63.

Valk, Sigizmunt N., ed. *Gramoty velikogo Novgoroda i Pskova.* Moscow: AN SSSR, 1949.

Vashkevich, Vladislav V., comp. *Sbornik uzakonenii kasaiushchikhsia evreev.* St. Petersburg, 1884.

Vasiliev, A. A. *The Russian Attack on Constantinople in 860.* Cambridge: Harvard University Press, 1946.

"Vekhi," kak znamenie vremeni: Sbornik statei. Moscow: "Zveno," 1910.

Vekhi: Sbornik statei o russkoi intelligentsii. 4th ed. Moscow: T. and I. N. Kushnerev, 1909. Reprint. Frankfurt-am-Main: Posev, 1967.

Vernadsky, George. *Bohdan, Hetman of Ukraine.* New Haven: Yale University Press, 1941.

———. *La Charte Constitutionelle de l'Empire russe de l'an 1820.* Paris: Librairie du Recueil Sirey, 1933.

———. "Juwaini's Version of Chingis-Khan's Yasa." *Annales de l'Institut Kondakov,* 11 (1939): 39, 42-44.

———. *Medieval Russian Laws.* New York: Columbia University Press, 1947. Reprint. New York: Octagon Books, 1955; New York: W. W. Norton, 1969.

———. *The Mongols and Russia.* George Vernadsky and Michael Karpovich, *A History of Russia,* vol. 3. New Haven: Yale University Press, 1953.

———. *The Origins of Russia.* Oxford: Clarendon Press, 1959.

Vigel', Filipp F. *Vospominaniia F. F. Vigelia.* 7 vols. in 3. Moscow, 1864-65.

———. *Zapiski.* Ed. S. Ia. Shtraikh. 2 vols. Moscow: Artel' Pisatelei Krug, 1928.

Vitte: See Witte.

Vol'noe Ekonomicheskoe Obshchestvo. *Istoriia Imperatorskogo Vol'nogo Ekonomicheskogo Obshchestva s 1765 do 1865.* Comp. A. I. Khodnev. St. Petersburg, 1865.

Vol'noe Ekonomicheskoe Obshchestvo. *Trudy Vol'nogo Ekonomicheskogo Obshchestva k pooshchreniiu v Rossii zemledeliia i domostroitel'stva.* 280 vols. St. Petersburg, various publishers, 1765-1915. See also Bolotov, Rychkov.

Von Laue, Theodore H. "A Secret Memorandum of Sergei Witte on the Industrialization of Imperial Russia." *Journal of Modern History,* 26 (March 1954): 60-74.

Voskresenskaia letopis'. Polnoe Sobranie Russkikh Letopisei, vols. 7-8. St. Petersburg, 1853.

Vossoedinenie Ukrainy s Rossiei: Dokumenty i materialy. 3 vols. Moscow: AN SSSR, 1954.

Vulliamy, C. E., ed. *The Letters of the Tsar to the Tsaritsa, 1914-1917.* Trans. A. L. Hynes. London: J. Lane, 1929.

Wallace, Donald Mackenzie. *Russia.* Rev. and enlarged ed. London: Cassell, 1912.

Walsh, Warren B., ed. *Readings in Russian History.* 3 vols. 4th ed. Syracuse, N.Y.: Syracuse University Press, 1963.

Weber, Friedrich Christian. *The Present State of Russia.* 2 vols. London, 1722-23.

Whitworth, Charles. *An Account of Russia As It Was in the Year 1710.* London, 1758.

Wiener, Leo, ed. *Anthology of Russian Literature from the Earliest Period to the Present Time.* 2 vols. New York: G. P. Putnam's Sons, 1902.

Wilhelm II. *The Kaiser's Letters to the Tsar.* Ed. N. F. Grant. London: Hodder and Stoughton, 1920.

Witte [Vitte], Sergei Iu. *Vospominaniia: Tsarstvovanie Nikolaia II.* 2 vols. Berlin: Slovo, 1922. See also: Yarmolinsky; Von Laue.

Wolf, L., ed. *The Legal Sufferings of the Jews in Russia.* London: T. F. Unwin, 1912.

Wormeley, Katherine Prescott, ed. and trans. *Prince de Ligne: His Memoirs, Letters and Miscellaneous Papers.* 2 vols. Boston: Hardy, Pratt, 1899.

Yarmolinsky, Abraham, ed. and trans. *The Memoirs of Count Witte.* Garden City, N.Y.: Doubleday, Page, 1921.

Zablotskii-Desiatovskii, Andrei P. *Graf P. D. Kiselev i ego vremia.* 4 vols. St. Petersburg, 1882.

Zaionchkovskii, A. M., comp. "Iz zapisnoi knizhki arkhivista v gody reaktsii." *Krasnyi arkhiv,* 8 (1925, no. 1): 240-43.

Zapadnorusskie letopisi. Polnoe Sobranie Russkikh Letopisei, vol. 17. St. Petersburg: Arkheograficheskaia Kommissiia, 1907.

Zemskii s''ezd 6-go i sl. noiabria 1904 g. Paris: Izd. Red. "Osvobozhdenie," 1905.

Zenkovsky, Serge A., ed. and trans. *Medieval Russia's Epics, Chronicles, and Tales.* New York: E. P. Dutton, 1963.

Zhurnal Ministerstva Iustitsii, 1917, nos. 2-3 (February-March), pp. 1-7.

Zhurnal Ministerstva Narodnogo Prosveshcheniia. 362 vols. St. Petersburg, 1834-1905; n.s. 72 vols., 1906-17.

Zisserman, Arnold L. *Fel'dmarshal Kniaz A. I. Bariatinskii, 1815-1877.* 3 vols. Moscow, 1888-91.

Zolkiewski, Stanislas. *Expedition to Moscow: A Memoir by Hetman Stanislas Zolkiewski.* Trans. M. W. Stephan. Intro. and notes by Jedrzej Giertych. Preface by Robert Bruce Lockhart. Polonica Series no. 1. London: Polonica Publications, 1959. See also Mukhanov.

PERMISSIONS

Permission to quote from the following copyrighted works is gratefully acknowledged.